MEDIEVAL POPULAR R

M000231333

READINGS IN MEDIEVAL CIVILIZATIONS AND CULTURES: II
series editor: Paul Edward Dutton

MEDIEVAL POPULAR RELIGION, 1000–1500

A READER

SECOND EDITION

edited by

JOHN SHINNERS

UTP

Previously published by Broadview Press 2007

LIBRARY AND ARCHIVES CANADA CATALOGUING IN PUBLICATION

Medieval popular religion, 1000–1500 : a reader / edited by John Shinners.—2nd ed.

(Readings in medieval civilizations and cultures; 2)
Index includes bibliographical references and index.

ISBN 13: 978-1-44260-106-2
PREVIOUS ISBN: 978-1-55111-698-3 (Broadview Press edition)

1. Europe—Religious life and customs—Sources. 2. Catholic Church—Europe—History—Sources. I. Shinners, John Raymond. 1954– II. Series.

BR252.M42   2006   282'40902   C2006-904506-2

We welcome comments and suggestions regarding any aspect of our publications—please feel free to contact us at news@utphighereducation.com or visit our Internet site at www.utphighereducation.com.

North America
5201 Dufferin Street
North York, Ontario, Canada, M3H 5T8

2250 Military Road
Tonawanda, New York, USA, 14150

ORDERS PHONE: 1-800-565-9523
ORDERS FAX: 1-800-221-9985
ORDERS EMAIL: utpbooks@utpress.utoronto.ca

UK, Ireland, and continental Europe
NBN International
Estover Road, Plymouth, PL6 7PY, UK
TEL: 44 (0) 1752 202301
FAX ORDER LINE: 44 (0) 1752 202333
enquiries@nbninternational.com

The University of Toronto Press acknowledges the financial support for its publishing activities of the Government of Canada through the Book Publishing Industry Development Program (BPIDP).

Book design and composition by George Kirkpatrick

PRINTED IN CANADA

For my family

CONTENTS

CHRONOLOGICAL TABLE OF CONTENTS

Bracketed numbers refer to the Documents.

1224 St. Francis dies (b. c. 1181)

c. 1224-37 **A tract on hearing confessions [4]**

1226 St. Louis IX (1214-70) crowned king of France

1231 Pope Gregory IX establishes the papal inquisition of heresy

1233 **The "Great Halleluia" in Italy [68]**

1230s **Jacques de Vitry's sermon to boys [6]**

mid-1230s **The Sign of the Cross explained [1]**

1244 Jerusalem's final fall to Muslims

mid-1200s **The spurious Saint Guinefort [72]**

mid-1200s **Thomas of Celano's *Dies irae* [77]**

1250 St. Louis IX taken captive while on Seventh Crusade

c. 1250-80 **The *Cantigas* of Holy Mary [23]**

1251 **The Shepherds' Crusade [67]**

c. 1260 **Jacob of Voragine's *Golden Legend*: Lives of St. Mary Magdalene and St. Nicholas [32]; the Rogations [49]**

1264 **Feast of Corpus Christi established [16]**

1274 Thomas Aquinas dies (b. 1225)

1280s **Giovanni de' Cauli's *Meditations on the Life of Christ* [14]**

1280s **German encounters with demons [38]**

c. 1286 **Durandus on the symbolism of church art [7]**

late 1200s **The *Stabat mater* [22]**

1290 Jews expelled from England

c. 1295 **Bishop Durandus's list of blessings [47]; Episcopal blessing for a new knight [48]**

1296 **An English bishop oversees popular piety [73]**

1300 **The Great Jubilee indulgence at Rome [64.1]**

1300s **Drama of the Annunciation from Padua [24]; Drama of the Visitation of the Sepulcher from Essen [51]**

1300s **The *Obsecro te* [26]**

1302 Boniface VIII issues the bull *Unam sanctam*

c. 1303 **The Eucharist and libels against the Jews [18]**

c. 1305-17 **Medical charms from the *Rosa medicinae* [53]**

1305-78 The Avignonese Papacy

1312 **The fraternity of the Blessed Virgin at Perugia [55]**

1312 The Council of Vienne suppresses the Knights Templar

1320 **Investigation of the French heretic Guillaume Austatz [75]**

1320 **A French peasant's theology of God [19]**

1321 Dante dies (b. 1265)

1323 Thomas Aquinas canonized

LIST OF ILLUSTRATIONS

PREFACE TO THE SECOND EDITION

Since it can be annoying to encounter a second edition that has assumed a brand new identity, I have tried to keep the contents of the first edition of *Medieval Popular Religion* largely intact here, preferring addition to subtraction. In a few places I have substituted texts that I think more richly evoke the sensibility of medieval religion than those they replace. For instance, the twelfth-century *Play of Adam* (Doc. 12) brings more psychological complexity to the Creation story than the *Play of Chester* it replaces. The new translation of the English peasant Thurkill's Grand Guignol vision of hell (Doc. 37) is a precocious precursor to Dante's later journey and far more evocative than the fairly dull tale from the *Gesta Romanorum* of the demons in the mountain that it replaces. At the suggestion of generous readers I have added excerpts from two pilgrims' travelogues to the Holy Land, one from the fourteenth century and, for comparison, the eccentric Margery Kempe's emotionally charged account from the early fifteenth century (Docs. 33 & 34). Also among the longer additions is a thirteenth-century handbook for confessors with its roll call of human vices and their remedies (Doc. 4) and two fifteenth-century explorations of sorcery, one theological (Doc. 44), the other a necromancer's dazzling recipe for a love spell (Doc. 45). I hope these additions help to highlight the unspoken theme that runs throughout the book: the intimacy and intensity of the impact that religious belief had on medieval people.

As well as adding ten new texts, I have also gone back over all my own translations and introductions, fine-tuning or correcting them where the light of hindsight has led me to reassess. I have also greatly increased the bracketed notes of explanation throughout the book and added reading questions at the end of most documents in the hope of making the book even more accessible. I offer my gratitude to those readers who have made many other thoughtful suggestions for improving *Medieval Popular Religion*. While my changes will doubtlessly fall short of expectations, I hope that old and new readers alike will judge this new edition to be largely a success as it tries to take us into the hearts of medieval Christians.

INTRODUCTION TO THE FIRST EDITION

What is medieval popular religion? This book's aim is to assemble enough documents for readers to answer the question for themselves. In the meantime, let this introduction venture one possible response.

Faced with this question, it is tempting to answer "What isn't it?" since religion suffused every aspect of medieval life. But *popular* religion typically suggests something else. Too often it has implied some quaint grab-bag of superstition, magic, and pious hooey clouding the minds of bumpkin peasants. Over the last several decades, however, scholars have realized that it is unfair to dismiss so quickly the religious experience of ordinary people and misleading to suggest that medieval lay people and the clergy, for all their distinctions, believed and behaved in significantly different ways in matters of religion. While historians have lately coined several phrases to describe popular religion – among them, "popular piety," "lay piety," "lay religion," "popular devotion," "local religion," and "traditional religion" – most of the religious observances they describe with these phrases were as likely to be as much a part of the devotional life of the typical bishop as the typical peasant.

In fact, by the twelfth century, medieval popular religion was, for many purposes, simply medieval religion. A literate, chiefly clerical audience could read scripture, theology, and devotional writings that most people could not, and men and women living under religious vows had stricter daily routines of prayer and demeanor. But all Christians, no matter their status, shared essentially the same religious world view and acted on it in similar ways. If for no other reason, most people learned their earliest religious lessons at the knees of their parents or other lay people, so almost everyone started from the same point. The everyday practices typically associated with popular religion – for instance, a preoccupation with miracles and prodigies, the enthusiastic veneration of saints, the recourse to quasi-magical prayers or charms, an acute concern for the fate of dead – were indeed *popular* because they were common and widespread, as vital a part of the religious life of most educated elites, clergy and lay alike, as they were the property of people at large. (With this all-encompassing meaning of "popular" in mind, I prefer the phrase "popular religion" to its alternatives.) There was, in fact, a constant and lively interplay of devotional ideas and practices between clergy and laity, high and low. For instance, one of the most popular feasts of the Middle Ages was the feast of Corpus Christi, which celebrated the institution of the eucharist at the Last Supper. It first sprouted up as a local devotion among groups of lay people in the early 1200s, gradually took hold in higher clerical circles, and ultimately was made a universal feast of the church by papal mandate in 1264. Thomas Aquinas, whose theology is one of the peaks of medieval high culture, then composed two Latin hymns in celebration of the new feast which in turn worked their way back down to ordinary people to become their favorite songs for the feast they had themselves created (see Doc. 16). In the case of the most characteristic component of medieval religion – the veneration of saints – the popular local acclamation of a person's sanctity was always far more important for making saints and sustaining their cults than papal approval, even after 1234 when Pope Gregory IX officially claimed the canonization of saints as the papacy's prerogative (see Doc. 72).

Medieval Christianity shares with all religions, ancient and modern, a need to make concrete and effective the perceived link between this world and some higher reality. Religious belief is an act of faith in things usually unseen; faith, by its nature, wavers between the poles of doubt and certainty. But popular belief craves certainty. It seeks to render concrete what must remain mysterious. Setting aside the intellectual subtleties toward which medieval theology could mount and the ravishing contemplations of medieval mystics, the daily religious preoccupation of medieval people was how most successfully to transact business with the denizens of the supernatural world. How to ward off sickness and disaster, how to win success in endeavors large or small, how to defend against demonic powers, how to gain the favor of God and his saints and thank them for their blessings, how to insure eternal happiness – how, in short, to live your life in order to save your soul with confidence and relative ease was the ever-present concern of all medieval Christians. To this degree there was (and is) something starkly functional about religion. But this business-like, expedient, literal-minded – and sometimes coarse – attitude of medieval Christians toward their everyday beliefs understandably arose from the simple human need to manifest nebulous ideas about the supernatural, life and death, and human celebration and tragedy in solid, understandable images and purposeful action.

Medieval Christians earnestly believed that a supernatural reality interwove their world. Popular religion sought tangible signs of that other reality and ways to tap and control its power. Thus, what we would now brand magical practices and assumptions, whether shaped by the Christian world view or transmitted and transmuted from extra-Christian traditions, played a regular role in the lives of most people, laity and clergy alike. Religion was a way of coping with the world; medieval people grabbed for whatever tools, natural or supernatural, that seemed to work best under the circumstances. It is easy enough to dismiss this magical character of medieval daily religion as gross superstition, at best the product of gullible and ignorant minds, at worst outright paganism and heresy. And to be sure, medieval believers sometimes teetered on the edge of or stumbled into doctrinal error and practice, a fact that left churchmen in a perpetual state of worry about the religious inclinations of the laity when left unguided by pastors. But superstition and delusion do not seem to have been the normal state of mind of most Christians. Despite the snares of superstition and heresy, the leaders of the medieval Christian church seem to have been largely, even remarkably, successful in instilling beliefs and habits in most people that were basically Christian, despite the extra layers of ornament with which local custom invariably dressed them. In large measure this was due to the church's talent for embodying and adapting Christianity's essential ideas in art and rituals that underscored through images, dramatic gesture, and ceremony what could not be grasped by lay people generally ignorant of Latin. In fact, popular religion, orthodox or not, almost always was rooted in some kind of expressive public or private rite.

Obedient to its own homespun logic, popular religious belief was never troubled by the need for intellectual consistency or doctrinal purity. From the point of view of prelates, theologians, and canonists, it was undisciplined, uncritical, and unorganized. This posed real dangers since charismatic leaders could coax believers, whose faith spoke more to the heart than to the head, into fanatical and unthinking attacks against Jews, Muslims, heretics, or even – when the leaders were themselves unorthodox – Christian clerics and the church. But from another perspective popular religion was free from the academically narrow categories placed on something as encompassing, amorphous, and mysterious as religious belief. Ordinary Christians took a broad-minded approach to religion, usually driven by custom and expediency. What worked, worked – as it had in the past. In this sense, they had a better grasp of religion's fluid boundaries than thinkers who restrained pious impulses by academic or doctrinal fetters.

Still, popular religion can seem too fixed in reciprocity ("Grant me x, save me from y, and I'll do z for you in return."), or too preoccupied with marvels and wonders at the expense of genuine piety and conversion of life. Yet we cannot ignore the deeply affective waves that regularly break the surface of everyday beliefs and practices. However contractual and crass the ordinary dealings between humans and the divine may occasionally appear, in their public and private devotions medieval people were often and reverently moved to pity, sorrow, joy, and terror. Popular religion addressed feelings of genuine need, so it came from the heart, was emotionally charged, and intensely human. To weigh the degree to which medieval popular Christianity was *really* Christian is to measure it by a standard against which modern

Christianity, in its multiple manifestations, would fare little better if at all. The City of God – a holy and loving assembly of all God's faithful – was no more easily apt to come to pass in the medieval Christian commonwealth than it is today. As medieval moralists stressed, pilgrims do not find rest and contentment until their journey ends. True enough, medieval believers in particular stuffed the scrip for their spiritual journey with an untidy array of beliefs, habits, and emergency provisions that were not always appropriate for the trip. But the evangelical mission of the medieval Christian church encompassed all Christian souls. Its greatest strength was its talent for being malleable, for offering outlets for religious expression that by and large provided for everyone's religious needs – from bishops, priests, monks, and nuns, to theologians, philosophers, and lawyers, to monarchs, nobles, merchants, burghers, and peasants. The typical medieval Christian's grasp of religion was surely a rough hodgepodge of ideas and actions shaped by rudimentary Christian instruction, communal tradition, hard experience, fertile imagination, and pressing need; it was probably always fuzzy on the details. But the very fact that Christianity successfully rooted, spread, and flourished across Europe's Middle Ages – that it became the cornerstone of medieval culture – suggests that, whatever adjustments it made for local custom or circumstance, at heart the Christian church succeeded in getting its basic message to the people meant to hear it.

This book draws together a variety of translated documents that illustrate the rich religious life of ordinary medieval Christians. The documents date from around the early eleventh century, when both social conditions and the church were settled enough and organized enough for there to be an emerging sense of a European Christendom, to the early sixteenth century, when that Christendom turned sectarian. For all it offers, there are many things necessarily missing, for the subject is too vast to be easily gathered in one volume, and this book must stick to basics. It cannot cover all the regional variations in belief and practice across Europe; it cannot do more than suggest some of the developments across time in the various subjects represented here. In fact, it must sweep rather recklessly across five centuries, offering only impressionistic portraits where sustained narratives would tell more. Conspicuously absent by and large are excerpts from works of Latin and vernacular literature, for though works of fiction reflect social realities and offer valuable insights into the religious mentalities of the Middle Ages, they are generally more easily at hand in translation than the works of non-fiction included here. Since this Reader contains so much material that has never or seldom been translated or collected before, I have sacrificed the literary record for the documentary. Likewise, the rich spiritual records of medieval mysticism are for the most part missing here. Mystics often attracted enthusiastic popular followings – Hildegard of Bingen or Dame Julian of Norwich come quickly to mind – and their impact on everyday religion needs to be weighed. But the mystical path to the divine was a sublimely narrow road that most people found unapproachable; it does not represent the typical medieval religious experience. Missing too are the popular religious traditions of Judaism and Islam, for these were marginalized cultures in medieval Europe.

Readers should bear in mind two caveats: first, and obviously, these documents are translations, which can never be mirror copies of their originals. Therefore no one should try to build arguments on a word or phrase which might more reflect the translator's compromise or ill-fated search for the *mot juste* than the writer's intended meaning. Second, almost all these documents have been filtered through the perspectives of clerical authors. They represent viewpoints colored by education, by literary, religious, historical, or legal commonplaces, and often by the authors' self-awareness that they were members of an elite that considered itself superior to lay people if only by virtue of a sacramental anointing. When these clerical go-betweens disapproved of what they described, that affected and slanted their accounts. Though the voices of unlettered believers sometimes sound in these texts – for instance in certain prayers or charms, or in the verbatim depositions of lay people haled before church tribunals – a literate, and usually clerical, intermediary always stands between what ordinary medieval people believed and did, and what we can learn of those beliefs and actions today.

Translations invariably mirror the speech of their day. While I hold my predecessors' work in great regard, I have taken the liberty of quietly updating the outdated turns of phrase in some of the older translations in order to make them ring a little more familiar to modern ears. Where I have had access to better editions than past translators, I have also emended the occasional mistranslation – I suspect I have added as many unwitting errors of my own as I have corrected others'. Words in square brackets represent my or other translators' explanatory additions to the text. Most biblical quotations cited here follow the Douai-Rheims translation which most closely captures the Latin Vulgate current in the Middle Ages.

★ ★ ★

My debt of thanks swelled as the pages of this book mounted. Especially helpful were Marina Smyth of the University of Notre Dame's Medieval Institute library; the staff of the Cushwa-Leighton Library at Saint Mary's

College, especially Robert Hohl; and Louis Jordan, head of Special Collections and the Ambrosiana Collection at Notre Dame. Ina Kahal and William Waymouth helped me prepare the illustrations. Many friends and colleagues lent me their guidance when I ventured into unfamiliar waters, among them Thomas Bonnell, William Dohar, Phyllis Kaminiski, Damian Leader, Daniel Mandell, Terence Martin, John Pauley, Jerry Rank, Marcia Rickard, John Van Engen, Mary Warnement, and Herold Weiss. As usual, any errors here are mine, not theirs. My friend and series editor Paul Dutton fed me a steady stream of advice and encouragement. The editorial staff at Broadview – Barbara Conolly, Mical Moser, Martin Boyne, and Julie Smith – were unstinting in their help, good advice, and patience. Finally, my thanks to my departmental colleagues Philip Hicks and Gail Mandell for their sustained interest and support during the course of my work.

CHAPTER ONE:

INSTRUCTION IN THE FAITH

Medieval Christianity, a "religion of the book," was founded on a written revelation augmented by the insights of great Christian thinkers and leaders which together comprised a deposit of faith accumulated over centuries and recorded in thousands of pages of writing. Though its core beliefs could be contained in the seventy-six Latin words of the Apostles' Creed, the Creed dealt only in basic doctrine; it did not set that doctrine in context or say how it was to be translated into a program for living. That task fell to an educated clerical caste who had to elaborate and disseminate Christianity's holy texts, its sacraments and other rituals, and its counsel on how to live a moral life and win salvation. Ordinary people, the vast majority of whom could not read Latin, encountered and cultivated their Christian faith only through these clerical intermediaries – at least officially. Church leaders expected lay people to know the rudiments of their faith. They were to memorize the Apostles' Creed, the Our Father, the Hail Mary, and how to make the sign of the cross. They were to participate in the church's sacraments: baptism at birth, confirmation in childhood, and matrimony in adulthood; extreme unction at the end of their lives or when seriously ill; and confession and holy communion at least once a year, though few lay people took communion more than three or four times annually. Sermons instructed them in the precepts of Christian life: the message of the Gospels, the Ten Commandments, the seven virtues (faith, hope, charity, justice, prudence, temperance, fortitude), the seven works of mercy (feed the hungry, give drink to the thirsty, clothe the naked, comfort the sick, visit the imprisoned, shelter strangers, bury the dead), and the seven deadly sins (pride, envy, anger, greed, lust, gluttony, sloth). Art and architecture – the unlettered person's "book" – embodied the faith in concrete images. Weighing the success of this program of instruction will always generate controversy among historians since the evidence is spotty and seldom reported firsthand from the experience of average Christians. But the four accounts at the end of this chapter, though admittedly about extraordinary people, hint at what typical Christians knew of their faith and how they acted on it.

Fig. 1.1. Preaching

A crowd sits listening to a barefoot friar who stands on a portable pulpit. Judging by their somber looks, he is preaching against vice and warning of judgment. A nineteenth-century copy reproduced in Charles Knight's *Old England: A Pictorial Museum of Regal, Ecclesiastical, Baronial, Municipal, and Popular Antiquities* (London: Charles Knight & Co., 1845), v. 1, p. 357 after an early fourteenth-century manuscript now in the British Library, MS Royal 14 E, iii.

1. BASIC CHRISTIAN PRAYERS

1. The Apostles' Creed

Three creeds embodying the basic tenets of Christian belief were in common use in the Middle Ages. The Nicene-Constantinopolitan Creed (originally issued at the Council of Nicaea in 325 and revised at succeeding early councils) was recited by the priest at mass. The Athanasian Creed (wrongly ascribed to St. Athanasius and usually known by its incipit Quicunque vult) *was a theological summary of beliefs about the Trinity and the Incarnation contained in the book of daily prayers for clerics called the breviary. But the Apostles' Creed (so called since according to legend each of the twelve apostles contributed one verse to it) was the most widespread creed: all Christians were required to know it by heart. Derived from early Christian baptismal oaths, its basic formula was fixed, except for minor variations, by the early eighth century, and it gained widespread acceptance as an essential statement of faith during the ninth-century Carolingian reforms of the Frankish church. Yet though it was mandatory and a fundamental summary of Christian doctrine, it does not seem to have played as large a role in popular devotions as the Lord's Prayer or Hail Mary; its length and the relative complexity of its ideas no doubt account for this. The explanatory preface to the Apostles' Creed below comes from the* Bobbio Missal *of the late seventh-early eighth century, which contains one of its earliest liturgical versions. The Creed itself is the traditional translation of the received text, which differs in a few insignificant details from the* Bobbio Missal's *version.*

Source: preface trans. J. Shinners from E.A. Lowe, *The Bobbio Missal: A Gallican Mass-Book*, Henry Bradshaw Society, v. 58 (London: Harrison & Sons, 1920), p. 56; Creed trans. traditional from Heinrich Denziger and A. Schönmetzer, *Enchiridion Symbolorum* (Freiburg: Herder, 32nd ed., 1963), p. 26. Latin.

The divine sacraments, most beloved brothers, should not so much be debated as believed, and not only believed but also feared. No one can keep the discipline of faith who will not accept its foundation of fear of the Lord. As Solomon says: "the beginning of wisdom is fear of the Lord" [Ps. 110 (111):10]. For whoever fears the Lord in everything that God says is a wise and faithful person. Today, therefore, you are about to hear the Creed, without which no one can proclaim Christ, keep the faith, or celebrate the grace of baptism. The Creed is a token of the Catholic faith, a symbol (*sacramentum*) of the eternal religion. Therefore prepare your senses suitably with all reverence; listen to the Creed that the holy Catholic church has passed down to you today in the mother tongue [Latin]:

I believe in God the Father Almighty, creator of heaven and earth; and in Jesus Christ, his only Son, our Lord; who was conceived by the Holy Spirit, born of the Virgin Mary, suffered under Pontius Pilate, was crucified, died, and was buried. He descended into hell; the third day he arose again from the dead; he ascended into heaven and sits at the right hand of God the Father Almighty. From thence he shall come to judge the living and the dead. I believe in the Holy Spirit, the holy Catholic church, the communion of saints, the forgiveness of sins, the resurrection of the body; and life everlasting. Amen.

2. The Lord's Prayer

Drawn from the gospels (Matt. 6:9-13; Luke 11:2-4), the Lord's Prayer or Paternoster *(Our Father) held a special place in Christian devotions since it was believed to represent the very words of Jesus. The prayer was such a part of ordinary life that it was commonly used to measure intervals of time; it is not unusual, for example, to find medieval recipes containing instructions to stir a dish "for as long as it takes to say the Our Father." Lay people were typically required to memorize the brief Latin of the Lord's Prayer, Hail Mary, and the Creed, though few would understand what they were saying without a vernacular translation. The word "patter," for instance, derives from the rapidly moving lips of someone mechanically reciting the* Paternoster. *Some clerics urged the laity to learn these prayers in the vernacular. The fourteenth-century English curate John Myrc argued that since people really understood what they prayed when they said the Our Father in English, it gave them more "lykyng and devocyn forto say it." The traditional translation below dates back to the late 1530s when Archbishop Thomas Cromwell was reforming the English liturgy under Henry VIII, but comparable English versions were circulating by the 1400s.*

Source: *Three Primers Put Forth in the Reign of Henry VIII*, ed. Edward Burton (Oxford: University Press, 1834), p. 459; slightly revised from the Primer of 1545. English.

Our Father, who art in heaven, hallowed be thy name. Thy kingdom come. Thy will be done, on earth as it is in heaven. Give us this day our daily bread. And forgive us our trespasses, as we forgive those who trespass against us. And lead us not into temptation, but deliver us from evil.... Amen.

3. The Hail Mary

The Ave Maria or Hail Mary (often called the "Angelic Salutation" in medieval documents) was in popular use in close to its modern form by the late eleventh century. Until the latter years of the fifteenth century it consisted of two verses from the Gospel of Luke joined together: the angel Gabriel's salutation to Mary (Luke 1:28: "Hail, full of grace, the Lord is with thee. Blessed art thou among women.") and Mary's cousin Elizabeth's greeting to her (Luke 1:42: "Blessed art thou among women and blessed is the fruit of thy womb."). Bishop Odo of Paris's synodal statutes of 1198 are apparently the first official document to require lay people to learn the Hail Mary, though it had already been in widespread popular use for at least a century. Its last verse ("Holy Mary, Mother of God, pray for us sinners now and at the hour of our death.") was added in stages during the later fifteenth and sixteenth centuries and papally ratified in 1568. Like the Lord's Prayer and the Creed, the Hail Mary would typically have been memorized and recited in Latin even by lay people who otherwise had no knowledge of that language. The anecdote below, from Hermann of Tournai's Restoration of St. Martin of Tournai (c. 1145), represents one of the earliest references to the Hail Mary in the form in which it was prayed during most of the Middle Ages.

Source: trans. Herbert Thurston, *Familiar Prayers, Their Origin and History* (Westminster, MA: Newman Press, 1953), p. 103. Latin.

A certain hermit, who dwelt alone in a neighboring wood which is called Broqueroy, saw, as he reported, not during his sleep but while wide awake at midday, the holy Mother of God seated in heaven upon a lofty throne like a queen, while the two saints [Waudru and Aldegund] whom I have just named, prostrated themselves at her feet and invoked vengeance upon Thierry of Avesnes, who had burned the churches dedicated to them. But when they made bitter complaint and demanded justice, the Blessed Virgin answered them in these terms: "Spare me, I pray you, and be not troublesome to me, because I am not willing at present to lay any grievous burden upon him. For his wife, the Lady Ada, renders me a certain service which binds me to her in such bonds of intimacy that I am unable to allow any harm to befall either her or her husband." And when the two saints sought to know what this service was, she answered: "That angelical salutation which was the beginning of all my joy on earth she repeats to me sixty times each day – twenty times while she lies prostrate, twenty times kneeling, twenty times standing upright, either in the church or in her chamber or in some [private] place, to wit: *Ave Maria, gratia plena, Dominus tecum, benedicta tu in mulieribus et benedictus fructus ventris tui* [Hail Mary, full of grace, the Lord is with thee, blessed art thou among women and blessed is the fruit of thy womb]."

4. The Sign of the Cross (mid-1230s)

Mentioned in sources from as early as the first decade of the third century, the sign of the cross is Christianity's most ancient ritual gesture and powerful symbol. Originally people traced the cross on their foreheads with thumb or fingers; it is unclear when they first started signing themselves with a large cross from forehead to chest and shoulder to shoulder, though literary evidence suggests that this gesture was in use by the eleventh century. Commentators typically encouraged using the thumb and first two fingers when making the sign in order symbolize the Trinity. The gesture was regarded as a universal protection against evil. Thus, people traced it in their hearth ashes at night, on their doors, over ailing parts of their bodies, on sick cattle, over food, and in the air when faced with supernatural danger. (See, for example, Docs. 41 & 44.) This account on how to make the sign of the cross, from Lucas, bishop of the Spanish city of Tuy (1239-49), dates from the mid-1230s.

Source: trans. Herbert Thurston, *Familiar Prayers, Their Origin and History* (Westminster, MA: Newman Press, 1953), p. 12. Latin.

A question occurs regarding the sign of the cross (*de consignatione*) whether when the faithful make the sign of the cross over themselves or others the hand ought to pass from the left to the right or from the right to the left. To which we answer, as we honestly believe and hold, that both methods are good, both holy, both able to overthrow the might of the enemy, providing only the Christian religion uses them in Catholic simplicity. Seeing, however, that many people presumptuously endeavor to put an end to one of these methods, maintaining that the hand ought not to pass from left to right, as has been handed down to us from our fathers, let us in the interests of charity say a few words on this subject. For when our Lord Jesus Christ for the redemption of the human race, mercifully blest the world, he proceeded from the Father, he came into the world, he descended, on the left hand as it were, into hell, and ascending to heaven he sitteth on the right hand of God. Now it is this which every faithful Christian seems to portray, when, on guarding his face (*faciem suam muniens*) with the sign of the cross, he raises three extended fingers on high, in front of his forehead (*contra frontem*) saying "In nomine Patris" [In the name of the father], then lowers them towards his beard with the words "et Filii" [and of the Son], then to the left saying "et Spiritus Sancti" [and of the Holy Spirit], and finally to the right as he utters "Amen."

If ordinary Christians knew the gist of these four prayers, what understanding of their faith would they have? To what extent do these prayers convey dogma and to what extent do they offer a plan for ethical living?

2. THE FOURTH LATERAN COUNCIL (1215)

In 1215 Pope Innocent III (1198-1216) gathered at Rome twelve hundred archbishops, bishops, abbots, and prelates from across Europe to discuss the state of the church. The decrees issued by this Fourth Lateran Council were a watershed in the history of medieval pastoral care. In fact, it is no exaggeration to say that the Council created the Christian church of the high Middle Ages since it defined the basic religious duties required of all Christians and established procedures for the administration of the church at the local levels of the diocese and parish. Canon 21, Omnis utriusque sexus, *was especially important: it obliged all adult Christians to make confession and receive holy communion at least once a year. This obligation, in turn, required priests themselves to be more meticulous in their exercise of the* cura animarum *or care of souls. In the decades following the Council a flurry of episcopal legislation and handbooks meant to better train the parish clergy for their pastoral duties circulated across Europe (see Docs. 3 and 4). Though the whole document repays study for students of popular religion, here are a few of the Council's canons especially concerned with everyday religious belief and conduct.*

Source: trans. H.J. Schroeder in *Disciplinary Decrees of the General Councils* (London: Herder, 1937), pp. 237-39, 251-52, 255-57, 259-60, 280-81, 286-87, 290-91. Latin.

Canon 1. We firmly believe and openly confess that there is only one true God, eternal and immense, omnipotent, unchangeable, incomprehensible, and ineffable, Father, Son, and Holy Ghost; three Persons indeed but one essence, substance, or nature, absolutely simple; the Father proceeding from no one, but the Son from the Father only, and the Holy Ghost equally from both, always without beginning and end. The Father begetting the Son, the Son begotten, and the Holy Ghost proceeding; consubstantial and coequal, co-omnipotent and coeternal, the one principle of the universe, Creator of all things visible and invisible, spiritual and corporeal, who from the beginning of time and by his omnipotent power made from nothing creatures both spiritual and corporeal, angelic, namely, and earthly, and then human, as it were, common, composed of spirit and body. The devil and the other demons were indeed created by God good by nature but they became bad through themselves; man, however, sinned at the suggestion of the devil. This holy Trinity in its common essence undivided and in personal properties divided, through Moses, the holy prophets, and other servants gave to the human race at the most opportune intervals of time the doctrine of salvation.

And finally, Jesus Christ, the only begotten Son of God made flesh by the entire Trinity, conceived with the cooperation of the Holy Ghost of Mary ever Virgin, made true man, composed of a rational soul and human flesh, one person in two natures, pointed out more clearly the way of life. Who according to his divinity is immortal and unable to suffer, according to his humanity was made able to suffer and mortal, suffered on the cross for the salvation of the human race, and being dead descended into hell, rose from the dead, and ascended into heaven. But he descended in soul, arose in flesh, and ascended equally in both; he will come at the end of the world to judge the living and the dead and will render to the reprobate and to the elect according to their works. Who shall rise with their own bodies which they now have that they may receive according to their merits, whether good or bad, the latter eternal punishment with the devil, the former eternal glory with Christ.

There is one universal church of the faithful outside of which there is absolutely no salvation. In which there is the same priest and sacrifice, Jesus Christ, whose body and blood are truly contained in the sacrament of the altar under the forms of bread and wine; the bread being changed (*transsubstantiatis*) by divine power into the body, and the wine into the blood, so that to realize the mystery of unity we may receive of him what he has received of us. And this sacrament no one can effect except the priest who has been duly ordained in accordance with the keys of the church, which Jesus Christ himself gave to the apostles and their successors.

But the sacrament of baptism, which by the invocation of each person of the Trinity, namely of the Father, Son, and Holy Ghost, is effected in water, duly conferred on children and adults in the form prescribed by the church by anyone whatsoever, leads to salvation. And should anyone after the reception of baptism have fallen into sin, by true repentance he can always be restored. Not only virgins and those practicing chastity, but also those united in marriage, through the right faith and through works pleasing to God, can merit eternal salvation....

Canon 10. Among other things that pertain to the salvation of the Christian people, the food of the word of God is above all necessary, because as the body is nourished by material food, so is the soul nourished by spiritual food, since "not in bread alone doth man live, but in every word that proceedeth from the mouth of God" [Matt. 4:4]. It often happens that bishops, on account of their manifold duties or bodily infirmities or because of hostile invasions or other reasons, to say nothing of lack of learning, which must be absolutely condemned in them and is not to be tolerated in the future, are themselves unable to minister the word of God to the people, especially in large and widespread dioceses. Wherefore we decree that bishops provide suitable men, powerful in work and word, to exercise with fruitful result the office of preaching; who in place of the bishops, since these cannot do it, diligently visiting the people committed to them, may instruct them by word and example. And when they are in need, let them be supplied with the necessities, lest for want of these they may be compelled to abandon their work at the very beginning. Wherefore we command that in cathedral churches as well as in conventual churches suitable men be appointed whom the bishops may use as coadjutors and assistants, not only in the office of preaching but also in hearing confessions, imposing penances, and in other matters that pertain to the salvation of souls. If anyone neglect to comply with this, he shall be subject to severe punishment....

Canon 14. That the morals and general conduct of clerics may be better reformed, let all strive to live chastely and virtuously, particularly those in sacred orders, guarding against every vice of desire, especially that on account of which the anger of God came from heaven upon the children of unbelief, so that in the sight of almighty God they may perform their duties with a pure heart and chaste body. But lest the facility to obtain pardon be an incentive to do wrong, we decree that whoever shall be found to indulge in the vice of [sexual] incontinence, shall, in proportion to the gravity of his sin, be punished in accordance with the canonical statutes, which we command to be strictly and rigorously observed, so that he whom divine fear does not restrain from evil, may at least be withheld from sin by a temporal penalty. If therefore anyone suspended for this reason shall presume to celebrate the divine mysteries, let him not only be deprived of his ecclesiastical benefices but for this twofold offense let him be forever deposed. Prelates who dare support such in their iniquities, especially in view of money or other temporal advantages, shall be subject to a like punishment. But if those, who according to the practice of their country [the Latin East] have not renounced the conjugal bond, fall by the vice of impurity, they are to be punished more severely, since they can use matrimony lawfully.

Canon 15. All clerics shall carefully abstain from drunkenness. Wherefore, let them accommodate the wine to themselves, and themselves to the wine. Nor shall anyone be encouraged to drink, for drunkenness banishes reason and incites to lust. We decree, therefore, that that abuse be absolutely abolished by which in some localities the drinkers bind themselves in their manner to an equal portion of drink and he in their judgment is the hero of the day who outdrinks the others. Should anyone be culpable in this matter, unless he heeds the warning of the superior and makes suitable satisfaction, let him be suspended from his benefice or office.

We forbid hunting and fowling to all clerics: wherefore, let them not presume to keep dogs and birds for these purposes.

Canon 16. Clerics shall not hold secular offices or engage in secular and, above all, dishonest pursuits. They shall not attend the performances of mimes, entertainers (*ioculatores*), or actors (*histriones*). They shall not visit taverns except in case of necessity, namely when on a journey. They are forbidden to play dice or games of chance or be present at them. They must have a becoming shaved crown and tonsure and apply themselves diligently to the study of the divine office and other useful subjects. Their garments must be worn clasped at the top and neither too short nor too long. They are not to use red or green [cloth] or [long sleeves, or embroidered or pointed] shoes or gilded bridles, saddles, breastplates for their horses, spurs, or anything else indicative of superfluity. At the divine office in the church they are not to wear cloaks with long sleeves, and priests and dignitaries may not wear them elsewhere except in case of danger when circumstances should require a change of outer garments. Buckles may under no condition be worn, nor [belts ornamented in] gold or silver, nor rings unless it be in keeping with the dignity of their office. All bishops must use in public and in the church outer garments made of linen, except those who were monks, in which case they must wear the habit of their order; in public they must not appear with open mantles, but these must be clasped either on the back of the neck or on the chest....

Canon 20. We decree that in all churches the chrism and the eucharist be kept in properly protected places provided with locks and keys, so that they may not be reached by rash and indiscreet persons and used for impious and blasphemous purposes. But if he to whom such guardianship pertains should leave them unprotected, let him be suspended from office for a period of three months. And if through his negligence an execrable deed should result, let him be punished more severely.

Canon 21. All the faithful of both sexes shall after they have reached the age of discretion [i.e., early teenage] faithfully confess all their sins at least once a year to their own [parish] priest and perform to the best of their ability the penance imposed, receiving reverently at least at Easter the sacrament of the eucharist, unless perchance at the advice of their own priest they may for a good reason abstain for a time from its reception; otherwise they shall be [barred from entering] the church during life and deprived of Christian burial in death. Wherefore, let this salutary decree be published frequently in the churches, that no one may find in the plea of ignorance a shadow of excuse. But if anyone for good reason should wish to confess his sins to another priest, let him first seek and obtain permission from his own priest, since otherwise the other priest cannot absolve or bind him.

Let the priest be discreet and cautious that he may pour wine and oil into the wounds of the one injured in the manner of a skillful physician, carefully inquiring into the circumstances of the sinner and the sin, from the nature of which he may understand what kind of advice to give and what kind of remedy to apply, making use of different means to heal the sick one. But let him exercise the greatest precaution that he does not in any degree by word, sign, or any other manner make known the sinner, but should he need more prudent counsel, let him seek it cautiously without any mention of the person. He who dares to reveal a sin confided to him in the tribunal of penance, we decree that he be not only deposed from the priestly office but also relegated to a monastery of strict observance to do penance for the remainder of his life....

Canon 27. Since the direction of souls (*regimen animarum*) is the art of arts, we strictly command that bishops, either themselves or through other qualified men, diligently prepare and instruct those to be elevated to the priesthood in the divine offices and in the proper administration of the sacraments of the church. If in the future they presume to ordain ignorant and uninformed men (a defect that can be easily discovered), we decree that both those ordaining and those ordained be subject to severe punishment. In the ordination of priests especially, it is better to have a few good ministers than many who are no good, "for if the blind lead the blind, both will fall into the pit" [Matt. 15:14]....

Canon 51. Since the prohibition of the conjugal union in the three last degrees [of family relationship] has been revoked, we wish that it be strictly observed in the other degrees. Whence, following in the footsteps of our predecessors, we absolutely forbid clandestine marriages [i.e., done without witnesses]; and we forbid also that a priest presume to witness such. Wherefore, extending to other localities generally the particular custom that prevails in some, we decree that when marriages are to be contracted they must be announced publicly in the churches by the priests during a suitable and fixed time, so that if legitimate impediments exist, they may be made known. Let the priests nevertheless investigate whether any impediments exist. But when there is ground for doubt concerning the contemplated union, let the marriage be expressly forbidden until it is evident from reliable sources what ought to be done in regard to it. But if anyone should presume to contract a clandestine or forbidden marriage of this kind within a prohibited degree, even through ignorance, the children from such a union shall be considered illegitimate, nor shall the ignorance of the parents be pleaded as an extenuating circumstance in their behalf, since they by contracting such marriages appear not as wanting in knowledge but rather as affecting ignorance. In like manner the children shall be considered illegitimate if both parents, knowing that a legitimate impediment exists, presume to contract such a marriage in the witness of the church in disregard of every prohibition. The parochial priest who deliberately neglects to forbid such unions or any regular [i.e., monastic] priest who presumes to witness them, let them be suspended from office for a period of three years and, if the nature of their offense demands it, let them be punished more severely. On those also who presume to contract such marriages in a lawful degree, a condign punishment is to be imposed. If anyone maliciously presents an impediment for the purpose of frustrating a legitimate marriage, let him not escape ecclesiastical punishment....

Canon 62. From the fact that some expose for sale and exhibit promiscuously the relics of the saints, great injury is sustained by the Christian religion. That this may not occur hereafter, we ordain in the present decree that in the future old relics may not be exhibited outside of a vessel or exposed for sale. And let no one presume to venerate publicly new ones unless they have been approved by the Roman pontiff. In the future prelates shall not permit those who come to their churches [for the sake of venerating relics] to be deceived by worthless fabrications or false documents as has been done in many places for the sake of gain. We forbid also that seekers (*quaestores*) of alms, some of whom, misrepresenting themselves, preach certain abuses, be admitted, unless they exhibit genuine letters either of the Apostolic See or of the diocesan bishop, in which case they may not preach anything to the people but what is contained in those letters. We give herewith a form which the Apostolic See commonly uses in granting such letters, that the diocesan bishops may model their own upon it. This is it:

> Since, as the Apostle says, "we shall all stand before the judgment seat of Christ" [Rom. 14:10] to exhibit what we have "done in the body, be it good or evil" [2 Cor. 5:10], we should prepare for the day of Last Judgment through the works of mercy, and, mindful of eternal things, we should sow on earth what we ought to reap in heaven – the Lord returning these fruits to us multiplied – holding the firm hope and trust that "He who soweth sparingly, shall also reap sparingly: and he who soweth in blessings, shall also reap blessings" for eternal life [2 Cor. 9:6]. Therefore, since its resources are insufficient to support the brothers of a certain hospice and the needy flocking there, we admonish and exhort all of you in the Lord and enjoin you in remission of

your sins that, from the goods God has given you, you give them pious alms and the welcome aid of charity so that through your help their need is looked after, and, through this and the other good deeds that you have done with the Lord's inspiration, you come to eternal joy.

Those who are assigned to collect alms must be upright and discreet, must not seek lodging for the night in taverns or in other unbecoming places, nor make useless and extravagant expenses, and must avoid absolutely the wearing of the habit of a false religious.

Since, through indiscreet and superfluous indulgences which some prelates of churches do not hesitate to grant, contempt is brought on the keys of the church, and the penitential discipline is weakened, we decree that on the occasion of the dedication of a church an indulgence of not more than one year may be granted, whether it be dedicated by one bishop only or by many, and on the anniversary of the dedication the remission granted for penances enjoined is not to exceed forty days. We command also that in each case this number of days be made the rule in issuing letters of indulgences which are granted from time to time, since the Roman pontiff who possesses the plenitude of power customarily observes this rule in such matters....

Canon 68. In some provinces a difference of dress distinguishes the Jews and Saracens from the Christians, but in others confusion has developed to such a degree that no difference is discernible. Whence it happens sometimes through error that Christians mingle with the women of Jews and Saracens, and, on the other hand, Jews and Saracens mingle with those of the Christians. Therefore, that such religious commingling through error of this kind may not serve as a refuge for further excuse for excesses, we decree that such people of both sexes (that is, Jews and Saracens) in every Christian province and at all times be distinguished in public from other people by a difference in dress, since this was also enjoined on them by Moses. On the days of Lamentation and on Passion Sunday they may not appear in public, because some of them, as we understand, on those days are not ashamed to show themselves more ornately attired and do not fear to amuse themselves at the expense of Christians, who in memory of the sacred passion go about attired in robes of mourning. That we most strictly forbid, lest they should presume in some measure to burst forth in contempt of the Redeemer. And, since we ought not be ashamed of him who blotted out our offenses, we command that the secular princes restrain presumptuous persons of this kind by condign punishment, lest they presume to blaspheme in some degree the one crucified for us.

What is the Council's ideal of the Christian church? What abuses in Christian life does it seek to correct? How does it strive to mold the clergy into a professional class? What are its expectations for lay people's participation in Christianity?

3. A HANDBOOK FOR PARISH PRIESTS (1385)

In the chain stretching from the leaders of the church to ordinary Christians, the parish priest was the crucial link. For most people in most places, he was the church's voice; his parishioners were apt to know no more about the finer points of Christianity than what he knew. Though there never was a uniform or universal program for educating medieval priests, the church's leaders knew that ignorant clergy threatened the Christian mission. One biblical verse was always on their lips: "If the blind lead the blind, both will fall into the ditch" [Matt. 15:14]. One remedy to priestly ignorance was brief handbooks encapsulating the core beliefs and practices of the faith. The English curate William of Pagula wrote a widely used manual of instruction for parish priests called the Oculus sacerdotis *(or* Priest's Eye*) between 1320-23. In the mid-1380s the following brief set of instructions was lifted from that much larger work and circulated independently. Though the work is English in origin, almost all of its admonitions are cited verbatim from the general canon law of church, so they represent knowledge that priests and parishioners across Europe were expected to know. Though William cites each admonition's source in canon law (Gratian's* Decretum, *the* Liber Extra, *the* Sext, *the* Clementines*), these are omitted in this translation, drawn from an early fifteenth-century manuscript.*

Source: trans. J. Shinners from Oxford, Bodleian Library MS Bodl. 424, ff. 155r-157v. Latin.

[1.] A parish priest should recommend as many things to his parishioners on Sundays as seem useful to him for their instruction, and he should repeat them often so they will not slip from memory. First he should teach them the formula for baptizing infants in the absence of a priest if it becomes necessary. This is the vernacular version: *I crysten thee in the name of the fadyr and the sone and the holyghost.* While saying this, sprinkle water over the child or immerse it in water three times or at the very least once. Anyone, whether cleric or lay person, may baptize a child in an emergency. Even the father of the child or its mother may do so without putting restrictions on their conjugal relations unless there is someone else present who knows how and wishes to do it. And if someone must baptize a child in an emergency using the above formula, he should speak the words distinctly and clearly only once, in no manner repeating the words of the rite or anything like them over the child. And if an infant baptized in this manner recovers, it should be taken to the church, and those who bring it should tell the priest that the child was baptized at home so that the priest will not baptize it again. But, excluding the immersion in water, he should perform the exorcism, the anointing, and the other customary actions that accompany baptism but were omitted. Let the priest teach his parishioners that they should baptize using only water, no other liquids. Likewise let him warn men and women who are appointed the godparents of children at baptism that, except in an emergency, they should not delay having their godchildren confirmed by a bishop. They should teach them or have them be taught the Lord's Prayer and the Creed, and admonish them when they reach adulthood or are capable of learning that they should guard their chastity, love justice, and practice charity.

The baptism of children born within eight days before Easter or Pentecost should be postponed for a week if it is convenient and they may be held back without danger, and then they should be baptized.

[2.] He should also warn them that anyone who has children who are not confirmed should make arrangements to have them confirmed by the time they are five years old if it is possible.

[3.] Also he should warn them that they should never put their children in bed with them in case through negligence they should roll over and smother them, which would be reckoned a case of homicide according to canon law. Nor should they thoughtlessly bind them in swaddling clothes or leave them alone by day or by night without someone watching them because of various dangers.

[4.] Also the priest should teach his parishioners that a spiritual kinship is established among godparents, godchildren, and the parents of the godchildren. The same is true for sponsors at confirmation. Because of this kinship, marriage between any of these parties is prohibited. A spiritual kinship is established among ten people in baptism and the same number in confirmation [i.e., the child, its parents, godparents, and immediate relatives].

[5.] He should also teach them that if a man and a woman shall have given their legitimate consent to contract a marriage by an exchange of words in the present tense (*verba de presenti*), even though there has been no betrothal but only an oath, and even though, as is the custom, no carnal relations have occurred, still they have contracted a true marriage — so much so that if afterwards one of them should contract a second marriage and even have carnal relations with the new partner, they should be separated and that person should return to the first marriage. Also he should teach them that marriages should not be contracted except in the presence of a priest and legitimate witnesses. Prior to the marriage ceremony banns should be solemnly published to the people in the church on three consecutive feast days. And any cleric or priest or other person who is present at a clandestine marriage [i.e., done without witnesses] shall be suspended from his office for three years.

[6.] Also he should warn them that boys and girls older than seven years should not lie together in the same bed because of the danger of fornication, nor should a brother share a bed with his sister because of the danger of incest.

[7.] Also he should publicly announce that any member of the faithful who has reached the age of discretion [twelve for girls, fourteen for boys according to William of Pagula] ought to confess all his sins to his own parish priest at least once a year and he should fulfill the penance imposed on him for his vices. During Eastertide he should receive the body of Christ unless, with the counsel of his priest, for some reason he should abstain; otherwise while he is alive he should be barred from entering a church, and when he dies he should be denied Christian burial. But if anyone does not wish to confess to his parish priest for a specific and well-founded reason, he should seek and obtain permission from his own priest to confess to another suitable priest.

[8.] Also he should teach them that pregnant women should be confessed beforehand so that they are prepared to receive the eucharist if life-threatening danger should arise during their delivery, since it would seem improper for the priest to stay with them [to hear their confession] during the course of their labor.

[9.] Also he should teach his parishioners that when the host is elevated during the consecration of the mass, they should genuflect if they can comfortably do so, and, adoring the host, they should say in a low voice: "Hail salvation of the world, Word of the Father, true sacrifice, living flesh, fully God, truly man" or "Glory to you Lord who is born" or the Lord's Prayer or some other devout words. And they should also do this when they see the body of Christ, preceded by lights and a ringing bell, carried to the sick [by a priest].

[10.] Also he should warn his parishioners that they should faithfully pay their tithes on goods legitimately acquired. For faithfully paying tithes brings a fourfold reward: the first is an abundance of crops; the second is bodily health according to Augustine; the third is the remission of sins; the fourth is reward in the kingdom of heaven. But those who tithe badly are punished in four ways: first because they transgress a divine commandment. Second because in the past those who tithed [voluntarily] from all their goods enjoyed an abundance; but now because they tithe badly, the tithe [is] enforced on them. Third, when tithes are poorly paid, God does not ward off locusts or other harmful things, nor does he dispel plagues or bring rain, except short-lived ones. Fourth, because of the failure to tithe, men rightfully collect taxes and tolls from the people since what Christ does not take, the royal treasury (*fiscus*) will. Besides, those who do not pay their tithes are cursed by God. And merchants and artisans as much as carpenters, blacksmiths, weavers, ale-wives and other such people, and all other hired laborers and boon laborers all ought to be admonished to pay tithes from their earnings or else reach a settlement with the rector of their church.

[11.] And the priest ought to announce to his people which days are feast days and which are days of fast.

[12.] Also he should instruct his parishioners that they should not practice magical arts, incantations, or sorcery since these things have no power to cure either man or beast and besides are utterly worthless and unlawful. Moreover clerics who do these things shall be degraded and lay people shall be excommunicated.

[13.] Also he should warn everyone not to lend money, grain, wine, oil or any other thing whatsoever by usury; namely by entering into a contract or having the intention to receive back more in repayment than he lent out. And if a cleric shall do this he shall be suspended from office; and a lay person shall be excommunicated until he makes restitution. To be sure, usury is forbidden in both the Old and the New Testaments.

[14.] He should also warn his parishioners that they should not wait in order to sell their goods at a higher price, for they are obliged to repay what they have gained by this type of withholding. Likewise they should not sell their goods to travelers, pilgrims, and other wayfarers for a higher price than they charge to their neighbors or than they can receive at market.

[15.] Let him also warn them that if anyone shall receive land or a dwelling as a pledge for a loan of money, after deducting his expenses, he should return the pledge; and if he receives more than that, it is to be reckoned as usury.

[16.] Also he shall publicly announce three times yearly that all those men who wish to enjoy the [legal] privileges of the clergy shall be duly tonsured, displaying the crown of their head suitably shaved especially in the presence of their ordinaries [clerical superiors] and in churches and in congregations of the clergy.

[17.] Also one day during Lent he should publicly preach the Creed, that is to say, the articles of faith.

[18.] And he should admonish his parishioners that they should enter church humbly and devoutly and should behave reverently, peacefully, and devoutly while in it. And when they hear named the name of Jesus they should genuflect at the very least in their hearts, or by bowing their head or striking their breast.

[19.] He should admonish them that no one should cause a disturbance or a disagreement, or hold discussions or idle and profane conversations in a church or its graveyard; nor should they provoke disputes or fights or anything else that could interrupt the divine services or dishonor the holiness of the place. Likewise business should not be conducted in the church or its graveyard and especially not fairs or markets, nor should courts, pleas, or secular judgments be held there. And dishonorable dances should not take place there, nor should improper songs be sung during the vigils of saints' days or at other times, nor should there take place anything else by which the church or the graveyard could be dishonored.

[20.] Also he should instruct them that neither a husband nor a wife should make an oath swearing to practice chastity, to fast, or to go on pilgrimage (except for a vow to go to the Holy Land) without the consent of the other. For a man and a wife are to be judged as equals in this regard.

[21.] He should also warn his parishioners that no one should harbor or defend in his home anyone who he knows has committed a known robbery.

How informed about their faith does this manual expect Christians to be? What sources of religious instruction does the manual assume are available to lay people? Is the manual more concerned with the dogmatic or the moral instruction of lay people? In general, to what kind of faults does the manual assume people are prone?

4. A TRACT ON HEARING CONFESSIONS
(c. 1224-37)

*In the wake of the Fourth Lateran Council's (Doc. 2) stress on the need for the professional training of parish priests, many leaders and thinkers of the church wrote short manuals of instruction intended to aid priests in performing their pastoral duties (Doc. 3). Since the Council mandated yearly confession for all Christians in its famous Canon 21, these pastoral manuals often addressed the subtleties of administering that sacrament successfully. Finesse in handling delicate matters of sin and repentance became even more important as the theory and practice of the sacrament evolved in the course of the twelfth century. Earlier handbooks for confessors, called penitentials, typically enumerated often fearsome lists of sins with a fixed penance prescribed for each one (Doc. 70). Newer manuals such as the following "Tract on [Hearing] Confessions" (*Quidam Tractatus de Confessionibus*) stressed the need to fit the penance to the character of the sinner, a task that demanded considerable psychological discernment. This tract was inserted into the statutes that Bishop Alexander Stavensby compiled for his diocese of Coventry and Lichfield in England around 1224-37. It suggests what sort of interrogation and spiritual counsel a lay person might hope to encounter with a well-trained pastor. It is worth noting that the confessional box with a partition between penitent and confessor that offered a degree of comforting anonymity was an innovation of the sixteenth century; medieval people confessed face-to-face to their priest, usually while he sat on a stool and they kneeled or sat on the floor at his feet.*

Source: trans. J. Shinners from F.M. Powicke and C.R. Cheney (eds.), *Councils & Synods with other Documents relating to the English Church* (Oxford: Clarendon Press, 1964), pt. II, v. 1, pp. 220-26. Latin.

A Certain Tract on Confessions

Since penance consists of three things – contrition of heart, confession by words, and satisfaction through works – the first thing to ask someone coming to confession is whether he is sorry that he sinned, because without contrition of the heart sin can never be remitted. If he says that he is sorry then the priest may proceed to hear the confession; if he says that he is not sorry he should be sent away as an obstinate sinner.

To hear a confession proceed in this manner, saying: "Brother or sister, you wish to be confessed of your sins. Do you have it in mind that hereafter, insofar as you can with the grace of God, you will not sin mortally?" If he says "I do not," then say to him that his confession is worthless. For thus says the wise man: "He that shall confess his sins, and forsake them, shall obtain mercy" [Prov. 28:13]. Someone may be understood to relinquish sin who has it in mind not to sin again with the grace of God.

Continue with the confession in this manner: Say to the penitent that there are chiefly three things that usually hinder someone from making a true confession: the pleasure of sin, the fear of the punishment that will follow, and shame. But a priest should explain how brief the pleasure of sin is due to which [the sinner] loses the reward of eternal joy. Against the fear of punishment that the penitent has, let the priest show him that unless he does penance in this life, his sin will be punished with eternal pains. Against his shame, show him that shame is the greatest part of penance. Therefore, he ought not to hold back because of his shame since he is telling his sin not to a man but to God who examines both the heart and the mind. Let him speak, therefore, in the Lord's name. Having heard all these things, the priest should ask him whether he has examined his conscience. If he says yes, then let him proceed to confess. If he says no, then the priest should supply those things that the penitent omits, just as it is written: "The just is first accuser of himself: his friend cometh and shall search him" [Prov. 18:17]. The just man (that is, the penitent) first ought to accuse himself. Afterwards his friend (that is, the priest) ought to inquire about those sins he omitted. If he is a layman, the priest should first ask whether he is married or single. If he is married, he should be asked whether he believes his marriage is legitimate – in other words, that between him and his wife there is no common paternity, consanguinity, or spiritual affinity, or any other marital impediment – and whether they legitimately contracted their marriage before the church. If he finds that this is not so, the priest should consult the archdeacon or the bishop.

Next the penitent should be asked what his occupation is. If he is a merchant – man or woman – he should see to it that he does not use false weights or measures. And if he has used false measures, he is bound to make restitution through the hands of the priest to the one he deceived. If he cannot remember whom he deceived, the ill-gotten money should be given to the poor at the discretion of the church. Lay people should generally be asked about their tithing because if they have tithed badly (as they are accustomed to do) they should seek pardon from the rector of the church either personally or through another if they are ashamed to do so themselves. A priest should particularly ask knights (*milites*) and those who are in charge of households (especially of poor servants) whether they have unjustly taken anything from those under them which they ought to give back. Priests should ask penitents, whether married or single, about the seven deadly sins and deal with them according to what is contained above in the tract on the seven sins [*omitted here*]. And everyone should especially be asked about bearing false witness. Women should be asked about using poisons and sorcery (*veneficiis et sortilegiis*). Single people should be asked whether they are willing to live chastely until they take a spouse; otherwise their confession has no value. Similarly, married people should be asked about the carnal sins they committed before they were married. They should be made aware that due to the obligation owed to nature, they should have relations with their wives; otherwise they sin against marriage.

A priest should make a brief interrogation of those whose flesh is weak in the following manner: "Either you knew that the woman whom you approached for sex was unmarried or you didn't. If you knew she was single, you are due a lesser penance; if you didn't know then you are obliged to do a greater penance because she might have been a married woman, a nun, or related to you through affinity, or she may have had relations with your father." (Likewise, prostitutes are prone to lie with lepers which can endanger their unborn children or their own health.) Also, they should be asked about the number of people they sinned with and the number of times if they can remember. Also whether they had sexual relations with widows who have taken religious vows, with virgins, with married people, or with nuns. Then they should be asked whether it was with a professed nun because those who have relations with nuns must be sent to the bishop for absolution since a bishop customarily excommunicates such people. If perhaps they do not wish to go to the bishop, the priest should go to the bishop and get his authorization. Likewise, if they had sexual relations with someone related to them by blood or through a spiritual affinity they should be asked in what degree they are related: removed or near. They should be asked whether they had sexual relations with a pregnant woman or a menstruating woman (which is dangerous due to the child that is born since a corrupted fetus is conceived by corrupted semen). Likewise, whether they had relations with a woman near childbirth, for then there is a danger that the infant could be killed. Also ask them whether they had relations with another man or with animals. And this penance should be enjoined on those who had relations with animals above and beyond any other penances that are enjoined: they must never eat that animal's meat. To sum it up briefly: Whenever semen is spilled it is a mortal sin except if it happens when one is sleeping or with one's own wife (and then this must be done legitimately according to the needs of nature). According to the diversity of the circumstances a variety of penances should be enjoined.

It is not proper to ask all of these questions of everyone, but the priest should make these inquiries as God inspires him. There should be one general rule: those consenting to commit mortal sins, whoever they are, sin mortally, although never so gravely as those actually committing the sin. But if restitution is appropriate, one who consents to the sin is obliged to make restitution; and someone who consents to fornication – whether man or woman – should be punished the same as someone committing [this] mortal sin.

Here is how to deal with gluttony and drunkenness. These conditions should be born in mind for gluttony: [eating food] too soon, too lavishly, too much, too eagerly, too daintily. Too soon means in the manner of Jonathan, son of Saul, who ate before the appointed hour and so sinned gravely [I Kings 14:27]. Too lavishly, as the Jews in the desert who, not content with manna, asked the Lord for meat [Num. 11:4-6]. Too much, as the Sodomites, whose sin was an abundance of bread [Ez. 16:49]. Too eagerly, as Esau, who ate a common thing (lentils) too eagerly and as a result sold his birthright [Gen. 25:34]. Daintily, as the sons of Eli, who were too painstaking over their food [I Kings 2:13-15]. These vices should always be avoided, but especially during Lent.

Drunkenness, if it is habitual, is a mortal sin. Thus, the Apostle says "Drunkards will not possess the kingdom of God" [I Cor. 6:10], that is, those habitually drunk. And learned men sensibly judge as drunk those whose wits or senses are scrambled due to too much drinking. In fact, certain authorities say that getting drunk even once is a mortal sin if someone deliberately, with immoderate excess, consumes more food or drink than he thinks useful for his nature; to the contrary, it burdens his nature. But I do not presume to define what this limit is. However, it should be noted that not every excess beyond what is licit is a mortal sin: only that which is immoderate and frequent is mortally sinful. This is what Augustine says in one book of his *Confessions*: "Who is the man who does not sometimes exceed the limits of what is necessary? If such a man exists, he is great; let him magnify God. I am not that kind of man; I am a sinner" [*Conf.* 10, 31].

Generally in every confession the circumstances that are noted in this phrase should be considered: *Who, what, where, with whose help, why, how, and when. Who* means to consider what sort of person [the sinner is], whether a cleric or a layman; if a cleric, whether regular [i.e., monastic] or secular; whether he holds some high office or not; whether he is in [major] sacred orders or not. If he is a member of a religious order, at what level of profession is he? Consider whether he is young or old, whether he is of servile status or free. *What* means that the type of sin must be considered: whether it is simple fornication, or adultery, or incest, whether it was committed with clerics, because the type of sin aggravates the gravity of the sin. *Where* means to consider where the sin was committed: on consecrated ground or not. *With whose help* means to consider which things were done willingly, which were compelled; whether something was done wholly from one's own will or whether with another's counsel or threat; whether it happened by chance or with deliberation. Many other things could be asked. *Why* means to consider the end for which something was done. Usually three ends can be distinguished: a useful one, an honest one, and an enjoyable one. Many people commit sins for useful ends; many people commit sins for enjoyable ones; but no one can commit a sin for an honest end. *How* means to consider the diverse means that accompany various types of sin. The diverse means that accompany sins of the flesh should be quite apparent from what was said above; inquiry is especially needed for these. *When* means to consider the time when the sin was committed: whether during Lent, whether on a feast day or on the eve of a feast. And if it happened on a feast day, consider that if it was during a major feast then there should be a suitable penance – for instance, that the penitent fast on bread and water during the vigil of the solemnity of the feast, especially if he committed a sin of the flesh.

The interrogation of a member of the clergy should proceed in this manner: The priest should determine whether the cleric was born from a legitimate marriage and is of free status. He should find out what sacred order [of the seven] he is in and how he received holy orders, whether legitimately, secretly, or through simony, and if he received them from his own bishop. If he received sacred orders secretly a bishop can give him dispensation unless he said "Under pain of excommunication we forbid anyone from receiving sacred orders who is not legitimately presented." Pope Innocent III considered a cleric to be excommunicated in this case only; in other instances it is a warning. A bishop cannot give dispensation to someone in the first case, nor can he dispense a simoniac; only the pope can do this. Also ask a cleric whether he received a benefice out of regard for God; if it was because of God, does he hold it in order to promote the salvation of souls? If not, he should cleanse his soul, and if he entered the benefice without the taint of simony, he may keep it, but he should be fearful nonetheless.

What follows concerns satisfaction. Because penances ought to be arbitrary, we will not define for you any specific penances which you should enjoin. Still, you should know that satisfaction chiefly has three elements: fasting, prayer, and almsgiving. Thus, Tobias says: "Prayer is good with fasting and almsgiving" [Tob. 12:8]. Prayer, if it has these two wings, fasting and almsgiving, is like a bird that flies on high. Fasting is valuable against carnal vices and should be imposed for sins of the flesh. Prayer should be directed for spiritual sins. Thus, [St.] Jerome says: "Fasting heals the plagues of the body; prayer, the plagues of the mind. Almsgiving avails against all sins." And thus says Daniel: "Redeem thou thy sins with alms" [Dan. 4:24]; it ought to be enjoined for all sins. You should take care, therefore, that you do not give leave to those foolish doctors who hope to cure every illness with one ointment: what does not heal the eye heals the foot. Indeed, just as we once yielded our members as slaves of iniquity unto iniquity, so now we should yield them as slaves of justice unto sanctification [see Rom. 6:19]. For instance, if someone sinned with his mouth by making false pleas or swearing falsely, he should be directed to pray and to defend the poor against those whom he helped defraud them in honest lawsuits. Or if someone sinned by being miserly, because of his greed he should be directed to give alms generously. If he sinned by wickedly fighting against the innocent, he should be directed to fight against the dangerous, namely heretics and Saracens. If he sinned through the loins, direct him to gird his loins with a leather belt [Mk. 1:6] and to fast and remove that which nourishes lust. And so for all types of sins, their opposites should be enjoined. Because the most common sin is gluttony, some kind of fasting should always be imposed as penance. And a priest should always ask all penitents whether they are under a sentence of excommunication for arson or for striking anyone in sacred orders [which incurred automatic excommunication]. However there are cases where striking a cleric does not incur the canonical sentence of excommunication; namely, if the cleric is a minor; if he is struck in a joking fashion; if a superior or a teacher strikes someone in order to discipline him; if the person struck is a degraded cleric; if an innocent person uses moderate force to repel an immoderate attack in self-defense; if someone discovers a cleric in a scandalous situation with his sister, mother, daughter, or wife and does not realize he is a cleric; if he is an apostate; if he is an agent administering the affairs of lay people; if a cleric interrupting the divine office is struck while being expelled from the church; if he is struck at the command of a clerical superior; or if he is struck while bearing arms in utter contempt of his clerical status. These distinctions should be made [in judging whether someone has violated the *privilegium canonis*]. Furthermore, in the following cases, a person who strikes a cleric may be absolved by someone other than the pope: if a door-keeper under the pretext of carrying out his office maliciously injures a cleric; if the person who strikes the cleric is old, a woman, weak, poor, blind, or lame; or if because of war or some other cause the person cannot go to the pope. (But when these causes have stopped, he should still go to the pope for absolution.) Likewise, a dying person may be absolved by someone other than the pope; so may a cleric who lightly strikes another cleric. A serf may be so absolved if he deceitfully strikes a cleric so that by going to Rome for absolution he may remove himself from obedience to his lord or cause the lord himself to suffer a loss because of the absence of his servant. Also, a person in poor health may be absolved by someone other than the pope, as long as he is warned that he must go to the pope when he has recovered his health.

People who are excommunicated should be especially avoided in five circumstances: at the dining table, during prayers, in greetings, at the kiss of peace [during mass], and in conversation. Regarding those occasions that do not lead to excommunication, there are four in which people having contact with those who are excommunicated do not themselves incur excommunication: occasions of necessity, piety, utility, and ignorance. There are two kinds of necessity, one domestic and one circumstantial. Domestic necessity applies to those people for whom Pope Gregory VII made exceptions in the canon *Quoniam multos* [*Decretum*, C. 11, q. 3, c. 103]. These are wives, children, servants, etc. Circumstantial necessity applies to a pilgrim passing through a place where people are excommunicated who can find no one else from whom to buy the necessities of life. [*The following sentences are highly abbreviated in the original text.*] [An occasion of] piety [does not incur excommunication], if someone [excommunicated is] about to perish [and] is saved through our help. [An occasion of] utility [does not incur the sentence], inasmuch as an excommunicated person should be admonished to make amends and those [wrong] things that he still upholds are discussed with [him]. [An occasion of] ignorance [means that someone may unknowingly have contact with an excommunicated person so long as his ignorance is] plausible [and not the result of] his indolence. Someone [has summed it up with these catchwords]: "Utility, wife, servant, law, humbly, things unknown and things necessary." All of these things are, without prejudice, the opinions of a quite sensible man. Amen.

If you were a penitent being confessed according to the instructions in this manual would you come away from the experience spiritually comforted? Is the approach to administering penance here more psychological, theological, or legal? Does the method outlined here confirm the adage that "confession is good for the soul"? What kind of knowledge about Christianity does this manual assume of ordinary Christians?

5. A SERMON ON THE ARTICLES OF FAITH
(c. 1410)

Sermons were the principal method the clergy used to instruct people in the rudiments of Christianity. The following outline of basic Christian belief comes from a book of sermons assembled at Oxford, probably in the first decade of the fifteenth century. Some are in Latin, some in Middle English; some are model sermons, others are tran-

scriptions of actual sermons. The twelve articles of faith, each attributed by medieval tradition to one of the apostles, could vary. Here, for example, there is no mention of the belief in the Holy Spirit as the third person of the Trinity.

Source: modernized by J. Shinners from Woodburn O. Ross, *Middle English Sermons*, Early English Text Society, Original Series, No. 209 (London: Humphrey Milford, Oxford University Press, 1940), pp. 12-15. Middle English.

"Attend, O my people, to my law" [Ps. 77:1].

Good men and women, our Lord God Jesus by his prophet commands all Christian people to understand and know his law, which all who shall come to heaven need in order to be saved, and by no other way. For Christ himself says in the Gospel, "He who believes in his law and follows it shall be saved, but he who will not believe shall be condemned" [see Mark 16:16]. This is God's own law, which we call Holy Writ; this law suffices to govern the people of God. In the Psalms, David writes of this law, "*Lex Domini immaculata*," etc. — "the law of our Lord," he says, "is without blemish, turning souls to good" [Ps. 18 (19):8]. This law should "be more desired than gold" or silver or any other precious thing, for it is "sweeter than any honey or the honeycomb." "Truly," says David furthermore, "all your servants keep this law, for in keeping it there is great reward" [see Ps. 18 (19):11-12]. This is the law that our Lord God, by the words of my theme, bids everyone to understand.

"Sir," perhaps you say, "you priests and prelates of the holy church forbid any uneducated man to meddle in Holy Writ." No sir, I say; but it is forbidden for any uneducated man to *misuse* Holy Writ, for God himself bids his people to understand it. If his people are to understand it, they must concern themselves with it; and if God bids you to know or understand it, truly, I dare not forbid you to meddle in it. You are bound to meddle in this law on pain of everlasting damnation, for you must know the Our Father, which is in the Gospel; the Hail Mary; the Creed; the Ten Commandments; and to fulfill the seven works of mercy, corporal and spiritual, to the best of your ability according to the determination of holy church. God give us grace, then, to know and keep his law well....

Sirs, understand that the words of my theme are the words of our Lord Christ Jesus, spoken to the people by the holy prophet Moses, and in English mean this: "My people, understand my law," as I said before.

I understand many things in this theme. First, he says, "My people" – that is, all you who have received baptism and become Christian men, for Christ is king of them all and they are his people. Furthermore he says, "Understand."

He does not say, "Read my law" only, but "understand it." For those who concern themselves with it without instruction and knowledge, understand it amiss. He also says, "My law shall be magnified above all man's law." Take this to mean that he is the chief lord, that his law surpasses all others. And therefore, David says in the first Psalm, "*Et in lege eius meditabitur die et nocte*" – "a righteous man," he says, "shall think about this law night and day."

But sir, but sir – insofar as God bids every Christian man and woman to understand his law, yet all cannot come to perfect understanding of it because of its subtlety and their worldly occupations by which they must get their sustenance, holy church has ordained that men must especially know and keep the twelve Articles of the Faith, which every Christian must believe; and the Ten Commandments, the seven works of mercy, the [proper use of] the five senses, and abstain from the seven deadly sins; [one must also know] the Our Father.

But inasmuch as St. James says that it is impossible to please God without faith, it is my purpose at this time to speak of the faith contained in the twelve articles. And I pray every man and woman to know and believe it, and I charge you [to know it] on pain of everlasting death if you fail to do so; and do not blame me if you fail.

The first is that God is one substance and three persons within himself, without beginning and end, and he made all things from nothing by his word.

The second is that the Son of God took on flesh and blood from the Virgin Mary through the Holy Ghost without carnal intercourse of man.

The third is that the same Jesus Christ, true God and true man, was born of the Virgin Mary who maintained her whole maidenhood before and after.

The fourth is that the same Jesus Christ, God and man, in the same flesh that he took from the Virgin Mary, suffered hard passion and true death without any damage to his godhood.

The fifth is that the holy body of Jesus Christ lay dead in his sepulcher without its soul until the third day, that he rose, but that the godhood departed neither from the body nor the soul.

The sixth is that when the soul of Jesus Christ departed from the body, it went down to hell and by the power of his godhood delivered the holy souls that were there.

The seventh is that on the third day he rose from death to life in body and soul, both God and man everlasting.

The eighth is this: that he truly ascended into heaven in the flesh of man and lifted mankind above all orders of angels, so that he [Jesus] is equal in his godhood with the Father of heaven in might and power.

The ninth is this: that at the end of the world he shall come and judge both those who are alive and those who are dead, both good and evil.

The tenth is this: that all those who ever lived shall rise in body and soul at the end of the world and they shall never die thereafter.

The eleventh is that the good shall have joy in body and soul everlasting; and the evil, pain without end.

The twelfth is faith in the sacraments of holy church, for every Christian man must believe that the sacraments of holy church have virtue and power to fulfill those things that they were ordained for.

Every Christian ought to believe these twelve articles and that which is contained in them on pain of everlasting damnation. Therefore Christ wishes every Christian to understand this law, as he says to you by the words of my theme: "My people, understand my law," as I said at the beginning.

Sirs, just as Christ is well pleased with every man who knows his law, and the more he knows the better he is pleased, so every uneducated man and laborer is permitted generally to believe all holy church does without further learning. But he may not excuse himself: he must diligently try to know and understand the twelve articles of faith, as I have said them; the Ten Commandments; the five senses; and the seven works of mercy, which God at Doomsday shall especially question us about. Therefore no Christian man may excuse himself from this; he must necessarily keep them and fulfill them. And if we do this truly, then truly at Doomsday we shall understand God's law face to face. May he who died on the Rood Tree grant us this. Amen.

How well does this sermon accomplish its goal? How well would it hold the attention of its audience? What vision of Christian living does it impart?

6. POPULAR SERMONS (1230s & c. 1400)

Though the most common means for lay people to receive regular religious instruction was the sermon, the question of how often they heard sermons is still unsettled. Before the thirteenth century people in the typical country parish had little opportunity to hear preaching since the occasions and techniques to train parish clergy were limited. The spread of the mendicant preaching orders in the early decades of that century broadened those opportunities; so did growing efforts by bishops to encourage their parish clergy to preach at least several times a year. In towns and cities preaching was more frequent.

Certainly by the late fourteenth century anyone living in a town of moderate size prob-
ably had little trouble hearing sermons. They were, for instance, the English religious
eccentric Margery Kempe's chief form of entertainment at the end of the fourteenth
century, as they were for countless other Christians. The two sermons below, one from
the 1230s, the other from the early 1400s, come from collections of sermons meant to
serve as models for preachers. They suggest the sort of subjects and the rhetorical style of
their treatment that more fortunate parishioners might hear. The first sermon, addressed
to children, is by the French bishop Jacques de Vitry (c. 1180-c. 1240), whose many
collected sermons became a gold mine of illustrative moral stories – called exempla *– for*
preachers for the rest of the Middle Ages.

Source: trans. J. Shinners from Jean-Baptiste Cardinal Pitra (ed.), *Analecta Novissima Spicilegii Solesmensis, Altera Continuatio*, v. 2 (Typis Tusculanis, 1888), pp. 439-42. Latin.

1. Sermon 73: For children and young people

The theme is from Proverbs 22: "It is a proverb: A young man according to his way, even when he is old he will not depart from it" [Prov. 22:6].

"The little ones have asked for bread, and there was none to break it unto them" [Lam. 4:4]. With these words, in the fourth chapter of his Lamentations, Jeremiah deplored the lack of learning and instruction that children (*pueri*) and young people – who are easily suited to learning – especially need, just as soft and pliable wax easily receives the impression of a seal. But there are few if any who will preach to them and break unto them the bread of learning. Thus, just as a body that lacks material bread fails, so too do the souls of little children grow weak and wither. As David says, "My heart is withered: because I forgot to eat my bread" [Ps. 101 (102):5].

Seek this bread every day from the Lord when you say, "Give us this day, our daily bread"; and whenever you go to a sermon, before it begins you should pray that God will open your heart to receive the words of life and learning, and you should say the Our Father.

Similarly, when you sit down at the dinner table, at the grace before the meal you should say the Our Father so that by the power of this prayer, accompanied by the sign of the cross, the Lord may guard you from the sin of gluttony. And when the meal is over, you should say the Our Father in thanks. People customarily thank their benefactors or even those who pass them a pitcher of wine; so it would be boorish indeed not to give thanks to the living God for all the good things he gives us.

In the same way, whenever you get into your bed to go to sleep, you should make the sign of the cross and say the Our Father so that while you sleep God will protect you from harassment by demons who unleash bad dreams and nightmares. Whenever children are discovered dead in their bed from sudden death, nothing bad would have happened to them if they had made the sign of the cross and said the Our Father.

When you get out of bed, you should make the sign of the cross and then say the Our Father so that this prayer will watch over everything you do during the whole day. As Jerome says, "For every action, for every undertaking, let your hand draw the cross."

Likewise, whenever you hear the bells toll for the dead, or when you pass by a graveyard, you should always say the Our Father for the souls of the dead, just as you would want someone to do for you if you were dead.

For we shouldn't live like animals but pay careful attention to how we pray. When you enter God's church, after making the sign of the cross you should immediately greet the Lord of the house by kneeling before the altar or the image of the Crucified and giving him thanks, saying, "We adore you, Christ, and we bless you, for by your holy cross you have redeemed the world." Say this five times in honor of him who bore the five wounds for us. And if you don't know how to say this greeting to the crucifix in Latin, say it in your native language.

After greeting the Lord of the house, next you should greet the Lady, kneeling before the image of the Blessed Virgin and saying seven times the angel's greeting, that is, "Hail Mary, full of grace" in honor of her who, filled sevenfold with the Spirit, conceived the Son of God. For she is courtly and kind, and she will return your greeting, perhaps not in words but in deeds.

When you have done this, offer your faith to God and say the Creed, and then any other prayers that God inspires in you.

The blessed [St.] Nicholas (see Doc. 32), who went to church daily with his parents, gives you an example of someone who frequently went to church as a child and young man. And it is said that when St. Martin was twelve years old, his soul was focused either on monasteries or churches.

But there are some people who are so crude and brutish that they go to church scarcely more than once a year when they are obliged to take communion; they don't know how to pray since they haven't learned either the Our Father, the Hail Mary, or the Creed. And when they grow up, they can never learn them thoroughly and completely. They answer just like a certain old stupid and foolish man who was asked if he knew the Our Father; he said, "I know up to the 'hallowed be thy name,' or maybe up to the 'forgive us our trespasses,' but I've never been able to get further than that."

But you should learn these prayers from a tender age. For the prayers of the innocent are especially pleasing to God. Thus, we read in St. Bernard that when he was riding one morning and saw some children in the meadows watching their sheep, he said to his monks, "Let us greet these children. For when they answer and bless us, we can travel safely today defended by the prayers of these innocents."

Therefore never forget these prayers, but say the Our Father frequently, just as I've told you above. And at the beginning of a sermon immediately say the Our Father so that God will open your heart to understand and retain these edifying words and the knowledge of salvation.

"It is a proverb: A young man, etc." It is not easy to break an old habit; it endures just as ancient proverbs last from generation to generation. This is why children should be taught faith and good works from the start, just as Tobias learned from infancy to fear God and avoid sin. In the [thirteenth] chapter of Daniel it says that the parents of Susanna, since they were just, taught her according to the law of Moses [Dan. 13:3]. Thus, Ecclesiasticus says, "Hast thou children? Instruct them, and bow down their neck from their childhood" [Ecclus. 7:25]. And chapter 41 also says, "The children will complain of an ungodly father because for his sake they are in reproach" [Ecclus. 41:10].

Ecclesiasticus 7: "Honor thy father and forget not the groanings of thy mother" [Ecclus. 7:29]. Remember because, except for them, you would not exist; and give back to them as they gave to you: not like the cuckoo who, after the little bird called the blue tit has raised it, kills its foster mother. "Of what an evil fame is he that forsakes his father; and he is cursed of God that angers his mother" [Ecclus. 3:18].

I once heard about a godless man who made his elderly father sleep in a stable and gave him one tattered cloak to wear. The godless man's son was heartbroken about his grandfather, so he went to his father and said, "Father, buy me a cloak." His father said, "Don't you already have enough fine clothes? What do want it for?" "I will store it away," he said, "and when you are old, I will dress you in it. I'll treat you just like you treat my grandfather, your father, who gave you life and raised you, and gave you whatever he had." May such children be blessed who do not consent to their parents' wrongdoing.

I have heard that there was a thief who was being taken to be hanged, hands bound behind his back. He saw his father who was following him weeping and wailing. Calling to him, he said, "My father, give me a kiss." But when he kissed his father, he bit him on the lips so hard that he drew blood, and said, "You are the cause of all my misfortunes because I was your son, and you knew when I started stealing and doing other bad things, but you never whipped or corrected me."

For it is good to teach children carefully from the start. [St.] Basil in particular testifies to this, saying "Just as someone cannot unlearn his native language, he likewise cannot unlearn an ingrained habit." As the verse [of Horace] says, "A new jug will long retain the taste of what it first contained."

Indeed, it is very difficult for children not to be corrupted by bad parents. We read about a certain good man who was quite simple, God-fearing, and worked every day in the field, living moderately from the labor of his hands. But his wife, who stayed at home, spent the whole day eating and drinking with her wantons. Whatever her husband managed to acquire, she spent living luxuriously. Now it happened that the husband died and his wife soon after. They left behind one daughter who began to ponder whether she should imitate her father's way of life or her mother's. The devil put before her eyes a vision of her father's life, which had been terribly rough and hard: he had always lived in travail and misery. But her mother had lived with great pleasures and delight. And now the daughter began leaning toward her mother's way of life. But the next night an angel of the Lord appeared to her in a dream and led her to a stinking and horrible place of torment where she saw her mother among the other damned souls, blackened and completely engulfed by an intolerable fire. Serpents gnawed and tore at all her limbs with the cruelest bites. Then the mother began to cry, almost howling, "Woe is me, daughter! Because of vile and fleeting pleasures, I will be tortured without end and will never have mercy. Take care, my daughter, that you do not follow my wretched and shameless life." After she had seen this, she was led to the loveliest, most glorious place where, in the company of the saints and the blessed spirits, she saw her father as splendid as the sun, crowned with glory and honor. The angel said to her, "Whose life do you want to imitate?" She said, "Sir, I swear and promise to you that I will never follow my mother's life; I will live out my life in penance and work." That morning she gave whatever she had to the poor and she shut herself away in a cave, living a life of great austerity.

Nature herself teaches us that, insofar as God allows us, we should obey our parents. Indeed, the mother of the wild goat, when she goes in search of food, strikes her kid with her hoof to keep him from going wandering about and to make him stay where he is. And he is so obedient that even if people come upon him, he will not move from the spot and allows himself to be captured.

Christ, as the epistle to the Philippians says, was obedient even to death [Phil. 2:8]. How much greater should your obedience be to God your father and your mother the church; and you should consecrate the flower of your youth to God:

> Without help, our goods vanish: pluck the flower,
> Which will fall to the ground unless it is picked.
> The years go past like flowing water;
> He who is not ready, will be less ready tomorrow.

It is said that it is the nature of the badger to dig a dwelling in a hillside with its teeth and claws. It is a very tidy animal that cannot stand any bad odors. The sly fox sees this and fouls the badger's burrow so that the badger abandons it. Thus, the fox inhabits a dwelling that it did not build.

This is how it is with God and the devil. For God created our souls and worked hard to redeem them. But after the devil fouls our dwelling, God, who cannot bear the stink, leaves and abandons the place to the devil.

Therefore keep your home clean and spotless for God, beloved sons, and do not welcome your enemies and betrayers into it. For you should not love him who killed your father. Yet the devil killed our First Parents; he ceaselessly kills our brothers every day; and he yearns to kill you too. He will never give you peace, so you must fight him boldly and you will conquer him, trampling him under your feet with the help of our Lord Jesus Christ.

What lessons would this sermon teach children? Is it well suited to its intended audience? What would they most remember about it?

2. Sermon for the dedication of a church (c. 1400)

The English curate John Myrc wrote several popular works intended to equip priests to minister to their parishioners. One of them was the Festiall, *a collection of sermons in English for Sundays and feast days written around 1400. Here Myrc offers a sermon to celebrate the day a local church was consecrated – along with Christmas, Easter, and the feast of the church's patron saint, one of the major celebrations of a parish's liturgical year.*

Source: modernized by J. Shinners from Theodor Erbe, [*John*] *Myrc's Festiall, A Collection of Homilies*, Pt. 1, Early English Text Society, Extra Series 96 (1905), pp. 277-81. Middle English.

Good men and women, on such a day, N[omen or Name], you shall celebrate your church's holy day. On that day you shall come to church to worship God, having in mind three reasons why the church is consecrated. The first is for cleansing the church; the second for devout praying; and the third for burying the dead. There are many other reasons why a church is hallowed, but at this time we shall speak of these three, as God gives us grace.

First, it was hallowed for our own cleansing. For the church is a place ordained for Christian people to come together in charity to worship God in rest and in peace, each one with the other. Then God is happy with them. He comes to them and gives them his blessing; he walks among them and is wonderfully happy with them; and he dwells with them while they are at rest and in peace with one another. But when the devil sees this he is sorry, and he shows all his malice to see if he might by himself or by any of his disciples bring them out of their charity, make strife and dissension among them, and thus drive God away from them. For I know well that God is not where strife and dissension are. And so, because our holy fathers knew the devil's ways and his malice, they ordained that the church be hallowed. Thus, by holy water and by hallowing she is cleansed of the devil and of his malice, and he has no power afterwards to come into the church. But it might happen that some wicked liar who is beloved by the fiend brings him into the church with him; for as long as a man or a woman lacks charity, the devil is in them and has power over them. Therefore to show you how the fiend is driven out of the church by hallowing, I will tell you some examples from what I find written in *The Golden Legend* and what St. Gregory [the Great] writes in his book called the *Dialogues*.

He says that once when a church was being blessed and relics of saints were brought into it, suddenly a swine ran among the people's feet here and there and then went out the church door and was seen no more afterwards. Thus God showed plainly how the fiend, by the hallowing of the church, was driven out of it. And to show how sorry he was to lose his dwelling, the fiend came again the night after, and he ran against the church with such noise that he scared all the people who heard it. And the second night he came again and made a more hideous noise; and the third night he made a noise that sounded as if the whole church was about to fall down, and then he left and came again no more.

The church is also hallowed for devout praying. I hope that you all pray well at home in your houses. For, as St. Augustine says, a good deed is a good prayer, so while a man does well he prays well. Yet when any of you wish to speak with a friend for any needed thing, you go to his house hoping that he will be in a better mood there than any other place. So when you wish to speak with God come to his house – that is, holy church – and speak with him there. For while a man prays he speaks with God, and while he reads God speaks with him.

Many of you don't know how you should pray to God, but the position of the church will tell you: it is set facing the east, teaching each man, when he prays, to have his heart toward the east and to consider that paradise is in the east. Therefore you should pray to God devoutly that he will have compassion on you, who have been exiled out of your heritage by the malice of your enemies, and that he will give you grace to discomfit your enemy, so that God shall send his angel when you die and fetch your souls into paradise again into that bliss that you lost due to your Old Father's [Adam's] trespass. Also you should think how Christ died in the east on the cross. Thus, you should pray devoutly to him that he gives you grace to remember his passion so that you may be worthy to be written among the number of those that he died for on the cross. Also think that Christ shall come out of the east to the Doomsday. Thus, you should pray to him to give you such contrition of heart for your misdeeds, that – after you have confessed your sins and made satisfaction – you may be sure to stand on Christ's right hand at the Last Judgment and escape the horrible rebuke that shall be done to those who will be damned because of their prideful heart which will not be sorry for its misdeeds nor ask for mercy in a time of mercy. For such devout prayers holy church was hallowed. For God himself says "My house is a house of prayer" [Isa. 56:7]. But more is the harm now that it is made a house of babbling, and of whispering and chattering, and of speaking of vanity and other filth.

Thus I read that, as a holy bishop was saying his mass, his deacon turned to bid the people bow for the blessing. Then he saw two women whispering together, and the devil sat on their shoulders writing on a long scroll as fast as he could. After mass, at the bidding of the bishop the deacon sent for these women and asked them how they had occupied the mass time. They said that they had said their Our Father. Then the bishop commanded the fiend to read what he had written, and when he had read all that they had talked about, they fell to the ground and begged for mercy.

The holy church is also hallowed for people's final resting. For when someone has died, then he is brought to the church to his final home. For, as [the liturgist] St. John Beleth [d. 1165] says, in past times rich men were buried on hilltops or at their foot or in their sides in tombs made in the rocks of the hill. But the smell and the odor of the corpses were too grievous to the living, so the holy fathers ordained that churchyards be made and the corpses be brought there to be buried for two reasons: first, so that they could be prayed for forever, since holy church prays for everyone buried inside the church or in the churchyard; second, so that the bodies of the dead should rest without being bothered or vexed by the fiend. Thus, the devil has no power to do anything to any body buried in a Christian grave. But sometimes it happens that someone has done such wrong that he is not worthy to be buried there. For John Beleth tells how no one should be buried inside the church except the patrons who defended the church, or priests or clerics who defended the church from spiritual enemies with their prayers, and other patrons who defended the church from bodily enemies. Thus, some people have been buried in a church and the next day their corpse has been found cast out of the church and all their clothes left in the grave.

Once an angel came to a churchwarden and bade him go to the bishop and tell him to remove from the church someone whom he had buried there or else he himself would be dead within thirty days. And so he was, for he would not do as he was told.

We read also in the *Deeds of the Franks* that an angel told holy Bishop Eucher how Charles [Martel], the King of France, was damned because he had deprived holy church of the rights that holy men had given her before. The angel bade him go and open his tomb and see the truth of it. The bishop took some men with him and when he opened the tomb a great dragon came out and flew forth and left the tomb burnt within as if it had been the mouth of a kiln. Thus, burying in a holy place does not help those that are worthy to be damned.

Also there are many men that walk about after they are dead and buried in a holy place. But this is not due to the vexations of the fiend, but rather the grace of God. For they are trying to get some aid for some sin that they are guilty of, and they may not have rest until they are helped. This happened near the abbey of Lilleshall when three men had stolen the abbot's ox and he excommunicated them. Two of them confessed and asked for mercy, but the third died unshriven. His spirit wandered about at night and so frightened the parishioners that no man dared go out of his house once the sun went down. Now the parish priest there, Sir Thomas Woodward, was taking the host to a sick woman after sunset. This spirit approached him and told him who he was and why he was wandering. He begged him to get his wife, go to the abbot of Lilleshall, and help see that he was shriven, or else he would have no rest. And so he went to Lilleshall, had the man shriven, and then he had rest.

Now pray to almighty God, since all goodness and grace is from him, to give you the grace of the Holy Ghost to worship him here in holy church, so that you may come to the rest he bought for you. Amen.

What is the message of this sermon? How well would an average Christian understand it? How well do its anecdotes illustrate its message?

7. DURANDUS ON THE SYMBOLISM OF CHURCH ART (c. 1286)

Art was one way to teach a largely unlettered laity. Though Guillaume Durand (c. 1230-96) – usually known by the Latinized Durandus – wrote for an educated clerical audience, his thoughts on the pedagogical value of art highlight his understanding of the popular religious mind: what is seen lasts longer than what is heard. They also illustrate some of the reigning artistic conventions of thirteenth-century liturgical art. Guillaume, the Bishop of Mende in France, was noted as both a canonist and a liturgist. He wrote his most famous treatise, the Rationale divinorum officiorum *(Rational of the Divine Offices), in the last decade of his life, and it quickly gained wide popularity in clerical circles. The "rational" of its title refers to the Hebrew high priest Aaron's breastplate, the "rational of judgment" (Exod. 28:29-30) on which was written doctrine and truth; for Guillaume wanted clerics to guard the knowledge of the church and its services that he imparted in his book "in the shrine of their breasts." This excerpt is from Book I, chapter 3.*

Source: John Mason Neale and Benjamin Webb, *The Symbolism of Churches and Church Ornaments, a Translation of the First Book of the* Rationale Divinorum Officiorum *by William Durandus* (London: Gibbings & Co., 1906), pp. 39-52; revised and corrected by J. Shinners from A. Davril and T.M. Thibodeau (eds.), *Guillelmi Duranti, Rationale Divinorum Officiorum I-IV, Corpus Christianorum Continuatio Mediaevalis* CXL (Turnhout: Brepols, 1995), pp. 34-41. Latin.

1. Pictures and ornaments in churches are the lessons and the Scriptures of the laity. Thus, [Pope] Gregory [the Great] says: "It is one thing to adore a picture, and another by means of a picture to learn a story that should be adored. For what writing supplies to those who can read, a picture supplies to those who are uneducated and look at it. Since they who are uninstructed thus see what they ought to follow, they 'read' by it even though they do not know letters." It is true that the Chaldeans worship fire and force others to do the same, burning other idols. But pagans adore images like icons and idols; Saracens do not, who neither will possess nor look on images, grounding themselves on that saying, "Thou shalt not make to thyself any graven image, nor the likeness of anything that is in heaven above, nor in the earth beneath, nor in the waters under the earth" [Exod. 20:4], and, drawing on this and other subsequent authorities, they greatly rebuke us about this. But we do not worship images, nor account them to be gods, nor put any hope of salvation in them; for this would be idolatry. Yet we venerate them for the memory and remembrance of things done long ago. Thus the verse,

Whenever you pass the image of Christ bow humbly,
Adoring not the image but him whom it represents.
It makes no sense to ascribe God's being
To material stone shaped by human hand.
The image you see here is neither God nor man,
He is God and man which this holy image represents.

2. The Greeks [Eastern Christians], moreover, employ painted representations [icons], painting them, it is said, only from the navel upwards and not lower so that all occasion of frivolous (*stulte*) thoughts may be removed. But they make no carved image for it is written in Exodus 20: "Thou shalt not make to thyself a graven thing nor the likeness of any thing." And in Leviticus 26: "You shall not make to yourselves any idol or graven thing." And in Deuteronomy 4: "Lest perhaps being deceived you might make you a graven similitude." And again: "You shall not make to yourselves gods of silver or gold" [Exod. 20:23]. See also the prophet: "Their idols are silver and gold, the work of man's hand. They that shall make them are like unto them: and so are all they that put their trust in them" [Ps. 113b (115):4, 8]. "Let them all be confounded that adore graven things, and that glory in their idols" [Ps. 96 (97):7]. Also, Moses says to the children of Israel: "Lest perchance ... being deceived ... thou adore and serve that which the Lord thy God created" [Deut. 4:19].

3. Thus also it was that Hezekiah, king of Judah, broke into pieces the brazen serpent which Moses set up, because the people, contrary to the precepts of the law, burned incense to it [see 4 Kings 18:4].

4. From these and other authorities, the excessive use of images is forbidden. For the Apostle [Paul] says in I Corinthians [8:4], "We know that there is no such thing as an idol in the world, and that there is no God but one." For those who are simple and weak may easily be perverted to idolatry by an excessive and indiscreet use of images. Thus, Wisdom 14 says: "Therefore there shall be no respect had even to the idols of the Gentiles: because the creatures of God are turned to an abomination, and a temptation to the souls of men, and a snare to the feet of the unwise." But there is no blame in a moderate use of pictures to depict how evil should be avoided and good followed. Thus, the Lord says to Ezechiel: "Go in and see the wicked abominations which they commit here. And he went in and saw every form of creeping things, and of living creatures, the abomination, and all the idols of the house of Israel, were painted on the wall" [Ezek. 8:9-10]. Of course, Pope Gregory says in Book II, chapter [10] of his *Pastoralia*: "When the shapes of external

objects are drawn inside, what is contemplated through these imagined pictures is, as it were, painted on the mind." Again God says to Ezechiel: "take thee a tile, and lay it before thee, and draw upon it the plan of the city of Jerusalem" [Ezek. 4:1].

But what was said above, that pictures are the letters of the laity, explains that saying in the Gospel, "They have Moses and the prophets: let them hearken to them" [Luke 16:29]. Of this, more later in Part Four. The Council of Agde [506 CE] forbids pictures in churches, and also that what is worshiped and adored should be painted on the walls. But Gregory says that pictures are not allowed to be destroyed with the excuse that they should not be worshiped. For painting appears to move the mind more than writing. Deeds are placed before the eyes in paintings, and so appear to be actually happening; but through writing the deed is done as it were by hearsay, which affects the mind less when called to memory. Thus it is that in churches we pay less reverence to books than to images and pictures.

5. Some pictures and images are on top of the church, as the cock and the eagle; some outside the church, namely at the entrance in front of the church, as the ox and the cow; others inside, as icons, statues, and various kinds of painting and sculpture, which are represented either on vestments, or on walls, or in stained glass. We have spoken about some of these in the treatise called *On the Church*, about how they are taken from the tabernacle of Moses and the temple of Solomon. For Moses made carved work, and Solomon made carved work and pictures, and adorned the walls with painted panels and pictures.

6. Bear in mind that the image of the Savior is appropriately depicted in churches three ways: as sitting on his throne, or hanging on the gibbet of the cross, or lying on the bosom of his mother. And because John the Baptist pointed to him, saying "Behold the Lamb of God," therefore some represented Christ in the form of a lamb. But because the shadow passed over and Christ is truly man, Pope Adrian says he must be represented in the form of a man. A holy lamb must not principally be depicted on the cross. But there is no objection when Christ has been represented as a man to paint a lamb in a lower or less prominent part of the picture, since he is the true lamb who "takes away the sins of the world."

7. The image of the Savior is painted in these and various other manners for a variety of meanings. Representing him in the cradle, the artist commemorates his nativity; on the bosom of his mother, his childhood; painting or carving him on the cross signifies his passion (and when he is on the cross, the sun and moon are represented as undergoing an eclipse). When he is

depicted on a flight of steps, his ascension is signified; when he is sitting on a throne or seat of dominion, we are taught about his present majesty, as he said, "All power in heaven and on earth has been given to me" [Matt. 28:18]; according to the saying, "I saw the Lord sitting on his throne" [Isa. 6:1], that is, the Son of God reigning over the angels, as the text says: "that sittest upon the cherubims" [Ps. 79 (80):2]. Sometimes he is represented as Moses, Aaron, Nadab, and Abihu saw him on the mountain; when "under his feet was as it were a work of sapphire stones, and as the heaven when clear" [Exod. 24:10]. And because as Luke says "they will see the Son of Man coming upon a cloud with great power and majesty" [Luke 21:27], sometimes he is represented surrounded by the angels that always serve him and stand by his throne, each being portrayed with six wings, according to what Isaiah said: "Upon it stood the seraphims: the one had six wings, and the other had six wings: with two they covered his face, and with two they covered his feet, and with two they flew" [Isa. 6:2].

8. The angels are also represented in the flower of youth, for they never grow old. Sometimes St. Michael is represented trampling the dragon, for according to John: "There was war in heaven: Michael fought with the dragon" [Rev. 12:7]. This battle represents the discord of the angels: the confirmation of those who were good, and the ruin of those that were bad, or the persecution of the faithful in the church militant. Sometimes the twenty-four elders are painted around the Savior, according to the vision of John, with "white garments and on their heads crowns of gold" [Rev. 4:4]. By these are signified the teachers of the Old and New Testaments, which are twelve on account of faith in the holy Trinity [i.e., *three*] preached through the *four* quarters of the world; or twenty-four on account of good works and the keeping of the Gospels. If the seven lamps [Rev. 1:12] are added, this represents the gifts of the Holy Spirit; if the sea of glass [Rev. 4:6], baptism.

9. Sometimes the four living creatures spoken of in visions of Ezechiel and the aforesaid John are represented: "the face of a man and the face of a lion on the right side, the face of an ox on the left, and the face of an eagle over all the four" [Ezek. 1:10; see Rev. 4:7]. These are the four Evangelists. They are painted with books by their feet because by their words and writings they have instructed the minds of the faithful and accomplished their own works. Matthew is assigned the figure of a man, Mark of a lion. These are painted on the right hand because the nativity and the resurrection of Christ were the general joy of all. Thus the Psalm says: "And gladness at the morning" [Ps. 29 (30):6].

But Luke is the ox because he begins with Zachary the priest and treats more specially of the passion and sacrifice of Christ, because the ox is an animal fit for the priest's sacrifice. He is also compared to the ox because of the two horns, containing, so to speak, the two testaments; and the four hoofs, which are, as it were, the words of the four Evangelists. By this Christ is also figured, who was offered for us as a sacrificial ox; and therefore the ox is painted on the left side (*a sinistris*) because the death of Christ was sinister for the apostles. Part Seven in the section on the Evangelists speaks about this and how blessed Mark should be depicted.

John has the figure of an eagle because, soaring to the utmost height, he says: "In the beginning was the Word" [John 1:1]. This also signifies Christ, "whose youth is renewed like the eagle's" [Ps. 102 (103):5] because, rising from the dead, he flourished and ascended into heaven. Here, however, it is not portrayed on the side but above, since it denotes the ascension and the word pronounced by God. How, since each of the living creatures has four faces and four wings, they can be depicted, shall be described more fully in Part Seven in the section on the Evangelists.

10. Sometimes painted around, or rather beneath, are the apostles, who were his witnesses by word and by deed to the ends of the earth. They are portrayed with long hair, as Nazarites, that is, holy persons. For the law of the Nazarites was this: from the time of their separation from the ordinary life of man, no razor passed over their heads [Num. 6:5]. They are also sometimes painted in the shape of twelve sheep because they were slain like sacrificial lambs for the Lord's sake; and sometimes the twelve tribes of Israel are so represented. When, however, more or less sheep than twelve are painted around the throne of majesty, then something other is signified, according to what St. Matthew says: "But when the Son of Man shall come in his majesty … then he will sit on the throne of his glory; … and he will separate them one from another, as the shepherd separates the sheep from the goats" [Matt. 25:31-32]. How Bartholomew and Andrew should be depicted is discussed in Part Seven.

11. And note that the patriarchs and prophets are painted with scrolls in their hands; and some of the apostles with books and some with scrolls. To be sure, before the advent of Christ the faith was set forth in metaphors, which made it confusing to many people. To represent this, the patriarchs and prophets are painted with scrolls to signify imperfect knowledge. But because the apostles were perfectly taught by Christ, the books, which are the emblems of this perfect knowledge, are open. But because some of them put their knowledge

into writing for the instruction of others, they are fittingly represented with books in their hands like teachers. So it is with Paul, the Evangelists, Peter, James, and Jude. But others, who wrote nothing which has lasted or been received into the canon by the church, are not portrayed with books, but with scrolls, as a sign of their preaching. Thus the Apostle to the Ephesians: "And the Lord himself gave some men as apostles, and some as prophets, others again as Evangelists, and others as pastors and teachers" [Eph. 4:11].

12. But sometimes the Divine Majesty is also portrayed with a closed book in the hands since no man was found worthy to open it except the Lion of the tribe of Judah [see Rev. 8:12]. And sometimes with an open book so that in it everyone may read that he is "the light of the world" [John 8:12], and "the way, the truth, and the life" [John 14:6], and the Book of Life. Why Paul is represented at the right and Peter at the left of the Savior is discussed in Part Seven.

13. Sometimes John the Baptist is painted as a hermit.

14. The martyrs [are painted] with the instruments of their torture (as St. Lawrence with the gridiron, St. Stephen with stones) and sometimes with palms to signify victory, according to the saying, "the just shall flourish like the palm tree" [Ps. 91 (92):13] – as a palm tree flourishes, so his memory is preserved. Thus it is that those who come from Jerusalem bear palms in their hands in token that they have been soldiers of that King who was gloriously received in Jerusalem with palms, and who afterwards, having in the same city subdued the devil in battle, entered the palace of heaven in triumph with his angels where the just shall flourish like palm trees and shall shine like stars.

15. Confessors are painted with their insignia (as bishops with their miters, abbots with their cowls) and some with lilies, which denote chastity. Doctors [i.e., teachers] [are painted] with books in their hands, virgins, according to the Gospel, with lamps [see Matt. 25:1].

16. Paul [is painted] with a book and a sword: with a book since he was a teacher, or because of his conversion; with a sword because he was a soldier....

17. Generally the effigies of the holy fathers are portrayed on the walls of the church, or on the back panels of the altar, or on sacred vestments, or in

various other places so that we may meditate continuously, not randomly or uselessly, on their holiness. Thus, in Exodus it is commanded by divine word that on the breast of Aaron, the breastplate of judgment should be bound with strings [Exod. 28:29] because fleeting thoughts should not occupy the mind of a priest, which should be girded by reason alone. In this breastplate also, according to Gregory, the names of the twelve patriarchs are commanded to be carefully inscribed.

18. To bear the fathers thus imprinted on the breast, is to meditate on the lives of the ancient saints without intermission. But the priest walks blamelessly when he gazes continually on the example of the fathers who have gone before, when he considers without ceasing the footsteps of the saints, and represses unholy thoughts, lest he put the foot of his works outside the bounds of prayer.

19. Consider also that the Savior is always depicted as crowned, as if he said, "Go forth, ye daughters of Sion, and see king Solomon in the diadem, wherewith his mother crowned him" [Song of Sol. 3:11]. But Christ was triply crowned. First by his mother, on the day of his conception, with a crown of pity, which is a double crown because of what he had by nature and what was given him; therefore it is called a diadem, which is a double crown. Secondly, by his step-mother [the Jews, symbolized by the synagogue] on the day of his Passion, with the crown of misery. Thirdly, by his Father on the day of his Resurrection, with the crown of glory; thus it is written, "thou hast crowned him with glory and honor, Lord" [Ps. 8:6]. Lastly, he shall be crowned by his whole family, in the last day of Revelation, with the crown of power. For he shall come with the judges of the earth to judge the world in righteousness. So also the saints are portrayed as crowned, as if they said: You children of Jerusalem, behold the martyrs with the golden crowns with which the Lord has crowned them. And in the book of Wisdom: "The just shall receive a kingdom of glory, and a crown of beauty at the hand of the Lord" [Wisd. 5:17].

20. But their crown is made in the fashion of a round shield because the saints enjoy the divine protection. Thus they sing with joy, "O Lord, thou hast crowned us as with a shield of thy good will" [Ps. 5:13]. But the crown of Christ is represented in the figure of a cross, and is thereby distinguished from that of the saints because by the banner of his cross he gained for himself the glorification of his flesh, and for us freedom from our captivity and the enjoyment of everlasting life. But when any living prelate or saint is portrayed,

the crown is not fashioned in the shape of a shield, but four-cornered so that he may be shown to flourish in the four cardinal virtues [fortitude, justice, prudence, and temperance] as is told in the story of blessed Gregory.

21. Again, sometimes paradise is painted in churches so that it may attract the beholders to follow after its rewards; sometimes hell so that it may terrify them by the fear of punishment. Sometimes flowers and fruit trees are portrayed to represent the fruits of good works springing from the roots of virtues.

22. Now the variety of pictures denotes the variety of virtues. For "to one through the Spirit is given the utterance of wisdom, and to another the utterance of knowledge" [1 Cor. 12:8], etc. The virtues are represented in the form of women because they soothe and nourish. Again, by the carved ceilings (called laquears) which are intended for the beauty of the house, the less educated servants of Christ are recognized, who adorn the church not by their learning but by their virtues alone. And the sculpted images that jut out appear to be emerging from the church's walls because when virtues become the habit of the faithful to such an extent that they seem to be naturally grafted to them, they are cultivated in all their many varieties.

How does Durandus argue for the value of religious art? How well do you think the average lay person would grasp the meaning of the symbols he describes? What kinds of lessons would the art he discusses teach?

8. THE FAITH OF PETER WALDES (1173)

While it is hardly typical of the average medieval Christian, the story of the conversion of the merchant Peter Waldes underscores the tension growing by the twelfth century between the forces of an emerging urban economy and a Gospel message that scorned wealth and celebrated poverty. It also illuminates the confidence that some ordinary lay people were gaining in directing their own spiritual lives, a confidence that would increasingly chip away at the traditional distinctions between clergy and laity. Writing several decades after Waldes's death, the Dominican inquisitor and preacher Etienne Bourbon adds an interesting detail that he learned from a fellow-priest, Bernard Ydros, who grew up in Lyons and worked as a scribe there when he was a young man. Waldes had hired Bernard and another priest to translate the Gospels into French for him since he knew no Latin but was eager to study them for himself. Eventually, they translated not only the Gospels, but several other books of the Bible and passages from the church fathers grouped by topic. Reading these translated texts led Waldes to his pursuit of evangelical perfection. Ultimately his insistence on following the Gospel literally and his criticism of the wealth and corruption of the leaders of the church led him into heresy. His followers, the Waldensians, advanced a sort of "proto-Protestant" critique of the institutional church. Although church leaders relentlessly pursued them as heretics, they were never completely suppressed. The minstrel's story of St. Alexis mentioned in this account is the legend of the wealthy young Roman who, on his wedding night, renounced his riches, fled to Syria, and became a beggar. Eventually returning home, Alexis lived beneath the stairs of his father's house unrecognized by his parents until just before he died. His tale was very popular in the Middle Ages.

Source: The *Chronicon universale anonymi Laudunensis* in Walter L. Wakefield and Austin P. Evans (trans. and eds.), *Heresies of the High Middle Ages* (New York: Columbia University Press, 1969), pp. 200–02. Latin.

In the course of the same year (that is, 1173) of our Lord's incarnation, there was at Lyons in Gaul a certain citizen named Waldes, who had amassed a great fortune through the wicked practice of lending at interest [usury]. One Sunday he had been attracted by the crowd gathered around a minstrel and had been touched by the latter's words. Wishing to talk to him more fully, he took him to his home, for the minstrel was at a place in his narrative in which Alexis had come peacefully to a happy end in his father's house.

On the following morning, the said citizen hastened to the school of theology to seek counsel for his soul's welfare and, when he had been instructed in the many ways of attaining to God, asked the master which was the most sure and perfect way of all. The master replied to him in the words of the Lord: "If thou wilt be perfect, go sell what thou hast" [Matt. 19:21], and so on. Waldes came to his wife and offered her the choice of keeping for herself all his property in either movable goods or real estate, that is, in lands, waters, woods, meadows, houses, rents, vineyards, mills, and ovens. Though greatly saddened by the necessity, she chose the real estate. From his movable goods, he made restitution to those from whom he had profited unjustly; another considerable portion of his wealth he bestowed upon his two small daughters, whom without their mother's knowledge he confided to the order of Fontevrault; but the greatest part he disbursed for the needs of the poor.

Now, a very severe famine was then raging throughout all Gaul and Germany. Wherefore Waldes, the citizen mentioned above, on three days a week from Pentecost to St. Peter in Chains [Aug. 1] gave bountifully of bread, vegetables, and meat to all who came to him. On the feast of the Assumption of the Blessed Virgin [Aug. 15], as he was in the streets distributing an appreciable sum of money among the poor, he cried out, "No man can serve two masters, God and mammon." Then all the citizens hurried to him, supposing that he had lost his senses, but he climbed to a commanding spot and addressed them thus: "My friends and fellow townsmen! Indeed, I am not, as you think, insane, but I have taken vengeance on my enemies who held me in bondage to them, so that I was always more anxious about money than about God and served the creature more than the Creator. I know that a great many find fault with me for having done this publicly. But I did it for myself and also for you: for myself, so that they who may henceforth see me in possession of money may think I am mad; in part also for you, so that you may learn to fix your hope in God and to trust not in riches."

As he was leaving the church on the following day, he asked a certain citizen, one of his former associates, to give him food for the love of God. The latter took him to his home and said, "As long as I live I will give you the necessities of life." His wife, on learning of this incident, was no little saddened. Like one beside herself, she rushed into the presence of the archbishop of the city to complain that her husband had begged his bread from another rather than from her. This situation moved all who were present to tears, including the archbishop himself. At the archbishop's bidding, the citizen brought his guest [Waldes] with him into his presence, whereupon the woman, clinging to her husband's garments, cried, "Is it not better, O my husband, that I, rather than strangers, should atone for my sins through alms to you?" And from that time forth, by command of the archbishop, he was not permitted in that city to take food with others than his wife....

[1177] Waldes, the citizen of Lyons whom we have already mentioned, having taken a vow to the God of heaven henceforth and throughout his life never to possess either gold or silver or to take thought for the morrow, began to gather associates in his way of life. They followed his example in giving their all to the poor and became devotees of voluntary poverty. Little by little, both publicly and privately, they began to declaim against their own sins and those of others.

9. THE FAITH OF ST. FRANCIS OF ASSISI (1203-09)

St. Francis of Assisi (born Francesco Bernardone, c. 1181-1226) is a central figure for grasping the religious devotions of the later Middle Ages. Most of the issues and impulses that drove popular piety also drove Francis, who shaped and directed them into a religious movement of enormous influence. His life and the following it inspired are sterling examples of the broad appeal for both lay people and religious orders of the vita apostolica *as the Middle Ages came to conceive it: a life dedicated to poverty and preaching in imitation of the early apostles. Ironically, Francis at first followed the path Peter Waldes trod: a well-to-do layman, left unsatisfied by material wealth, abandons it to pursue evangelical poverty. But although Francis conceived his life-changing plan while the Waldensian heresy was still an active threat to the church, his unconditional pledge of obedience to church superiors quelled any misgivings about his resemblance to Waldes. In 1209 Innocent III approved the Rule that Francis had drawn up for himself and his eleven companions and granted them permission to form the Order of Friars Minor, a company of itinerant preachers headquartered at Portiuncula just outside Assisi. Francis was popularly regarded as a saint in his lifetime, a verdict confirmed when Gregory IX canonized him just twenty-one months after his death. Thomas of Celano joined the fledgling order in 1214. The excerpt below is from his first version of the* Life of Francis, *started in 1228, perhaps the day after Francis' canonization, and completed by 1230. In it we discover the steps that led to his conversion, the means he took to follow the* vita apostolica, *and how his example affected the people around him. See Doc. 54 for the rule of life Francis wrote for lay people, and Doc. 68 for the pious movement called the "Great Halleluia" that reflected Franciscan religious impulses.*

Source: trans. Placid Hermann from Thomas of Celano, *Saint Francis of Assisi* (Chicago: Franciscan Herald Press, 1963), pp. 5-27. Latin.

Chapter 1. How Francis lived in the world before his conversion.

1. In the city of Assisi, which lies at the edge of the Spoleto valley, there was a man by the name of Francis, who from his earliest years was brought up by his parents proud of spirit, in accordance with the vanity of the world; and imitating their wretched life and habits for a long time, he became even more vain and proud. For this very evil custom has grown up everywhere among those who are considered Christians in name, and this pernicious teaching has become so established and prescribed, as though by public law, that people seek to educate their children from the cradle on very negligently and dissolutely. For, indeed, when they first begin to speak or stammer, children, just hardly born, are taught by signs and words to do certain wicked and detestable things; and when they come to be weaned, they are forced not only to speak but also to do certain things full of lust and wantonness. Impelled by a fear that is natural to their age, none of them dares to conduct himself in an upright manner, for if he were to do so he would be subjected to severe punishments. Therefore, a secular poet [Seneca] says well: "Because we have grown up amid the practices of our parents, we therefore pursue all evil things from our childhood on." This testimony is true, for so much the more injurious to their children are the desires of the parents, the more successfully they work out. But when the children have progressed a little in age, they always sink into worse deeds, following their own impulses. For from a corrupt root a corrupt tree will grow, and what has once become

wickedly depraved can hardly ever be brought into harmony with the norms of uprightness. But when they begin to enter the portals of adolescence, how do you think they will turn out? Then, indeed, tossed about amid every kind of debauchery, they give themselves over completely to shameful practices, inasmuch as they are permitted to do as they please. For once they have become the slaves of sin by a voluntary servitude, they give over all their members to be instruments of wickedness; and showing forth in themselves nothing of the Christian religion either in their lives or in their conduct, they take refuge under the mere name of Christianity. These miserable people very often pretend that they have done even worse things than they have actually done, lest they seem more despicable the more innocent they are.

2. These are the wretched circumstances among which the man whom we venerate today as a saint, for he is truly a saint, lived in his youth; and almost up to the twenty-fifth year of his age, he squandered and wasted his time miserably. Indeed, he outdid all his contemporaries in vanities and he came to be a promoter of evil and was more abundantly zealous for all kinds of foolishness. He was the admiration of all and strove to outdo the rest in the pomp of vainglory, in jokes, in strange doings, in idle and useless talk, in songs, in soft and flowing garments, for he was very rich, not however avaricious but prodigal, not a hoarder of money but a squanderer of his possessions, a cautious business man but a very unreliable steward. On the other hand, he was a very kindly person, easy and affable, even making himself foolish because of it; for because of these qualities many ran after him, doers of evil and promoters of crime. And thus overwhelmed by a host of evil companions, proud and high-minded, he walked about the streets of Babylon until the Lord looked down from heaven and for his own name's sake removed his wrath far off and for his praise bridled Francis lest he should perish. The hand of the Lord therefore came upon him and a change was wrought by the right hand of the Most High, that through him an assurance might be granted to sinners that they had been restored to grace and that he might become an example to all of conversion to God.

Chapter 2. How God touched the heart of Francis by sickness and by a vision.

3. For, indeed, while this man was still in the glow of youthful passion, and the age of wantonness was urging him on immoderately to fulfill the demands of youth; and while, not knowing how to restrain himself, he was stirred by the venom of the serpent of old, suddenly the divine vengeance, or, perhaps better, the divine unction, came upon him and sought first to recall his erring senses by visiting upon him mental distress and bodily suf-

fering, according to the saying of the prophet: "Behold I will hedge up thy way with thorns, and I will stop it up with a wall" [Hos. 2:6]. Thus, worn down by a long illness [in 1203], as man's stubbornness deserves when it can hardly be corrected except by punishments, he began to think of things other than he was used to thinking upon. When he had recovered somewhat and had begun to walk about the house with the support of a cane to speed the recovery of his health, he went outside one day and began to look about at the surrounding landscape with great interest. But the beauty of the fields, the pleasantness of the vineyards, and whatever else was beautiful to look upon, could stir in him no delight. He wondered therefore at the sudden change that had come over him, and those who took delight in such things he considered very foolish.

4. From that day on, therefore, he began to despise himself and to hold in some contempt the things he had admired and loved before. But not fully or truly, for he was not yet freed from the cords of vanity nor had he shaken off from his neck the yoke of evil servitude. It is indeed very hard to give up things one is accustomed to, and things that once enter into the mind are not easily eradicated; the mind, even though it has been kept away from them for a long time, returns to the things it once learned; and by constant repetition vice generally becomes second nature. So Francis still tried to flee the hand of God, and, forgetting for a while his paternal correction, he thought, amid the smiles of prosperity, of the things of the world; and, ignorant of the counsel of God, he still looked forward to accomplishing great deeds of worldly glory and vanity. For a certain nobleman of the city of Assisi was preparing himself in no mean way with military arms, and, puffed up by a gust of vainglory, vowed that he would go to Apulia to increase his wealth and fame. Upon hearing this, Francis, who was flighty and not a little rash, arranged to go with him; he was inferior to him in nobility of birth, but superior in generosity, poorer in the matter of wealth, but more lavish in giving things away.

5. On a certain night [in 1205], therefore, after he had given himself with all deliberation to the accomplishment of these things, and while, burning with desire, he longed greatly to set about the journey, he who had struck him with the rod of justice visited him in the sweetness of grace by means of a nocturnal vision; and because Francis was eager for glory, he enticed him and raised his spirits with a vision of the heights of glory. For it seemed to Francis that his whole home was filled with the trappings of war, namely saddles, shields, lances, and other things; rejoicing greatly, he wondered silently within himself what this should mean. For he was not accustomed to see such

things in his home, but rather piles of cloth to be sold. When, accordingly, he was not a little astonished at this sudden turn of events, the answer was given him that all these arms would belong to him and to his soldiers. When he awoke, he arose in the morning with a glad heart, and considering the vision an omen of great success, he felt sure that his journey to Apulia would come out well. He did not know what to say and he did not as yet recognize the task given him from heaven. Nevertheless, he might have understood that his interpretation of the vision was not correct, for while the vision bore some resemblance to things pertaining to war, his heart was not filled with his usual happiness over such things. He had to use some force on himself to carry out his designs and to complete the proposed journey. It is indeed quite fitting that mention be made of arms in the beginning and it is quite opportune that arms should be offered to the soldier about to engage one strongly armed, that like another David he might free Israel from the long-standing reproach of its enemies in the name of the Lord God of hosts.

Chapter 3. How, changed in mind but not in body, Francis spoke of the treasure he had found and of his spouse in allegory.

6. Changed, therefore, but in mind, not in body, he refused to go to Apulia and he strove to bend his own will to the will of God. Accordingly, he withdrew for a while from the bustle and the business of the world and tried to establish Jesus Christ dwelling within himself. Like a prudent business man, he hid the treasure he had found from the eyes of the deluded, and, having sold all his possessions, he tried to buy it secretly. Now since there was a certain man in the city of Assisi whom he loved more than any other because he was of the same age as the other, and since the great familiarity of their mutual affection led him to share his secrets with him he often took him to remote places, places well-suited for counsel, telling him that he had found a certain precious and great treasure. This one rejoiced and, concerned about what he heard, he willingly accompanied Francis whenever he was asked. There was a certain grotto near the city where they frequently went and talked about this treasure. The man of God, who was already holy by reason of his holy purpose, would enter the grotto, while his companion would wait for him outside; and filled with a new and singular spirit, he would pray to his Father in secret. He wanted no one to know what he did within, and taking the occasion of the good to wisely conceal the better, he took counsel with God alone concerning his holy proposal. He prayed devoutly that the eternal and true God would direct his way and teach him to do his will. He bore the greatest sufferings in mind and was not able to rest until he should have completed in deed what he had conceived in his heart; various thoughts succeeded

one another and their importunity disturbed him greatly. He was afire within himself with a divine fire and he was not able to hide outwardly the ardor of his mind; he repented that he had sinned so grievously and had offended the eyes of God's majesty, and neither the past evils nor those present gave him any delight. Still he had not as yet won full confidence that he would be able to guard himself against them in the future. Consequently, when he came out again to his companion, he was so exhausted with the strain, that one person seemed to have entered, and another to have come out.

7. One day, however, when he had begged for the mercy of God most earnestly, it was shown to him by God what he was to do. Accordingly, he was so filled with joy that he could not contain himself, and, though he did not want to, he uttered some things to the ears of men. But, though he could not keep silent because of the greatness of the joy that filled him, he nevertheless spoke cautiously and in an obscure manner. For, while he spoke to his special friend of a hidden treasure, as was said, he tried to speak to others only figuratively; he said that he did not want to go to Apulia, but he promised that he would do noble and great things in his native place. People thought he wished to take to himself a wife, and they asked him, saying: "Francis, do you wish to get married?" But he answered them, saying: "I shall take a more noble and more beautiful spouse than you have ever seen; she will surpass all others in beauty and will excel all others in wisdom." Indeed, the immaculate spouse of God is the true religion which he embraced; and the hidden treasure is the kingdom of heaven, which he sought with such great desire; for it was extremely necessary that the Gospel calling be fulfilled in him who was to be the minister of the Gospel in faith and in truth.

Chapter 4. Francis sold all his goods and despised the money given him.

8. Behold, when the blessed servant of the Most High was thus disposed and strengthened by the Holy Spirit, now that the opportune time had come, he followed the blessed impulse of his soul, by which he would come to the highest things, trampling worldly things under foot. He could not delay any longer, because a deadly disease had grown up everywhere to such an extent and had so taken hold of all the limbs of many that, were the physician to delay even a little, it would snatch away life, shutting off the life-giving spirit. He rose up, therefore, fortified himself with the sign of the cross, got his horse ready and mounted it, and taking with him some fine cloth to sell, he hastened to the city called Foligno. There, as usual, he sold everything he had with him, and, successful as a merchant, he left behind even the horse he was riding, after he had received payment for it; and, free of all luggage,

he started back, wondering with a religious mind what he should do with the money. Soon, turned toward God's work in a wondrous manner, and accordingly feeling that it would be a great burden to him to carry that money even for an hour, he hastened to get rid of it, considering the advantage he might get from it as so much sand. When, therefore, he neared the city of Assisi, he discovered a certain church along the way that had been built of old in honor of St. Damian but which was now threatening to collapse because it was so old.

9. When this new soldier of Christ came up to this church, moved with pity over such great need, he entered it with fear and reverence. And when he found there a certain poor priest, he kissed his sacred hands with great faith, and offered him the money he had with him, telling him in order what he proposed to do. The priest was astonished and, wondering over a conversion so incredibly sudden, he refused to believe what he heard. And because he thought he was being deceived, he refused to keep the money offered him. For he had seen him just the day before, so to say, living in a riotous way among his relatives and acquaintances and showing greater foolishness than the rest. But Francis persisted obstinately and tried to gain credence for what he said, asking earnestly and begging the priest to suffer him to remain with him for the sake of the Lord. In the end the priest acquiesced to his remaining there, but out of fear of the young man's parents, he did not accept the money; whereupon this true condemner of money threw it upon a window sill, for he cared no more for it than for the dust. He wanted to possess that wisdom that is better than gold and to acquire that prudence that is more precious than silver.

Chapter 5. How his father persecuted Francis and put him in chains.

10. So while the servant of the most high God was staying in the aforesaid place, his father went about everywhere, like a persistent spy, wanting to learn what had happened to his son. And when he learned that he was living in such a way at that place, "being touched inwardly with sorrow of heart," he was "troubled exceedingly" [Ps. 6:4] at the sudden turn of events, and calling together his friends and neighbors, he hurried to the place where the servant of God was staying. But he, the new athlete of Christ, when he heard of the threats of those who were pursuing him and when he got knowledge of their coming, wanting to give place to wrath, hid himself in a certain secret pit which he himself had prepared for just such an emergency. That pit was in that house and was known probably to one person alone; in it he hid so continuously for one month that he hardly dared leave it to provide

for his human needs. Food, when it was given to him, he ate in the secrecy of the pit, and every service was rendered to him by stealth. Praying, he prayed always with a torrent of tears that the Lord would deliver him from the hands of those who were persecuting his soul, and that he would fulfill his pious wishes in his loving kindness; in fasting and in weeping he begged for the clemency of the Savior, and, distrusting his own efforts, he cast his whole care upon the Lord. And though he was in a pit and in darkness, he was nevertheless filled with a certain exquisite joy of which till then he had had no experience; and catching fire therefrom, he left the pit and exposed himself openly to the curses of his persecutors.

11. He arose, therefore, immediately, active, eager, and lively; and, bearing the shield of faith to fight for the Lord, armed with a great confidence, he took the way toward the city; aglow with a divine fire, he began to accuse himself severely of laziness and cowardice. When those who knew him saw this, they compared what he was now with what he had been; and they began to revile him miserably. Shouting out that he was mad and demented, they threw the mud of the streets and stones at him. They saw that he was changed from his former ways and greatly worn down by mortification of the flesh, and they therefore set down everything he did to exhaustion and madness. But since a patient man is better than a proud man, the servant of God showed himself deaf to all these things and, neither broken nor changed by any of these injuries, he gave thanks to God for all of them. In vain does the wicked man persecute one striving after virtue, for the more he is buffeted, the more strongly will he triumph. As someone says, indignity strengthens a generous spirit.

12. Now when the noise and the shouting of this kind concerning Francis had been going on for a long time through the streets and quarters of the city, and the sound of it all was echoing here and there, among the many to whose ears the report of these things came was finally his father. When he heard the name of his son mentioned, and understood that the commotion among the citizens turned about his son, he immediately arose, not indeed to free him but rather to destroy him; and, with no regard for moderation, he rushed upon him like a wolf upon a sheep, and looking upon him with a fierce and savage countenance, he laid hands upon him and dragged him shamelessly and disgracefully to his home. Thus, without mercy, he shut him up in a dark place for several days, and thinking to bend his spirit to his own will, he first used words and then blows and chains. But Francis became only the more ready and more strong to carry out his purpose; but he did not abandon his patience either because he was insulted by words or worn out by chains. For

he who is commanded to rejoice in tribulations cannot swerve from the right intention and position of his mind or be led away from Christ's flock, not even by scourgings and chains; neither does he waver in a flood of many waters, whose refuge from oppression is the Son of God, who, lest our troubles seem hard to us, showed always that those he bore were greater.

Chapter 6. How Francis' mother freed him, and how he stripped himself before the bishop of Assisi.

13. It happened, however, when Francis' father had left home for a while on business and the man of God remained bound in the basement of the house, his mother, who was alone with him and who did not approve of what her husband had done, spoke kindly to her son. But when she saw that he could not be persuaded away from his purpose, she was moved by motherly compassion for him, and loosening his chains, she let him go free. He, however, giving thanks to almighty God, returned quickly to the place where he had been before. But now, after he had been proved by temptations, he allowed himself greater liberty, and he took on a more cheerful aspect because of the many struggles he had gone through. From the wrongs done him he acquired a more confident spirit, and he went about everywhere freely with higher spirits than before. Meanwhile his father returned, and not finding Francis, he turned to upbraid his wife, heaping sins upon sins. Then, raging and blustering, he ran to that place hoping that if he could not recall him from his ways, he might at least drive him from the province. But, because it is true that in the fear of the Lord is confidence, when this child of grace heard his [worldly] minded father coming to him, confident and joyful he went to meet him, exclaiming in a clear voice that he cared nothing for his chains and blows. Moreover, he stated that he would gladly undergo evils for the name of Christ.

14. But when his father saw that he could not bring him back from the way he had undertaken, he was roused by all means to get his money back. The man of God had desired to offer it and expend it to feed the poor and to repair the buildings of that place. But he who had no love for money could not be misled by any aspect of good in it; and he who was not held back by any affection for it was in no way disturbed by its loss. Therefore, when the money was found, which he who hated the things of this world so greatly and desired the riches of heaven so much had thrown aside in the dust of the window sill, the fury of his raging father was extinguished a little, and the thirst of his avarice was somewhat allayed by the warmth of discovery. He then brought his son before the bishop of the city, so that, renouncing all his

possessions into his hands, he might give up everything he had. Francis not only did not refuse to do this, but he hastened with great joy do what was demanded of him.

15. When he was brought before the bishop [in 1206], he would suffer no delay or hesitation in anything: indeed, he did not wait for any words nor did he speak any, but immediately putting off his clothes and casting them aside, he gave them back to his father. Moreover, not even retaining his trousers, he stripped himself completely naked before all. The bishop, however, sensing his disposition and admiring greatly his fervor and constancy, arose and drew him within his arms and covered him with the mantle he was wearing. He understood clearly that the counsel was of God, and he understood that the actions of the man of God that he had personally witnessed contained a mystery. He immediately, therefore, became his helper and cherishing him and encouraging him, he embraced him in the bowels of charity. Behold, now he wrestles naked with his naked adversary, and having put off everything that is of this world, he thinks only about the things of the Lord. He seeks now so to despise his own life, putting off all solicitude for it, that he might find peace in his harassed ways, and that meanwhile only the wall of flesh should separate him from the vision of God.

Chapter 7. How Francis was seized by robbers and cast into the snow, and how he served the lepers.

16. He who once wore fine garments now went about clad only in scanty garments. As he went through a certain woods singing praises to the Lord in the French language, robbers suddenly rushed out upon him. When they asked him in a ferocious tone who be was, the man of God replied confidently in a loud voice: "I am the herald of the great King. What is that to you?" But they struck him and cast him into a ditch filled with deep snow, saying: "Lie there, foolish herald of God!" But he rolled himself about and shook off the snow; and when they had gone away, he jumped out of the ditch, and, glad with great joy, he began to call out the praises of God in a loud voice throughout the grove. At length, coming to a certain cloister of monks, he spent several days there as a scullion, wearing a ragged shirt and being satisfied to be filled only with broth. But, when all pity was withdrawn from him and he could not get even an old garment, he left the place, not moved by anger, but forced by necessity; and he went to the city of Gubbio, where he obtained a small tunic from a certain man who once had been his friend. Then, after some time had elapsed, when the fame of the man of God was beginning to grow and his name was spread abroad among the people,

the prior of the aforementioned monastery recalled and realized how the man of God had been treated and he came to him and begged pardon for himself and for his monks out of reverence for the Savior.

17. Then the holy lover of complete humility went to the lepers (see Doc. 52) and lived with them, serving them most diligently for God's sake; and washing all foulness from them, he wiped away also the corruption of the ulcers, just as he said in his *Testament*: "When I was in sins, it seemed extremely bitter to me to look at lepers, and the Lord himself led me among them and I practiced mercy with them." So greatly loathsome was the sight of lepers to him at one time, he used to say, that, in the days of his vanity, he would look at their houses only from a distance of two miles and he would hold his nostrils with his hands. But now, when by the grace and the power of the Most High he was beginning to think of holy and useful things, while he was still clad in secular garments, he met a leper one day and, made stronger than himself, he kissed him. From then on he began to despise himself more and more, until, by the mercy of the Redeemer, he came to perfect victory over himself. Of other poor, too, while he yet remained in the world and still followed the world, he was the helper, stretching forth a hand of mercy to those who had nothing, and showing compassion to the afflicted. For when one day, contrary to his custom, for he was a most courteous person, he upbraided a certain poor man who had asked an alms of him, he was immediately sorry; and he began to say to himself that it was a great reproach and a shame to withhold what was asked from one who had asked in the name of so great a King. He therefore resolved in his heart never in the future to refuse any one, if at all possible, who asked for the love of God. This he most diligently did and carried out, until he sacrificed himself entirely and in every way; and thus he became first a practicer before he became a teacher of the evangelical counsel: "To him who asks of thee," he said, "give; and from him who would borrow of thee, do not turn away" [Matt. 5:42].

Chapter 8. How Francis built the church of St. Damian; and of the life of the Ladies who dwelt in that place.

18. The first work that blessed Francis undertook after he had gained his freedom from the hand of his [worldly] minded father was to build a house of God [in 1207]. He did not try to build one anew, but he repaired an old one, restored an ancient one. He did not tear out the foundation, but he built upon it, ever reserving to Christ his prerogative, though he was not aware of it, "for other foundation no one can lay, but that which has been laid, which is Christ Jesus" [1 Cor. 3:11]. When he had returned to the place where, as

has been said, the church of St. Damian had been built in ancient times, he repaired it zealously within a short time with the help of the grace of the Most High. This is the blessed and holy place, where the glorious religion and most excellent order of Poor Ladies and holy virgins had its blessed origin about six years after the conversion of St. Francis and through that same blessed man. Of it, the Lady Clare [c. 1194-1253], a native of the city of Assisi, the most precious and the firmest stone of the whole structure, was the foundation. For when, after the beginning of the Order of Brothers, the said lady was converted to God through the counsel of the holy man, she lived unto the advantage of many and as an example to a countless multitude. She was of noble parentage, but she was more noble by grace; she was a virgin in body, most chaste in mind; a youth in age, but mature in spirit; steadfast in purpose and most ardent in her desire for divine love; endowed with wisdom and excelling in humility; Clare by name, brighter in life, and brightest in character.

19. Over her arose a noble structure of most precious pearls, whose praise is not from men but from God's since neither is our limited understanding sufficient to imagine it, nor our scanty vocabulary to utter it. For above everything else there flourishes among them that excelling virtue of mutual and continual charity, which so binds their wills into one that, though forty or fifty of them dwell together in one place, agreement in likes and dislikes molds one spirit in them out of many. Secondly, in each one there glows the gem of humility, which so preserves the gifts and good things bestowed from heaven, that they merit other virtues too. Thirdly, the lily of virginity and chastity so sprinkles them with a wondrous odor that, forgetful of earthly thoughts, they desire to meditate only on heavenly things; and so great a love for their eternal Spouse arises in their hearts from the fragrance of that lily that the integrity of that holy affection excludes from them every habit of their former life. Fourthly, they have all become so conspicuous by the title of the highest poverty that their food and clothing hardly at all or never come together to satisfy extreme necessity.

20. Fifthly, they have so attained the singular grace of abstinence and silence that they need exert hardly any effort to check the movements of the flesh and to restrain their tongues; some of them have become so unaccustomed to speak that when necessity demands that they speak, they can hardly remember how to form the words as they should. Sixthly, with all these things, they are adorned so admirably with the virtue of patience, that no adversity of tribulations or injury of vexations ever breaks their spirit or changes it. Seventhly, and finally, they have so merited the height of contemplation that

in it they learn everything they should do or avoid; and happily they know how to be out of mind for God, persevering night and day in praising him and in praying to him. May the eternal God deign by his holy grace to bring so holy a beginning to an even more holy end. And let this suffice for the present concerning these virgins dedicated to God and the most devout handmaids of Christ, for their wondrous life and their glorious institutions, which they received from the lord Pope Gregory [IX], at that time Bishop of Ostia, requires a work of its own and leisure in which to write it.

Chapter 9. How Francis, having changed his habit, rebuilt the church of St. Mary of the Portiuncula, and how, upon hearing the Gospel, he left all things, and how be designed and made the habit the brothers wear.

21. Meanwhile the holy man of God, having put on a new kind of habit and having repaired the aforesaid church, went to another place near the city of Assisi, where he began to rebuild a certain dilapidated and well-nigh destroyed church, and he did not leave off from his good purpose until he had brought it to completion. Then he went to another place, which is called the Portiuncula where there stood a church of the Blessed Virgin Mother of God that had been built in ancient times, but was now deserted and cared for by no one. When the holy man of God saw how it was thus in ruins, he was moved to pity, because he burned with devotion toward the mother of all good; and he began to live there in great zeal. It was the third year of his conversion when he began to repair this church. At this time he wore a kind of hermit's dress, with a leather girdle about his waist; he carried a staff in his hands and wore shoes on his feet.

22. But when on a certain day [in 1208?] the Gospel was read in that church, how the Lord sent his disciples out to preach, the holy man of God, assisting there, understood somewhat the words of the Gospel; after mass he humbly asked the priest to explain the Gospel to him more fully. When he had set forth for him in order all these things, the holy Francis, hearing that the disciples of Christ should not possess gold or silver or money; nor carry along the way scrip, or wallet, or bread, or a staff; that they should not have shoes, or two tunics [Matt. 10:9-11]; but that they should preach the kingdom of God and penance, immediately cried out exultingly: "This is what I wish, this is what I seek, this is what I long to do with all my heart." Then the holy father, overflowing with joy, hastened to fulfill that salutary word he had heard, and he did not suffer any delay to intervene before beginning devoutly to perform what he had heard. He immediately put off his shoes from his feet, put aside the staff from his hands, was content with one tunic,

and exchanged his leather girdle for a small cord. He designed for himself a tunic that bore a likeness to the cross, that by means of it he might beat off all temptations of the devil; he designed a very rough tunic so that by it he might crucify the flesh with all its vices and sins; he designed a very poor and mean tunic, one that would not excite the covetousness of the world. The other things that he had heard, however, he longed with the greatest diligence and the greatest reverence to perform. For he was not a deaf hearer of the Gospel, but committing all that he had heard to praiseworthy memory, he tried diligently to carry it out to the letter.

Chapter 10. Of his preaching of the Gospel and his announcing peace and of the conversion of the first six brothers.

23. From then on he began to preach penance to all with great fervor of spirit and joy of mind, edifying his hearers with his simple words and his greatness of heart. His words [were] like a burning fire, penetrating the inmost reaches of the heart, and it filled the minds of all the hearers with admiration. He seemed completely different from what he had been, and, looking up to the heavens, he disdained to look upon the earth. This indeed is wonderful, that he first began to preach where as a child he had first learned to read and where for a time he was buried amid great honor, so that the happy beginning might be commended by a still happier ending. Where he had learned he also taught, and where he began he also ended. In all his preaching, before he proposed the word of God to those gathered about, he first prayed for peace for them, saying: "The Lord give you peace." He always most devoutly announced peace to men and women, to all he met and overtook. For this reason many who had hated peace and had hated also salvation embraced peace, through the cooperation of the Lord, with all their heart and were made children of peace and seekers after eternal salvation.

24. Among these, a certain man from Assisi, of pious and simple spirit, was the first to devoutly follow the man of God. After him, Brother Bernard [of Quintavalle], embracing the delegation of peace, ran eagerly after the holy man of God to purchase the kingdom of heaven [in 1209]. He had often given the blessed father hospitality, and, having had experience of his life and conduct and having been refreshed by the fragrance of his holiness, he conceived a fear and brought forth the spirit of salvation. He noticed that Francis would pray all night, sleeping but rarely, praising God and the glorious Virgin Mother of God, and he wondered and said: "In all truth, this man is from God." He hastened therefore to sell all his goods and gave the money to the poor, though not to his parents; and laying hold of the title to the way

of perfection, he carried out the counsel of the holy Gospel: "If thou wilt be perfect, go, sell what thou hast, and give to the poor, and thou shalt have treasure in heaven; and come, follow me" [Matt. 19:21]. When he had done this, he was associated with St. Francis by his life and by his habit, and he was always with him until, after the number of the brothers had increased, he was sent to other regions by obedience to his kind father. His conversion to God was a model to others in the manner of selling one's possessions and giving them to the poor. St. Francis rejoiced with very great joy over the coming and conversion of so great a man, in that the Lord was seen to have a care for him by giving him a needed companion and a faithful friend.

25. But immediately another man of the city of Assisi followed him; he deserves to be greatly praised for his conduct, and what he began in a holy way, he completed after a short time in a more holy way. After a not very long time, Brother Giles [of Assisi] followed him; he was a simple and upright man, and one fearing God. He lived a long time, leading a holy life, justly and piously, and giving us examples of perfect obedience, manual labor, solitary life, and holy contemplation. After another one had been added to these, Brother Philip [the Long] brought the number to seven. The Lord touched his lips with a purifying coal that he might speak pleasing things of him and utter sweet things. Understanding and interpreting the sacred Scriptures, though he had not studied, he became an imitator of those whom the leaders of the Jews alleged to be ignorant and unlearned.

Chapter 11. Of the spirit of prophecy of St. Francis and of his admonitions.

26. Therefore the blessed father Francis was being daily filled with the consolation and the grace of the Holy Spirit; and with all vigilance and solicitude he was forming his new sons with new learning, teaching them to walk with undeviating steps the way of holy poverty and blessed simplicity. One day, when he was wondering over the mercy of the Lord with regard to the gifts bestowed upon him, he wished that the course of his own life and that of his brothers might be shown him by the Lord; he sought out a place of prayer, as he had done so often, and he persevered there for a long time with fear and trembling standing before the Lord of the whole earth, and he thought in the bitterness of his soul of the years he had spent wretchedly, frequently repeating this word: "O God, be merciful to me the sinner" [Luke 18:13]. Little by little a certain unspeakable joy and very great sweetness began to flood his innermost heart. He began also to stand aloof from himself, and, as his feelings were checked and the darkness that had gathered in his heart because of his fear of sin dispelled, there was poured into him a certainty that

all his sins had been forgiven and a confidence of his restoration to grace was given him. He was then caught up above himself, and absorbed in a certain light; the capacity of his mind was enlarged and he could see clearly what was to come to pass. When this sweetness finally passed, along with the light, renewed in spirit, he seemed changed into another man.

27. And then, coming back, he said with joy to his brothers: "Be strengthened, dear brothers, and rejoice in the Lord, and do not be sad because you seem so few; and do not let either my simplicity or your own dismay you, for, as it has been shown me in truth by the Lord, God will make us grow into a very great multitude and will make us increase to the ends of the world. For your profit I am compelled to tell you what I have seen, though I would much rather remain silent, were it not that charity urges me to tell you. I saw a great multitude of men coming to us and wanting to live with us in the habit of our way of life and under the rule of our blessed religion. And behold, the sound of them is in my ears as they go and come according to the command of holy obedience. I have seen, as it were, the roads filled with their great numbers coming together in these parts from almost every nation. Frenchmen are coming, Spaniards are hastening, Germans and Englishmen are running, and a very great multitude of others speaking various tongues are hurrying." When the brothers had heard this, they were filled with a salutary joy, both because of the grace the Lord God gave to his holy one and because they were ardently thirsting for the advantages to be gained by their neighbors, whom they wished to grow daily in numbers and to be saved thereby.

10. THE FAITH OF JOAN OF ARC (1431)

We know more about the extraordinary life of Joan of Arc (1412-31) than any other medieval woman of her social class through the detailed transcripts – in French and Latin – taken during the course of her trial for heresy. Joan's intense and abiding belief in saintly voices sent from God to guide her in expelling the English from France was hardly a routine religious experience. But her description of her childhood formation in Christian belief and practice was probably typical of Christian life in most villages. Those sections from the trial deposition touching on Joan's early religious education, her own understanding of faith, and some of her descriptions of her voices are extracted below.

Source: trans. J. Shinners from *Procès de Condamnation de Jeanne d'Arc*, eds. Pierre Tisset and Yvonne Lanhers, (Paris: Librairie C. Klincksieck, 1960), v. 1., pp. 40-41, 46-48, 57-60, 62, 65-67, 69-74, 101, 103-06, 159. Latin.

[*February 21, 1431*] After taking this oath [to speak truthfully], Jeanne was interrogated by us about her name and surname. To which she answered that in her own region she was called Jeannette; but after she came into France she was called Jeanne. She said that she knew nothing about her surname. Asked about her place of origin, she answered that she was born in the village of Domrémy, which is one with the village of Greux; the principal [parish] church is at Greux.

Asked about the name of her father and mother, she said that her father was called Jacques d'Arc; her mother, Ysabelle.

Asked where she was baptized, she said in the church of Domrémy.

Asked who were her godfathers and godmothers, she responded that one of her godmothers was called Agnes, one Jeanne, and the other Sibylle. One of her godfathers was called Jean Lingué, another Jean Barrey. She heard from her mother that she had several other godmothers.

Asked what priest baptized her, she answered that she believed [it was] Reverend (*dominus*) Jean Minet. Asked if he was still alive, she said she believes so.

Asked how old she was, she answered that it seems to her that she is about nineteen years old. She further said that she learned the Our Father, Hail Mary, and Creed from her mother; she had learned no other beliefs except from her mother.

We asked her to say the Our Father. She answered that we should hear her confession [the sacrament of penance] and she would willingly say it. When we asked her several more times about this, she answered that she would not say the Our Father, etc. unless we heard her confession. But then we told her that we would willingly send her one or two well-regarded men who spoke French, before whom she could say the Our Father, etc. To this the said Jeanne answered that she would not say them unless they heard her confession....

[*February 22*] Asked whether she confessed her sins each year, she answers yes, to her own parish priest; and when he was busy, she confessed to another priest with his permission. Sometimes she also confessed to the mendicant friars – two or three times, she believes; this was at Neufchâteau. And she received the sacrament of the Eucharist during Eastertime.

Asked whether she had received the sacrament of the Eucharist at any other feast than Easter, she told the questioner that he should move on to something else. She further states that when she was thirteen years old, she received a voice from God to help guide her. The first time [that she heard it] it caused her great fear. This voice came to her around midday, in the summer, in her father's garden. The said Jeanne had not fasted the day before. She heard this voice at her right side, towards the church; and she rarely heard it without [an accompanying] light. This light comes from the same side the voice is heard from, but usually there is a great light there. And when the said Jeanne came into France she often heard this voice.

She was asked how she could see this light that she said was there since the light was at her side. She did not answer this, but went on to something else. She then said that if she were in a grove, she could clearly hear the voices coming to her. She also said it seemed to her to be a worthy voice, and that she believes that this voice was sent from God. After she heard it for the third time, she recognized that it was the voice of an angel. She also said that this voice had always guarded her well, and that she understood it well.

She was asked what kind of lesson the voice taught her regarding the salvation of her soul. She said that it instructed her to behave well and to go to church often; and it told the said Jeanne that it was necessary for Jeanne to come into France. The said Jeanne added that, for the time being, the questioner would not learn from her in what form this voice appeared to her. She further said that this voice said to her two or three times a week that Jeanne must leave and go into France, and that her father knew nothing about her departure. She said that the voice told her to go into France; she could no longer stay where she was. The voice also told her to lift the siege made on the city of Orleans....

[*February 24*] Asked the last time she had heard the voice that comes to her, she responded: "I heard it yesterday and today."

Asked at what hour yesterday she heard that voice, she answered that she heard it three times that day: once in the morning, once at vespers, and again when the bells [the angelus bell] were rung for [saying] the Hail Mary in the evening; and she hears it many more times than she could say.

Asked what she was doing yesterday morning when the voice came to her, she said that she was sleeping and the voice woke her.

Asked if the voice woke her by touching her arm, she said that the voice woke her without touching her.

Asked if that voice was in her room, she said she does not know, but it was in the castle.

Asked if she thanked that voice and kneeled, she said that she thanked it while sitting there on her bed, and she joined her hands. This was after she asked for its help. But the voice told Jeanne that she should answer boldly.

Asked what the voice said to her when it woke her, she answered that she asked the voice advice about how she should answer, telling the voice to seek the Lord's counsel about this. And the voice told her that she should answer boldly, and that God would help her.

Asked whether the voice said any other words to her before she asked it, she said that the voice said other things, but that she did not understand it all. Nevertheless, once she was waked from sleep, the voice told her to answer boldly.

Then she said to us, the bishop: "You say you are my judge. Be careful what you are doing; for in truth I am sent from God, and you place yourself in great danger" – in French, *en grant dangier.*

Asked whether this voice had ever changed its advice, she answered that she never found it to offer two contrary actions. She also said that that night she heard it telling her that she should answer boldly....

Asked if the voice that she said appears to her is an angel, or comes directly from God, or is the voice of a male or female saint, she responded: "The voice comes from God; and I believe that I do not tell you completely what I know: I have a greater fear of failing by telling you something that would displease these voices than I have of answering you. And regarding this question, I ask you to give me a delay [in answering]."...

Then she was asked whether the voice from which she seeks advice has a face and eyes. She responded: "You will not get that from me yet." And she said that there is a saying of little children that sometimes men are hanged for telling the truth.

Asked whether she knows if she is in the grace of God, she responded: "If I am not, may God put me there; if I am, may God keep me there. I would be the saddest person in the whole world if I knew that I was not in God's grace." She said further that if she was in a state of sin, she believes that the voice would not come to her; and she wished that anyone could perceive it as clearly as she did....

She was asked about a certain tree located near her village. To which she responded that fairly nearby Domrémy there is a certain tree called "The Ladies' Tree" (*l'Arbre des Dames*); others call it "The Fairies' Tree" – in French, [*l'Arbre*] *des Fees* – next to which there is a spring; and she had heard it said that people sick with fevers drink from the spring and go there seeking its water to be healed. She herself has seen this; but she does not know whether they were healed. Also, she said that she has heard that the sick, when they can get up, go to this tree and stroll around it. It is a big tree, called a beech, from which comes the "may" (*mayum*) – in French, *beau may* [a decorative garland]. By custom it belongs to the knight, Seigneur Pierre de Bourlement. She said that sometimes she went there walking around with other girls, and at that tree she made a garland for the image of Blessed Mary of Domrémy. Many times she has heard from old folks – but not related to her – that the lady fairies dwell around this tree. And she has heard it said by the woman named Jeanne – one of Jeanne's godmothers and the wife of Aubery, the mayor of that village [of Domrémy] – that she has seen the lady fairies there;

but she does not know whether this is true or not. She said that, as far as she knows, she has never seen the fairies at the tree; but if she saw them elsewhere, she does not know whether she saw them or not. She said that she saw the young girls putting garlands on the branches of this tree, and she herself has sometimes put them there with the other girls; sometimes they took them with them, sometimes they left them. She said that once she knew that she had to come into France, she did little playing and strolling about, much less than she could have. She does not recall that, once she reached the age of discretion, she ever danced there at the tree. Sometimes she really did dance there with the children, though she sang more than she danced. She also said that there is one grove there called the Oakwood – in French, *le Bois Chenus* – which is visible from her father's door; it is not more than half a league away. She does not know and has never heard if the lady fairies dwell there; but she heard it said by her brother that it is said in the land that Jeanne began her mission at the Lady Fairies' Tree. But she said that she had not done this, and she told him the contrary. She further said that, when she went to her king, some people asked her whether there was not in her land a grove called in French *le Bois Chenus*, because there were prophecies saying that from around this grove would come a maid who would do marvelous things. But Jeanne said that she put no faith in this....

[*February 27*] Asked whether she fasted every day of Lent, she responded by asking: "Is this part of your case?"

When she was told this pertained to the case, she answered; "Yes, indeed. I have fasted every day during this Lent."

Asked whether it was the voice of an angel which spoke to her, or whether it was the voice of a male or female saint, or of God speaking directly, she responded that it was the voice of Saint Catherine and of Saint Margaret. And their figures are encircled with beautiful crowns, very rich and precious. "And I have permission from the Lord," she said, "to tell you this. But if you have a doubt about this, send to Poitiers, where I was examined previously" [at the start of her mission in 1429 by Charles VII's counselors].

Asked how she knew there were two saints, and how well she could tell one from the other, she answered that she knows quite well who they are and knows well how to tell one from the other.

Asked how she knows one from the other well, she answered that she knows them by the greeting they give her. She added that seven years have now passed since they began guiding her. She said she knows these saints well for this reason: they named themselves to her.

Asked whether these two saints are dressed in the same material, she responded: "I will tell you no more for now; I do not have permission to reveal it. If you do not believe me, go to Poitiers." She also said that there are some revelations which go to the king of France and not to those who are questioning her.

Asked whether these saints are the same age, she answered that she did not have permission to speak about this.

Asked whether the saints speak together or one after the other, she answered: "I do not have permission to speak about this; but, I have always had counsel from both of them."

Asked which of them appeared to her first, she responded: "I did not recognize them so quickly; I knew this well enough once, but I have forgotten. If I had permission, I would willingly tell you; it is contained in the register at Poitiers." Next, she also said that she received comfort from Saint Michael.

Asked which of these appearing to her came first, she answered that Saint Michael came first.

Asked whether much time passed after she first received the voice of Saint Michael, she responded: "I did not mention the voice of Saint Michael to you by name; but I speak about [his] great comfort."

Asked what was the first voice that came to her when she was about thirteen, she answered that it was Saint Michael, whom she saw before her eyes; and he was not alone, but was joined by angels from heaven....

Asked whether she saw Saint Michael and these angels physically and really, she responded: "I saw them with my bodily eyes as clearly as I see you; and when they left, I cried and truly wished that they had taken me with them."...

[*March 15*] Asked whether, since offerings of candles are commonly made to the saints in paradise, she has made an offering of lighted candles or other things in church or elsewhere to the saints who come to her or had masses said, she responded no, except for the one that ought to be offered in the hands of the priest during mass to honor Saint Catherine; and she believes that she is one of the saints who appear to her. She has not burned as many candles as she would freely wish to offer to Saint Catherine and Saint Margaret, who are in paradise, who she firmly believes to be the ones who come to her.

Asked whether, when she put candles before the image of Saint Catherine, she put them there in honor of the one who appears to her, she responded: "I do this in honor of God, of Blessed Mary, and of Saint Catherine who is in heaven, and of the one who reveals herself to me."

Asked whether she placed candles like this in honor of that Saint Catherine, who has revealed herself to her or who has appeared to her, she responded yes, and that she makes no distinction between the one who appears to her and the one who is in heaven....

The transcript also depicts the religious beliefs of the people around Joan:

[*March 3*] .... Asked whether the women of that town [Rheims] had not touched their rings on that ring that Jeanne wore on her finger, she responded that, "Many women touched my hands and my rings; but I do not know their reason or their intention."...

Asked how old the boy was that she revived at Lagny, she responded that the boy was three days old. He was brought before the image of Blessed Mary of Lagny. Jeanne was told that the girls of the village were [praying] before this image, and that she might want to go pray to God and Blessed Mary that life be given to the infant. Then she went and prayed with the other girls; and finally life returned to the boy who gave three yawns and then was baptized. He soon died and was buried in consecrated ground. It was said that three days had passed during which no life appeared in the boy; he was as black as Jeanne's coat. But after he yawned, his color began to return. And Jeanne was with the other girls kneeling in prayer before Our Lady.

Asked if it was said in that town that she had caused this resuscitation to occur, and that this happened through her prayer, she responded that she did not ask about it.

Asked whether she knew or had seen Catherine de La Rochelle [a rival visionary who later testified against Joan], she said yes, at the town of Jargeau and at Montfaucon in the duchy of Berry. Asked whether this same Catherine had shown her a certain lady dressed in white, who she said sometimes appeared to her, she answered no.

Asked what this Catherine said to her, she said that this Catherine told her that a certain White Lady [*domina alba*], dressed in cloth-of-gold, came to the said Catherine telling her that she should go through the good [i.e., loyal] towns, and that her king would give her heralds and *tubicines* or trumpets to proclaim that whoever had gold, silver, or treasure hidden away should immediately bring it out, for Catherine would clearly know whether anyone had anything hidden and did not bring it out, and she would clearly know where to find that treasure. And with these she would pay Jeanne's men-at-arms. To this, Jeanne told Catherine that she should go back to her husband, do her household duties – in French, *son mesnage* – and raise her children. To know for certain about the doings of this Catherine de La Rochelle, Jeanne spoke to St. Catherine and St. Margaret, who told her that the actions of this Catherine were nothing but foolishness and amounted to nothing....

Also, she said that she asked this Catherine whether this White Lady who appeared to her came to her every night, telling her that if this were the case she wished to stay in the same bed with her [in order to see the lady]. To do this, Jeanne stayed awake in bed with her until the middle of the night; but she saw nothing there and so went to sleep. When morning came, she asked this Catherine whether the White Lady came to her. She said yes, while Jeanne was sleeping but she was unable to wake her up. Then Jeanne asked her whether the lady would come the following night; Catherine said yes, so because of this Jeanne slept that day so that she could stay awake all the next night. She lay in bed with Catherine the whole night watching, but she saw nothing, even though she often asked Catherine whether the lady was coming, and Catherine replied, "Yes, soon."

11. THE FAITH OF THE SPANISH PEASANT, JUAN DE RABE (1518)

A Spanish example from the early sixteenth century offers an interesting counterpoint to Joan of Arc. Here, too, the peasant Juan de Rabe sees visions, but their character, his character, and the outcome of the investigation differ markedly. Both St. Sebastian and St. Roch, who figure in this peasant's second vision, were invoked against the plague.

Source: trans. William A. Christian, Jr., *Apparitions in Late Medieval and Renaissance Spain* (Princeton, NJ: Princeton University Press, 1981), pp. 153-56. Spanish.

[*February 18, 1518*] Juan de Rabe, citizen of La Mota, was ordered called in by their Reverences to the hearing room, being a prisoner in the jail of the Holy Office [of the Inquisition] by their order. And when he was sworn in by the inquisitor Juan Yañes he was asked by his Reverence what his name was. He said he was Juan de Rabe, and his parents were Juan de Rabe and Ynes Rodríguez, both deceased, inhabitants and natives of Villaverde and full-blooded Old Christians. His only sister lives in La Mota. She is named María de Rabe and is married to Pedro García, laborer, inhabitant of La Mota.

Asked if he is married or ever has been, he said no, and that he is about fifty years old. Asked why he did not marry, he said it was because he could not find a good match. Asked what property he owned, he said he owned nothing, that he maintained himself by working, by digging, plowing, and sometimes herding sheep, as he did last year. Asked where he has lived in the past few years, he said in La Mota and in Santa María de los Llanos. Asked if he knows what year it is, he said he does not know, but that he does know that it is the month of February.

He was asked by his Reverence if he knew the *Credo* and the *Salve Regina*;

he said he did not. Asked if he knew the *Pater Noster* and the *Ave Maria*; he said he did. He was ordered to say them. He said the entire *Ave Maria*, and the *Pater Noster* he said in its entirety but he did not know it well. He was asked by his Reverence if he confessed every year as Holy Mother Church mandates. He said that he has confessed every year at Lent with the old priest in the town of La Mota, and that every time he confessed he received the most holy sacrament.

Asked if he knew the Ten Commandments and the Articles of Faith and the seven deadly sins and the five senses, he said he did not know any of these in whole or in part. Asked by his Reverence what it was he confessed, if he did not know the seven deadly sins or the Ten Commandments or the five senses, he said he confessed what he did know about. He was asked if pride or envy or lust or the killing of a man or insulting someone with offensive words was a sin, and to each of these he replied he did not know. He was asked if theft was a sin, and he said that, God preserve us, theft was a very great sin.

He was asked what things he did confess, since he did not confess any sins at all. He said that about four years ago he was on his way alone to turn over the soil in a vineyard at Santa María de los Llanos that belonged to his cousin, Francisco Martínez. He was carrying a hoe, a wineskin, and bread for his lunch. On the road he heard a loud bolt of thunder in the sky and said to himself, "God in heaven help me! The sky is clear, why does it thunder?" He said he looked toward town and heard another thunderclap, and since the sky was clear he said, "God help me! What is this about?" Then he looked down, and he said he saw next to his feet Our Lady the Virgin Mary. She seemed to him like a tiny girl, and that she was riding on a tiny burro and dressed in white.

Asked what color the burro was, he said it was very pretty but he does not know what color it was.

Asked who came with her, he said that no one else came with her.

Asked how he knew or who told him that the girl he referred to was Our Lady, he said that she herself told him so. And that she said to him, "O how many bad people there are in this town of yours who do nothing but blaspheme and foreswear my son," and that it was not enough that men should do this, but that the women did it too. And that he should tell the whole town and the priest to take the cross and go in procession to the holy calvary in El Pedernoso or on the way to Pedernoso, and that they erect a cross where she came and appeared to this witness.

And so later he went to tell everybody about it, and they came afterwards with a cross and put it where this witness told them Our Lady had appeared to him. And from there they went to the holy calvary, which may be more than four crossbow shots from there. And afterwards they went back in procession to the town. And that before he went to tell the people all this she disappeared, and he never saw her again. And that this took place on a Saturday morning, and that she told him not to report it until the afternoon, which is what he did. And the priest would not absolve him until he said it out loud in front of everyone in church.

Asked if Our Lady, she who he says he saw, carried a baby in her arms, he said all he saw was that she was seated on the little burro.

Asked if he knows if it was a little burro or a little mule, he said he does not know, just that it seemed like a little burro to him, and very pretty. And that on no other occasion did she appear to him, but that another time two years later Saint Sebastian appeared to him in Los Llanos de la Casa Sola wearing a brown garment and his arrows with blood and a crown of gold like a star. He was about half as tall as this witness, and he came alone. This took place in the morning before the witness had breakfasted, when he was tending the animals of Christobal Sánchez of la Mota. And he told him he was Saint Sebastian, and that he should go to El Toboso because at that time many people were dying of the plague and tell them to build two chapels. One was to be in the Cerro Espartoso, which Our Lady had ordered them to build and which they had not seen fit to build until the epidemic returned as they had had it before when she ordered it. The other was to be below Saint Peter, which has been started. And that he does not know to what saint except that he ordered them that the one on the Cerro Espartoso should be dedicated to Saint Roch.

His inquisitors rejected Juan de Rabe's visions as vanities and ordered him to be publicly whipped a hundred times, incarcerated until he received adequate religious instruction, and then released.

Compare the level of religious knowledge of Peter Waldes, Francis of Assisi, Joan of Arc, and Juan de Rabe. What avenues of instruction did they have available to them and how well did they each understand their faith? Was their faith just the result of effective Christian propaganda or did they internalize the Christian message? How free was each of them to explore and develop their personal religious interests?

CHAPTER TWO: GOD

The Christian idea of God confronted believers with a dazzlingly subtle concept: a single God who eternally existed as a trinity of three separate persons, and a Son of God who was both utterly human and utterly divine. A religious riddle puzzling to even the most erudite theologian, it certainly baffled plenty of ordinary people. One medieval anecdote tells of a shepherd who, when asked about the Trinity, recognized the Father and the Son, but couldn't quite place "that third fellow"! Yet it is worth bearing in mind that Christians of every age have struggled to grasp in even the dimmest way the mystery of the Trinity. Since popular religion always prefers the concrete to the abstract, it is not surprising that the Son of God, whose human biography could be clearly recounted, overshadowed the Father and the Holy Spirit in popular belief. One of the most interesting developments in the medieval idea of God was the emerging emphasis on Jesus' humanity, a trend spurred on by twelfth-century Cistercian and, especially, thirteenth-century Franciscan devotions. Jesus remained intimidating in his role as Last Judge, but the focus on his manhood helped stir people's compassion for and identification with the palpable human experience of their God. It is a development seen most vividly as western artists rejected the stately, stoic, robed Christ of Syrian-influenced crucifixions typical of early medieval art, and opted for the slumped, suffering, naked Jesus typical of the later Middle Ages.

Fig. 2.1. Judgment Day

The most fearsome image of Christ was as the Last Judge. Here, as Mary and St. John plead before him, he sits in majesty judging the world, flanked by angels holding the nails, spear, cross, and crown of thorns from his passion. More angels sound the last trumpet to wake the dead. St. Peter with his key admits the souls of the righteous into heaven while devils plunge the damned into a hissing cauldron. From a treatise on the ten commandments written for France's Philip III in 1278; Milan, Ambrosian Library, MS H 106 sup., fol. 23v.

12. *THE PLAY OF ADAM* (c. 1125-75)

Mystery plays (enacting episodes from the Old and New Testaments) and morality plays (dramatizing allegorical contests of good and evil) offer modern readers one avenue into the religious knowledge of ordinary medieval people. Typically organized and performed by urban guilds on pageant wagons pulled through town streets or, as in this play, on church porches or stages erected for the purpose, these plays were public and popular recreations of Christian history. They were usually composed by men of some kind of clerical status; but they were specifically meant for popular consumption, so they were typically written in the vernacular and dealt with sacred matters in ways readily grasped by people of little or no education. The authors of these plays drew their material from the Bible, but they also freely adapted legendary material from the apocryphal gospels and popular collections such as Jacob of Voragine's thirteenth-century Golden Legend *(see Doc. 32). Since medieval pastoral theology seldom focused distinctly on either God the Father or God the Holy Spirit, and since vernacular translations of the Bible were usually discouraged, theatrical representations were one of the few ways that ordinary people learned about God as Creator. Elaborate stage effects depicting God in glory, typically part of the spectacle, would heighten the dramatic impression. (In this play God is always called "the Figure of God" presumably to avoid ensnaring the audience in idiolatry.) This excerpt is from the earliest surviving play in French, the three-part* Play of Adam *(Ordo representacionis Ade or Le Jeu d'Adam), written sometime between 1125 and 1175 either in Normandy or England. The dialogue is in Norman French; the italicized stage directions and the choir's songs are in Latin. The dramatic action is based on chapters two and three of the Book of Genesis, but the feudal terminology woven into the play is one of its noteworthy features. The end of the play, omitted here, recounts the story of Cain and Abel and the Procession of the Prophets.*

Source: *The Play of Adam (Ordo Representacionis Ade)*, trans. Carl J. Odenkirken (Brookline, MA: Classical Folia Editions; Leyden: Brill, 1976), pp. 43-109. Norman French and Latin.

[Stage directions in Latin:] *Paradise is to be set up on a somewhat higher level, with curtains and silk panels placed around at such a height that the actors in paradise are visible down to their shoulders. Fragrant flowers are to be intertwined with foliage; inside, there are to be different varieties of trees, and fruit suspended from them, so that it will seem a most delightful place. Now the Savior is to enter, clothed in a dalmatic; Adam and Eve are to take their places before him. Adam is to wear a red tunic, Eve a white, woman's garment, a white silk robe. Both must stand before the Figure of God, Adam somewhat closer, his features quite composed, while Eve is to have a rather more timid look. Adam is to be well trained in the timing of his lines, so that he will answer neither too quickly nor too slowly. And not only he, but all the actors must be trained to speak with deliberation, and to make gestures that are in keeping with what they are saying; they must not add or take away a syllable in their lines, but rather pronounce them all distinctly, and deliver everything they have to say in the proper order. Every time someone mentions paradise he is to look at it and point it out with his hand.*

Now let the lesson begin: "In the beginning God created heaven and earth ..." [Gen. 1:1] *and when this is finished, the choir is to sing* [in Latin]: *"The Lord therefore shaped ..."* [Gen. 2:7] *and when this is finished, the* FIGURE OF GOD *is to say:* Adam!

And he is to answer: My Lord!

FIGURE OF GOD: I have given you form *de limo terre* [i.e., from the clay of the earth].

ADAM: Well I know it.

FIGURE OF GOD: I have formed you according to my likeness [*gap in manus-ript*]. Out of earth after my own image I have made you; you must never start a war with me.

ADAM: That I shall not do; no, indeed; I shall believe in you. I shall obey my creator.

FIGURE OF GOD: I have given you a good companion; she is your wife, her name is Eve. She is your wife and your equal; you are to be most faithful to her. Love her, and let her love you; then both of you will be loved by me. She is to be subject to your command, and both of you subject to my will. From your rib I have created her; she is no stranger, she was born from you. I fashioned her from your body, she came out of you, not from elsewhere. Guide her with reason. Let there never be any quarrel between you, but rather great love, great mutual support; let such be the rule of your household.

Now I shall speak to you, Eve! Mark this closely, do not treat it lightly! If you agree to do my will, you shall keep the goodness you have within you. Love me, and honor your creator; acknowledge me as your lord. Apply all your thought, all your strength, and all your mind to my service. Love Adam, and hold him dear; he is the husband and you are his wife. Be subject to him always, and do not fail in your obedience to him. Serve him and love him with an upright heart, for this is the law of marriage. If you are a good helpmate to him, I shall place you together with him into eternal glory.

EVE: That I shall do, Lord, according to your wishes; I shall never have the desire to depart from it. I shall acknowledge you as lord, him as my equal and as the stronger. I shall at all times be faithful to him; from me he will receive good counsel. I shall please you, I shall serve you, lord, in every way.

Then the FIGURE OF GOD *is to beckon Adam to come closer, and say even more in-sistently to him:* Listen, Adam, and pay attention to my words. I created you, and now I shall make you a gift as follows: you can live forever, if you obey my word; you will forever, enjoy health, never will you be afraid. You will never be hungry, nor will you drink because you need to, never will you be cold, nor will you feel heat; you will live in joy without ever feeling weary, and in your pleasure you will never know pain.

Your whole life you will spend in joy; it will last forever, and that is not something of little worth! I say this to you, and I want Eve to hear it, too. If she does not pay attention to it, she will indeed be a fool.

You have mastery over all the earth; over birds, beasts, and over the rest of the earth's inhabitants. If anyone envies you, consider him of little importance, for the whole world will be subject to you.

Within you I place both good and evil; he who possesses such a gift is not chained to a post. Now weigh everything on the scales impartially; follow only such advice as may be loyal to me.

Leave aside evil, and hold on to what is good; love your lord and be on his side; because of no other counsel must you disregard mine; if you do all this you will not sin in anything.

ADAM: I give great thanks to your generosity, to you who created me, and who now even grants me power over good and evil. To your service I shall apply my will. You are my lord, I am your creature; you gave me form, and I am the work of your hands. Let my will never be so stubborn that not all my concern be directed towards serving you.

Thereupon let the FIGURE OF GOD *point out paradise to Adam with its hand, saying:* Adam!

ADAM: My Lord.

FIGURE OF GOD: I shall tell you of my plans. Do you see this garden?

ADAM: What is its name?

FIGURE OF GOD: Paradise.

ADAM: It is most beautiful.

FIGURE OF GOD: I planted it and found a place for it. Whoever lives in it will be my friend. I entrust it to you, to live in and to take care of.

Thereupon the FIGURE OF GOD *will place them into paradise, saying:* I now place you inside.

ADAM: Can we stay?

FIGURE OF GOD: To live forever. You need fear nothing here; you can neither die nor fall ill. *The choir is to sing: "The Lord therefore took the man
...*" [*Gen. 2:15*]. *Then the* FIGURE OF GOD *will extend its hand towards
paradise, saying:* I shall tell you what the nature of this garden is: you
will find no delight that is lacking. There is not a good in the world
that any creature might long for that each could not find here in full
measure. Here woman will not have cause for anger against man, nor
will man feel shame or fear of woman. Here the act of procreation does
not make a sinner of man, nor does a woman feel pain when giving
birth. You will live forever, so fine a dwelling place it is; you cannot
grow older. Here you will not fear death, it will not do you harm. I do
not want you to leave: here you will make your home.

The choir is to sing: "The Lord said to Adam ..." [*Gen. 2:16*]. *Thereupon the*
FIGURE OF GOD *is to point out to Adam the trees of paradise, saying:* Of all
this fruit you can eat at your pleasure; – *and is to show him the forbidden
tree and its fruit, saying:* This one is forbidden to you, do not seek any
other satisfaction from it. If you eat of it, you at once shall feel death;
you shall lose my love, and your fortune you shall change from good
to bad.

ADAM: I shall fully respect your commandment; neither I nor Eve shall
evade it in any respect. If I should lose such a dwelling-place for a
single fruit, I deserve to be cast out, at the mercy of the wind.
If I ever in my life throw away your love for one apple, whether in
sound or unsound mind, I must be judged by the law that applies to a
traitor who swears falsely and betrays his lord.

*Then the Figure of God is to go to the church, and Adam and Eve are to stroll about
in paradise, virtuously enjoying themselves. In the meantime devils are to run
about through the square with suitable antics; each is to come up to paradise and
show Eve the forbidden fruit, as though persuading her to eat it. Then the Devil
will come up to Adam and say to him:* What are you doing, Adam?

ADAM: I'm living here and enjoying myself greatly.

DEVIL: You're getting along all right?

ADAM: I don't notice anything bothering me.

DEVIL: You could have it better.

ADAM: I wouldn't know how.

DEVIL: You want to know?

ADAM: Sure, I'd like that very much.

DEVIL: I know how.

ADAM: But why does that concern me?

DEVIL: Why not?

ADAM: It's of no use to me.

DEVIL: It's going to be.

ADAM: I wouldn't know when.

DEVIL: I'm not going to tell you this way, on the run.

ADAM: Come on, tell me.

DEVIL: I won't; first, I'd rather see you tired out from begging me.

ADAM: I don't really have to know it.

DEVIL: Well then you don't deserve to own anything good; you've got something good, but you don't know how to enjoy it.

ADAM: How's that?

DEVIL: You want to hear? I'll tell you in strict confidence.

ADAM: [*gap in manuscript*] for sure.

DEVIL: Listen, Adam, pay close attention; it'll be to your advantage.

ADAM: Agreed.

DEVIL: Are you going to believe me?

ADAM: Yes, I certainly will.

DEVIL: In every respect?

ADAM: With one exception.

DEVIL: What's that?

ADAM: Well, I'll tell you: I'm not going to sin against my creator.

DEVIL: You fear him that much?

ADAM: To tell the truth, yes. I love him and I fear him.

DEVIL: That's not very smart. What can he do to you?

ADAM: Both good and evil.

DEVIL: You're acting like a fool, when you believe that evil could befall you. Are you not immortal? You can't die!

ADAM: God has told me that I will die when I break his law.

DEVIL: What is this great law-breaking all about? Don't hold anything back – I want to hear it.

ADAM: I'll tell you just the way it is. He gave me a commandment: I can eat of all the fruit in paradise – that's what he said – except just one. That one's forbidden. I won't even lay a hand on it.

DEVIL: Which one is that?

Then ADAM *is to raise his hand and show him the forbidden fruit saying:* You see it over there? He very strongly forbade me to eat that one.

DEVIL: Do you know the reason?

ADAM: I? Certainly not.

DEVIL: Well, I'll tell you his motive; he doesn't care about the rest of the fruit *(and with his hand he is to show him the forbidden fruit, saying:)* except that one hanging high up there. That is the fruit of wisdom; it gives you mastery of all knowledge. If you eat it, you'll be doing yourself a favor.

ADAM: If I did, how would that be?

DEVIL: You'll see. Right away your eyes will be opened; whatever is yet to be will be revealed to you. You can do anything you want. It'll make you feel good just to pull it down to you. Eat it, you'll be doing yourself a favor! You'll no longer fear your God in any way; instead you'll be completely his equal. That's why he thought of forbidding it to you. You believe me, don't you? Taste the fruit!

ADAM: I won't!

DEVIL: What a joke! You're not going to do it?

ADAM: No.

DEVIL What a fool you are! Well, you'll yet remember my words.

Then the Devil will withdraw, and he will go over to the other demons, and he will run around the square; and after a short interval he will come back all cheerful and happy to continue tempting Adam, and he will say to him: Adam, what now? Are you going to change your mind? Are you still sticking to your foolish resolve? Didn't I tell you last time that God had assumed the responsibility of feeding you here? He put you here to eat this fruit. Do you have any other diversions?

ADAM: Indeed I do; [there is nothing] I don't have.

DEVIL: Aren't you ever going to get up in the world? You can really think of yourself as important, when God has made his gardener out of you! God has put you in charge of his garden; aren't you going to look for any other satisfactions? Did he create you just so you could stuff your belly? Other rewards don't attract you? Listen, Adam, pay attention; I'll give you some advice in all good faith: you can be your own man, and be the creator's equal. I'll give you the long and short of it: if you eat the apple *(here he will raise his hand towards paradise)* you will reign in majesty. You will share power with God.

ADAM: Get away from here!

DEVIL: What are you saying, Adam?

ADAM: Get away from here! You're Satan; you're giving evil counsel!

DEVIL: How could I do that?

ADAM: You want to deliver me to eternal torment, you want to put me at odds with my lord, take away my joy, place me into pain. I will not believe you! Get away from here; don't be so rash as ever to show up here again! You're a traitor, your word is not to be trusted.

Then [the Devil] will sadly leave Adam, with downcast face, and he will go up to the gates of hell and will confer with the other demons, after which he will run about through the audience. From that direction he will approach paradise on Eve's side, and with a happy face and in a wheedling manner he will address her as follows:

DEVIL: Well, Eve, I've come to see you.

EVE: Tell me, Satan, why did you?

DEVIL: I'm looking out for what's to your advantage, what will get you up in the world.

EVE: God grant it!

DEVIL: Don't be afraid. I found out all the secret plans of paradise a long time ago. I'll tell you some of them.

EVE: Well, go ahead; I'll listen.

DEVIL: Are you really going to listen?

EVE: Indeed I will; I won't do anything to make you angry.

DEVIL: Will you keep the secret?

EVE: Yes, I give you my word.

DEVIL: Will it get known?

EVE: Not through me.

DEVIL: I'm going to put myself into your trust; I want no other pledge from you.

EVE: You can depend on my word.

DEVIL: You've been to a good school. I talked to Adam, but he's just too big a dunce.

EVE: He's a little hard.

DEVIL: We'll soften him! He's harder than hell itself.

EVE: He's quite noble-minded.

DEVIL: I'd call him very boorish! He refuses to look out for himself; why doesn't he at least look out for you? You're a fragile and tender thing; you're fresher than a rose, you're whiter than crystal, than the snow that falls on the ice in a valley. The creator made an ill-assorted couple out of you two; you're too tender, and he's too hard. But you are wiser than he all the same; you've gotten into the habit of great good common sense. That's why it's a pleasure to come and see you. I want to talk to you.

EVE: Well then, let's trust each other.

DEVIL: Nobody is to find out!

EVE: Who should find out?

DEVIL: Not even Adam!

EVE: He won't from me!

DEVIL: I'll tell you, and you listen closely. There are only the two of us on this path, and Adam, over there where he can't hear us.

EVE: Speak out loud, he won't know a thing.

DEVIL: Let me call your attention to a big trick that is being played on you in this garden: the fruit that God gave you has hardly any good in it; but the one he has so strongly forbidden you, that's the one which contains great power. In it is the gift of life, of sovereignty, of all knowledge, good and evil.

EVE: How does it taste?

DEVIL: Heavenly! With your beautiful body, your shapely form, you deserve the chance to be mistress over the whole world, of heaven and of hell, and to know all that is yet to be; the chance to be a first-rate ruler of the universe.

EVE: Is that what the fruit is like?

DEVIL: Yes, indeed it is.

Then EVE *will look attentively at the forbidden fruit. After having looked at it for some time, she will say:* Why I already feel good just looking at.

DEVIL: What harm would there be in eating it?

EVE: How do I know?

DEVIL: Aren't you going to believe me? You take it first, then give it to Adam. Right away you two will be given the crown of heaven; you'll be the creator's equal. He'll no longer be able to hide his secrets from you, as soon as you've eaten the fruit. Right away your hearts will be changed; you'll dwell with God, no doubt about it, his equal in merit, his equal in power. Taste the fruit!

EVE: I'm considering it.

DEVIL: Don't believe Adam.

EVE: I'll do it!

DEVIL: When?

EVE: Give me time until Adam has gone away for his nap.

DEVIL: Eat it! Don't be afraid! It's childish to wait!

Then the Devil will leave Eve, and return to hell. ADAM *will now approach Eve, angry because the Devil has talked to her, and he will say to her:* Tell me, wife, what did that evil Satan want from you? What was he after?

EVE: He talked to me about our position in the world.

ADAM: Don't ever believe the traitor, for that's what he is.

EVE: I know that quite well.

ADAM: How do you know?

EVE: Well, I heard what he had to say. So, why should I worry about just seeing him?

ADAM: He'll change your mind for you.

EVE: No he won't, for I won't believe him in anything he tells me as long as I'm wise to it.

ADAM: Don't ever let him approach you again, for his word stinks. Already once before he wanted to betray his lord, and take up arms against God on high. Such a scoundrel, one who did that, I don't want to have anything to do with you.

Now a skillfully constructed serpent will climb up along the trunk of the forbidden tree. Eve will bring her ear closer, as though listening to the serpent's words; after which Eve will accept the apple, will offer it to Adam. Adam will however not immediately take it, and EVE *will say to him:* Eat, Adam, you don't know what it's like. Let's take this gift that's offered us.

ADAM: Is it that good?

EVE: You'll find out. But you won't find out if you don't taste it.

ADAM: I have my doubts.

EVE: Let it go, then.

ADAM: No, I won't!

EVE: You're stalling, like a coward!

ADAM: All right then, I'll take it!

EVE: Eat some of it! That way you'll know both good and evil. I'll eat first.

ADAM: And I'm next.

EVE: Are you sure?

Then Eve will eat part of the apple, and she will say to Adam: I've tasted it. My God, what a flavor! I have never before tasted such sweetness – such a flavor does this apple have.

ADAM: What flavor is that?

EVE: Like nothing ever tasted before by man. My eyes now see so clearly, I am like God the all-powerful. Whatever has been, whatever is yet to be, I know in its entirety. I am indeed mistress over it all. Eat, Adam! Don't hesitate! This is the right moment to take it!

Now ADAM *will take the apple from Eve's hand, saying:* I'll take your word for it. You are my wife.

EVE: Eat! You can't still be afraid!

And now Adam is to eat part of the apple. And when he has eaten it, he will at once recognize his sin, and he will stoop over, so that he cannot be seen by the audience. And he will take off his festive garments, and will put on wretched garments sewn together from the leaves of figs, and assuming the appearance of very great grief, he will begin his lament:

ADAM: Alas, sinner that I am, what have I done? I am dead, there is no retreat; irrevocably am I dead, such ill has fallen to my lot. My fortune has changed for the worse; just a little while ago it was still good, it now is very harsh. I have rejected my creator because of the counsel given by an evil wife. Alas, guilty of sin as I am, what shall I do? How shall I await and face my creator, how shall I face my creator whom I have rejected in my folly? I have never struck so bad a bargain; I know now what it is to sin. Ah, Death, why do you let me live, why isn't the world rid of me? I must seek out the depths of hell; hell will be my dwelling-place; until he arrives who can deliver me, I shall spend my life in hell. Where will help come from, down there? From where will rescue come? Who will free me from such suffering? Why did I sin against my lord? No one can be my friend now. There is no one anywhere strong enough; I am lost, there is no doubt. I have so sinned against my lord that I cannot go to court with him, for I am in the wrong and he is in the right. Oh God, what a poor case have I! Who will ever give me another thought, as I have so sinned against the king of glory? I have so sinned against the king of heaven that I cannot offer him a shred of justification. I have no friend, no neighbor who will in the end free me from this action at law. Whom shall I now entreat to help me, when my very wife has betrayed me, whom God gave me as my equal? It was she who gave me the evil counsel. Ah, Eve!

Then he will look at Eve his wife and he will say:

Woman so gone astray, what a misfortune that you were born of me! If only this rib had been burned, which has brought me into such a miserable state; if only fire had consumed this rib, which has built up such great strife for me! When he took this rib from me, why did he not burn it up and kill me off? The rib has betrayed the whole body, plunged it into madness, and sorely misused it. I don't know what to say or what to do. If pardon does not come to me from heaven, I cannot be delivered from my punishment. Such is the evil that has me in its grip. Ah, Eve, how great is our misfortune now! What great suffering overcame me, once you were made my equal. I am destroyed now, because of your advice; because of your advice I'm thrown into misfortune. From the heights I've been cast into the depths. I cannot be rescued by any man born, except by God, the God of majesty. Alas, what am I saying? Why did I call his name? He'll help me! But I have angered him. No one will ever bring me any help, except the son to be born of Mary. I do not know how to take measures for our protection, when we did not keep our word to God. Now let everything be as may please God. There is only one way, and that is to die.

Then the choir is to begin: "While he was walking ..." [Gen. 3:8]. With this com-pleted, the Figure of God will appear, wearing a stole; it will enter paradise, looking all about as though trying to discover where Adam might be. Adam and Eve will be hiding in a corner of paradise, as though aware of their wretchedness, and the FIGURE OF GOD *will say:* Adam, [where are you]?

Then both will stand up, facing the Figure of God, not entirely erect, however, but somewhat bent over because of the shame they feel through their sin; they are in great sadness, and ADAM *is to answer:* Here I am, my lord. I went into hiding because of your anger. And because I am stark naked, I concealed myself here like this.

FIGURE OF GOD: What have you done? How did you go astray? Who has deprived you of your state of innocent goodness? What have you done? Why are you ashamed? How shall I ask you for an accounting? The other day you had nothing that you needed to be ashamed of. Now I see you very sad and dejected. There is little joy in a life lived this way!

ADAM: I feel such shame before you, lord.

FIGURE OF GOD: Why is that?

ADAM: So great a feeling of shame constricts me, I dare not look you in the face.

FIGURE OF GOD: Why did you overstep my prohibition? Did you in any way profit from it? You are my serf and I am your lord!

ADAM: In this I cannot contradict you.

FIGURE OF GOD: I gave you shape after my own likeness; why did you vio-late my commandment? I molded you exactly according to my image; is that why you committed such an outrage against me? My prohibition you did not observe in the slightest; you wantonly overstepped it; you ate the fruit I had forbidden you – and I had even reminded you! Did you think you were going to be my equal that way? Are you perhaps intent on an idle boast?

Here ADAM *will stretch out his hand towards the Figure of God, then towards Eve, saying:* The woman that you gave me, she was the first to commit this sin. She gave it to me, and I ate. Now I see that it has turned to woe for me. What a misfortune that I got to know this food! I have sinned through my wife.

FIGURE OF GOD: You believed your wife more than me; you ate the fruit without my consent. Now hear how I shall reward you. The earth shall lie under a curse; wherever you may wish to plant your grain, it will always fail to come to harvest. Under your hand, the earth is accursed; you will till it in vain. It will refuse its fruit to you, it will give you back thorns and thistles. It will seek to ruin what you have planted; it will be ill-disposed toward you, and this is to be your punishment. With great toil, with great effort will you eat your bread; with much pain, with much sweat will you live both night and day.

Now the FIGURE OF GOD *will turn against Eve, and with a threatening expression it will say to her:* And you, Eve, wicked woman, you started war with me all too soon! You did not observe my commandments very long.

EVE: It was the evil serpent that tricked me.

FIGURE OF GOD: Was it through him that you sought to be my equal? Do you still think you can foretell the future? Once you had mastery over every living thing. How soon you lost it! Look at you now, how afflicted and unfortunate you are! Did you gain or lose? I shall give you your just deserts; I shall pay you according to services rendered! Every form of misfortune shall befall you: in pain you shall bring forth your children, and they shall suffer all their years long; your children shall be born in sorrow, and they shall end in great anguish. Such is the struggle, such is the ruin into which you have plunged yourself and your descendants. All those of your lineage shall weep for your sin.

And EVE *will answer, saying:* I have sinned; it was through my folly. For an apple I shall suffer so great a ruin that I am inflicting hell's punishment on both myself and my descendants. For a little profit, how I am obligated to heavy service!

If I sinned, it was no great wonder, when it was the serpent that betrayed me with his seductive ways. He is well versed in evil, he seems no innocent lamb; if you seek out his advice you will find yourself in a sorry state.

I took the apple — I now know that I committed an act of folly — contrary to your prohibition; in this I committed a grievous wrong. To my misfortune I tasted it; now I am the object of your hatred. For a little bit of fruit I must lose my life.

Then the FIGURE OF GOD *will threaten the serpent, saying:* And you, Serpent, be accursed! I shall, you may be sure, make good my claim against you. You shall drag yourself along on your belly all the days of your life. Dust shall forever be your food, in woods, on plain, on heath. Woman shall bear you hatred: she shall at all times be a hostile neighbor to you. You shall keep a sharp lookout for her heel; she shall crush you to the ground. She shall strike your head with such a blow as to cause you the greatest pain. And she will take still further steps; see how she can avenge herself on you. It was to your misfortune that you made her acquaintance; she will force you to hold your head bent low. Moreover a root will come from her which will confound all your strength.

Then the FIGURE OF GOD *will drive them out of paradise, saying:* Now get out of paradise! It's a poor exchange of home you've made! You will build a house on earth; you have no further business in paradise. You have no grounds for an appeal; you are getting out, without hope of return. You own nothing here, that is the judgment of the court. Find lodgings elsewhere now: you are leaving a good shelter against the night. You shall never be without hunger or fatigue, you shall never be without grief or pain any day of the week. On earth your stay shall be wretched, and then, in the end you shall die! After you have tasted death you shall go to hell without delay. Here on earth your bodies shall suffer exile, in hell your souls shall go under. Satan shall have you in his power. There is no man who can come to your aid; by whom will you be ransomed, if I do not take pity on you?

Let the choir sing: "In the sweat of your countenance ..." [Gen. 3:19]. During this an angel dressed in white will appear, carrying a flashing sword in his hand; the FIGURE OF GOD *will station him at the gate of paradise and will say to him:* Guard paradise well for me, so that this ill-fated wretch can never again come in; let him never again have power or command here, nor touch the fruit of life. With this sword that shines so brightly, completely forbid him the way!

As soon as they are outside paradise, as though dejected and confused they will hunch over to the ground on their heels, and the Figure of God will point them out with its hand, while facing paradise. And the choir will begin: "Behold Adam, like one ..." [Gen. 3:22]. When this is concluded, the Figure of God will return to the church. Then Adam will pick up a spade, and Eve a rake and they will begin to till the earth, and will plant wheat. After their planting is finished, they will go and find a place to sit down for a short while, as though tired from their labors, and in tears they will often look back at paradise, while they beat their breasts. During this the Devil will come and sow thorns and thistles in their field, then leave. When Adam and Eve return to their field and see the thorns and thistles that have sprung up, they will fall prostrate to the ground, struck with violent grief; and then, as they sit up they will strike their breasts and their thighs, showing the grief they have suffered. And [ADAM] will begin his lament: Alas, miserable wretch that I am, what a misfortune it was, that I ever saw the hour when my sins overwhelmed me, when I rejected the lord that men adore. Whom can I from now on call upon to come to my aid?

At this point Adam will look back at paradise, and he will lift up his hands in its direction, and reverently bowing his head he will say: Ah paradise! So beautiful a dwelling place! Garden of eternal glory! How good it is to look at you! I have been cast out because of my sin — it's only too true; I have lost all hope of regaining it.

I once was inside, I did not know how to enjoy it; I accepted advice which soon forced me to leave; now I repent, I have the right to show how I feel; but it's too late, my sighs avail me nothing.

Was I bereft of my senses? Was my memory so short that for Satan I cast aside the King of Glory? Now I torment myself, but it helps me very little; history will record my sin.

Then he will lift up his hand against Eve, who will be at a slight distance from him, and shaking his head in great indignation he will say to her: Ah, evil woman, full of treachery, how quickly you consigned me to eternal damnation, when you deprived me of my reason and my common sense. Now I repent; but there is no pardon for me.

Unhappy Eve, how you surrendered to evil, when you so quickly followed the advice of the snake! Through you I am a dead man, for I have lost my life; your sin will be duly recorded. Do you see the signs of the great upheaval? The earth senses the curse that is upon us; we planted wheat, and thistles spring up.

You have seen the beginnings of our misfortune; this is great suffering for us, but greater suffering awaits us. We shall be taken into hell! There, make no mistake, we'll be spared neither pain nor torment.

Eve, wretched woman, what do you think of all this? It's what you have won for me, it's what's given to you as your dowry. You'll never be capable of bringing anything good to man, but you'll always be the enemy of common sense. All those born of our lineage will suffer the penalty of your transgression. You committed a criminal act; the penalty will be adjudged on them all. He who can commute it will be long in coming.

Then let EVE *reply to Adam:* Adam, my lord, you have heaped blame on me, you have recounted my infamy and have reproached me for it. If I committed a crime, it is I who am suffering the punishment. I am guilty, I shall be judged by God.

I have offended greatly against God and against you; my offense will be talked about for a long time to come. My guilt is great, my sin sickens me, I am poverty-stricken, deprived of everything that was mine.

There are no grounds on which I could defend myself before God, that I should not give myself up as a guilty sinner. Forgive me, as I cannot make amends; if I could, I would do it through some sacrificial offering.

Ah, sinful, weary, and wretched that I am! Because of my transgression, how rebellious am I against God! Death, take me! Do not let me go on living! I am in mortal danger, I cannot reach the shore.

The treacherous serpent, that snake of evil origin, with hostile intent made me eat the apple. I gave you part of it; I thought I was doing right, but I plunged you into sin, from which I cannot rescue you.

Why was I not obedient to my creator? Why, lord, did I not observe your commands? You sinned, but I am the root of your sin. The remedy for our sickness will be long in coming. The heavy cost of my sin, of my misfortune, our descendants will share. The fruit was sweet, the punishment is harsh. What a misfortune that it was eaten; ours will be the cost.

And yet my hope is in God; for this sin full settlement will be reached. God will restore me to his grace, and will make it manifest; he will, through his might, free us from hell.

Then the Devil will come, and three or four other devils with him, bearing in their hands chains and iron bonds, which they will put around the necks of Adam and Eve. And several will push, others will pull them, towards hell; other devils will come to meet them as they approach hell, and they will start a loud argument as to what their eternal punishment should be; and a few other devils will one by one point out Adam and Eve approaching, and they will take them and put them into hell. Inside, they will cause great quantities of smoke to rise up, and they will shout to one another while they rejoice in hell, and they will strike pots and kettles against each other so that they can be heard outside. After a brief pause devils will come out and run about through the square, but some will remain in hell.

What image of God does the play convey? On whom does the play place blame for the Fall of Adam and Eve? What image of women does the play depict? What image of the devil? Is the play more successful as a teaching tool or as entertainment?

13. ST. FRANCIS OF ASSISI AND THE CHRISTMAS CRÈCHE (1223)

Fueled by Cistercian piety in the twelfth century and Franciscan piety in the thirteenth, devotion to the human Jesus, in all his infant frailty and adult suffering, created an image of God truly made man that could tap the deepest wells of an ordinary Christian's compassion. While St. Francis probably did not invent the Christmas manger scene, his personal devotion to it as an aid to meditation on the incarnated humanity of Jesus helped popularize its use. Rather like medieval drama, the crib and its trappings offered the sort of concrete images of spiritual ideas that always appealed to the popular religious imagination. This account is from Thomas of Celano's first version of the life of St. Francis, completed between 1229 and 1230. Greccio, where Francis had the manger constructed, is about forty-five miles south of Assisi.

Source: trans. Placid Hermann from Thomas of Celano, *Saint Francis of Assisi* (Chicago: Franciscan Herald Press, 1963), pp. 75-78. Latin.

Chapter 30. Of the manger Francis made on the day of the Lord's birth.

84. Francis' highest intention, his chief desire, his uppermost purpose was to observe the holy Gospel in all things and through all things and, with perfect vigilance, with all zeal, with all the longing of his mind and all the fervor of his heart, "to follow the teaching and the footsteps of our Lord Jesus Christ." He would recall Christ's words through persistent meditation and bring to mind his deeds through the most penetrating consideration. The humility of the incarnation and the charity of the passion occupied his memory particularly, to the extent that he wanted to think of hardly anything else. What he did on the birthday of our Lord Jesus Christ near the little town of Greccio in the third year before his glorious death [in 1226] should especially be noted and recalled with reverent memory. In that place there was a certain man by the name of John, of good reputation and an even better life, whom blessed Francis loved with a special love, for in the place where he lived he held a noble and honorable position inasmuch as he had trampled upon the nobility of his birth and pursued nobility of soul. Blessed Francis sent for this man, as he often did, about fifteen days before the birth of the Lord, and he said

to him: "If you want us to celebrate the present feast of our Lord at Greccio, go with haste and diligently prepare what I tell you. For I wish to do something that will recall to memory the little Child who was born in Bethlehem and set before our bodily eyes in some way the inconveniences of his infant needs, how he lay in a manger, how, with an ox and an ass standing by, he lay upon the hay where he had been placed." When the good and faithful man heard these things, he ran with haste and prepared in that place all the things the saint had told him.

85. But the day of joy drew near, the time of great rejoicing came. The brothers were called from their various places. Men and women of that neighborhood prepared with glad hearts, according to their means, candles and torches to light up that night that has lighted up all the days and years with its gleaming star. At length the saint of God came, and finding all things prepared, he saw it and was glad. The manger was prepared, the hay had been brought, the ox and ass were led in. There simplicity was honored, poverty was exalted, humility was commended, and Greccio was made, as it were, a new Bethlehem. The night was lighted up like the day, and it delighted men and beasts. The people came and were filled with new joy over the new mystery. The woods rang with the voices of the crowd and the rocks made answer to their jubilation. The brothers sang, paying their debt of praise to the Lord, and the whole night resounded with their rejoicing. The saint of God stood before the manger, uttering sighs, overcome with love, and filled with a wonderful happiness. The solemnities of the mass were celebrated over the manger and the priest experienced a new consolation.

86. The saint of God was clothed with the vestments of the deacon [the second highest of the seven holy orders, just below priest], for he was a deacon, and he sang the holy Gospel in a sonorous voice. And his voice was a strong voice, a sweet voice, a clear voice, a sonorous voice, inviting all to the highest rewards. Then he preached to the people standing about, and he spoke charming words concerning the nativity of the poor King and the little town of Bethlehem. Frequently too, when he wished to call Christ *Jesus*, he would call him simply the *Child of Bethlehem*, aglow with overflowing love for him; and speaking the word *Bethlehem*, his voice was more like the bleating of a sheep. His mouth was filled more with sweet affection than with words. Besides, when he spoke the name *Child of Bethlehem* or *Jesus*, his tongue licked his lips, as it were, relishing and savoring with pleased palate the sweetness of the words. The gifts of the Almighty were multiplied there, and a wonderful vision was seen by a certain virtuous man. For he saw a little child lying in the manger lifeless, and he saw the holy man of God go up to it and rouse the child as from a deep sleep. This vision was not unfit-

ting, for the Child Jesus had been forgotten in the hearts of many; but, by the working of his grace, he was brought to life again through his servant St. Francis and stamped upon their fervent memory. At length the solemn night celebration was brought to a close, and each one returned to his home with holy joy.

87. The hay that had been placed in the manger was kept, so that the Lord might save the beasts of burden and other animals through it as he multiplied his holy mercy. And in truth it so happened that many animals throughout the surrounding region that had various illnesses were freed from their illnesses after eating of this hay. Indeed, even women laboring for a long time in a difficult birth were delivered safely when some of this hay was placed upon them; and a large number of persons of both sexes of that place, suffering from various illnesses, obtained the health they sought. Later, the place on which the manger had stood was made sacred by a temple of the Lord, and an altar was built in honor of the most blessed father Francis over the manger and a church was built, so that where once the animals had eaten the hay, there in the future men would eat unto health of soul and body the flesh of the lamb without blemish and without spot, our Lord Jesus Christ, who in highest and ineffable love gave himself to us, who lives and reigns with the Father and the Holy Spirit, God, eternally glorious, forever and ever. Amen. Alleluia, Alleluia.

What is Francis's feeling toward the infant Jesus? Do other people share it? Does Francis seem out of the ordinary in his reactions here? What does the way in which ordinary people incorporate this episode into their religious practices tell us about popular religion?

14. THE PASSION NARRATIVE FROM GIOVANNI DE' CAULI'S *MEDITATIONS ON THE LIFE OF CHRIST* (LATE THIRTEENTH CENTURY)

Nowhere is popular empathy for the humanity of Jesus better captured than in the Meditations on the Life of Christ *(Meditationes vitae christi) which became a veritable medieval best-seller soon after it first appeared near the end of the thirteenth century. Its author, once wrongly thought to be St. Bonaventure, was plausibly Giovanni de' Cauli, a Franciscan friar from Tuscany. Writing these meditations for a nun of his sister order of Poor Clares to aid her spiritual contemplation, he combined the four Gospels to retell the story of the life of Jesus. But he drew on an array of other medieval authorities to fill his narrative with the emotionally evocative detail that makes*

the work so appealing: the Lives of the Desert Fathers, *Jacob of Voragine's* Golden
Legend *(a thirteenth-century collection of saints' lives), the sermons and letters of
Bernard of Clairvaux, the vast biblical explication called the* Glossa ordinaria, *Peter
Comestor's* Historia scholastica *(a School History compiled from biblical stories),
and Christian pilgrims' accounts of their travels in the Holy Land. Written originally
in Latin, the* Meditations *was quickly translated into most of Europe's vernacular
languages (including Gaelic) and spread across the continent. Well over 200 manuscript
copies, about 20 of them illustrated, still survive, though few of these contain the whole
text, which is almost 400 pages long in its most recent English translation. The influence of what has been called "the fifth Gospel" was profound: many of the non-biblical
details that people still associate with the life of Jesus – the angel kneeling before Mary
at the Annunciation, one of the three Wise Men kissing the infant's foot, Jesus and
John the Baptist playing together as children, the two ladders propped against the cross
after Jesus' death – were imagined by the author of the* Meditations *and popularized
through artists inspired by his powerful verbal imagery. The author's persistent effort
to have his reader visualize the details of the story in order better to empathize with its
actors is a hallmark of Franciscan spirituality. The excerpt below is from the Passion
narrative, which often circulated independently of the rest of the* Meditations. *It can
be compared with the depiction of the Passion in the York Cycle (Doc. 57), pilgrims'
impressions of sites associated with the Passion (Docs. 33 and 34), and Fig. 6.1.*

Source: trans. Isa Ragusa and Rosalie Green, *Meditations on the Life of Christ, An Illustrated
Manuscript of the Fourteenth Century* (Princeton, NJ: Princeton University Press, 1961), pp. 317-
19, 327-38, 345-47. Latin.

Chapter 74. Meditation on the Passion of the Lord, in General

We must now treat of the Passion of our Lord Jesus. He who wishes to glory in
the Cross and the Passion must dwell with continued meditation on the mysteries and events that occurred. If they were considered with complete regard
of mind, they would, I think, lead the meditator to a (new) state. To him who
searches for it from the bottom of the heart and with the marrow of his being,
many unhoped-for steps would take place by which he would receive new
compassion, new love, new solace, and then a new condition of sweetness that
would seem to him a promise of glory. I, as an ignorant person and a stam-
merer, believe that in attaining this state it is therefore necessary to be directed
by the whole light of the mind, by the eyes of the watchful heart, having left all
the other extraneous cares that man keeps for himself for all those things that
occur around this Passion and Crucifixion of the Lord, by desire, wisdom, and
perseverance, not with slothful eyes or with omissions or with tedium of the
soul. Therefore I exhort you that, if you have studiously considered the things

said above on his life, you much more diligently concentrate the whole spirit and all the virtues, for here is shown more especially this charity of his that should kindle all our hearts. Therefore take all the things, that is, what can be as piously meditated as I think I am telling you, with the accustomed meditation. I do not intend to affirm anything in this little book that is not asserted or said by Holy Scripture or the word of the saints or by approved opinion. It appears to me that one can say not improperly that not only that penal and mortal Crucifixion of the Lord, but also that suffering that went before, is cause for strong compassion, bitterness, and stupor. What should we think that our Lord, blessed God above all things, from the hour of his capture at night until the sixth hour of his Crucifixion, was in a continuous battle, in great pain, injury, scorn, and torment, that he was not given a little rest! But in what battle is he tormented? You will hear (and see). One of them seizes him, (this sweet, mild, and pious Jesus,) another binds him, another attacks him, another scolds him, another pushes him, another blasphemes him, another spits on him, another beats him, another walks around him, another questions him, another looks for false witnesses against him, another accompanies the one that searches, another gives false testimony against him, another accuses him, another mocks him, another blindfolds him, another strikes his face, another goads him, another leads him to the column, another strips him, another beats him while he is being led, another screams, another begins furiously to torment him, another binds him to the column, another assaults him, another scourges him, another robes him in purple to abuse him, another places the crown of thorns, another gives him the reed to hold, another madly takes it away to strike his thorn-covered head, another kneels mockingly, another salutes him as king. These and many similar things were done to him, not just by one but by many. He is led back and forth, scorned and reproved, turned and shaken here and there like a fool and an imbecile; like a thief and a most evil malefactor he is led now to Annas, now to Caiaphas, now to Pilate, now to Herod, and again to Pilate, now in, now out. O my God, what is this? Does this not seem a most hard and bitter battle? But wait a while and you will hear harsher things....

[*The narrative recounts Jesus' agony at prayer in the garden of Gethsemane, his betrayal by Judas with a kiss, and his arrest.*]

Chapter 76. Meditation on the Passion of Christ at the First Hour

Early in the morning, the chiefs and elders of the people returned and had his hands tied behind his back, saying, "Thief, come with us; come to judgment. Today your evil deeds are to be fulfilled; now your wisdom shall appear." And they led him to Pilate; and he followed them as if he were a criminal, he who was the most innocent Lamb. When his mother, John, and her companions – for these had gone outside the walls at dawn in order to come to him – met him at the crossroads and saw him thus vituperatively and outrageously led by such a multitude, they were filled with more sorrow than can be expressed. Moreover in this meeting there was the most vehement grief on both sides, for the Lord was deeply moved by his compassion for his own, and especially for his mother. He knew that they grieved on his account until their souls were torn from their bodies. Consider and contemplate each thing diligently: there are certainly very many, indeed very great causes for compassion.

He is led, then, to Pilate; and these women who cannot draw near follow at a distance. At this time he was accused by them of many things; and Pilate sent him to Herod. Herod, longing in truth to see miracles performed by him, rejoiced; but was unable to obtain a miracle or even a word. Therefore, thinking him a fool, in derision he had him dressed in white, and sent him back to Pilate. Thus you see how he was regarded by everyone not only as a criminal but as a fool; but he bore everything most patiently. Look at him again while he is led hither and thither with downcast gaze and shamefaced walk, hearing all the shouts, insults, and mockeries, perchance struck by a stone or enduring indecencies and filth. See also his mother and the disciples standing apart in unspeakable sorrow and then following him as he is brought back to Pilate. Those dogs prosecute their accusations with great audacity and constancy; but Pilate, not finding cause for death in him, tried to release him. Thus he said, "I will chastise him and release him." O Pilate! Do you castigate your Lord? You do not know what you are doing, for he deserves neither death nor scourges. You would act rightly if you chastised yourself at his bidding. However, he orders him most harshly scourged.

The Lord is therefore stripped and bound to a column and scourged in various ways. He stands naked before them all, in youthful grace and shame-facedness, beautiful in form above the sons of men, and sustains the harsh and grievous scourges on his innocent, tender, pure, and lovely flesh. The flower of all flesh and of all human nature is covered with bruises and cuts. The royal blood flows all about, from all parts of his body. Again and again, repeatedly, closer and closer, it is done, bruise upon bruise, and cut upon cut, until not only the torturers but also the spectators are tired; then he is ordered untied. The *Historia* says that the column to which he was bound shows the traces of his bleeding. Here, then, consider him diligently for a long time; and if you do not feel compassion at this point, you may count yours a heart of stone. Now is fulfilled what Isaiah the prophet said. "We saw him," he says, "and there was no beauty, and we thought of him as a leper and one humiliated by God" [Isa. 53:2,4]. O Lord Jesus! Who was so audacious and so bold as he who stripped you? And who was the more audacious one who bound you?

But who was the most audacious one who scourged you so cruelly? But you, Sun of Justice, withheld your rays, and therefore the darkness came, and the power of darkness. All are more powerful than you. Your love and our sin made you feeble. Cursed be such sin, for which you are so afflicted!

Releasing the Lord from the column, they led him thus naked and beaten through the house, seeking his clothes, which had been cast aside in the house by those who had despoiled him. See him thus harshly afflicted and trembling most severely, for it was very cold, as the Gospel says [John 18:18]. When he wished to clothe himself again, some most impious men contended with him, saying to Pilate, "Lord, here he made himself king. Let us clothe him and crown him with kingly honor." And taking a sort of robe of dirty red silk, they clothed him; and they crowned him with thorns. Look at him in each of his actions and afflictions, for he does and endures all that they wish. He bears the purple; he wears the crown of thorns on his head; he carries the reed in his hand; and he holds his peace and most patiently remains silent before those who bow and salute him as king. Look at him now in bitterness of heart, especially at his head, full of thorns, often struck by the reed. And see how, with bent neck, he painfully receives the sharp and heavy blows. For those sharpest of thorns pierced his most sacred head until they made it run with blood. O wretches! How terrible that royal head that you are striking now will appear to you yet! They mocked him as though he wished to rule but did not have the power. He bore all things, for their cruelty was excessive. Indeed, not only did he endure their gathering together the whole company for great mockery, but also their leading him before Pilate and all the people to mock him publicly, wearing the crown of thorns and the purple robe. Behold him now, for God's sake, how he stands with face bowed toward the ground before the multitude shouting and crying, "Crucify him," and moreover deriding and insulting him as though they were wiser than he; and how he seems to have acted foolishly toward the chiefs and Pharisees who had him taken and who lead him to such an end. Thus he received not only pain and punishment from them, but disgrace as well.

Chapter 77. Meditation on the Passion of Christ at the Third Hour

Then the whole multitude of Jews demands that he be crucified; and thus he is condemned by Pilate, the miserable judge. His benefits and works are not remembered by them, nor are they moved by his innocence; and what is most cruel to see is that they are not drawn back by the afflictions they have already caused him; but the chiefs and elders rejoice that their wicked intentions have been accomplished. They laugh and mock at him who is the true and eternal God, and hasten his death. He is led back inside, stripped of the purple, and stands before them nude, not given leave to reclothe himself. Pay diligent attention to this and consider his stature in every part. And to make yourself more deeply compassionate and nourish yourself at the same time, turn your eyes away from his divinity for a little while and consider him purely as a man. You will see a fine youth, most noble and most innocent and most lovable, cruelly beaten and covered with blood and wounds, gathering his garments from the ground where they were strewn and dressing himself before them with shame, reverence, and blushes however much they jeer, as though he were the meanest of all, abandoned by God, and destitute of all help. Look at him diligently, therefore, and be moved to pity and compassion: now he picks up one thing, now another, and dresses himself before them. Next return to his divinity and consider the immense, eternal, incomprehensible, and imperial majesty incarnate, humbly bowing down, bending to the ground to gather his garments together, dressing himself with reverence and blushes as if he were the vilest of men, indeed the servant under their domination, corrected and punished by them for some crime. Look at him diligently and admire his humility, again having compassion on him for the considerations you held when he was tied to the column and beaten so excessively. When he is clothed they lead him outside, so as not to postpone his death any longer, and then place on his shoulders the venerable wood of the long, wide, very heavy cross, which the most gentle Lamb patiently takes and carries. As it is told in the *Historia*, the cross of the Lord is supposed to have been fifteen feet high. Then he is led and hurried and saturated with taunts, as told above at the beginning of the events of the morning. Moreover he was led outside with his companions, the two thieves. Behold, this is his company! O good Jesus! How much shame these friends of yours cause you! They associate you with thieves, yet make you their inferior, for they impose on you the carrying of the cross, which we do not read was done to the thieves. Thus you are not only "numbered with sinners," according to Isaiah [Isa. 53:12], but as more sinful than sinners. Your patience, Lord, is indescribable.

Look at him well, then, as he goes along bowed down by the cross and gasping aloud. Feel as much compassion for him as you can, placed in such anguish, in renewed derision. And because his sorrowful mother could not approach him or even see him, on account of the multitude of people, she went with John and her companions by another, shorter road, so that, preceding the others, she could draw near to him. When, however, outside the gate of the city, at a crossroads, she encountered him, for the first time seeing him burdened by such a large cross, she was half dead of anguish and could not say a word to him; nor could he speak to her, he was so hurried along by those who led him to be crucified. But after going a little farther on, the Lord turned to the weeping women and said to them, "Daughters of Jerusalem, do not weep for me but for yourselves" etc., as is more fully related in the Gospel [Luke 23:28]. And in these two places there are the remains of churches that were built there within the memory of man, as I heard from a brother of ours who saw them. He also said that Mount Calvary, where Christ was crucified, was as far from the gate of the city as our place is from the Gate of Saint Germanus. Therefore the carrying of the cross took excessively long. When they had gone a bit farther, and he was so tired and broken that he could not carry it any longer, he laid down the cross. Those wicked ones, however, unwilling to defer his death, fearing that Pilate might revoke his sentence – for he had shown a wish to dismiss him – had someone else carry the cross, thereby releasing him; and they led him bound, like a thief, to the place of Calvary. Do not the events that took place at matins and the first and third hours appear to you to be most vehement and bitter sorrows, and exceedingly shocking horrors, even without the Crucifixion? I certainly consider them as such, and as reasons for compassion and most intense feelings. This seems to complete what there is to say at the present time about these three hours. Let us now see what happened at his Crucifixion and death, that is to say, at the sixth and ninth hours; then we shall see what happened after his death, that is, at the hours of vespers and compline.

Chapter 78. Meditation on the Passion of Christ at the Sixth Hour

When the Lord Jesus, led by impious men, reached that foul place, Calvary, you may look everywhere at wicked people wretchedly at work. With your whole mind you must imagine yourself present and consider diligently everything done against your Lord and all that is said and done by him and regarding him. With your mind's eye, see some thrusting the cross into the earth, others equipped with nails and hammers, others with the ladder and other instruments, others giving orders about what should be done, and others stripping him. Again he is stripped, and is now nude before all the multitude for the third time, his wounds reopened by the adhesion of his garments to his flesh. Now for the first time the mother beholds her son thus taken and prepared for the anguish of death. She is saddened and shamed beyond measure when she sees him entirely nude: they did not leave him even his loincloth. Therefore she hurries and approaches the son, embraces him, and girds him with the veil from her head. Oh, what bitterness her soul is in now! I do not believe that she could say a word to him: if she could have done more, she would have, but she could not help him further. The son was torn furiously from her hands to the foot of the cross.

Here pay diligent attention to the manner of the crucifixion. Two ladders are set in place, one behind at the right arm, another at the left arm, which the evil-doers ascend holding nails and hammers. Another ladder is placed in front, reaching to the place where the feet are to be affixed. Look well now at each thing: the Lord Jesus is compelled to ascend the cross by this small ladder; without rebellion or contradiction he humbly does what they require. When he reaches the cross, at the upper part of this small ladder, he turns himself around, opens those royal arms, and, extending his most beautiful hands, stretches them up to his crucifiers. He looks toward heaven, saying to the Father, "Behold, I am here, my Father. For love and the salvation of mankind you wished me humbled as far as the cross. It pleases me; I accept; and I offer myself to you for those whom you gave to me, wishing them to be my brothers. Therefore, Father, accept, and for love of me be pleased to wipe away and remove all the old stains from them: I offer myself to you for them, Father." Then he who is behind the cross takes his right hand and affixes it firmly to the cross. This done, he who is on the left side takes his left hand and pulls and extends it as far as possible, puts in another nail, drives it through, and hammers it in. After this, they descend from the ladders, and all the ladders are removed. The Lord hangs with the weight of his body pulling him down, supported only by the nails transfixing his hands. Nevertheless, another one comes and draws him down by the feet as far as he can, and while he is thus extended, another most cruelly drives a nail through his feet. There are, however, those who believe that he was not crucified in this manner, but that the cross was laid on the ground and that they then raised it up and fixed it in the ground. If this suits you better, think how they take him contemptuously, like the vilest wretch, and furiously cast him onto the cross on the ground, taking his arms, violently extending them, and most cruelly fixing them to the cross. Similarly consider his feet, which they dragged down as violently as they could.

Behold, the Lord Jesus is crucified and extended on the cross so that each of his bones can be numbered, as he complained by the prophet [Ps. 21 (22):18]. On all sides, rivers of his most sacred blood flow from his terrible wounds. He is so tortured that he can move nothing except his head. Those three nails sustain the whole weight of his body. He bears the bitterest pain and is affected beyond anything that can possibly be said or thought. He hangs between two thieves. Everywhere are torments, everywhere injuries, everywhere abuses. For though he is in such anguish, they do not refrain from abuse. Some blaspheme, saying, "Ah! You who destroy the temple of God," or "himself he cannot save." Others make abusive remarks: "If he be the Son of God, let him descend from the cross, that we may believe in him" [Matt. 27:40,42]. And the soldiers that crucified him divided his clothing for themselves in his presence.

And all this is said and done in the presence of his most sorrowful mother, whose great compassion adds to the passion of her son, and conversely. She hung with her son on the cross and wished to die with him rather than live any longer. Everywhere are tortures and torments that can be sensed but in truth hardly described. The mother stood next to his cross, between the crosses of the thieves. She did not turn her eyes away from her son; she was in anguish like his; and with her whole heart she prayed to the Father, saying, "Father and eternal God, it pleases you that my son should be crucified: it is not the time to ask him back from you. But you see what anguish his soul is in now: therefore I beg you to lessen his suffering, if it please you. Father, I recommend my son to you." And the son similarly prayed to the Father for her and silently said, "My Father, see how afflicted my mother is. I ought to be crucified, not she, but she is with me on the cross. It is enough that I, who bear the sins of all the people, am crucified; she does not deserve the same. See how desolate she is, consumed with sadness all the day. I recommend her to you: make her sorrow bearable." Near the cross, with the Lady, there were also John and the Magdalen, and the Lady's two sisters, that is, Mary Jacobi and Salome, and perhaps others as well, all of whom, especially the Magdalen, beloved disciple of Jesus, wept vehemently, nor could they be comforted for their beloved Lord and Master. They suffered for the Lord and the Lady, and for each other. Their sorrow was often renewed, for their compassion was renewed whenever abuses or deeds added anew to the passion of their Lord.

Chapter 79. Meditation on the Passion of the Lord at the Ninth Hour

While he was hanging on the cross, however, until the departure of his spirit, the Lord was not idle, but did and taught useful things for us. From there he spoke the seven words that are found written in the Gospel.

The first was during the act of his crucifixion, when he prayed for his crucifiers, saying, "Father, forgive them, for they do not know what they are doing" [Luke 23:34], which word gives a token of great patience and great love, and indeed came of indescribable charity.

The second was to the mother, when he said, "Woman, behold your son," and to John, "Behold your mother" [John 19:26,27]. He did not call her "mother," in order that the tenderness of vehement love might not grieve her the more.

The third was to the penitent thief, when he said, "Today you shall be with me in Paradise" [Luke 23:43].

The fourth was, "Eli, Eli, lamma sabacthani?" This is, "My God, my God, why have you forsaken me?" [Matt. 27:46], as if he said, "Father, you loved the world so much that, while you delivered me up for it, you seem to have forsaken me."

The fifth was when he said, "I am thirsty" [John 19:28], in which word there was the great compassion of the mother and her companions, and John, and the great pleasure of those wicked men. Now one could show that he was thirsty for the salvation of souls; yet in truth he thirsted because he was inwardly drained by loss of blood, and was dried out. And when those wretches were unable to think how they could injure him further, they found a new manner of ill-treating him and gave him vinegar mixed with gall to drink. Cursed be their fury, for it was persistent; and they did as much harm as they could.

The sixth word was, "It is consummated" [John 19:30], as if he said, "Father, I have completed perfectly the obedience that you imposed on me. Yet, Father, whatever you still wish, command of me, your son. I am ready for whatever remains to be fulfilled. 'For I am ready for the scourge' [Ps. 37 (38):18]. But all that is written about me is consummated. If it please you, Father, call me back to you now." And the Father said to him, "Come, my most beloved son. You have done everything well. I do not wish you to be troubled any further. Come, for I will receive you to my breast and embrace you." And from that time on, he began to weaken, in the manner of the dying, now closing his eyes, now opening them, and bowing his head, now to one side, now to the other, all his strength failing.

At length he added the seventh word, with a loud cry and tears, saying, "Father, into your hands I commend my spirit" [Luke 23:46]. And saying this, he sent forth his spirit: with his head bowed on his breast toward the Father, as though giving thanks that he had called him back, he gave up his spirit. At this cry, the centurion that was there was converted, and said, "Truly this was the Son of God" [Matt. 27:54] on hearing that he expired with a loud cry; for other men, when dying, are not able to cry out; therefore he believed in him. So great was that cry that it was heard even in hell. Oh, what was the soul of the mother like, then, when she saw him thus painfully weaken, faint, weep, and die! I believe that either she was so absorbed by the multitude of her sorrows as to be insensible or was half dead, now even more so than when she met him carrying the cross. What did the faithful Magdalen, the beloved disciple, what did John, beloved above all, what did the other two sisters of the Lady, do now? What could they do, filled with bitterness, overwhelmed with sorrow, drunk with wormwood? Everyone wept unconsolably. Behold, then, the Lord hangs dead on the cross; the whole multitude departs; the most sorrowful mother remains with those four. They seat themselves near the cross, contemplating their beloved, looking for help from the Lord as to how they can take him down and bury him. But you, if you will contemplate your Lord well, will consider that from the sole of his foot to the crown of his head there is no health in him: there is not one member or bodily sense that has not felt total affliction or passion. Therefore you have his crucifixion and death, and the events of the sixth and ninth hours that appear at the present time, written according to my modest means and your inexperience. Study devoutly, faithfully, and solicitously to meditate on all this. Now we shall speak of what happened after his death.

Chapter 80. Of the Opening in the Side of Christ

While our reverend Lady Mary, as well as John, the Magdalen, and the sisters of the mother of the Lord, remained, sitting to one side of the cross, unceasingly observing the Lord Jesus hanging thus on the cross between the thieves, naked, afflicted, dead, deserted by all, behold, many armed men came toward them from the city, sent to break the legs of the crucified, to kill and bury them, so that no body should remain hanging on a cross on the great day of the sabbath. Then the Lady and all of them rise and look up and see them, and they do not know what is happening. Their sorrow is renewed and their fear and trembling increase. Indeed, the mother is much afraid and does not know what might happen and, turning toward her dead son, says, "My most beloved son, why do these men return? What more do they wish to do to you? Have they not killed you? My son, I believed them to be satisfied with you, but I see that you are persecuted even after death. My son, I do not know what to do. I could not defend you from death, but I shall come and stand at your feet near your cross. My son, beg your Father to make them gentle with you. I too shall do what I can." And then all five come weeping and place themselves before the cross of the Lord Jesus. The men approach with great fury and noise and, seeing the thieves still alive, break their legs and kill them, and take them down and throw them hastily into some ditch. As they came back to the Lord Jesus, however, the mother, fearing that they would do the same to her son, moved by the inward sorrow of her heart, thought of her usual weapon, that is, her innate humility. And down on her knees, arms crossed, with tear-stained face and hoarse voice, she addressed them, saying, "Men, brothers, I beg you in the name of God the most high, do not wish to injure me further in my most beloved son. For I am his most sorrowful mother, and you know, brothers, that I have never offended you or injured anybody. And if my son seemed to be opposed to you, you have killed him; and I forgive you for all injuries and offenses and the death of my son. Have mercy upon me and do not strike him; let me at least bury him whole. It is not necessary that his legs be broken, for you see that he is already dead and departed." For this was after he had gone. John, the Magdalen, and the sisters of the mother of the Lord stayed kneeling with her, and all wept most bitterly. O Lady, what are you doing? You stay at the feet of the most wicked of men; you pray to the inexorable. Do you think that pity will move the cruellest and most impious, and humble the proud? Humility is an abomination to the proud: you labor in vain. One, more-over, Longinus by name, then impious and proud, though later converted, a martyr and saint, extending his lance from a distance, scorning their prayers and entreaties, opened a great wound in the right side of the Lord Jesus; and blood and water came forth. Then the mother, half dead, fell into the arms of the Magdalen. John, urged on by sorrow, took action and rose against them, saying, "Most wicked men, why do you do these impious things? Can you not see that he is dead? Do you wish to kill his most sorrowful mother? Go away, for we shall bury him." Then as it pleased God, the men departed. The Lady was aroused, getting up as if awakening, asking what was done to her beloved son. They answered, "Nothing was done to him." After that, she sighed and was grieved, and, looking at the wounds of her son, was weakened by the sorrow of death. Do you see how often she is near death today? Certainly as often as she saw new things done against her son. In truth there was fulfilled in her what Simeon had said to her. "Your own soul," he said, "will be transfixed by a sword" [Luke 2:35]. For now, truly, the sword of that lance pierced the body of the son and the soul of the mother. Then they all return and sit down near the cross, not knowing what they ought to do. For they cannot take the body down and bury it, because they do not have enough force, nor implements with which they might lower him. Thus they remain, not daring to depart, yet unable to remain long, with night approaching. You see what perplexity they are in. O benign God, how do you permit your own, chosen of all women, mirror of the world and our resting-place, to be thus tried? ....

[*Jesus' mother Mary, Mary Magdalen, the apostle John, and their companions remove the body from the cross and bury it; but Mary cannot bear to leave his tomb.*]

As night was approaching, John said to the Lady, "It is not proper to remain here too long or return to the city by night. On that account, if it please you, Lady, let us withdraw." Then the Lady, rising and kneeling, embracing and blessing the sepulcher, said, "My son, I cannot stay with you any longer: I recommend you to your Father." Then, with eyes raised to heaven, she said tearfully, with great feeling, "Eternal Father, I recommend to you my son and my soul, which I leave behind me." And then they began to withdraw. When they reached the cross, she knelt and adored it, saying, "Here my son rested, and here is his most precious blood." And all did similarly. Think as well as you can that she was the first to adore the cross. After this they withdrew toward the city, and on the road she often turned around to look back. When they reached the last place from which they could see the sepulcher and the cross, she turned, bowed, and knelt in devout adoration. And all did similarly. When they approached the city, the sisters of the Lady veiled her as a widow, enveloping almost her whole face, and went on ahead. Thus veiled, the Lady followed most sorrowfully, between John and the Magdalen. Then the Magdalen, wishing on entering the city to take the road that led to her house and lead them there, looked ahead and said, "My Lady, I pray you, for love of my Master, to come to our house. There we shall be better off. You know how gladly he came to it. It is yours, and everything of mine is yours. I pray you to come." And they began to lament. But the Lady kept silent and indicated John, so the Magdalen went on pleading with him. He answered, "It is more fitting that we go to Mount Sion, mainly because we can meet our friends that way, and it is better for you to come with her." The Magdalen answered, "You know well that I will come with her wherever she goes and never leave her." At the entrance to the city, they met on all sides virgins and good matrons, who, as soon as they could reach her, accompanied her on the road for consolation; but great was the lamentation. And some good men felt compassion for her as they passed and were moved to grief, saying, "Surely a great injustice was done today by the rulers against the son of this lady, and God manifested great signs for him. Let them beware of what they have done!" When they came to the house, she turned toward the ladies, thanked them, and bowed most devotedly. They too bowed and knelt, all beginning to lament greatly. Thus the Lady entered the house with the Magdalen and her sisters. John, placing himself at the door, begged everyone to return home, for the hour was late; and thanking them he closed the door. Then the Lady, looking around the house, spoke thus: "My sweetest son, where are you, that I do not see you here? O John, where is my son? O Magdalen, where is your Father, who loved you so tenderly? O beloved sisters, where is our son? Our joy, our sweetness, and the light of our eyes has gone; but he has gone, you know, in great anguish. And this is what adds greatly to my sorrow, that he went wholly lacerated, wholly straitened and athirst, goaded, oppressed, and outraged; nor could we help him in any way. Everyone abandoned him, and his Father, omnipotent God, did not wish to help him. In what quick order this was done to him, you saw. Whose condemnation, at any time, even that of the wickedest of men, was so hasty and fulminating? O son, in this night you were captured, perfidiously betrayed; in the morning, at the third hour, condemned; and at the sixth hour crucified; and so you died. O son, how bitter is the separation from you and the memory of your most shameful death!" At last John begged her to desist, and consoled her. If you will use your powers, you too will know how to obey, serve, console, and comfort her, so that she may eat a little, and comfort the others in doing so, for they have all fasted up to now. Afterwards you may receive a blessing from the Lady and each of the others, and withdraw.

What reactions to the Passion do Giovanni de' Cauli's Meditations strive to evoke? How do they stimulate compassion for Jesus' suffering? To what extent is this work aimed at the heart and to what extent at the head? What are its most memorable passages? Why? What literary and rhetorical effects does Giovanni employ to achieve his goals?

15. CAESARIUS OF HEISTERBACH'S MIRACLES OF THE EUCHARIST (c. 1220-35)

As the theology of the Eucharist evolved in the eleventh and, especially, the twelfth century, the emphasis on Jesus' real presence in this sacrament had profound consequences for liturgical practice and popular belief. By the late twelfth century, the communion wine was withdrawn from lay people since theologians had decided that the bread alone contained both Jesus' flesh and blood. Along with the words of consecration, the elevation of the host became an essential ritual of the mass, so much so that merely seeing the elevated host was deemed to convey a sacramental power. Perhaps most important for popular religion, lay people stopped receiving communion regularly since, if Jesus was really present in the host, receiving it became an event of awesome importance not to be trivialized by routine reception. Thus, the Fourth Lateran Council (1215), which dogmatically defined Jesus' real presence in the consecrated elements of bread and wine, judged that it was sufficient for lay people to communicate just once a year (see Doc. 2.21). All of this meant that the host acquired a central place in the pious imagination, and Jesus' real presence in the host and its consequent power were persistent themes in devotional literature and popular belief from the twelfth century onwards. The miracle stories of Caesarius of Heisterbach (c. 1180-c. 1240) neatly make the point. Educated at the cathedral school of Cologne, from there he entered the Cistercian monastery at Heisterbach near Bonn. In his role as instructor of novices, he wrote the Dialogue on Visions and Miracles *(Dialogus magnus visionum atque miraculorum, c. 1220-35), divided into twelve books covering such topics as conversion, confession, temptation, demons, visions, and miracles. The* Monk *and the* Novice *in these conversations represent Caesarius himself and a student monk. His stories of miracles of the Eucharist, which tangibly reinforced the idea of the real presence, would have easily entered the popular imagination through sermons since his* Dialogue *was very popular and filled with the sort of vivid examples that characterized medieval homiletics. But as this excerpt from Book Nine on the Eucharist indicates, many of Caesarius' stories were just as easily originally culled from miraculous tales told by lay people who were likewise eager to endorse the wondrous power of the host. (Theologians, on the other hand, took a more cautious approach. A generation after Caesarius, Thomas Aquinas in his* Summa theologiae *[III, q. 76, art. 8] was skeptical that people could actually see physical attributes of Jesus in bread and wine.) The pyx mentioned in several of these stories was a small, usually round receptacle used either to store the consecrated host or carry it to the sick.*

Source: trans. H. von E. Scott and C.C. Swinton Bland in Caesarius of Heisterbach, *The Dialogue on Miracles* (London: George Routledge & Sons, 1929), v. II, pp. 111-19; revised. Latin.

Book 9, Chapter 3. Of Adolph, the priest who saw the host transform itself into the Virgin and Child and then into a lamb, and last of all into the crucified.

When the lord abbot, on his way to Friesland to make a visitation, had told the aforesaid vision [of the infant Jesus appearing in a host] to a certain knight, the latter repeated the story to Adolph, priest of Dieveren. And when he heard it, he sighed and said: "To what purpose does the Lord God show such visions to holy men who are perfect in the faith? They ought to be revealed to a sinner and others like me who often have doubts about this sacrament."

One day when this Adolphus was celebrating mass and before the *Agnus dei* had lifted up the host to break it, he saw the Virgin in the host itself, sitting upon a throne and holding the infant to her breast. Wishing to know what was on the other side, as soon as he turned the host he saw a lamb in it, and when he again turned it he saw in it, as if through a glass, Christ hanging on the cross with bent head. When he saw this, the priest was terrified and stood for a long time thinking whether he ought to stop there or finish the service. When he had appeased the Lord with his tears, the sacrament took again its former appearance and he completed the service. And when the congregation wondered at the delay, he went up into the pulpit and told the people the vision with many tears and that very hour fifty men took the cross [i.e., vowed to go on crusade] at his hands. For it was the octave of the apostles Peter and Paul....

The Savior condescends, as I said in the beginning, to show the reality of his body in this sacrament to good priests in order that they may be comforted; to those who are wavering in their faith that they may be strengthened; to those who are living ill that they may be warned. Here are examples....

Chapter 5. Of the priest of Wickindisburg who felt a doubt in saying the canon and beheld raw flesh.

And it is less than two years ago since a priest who was in doubt about the sacrament of the body of Christ celebrated in the castle which is called Wickindisburg, and when at the canon he was hesitating about so wonderful a change of the bread into the body of Christ, the Lord showed him raw flesh in the host. When also this was seen by a nobleman named Widekin who was standing behind him, after the mass was over, he drew the priest apart and confessed that he also had been in doubt about the sacrament at that very time. And each told the other how he had seen raw flesh in the host. This Widekin had a daughter, married to Syfrid of Runkel, [and] a niece, a daughter of his sister the abbess of Rheindorf who told me that she had seen the same vision the year before.

Monk. Would you like to hear how the Lord shows two priests of evil life that he is crucified by them?

Novice. Very much.

Monk. Listen then to this terrible vision.

Chapter 6. Of a priest who keeping the host in his mouth with wicked intent, found himself unable to leave the church.

A certain licentious priest made love to a woman, and when he could not gain her consent, while saying mass, he kept in his mouth the most pure body of the Lord, hoping if he were to kiss her that her will would be bent to his by the power of the sacrament. But the Lord whom we find saying by Zacharias that prophet about such priests, "And you people crucify me all day," prevented his wickedness in the following way.

When he desired to go out of the door of the church, he seemed to have grown in such a way that he knocked against the ceiling of the church with his head. The unhappy man in terror drew the host from his mouth, and because he was nearly out of his mind, tried to bury it in the corner of the church. In fear that divine vengeance would quickly fall upon him, he confessed his sacrilege to a friend of his who was a priest. Both priests went together to the spot and moving away the dust, found not the species of bread, but the figure of a man hanging upon a cross, small indeed in size but wholly composed of flesh and blood. What they afterwards did with it or what the priest did, I do not relate, because it was a long time since these things were told to me by the precentor Herman who knew the story well. That man was worse than those who crucified Christ actually.

Monk. It is true that if they had known, they would never have crucified the Lord of glory. This man showed contempt for him whom he knew and by his contempt re-crucified him. I think I have shown you enough that the true body of Christ lies under the form of bread and that the transubstantiation takes place as much at the hands of evil priests as of good.

Novice. If all priests knew this story and believed what they heard, I think that they would honor more than they do now the God-made sacraments.

Monk. It is a very miserable thing that this sacrament which was instituted for us men and for our salvation, should find us so lukewarm about it when the brute beasts, and even the worms and reptiles, recognize the creator in it.

Chapter 7. Of the body of the Lord which was stolen from a church and its place of concealment revealed by oxen in the field.

In a small town called Comede some thieves by night broke into a church and among other things carried off the vessel containing the body of the Lord. But when they found in it nothing but relics and the pyx with the sacrament, they took no more care of it and laying down the pyx in a furrow on a field close to the town they went off in confusion. When in the morning a peasant was plowing the same field with oxen and the animals came near to the pyx, they stood still in terror. And when the plowman urged them forward and they would not go, sometimes drawing back and sometimes wheeling out of the way, he cried angrily: "What devil has gotten into these oxen?" For he could not see plainly because he was working at dawn. But when he looked more carefully, he discovered the pyx just in front of the feet of the oxen and close by it the vessel from the church. Then understanding the cause of their rebellion he let them loose in the field and ran back to the town and told all that had happened, both to the priest and to everybody else. A troop of asses showed him a similar honor by coming down from the road into the mud, as I remember I related in the ninety-eighth chapter of the fourth book. Hear now visions glorious enough about tiny creatures.

Chapter 8. Of bees who built a shrine for the body of the Lord.

Once a woman kept a large number of bees, which were no profit to her, but kept dying off. When she tried to find a remedy for this misfortune, she was told that if she placed the Lord's body among them, the plague would quickly be stayed. She therefore went to the church, and pretending that she wished to communicate, she received the Lord's body, which she immediately withdrew from her mouth when she returned from the altar, and placed it in one of the hives. Wonderful power of God! The insects recognized their creator, and built a most beautiful chapel with wonderful skill from the sweetest honeycomb for their most gracious guest, and placed it in an altar of the same material, and laid upon it the most sacred body. And the Lord gave his blessing to all their work. And when in course of time the woman opened the hive, and saw the aforesaid shrine, she was terrified, and ran to the priest, and confessed to him all she had done and seen. Thereupon he took with him his parishioners and they came to the hive, drove away the bees flying round and buzzing loudly to the praise of the creator, while they admired the walls of the chapel, its windows, roof, bell tower, porch, and altar, and carried back to the church the Lord's body with songs of praise and thanksgiving. For although God is marvelous in his saints, he is shown yet more wonderful in these the least of his creation. Lest anyone should show such presumption in the future, I will tell you a terrible happening, which was related to me last year by the abbess of the Island of St. Nicholas.

Chapter 9. Of a woman who was stricken with paralysis because she had spread the Lord's body over her cabbages.

In the same island there was a girl possessed of a devil; she was a lay woman, and I myself saw her there. When the devil was asked by a priest why he so cruelly tormented Hartdyfa de Cochem for so long a time, he replied by the girl's mouth: "Because she has deserved it over and over again. She has spread the Most High himself over her vegetables." And when the priest did not fully understand what he meant, but the other was unwilling to explain, he went to the woman and told her what the devil had said about her, urging her not to deny if she understood. And she immediately confessed her fault and said: "I quite well understand what he meant, a thing which I have never disclosed to any man before now. When I was a young girl and undertook the duty of cultivating the garden, one night I took in a vagabond woman and gave her hospitality. When I had put before her the losses of my garden, telling her that all my vegetables were devoured by caterpillars, she replied: 'I can tell you of a good remedy. Take the Lord's body and break it up small and sprinkle it over the vegetables, and immediately the plague will be stayed.' Foolish woman that I was, I was more anxious about my garden than about the sacrament, and when on Easter Day I received the Lord's body and took it out of my mouth and did with it as I had been told, it became a torment to me as well as a remedy for the cabbages, as the devil can witness."

Novice. This woman was more cruel than Pilate's servants, who spared the Lord when dead, that a bone of him might not be broken.

Monk. That is why even to this day she is atoning for her terrible sin, and suffers unheard of pain. Let those who use the divine sacraments for worldly gain, or what is worse wickedness, for wrong doing, consider not the guilt but its punishments. If even insects forget the reverence due to the sacrament, they will one day pay the penalty.

Chapter 10. Of the fly which hovered over the Lord's body at the hour of reception and was punished with death.

Last year one of our priests was celebrating the daily mass in honor of Our Lady in the presence of the Bishop Theodoric, and a big fly began to hover over the chalice so importunately at the very moment of consecration that it seemed almost determined to enter the chalice by force. The priest trembling and fearing since he had his hands occupied and failed in his attempt to blow away the fly again and again by a cough, called to his aid Henry the deacon, who at that moment was giving the kiss of peace to the bishop. Then the fly rising higher in swift flight, there paid the penalty of its presumption because soon afterwards when the reception and the absolution were over and the priest whom it had annoyed was still looking on, it fell dead like a stone between the corporal and the chalice. And the deacon threw it away from the altar.

Novice. I am greatly pleased with this account....

[*Monk.*] So great is the glory of this sacrament that not only animals who possess a moving life, but even the invisible elements feel its power. Here is an example.

Chapter 12. Of the Lord's body which when cast into the river drowned some heretics.

At that time when the Albigensian heresies began to show themselves, some wicked men supported by the power of the devil displayed certain signs and wonders by which they bolstered up these heresies and overthrew the faith of many. They walked upon the waters and did not sink. A man of sound faith and religious life perceiving this and knowing that true signs could not co-exist with false doctrine carried the Lord's body in the pyx to the river where these men were to display their power to the people, and he said in the hearing of everybody: "I adjure thee, O devil, by him whom I carry in my hands that you exercise no tricks on this river to pervert this people by means of these men." After these words the priest much troubled cast the Lord's body into the stream on whose waters these men were walking. Behold the wonderful power of Christ. As soon as the sacrament touched the elements, trickery gave way to truth, and those false saints went down like lead into the deep and were drowned. And immediately the pyx containing the sacrament was carried away by angels. When the priest saw all these things, he rejoiced indeed over the miracle but grieved at the loss of the sacrament. Passing all that night in tears and lamentations in the morning he found the pyx with the sacrament on the altar. This story was told me at the time it happened. Another miracle happened in the sea regarding the Lord's body and I will not pass it over in silence.

Chapter 13. Also of the Lord's body which when a ship was wrecked, floated to the other ships.

When in that great expedition ships collected from all parts of Germany entered upon their voyage, the priests were ordered for various reasons not to have the Lord's body in any of the ships. And all obeyed these orders, one ship only of the Frisians refusing to obey, and quickly paid the penalty of its disobedience. It was wrecked as if by a judgment of God and the pyx containing the Lord's body with everything else which had been placed in the ship. But the men were saved by the other ships which came to their help. And behold they saw at a distance the pyx floating in the sea, and it came to the ships with so swift a motion that it seemed to have been driven by sails. And when it had been taken up into one of the ships, another miracle was seen to take place. Though its lid was open and unfastened by any hand, yet not even a drop of water got in among all those stormy waves. Herman, dean of Gereon in Cologne, who was there and saw all this, used to tell the story as if it were a great miracle. The earth itself recognized its creator in the sacrament.

Are these stories meant to inspire faith or to quell doubts? What effect would they have on their audience? What impression of the Eucharist and God do they convey? If they seem incredible to us now, what made them believable to their medieval audience?

16. TWO HYMNS FOR THE FEAST OF CORPUS CHRISTI (1264)

One of the most popular medieval feasts was Corpus Christi celebrating Christ's real presence in the Eucharist. The devotion – born in Liège in the early 1200s and championed by St. Juliana of Cornillon (d. 1258) whose visions partly inspired it – was officially declared a universal feast of the church in 1264, though it became widely observed only in the fourteenth century. Celebrated on the Thursday after Trinity Sunday (which could fall between May 21 and June 24), this summer feast was marked across Europe by solemn processions of people through their villages, neighborhoods, or towns led by clergymen carrying the consecrated host. Long tradition ascribes the mass sequences and hymns written for Corpus Christi to Thomas Aquinas (c. 1224-74), an ascription which recent scholarship supports. Whoever their author, two Corpus Christi hymns became enormously popular by the fourteenth century: the Pange lingua, *and the* Lauda sion. *Both of them were sung during public processions of the Eucharist, and both of them encapsulated boilerplate doctrine about the real presence. The church's eucharistic theology was further distilled and popularized in vernacular sermons written for Corpus Christi and, especially in England, in Corpus Christi pageant plays. The verse translation of the Pange lingua below is Edward Caswall's familiar nineteenth-century version, which preserves both the sense and the cadences of the medieval Latin.*

Source: (1) trans. Edward Caswall, *Hymns and Poems, Original and Translated* (London: Burns, Oates, & Co., 1873), pp. 65-66; (2) trans. Joseph Connelly, *Hymns of the Roman Liturgy* (Westminster, MA: Newman Press, 1957), pp. 124-26; revised. Latin.

1. Pange lingua

Sing, my tongue, the Savior's glory,
Of his flesh the mystery sing;
Of the blood, all price exceeding,
Shed by our immortal king,
Destined for the world's redemption,
From a noble womb to spring.

Of a pure and spotless virgin
Born for us on earth below,
He, as man, with man conversing,
Stayed, the seeds of truth to sow;
Then he closed in solemn order
Wondrously his life of woe.

On the night of that last supper
Seated with his chosen band,
He, the paschal victim eating,
First fulfills the law's command;
Then as food to all his brothers
Gives himself with his own hand.

Word made flesh, the bread of nature
By his word to flesh he turns;

Wine into his blood he changes:
What though sense no change discerns?
Only be the heart in earnest,
Faith her lesson quickly learns.

Down in adoration falling,
Lo, the sacred host we hail;
Lo, o'er ancient forms departing,
Newer rites of grace prevail;
Faith for all defects supplying,
Where the feeble senses fail.

To the everlasting Father,
And the Son who reigns on high,
With the Holy Ghost proceeding
Forth from each eternally,
Be salvation, honor, blessing,
Might, and endless majesty.

2. Lauda Sion

Sion, praise your Savior.
Praise your leader and shepherd
In hymns and canticles.
Praise him as much as you can,
For he is beyond all praising,
And you will never be able to praise him as he merits.

A theme worthy of particular praise –
The living and life-giving bread –
Today is put before us;
That, without any doubt,
Was given to the Twelve at table
During the holy supper.

Therefore let our praise be full and resounding,
And our soul's rejoicing
Full of delight and beauty,
For this is the festival day
To commemorate the first institution
Of this table.

At this table of the new King,
The new law's new Pasch
Puts and end to the old Pasch.
The new displaces the old,
Reality the shadow,
And light the darkness.

Christ wanted what he did at the supper
To be repeated
In his memory.
And so we, in accordance with his holy directions,
Consecrate bread and wine
To be salvation's Victim.

Christians know by faith
That bread is changed into his flesh
And wine into his blood.
You cannot understand this, cannot perceive it;
But a lively faith affirms that the change,
Which is outside the natural order of things, occurs.

Under the different species,
Which are now signs only and not their own reality,
There lie hidden wonderful realities.
His body is our food, his blood our drink.
And yet Christ remains entire
Under both species.

The complete Christ,
Uncut, unbroken, and undivided,
Is what the communicant receives.
Whether one receive or a thousand,
The one receives as much as the thousand,
Nor is Christ diminished by being received.

The good and the wicked alike receive him,
But with the unlike destiny
Of life or death.
To the wicked it is death, but life to the good.
See how different is the result,
Though each receives the same.

Last of all, if the sacrament is broken,
Have no doubt; but remember
There is as much in a fragment,
As in an unbroken host.
There is no division of the reality,
But only a breaking of its sign;
Nor does the breaking diminish the condition or size
Of the One hidden under the sign.

17. CATHERINE OF SIENA ON RECEIVING THE EUCHARIST (c. 1378)

Whatever its source, direct knowledge of God and communion with him through mystical experience was one path of medieval religious experience; but the mystic's interior vision of God was hardly typical. Not that mystics were unpopular: visionaries like Hildegard of Bingen, Bridget of Sweden, Catherine of Siena, or Julian of Norwich, to mention just a few, gained devoted followers during their lifetimes, and written accounts of their revelations and spiritual counsels circulated among the more elite circles of the devout. Still, the official church remained wary of mystics – especially women mystics – and carefully weighed their orthodoxy since their personal revelations from God could threaten the customary sources of Christian revelation through scripture and tradition. Catherine of Siena (1347-80) was medieval Europe's most public mystic. Born Catherine Benincasa to a Sienese wool-dyer and his wife, she was the twenty-fourth of their twenty-five children. Her early ascetic leanings found an outlet in her middle-teens when she became a tertiary of the Dominican order, and soon she began to undergo mystical experiences. Unlike many mystics who sought solitude, Catherine preferred to engage the world. In fact, she was one of the most outspoken people of her day, scolding – sometimes gently, sometimes not – two popes, the king of France, the queen of Naples, and countless officials of the city-states of Siena and Florence for failing to be as Christian as they could. Addressed to the mighty and the lowly, the clergy and the laity, family, friends, and strangers, 382 of her letters survive, mostly written in the last decade of her brief life, including the following letter written to Ristoro Canigiani, the father of one of her secretaries – she dictated all her letters – who was having scruples about receiving communion unworthily. In it we see her distilling mystical wisdom to answer a layman's spiritual anxiety with heartfelt piety and straightforward, level-headed counsel.

Source: trans. Vida Scudder, *Saint Catherine of Siena as seen in her Letters* (London: J.M. Dent, 1926), pp. 199-205; revised. Italian.

In the name of Jesus Christ crucified and of sweet Mary:

Dearest son in Christ sweet Jesus. I Catherine, servant and slave of the servants of Jesus Christ, write to you in his precious blood with desire to see you free from every particle of self-love, so that you may not lose the light and knowledge which come from seeing the unspeakable love which God has for you. And because it is light which makes us know this, and false love is what takes light from us, therefore I have very great desire to see it quenched in you. Oh, how dangerous this self-love is to our salvation! It deprives the soul of grace, for it takes from it the love of God and of its neighbor, which makes us live in grace. It deprives us of light, as we said, because it darkens the eye of the mind, and when the light is taken away we walk in darkness, and do not know what we need.

What do we need to know? The great goodness of God, and his unspeakable love toward us; the perverse law which always fights against the spirit, and our own wretchedness. In this knowledge the soul begins to render his due to God; that is, glory and praise to his name, loving him above everything, and the neighbor as one's self, with eager desire for virtue; and the soul bestows hate and displeasure on itself, hating in itself vice, and its own sensuousness, which is the cause of every vice. The soul wins all virtue and grace in the knowledge of itself, abiding therein with light, as was said. Where shall the soul find the wealth of contrition for its sins, and the abundance of God's mercy? In this house of self-knowledge.

Now let us see whether we find it in ourselves or not. Let us talk somewhat about it. For, as you wrote me, you have a desire to feel contrition for your sins, and not being able to feel it, you give up for this reason Holy Communion. Now we shall see whether you ought to give it up for this.

You know that God is supremely good, and loved us before we were, and is Eternal Wisdom, and his power in virtue is immeasurable. So for this reason we are sure that he has power, knowledge, and will to give us what we need. Well we see, in proof, that he gives us more than we know how to ask, and that which was not asked by us. Did we ever ask him that he should create us reasonable creatures in his own image and likeness, rather than brute beasts? No. Or that he should create us by grace by the blood of the Word, his only-begotten son, or that he should give us himself for food, perfect God and perfect man, flesh and blood, body and soul, united to deity? Beyond these most high gifts, which are so great, and show such fire of love toward us, that there is no heart so hard that its hardness and coldness would not melt by considering them at all: infinite are the gifts and graces which we receive from him without asking.

Then, since he gives so much without our asking – how much the more will he fulfill our desires when we shall desire a just thing of him? Nay, who makes us desire and ask it? Only he. Then, if he makes us ask it, it is a sign that he means to fulfill it, and give us what we seek.

But you will say to me: "I confess that he is what you say. But how does it happen that many times I ask both contrition and other things, and they seem not to be given me?" I answer you: It may be that it is through a defect in him who asks, asking imprudently, with words alone and not with his whole heart – and of such as these our Savior said that they call him Lord, Lord, but shall not be known by him – not that he does not know them, but for their fault they shall not be known by his mercy. Or the man who prays asks for something which, if he had it, would be injurious to his salvation. So that when he does not have what he asks, he really has it, because he asks for it thinking that it would be for his good; but if he had it, it would be to his harm, and it is for his good not to have it. So God has satisfied the intention with which he asked it. So that on God's side we always have our prayer; but this is the case, that God knows the secret and the open, and is aware of our imperfection; so he sees that if he gave us the grace at once as we ask it, we should do like an unclean creature, who, rising from the sweetest honey, does not mind afterwards lighting on a fetid object. God sees that we do so many a time. For, receiving his graces and benefits, sharing the sweetness of his charity, we do not mind afterwards alighting on miserable things, turning back to the filth of the world. Therefore God does not sometimes give us what we ask as soon as we should like to make us increase in the hunger of our desire, because he rejoices and pleases himself in seeing the hunger of his creatures toward him.

Sometimes he will do us the grace by giving it to us in effect though not in feeling. He uses this means with foresight, because he knows that if a man felt himself to possess it, either he would slacken the pull of desire or would fall into presumption; therefore he withdraws the feeling, but not the grace. There are others who both receive and feel, according as it pleases the sweet goodness of our physician to give us sick folk; and he gives to everyone in the way that our sickness needs. You see, then, that in any case the yearning of the creature, with which it asks of God, is always fulfilled. Now we see what we ought to seek and how prudently.

It seems to me that the sweet primal truth teaches us what we ought to seek when in the holy Gospel, reproving man for the intemperate zeal which he bestows on gaining and holding the honors and riches of the world, he said: "Take no thought for the morrow. Its own care suffices for the day." Here he shows us that we should consider prudently the shortness of time.

Then he adds: "Seek first the kingdom of heaven; for your heavenly father knows well that you have need of these lesser things." What is this kingdom, and how is it sought? It is the kingdom of eternal life, and the kingdom of our own soul, for this kingdom of the soul, unless it is possessed through reason, never becomes part of the kingdom of God. With what is it sought? Not only with words – we have already said that such as these are not recognized by God – but with the yearning of true and real virtues. Virtue is what seeks and possesses this kingdom of heaven; virtue, which makes a man prudent, so that he works for the honor of God and the salvation of himself and his neighbor, with prudence and maturity. Prudently he endures his neighbor's faults; prudently he rules the impulse of charity, loving God above everything, and his neighbor as himself. This is the rule: that he hold him ready to give bodily life for the salvation of souls, and temporal goods to help the body of his neighbor. Such a rule is set by prudent charity. Were he imprudent, it would be just the opposite as with many who use a foolish and crazy sort of charity, who many a time, to help their neighbor – I speak not of his soul, but of his body – are ready to betray their own souls, by publishing abroad lies, giving false witness. Such men as these lose charity, because it is not built upon prudence.

We have seen that we must seek the kingdom of heaven prudently. Now I answer you about the attitude we should hold toward Holy Communion, and how it befits us to take it. We should not use a foolish humility, as do secular men of the world. I say it befits us to receive that sweet sacrament because it is the food of souls without which we cannot live in grace. Therefore no bond is so great that it cannot and must not be broken that we may come to this sweet sacrament. A man must do on his part as much as he can, and that is enough. How ought we to receive it? With the light of most holy faith, and with the mouth of holy desire. In the light of faith you shall contemplate all God and all man in that host. Then the impulse that follows the intellectual perception receives with tender love and holy meditation on its sins and faults, where it arrives at contrition and considers the generosity of the immeasurable love of God, who in so great love has given himself for our food. Because someone does not seem to have that perfect contrition and disposition which he himself would wish, he must not therefore turn away; for goodwill alone is sufficient, and the disposition which exists on his part.

Again I say that it befits us to receive as was depicted in the Old Testament, when it was commanded that the lamb should be eaten roasted and not simmered; whole and not in part; girded and standing, staff in hand; and the blood of the lamb should be placed on the throne of the threshold. Thus it befits us to receive this sacrament: to eat it roasted, and not simmered; for if it were simmered there would be interposed earth and water – that is, earthly affections and the water of self-love. Therefore it must be roasted, so that there shall be nothing between. We take it this way when we receive it straight from the fire of divine charity. And we ought to be girded with the girdle of conscience, for it would be very shocking that one should advance to so great cleanliness and purity with mind or body unclean. We ought to stand upright, that is, our heart and mind should be wholly faithful and turned toward God; with the staff of the most holy cross, where we find the teaching of Christ crucified. This is the staff on which we lean, which defends us from our foes, the world, the devil, and the flesh. And it befits us to eat it whole and not in part: that is, in the light of faith, we should contemplate not only the humanity in this sacrament, but the body and the soul of Christ crucified, wrought into unity with deity, all God and all man. We must take the blood of this lamb and put it on our forehead – that is, confess it to every rational being, and never deny it, for pain or for death. Thus sweetly it befits us to receive this lamb, prepared in the fire of charity upon the wood of the cross. Thus shall we be found sealed with the sign of Tau [the cross-shaped, Greek letter *T*], and shall never be struck by the avenging angel.

I said that it did not befit us, nor do I wish you, to do as many impudent laymen, who pass over what is commanded them by holy church, saying: "I am not worthy of it." Thus they spend a long time in mortal sin without the food for their souls. Oh, foolish humility! Who does not see that you are not worthy? At what time do you expect worthiness? Do not expect it, for you are just as worthy at the end as at the beginning. For with all our just deeds, we shall never be worthy of it. But God is he who is worthy, and makes us worthy with his worth. His worth grows never less. What should we do? Make us ready on our part, and observe his sweet commandment. For if we did not do so, giving up communion, believing in this way to flee from fault, we should fall into fault.

Therefore I conclude, and will that such folly be not in you; but that you make yourself ready, as a faithful Christian, to receive this Holy Communion as I said. You will do it just as perfectly as you are in true knowledge of yourself, not otherwise. For if you abide in that knowledge, you will see everything clearly. Do not slacken your holy desire, for pain or loss, or injury or ingratitude of those whom you have served; but manfully, with true and long perseverance you shall persevere till death. Such I beg you to do by the love of Christ crucified. I say no more. Remain in the holy and sweet grace of God. Sweet Jesus, Jesus love.

What spiritual difficulty does Ristoro find himself in here? What counsel does Catherine offer him? How does she argue her case and what metaphors does she employ? Is this good, clear advice?

18. THE HOST AND LIBELS AGAINST THE JEWS
(c. 1303)

The doctrine of the real presence of Jesus in the consecrated bread and wine – rati-
fied both theologically and in the popular mind – could be put to impious purposes.
Rudolf of Schlettstadt, a Dominican living in the Upper Rhine at the turn of the
fourteenth century, is the elusive author credited with a collection of fifty-six stories
about Jewish sacrilege, demonic possession, and ghostly apparitions that now survives in
a single manuscript copied from the original in the mid-sixteenth century. Among other
things, his work preserves a dark side of popular Christianity: its easy scapegoating
of Jews. By the thirteenth century the Christian complaint against the Jews was both
the ancient libel that they killed Christ and that they had divinely revealed proof of
the truth of Christianity but obstinately rejected it. Fueling Christian anti-Semitism
were widespread rumors prevalent since the mid-twelfth century that Jews were killing
Christian children and using their blood in their sinister rituals – the infamous "blood
libel." Rudolf himself relished the more recent allegations that Jews were desecrating
consecrated hosts. Neither accusation rested on a shred of rational evidence. But these
stories about profaned hosts both underscored Christian awe for the Eucharist, while
helping to relieve doubts about the mystifying concept of the real presence, and provided
ammunition for pillorying religious enemies. These themes were later dramatized for
public performance in plays such as the English Play of the Sacrament *from Croxton*
or the French Mistere de la Sainte Hostie, *both written in the fifteenth century and*
both about alleged Jewish desecrations of the host.

Source: trans. J. Shinners from Rudolf von Schlettstadt, *Historiae Memorabiles, Zur Dominikanerliteratur und Kulturgeschichte des 13. Jahrhunderts,* ed. Erich Kleinschmidt (Cologne: Böhlau-
Verlag, 1972), pp. 41-44; 51-53. Latin.

[1] In 1298 Lord Kraffto of Hohenloe had contracted large debts from the
Jews which he was unable to pay without great loss of his property. The
Jews who lived in his domain, fearing Lord Kraffto, went suppliantly to
the bishop of Würzburg asking him to compel their Lord Kraffto to stand
by the Christian oath he made to them that he would harass no Jew in
either possessions or body. The lord bishop assented to their request, went
to Lord Kraffto, interceded humbly for the Jews, and what he asked for he
effectively got. By virtue of this success, the Jews grew bolder in making
their contracts. Whatever it occurred to them to do they readily attempted.
During this same time there were many Jews living at Castle Wickersheim,
which was in the domain of Lord Kraffto. By price or plea they persuaded
a bellman or sacristan to open the church for them on Holy Thursday night
before matins and let them go inside freely and do whatever they wanted to

do. When the Jews went to the church on Holy Thursday night and found it open, with great glee they ran up to the altar, took the sacrament (that is, the hosts), tossed them on the altar and stuck them with knives and heaped whatever abuse on them they were able. The hosts wounded by the blades shed the purest blood from their wounds and bled profusely so that the blood stained the Jews' hands and palms and spotted the pavement in many more places. With a loud cry the hosts shouted over and over the words of Christ as he hung on the cross: *Hely, hely lamma sabacthani?* that is, "My God, my God, why hast thou forsaken me?" [Matt. 27:46]. They made such an uproar that nearly everyone in the neighborhood was terrified, and they all alike got up and went outside their houses where they all heard great shouting and horrifying voices inside the church. But those inside the church – the Jews – through Christ's permission could hear neither the shouting nor anything else. The people all together followed the crying and shouting to the church and found it open. Going inside they saw the Jews standing near the altar throwing hosts here and there and the blood flowing from the wounds. When the neighborhood poor saw this, they all seized the Jews and put them in custody. But the local priest seeing and hearing this, ran to the Lord of Hohenloe and told him what they had done. The lord said to the priest, "At the behest of my lord the bishop, I promised that no harm would come to the Jews and I mean strictly to abide by this. But I will confer with the lord bishop and whatever he counsels me to do, I will do it." However after the lord went to the bishop and faithfully related all of the above, the bishop said: "It is written: Judge justly the sons of man. If a man kills a man, you know his punishment and you have often inflicted it. But what punishment is worthy for those who crucify our Lord Jesus Christ, son of the Virgin Mary, true God and man, our creator, redeemer, and judge in his sacramental form? – I cannot say. So this is my advice: judge your Jews in such a way that you will not eternally suffer the Almighty's punishment." After the Lord of Hohenloe heard the lord bishop's response, he returned to his own place, seized all the Jews he could find, and, as best he could, he burned them all to ashes.

[2] Near the town of Möckmühl a river flowed that had formed a sort of island on which no one lived except paupers and prostitutes who concealed their excesses [there]. On this island burning lights appeared several times to some men, which greatly frightened them. When this was reported to the governors of the town, some of them were told to visit the place and carefully investigate and inquire where the lights had been seen. For there was a great suspicion that the Jews, who had lived on the island shortly before, had perpetrated some crime that God wished to reveal. The next day the men deputized on the order of their superiors to discharge their wishes went to

the island. They carefully probed around with a shovel and saw turned earth in many places and they found new dirt carelessly replaced. They re-opened these holes and in each hole they found hosts or pieces of the Lord's sacrament stolen by the Jews. They lifted these up with awe and reverently carried them back to the church....

[8] Concerning the revelation of Christ's Body through boys.

When the Jews suffered persecution by [the nobleman] Rindfleisch through all Franconia [in 1298], some of them deserted their houses and took themselves and their movable goods to safer places. Among them, one Jew from Iphofen abandoned his house and left for the time being. This Jew had a Christian neighbor who had two boys whom he dearly loved. These boys often played together, as boys are wont to do, in front of the deserted house of the absent Jew and passed their time there. Now and then they even peeked through the chinks into the house and one time they saw inside a lovely little boy scampering about. When they saw this, they quickly dashed to their father and shouted with a loud voice, saying, "Father, father! We saw a lovely little boy in the Jew's house!" The father did not believe that his boys had seen anything and said, "He's gone [now] and we can't catch him." The boys went back and again saw the child in the Jew's house just as they had the first time. They returned to their father and told him that they had seen the boy again. Then the father said to them: "Let's go there and get him." Saying this, he went with the boys to the Jew's house, asking them exactly where they had seen the boy. But when he saw nothing there, he harshly scolded the boys and went back to tending his garden and the boys went back to their father's house. But several days later the boys again carefully looked around the Jew's house (since it was in their neighborhood). Then they saw through the chinks a woman dressed in the most beautiful attire with the handsomest boy walking around her. Again they swiftly ran with joy to their father, saying, "Father, father! We have seen our auntie in the Jew's house wearing the most beautiful clothes while a boy walks around her." The father was disturbed and amazed and said: "Let's go see this marvel." And when they got to the spot the boys showed him, just as the last time he saw absolutely none of the things that the boys had seen. Thinking that his boys were playing tricks on him, he said to his neighbors, "My boys have made a fool of me. They told me they saw a handsome boy resting in that house and their aunt wearing the loveliest clothes and taking care of the boy." His neighbors said: "No doubt about it – the Lord's sacrament is hidden in that house. So let's call the priest and carefully look about; for God wants to reveal to us his power and marvels." When the priest arrived, all the neighbors gathered around him telling him what they heard from their rustic neighbor. Then the father began to recount everything above in the order it happened. The priest summoned both boys and questioned them, and they told him just what they told their father. Then the priest ordered the door of the Jew's house to be opened, and in the presence of everyone he asked them where and in what spot they had seen the boy resting. The boys said, "Here!" pointing their fingers at the spot. Then the priest dug into the ground with a stick and discovered three hosts of the Lord's sacrament. The priest called for his sacristan to bring large candles, clean corporal-cloths, and incense in a thurible, and to have the bells rungs and the people called together. When the people had gathered, the priest had the above story recited and asked for advice as to what should be done about it. Everyone advised that the Lord's Body should be left lying there in order to prove the malice and envy of the Jews and Christ's suffering. After this the priest and people set up some people around the Body who would defend and guard it day and night so that no one would have free access to the Lord's Body. For a priest and two worthy lay men were always present there; and it was so arranged that whenever they wished to leave, two others would quickly take their place while they were gone. And they faithfully considered how to build a church on that spot.

How are the Jews in these stories depicted? What kind of relations do they have with Christians? What effect would these stories have on their audience? How do these stories compare with Caesarius of Heisterbach's miracles of the Eucharist in Doc. 15?

19. A FRENCH PEASANT'S THEOLOGY OF GOD
(1320)

From 1318-25, Bishop Jacques Fournier conducted an extensive inquisitorial sweep of his diocese of Pamiers to root out the vestiges of Cathar or Albigensian beliefs that had surfaced and flourished in the south of France a century earlier. The core of the Cathar creed was dualism, the belief that one god created spiritual things, which were good, and another god created material things, which were evil. The records of Fournier's inquisitions are invaluable documents of the religious beliefs, whether orthodox or heretical, of ordinary men and women (see Doc. 75). Though the testimony of Arnaud Cogul ultimately betrayed his vaguely Cathar cosmology (here called "Manichaean"), his honest difficulty in grappling with the age-old problem of theodicy – how a good God could allow evil – gives a glimmer of an idea about how ordinary Christians may have conceived God.

Source: trans. J. Shinners from Jean Duvernoy, *Le Registre d'Inquisition de Jacques Fournier, Évêque de Pamiers (1318-1325)*, v. 1 (Toulouse: Édouard Privat, 1965), pp. 378-80. Latin.

Against Arnaud Cogul of Lordat

December 5, 1320. It came to the attention of the reverend father in Christ Jacques [Fournier], by the grace of God bishop of Pamiers, that Arnaud Cogul of Lordat had said and asserted before many people that God had not made the devil or the wolf, or anything else harmful to human beings; and that the devil and the wolf had their being through themselves and were not created by anyone else; and also that he had said many other things that related to the Manichaean sect, which made him appear to be a believer in that sect. The bishop also heard that some time past he had been friends with these heretics and had great familiarity with their adherents, and that he joked about the inquisitors investigating heretical depravity and laughed at them since when they summoned him to inquire about a matter of faith he chose to confess nothing to them. Wishing to question him about these above matters and others pertaining to the Catholic faith, the bishop, with the assistance of Frère Gaillard de Pomiès who was acting as the deputy of the lord inquisitor of Carcassone, summoned the said Arnaud to come before him in his episcopal residence at Pamiers, who swore on the four holy Gospels of God that he would simply and purely tell the truth about the above matters, both about himself as principal and about others living and dead as he testified.

After he had sworn the oath, he said that for about six years he had believed that, since God is good and one, in whom no evil can exist, he did not make the devil or his demons. Also, he owned cows and sheep, some of which a wolf had once snatched and eaten; and he believed at that time that God would not have made such an evil animal as the wolf.

Also he said that during that time he believed that the devil had been created neither by God nor anyone else, but that he existed through himself, being neither created nor produced.

Also he said that during that time, though he did believe that one wolf nowadays produced another wolf, still he believed that in the beginning there was a first wolf which came into being through itself, not being made by any other being. But he believed that it came into the world in this way since no one knows where this wolf came from or who sent it. Nevertheless, so he said, he believed and still believes that God made all other physical and spiritual things, such as the good angels, heaven, earth, the waters, human bodies and in general all other bodies and things.

Also he said that, though he believed that on Judgment Day human souls would return to the flesh and bones in which they dwell while alive, yet, so he said, once Judgment Day ended, all human bodies would be shed or dissolved into earth, just as it now happens that after death a human body is reduced to earth.

Also he said that he had always believed that God always was and always will be, and that he entered the womb of the Blessed Virgin Mary and remained in her womb for nine months until he was born on Christmas Day. But though he appeared to be a man and looked human, in fact he was not a real man though he was really God; nor did he eat or drink anything other than God's grace.

He was carefully questioned about all the articles of faith and the articles of the Manichaean sect. He responded to all them suitably and according to Catholic belief.

Afterwards in the same year on December 11, the said Arnaud, standing for judgment before the lord bishop in his episcopal residence at Pamiers, with the assistance of Frère Gaillard de Pomiès and the witnesses written below, was read the preceding confession intelligibly and in his own language by the lord bishop. He was asked there if he had believed the things contained in the confession during the time he testified he had believed in them. He responded that he had, and that he wished to stand by the confession. He said that he had believed the said things because he had no one to instruct him about what the Roman church held and preached about the Catholic faith and about contrary beliefs during the time he had believed the heretical articles he had confessed even though he had believed them for forty years; and he said that he was terribly sorry that he had believed such things. But now, so he said, with the instruction of the lord bishop, he believed and would henceforth believe that God made all things: the good angels and the bad angels or demons, heaven, earth, the waters, and all creatures in general – even wolves – and all human spirits. Also, he said that he believed and would henceforth believe that the devil and also the wolf were made by God, and did not bring themselves into being, and there were no other creatures not made by God. Also, he said that he believed and would henceforth believe that after the Last Judgment, human bodies would not reduce or dissolve into earth but would remain eternally incorruptible, either in glory or in pain, and that they will remain forever after inseparably reunited with their own souls. Also, he said that he believed and would henceforth believe that, though God the Son was always and only God before the Incarnation, after the Incarnation he was truly God and truly man, having a real human body and a real rational soul like other humans. Also, he said that he believed and would henceforth believe that while Christ dwelled with us in this mortal life, he ate and drank natural, physical, tangible food and drink, and he grew hungry and thirsty, slept, woke up, and bore other human necessities, though he bore them voluntarily.

Asked if he had learned or been informed about the preceding errors that he said he had believed from a heretic of the Manichaean sect or from one of its adherents, he answered no. Asked if any other man or woman had taught him these things, he answered no. Asked how he had fallen into the preceding errors, he answered that it was through himself and his own foolishness. Asked whether he had taught or instructed anyone else about these things, he said no. Asked whether he had seen any heretics or heard them speaking, he said there was no one that he knew to be a heretic. But he said that he had seen the heretics Guillaume and Pierre Authié before they had fled, leaving this region to go to Lombardy. But they said nothing to him about the preceding matters.

Arnaud made the preceding confession freely and willingly; he was not jailed, though he was detained by the said lord bishop, able to go about the city of Pamiers and its boundaries.

Done in the presence of the lord bishop, Frère Gaillard de Pomiès, Frère Arnaud de Caslar of the Dominican Order at Pamiers, Frère David, monk of Fontfroide, and me, Guillaume Pierre Barthe, the bishop's notary, who wrote this document.

Does Arnaud Cogul's image of God make sense? Has he willfully embraced heresy or has he just been poorly educated? If you were his judge, would you believe his explanation?

CHAPTER THREE: THE VIRGIN MARY

Mary's place in popular religion was fundamental, often even at the expense of God. No other figure played such multiple roles in people's devotional lives. She was heavenly healer, merciful intercessor, devoted mother, reliable friend, swift avenger, stern judge, and trustworthy advocate. Perhaps above all she stood as a pliant mediatrix between Christians and her son, whose judgments, like a distant king's, could seem severe. But Mary was like a kind-hearted noblewoman who could bend her son's ear in favor of her clients and shower them with his gifts. The very names by which medieval Christians addressed her – Our Lady, Notre Dame, Madonna – were the deferential titles accorded noble women, designations for her that date from the eleventh century. Though she functioned in the popular imagination much like a goddess – almost a fourth member of the Trinity – the details of her history and the role she played in daily Christian life let her retain something intimately human with which ordinary people easily identified. It would not stretch the truth to argue that medieval popular religion pivoted around Mary and her son.

Fig. 3.1. The Annunciation

As God looks down, the angel Gabriel gives Mary his salutation: "*Ave [Maria] gratia plena. Dominus tecum* – Hail [Mary], full of grace. The Lord is with you." From a late fourteenth-century French Book of Hours; Milan, Ambrosian Library, MS I 7 sup., fol. 19r.

20. FOUR ANTIPHONS OF THE VIRGIN (ELEVENTH TO TWELFTH CENTURIES)

Born in monastic devotions, by the twelfth century the Virgin Mary's growing cult as the queen of heaven enshrined her in the popular religious imagination as an intercessor so powerful and so appealing that she often threatened to supplant God. Religious art, architecture, literature, and especially private and public prayer all celebrated her nurturing role as the mother of God and patroness of humanity. These qualities are celebrated in these four Marian antiphons, one of which was always sung during the course of the daily monastic divine office, after Compline and usually after Lauds. The Alma redemptoris mater *probably belongs to the middle eleventh century and with great uncertainty has been attributed to the monk Hermannus Contractus (1013-54). The* Salve regina, *probably the most famous medieval Marian verse, dates from the latter half of the eleventh century; the* Ave regina caelorum *comes from the twelfth century. A late edition to the antiphons, the* Regina caeli *is an adaptation of a twelfth-century Christmas hymn and first appears in a manuscript from the early thirteenth century. The earliest written witness of these four prayers joined together as a quartet is a letter of 1249 describing their use among Franciscans. But many lay people apparently could sing these Latin hymns, even if they did not completely understand them. The* Salve regina, *for instance, was a favorite hymn of sailors: it was frequently on the lips of Columbus's crew during their voyage to the New World. And Chaucer's seven-year-old "litel clergeoun" sang the* Alma redemptoris mater *by heart as he went back and forth to school in the* Prioress's Tale *of* The Canterbury Tales.

Source: trans. Joseph Connelly, *Hymns of the Roman Liturgy* (Westminster, MA: Newman Press, 1957), pp. 44-47; revised. Latin.

The *Alma redemptoris mater*

Loving Mother of the Redeemer,
Open door to heaven and star of the sea,
Come quickly to the aid of your people,
Fallen indeed but striving to stand again.
To nature's astonishment you were the mother of your holy Creator
Without ceasing to be a virgin, and heard from Gabriel
That greeting "Hail." Have pity on us sinners.

The *Salve regina*

Hail queen and mother of mercy,
Hail our life, comfort, and hope.

Exiled children of Eve, we cry to you.
We sigh weeping and wailing to you,
In this valley of tears.
Come then, our advocate,
And turn those eyes of pity towards us now.
When this time of exile is past,
Show us Jesus, the blessed fruit of your womb,
O clement, O pious, O sweet Virgin Mary.

The *Ave regina caelorum*

Hail, queen of heaven;
Hail mistress of the angels;
Hail, root of Jesse; hail, the gate
Through which the Light rose over the earth.
Rejoice, virgin most renowned
And of unsurpassed beauty.
Farewell, lady most comely.
Prevail upon Christ to pity us.

The *Regina caeli*

Queen of heaven, rejoice, alleluia,
The Son whom it was your privilege to bear, alleluia.
Has risen as he said, alleluia.
Pray God for us, alleluia.

21. ELISABETH OF SCHÖNAU'S VISION OF THE ASSUMPTION (c. 1157)

The New Testament offered only the sketchiest picture of the life of Mary. What was missing had to be filled in from apocryphal texts, creative interpolations from Old Testament prophecy, and outright legend. Spiritual visions offered another source, like this one from the German Rhineland mystic, Elisabeth Schönau (1129-65). A younger friend of the gifted abbess Hildegard of Bingen, Elisabeth entered the Benedictine monastery at Schönau when she was about twelve. Delicate in health and prone to depression, in 1152 she began having ecstatic visions in both Latin and German which her brother compiled for her in the Book of the Paths of God. *She soon gained a local reputation as a holy woman and seer. Her revelations about Mary's bodily Assumption occurred over a three-year period. Since they offered new details about*

Mary's life – in particular that her Assumption came forty days after her death – they spread quickly and were translated into several vernacular languages including French, German, Icelandic, and Anglo-Norman. Jacob of Voragine quoted Elisabeth directly when he narrated the story of the Assumption in his authoritative collection of saints' lives, The Golden Legend, *a century later. (For other apocryphal details of her life, see Doc. 62.49.)*

Source: trans J. Shinners from F.W.E. Roth, *Die Visionen der Hl. Elisabeth und die Schriften der Äbte Ekbert und Emecho von Schönau* (Brünn: Raigerner Benedictiner Druckerai, 1884), pp. 53-55. German.

Book II, chapter 31. Elisabeth's vision concerning the resurrection of the Blessed Virgin, mother of the Lord.

In the year the angel announced the *Book of the Paths of God* to me [c. 1155], on the day [August 22] on which the church celebrates the octave of Our Lady's Assumption, during the holy sacrifice of the mass I fell into an ecstasy and that comforter, my Lady of heaven, appeared to me in her usual manner. Then, following the advice of one of our superiors, I asked her: "My benevolent Lady, may it please you to make known to us whether you were assumed into heaven only in spirit or also in the flesh?" I mentioned this because, as they say, there is uncertainty about it in the books the [church] fathers wrote. She said to me: "What you ask you may not know until the future when it shall be revealed through you." For the space of a whole year I dared ask nothing more about this either from the angel who was my spiritual companion or from her when she revealed herself to me. But the brother who had urged me to ask the question put many requests to me to ask her for a revelation in answer to it. After a year had passed, as the feast of her Assumption again approached, I languished sick for many days. But as I was lying in my small bed during the holy sacrifice of the mass I fell, with great effort, into an ecstasy. And I saw in a very distant place a sepulcher surrounded by many lights with what appeared to be the shape of a woman inside it, and a great band of angels encircled it. After a bit, she was raised up from the sepulcher and along with that throng surrounding her, she was lifted on high. And when I had seen this, behold, coming to meet her from the heavenly heights was a man glorious beyond estimate, carrying in his right hand the sign of the cross on which there was a banner, whom I knew to be the Lord Savior, and infinite thousands of angels accompanied him. Eagerly greeting her they carried her to the pinnacle of heaven with great harmonious song. When I had observed this, after a while my Lady approached me through the door of light in which I usually saw her, and standing there, she revealed to me her glory. In that same hour an angel of the Lord attended me, who came to tell me the tenth discourse of the aforementioned book, and I asked him, "Sir, what does this great vision I have seen mean?" He answered, "Through this vision, you were shown how Our Lady was assumed into heaven in body as well as spirit." Later, on the eighth day [after the feast] I asked the angel (who had also come to me to state the conclusion for the book) how many days after her death did her physical resurrection occur. Again, he kindly assured me, saying, "Since she passed from this life on the day on which her Assumption is now celebrated [August 15], she rose from the dead forty days after that on September 23. The holy fathers, who ordered the church to celebrate the feast of the Assumption, were uncertain about her physical assumption, so they set the feast on the day of her death which they called her Assumption even though they really did believe that she had also been bodily assumed." Afterwards, when I hesitated to make this revelation known in writing, fearing I would be considered the inventor of novelties, when two years had passed and it was again the feast of her Assumption, my Lady appeared to me. I asked her: "Lady, may we not make public the news you revealed to me about your resurrection?" But she said, "This is not to be made known to the people, for the world is wicked, and those who would hear it are ensnared in it and do not know how to untangle themselves." Again I said: "Do you wish us to erase completely what we have written about this revelation?" She answered: "These things were not revealed to you for you to erase them and consign them to oblivion, but for my glory to be multiplied among those of you who especially love me. Let them be revealed by you to those in my service; they will be open to those who open their heart to me. Through this let them show me special praise and they will receive a special reward from me. For there are many people who will hear this news with great rejoicing and veneration." Because of these words, we celebrated that feast in our community on the day mentioned above the best way we could, offering devout praises to our venerable Lady. And as the mystery of the divine office was being celebrated, she appeared to me as was her custom, and I asked her: "My Lady, how long did you live on earth after the Lord's Ascension? Were you assumed into heaven in the same year as his Ascension? She responded gently to my words, saying, "After the Lord's Ascension, I remained on earth in this mortal life for a full year and as many days as there are between the feast of the Ascension and the day my Assumption is celebrated." I asked further, "Did the Lord's apostles carry you to your sepulcher?" She answered, "All of them carried my body with great reverence and committed it to the earth."

Chapter 32. It was while we were celebrating the feast of the Lord's Annunciation [March 25] when my Lady again showed me her glorious face that I was bold enough to ask her how old she was when, at the angel's news, she conceived the Word of God in her virgin womb. She deigned to give me this answer to my question: "I had lived fifteen years," she said, "from the time of my birth to the feast of the Lord's Annunciation."

What image of Mary does Elisabeth construct here? What would be its appeal? Why would it carry authority?

22. THE *STABAT MATER* (LATE 1200s?)

Just as, by the early thirteenth century, popular piety accentuated the suffering of Jesus, it also highlighted his mother's grief for her son's torment. By the late fourteenth century this image of Mary as Our Lady of Pity – the Pietà – had a sure hold on popular devotions, serving as a poignant counterpoint to earlier images of the Mother and Child. Allied to the Pietà was the growth in the fifteenth century of devotions to the Seven Sorrows of the Virgin (namely, Simeon's prophecy, the flight into Egypt, losing the boy Jesus in the Temple, the meeting on the road to Calvary, standing at the foot of the cross, the descent from the cross, and Jesus' burial). One of the most famous medieval hymns commemorating the Mater dolorosa, or Sorrowful Mother, was the Stabat mater, which meant to stir the listener to compassion by tenderly sketching Mary sunk in sorrow at the foot of her son's cross. Its author was probably the Franciscan Jacopone da Todi (d. 1306), a former lawyer who wrote many other devotional hymns, though some ascribe it to Pope Innocent III. The hymn, originally a sequence sung before the Gospel during Lent and Passion week, grew popular among lay people by the fourteenth century. Witnesses record that during the Black Death, some penitent bands sang it while they walked in procession (see Doc. 69). It endured long past the Middle Ages, and many later composers set it to music, including Pergolesi, Haydn, Schubert, Rossini, Dvořák, and Verdi. Edward Caswall's nineteenth-century translation, famous in its own right as a well-known Catholic hymn, captures both the meter and the pathos of the medieval Latin.

Source: trans. Edward Caswall, *Hymns and Poems, Original and Translated* (London: Burns, Oates, & Co., 1873), pp. 76-77. Latin.

At the cross her station keeping
Stood the mournful mother weeping,
Close to Jesus to the last.
Through her heart, his sorrow sharing,
All his bitter anguish bearing,
Now at length the sword has passed.

Oh, how sad and sore distressed
Was that mother highly blest
Of the sole-begotten one.
Christ above in torment hangs;
She beneath beholds the pangs
Of her dying glorious son.

Is there one who would not weep,
Whelm'd in miseries so deep
Christ's dear mother to behold?
Can the human heart refrain
From partaking in her pain,
In that mother's pain untold?

Bruised, derided, cursed, defiled,
She beholds her tender child
All with bloody scourges rent;
For the sins of his own nation,
Saw him hang in desolation,
Till his spirit forth he sent.

O thou mother, fount of love,
Touch my spirit from above,
Make my heart with thine accord.
Make me feel as thou hast felt;
Make my soul to glow and melt
With the love of Christ my Lord.

Holy mother, pierce me through;
In my heart each wound renew
Of my Savior crucified.
Let me share with thee his pain,
Who for all my sins was slain,
Who for me in torments died.

Let me mingle tears with thee,
Mourning him who mourned for me,
All the days that I may live.
By the cross with thee to stay;
There with thee to weep and pray,
Is all I ask of thee to give.

Virgin of all virgins best,
Listen to my fond request:
Let me share thy grief divine;
Let me, to my latest breath,
In my body bear the death
Of that dying son of thine.

Wounded with his every wound,
Steep my soul till it has swooned
In his very blood away;
Be to me, O Virgin, nigh,
Lest in flames I burn and die,
In his awful Judgment Day.

Christ, when thou shall call me hence,
Be thy mother my defense,
Be thy cross my victory;
While my body here decays,
May my soul thy goodness praise,
Safe in paradise with thee.

23. THE *CANTIGAS DE SANTA MARIA* OF ALFONSO X (c. 1250-80)

The Cantigas de Santa Maria *or* Songs of Holy Mary *was a lavishly illuminated collection of more than 400 songs in praise of Mary (written in Galician-Portuguese) compiled at the command of the king of Castile and Leon, Alfonso X "the Wise" (1221-84), a great patron of law, science, and the arts; in fact, he may have composed some of the songs himself. In the collection, assembled around 1250 to 1280, miracles of the Virgin drawn both from local history and legends and from miracle stories in circulation across Europe were interspersed with songs honoring Mary composed in the spirit of troubadour poetry celebrating the lady of courtly love. The following translations abandon the rhyme and meter of the* cantigas, *which were meant to be sung, often to the accompaniment of the many musical instruments illustrated in the manuscript.*

Source: trans. J. Shinners from Walter Mettmann, (ed.), *Alfonso X, O Sabio, Cantigas de Santa Maria*, Acta Universitatis Conimbrigensis (Coimbro: 1959, 1961), v. I, pp. 7, 100; v. II, p. 159; cantiga 228 trans. John E. Keller, in *Mediaeval Age: Specimens of European Poetry from the Ninth to the Fifteenth Century*, ed. Angel Flores (New York: Dell, 1963), pp. 278-79. Galician-Portuguese.

7. This is how Holy Mary delivered a pregnant abbess who fell asleep weeping before her altar.

We should offer great love to Holy Mary, and pray that she covers us with her grace so that the devil does not shamelessly lead us into error and sin.

That is why I will tell you about a miracle I heard that the Mother of the Great King did for an abbess who was completely devoted to her, as I learned. But the devil had led her into sin, for she got pregnant by a man from Bologna who was careful to hide his deed and her distress.

We should offer great love to Holy Mary, etc.

The nuns, learning what she had done, were quite happy, for she never let them do anything wrong, and they bore her malice. They complained to the bishop of the diocese who came to the abbey from Cologne. When he summoned her, she went without hesitating, happy and smiling.

We should offer great love to Holy Mary, etc.

The bishop said this to her: "Lady, from what I understand, you have behaved badly, and I have come here in order for you to make amends before me." But without a pause the lady went and prayed to the Mother of God, and, as if in a dream, Holy Mary took the child from her and had it brought up in Soissons.

We should offer great love to Holy Mary, etc.

When the lady woke up and found herself delivered, she quickly went to the bishop, who looked at her carefully and made her disrobe. After he had seen her body, he began praising God and rebuking the nuns (who were of the order of Onna), saying: "God save me, she is in God's grace. I do not know what to accuse her of."

We should offer great love to Holy Mary, etc.

100. Song

Holy Mary, Morning star,
Show us the way to God,
And guide us.
For you make clear the errors of those
Who would all be lost through their sins,
And you make them realize their fault.
But through you they are pardoned

For the reckless things
Their folly makes them do
That they should not have done.
Holy Mary, Morning star, etc.
Show us the way by which
We may most surely gain
That light, true and unequaled,
That you alone can offer us
Which God offered you
And willingly offers through you.
Holy Mary, Morning star, etc.
By your light you can guide us,
Better than any other thing, to paradise,
Where God always keeps joy and laughter
For those who believe in him.
And my joy will be unmatched
If it pleases you for my soul
To be welcomed into such company.
Holy Mary, Morning star, etc.

159. How Holy Mary revealed a steak stolen from some pilgrims on the
way to Rocamador.

Holy Mary does not allow those who go on pilgrimage to suffer losses.

This is a miracle, told to me, which I want to tell you about what Holy
Mary did for nine pilgrims who were going to Rocamador to pray simply
and humbly as good Christians.

Holy Mary does not allow, etc.
They entered the town, searched out an inn, and ordered some steaks and
bread and wine for dinner. Meanwhile, they went to the Virgin praying that
she ask her son to hear their pious prayers ...

Holy Mary does not allow, etc.
... and intercede in their favor and to ask forgiveness for their sins. When
they had finished praying, they quickly went back to the inn where they
waited for dinner impatiently.

Holy Mary does not allow, etc.
They had ordered nine steaks to be put in the pot, God save me, since there

were so many of them. But when they came to be served, they discovered one steak was missing, stolen by a serving girl; thus all of them were now greatly complaining.

Holy Mary does not allow, etc.
They searched the whole inn to try to find it, asking Holy Mary to show them what they sought. Just then they heard the missing steak inside a trunk and rushed over to it.

Holy Mary does not allow, etc.
They quickly opened the trunk and found the steak hopping around inside it. They rushed out into the street to call people to witness this miracle, which was one of the most marvelous ...

Holy Mary does not allow, etc.
... that the glorious Virgin had done there. Then they took the steak and hung it by a silken string before her holy altar, praising Holy Mary who works noteworthy miracles.

Holy Mary does not allow, etc.

228. How a farmer owned a mule that was paralyzed in both legs, and how he ordered it skinned by a servant, and how, while the servant was eating, the mule got up and went to church.

So great is the mercy and kindness of the Virgin that she even demonstrates her piety to dumb beasts.
The Holy Virgin Mary wrought in Terena a miracle for a man whose mule had its hindquarters so paralyzed that it dragged them behind. This mule was cured because of its faith. Listen well to the story.

So great is the mercy, etc.
The infirmity attacked the mule with a pain in its legs; therefore, for a long time it had stayed in the stable being scarcely able to move.

So great is the mercy, etc.
When the owner saw it so, he was very sad, but in order to rid himself of the animal he ordered one of his servants to skin it. While the servant was eating his lunch, the mule was struggling to its feet in spite of its ailment.

So great is the mercy, etc.

It went past the house and toward the church, walking weakly and wearily; but she who is blessed, as soon as the mule had approached and had lain down close by, performed a wondrous miracle, for she immediately made it sound and free from sickness.

So great is the mercy, etc.

The servant whom the master ordered to skin the mule, when he did not see it, followed after the beast to the place which it had gone. He saw it at the church, but not as he had left it. At this he marveled and said to the people: "Look and see!"

So great is the mercy, etc.

"A strange marvel has been performed in this mule's behalf. Beforehand it was unsound in both hindquarters and now it is sound and walks and runs quickly as we now behold it! Come with me and see this!"

So great is the mercy, etc.

Straightaway all who were present went to see the mule and they had difficulty in recognizing it after they had examined it. The Virgin healed it out of charity.

So great is the mercy, etc.

And there where they watched, the mule went very quickly three times around the church of the Virgin, the Holy Queen; and the folk who then believed, saw how it entered the church showing great piety.

So great is the mercy, etc.

And before the high altar it bent its knees. Then it went to its owner's house where all were amazed. Many prayers were said to Saint Mary, the Holy One.

So great is the mercy, etc.

What image of Mary do the Cantigas *offer? What would be its appeal? What insights do the* Cantigas *yield into the religious concerns of ordinary Christians?*

24. A LITURGICAL DRAMA OF THE ANNUNCIATION (FOURTEENTH CENTURY)

The biblical episode of the angel Gabriel's news to Mary that she would bear the Son of God lent itself well to dramatic adaptation, and by the thirteenth century many churches across Europe were staging the scene during mass, at some places on the feast of the Annunciation (March 25), at others during Advent. Congregations witnessing this dramatic interlude would have been impressed since the stagecraft surrounding the representation could be elaborate: at Tournai, a replica of a dove representing the Holy Spirit descended from the roof; at Parma, Gabriel himself was lowered from a hole in the cathedral vault. The staging instructions below (with the script taken verbatim from Luke 1: 26-48) come from a fourteenth-century manuscript from the cathedral of Padua. The moment of Mary's conception by the Holy Spirit is cleverly represented by "Mary" concealing a dove under her costume.

Source: trans. J. Shinners from Karl Young, *The Drama of the Medieval Church* (Oxford: Clarendon Press, 1933), II, pp. 248-50. Latin.

On the day of the feast of the Annunciation, after dinner, let the great bell be rung at the usual time, and meanwhile let the clergy gather at the church; they should prepare themselves in the main sacristy, some of them wearing their copes and other required things. In this sacristy [the actors] Mary, Elizabeth, Joseph, and Joachim should stand ready with a deacon and a subdeacon holding silver books. At the appointed time they should leave the sacristy in procession and make their way to the place prepared for them. Leaving them there, the procession should continue to the baptistery where a boy should be waiting seated on a chair dressed as Gabriel. Let him be lifted up on the chair and carried from the baptistery into the church along the side aisle and taken up the steps next to the choir. The clergy should stand in the middle of the church arranged like a chorus. Meanwhile the subdeacon should begin the prophetic epistle: "The Lord spoke again to Achaz" [Isa. 7:10]. After the prophecy is finished, the deacon should start the Gospel: "The angel Gabriel was sent" [Luke 1:26 ff.] and proceed up to the words "And when the angel had come to her, he said." At that point, Gabriel, kneeling with two fingers of his right hand upraised, should begin singing this antiphon in a loud voice: "Hail, Mary, full of grace, the Lord is with thee; blessed art thou among women." When this antiphon is finished, the deacon should continue reciting the Gospel up to the words "And the angel said to her." Then the Angel, again standing with his right hand completely open, should begin this antiphon: "Do not be afraid, Mary, for thou has found grace with God. Behold, thou shalt conceive in thy womb and shalt bring forth a son."

When this antiphon is finished, the deacon should continue reciting up to the words "But Mary said to the angel." Then Mary should answer in a clear voice with this antiphon: "How shall this happen, angel of God, since I do not know man?" When this antiphon is finished, the deacon should continue reciting up to the words "And the angel answered and said to her;" and the Angel should again begin this verse: "Listen, Mary, virgin of Christ, the Holy Spirit shall come upon thee and the power of the Most High shall overshadow thee." But when he comes to the words "the Holy Spirit shall come upon thee," let him hold out a dove a little way from him. When this verse is finished, the deacon should continue reciting up to the words "But Mary said to the angel." When this is finished, Mary should stand up with her arms outstretched and begin saying in a loud voice, "Behold the handmaid of the Lord." Before the end of this antiphon, he should let go of the dove and Mary should take it and put it under her cloak. Antiphon: "Behold the handmaid of the Lord; be it done to me according to thy word."

When all this is ended, the deacon should continue on to the next verse, "Now in those days Mary arose and went with haste into the hill country" up to the words "And Elizabeth cried out with a loud voice, saying." Meanwhile, Mary should descend from her place and go over to where Elizabeth and Joachim are. Both of them should receive her according to the description in the Gospel. Having done this, Elizabeth should kneel, touch Mary's body with both hands, and begin this antiphon with a humble voice: "Blessed art thou among women and blessed is the fruit of thy womb!" When the antiphon is finished, Elizabeth should get up and, standing again, say this antiphon: "And how have I deserved that the mother of my Lord should come to me? For behold, the moment that the sound of thy greeting came to my ears, the babe in my womb leapt for joy. And blessed is she who has believed because the things promised her by the Lord shall be accomplished." When this is finished, the deacon should again continue up to "And Mary said." Then Mary should turn and face the people and in a loud voice sing at the eighth tone these three verses [i.e., the Magnificat]: "My soul magnifies the Lord, and my spirit rejoices in God my Savior; because he has regarded the lowliness of his handmaid; for, behold, henceforth all generations shall call me blessed." When this is finished, the organ should answer with one verse, and the choir with the next, and so on until the end. When this is all done, let everyone return to the sacristy.

What image of Mary would this dramatic interlude convey to an audience? What is the balance between instruction and entertainment in this scene?

25. JOHANNES HEROLT'S MIRACLES OF THE VIRGIN MARY (c. 1435-40)

Nothing better illustrates the cult of Mary in medieval popular religion than the hundreds of stories of the miracles she worked for her supplicants. Those collected by Johannes Herolt are typical. A Dominican from Basel, he wrote several popular books of sermons and sermon exempla, *perhaps none more popular than his* Pupil's Storehouse of Miracles of the Blessed Virgin Mary (Promptuarium Discipuli de Miraculis Beate Marie Virginis), *which he wrote "to strengthen in love for her the hearts of the faithful." Compiled around 1435-40, this collection of a hundred miracle stories is the culmination of medieval tales about Mary, drawing all its material from earlier authorities. Herolt's chief sources were from the mid- to late thirteenth century: Caesarius of Heisterbach's* Dialogue on Miracles *(see Doc. 15),* Vincent of Beauvais's Speculum maius *(The Great Mirror),* Jacob de Voragine's Golden Legend *(see Doc. 32), and Thomas de Cantimpré's* The Commonwealth of Bees *(Bonum universale de apibus). But he also took stories from other noted preachers and writers such as Gregory of Tours, Peter Damian, Guibert of Nogent, Jacques de Vitry, and Étienne de Bourbon. The selections from his book offered here represent a few of the venerable and more often-repeated stories about Mary. The first nine stories derive from an influential collection of Marian miracles gathered in the first decades of the twelfth century by Anselm, abbot of Bury St. Edmund's, the nephew of the famous theologian, Anselm of Canterbury. Most later collections of Marian miracles contained them. The opening tale of Theophilus' oath to the devil is one of the very oldest miracle stories associated with Mary, traceable to sixth-century Byzantine sources. It circulated in dozens of versions during the Middle Ages, finding its way into secular literature, drama, and art; in it is a glimmer of the Faust legend. Bracketed numbers below refer to the number of the story in Herolt's collection, which is rearranged here to reflect roughly the chronological order of the composition of the original stories.*

Source: trans. C.C. Swinton Bland from Johannes Herolt, *Miracles of the Blessed Virgin Mary* (London: Routledge, 1928), pp. 22-23, 31-32, 35, 43-47, 66-69, 76-78, 80-81, 86-89, 98-99, 110-13, 118-21; revised. Latin.

1. [Story 42]. There was a certain noble named Theophilus who became impoverished and was at a loss what to do. At last he thought of going to the crossroads and talking with the devil, to get him to aid in his worldly affairs. This he did, but when Theophilus beseeched the devil with prayers to restore his wealth to him, he asked Theophilus if he could and would do what he proposed. He replied that he would, and took the oath. Going there three nights in succession, on the first night he renounced his baptism, on the second his Creator, on the third even the Mother of Mercy.

But the devil considering his love for the last, said: "If you will confirm this oath in an indenture written in your blood, then all is complete." This was accordingly done, the indenture written in the blood of Theophilus being confirmed by the devil's seal.

It happened that one day Theophilus, stung with remorse, began to weep, and, as he wept, to prostrate himself before the image of the Blessed Virgin Mary, calling on the Blessed Virgin earnestly. But the Blessed Virgin was ever pitiful, and in her kindly pity for him she pardoned what he had done. And when Theophilus, prostrate before the altar, was weeping bitterly and praying to the image of the Blessed Virgin Mary, the image of God, as if in anger, would not listen to him and turned his face away.

Seeing this the Blessed Virgin placed her son's image on the altar and with Theophilus went to the devil. Thus was he brought back to the grace of God, and the devil ordered by her to return the indenture of renunciation which Theophilus had given to him, and thus Theophilus was converted and at last entered into the joys of heaven.

2. [Story 27.] A certain young knight in the flower of his youth and of unstained chastity was vassal to another knight, his lord, and lived with him.

Now, through the devil's malice he began to be hotly tempted with love of his lord's wife. And, after enduring this for a whole year, he put away his shame and revealed his passion to the lady. Rejected by her, he was afflicted more than ever, for the matron was chaste and faithful to her husband. The knight went, therefore, to a hermit and with tears confessed to him his passion.

The holy man assured him in reply: "I will give you counsel which will cure you. All this year and every day you shall salute the Blessed Virgin Mary with the angel's words [the Hail Mary] a hundred times, and whatever you wish, you will obtain through her." For he knew that she who loved chastity would not deny a chaste youth.

And while the young man with singleness of heart was paying worship to the Virgin Mary, as he had been taught, one day, while sitting at the table of his lord, he remembered that that was the last day of the year. Rising at once and mounting his horse, he entered a neighboring church and repeated his usual prayers.

And as he was leaving the church, he saw a very beautiful matron, whose beauty exceeded that of other women, pass in front of his horse and grasp the reins. As he wondered who she was, she said: "Does my beauty please you?" And when he said: "I have never seen one more beautiful," she answered: "I will be your wife. Come to me." And, kissing him, she said: "This is our betrothal. On a certain day in the presence of my son the nuptials shall be completed."

From that he knew she was the Mother of the Lord, whose purity delights in human chastity. From that hour he was fully delivered from temptation, so that even the wife of his lord wondered. When he had recounted these things to the hermit, the latter, praising the goodness of God, said: "May I be present on the day of those nuptials." And, when the day came that had been fixed in the presence of the hermit, the soldier in his death-agony breathed out his soul, and in his heavenly home entered upon the promised marriage.

3. [Story 5.] There was once a very great robber [called Eppo], a most wicked man, who thought of nothing but the service of the devil. Yet he had this good in him that he scrupulously fasted on bread and water during the vigil of the Blessed Mary; and when he went out to rob he used to salute her with such devotion as he could, asking her not to allow him to die in mortal sin.

But, being caught and brought to the gallows, he hung there for three days and could not die. And when he called to those passing by and asked them to bring a priest, one came with the judge and the people and he was taken down from the gallows. Then he said that it was the Blessed Virgin who kept him alive; and so he was set free, and afterwards he finished his life in praiseworthy fashion.

4. [Story 93.] There was a certain half-witted priest who knew no mass but that of the Blessed Lady Mary. Celebrating this mass every day and being accused of so doing, he was forbidden by the bishop to celebrate any mass in the future.

Being in trouble and need, he called upon the Blessed Virgin and she appeared to him saying: "Go to the bishop and tell him from me to restore your office to you." The priest replied: "Our Lady, I am a poor man and a person of no account. He will not listen to me, nor shall I be allowed to approach him." Then the Blessed Virgin added: "Go, and I will prepare the way for you." He said: "O Lady Virgin Mary, he will not believe me." And she replied: "You shall say to him, as a sign, that at such an hour and in such a place, while he was mending his hair shirt, I held it on one side to help him, and he will at once believe you."

In the morning entering without hindrance the priest came to the bishop carrying the message of the Blessed Mother of God. When he said: "How am I to believe that you are sent by her," he added that sign referring to the hair shirt. Hearing this, the prelate in amazement and alarm replied: "Behold I allow you again to celebrate and repeat the mass for Our Lady the Blessed Virgin and that alone; and pray for me."

5. [Story 40.] A certain abbot was caught in the midst of the British seas with others in a very great storm sent by God, so that all despaired of their lives. And so some were calling upon the Blessed Nicholas, some on the Blessed Andrew or any other saint, for everyone in his need invoked his own patron saint in familiar terms.

But when the abbot saw them calling on all these less powerful saints, but no one naming the Mother of Mercy, who has power over heaven and earth and sea, he said: "What are you doing, my brothers? Why do you call on those other saints, who have less power, and omit one who has more power than all of them? Indeed you do well, but you would do much better if with one voice you all acclaimed the Mother of Mercy."

Being thus counseled, all with one voice invoked the Mother of God, and all cried out to her to have pity on them. The abbot himself, who had had nothing to eat except one apple, and who for two days and two nights was in such sore distress that he could hardly draw breath, began with his monks to chant most earnestly the responsory, "Blessed, etc.," with its verse *Ora pro populo.*

Scarcely had the people and the monks sorrowfully finished the prayer with much devotion, when, behold, at the top of the mast a great light appeared like a candle, chasing away the darkness of night and flooding all the boat with its brightness. And the storm ceased entirely on the sea, and at the command of the Queen of heaven there was a calm. And not long after there dawned a fine day and the ship came to the land to which it was sailing.

6. [Story 51.] There was certain man of the world engaged in rural work and occupied with worldly cares. He, being ensnared in many wicked acts, also when plowing his land stole as much as he could from his neighbors, and by crossing their landmarks with his plowshare secretly joined the land of others to his own. He kept the holy Mother of God in mind, however, and often saluted her with devotion.

And so, when he died, the devils gathered together, assured of carrying off his soul. Two angels came there to put forward the good deeds done by him. The devils on the contrary began to bring up his countless evil deeds. And when in joy at this they thought they were victorious, one of the angels added that he was accustomed with much devotion to salute Mary, the holy Mother of God. Hearing this, the foul spirits relinquished the man's soul and fled from it in confusion.

And so that soul, being rescued from the power of its adversaries by the grace of God, escaped everlasting damnation through the merits of his Mother. Blessed be she with him for evermore.

7. [Story 84.] There is another church of the Mother dedicated to St. Michael on the Mount [Mont-Saint-Michel], which is called Tumba. Now it happened one time that that church was set on fire by the judgment of God through lightning that fell on it from heaven. Moreover, in it was an image of the Blessed Virgin made of wood having a head-covering like a miter.

When, therefore, the fire reached the place where the image was, it consumed everything in a circle round it. But the image itself was left altogether untouched, as though the fire was afraid of it, so that even the white covering it wore on its head could by no means be darkened by the vapor of the smoke. Actually a single feather from the wings of a peacock escaped, that was caught in the image, a very sufficient proof of the miracle, that she protected its image from fire, showing that she can easily deliver her servants from everlasting fire.

8. [Story 18.] In Bourges once when the Christians were communicating at Easter, among the Christian boys a Jew went up to the altar and received the Body of the Lord with them. Returning to his parents and being asked where he had been he replied that he had gone with his friends to the church and had taken communion with them.

Then his father, being exceedingly angry, threw the boy into the fire, from which however, the Blessed Virgin Mary saved him unhurt. But the mother of the boy by her cries collected many Christians and Jews together, who, seeing the boy alive in the fire, asked him, after he had been taken out, how it was he felt no pain. And he replied that she who was above the altar of the Christians had appeared to him and driven off all the flames with her cloak. Then understanding that it was the image of the Blessed Mary, they threw the father of the boy into the fire and he being at once consumed, many became more fervent in the faith.

9. [Story 70.] There was a certain clerk who did nothing good, but rather was full of vices. This was the only good in him: that he regularly and devoutly said the Hours of the Virgin Mary.

But when one day he was crossing a river intending to gratify his desires, because he had not offered his morning praises, he began to say: "Hail Mary, full of grace," and then fell into deep water, and after that uttered no more salutations, but when he came to the words: "The Lord is with thee," he was drowned and seized by demons. But in spite of them he was defended by the Blessed Virgin and through her merits brought before Christ for trial, where after much disputing the Virgin asserted: "My son, you have said 'Where I find you, there will I judge you. You shall also be justified by your words.' Therefore, my son, although this man has lived a bad life, in the end he passed away praising me, in which he was ever diligent in his life. I beg that he might find favor in your sight. If the demons will not believe me that this is so, let them look into his mouth." The demons, doing so, found printed in golden letters "Hail Mary, full of grace" and thereupon in confusion they departed. The Judge commanded the soul to return to the body and to change its life for the better, which it did.

10. [Story 14.] A certain woman of simple and upright life used to worship the holy Mary, Mother of God, often strewing flowers and herbs before her image.

Now it chanced that the woman's only son was taken prisoner. And the mother weeping for him would not be comforted, and prayed with all her heart to the Blessed Virgin Mary for her son's deliverance. But seeing it was all in vain, she entered the church and thus addressed the image of the Blessed Virgin: "O Blessed Virgin Mary, I have often asked you for deliverance of my son and you have not heard me. Therefore, as my son was taken from me, so will I take away yours and will put him in duress as a hostage for mine."

And taking the image of the Child from the bosom of Mary, she went home, wrapped him up in a clean cloth, and shut him up carefully in a chest. And, behold, the following night the Blessed Mary appeared to the captive youth bidding him to go forth and said to him: "Tell your mother to give me my son." And he coming to his mother, described how he had been set free. But she with great rejoicing carried back the image of Jesus to Mary and gave her thanks. [*From The Golden Legend.*]

11. [Story 25.] In a certain convent of nuns many years ago there lived a nun named Beatrice under the vow of chastity. Beautiful, devout in soul, and a zealous servant of the Mother of God, she counted it her greatest joy to offer up her prayers to her in private and, when she was made custodian, her devotion increased with her greater freedom. A certain cleric, seeing her and desiring her, began to use enticements. When she scorned his wanton talk, he became so much the more eager, and the old serpent hotly tempted her, so that her heart could no longer endure the fires of passion, but going to the altar of the Blessed Virgin Mary, who was the patron saint there, she said: "Lady, I have served you as faithfully as I could; but now I resign to you your keys. I can no longer withstand the temptations of the flesh." Placing the keys on the altar she went in secret after the cleric, and he, after dishonoring her, within a few days deserted her. And she having no means of living and being ashamed to return to the cloister, became a harlot.

Having lived publicly for many years in this wickedness, one day she came in her secular dress to the gate of the convent, and said to the gatekeeper: "Do you know one Beatrice, formerly the custodian of this convent?" And he replied: "Yes, she is a very worthy lady, holy and without reproach from her childhood, who has lived in this convent to this day."

She, hearing these words but not weighing their meaning, was about to go away when the Mother of Mercy appeared to her in the form of a woman and said: "For fifteen years I have filled your office in your absence. Return now to your home and do penance, for no one knows of your departure." The Mother of God had actually in her shape and dress taken her place as guardian. At once she returned, and as long as she lived she gave thanks to the Virgin Mary, and in confession made known to her confessor all that had happened to her. [*From Caesarius of Heisterbach.*]

12. [Story 83.] A certain painter painted the devil with horns and other members as ugly as he could and still more dreadful. But the image of the Blessed Virgin Mary he painted as comely and as beautiful as he could in different colors.

Now the devil being enraged at this and envious, went in haste to the painter and asked him why he painted him so dreadfully ugly and the Virgin so comely and beautiful. He replied that the reality was as shown in the painted picture. But the devil in his rage one day was going to hurl the painter from the height, where he painted the image of the Blessed Virgin Mary, and he broke up the wooden scaffold on which the painter stood, who began to fall, but at once the image of the gracious Virgin stretched forth its hand to the painter and firmly held him from falling and so protected him from the demon. [*From Vincent of Beauvais.*]

13. [Story 82.] There is a certain township near the city of Orleans which is called Avignon, where the citizens have built a church in honor of the Blessed Virgin Mary. Once when they were besieged by the enemy and were distressed within the town, putting their trust rather in the aid of Mary the Mother of God than in their own strength, they went to the church with their little children and the women, and, standing devoutly before the image of the holy Virgin Mary, with cries from heart and lips implored her help and when they had finished their tearful prayers, they returned to carry her image away and set it up in the gate to protect them and terrify their enemies.

Now, one of the citizens, standing guard at the gate and from behind the image shooting arrows against the foe, caused much slaughter among the enemy. He being espied in his hiding-place by one of them, the enemy said wickedly: "You shall not escape death, nor shall the image be able to help you any longer, unless you desert the gate and make haste to throw open the city." And when this enemy hurled his javelin against the archer citizen, wonderful to say, the image raised its knee and putting it in the way of the javelin stopped it and thus protected the man devoted to her from the enemy's attack. Rejoicing at his wonderful delivery by the Virgin, he at once aimed an arrow at his foe and struck down the blasphemer.

The rumor of the miracle spread through the people and even reached the enemy. By the acclamations of all it was asserted that the holy Mother of God was fighting for the citizens of the place. Hearing this, the enemy consented to a peace. They visited the church of Our Lady, offering rich gifts and declared before witnesses that in future they would do no harm to that place, and to this day that image protects them, and it remains in the same place, still carrying the javelin on its raised knee. [*From Vincent of Beauvais.*]

14. [Story 62.] There was a certain priest of a parish who had power in the world and repute, but was given up both to vice and to the getting of riches. This man had in his cure a rich nobleman and a poor widow.

One time, as they were going to rest, they both received the summons of death. The priest was called to visit the dying rich man, and, having heard his confession, he gave him the sacrament to commend the departing soul to God. But he was too anxious to get the fleece to trouble about the sheep. When he received the rich man's message, he hastened to go, entered his palace, passed into his bedchamber. The rich man was lying clad in purple silk and covered with jewels, reclining on soft down cushions. There also he found a crowd standing round offering comfort to the rich man in wheedling flatteries. His wife and sons and all his family were mourning for their lord.

Meantime there came someone on behalf of the widow, who said that she, being on the point of death, asked for the sacrament of a Christian's salvation. The priest, entirely occupied in cajoling the sinner, made no reply. But the deacon, standing by and speaking earnestly, said, on behalf of the lonely woman: "It will be a great crime for us and perilous for the woman if it should so happen that by our negligence she passes away without partaking of confession and the sacred mystery."

And the priest's anger being roused, he replied: "What a madman's idea to leave a noble patron for a humble widow!"

"Be not vexed," said the deacon. "If you bid me, I will visit the sick woman." The priest approving of this, the deacon quickly departed. And, taking the life-giving host, he came to the hovel of the widow, who, poor in all worldly possessions yet full of good works, lay prostrate on the hard ground, her emaciated limbs covered with a little straw.

And so the deacon, approaching the house of the poor woman with the sacrament of the eucharist, stood at the door, and lifting up his eyes saw guardian angels from heaven standing by the servant of Christ, as she lay. For Mary the Mother of Jesus stood there with her band of virgins, and brought a linen cloth and was busy wiping the sweat from the face of the sick woman in close attendance.

Amazed at seeing this, the deacon stood afar off, but the Queen of heaven looked kindly on him in his wonder, and, seeing the body of God and her son, she prostrated herself on the ground with her virgins and adored the host. And when they stood up, the man of God took confidence and entered. Then Mary putting a seat for him and bidding him not to be afraid, he sat down. Next he received the widow's confession, gave her the sacrament, and with psalms fortified her against death.

After that he hastened with joy to the house of the rich man. And, standing on the threshold, he saw black cats running around the bed of the rich man, who, seeing them and knowing them to be bitter enemies, bellowed loudly: "Take the cats away, take them away; help a miserable man!" Finally, a black man threatened him, and with a dreadful look plunged a hook, which he was carrying in his hand, into his throat. The unhappy soul, finding in his conduct no comfort for his conscience, was in fear and trembling, and death little by little seized upon the poor wretch. Then the black man in a rage drew out his hook from his quivering throat, and uttering a dreadful cry, the sick man gave up his unhappy soul. Rushing on the sinning soul, the rest of those confederates in malice wounded it with their scourges and plunged it into the place of gloom and the lake of eternal death.

Seeing this, the deacon was seized with trembling, and falling down lost his senses; but soon the Mother of the King of glory appearing to him, said: "Fear not, beloved one, the malice of the devil shall not hurt you, for whom is prepared the happiness of heaven." Restored by these gentle words, after he had recovered he rendered thanks to his comforter, and from that vision profited not a little. [*From Thomas de Cantimpré.*]

15. [Story 55.] Three brothers were totally dispossessed by a knight, lord of a castle, and hence lurking in a neighboring forest, did much damage to travelers. Consequently the knight seized and hanged two of them. The third, exasperated by this and yet extremely afraid that if he should be taken, no one would spare him, opened his heart to a certain monk. The monk told him to give up robbing, but he replied that he could not stop until he had first struck down the knight with arrow or sword to avenge his brothers.

"Yet," he said, "I have resolved to keep the four fasts of the Blessed Mary – namely, the Purification, the Annunciation, the Assumption, and the Nativity – with bread and water, so that the Blessed Virgin may not allow me to die without confession and the viaticum [the eucharist]." To this the monk replied: "It is good, but little or no advantage to you since you are not giving up your intention of sinning."

Departing, soon after he was seized by that knight and his squires, and in their rage his body was cut to pieces, and when, although he was entirely dismembered, he could not lose his speech, he said: "In vain do you exert yourselves, for you cannot kill me until I have first confessed and communicated." They went for a priest, who at once came, and, after he had confessed and received the viaticum, forthwith he expired. [*From Étienne de Bourbon.*]

16. [Story 90.] A woman who was in peril of childbirth for seven days and turning black had been given up by everyone; she made a vow to Blessed Francis [of Assisi] and with her dying breath began to implore his aid.

Now uttering this prayer she fell asleep, and in her sleep she saw the Blessed Francis addressing her kindly words and asking whether she knew his face and if she knew how to recite the *Salve Regina* in honor of the glorious Virgin. When she replied that she had knowledge of both, St. Francis began that antiphon of the glorious Virgin that is the *Salve Regina*. And as she uttered in prayer the words "the fruit which the Virgin brought forth," at once she was delivered from all her pains, and she brought forth a fine child and she offered thanksgiving to the Queen of heaven who through the merits of the Blessed Francis deigned to pity her.

17. [Story 50.] There was a certain monk who was religious in name only, but, wherever true religion was concerned, hard-hearted and careless. He was, however, in the habit of praying to the Blessed Virgin and saying once every day a hundred Hail Marys. Coming near his end, he was carried away in an ecstasy, and devils charged him before the Great Judge seeking a sentence that would rule him to be theirs. God, therefore, knowing his many sins, said that he must be condemned.

Meantime the Blessed Virgin came offering schedules in which were contained all the Hail Marys, and begging her son to allow him to receive a milder sentence. But the devils brought many books full of his sins. The books on both sides were put into the scales, but the sins weighed most. Then the Blessed Virgin, seeing she was doing no good, earnestly pleaded with her son, saying: "Remember, beloved, that you received from my substance visible, sensible, and tangible substance; give to me one drop of your blood shed for sinners in your passion." And he replied: "It is impossible to deny you anything. Yet know that one drop of my blood weighs heavier than all the sins of the whole world. Receive therefore your request." Receiving it, she placed it in the scales, and all the sins of the monk weighed against it as light as ashes.

Then the devils departed in confusion, crying out and saying: "The Lady is too merciful to Christians; we fail as often as she comes to contend with us." And so the man's spirit returned to his body, and on recovery he related the whole tale and became a true monk.

What various roles does Mary play in these stories? Do the stories encourage people to equate her in power to God? To what degree are these stories theologically sophisticated and to what degree are they fixated on miracle-working? What lessons do they teach? How might these various images of Mary color people's opinion of ordinary women? Compare these stories to the miracles of Mary that Guibert of Nogent recounts in Doc. 28.

26. THE *OBSECRO TE* (FOURTEENTH CENTURY)

This prayer, summing up many of Mary's most admired attributes, was often inserted into Books of Hours, prayer books containing psalms and other prayers usually meant for literate laity.

Source: trans. Roger S. Wieck from *Time Sanctified, The Book of Hours in Medieval Art and Life* (New York: George Braziller, 1988), pp. 163-64. Latin.

I beseech you, Mary, holy lady, mother of God, most full of piety, daughter of the greatest king, most glorious mother, mother of orphans, consolation of the desolate, the way for those who stray, salvation for those who hope in you, virgin before giving birth, virgin while giving birth, virgin after giving birth, fountain of pity, fountain of salvation and grace, fountain of piety and joy, fountain of consolation and kindness, through that holy, unutterable joy with which your spirit rejoiced in that hour when the Son of God was announced to you by the archangel Gabriel and was conceived, and through that divine mystery that was then worked by the Holy Spirit; and through that holy unutterable piety, grace, mercy, love, and humility through which your son descended to accept human flesh in your most venerable womb and which he saw in you when he commended you to St. John the Apostle and Evangelist and when he exalted you over the angels and archangels; and through that holy inestimable humility in which you responded to the archangel Gabriel, "Behold the handmaiden of the Lord, be it done unto me according to thy word"; and through those most holy fifteen joys that you had in your son, our Lord Jesus Christ; and through that holy, great compassion and that most bitter sorrow in your heart that you had when you saw your

Fig. 3.2. The Virgin and Child

Two nineteenth-century etchings by Guillaumde and Mouard (after Viollet-le-Duc's drawings) of statues from Amiens cathedral show the evolving naturalism in images of Mary and her child, a development that increasingly humanized them. The stately statue on the left (from the west portal) was carved around 1225; the famous Vierge dorée on the right (from the south portal) was created around 1260. Reproduced in M. Viollet-le-Duc's *Dictionnaire raisonné de l'architecture française du XI^ au XVI^ siècle* (Paris: A. Morel, 1868), v. 9, pp. 369, 370.

son, our Lord Jesus Christ, nude and lifted up on the cross, hanging cruci-fied, wounded, thirsty but served gall and vinegar, and you heard him cry "Eli" and you saw him dying; and through the five wounds of your son and through the collapse of his flesh because of the great pain of his wounds; and through the sorrow that you had when you saw him wounded; and through the fountains of his blood and through all his suffering; and through all the sorrow of your heart and through the fountains of your tears; with all the saints and elect of God. Come and hasten to my aid and counsel, in all my prayers and requests, in all my difficulties and needs, and in all those things that I will do, that I will say, that I will think, in every day, night, hour, and moment of my life. And secure for me, your servant, from your esteemed son the fullness of all mercy and consolation, all counsel and aid, all help, all blessings and sanctification, all salvation, peace, and prosperity, all joy and gladness, and an abundance of everything good for the spirit and the body, and the grace of the Holy Spirit so that he might set all things in good order for me, guard my soul, rule and protect my body, lift up my mind, direct my course, preserve my senses, control my ways, approve my actions, fulfill my wishes and desires, instill holy thoughts, forgive the evils I have done in the past, correct those of the present, and temper those of the future, grant me an honest and honorable life, and grant me victory over all the adversities of this world, and true peace for my spirit and body, good hope, charity, and faith, chastity, humility, and patience, rule and protect my five bodily senses, make me fulfill the seven works of mercy, make me firmly believe in and hold to the twelve articles of faith and the Ten Commandments of the law, and from the seven deadly sins keep me free and defend me until my end. And at the end of my life show me your face, and reveal to me the day and hour of my death. Please hear and receive this humble prayer and grant me eternal life. Listen and hear me, Mary sweetest virgin, Mother of God and of mercy. Amen.

27. AN APPARITION OF THE VIRGIN MARY IN CASTILE (1399)

While Mary frequently appeared physically in the hundreds of miracle stories told about her, apparitions of Mary resembling those claimed at modern sites like Lourdes, Fatima, or Medjugorje only surface in the late Middle Ages. The single manuscript recording this vision of 1399 dates from about 1471 and seems to have been meant for display at the shrine established on the site, since at the bottom of the manuscript there is the text of an indulgence for visitors coming to the shrine. Another indulgence issued by Pope Benedict XIII in 1404 confirmed that pilgrims were visiting the site of the apparition and that many miracles were said to have happened there. The Benedictine monastery that the Virgin requested was founded at Santa Gadea del Cid in Burgos about a decade after the vision took place (after a few years of legal wrangling with another neighboring Benedictine house). But the long gap between the vision and the document first describing it raises the question of whether the account's details are genuine or the fruit of a pious imagination hoping to invest the shrine with special credibility. As historian William A. Christian notes, some features of the story match elements of the Passion story perhaps too conveniently: Pedro and Juan could represent the apostles Peter and John, the vision occurs during Holy Week, and Pedro, like Peter, initially denies the Virgin's request. The "infidels" accused of massacring Christians here were, of course, Spain's early Muslim conquerors who had not posed a threat to the area for 300 years. This apparition can be compared to Doc. 11.

Source: trans. William A. Christian, Jr., *Apparitions in Late Medieval and Renaissance Spain* (Princeton, NJ: Princeton University Press, 1981), pp. 27-32. Spanish.

This is a copy of testimony taken in the town of Santa Gadea as written on parchment and signed by a notary public.

In Santa Gadea, Sunday, April 20, in the year of the birth of our saviour Jesus Christ 1399. This day in the church of Saint Peter of the town of Santa Gadea in the presence of Ruy Martínes and Juan Pérez de Río, parish priests of the church; the other clergy and cabildo [chapter]; the alcalde [mayor] Diego García de Arbolancha; the procurador; the governors; the council of the town gathered by ringing the bell; in my presence, Juan Martínes of Santa Gadea, scrivener and notary public for our lord the King; and the witnesses whose names are written at the end of this testimony; there appeared a youth from this town named Pedro, the son of Yñigo García de Arbe, a citizen of this town.

He said that on the day of Saint Mary of March of this present year [March 25] he was watching his father's sheep with Juan, the son of Juan de Enzinas, in the jurisdiction of this town near a church called Sant Millán. In an oak tree in the cemetery of the church they found a hive of bees, and through an opening in the trunk they saw much honey and wax. They agreed that on Wednesday of Holy Week, once their flock was stabled in town and their parents had gone to the matins ceremony, they would come to gather the honey and wax from the tree.

When the day came they set out to do it. When they went to the oak and began to take out the honey and wax, they saw many people with white garments gathered around a very big hawthorn tree, holding three lights that lit up everyone quite clearly. And they saw a lady on top of the hawthorn tree who shone brighter than the sun, so they could not look at her without being blinded. And then they heard a voice from the people there calling out, "Come to matins"; and at this call there appeared from the direction of Santa María de Guinicio a great number of people as if in a procession in white garments; and most of them wore red garments with white stripes on top, and many other colors. They carried in their hands branches like palms and two torches that lit up the entire procession as if it were daytime. This procession came to join the people around the lady; and the brightness went up as far as the sky; and around her were three torches like big candles, so powerful they lit up all of the landscape; and it seemed that they went up as far as the sky. And they heard singing, like priests chanting the hours, and frightened by the voices they stopped gathering their honey and fled toward town. When they reached the flat place that is halfway, they looked back and saw all the lights join in one; and the singing went up to the heavens, so much that they did not dare go back.

The following Thursday [March 27] Pedro was keeping the sheep of his father, Yñigo García de Arbe, near the same spot in the village territory. Suddenly there appeared to him a lady so resplendent that he could not look at her directly, but only in parts. She told him he should tell of his vision to the parish priests, clergy, and council of Santa Gadea. And that people everywhere should know that she whom he had seen on the hawthorn tree was the Virgin Mary glorified in person; and the people he had seen around her were the angels of heaven, that very pure company. And that they should know that her coming was willed by her precious son, the redeemer of the human race. And that "at the time of the destruction of Spain there had been a town at that place called Montañana la Yerma and a church in my name in which, and in whose cemetery, refugees from said town of Montañana la Yerma were forced to take shelter from a great onslaught of infidels. In the church and cemetery they were surrounded and taken by force of arms; and because they would not convert to their religion, they were all martyred by beheading, and the entire church and cemetery and its surroundings were bathed in the blood of the glorious martyrs.

"And since the memory of this mystery was dying, at the constant and assiduous urging of the martyrs and virgins who perished there long ago and at their supplication, my glorious son, redeemer of the human race, had to give in to their prayers. It was his will that I come glorified in person with the angels to celebrate the office of matins of Holy Week and that those glorious souls be present with me to visit the bodies that on a day like this one they had left behind.

"Just as God the Father came to Moses in the briarbush, which was not consumed by fire for the good of his people, so I was sent in the hawthorn for the good of the souls and bodies of the faithful of the human race. You will find that the hawthorn is not burned or damaged in any way; it will serve as medicine for the diseases that people have here. The voice you heard calling to matins was that of the Angel Saint Michael. Just as he was present in that place to receive the souls of the glorious martyrs and take them to glory at the time of their martyrdom, so his was the voice that called them into being to celebrate that solemn office, and our Lord saw fit that they should respond quickly in the form of a very glorious procession, as you saw. One of the two torches they carried signified the crown of holy martyrdom, and the other the virginity of the many virgin girls who had perished there. The other three torches you saw around me signified the three persons of the Father, the Son, and the Holy Spirit. The voices you heard were the sweet voices of the angels who performed the office. And when at the end of the ceremony the torches were consumed in one it signified the unity with which we all went up to glory, each to his established seat and place.

"I order you to explain that this place is holy and occupied by the many relics of the bodies that perished here by martyrdom. I also order you to say that it is the will of my glorious son that a monastery and church of the order of Saint Benedict be built to revive the memory of this secret. You must say that all the people who come or send their help or alms to build the church and monastery and support the monks who will live in it will have remission of their sins. Their souls will be in the company of the said martyrs, and their bodies and property will be helped and protected whenever they commend themselves with great devotion to me. In memory of my apparition in this hawthorn tree [whoever] carries a depiction of my apparition on his person will be freed from the power of the devil, and the devil will be powerless to harm him when he sees my emblem. Also, if carried with great devotion, it will ward off pestilence and all disease. I also order you to tell the parish priests, clergy, alcalde, procurador, and governors of the town of Santa Gadea gathered in council that, if they want their town and its people to prosper and their souls to grow in grace, they should immediately clean out the weeds and brush in and around the church where you had the apparition. Let them know that just as the harshness and wildness of the place has led to anger and thefts, so it will become a place of refreshment for the body and health for the soul. If they want to have their just desires met, they should begin to build the church and the monastery. As long as they do so, and they put their devotion into practice, things will improve for them and for all the towns and people wherever they are from.

"I order you to keep on declaring this publicly to the parish priests, clergy, alcaldes, and governors of the council of the town of Santa Gadea and to all the districts and regions for the remainder of the short time you have to live. You must take as your name Pedro de Bueno Ventura [Peter of Good

Fortune], for truly you deserve it. And you must tell your companion Juan that he should soon take up the arms of the knights of the blessed virgin Saint Catherine, for he will die in them. His end will come nine days after he arrives at the grave of Saint Catherine from Jerusalem. I order you to make this known at once. Do not delay out of timidity, or else in my presence you will be punished as you will see." And with this she disappeared.

Out of timidity and fear he would not be believed, Pedro did not mention the apparition to anybody. The following Sunday night [March 30, Easter Sunday] at the hour of the second cock crow, when Pedro was in bed near that of his father, the Virgin Mary came to it in the form that he had seen her the previous Thursday, and she brought with her two torches and two men dressed as monks. One of them took him by the arm and pulled him out of bed, and the other took his belt and struck him many blows and wounds. Neighbors heard his loud cries and got up, especially the alcalde Diego García de Arbolancha and his household. With others of the neighborhood they called out loudly at the doors of Yñigo García's house. No one answered them, and because of Pedro's cries, they knocked down the doors of Yñigo García's house. When they went up the stairs, they saw the house was as bright as at noonday, but the brightness ended when they got to the top. With the candles that the women carried they found Pedro lying in shock (*muy fatigado*) with many whip marks on the floor of the room.

At this point Yñigo García, his wife, and the other people in the house were roused. [Yñigo] angrily demanded what they wanted in his house at such an hour and in such a way. Diego García de Arbolancha replied that they had come to help the youth because he had been treated with great cruelty. The father replied that nothing of the kind had ever taken place in his house. Then Pedro spoke up and said that neither his father nor anyone else in the house was responsible and asked them, and in particular Diego García de Arbolancha in his capacity as alcalde, to order the parish priests and clergy and governors and council to gather in the church, and that he himself be carried there so he could declare what had happened. When the sun came up the mayor did this, and after the entire town had gathered Pedro was brought in. They all saw the welts and injuries, and he himself told them all that has been told above.

I the scrivener bear witness that I have seen the marks and wounds on Pedro and heard from his own mouth all the testimony given.

How does this vision compare with the other miraculous stories about Mary in this chapter? Does the social status of the various people in the story affect how the story is told? Assuming Pedro didn't really see such a vision, what would be his motives for creating this story? What do its details reveal about his religious life?

CHAPTER FOUR: SAINTS, RELICS,
AND PILGRIMAGE

The origin and evolution of the Christian cult of saints and its role in medieval religious life are, to say the least, intricate subjects. Yet whatever else they were, in simplest terms saints were intercessors between the earthly and heavenly realms. Their holy lives won them the reward of heaven where they could plead on behalf of their fellow humans before God. Their earthly remains — both bodies and material possessions — became the conduits through which God worked miracles out of regard for the merits of his saints. By virtue of this wonder-working, saints' shrines were potent places of intersection between this world and the next. Christian pilgrims flocked there seeking favors from their powerful patrons before God. Saints' legends were always on the lips of preachers and other storytellers, with double-edged results. For church leaders the saints were exemplars of Christian living whose lives could inspire ordinary people to follow them. For typical Christians, saints may have been role models, but they were more. Believing in sympathetic magic, where like affects like, most people used what they knew of saints' legends (which were sometimes adapted tales of Greco-Roman deities and even when authentic were usually highly embellished legends) to assign them specialized areas of miraculous expertise. For example, St. Elmo, who was disemboweled, was invoked against intestinal cramps; St. Margaret, who, when swallowed by a demonic dragon, grew until she burst from its stomach, was the patroness of women in childbirth; and St. Lawrence, roasted alive on a gridiron, was the patron saint of cooks. Through their legends and miracle-working, the scores of Christian saints served for medieval believers as a sort of popular pantheon of demigods who could be called upon to help weather most of life's troubles.

28. THE TRAVELING RELICS OF LAON
CATHEDRAL (1112)

This excerpt from the extraordinary memoirs of abbot Guibert of Nogent (c. 1055-c. 1125) illustrates the great regard people held for relics. In late April 1112 during Easter, the commune of Laon rebelled against the oppression of its bishop, killed him, and burned down the cathedral church and the episcopal palace. Guibert's story of the cathedral's efforts to raise money for rebuilding by sending its relics on tour – a pious medicine show of sorts – offers a memorable instance of how the veneration of saints could build a bridge between spiritual and earthly commerce. But it is hardly unique: exceptional relics always reaped exceptional favors and income in the Middle Ages, and there are many cases of churches sending their relics around the region both to kindle piety and raise funds.

Source: John F. Benton (ed.) and C.C. Swinton Bland (trans.) in *Self and Society in Medieval France, The Memoirs of Abbot Guibert of Nogent* (New York: Harper & Row, 1970), pp. 191-97. Latin.

Book III, Chapter 12.... Meanwhile, following the customary way, such as it is, of raising money, [the monks] began to carry around the feretories and relics of the saints. And so it came to pass that the gracious Judge, who comforts with his pity in heaven those whom he reproves below, showed many miracles where they went. Now they were carrying, along with some box of undistinguished memory, a splendid little reliquary which contained parts of the robe of the Virgin Mother and of the sponge lifted to the lips of the Savior [see John 19:29] and of his Cross. Whether it contained some of the hair of Our Lady, I do not know. It was made of gold and gems, and verses written on it in gold told of the wonders within.

On their second trip, coming to the district of Tours, they reached the town of Buzançais, which is held by a certain robber. There they preached to the people, among other things, about the disaster to their church. When our clergy saw that the lord and his garrison were listening to them with evil in their hearts and were planning to plunder them as they left the castle, the man who had the responsibility of speaking was placed in a difficult position. Although he did not believe his promises, he said to the people standing there, "If there is an infirm soul among you, let him come to these holy relics, and, drinking the water which the relics have touched, he will assuredly by healed."

Then the lord and the men of his castle were glad, thinking they must be caught for liars out of their own mouths, and they brought forward to him a

Fig. 4.1. A procession of relics

A nineteenth-century copy of a thirteenth-century drawing (c. 1250) by Matthew Paris depicting a procession of the relics of England's legendary proto-martyr St. Alban shortly after King Offa discovered them in the early eighth century. Led by a cleric sprinkling the way with holy water as other clerics hold a processional cross and candles, the feretory is shouldered by four tonsured monks and followed by two others singing from a small hymnal. King Offa looks on. Two lame men – one carrying a small tripod to scoot along the ground – strain to touch the reliquary hoping for a miraculous cure. Reproduced in Charles Knight's *Old England: A Pictorial Museum of Regal, Ecclesiastical, Baronial, Municipal, and Popular Antiquities* (London: Charles Knight & Co., 1845), v. 1, p. 357 after British Library MS. Nero D i, fol. 22r.

servant about twenty years old, who was deaf and dumb. At that the danger and dismay of the clergy cannot be described. After they had prayed with deep sighs to the Lady of all and her only son, the Lord Jesus, the servant drank the holy water and the trembling priest asked him some question or other. He immediately replied, not with an answer to the question but with a repetition of the exact words which the priest had used. Since he had never before heard what was said to him, he was ignorant of any words but those just used. Why prolong the story? In that poor town their hearts suddenly became larger than their means. The lord of the town immediately gave the only horse he had, while the liberality of the rest went almost beyond their powers. And so the men who had planned to be their attackers became their advocates, with many tears praising God as their helper, and they freed the youth who had been cured so that he could stay with the holy relics forever. I saw this man in our church of Nogent, a person of dull intellect, awkward in speech and understanding, who faithfully carried round the tale of such a miracle and died not long afterward in the discharge of that duty.

In the city of Angers, there was a woman who had married as a little girl, and had worn the ring placed on her finger at that early age day and night, as she said, without ever taking it off. As years went by and the girl grew larger in body, the flesh rising up on each side of the ring had almost covered the metal, and consequently she had given up all hope of getting it off her finger. When the holy relics came there and she went with other women after the sermon to make her offering, as she held out her hand to place the money she had brought on the relics, the ring cracked and slipped from her hand before them. When the people, and especially the women, saw that the Virgin Mother had granted the woman such a favor, something she had not dared to ask for, the offerings of money by the people and of rings and necklaces by the women were beyond description. Touraine took much joy from the showering of the sweet odor of the merits of Our Lady, who is common to all, but the people of Anjou boasted that in a special sense they had the Mother of God at hand.

At another place – I cannot exactly say in what town it happened, but in the same diocese – at her own urgent prayer the relics were taken by the clergy to a certain honorable lady, who had long been in the grasp of a lasting and hopeless infirmity. And when she had adored the relics with all her heart and had drunk the holy water prepared from them, at once by Mary's healing she was restored to health. After she had done honor with due offerings to God's sacred relics and their bearer had left the threshold of her house, suddenly a boy came up on a horse, drawing a wagon which filled the middle of the narrow lane through which he had to pass. The cleric said to him, "Halt, until the holy relics pass by." And when the bearer had passed and the boy began to urge his horse forward, he was unable to continue his journey. The man who bore the relics then looked back that way and said, "Go on, in the name of the Lord." Once that was said, the horse and cart moved on. See what power you do grant in Mary and what respect she demands for herself!

In the third journey, they came to the castle of Nesle. Now Raoul, the lord of the castle, had in his house a deaf-and-dumb youth who supposedly knew the art of divination, learned no doubt from devils, and whom he was therefore said to love greatly. The relics were brought into the castle and honored by the people with quite small gifts. The deaf-and-dumb man, who had been informed by signs of the curing of the other deaf-mute and who now actually saw him, gave his shoes to a poor man and, barefooted and with a penitent heart, followed the relics to the monastery of Lihons. As he lay during the day under the reliquary, it happened to be the hour for dinner; most of the clergy went to their meal and only a few remained to guard the relics. These men went for a short walk outside the church, and when they returned, they found the man stretched on the ground in great distress, with blood flowing from his mouth and ears with a great stench. When they saw this, the clerics called their companions who had gone to dinner to run to the scene of such a wonder. As the man came out of his fit, the clerics tried to ask him somehow or other if he could speak. Immediately he replied in the same words as he had heard his questioner use. They offered praise without limit and indescribable jubilation to God on high. At last by all sorts of prayers they were compelled to return to the town of Nesle, so that the poor first offering to the relics might be amply increased. And that was done to a wonderful degree. Here, too, Our Lady glorified herself, when her Divine Son made whole the gifts of nature which up to then he had held back.

Chapter 13. From here they sought lands overseas. When they had traveled to the Channel, they found certain wealthy merchants with ships for that voyage and were carried across calmly, as far as the winds were concerned. But suddenly they saw the galleys of pirates, whom they greatly feared, coming on directly against them. Steering toward them with oars sweeping the waters and their prows cutting through the waves, they were soon scarcely a furlong off. As the carriers of the relics were terribly afraid of those marine soldiers, one of our priests arose from their midst and lifted on high the reliquary in which the relics of the Queen of heaven were kept, forbidding their approach in the name of the Son and of the Mother. At that command the pirate craft immediately fell astern, driven off as speedily as they had with eagerness approached. Then there was thanksgiving among the delivered and much glorification, and the merchants with them offered many gifts in thanks to the gracious Mary.

They had a fair voyage then to England, and when they came to Winchester, many miracles done there brought renown. At Exeter similar events occurred and produced many gifts. Let me pass over the ordinary healing of sickness and touch only on exceptional cases. We are not writing their travel book – let them do that themselves – or what happened to each person, but are picking out examples useful for sermons. In almost all places, they were received with reverence, as was fitting, but when they came to a certain hamlet they were not admitted by the priest within the church, or by the peasants within their dwellings. They found two buildings without inhabitants and in one they bestowed themselves and their baggage and fitted up the other for the holy relics. Since that wicked crowd persisted in their obstinacy against the holy things, the next morning after the clergy left that place, suddenly, with a crash of thunder, a terrible bolt of lightning struck from the clouds and in its descent blasted their town, burning all the dwellings to ashes. But what a marvelous distinction God made! Although those two houses were in the midst of those that were burned, they remained as a manifest testimony by God that those unhappy men had suffered their fire because of the irreverence they had shown toward the Mother of God. The wicked priest, who had inflamed the cruelty of the barbarians instead of teaching them, gathered up the goods he was able to save from the heaven-sent fire and carried them away, either to the river or the sea, intending to cross over. But there all the property he had gathered together to take across was destroyed on the spot by lightning. Thus these country people, uninstructed in the understanding of the mysteries of God, were taught by their own punishment.

They came to another town in which the great fervor of offerings to the sacred relics corresponded to their reputation and the evidence of the miracles. A certain Englishman standing in front of the church said to his companion, "Let's go drink." But the other said, "I don't have the money." Said the first, "I will get some." "Where will you get it?" said he. "I am thinking about those clerics," said the first, "who by their lying and their tricks get so much money out of the silly people. I will certainly manage in some way or other to get out of them the expense of my entertainment." After saying this, he entered the church and went to the platform on which the relics were placed, and, pretending that he wished to show his reverence for them by kissing them, he put his mouth against them with his lips open and sucked up some coins that had been offered. Then he went back to his companion and said, "Come on, let's drink, for we have enough money now for our drinking bout." "Where did you get it" said he, "when you had none before?" "I got it," he said, "by carrying away in my cheek some of the money given to those cheats in the church." "You have done something bad," said the other, "since you took it from the saints." "Be quiet," replied he, "and get along to the nearest tavern." Why am I running on? They almost drank the sun down into the ocean. When evening came on, the man who had stolen the money from the holy altar mounted his horse and said he was going home. And when he had reached a nearby wood, he made a noose and hanged himself on a tree. Dying a miserable death, he paid the penalty for his sacrilegious lips. Out of the many things which the queenly Virgin did in England, it should be enough to have culled these instances.

After they had returned to Laon from collecting money, I have been told by a cleric of good character, who was given the job of carting wood for the repair of the roof of the church, that in ascending the mountain of Laon one of the oxen broke down from exhaustion. The cleric was exasperated, because he could not find another ox to put in its place, when suddenly an ox ran up to offer itself to him, coming as if it intended to help in the work. When he and the others had speedily drawn their carts right up to the church, the cleric was very anxious to know to whom he should return the strange ox. But as soon as the ox was unyoked, it did not wait for an oxherd or driver, but returned quickly to the place from which it came....

How broad a spectrum does Guibert's idea of what constitutes a miracle cover? Is his belief in miracles uncritical? What kinds of reactions do people have to the monks and their traveling relics? What do these adventures reveal about Guibert's beliefs?

29. ACCOMMODATING PILGRIMS AT THE CHURCH OF ST.-DENIS (c. 1144-47)

Prominent relics could attract throngs of worshipers. If a shrine became popular enough, churches frequently had to adapt their architecture for crowd control, usually by building ambulatory aisles around the sanctuary with radiating chapels housing the relics. The most famous account of this kind of redesign comes from Abbot Suger (c. 1081-1151), whose renovations to his abbey church of St.-Denis marked an early step in Gothic architecture. His description (c. 1144-47) vividly evokes the crush of devout pilgrims shoving their way to the heart of a shrine.

Source: trans. Erwin Panofsky (ed.), *Abbot Suger on the Abbey Church of St.-Denis and Its Art Treasures* (2nd ed., Gerda Panofsky-Suerel; Princeton, NJ: Princeton University Press, 1946, 1979), pp. 87-89. Latin.

When the glorious and famous King of the Franks, Dagobert [d. 639], notable for his royal magnanimity in the administration of his kingdom and yet no less devoted to the church of God, had fled to the village of Catulliacum [St.-Denis] in order to evade the intolerable wrath of his father Clothaire the Great, and when he had learned that the venerable images of the holy martyrs who rested there – appearing to him as very beautiful men clad in snow-white garments – requested his service and unhesitatingly promised him their aid with words and deeds, he decreed with admirable affection that a basilica of the saints be built with regal magnificence. When he had constructed this [basilica] with a marvelous variety of marble columns he enriched it incalculably with treasures of purest gold and silver and hung on its walls, columns, and arches tapestries woven of gold and richly adorned with a variety of pearls, so that it might seem to excel the ornaments of all other churches and, blooming with incomparable luster and adorned with every terrestrial beauty, might shine with inestimable splendor. Only one thing was wanting in him: that he did not allow for the size that was necessary. Not that anything was lacking in his devotion or good will; but perhaps there existed thus far, at that time of the early church, no [church] either greater or [even] equal in size; or perhaps [he thought that] a smallish one – reflecting the splendor of gleaming gold and gems to the admiring eyes more keenly and delightfully because they were nearer – would glow with greater radiance than if it were built larger.

Through a fortunate circumstance attending this singular smallness – the number of the faithful growing and frequently gathering to seek the intercession of the saints – the aforesaid basilica had come to suffer grave inconveniences. Often on feast days, completely filled, it disgorged through all its doors the excess of the crowds as they moved in opposite directions, and the outward pressure of the foremost ones not only prevented those attempting to enter from entering but also expelled those who had already entered. At times you could see, a marvel to behold, that the crowded multitude offered so much resistance to those who strove to flock in to worship and kiss the holy relics, the Nail and Crown of the Lord, that no one among the countless thousands of people because of their very density could move a foot; that no one, because of their very congestion, could [do] anything but stand like a marble statue, stay benumbed or, as a last resort, scream. The distress of the women, however, was so great and so intolerable that you could see with horror how they, squeezed in by the mass of strong men as in a winepress, exhibited bloodless faces as in imagined death; how they cried out horribly as though in labor; how several of them, miserably trodden underfoot [but then] lifted by the pious assistance of men above the heads of the crowd, marched forward as though upon a pavement; and how many others, gasping with their last breath, panted in the cloisters of the brethren to the despair of everyone. Moreover the brethren who were showing the tokens of the Passion of our Lord to the visitors had to yield to their anger and rioting and many a time, having no place to turn, escaped with the relics through the windows. When I was instructed by the brethren as a schoolboy I used to hear of this; in my youth I deplored it from without; in my mature years I zealously strove to have it corrected. But when it pleased him who separated me from my mother's womb, and called me by his grace, to place insignificant me, although my merits were against it, at the head of the so important administration of this sacred church; then, impelled to a correction of the aforesaid inconvenience only by the ineffable mercy of Almighty God and by the aid of the holy martyrs our patron saints, we resolved to hasten, with all our soul and all the affection of our mind, to the enlargement of the aforesaid place – we who would never have presumed to set our hand to it, nor even to think of it, had not so great, so necessary, so useful and honorable an occasion demanded it.

30. THE MIRACLES OF ST. THOMAS BECKET
(1170s)

At the shrines of renowned saints, clerics customarily kept a written record of the miracles that the resident relics produced either there or elsewhere through the saint's intervention. These accounts both corroborated and advertised the saint's prodigies. Naturally, they are gold mines of information for historians wishing to track medieval people's perceptions of the miraculous, their attitudes toward the saints, and the religious interests, social status, medical maladies, and geographical origins of pilgrims, among other things. The largest collection of miracles connected to one saint is that compiled at the shrine of the archbishop of Canterbury, Thomas Becket (c. 1118-70), murdered by four knights of King Henry II on December 29, 1170. He was formally canonized in 1173, but a cult sprang up around him just hours after his death, and by that spring his shrine was attracting crowds of pilgrims. Especially in the first decade after his martyrdom, miracles seemed to pour from his relics. Two monks sat near his shrine keeping track of them: Benedict of Canterbury recorded 265 miracles from early 1171 until the late 1170s; his colleague William of Canterbury wrote down another 438 (with some overlap with Benedict) between 1172 and 1179. Below is a sample of the miracles from Benedict's eyewitness accounts. The first group comes from around Easter (on March 28) of 1171, just three months after Thomas's death; the second group of longer stories probably dates from around 1173.

Source: miracles of 1171 trans. J. Shinners from James C. Robertson, *Materials for the History of Thomas Becket, Archbishop of Canterbury*, Rolls Series no. 67 (London: Longman & Co., 1876), v. II, pp. 61-69, 74; miracles of 1173 trans. Edwin A. Abbott, *St. Thomas of Canterbury, His Life and Miracles* (London: Adam & Charles Black, 1898), v. II, pp. 80-102, 113-15, 146-60, 162-69, 190-95, revised with additional trans. J. Shinners. Latin.

[Miracles of 1171]

Book II, Chapter 7. Edilda, a woman from Canterbury, was left at the shrine, carried with the help of three women. It had now been about a year and half since she could stand on her foot. During that whole time she had lived as if on the brink of death, confined to bed. The disease was especially severe in her left knee, which through the contraction of the muscles prevented her from walking. Her knee reeled with pain if the woman happened to touch it even lightly with her hand. She was carried to the martyr by three women, as we said, and propped on a staff; she returned home with her pain relieved. In witness of her recovered health, before us all with her upraised fist she struck her knee a hard blow, which since the second year of her illness she could not touch because of the pain. The people saw her walking about and praising the Lord; they were filled with wonder and amazed over what had happened to her. But we refrain from discussing why she remained lame and did not regain complete health, considering it more prudent to keep totally silent about God's secret judgments than to draw rash conclusions from them.

Chapter 8. But we know that he who strengthened that woman's weak knee was capable of making her feet and soles completely firm so that she could have walked normally, just as we have no doubt that he did grant this to Wlviva, a woman from Canterbury. Satan had bound her for three years already, and she was bent over, unable to walk anywhere without a crutch. She fell down before the saint for a short prayer and, with the pain gone from her loins, she rose standing straight up without her crutch, wanting no longer to carry the thing that had once supported her.

Chapter 9. Edmund, a young man born in Canterbury and well known there, brought himself to the shrine guided by one eye alone: he had only the appearance of a left eye for it had no power of vision. On his left side he also had something growing inside that seemed congealed and very heavy, which, shifting up and down, had tormented him for nearly two years causing him unbelievable stabs of pain and amazing torture. It was pushing him toward death, which was apparent just by his pale and withered look. A drop of [Becket's] most holy blood was put in his eye, and he drank an infusion of the blood and water. Miraculous power of that drink! Going a good distance away from the tomb, he threw himself down on his face; he turned himself on his side and began thrashing around and screaming; he kept getting up but could not stand because of his weakened gait. He sunk down on his face, dashing it against the stone, and it seemed as if he had come there only to his harm. Whom divine power was healing you would have thought insane. Finally he collapsed into sleep. He lay on his back sleeping. The saint of God stood next to him while he slept and, grabbing him by the shoulder, shook him and said, "Get up, go on." He instantly awoke and felt that the shifting thing that had been twisting inside him was being forced up to the bottom of his throat. Nearly choking, he threw his hand to his throat, wanting to feel what it was. Then instantly, as if some small inner sack had burst, by some divine power it was expelled from his mouth. It seemed to him to have the taste of bitter gall. Immediately he got up, threw down his cloak, and proceeded to the martyr's tomb to give thanks. Having received a complete cure of his eye and his body, through love of the martyr he took the cross [i.e., vowed] that he would go to Jerusalem, and all the people who saw it praised God.

Chapter 10. We realize that what happened to a woman named Muriel deserved no less praise or glory. Debilitated by a grave illness for two years or more, she thought that only the remedy of death would put an end to her suffering. When her husband realized the things that God's martyr was gloriously doing, he offered his sick wife a drink of that health-giving drink [Becket's blood mixed with water]. She drank it, and by degrees over the course of three days began to suffer more than usual from weakness. By the third day she had weakened to the point of death, so much so that she was taken out of her bed lest, contrary to the custom of the Christian religion, she die lying on a comfortable feather bed. A priest was summoned with the greatest haste to administer extreme unction to her. But she suddenly was nauseous and vomited up what was making her sick; for that whole day at regular intervals she did not stop vomiting. It was discovered that she was spitting up an enormous number of cherry stones, plum pits, and acorns – cooled in the woman's stomach, some of them had even sprouted! Some of these were shown to us, which left us awestruck both that the woman had carried the pits of these fruits in her stomach for such a long time and that the pits could germinate there. There can be no doubt that they would have hastened her death if the draft of that holy liquid had not come to her aid. Thus the woman was cured, snatched, as it were, from the very jaws of death. And though, as we said, she was so incapacitated that she had been unable to set foot out of her house for more than two years, the next day, through the strength bestowed on her by God, she went on foot to the martyr. And all the people rejoiced together at the things he had gloriously done.

Chapter 11. The Lord added another miracle to this one, though for a less serious illness. (Why do I say less serious? The sickness someone endures never seems small.) We knew a certain lady named Ethelburga, full of good works and charity, who had suffered for many days from a serious gout in her left arm and shoulder. Deprived of the use of her left arm, she arranged to have a candle made to the measure of the arm's length in honor of the martyr. You should have seen how the martyr responded to the woman through the action of grace, because the Lord promised to those turning to him, "Before you can call me, I will say to you, 'Look, here I am'" [see Is. 58:9]. For she had scarcely begun to measure her arm with a thread than she announced that she felt all the pain receding. And so she had the candle made, offered it to the martyr, and regained full health.

Chapter 12. Robert, a blacksmith from the Isle of Thanet, also found the grace of healing, but the vision that preceded the gift of his cure is no less wonderful. He had been blind for at least two years; the loss of his livelihood troubled him more than his lost sight. But then, after our venerable father had been called home from exile, around the time when he was called to heaven from the exile of this world [Dec. 29], this man heard this oracle in a dream: "Go, Robert, to Christ Church Canterbury; a monk will put milk in your eyes and you will recover your sight." But at first he thought he was deluded; he neither believed the promise nor obeyed the command. Yet later, when he heard that God's saint practically glittered with miracles, he recalled what he had heard and, equating this sweetest lamb's innocent blood to milk's sweetness, he began to hope for a cure. With the guidance of his wife and daughter (for we understand they accompanied him), he arrived where he had been ordered to go. After daubing his eyes with the longed-for blood of the martyr, he prostrated himself in prayer. While facedown, he felt his head racked by what seemed like a loud thunderclap and he regained his sight. Getting up, he publicly preached God's grace.

Chapter 13. But what is easier: to restore health to the body or the mind? He who restored sight to physical eyes restored sanity to the young man, Henry of Fordwich. He had been insane for some days and had accidentally wounded his friends due to his pain. With his hands bound behind him, he was dragged to the saint. He was presented to the saint even though he was struggling and shouting. He remained there insane for the whole day, but as the light of the sun waned, he started gradually to recover the light of reason. He spent the night in the church and went back home in the morning completely recovered.

Chapter 14. We received a woman from the vicinity of the same town who not only could not hear but was also troubled by an unbearable pain in the head. That universal medicine of the sick – water mixed with the blood – was poured into her stopped ears; she was also given some to drink, and then she threw herself into prayer. While she prayed she suffered more bitterly than before and she thought [she heard] many twigs being snapped in pieces inside her head. She asked those standing around whether they heard the noise in her head. But while she was being racked this way, she cried out to the Lord and he heard her. For as she shouted, a great deal of matter flowed out of her ears, as if some inner abscess had ruptured. The matter was followed by blood, and the blood by the gift of her lost hearing.

Chapter 15. Eilward, a man from Tenham, for some years had lost the pleasures of the sense of smell and could smell absolutely nothing. He entered that place where rests that good odor of the anointed one, that sweet victim, that scented tree, whose aroma the whole world now senses; but before he had reached that fragrant flower of England, there came to him the sweetest perfume filling his nostrils, and he rejoiced to recover his smelling.

Chapter 16. We think that it should not be forgotten that, while many people obtained a longed-for healing, one person was denied outright. For the holy father [Becket] came to a crippled boy who had gone seeking a favor from the martyr and had fallen asleep with his head resting on top of the tomb. "Why are you lying on me?" he asked. "You certainly will not be healed. Go away. I'll do nothing for you." These words woke him up and he told us and his mother what he had heard with great sadness of heart. Convinced by the adamancy of the [saint's] words, he had himself taken elsewhere. Still, we urged him to press on with his prayers, and he agreed; but time passed and he did not regain his health....

Chapter 18. With regard to these other cures, it first occurs to us to speak about what Agnes, a Canterbury woman, gained from the Water of St. Thomas — for this is what the people of the surrounding region called it: "St. Thomas's Water," or "Canterbury Water." Thus, an uncontrollable pain seized this woman's face, and a horrible tumor disfigured it; her mouth, twisted on one side, betrayed the shape of nature corrupted. An excess of phlegm constantly and copiously flowing from her mouth caused her much embarrassment without any relief from the pain or the tumor. At last the inner part of her face became infected, with the result that it was necessary for the woman to have milk instead of solid food. Since she was unable to eat food, she sustained herself with little sips of liquid. But for the last three days she had stopped drinking even these since she was so squeezed by pain. You would not have endured the stink that issued from her putrefying face. Into her fifth week of pain, the woman was thirsty and drank some of the saint's water. O miraculous water, which quenched not only the thirst but the pain of its drinker! O miraculous water, which quenched not only the pain but shrunk the tumor! I am about to tell you something astonishing. A basin used to be put to the woman's mouth to catch the phlegm. Lying prone with her mouth open, the woman was being coaxed to take care of the phlegm running out of her mouth. But when she lay back down after a swallow of water, from her mouth appeared the rather large head of a worm shaped like a red-hot coal, one and half inches long with a tail like a very sharp awl and crawling on four feet. By its speed it showed such tenacity that some said it had come from the Enemy. It was drowned in the bowl of phlegm, so it was thought, but when [the bowl was] put up to an upper window, it was not visible. Thus the patient's pain ceased and in a brief time her swollen face returned to its normal state....

Chapter 24. What are we to say about Saxeva of Dover? Did not her joy wane as her pain waxed? From Christmas to Easter she continually experienced what the opposite of health is through a cramp in her bowels and a pain in her arm. A mental pain afflicted her as much as her physical suffering, for she was unable to work but ashamed to beg. Her spirit grew weary of life. She fled to the martyr, prayed to him, and slept. The martyr revealed his presence to the sleeper. "Rise," he said, "offer your candle." Leaping up, she discovered herself cured. She obeyed his order and showed herself so healthy and agile that she said with exaggeration that she was strong enough to fly.

[Miracles of c. 1173]

Book III, Chapter 2. There was a man of the common folk, Eilward by name, in the king's town of Weston in the county of Bedford. One of his neighbors, Fulk, owed him two pennies of rent for a portion of plow-land; he had paid part but put off paying the rest until the following year with the excuse that he did not have the money. One day after the feast of the passion of the blessed martyr [Thomas] when they were both by chance going to the alehouse together (for it is the English custom to indulge in feasting and drinking on feast days, which makes them seem to be enemies and scorners of their holy days), Eilward asked for his money and Fulk swore that he did not owe him. Eilward asked him to pay half, as he was going to have some beer, and keep the other half for himself, likewise for beer. When Fulk completely denied that he was in debt to him, the other said that he would get even with him.

After both of them got drunk at the tavern, getting up on some pretext, Eilward left before Fulk and turned aside to Fulk's cottage, tore away the bar to the door, and broke into the house, turned burglar as much through rashness as through drunkenness. Going through the house looking for what he could take, he stumbled upon a large grindstone and some gloves which country people are wont to wear on their hands to protect them from the sharp points of thorns. The poor robber stole these, both of them together scarcely worth a penny. The boys playing together in the yard of the house cried out, and running to the tavern, called out to their father to come get his property back. Striking him, Fulk wrenched the grindstone from him and, brandishing it over the robber's head, he as much broke the grindstone with Eilward's head as he smashed his head with the grindstone. Baring a sharp-pointed knife he carried, he stabbed him in the arm. Overcoming him, he bound the miserable man and led him as a thief and robber back to the house he had broken into. He summoned Fulk the town beadle to find out what he should do with the prisoner. "The charge for which he has been seized," he said, "is not serious enough and insufficient. But if you make the robbery more serious by producing him loaded with other things that appear stolen, you can prosecute him to be punished for the crime." Fulk agreed and fastened around his prisoner's neck an awl, a two-edged axe, a net, and some clothes together with the grindstone and the gloves, and on the following day brought him thus before the king's officers.

Having been thus taken to Bedford, he was kept in prison there for a month. He sent for a priest, the reverend Paganus, so that, faced with the ultimate danger, he could prepare himself for death – or rather for life; and going over all the secrets of his conscience, whatever he found contrary to his salvation, he poured into the safely-sealed ears of the priest. Putting his trust in divine mercy for the deliverance of his body, he said, "Dearest sir, if I escape this moment of danger, I will go on foot to the land that the Son of God, our Lord Jesus made holy by his life on earth and death [i.e., the Holy Land]. And so I beg to have the sign of the cross branded on my right shoulder with a hot iron so that no one has the power to strip it from me even though my clothes are stripped away." The priest branded him accordingly, but also suggested that he should devoutly seek the protection of the saints, and especially of the glorious martyr St. Thomas whom the Lord magnified by such glorious signs. Moreover, he measured the length and breadth of his body with a thread with which to make a candle to be offered to the martyr for his release. He also gave him a scourge made of branches, say-ing, "Take these branches and five times a day before you take a little food, become your own torturer, and do not cease day and night to kneel to the martyr and call upon him except when, overcome by the annoyance of sleep, you are compelled to succumb to the weakness of human nature." Thus carefully instructing him, he left him, saying that the judges had forbidden any priest to have further access to him. However, he sent for him many times and he secretly announced himself at the window either to rouse him from negligence [in his prayer and devotions] or to further kindle his zeal. Also, Galfrid, the prior of the canons of Bedford (whose witness we have for this admirable miracle) often supplied him with needed food, visited him in prison, and – for him to have at least an hour of fresh air – took him from the jail and had him walk around under the open sky.

When four weeks had passed and the fifth begun, this poor man was led from jail and taken before the court for trial. His accuser charged him with the crime of theft; he consistently denied the charge, further objecting that he had taken none of the things hanging around his neck except for the grindstone and the gloves which he admitted taking, but only as a pledge for Fulk's debt, which had motivated the theft and the crime. The judgment was put off so he was again remanded into custody.

Brought out again in the fifth week and taken before the court, he was now charged by his accuser only with the theft of the grindstone and the gloves. For his accuser feared to undergo the trial by combat demanded by the accused, and his silence condemned all his previous charges; but – having the viscount and the judges on his side – he managed to free himself from the obligation to fight, and to arrange that the accused should be tried by the ordeal of water.

Now it was the Sabbath, and the examination was put off until the third day of the following week, he himself being kept again in prison. The cruelty of his keeper forbade him to keep vigil in the church – a right conceded by the compassion of religion to all who are to purge themselves by ordeal from criminal charge. In prison, however, he devoutly kept the watch that he was not allowed to keep in the church.

When brought out to the water [for the ordeal], he was met by the priest Paganus, mentioned earlier, who exhorted him to bear everything patiently in remission of his sins, to hold no hatred and anger in his heart, to forgive sincerely all his enemies for all they had done to him, and not to despair of God's mercy. And he replied, "May the will of God and of the martyr Thomas be done in me."

After being plunged into the water, he was found guilty. The beadle Fulk now seized him, saying, "Follow me, rascal, follow me!" "Thanks be to God," he replied, "and to the holy martyr Thomas." Dragged to the place of punishment, he was deprived of his eyes and his genitals were lopped off. As for his left eye, they at once extracted that whole; but his right eye, after being sliced and cut in pieces, was at last with difficulty gouged out. The members which they had chopped off him they hid under the sod; and – like what is read about the man who "fell in with robbers" – "after both stripping him and beating him" (as described above) "they went their way, leaving him half-dead" [Luke 10:30].

His accuser Fulk and the official of the same name (by whose suggestion and advice this man is believed to have been brought into this misery) and also two other executioners with them mutilated him. When, however, they asked [his] pardon for the love of God and St. Thomas the martyr, he willingly forgave them, crying aloud with a wonderful faith that he would go to the martyr's memorial, blind though he was, and he would not despair of the martyr's holiness and power, knowing that it was more glorious for the martyr to restore eyes that had been taken away than to preserve them when not taken.

He was escorted only by his twelve-year-old daughter, who had also begged food for him while he was incarcerated. For all his goods were confiscated, all his friends spurned him, and there was not one of all those dear to him to console him. Such a great amount of blood gushed from his wounds that, in fear of his death, those who were present sent for a priest to whom he confessed. By degrees, however, when the flow of blood was assuaged, led by the little girl, he returned to Bedford, where he threw himself down against the wall of a house; and all that day, until evening, no man showed him kindness. But at nightfall, one Eilbrict took compassion on him, especially since the weather was inclement and he was lying there vexed by a downpour of rain. He welcomed him rejoicing into his house.

He lay there in darkness for ten days, offering prayers and vigils. But at the first watch of the tenth night, after mourning, groaning, and sighing, as he relaxed in sleep he whom he had invoked appeared to him, clothed in snow-white garments. With his pastoral staff he painted the sign of the cross on his forehead and eyeless sockets and appeared to depart in silence. Waking up and disregarding the vision, he flung himself down again and went back to sleep. A second time before dawn he, who washed his garments in the blood of the Lamb, returned dressed in white. He said to the man, "Good man, are you sleeping?" When he acknowledged that he was awake, the man in white said, "Do not sleep, do not sleep, but watch and press on with your prayers. Do not despair but put your hope in God, the Blessed Virgin Mary, and St. Thomas who comes to visit you. If, tomorrow night, you keep watch with a waxen light before the Virgin's altar in the church of the Blessed Mary close by, and devote yourself in faith to praying, and have no doubts, you shall rejoice in the restoration of your eyes." Rousing from sleep, the man silently thought about what such a vision could mean – or rather whether once the hidden meaning was uncovered, the saint's promise would be fulfilled. Mulling over such a mysterious thing, taking it as news of a good omen, the maid-servant said, "Tonight, Eilward, I dreamed that you recovered sight in both your eyes." And he said, "So it may be when it shall please God and his blessed martyr Thomas."

When it was getting on toward evening, and daylight was declining, the eyelids of his left eye started itching. In order to scratch them, he removed a wax poultice which had been applied either to draw out the purulent matter in the empty orbs, or to close the eyelids themselves. Opening his eyelids, by the marvelous power of God it appeared to him as if a bright lantern were shining on the opposite wall of the house – it was the red sunlight, since the sun was by this time verging on setting. But he, ignorant of the truth and distrusting himself about the matter, called the master of the house and pointed out to him what he thought he saw. "You are mad, Eilward, you are mad," replied his host, "Be quiet. You don't know what you are saying." "I am not the least bit mad, sir," he said, "but I do seem to see what I say with my left eye." Shaken in his mind and anxious to ascertain the truth, his host spread out his hand before his eyes and said to him, "Do you see what I'm doing?" He answered, "I think your hand is waving before my eyes, moving back and forth." Then, starting with the beginning of the first vision, he told Eilbrict step by step what he had seen and what he had been ordered and promised.

Word about this spread among the neighborhood, and this novelty of novelties attracted not a small multitude of people. The deacon Osbern, lord – or rather, minister – of the church mentioned earlier comes running. When he hears about the vision from the man, he takes him to the church, brings him before the altar of the Blessed Virgin, and instructs and strengthens his faith. Putting a light in his hand, he declares that he distinctly sees the altar cloth, then the image of the Blessed Virgin Mary, and then any other objects of smaller size.

People's amazement grows over how this man was favored with sight. Thus, when the strength of the vision in his new eyes (or rather empty sockets without pupils) proceeds to be put to the test, they detect two small pupils concealed deeply in his head, scarcely equal in size to the pupils of a small bird, which, still constantly growing, prolonged by their gradual increase in size the ineffable and incredible wonder of those beholding them.

The shouts of the people rise up to heaven; due praises are paid to God; church bells are rung; crowds flock in who were just about to go to bed, and sleepless they await the sunlight with the man restored to light.

In the morning a crowd of the whole town massed together. Closely examining him in the bright light, they noticed that one eye was parti-colored, the other quite black, though from birth both his eyes had been parti-colored. Now among others the priest from the church of St. John, who had heard his confession after the mutilation, ran up. Seeing this miracle of God's power he said, "Why are we waiting for papal instructions? No more delaying for me! This very moment I will begin and conduct to the end a solemn service in the name of Thomas, the glorious friend of God, indeed, the martyr beyond price. Who can hesitate to give the name martyr to one who does such mighty and such merciful deeds?" So he ran to the church, set the bells ringing, and was as good as his word.

This man, however, now no longer bereft of light but bedecked with it, as he had been dragged in disgrace through the middle of the town to be punished, so now through the selfsame street, amid the praise and applause of the people, he is led back to the church of St. Paul where he also passed the eve of the Lord's day in vigil. Departing from there he hastened on the way toward St. Thomas, the author of his healing. Wherever he passed, a great multitude of people followed him, for his fame flying along in front of him excited anyone on his way. Whatever gifts they gave him, he gave to the poor out of love for the martyr. He had completed about four miles of his journey when he started to scratch an itch on the bag of his testicles with his near hand, and he discovered that those members had also been restored to him, very small indeed but growing bigger, which he even did not refuse to anyone who wanted to feel them.

On his coming to London, he was received with congratulations by Hugh, Bishop of Durham [1153-95], who would not let him leave him until he had sent a messenger to Bedford to make careful inquiry and had been made certain of the facts.

But even after we had received him in our house [at Canterbury], although he had been preceded by the testimony of very many witnesses, we did not feel satisfied until we heard the substance of the above-written statements confirmed by the letter and testimony of the citizens of Bedford. For they sent letters to us, the contents of which were as follows:

"The burgesses of Bedford to the convent of Canterbury and to all the faithful in Christ, greetings. Be it known to the convent of Canterbury and also to all Catholics that God has worked a wonderful and excellent miracle by the merits of the most holy martyr, Thomas. For it happened that a certain countryman of Weston by the name of Eilward was seized and taken before the viscount of Bedford and knights of the county for a theft valued at only a penny. He was publicly condemned by them and deprived of his eyes and genitals in the presence of clergy, men, and women. The chaplain of St. John of Bedford, to whom the aforesaid countryman confessed [after his mutilation] also testifies to this. And this same is testified by his host, named Eilbrict, in whose house he was afterwards received: namely that he was entirely without eyes or testicles when he was first received in his house. And afterwards, often invoking the merits of St. Thomas the martyr, by an apparition of the aforesaid martyr he was gloriously and miraculously restored to health.".…

Book IV. Chapter 45. Eilwacher of Dover was sailing to lesser Britain [Brittany]. A storm arose and he cast out three anchors but lost all of them through the cables breaking. However, he made it back to land after invoking the martyr. On the return of fair weather he returned with his companions to the sea to seek the anchors, for the place where he had lost them was not far from the land. For three days they searched and found nothing, so one of them said, "Let's also promise to the martyr of Canterbury a wax anchor [to be offered at the shrine] so that he will give us back our iron ones." All agreed, and straightaway letting down into the water the instrument with which they were searching the bottom, they drew out all of the anchors. So they turned back to England and came to the martyr. They brought to him the gift they had promised.…

Chapter 65. Now, in the diocese of Norwich, a girl about fifteen years old named Cecilia, the daughter of one Jordan of Plumstead, was stricken with cancer.

While maidenly modesty induced her to bear her pain rather than reveal what caused her shame, the disease gradually spread until it ate away her thighs and buttocks so that the joints of the bones and the muscles were exposed. At length her pale face showed that she was not well. Her parents asked what was wrong with her and were told of her great suffering.

The ulcers were a foot wide, emitting such a stench that even her mother desired her death and her friends avoided her presence. The neighbors loathed to enter the house where she lay. The ulcers of the devouring cancer were wrapped in cloths that had to be changed every hour due to the mass of putrid matter issuing from them. She could neither sit nor lie down, but leaning on her knees or forearms, she bent forward on her face.

Suffering like this from harvest-time up to the month of March, she was at last brought to the end. For three or four days she took no food or drink but stayed in bed; leaning against the wall with her knees drawn together, her eyelids open and unblinking, she seemed to present the aspect of someone neither living nor dead.

When people regarded her, they thought she had been carried [in ecstasy] out of her body, calling to mind a woman in the neighborhood named Agnes who, a few days before when she had fallen asleep had been taken up in the spirit and, with the guidance and revelation of St. Catherine, had beheld the rewards and punishments of the departed. So, thinking that she too, like Agnes, had been led out of the body, they watched her in the hope of her return (see Doc. 37).

But it happened that, while the girl stayed motionless, toward nightfall a woman from the neighborhood came to see her who loved her very dearly. Believing her to be really dead, she exclaimed, "What a sin it was for you to let this girl die in her bed! Why was she not laid out on a haircloth as is the custom for dying Catholics? You have acted foolishly."

Then she was carried into an outer building and laid on the floor – her limbs stiff, her body cold, and eyes wide open, the muscles of her knees contracted stiff and quite hard like a dead person's. Her legs could not be straightened out or stretched. A linen sheet was spread over the corpse and, following funeral custom, tapers were lighted.

But her father, who had collapsed in sleep, worn out both by sorrow and work, woke up and rushed in shouting, "Is my daughter really dead?" "Indeed," his wife said, "she is dead." Then he said, "O St. Thomas, martyr of God, return me now my service which in the past I zealously paid you. Return me now my service. Now I really need you. Once I served you diligently before you were exalted with this world's honors. Return me my service! Remember, blessed martyr, how you were sick long ago in Kent in Turstan the clerk's house, and what good service I gave you there. You could not touch wine, or spirits, or beer, or any other strong liquor, and I used to scour the whole neighborhood to find you whey to drink. Return me my service! Then you had only one horse, and I had charge of that too. Return me my service, bearing in mind all the trouble I bore waiting on you. Return me my service! You surely do not wish for me to have served you for free."

The man spent almost half the night in such outcries. And when he had repeated "Return me my service" so often that hoarseness shut his windpipe, the pity of the martyr assented to the prayers of the suppliant and, so that he would not appear ungrateful for all his services, he restored his daughter to her original health. For straightaway under the sheet with which she lay covered, she drew back her outstretched hand; but though she tried to speak, she could utter nothing intelligible due to her excessive weakness. The next morning food and drink revived her. Even her cancerous thighs had dried up within three days, and had recovered in three weeks without any medicine of this world.

After this wonderful conclusion, the man mentioned above, the girl's father, sought the presence of William, bishop of Norwich [1146-74], informing him of the event and requesting a letter of testimony. The bishop did not at once put faith in the story, but called the priest and eye-witnesses, and ascertained all the facts in order, so that, when certified by their testimony, he might stand as a witness. Also, after calling in two respectable matrons to examine any traces of cancer, he proved that the girl was now in perfect health. So he addressed a letter to us sealed with his seal testifying that she had been laid out on the floor as if dead, but touching too briefly on the points treated by us, as we believe, with sufficient fullness. The tenor of the letter is as follows:

"William, by the grace of God bishop of Norwich, to his venerable brothers in the Lord, the prior and sacred convent of Canterbury, eternal salvation in Christ. The wonderful works of God, which in our diocese come to pass concerning those afflicted with various illnesses, from their earnest devotion to St. Thomas, and from the pure invocations of their hearts, which of their free will they proffer – these we desire with all our heart to make known to you. For how shall man presume to keep secret what God, glorifying his saint, does not wish to remain hidden? Since, therefore, we have received from the testimony of William, a priest in our domain, and of very many of our men, the bearer of [this letter], Cecilia, daughter of one who is our vassal, having long been kept to her bed by the disease of cancer, while that disease was painfully creeping around her thighs, at last, under the increasing pressure of the disease, was brought so low that she was thought to be lifeless, and was laid out on the floor as if dead. Then her father's soul, turned to bitterness, yet still trusting in the divine compassion and in the merits of the most blessed martyr, bursting out into exclamations of sorrow, invoked the saint of the Lord with perfect devotion of heart; and through the cooperation of divine grace, [she] obtained the restoration of her original health by the merits of the most blessed martyr, [and] is sent by us to you together with the testimony of our writing, because of the glory of this great miracle. Farewell."

Chapter 66. In the manor of the county of Warwick called Benedega, Hugh Scot has the witness of his neighbors in the county to be of good name and unblemished reputation. His son Philip, about eight years old, while by a deep pool in an ironstone quarry, overwhelming with stones (as boys will do) the frogs that rose up to the surface, happened to fall in, and was himself overwhelmed by the waters.

When his father, on coming home, could not find the boy, he looked for him everywhere. At last he finds him under the water and draws him out while the sun was setting, distended by the abundance of the water [he had swallowed], and, as he [still] believes, lifeless. The corpse is carried into the house. The people flock in, expressing sympathy with the agonizing grief of the parents. They try, but all in vain, to see if human efforts might possibly help the child in some way.

The boy's coat, which happened to be quite wide, big enough for two boys – since it could not be taken off, being so tightly stretched by the distension of his stomach – they rip from top to bottom. They hang him up head downwards and beat the soles of his feet. But no water flowed out so they gave up hope. Finally the boy was stretched out on a table, a fire was lit at each end of the room, and watch was kept till morning.

But at sunrise, at the mother's advice, they sent to a near village and fetched the Water of St. Thomas the martyr. Opening the closed mouth and the fast-clenched teeth with a spindle or some such thing, she happened to put in her finger; and, as the spindle slipped out, her finger was caught fast and almost pierced to the bone by the clenching teeth. Hearing her cry out, the father placed a small knife between the teeth; but before he could extricate her finger from their grip, he had to break the two front teeth called the incisors.

Others, who were standing by, desired to have a priest called to say a funeral mass for the boy so that he could be buried; but the father loudly refused, saying, "So may God help me, unless the blessed Thomas restores him to me alive here, he shall have him at Canterbury dead. For I will either lead him there alive or carry him dead. He will absolutely not be buried here."

But the Water poured once and then a second time into the mouth flowed back out again, finding no open passageways. On the third injection, by divine will, it went down into the inner parts, and suddenly the muscles seemed to move. The boy unfolds his hand, which was clenched before; after unfolding it, by degrees he draws it toward him; he opens one eye. With inexpressible joy his father cried, "My son do you wish to live?" "Father," he replied, "I do."

Those who were present crowded around, still lamenting, however, the frightful inflation of his stomach; but gradually the stomach subsided and recovered its natural symmetry and condition before the eyes of all, and this though not a drop of water flowed forth from the body above or below. That this boy, therefore, was undoubtedly dead, we have ascertained not only from the testimony of the father but also from that of very many others – and indeed by a letter of testimony from his priest....

Chapter 88. I know a respected man in the city of Winchester, whose son Geoffrey, about a year and a half old, was delivered by the Water of Canterbury from acute disease. But after some days, when the boy's mother was sitting alone in the house, and he, opposite her, quiet in the cradle, a large stone party-wall fell with a crash, burying the child in a heap of rubble.

The mother cried out, "My lord St. Thomas, save my son whom you just lately restored to me." Then she fainted from excessive grief. But some of the house servants came in, and, seeing her lying on the floor as if dead, they applied the usual remedy of cold water. When she came to herself and sat up, they said, "What's wrong, mistress?" "Woe is me," she answered, "my son is dead. See! He lies crushed to pieces beneath that heap of rubble and stones."

Invoking the name of God and the martyr and calling plenty of men to help, they tear the mound apart, and at last reaching the boy, though not without much effort, they find him not only unhurt but actually laughing – and this even though the boy's cradle, which was made of stout and solid boards, had been shattered and splintered into eighteen parts. But the infant's tender body was absolutely unharmed with the exception of a very slight blueness under the eye, though laying just over the infant was a stone bigger than the infant himself. Those seeing this were amazed and seized by wonder.

What do these stories reveal about the role that saints played in medieval life? What conception do ordinary people seem to have of saints? To what extent are these stories believable to modern readers? Which ones strain your credibility and why? How would you explain them? What details of ordinary people's religious life are contained in these stories?

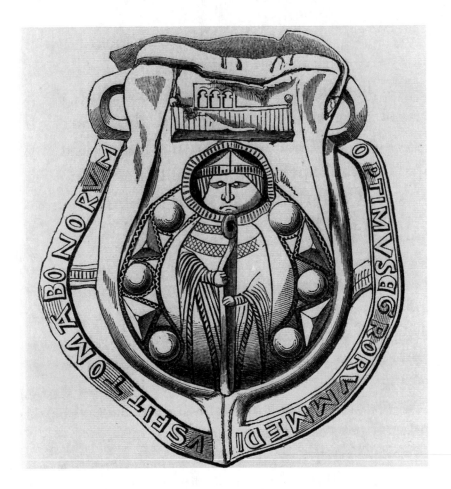

Fig. 4.2. An ampule for Canterbury Water

Purchased by pilgrims at his shrine, this thirteenth-century lead ampule – part cura-
tive, part souvenir – held water infused with the blood of St. Thomas Becket or dust
from his tomb. It was filled from a hole at the top and loops on both sides let pilgrims
hang it around their neck with a cord. On one side was a picture of the shrine in
Canterbury cathedral; on the other, this effigy of the saint bordered by the Latin
motto: OPTIMVS EGRORVM MEDI[C]US FIT TOMA BONORVM, or "Thomas
makes the best doctor for the worthy sick." Reproduced in Daniel Rock's *Church of
Our Fathers* (London: C. Dolman, 1852), v. 3, pt. 1, p. 418 after the original in the
former Museum of Antiquities, York.

31. BISHOP HUGH OF LINCOLN'S DEVOTION TO RELICS (1186-1200)

England's King Henry II handpicked the Carthusian monk, Hugh of Avalon (c. 1135-1200) to head the Charterhouse he founded at Witham, Somerset as part of his penance for Becket's murder. In 1186 Hugh was elected bishop of Lincoln, where he ruled effectively and affectionately for the next fourteen years – so effectively that he himself was canonized twenty years after his death. Devout, learned, an upright judge, an equal friend to both the poor and three English kings, and owner of a pet swan, he was perhaps the best man of his day. The nineteenth-century English art critic and reformer John Ruskin called him "the most beautiful sacerdotal figure known to me in history." His biographer Adam of Eynsham described the saint's passion for relics, a passion most medieval people shared.

Source: trans. Decima. L. Douie and Hugh Farmer from *Adam of Eynsham's Magna Vita Sancti Hugonis* (London: Thomas Nelson, 1962), v. 2, pp. 167-71. Latin.

He had amongst his treasures a silver casket which it was his custom to carry in his hands when he consecrated churches. This contained innumerable relics of saints of both sexes, which had been acquired in very many different places either by himself or by his monk chaplain who had the custody of his treasury. The bishop gave those he had obtained himself to the very devout sacrist at Chartreuse in the presence of the prior and brethren [in 1200], to be preserved there, and handed over to the monk his own acquisitions to take to his own monastery.

Whilst I am on the subject of the relics of the saints it would not be amiss to give certain anecdotes which contribute to their glory and to the edification of the reader. The bishop had ordered to be made for him a ring of the finest gold set with precious stones, which had in the part which encircled the outside of his finger a kind of hollow jewel which he intended to use as a repository for relics. The receptacle was about the width of four fingers, and in it he had collected thirty relics of the saints.

Although he tried with deep devotion and earnestness to acquire these priceless treasures, he wanted most of all to obtain a portion of the body of that great confessor of Christ and patriarch and lawgiver of monks, Benedict [of Nursia]. This ardent desire caused him to dispatch a pleading letter to the venerable abbot and monks of the monastery of Fleury where the most holy bones of the saintly father repose. He sent this by one of their own monks and brethren, the warden of certain estates held by them near Lincoln, beseeching them earnestly to give him some portion of their immense treasure. The sequel was that the bearer of the letter returned at last, and brought to the man of desires [see Dan. 9:23] the reward of his prayers and longings, namely one of the teeth of the saint and a large portion of the cloth in which his remains had been wrapped. He also brought a letter in reply from those to whom he had been sent, in which the greeting and compliments of the venerable bishop were courteously returned, and sure proof was furnished as to the genuineness of the gifts which had been dispatched. Having received and read these, the man of God was filled with gladness, and immediately summoned his goldsmith who lived in his town of Banbury, since when these events took place the bishop was at his manor at Dorchester, which is almost thirty miles from the place I have just mentioned.

Lo, whilst he was giving instructions to the messenger who was to fetch the goldsmith, to tell him to bring tools with him in order to open and then close up again the bishop's sacramental ring (he gave it this name because he often used it at ordination and consecration ceremonies as an incentive to devotion), the craftsman he was sending for suddenly arrived. This unexpected and wished-for arrival equally amazed and rejoiced the company. When questioned why he had come he related how about midnight a person had appeared to him in his sleep and ordered him to go at once to the bishop. "Some very valuable relics have been sent to him which you must insert in his ring. Get up immediately and start your journey to him." "Being awakened by these words, my mind was so disturbed that I could not concentrate on work of any kind but had to come and tell you these things to find out for myself whether what I heard was true, so here I am with my tools, make what use you please of my skills." All those who were present and heard the goldsmith's account of his vision had their faith strengthened and their joy enhanced. The bishop, out of his unbound generosity, distributed small fragments of the cloth which he had received to the abbots and monks who were there. He frequently kissed the tooth with deep devotion before having it placed in his ring.

When he was at the celebrated monastery of Fécamp, he extracted by biting two small fragments of the bone of the most blessed lover of Christ, Mary Magdalen. This bone had never been seen divested of its wrappings by the abbot or any of the monks who were present on that occasion, for it was sewn very tightly into three cloths, two of silk and one of ordinary linen.

They did not dare to accede even to the bishop's prayer to be allowed to see it. He, however, taking a small knife from one of his notaries, hurriedly cut the thread and undid the wrappings. After reverently examining and kissing the much venerated bone, he tried unsuccessfully to break it with his fingers, and then bit it first with his incisors and finally with his molars. By this means he broke off the two fragments, which he handed immediately to the writer, with the words, "Take charge of this for me with especial care."

When the abbot and the monks saw what had happened, they were first overcome with horror, and then became exceedingly enraged. They cried out, "What terrible profanity! We thought that the bishop had asked to see this holy and venerable relic for reasons of devotion, and he has stuck his teeth into it and gnawed it as if he were a dog." He mollified their anger with soothing words. Part of his speech is worth recording. "If, a little while ago I handled the most sacred body of the Lord of all the saints with my fingers, in spite of my unworthiness, and when I partook of it, touched it with my lips and teeth, why should I not venture to treat in the same way the bones of the saints for my protection, and by this commemoration of them increase my reverence for them, and without profanity acquire them when I have the opportunity?"

On another occasion at Peterborough where the arm of the glorious king and martyr Oswald [d. 642] is displayed with the bones and skin, and flesh still bloody as if recently severed from a living body, he severed with a knife a protruding sinew which was pliable and flexible enough to be drawn out by whoever handled it. This he kept and preserved with great devotion. It and other holy relics which it would take too long to describe he placed in the ring I have mentioned so often. Once, returning to Lincoln from abroad, he solemnly offered the ring at the altar of the Blessed Virgin, as a final bequest. Afterwards he forgot this oblation, and ordered that the said ring should be given to the Carthusians along with the rest of his relics. When his monk who had the custody of them reminded him of his previous gift, he ordered the ring to be restored to the church of Lincoln. He had sent to them, however, as a present the golden casket studded with precious stones which was in his treasury at Lincoln so that they could keep it in the collection of the relics of the saints which he had given them. This was done after the death of the saint [i.e., Hugh], owing to the efforts of the same monk.

32. ST. MARY MAGDALENE AND ST. NICHOLAS FROM THE *GOLDEN LEGEND* (c. 1260)

The Golden Legend *(Legenda Aurea) was the quintessential work of medieval hagiography. Containing brief lives of close to two hundred saints as well as stories about Jesus, the Virgin Mary, and all the major feasts of the Christian year, in the late Middle Ages its popularity was probably rivaled only by the Bible. Written in Latin around 1260 and soon translated into almost every Western European language, it survives in at least a thousand manuscripts, an astonishing number for a medieval book. It appeared in over 150 editions within the first century of printing; in fact, it was more frequently published than the Bible in the early years of printing. The*

Dominican Jacob de Voragine (Jacopo de Varazze; c. 1230-1298), who finished his life as archbishop of Genoa, compiled the work from over 100 different authorities stretching from the earliest church fathers to his own day. Though he probably intended it as a book of source material for preachers, it also struck a chord with clergy and literate lay people as a devotional aid since it served up almost all of Christian doctrine in stories that were both informative and typically very readable. Chaucer, for example, knew it well. It is an essential source for students of medieval popular religion since there are few facets of the subject that Jacob does not touch upon somewhere in his enormous book, which runs close to 800 pages in its most recent English translation. At the least it encapsulates most of the nuances of the medieval concept of sainthood. Only the briefest representative excerpt can be offered here: the lives of two of the most popular saints of the Middle Ages, Mary Magdalene and Nicholas. The most frequently mentioned woman in the New Testament after Jesus' mother, and his most prominent female disciple, Mary Magdalene gained her tarnished reputation as a redeemed prostitute when Pope Gregory the Great conflated Mary of Magdala, Mary of Bethany (the sister of Martha and Lazarus) and an unnamed woman sinner (Luke 7:37-50) in a sermon he preached in 591. But in the Middle Ages she was highly regarded for her un-rivaled penitence, her devotion to Jesus, and, remarkably, for her preaching even though medieval women were not allowed to preach. For Mary Magdalene first brought the news of the Resurrection to the apostles on the first Easter morning and was therefore considered the "apostola apostolorum" — the apostle to the apostles. St. Nicholas, a fourth-century bishop, is, of course, the inspiration for Santa Claus. He was the patron saint of, among others, bankers and pawnbrokers, merchants, mariners, fishermen, brides, dozens of cities, and, obviously, children.

Source: trans. William G. Ryan, *Jacobus de Voragine's Golden Legend, Readings on the Saints* (Princeton, NJ: Princeton University Press, 1993), v. 1, pp. 21-27, 374-83. Latin.

1. Saint Mary Magdalene

The name Mary, or Maria, is interpreted as *amarum mare*, bitter sea, or as illuminator or illuminated. These three meanings are accepted as standing for three shares or parts, of which Mary made the best choices, namely, the part of penance, the part of inward contemplation, and the part of heavenly glory. This threefold share is what the Lord meant when he said: "Mary has chosen the best part, which shall not be taken away from her." The first part will not be taken away because of its end or purpose, which is the attainment of holiness. The second part will not be taken because of its continuity: contemplation during the earthly journey will continue in heavenly contem-plation. And the third part will remain because it is eternal. Therefore, since Mary chose the best part, namely, penance, she is called bitter sea because in her penances she endured much bitterness. We see this from the fact that she shed enough tears to bathe the Lord's feet with them. Since she chose the best part of inward contemplation, she is called enlightener, because in contemplation she drew draughts of light so deep that in turn she poured out light in abundance: in contemplation she received the light with which she afterwards enlightened others. As she chose the best part of heavenly glory, she is called illuminated, because she now is enlightened by the light of perfect knowledge in her mind and will be illumined by the light of glory in her body.

Mary is called Magdalene, which is understood to mean "remaining guilty," or it means armed, or unconquered, or magnificent. These meanings point to the sort of woman she was before, at the time of, and after her conversion. Before her conversion she remained in guilt, burdened with the debt of eternal punishment. In her conversion she was armed and rendered unconquerable by the armor of penance: she armed herself the best possible way – with all the weapons of penance – because for every pleasure she had enjoyed she found a way of immolating herself. After her conversion she was magnificent in the superabundance of grace, because where trespass abounded, grace was superabundant.

Mary's cognomen "Magdalene" comes from Magdalum, the name of one of her ancestral properties. She was wellborn, descended of royal stock. Her father's name was Syrus, her mother was called Eucharia. With her brother Lazarus and her sister Martha she owned Magdalum, a walled town two miles from Genezareth, along with Bethany, not far from Jerusalem, and a considerable part of Jerusalem itself. They had, however, divided their holdings among themselves in such a way that Magdalum belonged to Mary (whence the name Magdalene), Lazarus kept the property in Jerusalem, and Bethany was Martha's. Magdalene gave herself totally to the pleasures of the flesh and Lazarus was devoted to the military, while prudent Martha kept close watch over her brother's and sister's estates and took care of the needs of her armed men, her servants, and the poor. After Christ's ascension, however, they all sold their possessions and laid the proceeds at the feet of the apostles.

Magdalene, then, was very rich, and sensuous pleasure keeps company with great wealth. Renowned as she was for her beauty and her riches, she was no less known for the way she gave her body to pleasure – so much so that her proper name was forgotten and she was commonly called "the sinner." Meanwhile, Christ was preaching here and there, and she, guided by the divine will, hastened to the house of Simon the leper, where, she had learned, he was at table. Being a sinner she did not dare mingle with the righteous, but stayed back and washed the Lord's feet with her tears, dried them with her hair, and anointed them with precious ointment [Luke 7:36-

50]. Because of the extreme heat of the sun the people of that region bathed and anointed themselves regularly.

Now Simon the Pharisee thought to himself that if this man were a prophet, he would never allow a sinful woman to touch him; but the Lord rebuked him for his proud righteousness and told the woman that all her sins were forgiven. This is the Magdalene upon whom Jesus conferred such great graces and to whom he showed so many marks of love. He cast seven devils out of her [Luke 8:2], set her totally afire with love of him, counted her among his closest familiars, was her guest, had her do the housekeeping on his travels, and kindly took her side at all times. He defended her when the Pharisee said she was unclean, when her sister implied that she was lazy, when Judas called her wasteful. Seeing her weep he could not contain his tears. For love of her he raised her brother, four days dead, to life, for love of her he freed her sister Martha from the issue of blood she had suffered for seven years, and in view of her merits he gave Martilla, her sister's handmaid, the privilege of calling out those memorable words: "Blessed is the womb that bore you!" Indeed, according to [St.] Ambrose, Martha was the woman with the issue of blood, and the woman who called out was Martha's servant. "She [Mary] it was, I say, who washed the Lord's feet with her tears, dried them with her hair and anointed them with ointment, who in the time of grace did solemn penance, who chose the best part, who sat at the Lord's feet and listened to his word, who anointed his head, who stood beside the cross at his passion, who prepared the sweet spices with which to anoint his body, who, when the disciples left the tomb, did not go away, to whom the risen Christ first appeared, making her an apostle to the apostles."

Some fourteen years after the Lord's passion and ascension into heaven, when the Jews had long since killed Stephen and expelled the other disciples from the confines of Judea, the disciples went off into the lands of the various nations and there sowed the word of the Lord. With the apostles at the time was one of Christ's seventy-two disciples, blessed Maximin, to whose care blessed Peter had entrusted Mary Magdalene. In the dispersion Maximin, Mary Magdalene, her brother Lazarus, her sister Martha, Martha's maid Martilla, blessed Cedonius, who was born blind and had been cured by the Lord, and many other Christians, were herded by the unbelievers into a ship without pilot or rudder and sent out to sea so that they might all be drowned, but by God's will they eventually landed at Marseilles. There they found no one willing to give them shelter, so they took refuge under the portico of a shrine belonging to the people of that area. When blessed Mary Magdalene saw the people gathering at the shrine to offer sacrifice to the idols, she came forward, her manner calm and her face serene, and with well-chosen words called them away from the cult of idols and preached Christ fervidly to them. All who heard her were in admiration at her beauty, her eloquence, and the sweetness of her message ... and no wonder, that the mouth which had pressed such pious and beautiful kisses on the Savior's feet should breathe forth the perfume of the word of God more profusely than others could.

Then the governor of that province came with his wife to offer sacrifice and pray the gods for offspring. Magdalene preached Christ to him and dissuaded him from sacrificing. Some days later she appeared in a vision to the wife, saying: "Why, when you are so rich, do you allow the saints of God to die of hunger and cold?" She added the threat that if the lady did not persuade her husband to relieve the saints' needs, she might incur the wrath of God; but the woman was afraid to tell her spouse about the vision. The following night she saw the same vision and heard the same words, but again hesitated to tell her husband. The third time, in the silence of the dead of night, Mary Magdalene appeared to each of them, shaking with anger, her face afire as if the whole house were burning, and said: "So you sleep, tyrant, limb of your father Satan, with your viper of a wife who refused to tell you what I had said? You take your rest, you enemy of the cross of Christ, your gluttony sated with a bellyful of all sorts of food while you let the saints of God perish from hunger and thirst? You lie here wrapped in silken sheets, after seeing those others homeless and desolate, and passing them by? Wicked man, you will not escape! You will not go unpunished for your long delay in giving them some help!" And, having said her say, she disappeared.

The lady awoke gasping and trembling, and spoke to her husband, who was in like distress: "My lord, have you had the dream that I just had?" "I saw it," he answered, "and I can't stop wondering and shaking with fear! What are we to do?" His wife said: "It will be better for us to give in to her than to face the wrath of her God whom she preaches." They therefore provided shelter for the Christians and supplied their needs.

Then one day when Mary Magdalene was preaching, the aforesaid governor asked her: "Do you think you can defend the faith you preach?" "I am ready indeed to defend it," she replied, "because my faith is strengthened by the daily miracles and preaching of my teacher Peter, who presides in Rome!" The governor and his wife then said to her: "See here, we are prepared to do whatever you tell us to if you can obtain a son for us from the God whom you preach." "In this he will not fail you," said Magdalene. Then the blessed Mary prayed the Lord to deign to grant them a son. The Lord heard her prayers and the woman conceived.

Now the husband began to want to go to Peter and find out whether what Magdalene preached about Christ was the truth. "What's this?" snapped his wife. "Are you thinking of going without me? Not a bit of it! You leave, I leave. You come back, I come back. You stay here, I stay here!" The man replied:

"My dear, it can't be that way! You're pregnant and the perils of the sea are infinite. It's too risky. You will stay home and take care of what we have here!" But she insisted, doing as women do. She threw herself at his feet, weeping the while, and in the end won him over. Mary therefore put the sign of the cross on their shoulders as a protection against the ancient Enemy's interference on their journey. They stocked a ship with all the necessaries, leaving the rest of their possessions in the care of Mary Magdalene, and set sail.

A day and a night had not passed, however, when the wind rose and the sea became tumultuous. All aboard, and especially the expectant mother, were shaken and fearful as the waves battered the ship. Abruptly she went into labor, and, exhausted by her pangs and the buffeting of the storm, she expired as she brought forth her son. The newborn groped about seeking the comfort of his mother's breasts, and cried and whimpered piteously. Ah, what a pity! The infant is born, he lives, and has become his mother's killer! He may as well die, since there is no one to give him nourishment to keep him alive! What will the Pilgrim do, seeing his wife dead and the child whining plaintively as he seeks the maternal breast? His lamentations knew no bounds, and he said to himself: "Alas, what will you do? You yearned for a son, and you have lost the mother and the son too!"

The seamen meanwhile were shouting: "Throw that corpse overboard before we all perish! As long as it is with us, this storm will not let up!" They seized the body and were about to cast it into the sea, but the Pilgrim intervened. "Hold on a little!" he cried. "Even if you don't want to spare me or the mother, at least pity the poor weeping little one! Wait just a bit! Maybe the woman has only fainted with pain and may begin to breathe again!"

Now suddenly they saw a hilly coast not far off the bow, and the Pilgrim thought it would be better to put the dead body and the infant ashore there than to throw them as food to the sea monsters. His pleas and his bribes barely persuaded the crew to drop anchor there. Then he found the ground so hard that he could not dig a grave, so he spread his cloak in a fold of the hill, laid his wife's body on it, and placed the child with its head between the mother's breasts. Then he wept and said: "O Mary Magdalene, you brought ruin upon me when you landed at Marseilles! Unhappy me, that on your advice I set out on this journey! Did you not pray to God that my wife might conceive? Conceive she did, and suffered death giving birth, and the child she conceived was born only to die because there is no one to nurse him. Behold, this is what your prayer obtained for me. I commended my all to you and do commend me to your God. If it be in your power, be mindful of the mother's soul, and by your prayer take pity on the child and spare its life." Then he enfolded the body and the child in his cloak and went back aboard the ship.

When the Pilgrim arrived in Rome, Peter came to meet him and, seeing the sign of the cross on his shoulder, asked him who he was and where he came from. He told Peter all that had happened to him, and Peter responded: "Peace be with you! You have done well to trust the good advice you received. Do not take it amiss that your wife sleeps and the infant rests with her. It is in the Lord's power to give gifts to whom he will, to take away what was given, to restore what was taken away, and to turn your grief into joy."

Peter then took him to Jerusalem and showed him all the places where Christ had preached and performed miracles, as well as the place where he had suffered and the other from which he had ascended into heaven. Peter then gave him thorough instruction in the faith, and after two years had gone by, he boarded ship, being eager to get back to his homeland. By God's will, in the course of the voyage they came close to the hilly coast where he had left the body of his wife and his son, and with pleas and money he induced the crew to put him ashore. The little boy, whom Mary Magdalene had preserved unharmed, used to come down to the beach and play with the stones and pebbles, as children love to do. As the Pilgrim's skiff drew near to the land, he saw the child playing on the beach. He was dumbstruck at seeing his son alive and leapt ashore from the skiff. The child, who had never seen a man, was terrified at the sight and ran to his mother's bosom, taking cover under the familiar cloak. The Pilgrim, anxious to see what was happening, followed, and found the handsome child feeding at his mother's breast. He lifted the boy and said: "O Mary Magdalene, how happy I would be, how well everything would have turned out for me, if my wife were alive and able to return home with me! Indeed I know, I know and believe beyond a doubt, that having given us this child and kept him alive for two years on this rock, you could now, by your prayers, restore his mother to life and health."

As these words were spoken, the woman breathed and, as if waking from sleep, said: "Great is your merit, O blessed Mary Magdalene, and you are glorious! As I struggled to give birth, you did me a midwife's service and waited upon my every need like a faithful handmaid." Hearing this, the Pilgrim said: "My dear wife, are you alive?" "Indeed I am," she answered, "and am just coming from the pilgrimage from which you yourself are returning. And as blessed Peter conducted you to Jerusalem and showed you all the places where Christ suffered, died, and was buried, and many other places, I, with blessed Mary Magdalene as my guide and companion, was with you and committed all you saw to memory." Whereupon she recited all the places where Christ had suffered, and fully explained the miracles and all she had seen, not missing a single thing.

Now the Pilgrim, having got back his wife and child, joyfully took ship and in a short time made port at Marseilles. Going into the city they found blessed Mary Magdalene with her disciples, preaching. Weeping with joy, they threw themselves at her feet and related all that had happened to them, then received holy baptism from blessed Maximin. Afterwards they destroyed the temples of all the idols in the city of Marseilles and built churches to Christ. They also elected blessed Lazarus as bishop of the city. Later by the will of God they went to the city of Aix, and, by many miracles, led the people there to accept the Christian faith. Blessed Maximin was ordained bishop of Aix.

At this time blessed Mary Magdalene, wishing to devote herself to heavenly contemplation, retired to an empty wilderness, and lived unknown for thirty years in a place made ready by the hands of angels. There were no streams of water there, nor the comfort of grass or trees: thus it was made clear that our Redeemer had determined to fill her not with earthly viands but only with the good things of heaven. Every day at the seven canonical hours she was carried aloft by angels and with her bodily ears heard the glorious chants of the celestial hosts. So it was that day by day she was gratified with these supernal delights and, being conveyed back to her own place by the same angels, needed no material nourishment.

There was a priest who wanted to live a solitary life and built himself a cell a few miles from the Magdalene's habitat. One day the Lord opened this priest's eyes, and with his own eyes he saw how the angels descended to the already mentioned place where blessed Mary Magdalene dwelt, and how they lifted her into the upper air and an hour later brought her back to her place with divine praises. Wanting to learn the truth about this wondrous vision and commending himself prayerfully to his Creator, he hurried with daring and devotion toward the aforesaid place; but when he was a stone's throw from the spot, his knees began to wobble, and he was so frightened that he could hardly breathe. When he started to go away, his legs and feet responded, but every time he turned around and tried to reach the desired spot, his body went limp and his mind went blank, and he could not move forward.

So the man of God realized that there was a heavenly secret here to which human experience alone could have no access. He therefore invoked his Savior's name and called out: "I adjure you by the Lord, that if you are a human being or any rational creature living in that cave, you answer me and tell me the truth about yourself!" When he had repeated this three times, blessed Mary Magdalene answered him: "Come closer, and you can learn the truth about whatever your soul desires." Trembling, he had gone halfway across the intervening space when she said to him: "Do you remember what the Gospel says about Mary the notorious sinner, who washed the Savior's feet with her tears and dried them with her hair, and earned forgiveness for all her misdeeds?" "I do remember," the priest replied, "and more than thirty years have gone by since then. Holy Church also believes and confesses what you have said about her." "I am that woman," she said. "For the space of thirty years I have lived here unknown to everyone; and as you were allowed to see yesterday, every day I am borne aloft seven times by angelic hands, and have been found worthy to hear with the ears of my body the joyful jubilation of the heavenly hosts. Now, because it has been revealed to me by the Lord that I am soon to depart from this world, please go to blessed Maximin and take care to inform him that next year, on the day of the Lord's resurrection, at the time when he regularly rises for matins, he is to go alone to his church, and there he will find me present and waited upon by angels." To the priest the voice sounded like the voice of an angel, but he saw no one.

The good man hurried to blessed Maximin and carried out his errand. Saint Maximin, overjoyed, gave fulsome thanks to the Savior, and on the appointed day, at the appointed hour, went alone into the church and saw blessed Mary Magdalene amidst the choir of angels who had brought her there. She was raised up a distance of two cubits above the floor, standing among the angels and lifting her hands in prayer to God. When blessed Maximin hesitated about approaching her, she turned to him and said: "Come closer, father, and do not back away from your daughter." When he drew near to her, as we read in blessed Maximin's own books, the lady's countenance was so radiant, due to her continuous and daily vision of the angels, that one would more easily look straight into the sun than gaze upon her face.

All the clergy, including the priest already mentioned, were now called together, and blessed Mary Magdalene, shedding tears of joy, received the Lord's Body and Blood from the bishop. Then she lay down full length before the steps of the altar, and her most holy soul migrated to the Lord. After she expired, so powerful an odor of sweetness pervaded the church that for seven days all those who entered there noticed it. Blessed Maximin embalmed her holy body with aromatic lotions and gave it honorable burial, giving orders that after his death he was to be buried close to her.

Hegesippus (or, as some books have it, Josephus) agrees in the main with the story just told. He says in one of his treatises that after Christ's ascension Mary Magdalene, weary of the world and moved by her ardent love of the Lord, never wanted to see anyone. After she came to Aix, she went off into the desert, lived there unknown for thirty years, and every day at the seven canonical hours was carried up to heaven by an angel. He added, however, that the priest who went to her found her closed up in a cell. At her request he reached out a garment to her, and when she had put it on, she went with him to the church, received communion there, and, raising her hands in prayer beside the altar, died in peace.

In Charlemagne's time, namely, in the year of the Lord 769, Gerard, duke of Burgundy, being unable to have a son of his wife, openhandedly gave away his wealth to the poor and built many churches and monasteries. When he had built the monastery at Vézelay, he and the abbot sent a monk, with a suitable company, to the city of Aix in order to bring back the relics of Saint Mary Magdalene, if possible. When the monk arrived at the aforesaid city, however, he found that it had been razed to the ground by the pagans. Yet by chance he discovered a marble sarcophagus with an inscription which indicated that the body of blessed Mary Magdalene was contained inside, and her whole story was beautifully carved on the outside. The monk therefore broke into the sarcophagus by night, gathered the relics, and carried them to his inn. That same night blessed Mary appeared to him and told him not to be afraid but to go on with the work he had begun. On their way back to Vézelay the company, when they were half a league from their monastery, could not move the relics another step until the abbot and his monks came in solemn procession to receive them.

A certain knight, whose practice it was to visit the relics of Saint Mary Magdalene every year, was killed in battle. As he lay dead on his bier, his parents, mourning him, made pious complaint to the Magdalene because she had allowed her devotee to die without making confession and doing penance. Then suddenly, to the amazement of all present, the dead man rose up and called for a priest. He made his confession devoutly and received viaticum, then returned to rest in peace.

A ship crowded with men and women was sinking, and one woman, who was pregnant and saw herself in danger of drowning, called upon Magdalene as loudly as she could, and vowed that if by Mary's merits she escaped death and bore a son, she would give him up to the saint's monastery. At once a woman of venerable visage and bearing appeared to her, held her up by the chin, and, while the rest drowned, brought her unharmed to land. The woman in due time gave birth to a son and faithfully fulfilled her vow.

There are some who say that Mary Magdalene was espoused to John the Evangelist, who was about to take her as his wife when Christ called him away from his nuptials, whereupon she, indignant at having been deprived of her spouse, gave herself up to every sort of voluptuousness. But, since it would not do to have John's vocation the occasion of Mary's damnation, the Lord mercifully brought her around to conversion and penance; and, because she had had to forgo the heights of carnal enjoyment, he filled her more than others with the most intense spiritual delight, which consists in the love of God. And there are those who allege that Christ honored John with special evidences of his affection because he had taken him away from the aforesaid pleasures. These tales are to be considered false and frivolous. Brother Albert [Magnus], in his introduction to the Gospel of John, says firmly that the lady from whose nuptials the same John was called away persevered in virginity, was seen later in the company of the Blessed Virgin Mary, mother of Christ, and came at last to a holy end.

A man who had lost his eyesight was on his way to the monastery at Vézelay to visit Mary Magdalene's body when his guide told him that he, the guide, could already see the church in the distance. The blind man exclaimed in a loud voice: "O holy Mary Magdalene, if only I could sometime be worthy to see your church!" At once his eyes were opened.

There was a man who wrote a list of his sins on a sheet of paper and put it under the rug on the Magdalene's altar, asking her to pray that he might be pardoned. Later he recovered the paper and found that his sins had been wiped out.

A man who lay in chains for having committed the crime of extortion called upon Mary Magdalene to come to his aid, and one night a beautiful woman appeared to him, broke his fetters, and ordered him to be off. Seeing himself unshackled, he got away as fast as possible.

A clerk from Flanders, Stephen by name, had fallen into such a welter of sinfulness that, having committed every sort of evil, he could do no works of salvation nor even bear to hear of them. Yet he had deep devotion to blessed Mary Magdalene, observed her vigils by fasting, and celebrated her feast day. Once when he was on a visit to her tomb and was half asleep and half awake, Mary Magdalene appeared to him as a lovely, sad-eyed woman supported by two angels, one on either side, and she said to him: "Stephen, I ask you, why do you repay me with deeds unworthy of my deserts? Why are you not moved with compunction by what my own lips insistently say? From the time when you began to be devoted to me I have always prayed the Lord urgently for you. Get up, then! Repent! I will never leave you until you are reconciled with God!" The clerk soon felt so great an inpouring of grace in himself that he renounced the world, entered the religious life, and lived a very holy life thereafter. At his death Mary Magdalene was seen standing with angels beside the bier, and she carried his soul, like a pure-white dove, with songs of praise into heaven.

2. Saint Nicholas

The name Nicholas comes from *nicos*, which means victory, and *laos*, people; so Nicholas may be interpreted as meaning victory over a people, that is, either victory over vices, which are many and mean, or as victory in the full sense, because Nicholas, by his way of life and his doctrine, taught the peoples to conquer sin and vice. Or the name is formed from *nicos*, victory, and *laus*, praise – so, victorious praise – or from *nitor*, shining whiteness, and *laos*, people, as meaning the bright cleanness of the people. Nicholas had in him that which makes for shining cleanness, since, according to Ambrose, "the word of God makes clean, as do true confession, holy thoughts, and good works."

The life of Saint Nicholas was written by learned men of Argos, called Argolics, Argos being, according to Isidore [of Seville], a town in Greece, so the Greeks are also called Argolics. Elsewhere we read that his legend was written in Greek by the patriarch Methodius and translated into Latin by John the Deacon, who added much to it.

Nicholas, a citizen of Patera, was born of rich and pious parents. His father was named Epiphanes, his mother, Johanna. When, in the flower of their youth, they had brought him into the world, they adopted the celibate life thenceforth. While the infant was being bathed on the first day of his life, he stood straight up in the bath. From then on he took the breast only once on Wednesdays and Fridays. As a youth he avoided the dissolute pleasures of his peers, preferring to spend time in churches; and whatever he could understand of the Holy Scriptures he committed to memory.

After the death of his parents he began to consider how he might make use of his great wealth, not in order to win men's praise but to give glory to God. At the time a certain fellow townsman of his, a man of noble origin but very poor, was thinking of prostituting his three virgin daughters in order to make a living out of this vile transaction. When the saint learned of this, abhorring the crime he wrapped a quantity of gold in a cloth and, under cover of darkness, threw it through a window of the other man's house and withdrew unseen. Rising in the morning, the man found the gold, gave thanks to God, and celebrated the wedding of his eldest daughter. Not long thereafter the servant of God did the same thing again. This time the man, finding the gold and bursting into loud praises, determined to be on the watch so as to find out who had come to the relief of his penury. Some little time later Nicholas threw a double sum of gold into the house. The noise awakened the man and he pursued the fleeing figure, calling out, "Stop! Stop! Don't hide from me!" and ran faster and faster until he saw that it was Nicholas. Falling to the ground he wanted to kiss his benefactor's feet, but the saint drew away and exacted a promise that the secret would be kept until after his death.

Some time later the bishop of Myra died, and all the bishops of the region gathered to choose a successor. Among them was one bishop of great authority, upon whose opinion the decision of the others would depend. This prelate exhorted the others to fast and pray; and that very night he heard a voice telling him to post himself at the doors of the church in the morning, and to consecrate as bishop the first man he saw coming in, whose name would be Nicholas. In the morning he made this known to his colleagues and went outside the church to wait. Meanwhile Nicholas, miraculously guided by God, went early to the church and was the first to enter. The bishop, coming up to him, asked his name; and he, filled with the simplicity of a dove, bowed his head and answered, "Nicholas, the servant of your holiness." Then all the bishops led him in and installed him on the episcopal throne. But he, amidst his honors, always preserved his former humility and gravity of manner. He passed the night in prayer, mortified his body, and shunned the society of women. He was humble in his attitude toward others, persuasive in speech, forceful in counsel, and strict when reprimands were called for. A chronicle also states that Nicholas took part in the Council of Nicaea.

One day some seamen, threatened by a violent storm at sea, shed tears and prayed as follows: "Nicholas, servant of God, if what we have heard about you is true, let us experience your help now." At once there appeared before them a figure resembling the saint, who said to them: "You called me, here I am!" And he began to assist them with the sails and ropes and other rigging of the ship, and the storm died down immediately. The sailors eventually came to the church where Nicholas was and recognized him instantly, although they had never seen him in the flesh. They thanked him then for their deliverance, but he told them to thank God, since their rescue was due not to his merits, but only to the divine mercy and their own faith.

There came a time when Saint Nicholas's province was beset by a famine so severe that no one had anything to eat. The man of God learned that several ships laden with grain were anchored in the harbor. He hastened there promptly and begged the ships' people to come to the aid of those who were starving, if only by allowing them a hundred measures of wheat from each ship. But they replied: "Father, we dare not, because our cargo was measured at Alexandria and we must deliver it whole and entire to the emperor's granaries." The saint answered: "Do what I tell you, and I promise you in God's power that the imperial customsmen will not find your cargo short." The men did so, and when they arrived at their destination, they turned over to the imperial granaries the same quantity of grain that had been measured out at Alexandria. They spread news of the miracle and glorified God in his saint. Meanwhile the grain they had relinquished was distributed by Nicholas to each according to his needs, and so miraculously that not only did it suffice to feed the whole region for two years but supplied enough for the sowing.

In the past this region had worshiped idols; and even in Saint Nicholas's time there were rustics who practiced pagan rites under a tree dedicated to the wicked goddess Diana. To put a stop to this idolatry the saint ordered the tree cut down. This infuriated the ancient enemy, who concocted an unnatural oil that had the property of burning on water or on stone. Then, assuming the form of a nun, he came alongside a ship carrying people on their way to visit the saint and called to them: "I wanted so much to come with you to the holy man of God, but I cannot. May I ask you to offer this oil at his church and to paint the walls with it in memory of me." And forthwith he vanished. Then they saw another craft nearing them with honest people aboard, including one person who bore a striking likeness to Saint Nicholas, and this one asked them: "What did that woman say to you and what did she bring to you?" The people gave a full account of what had taken place. "That was the shameless Diana herself," he replied, "and if you want proof of it, throw that oil out over the water." They did so, and a huge fire flared up on the sea and, contrary to nature, burned for hours. When the travelers finally came to the servant of God, they said: "Truly you are the one who appeared to us at sea and delivered us from the wiles of the devil."

About that time there was a tribe that had risen in rebellion against the Roman Empire, and the emperor sent three princes, Nepotian, Ursus, and Apilion, to put them down. The three were forced by adverse winds to put in at an Adriatic port, and Nicholas, anxious to have them restrain their men from robbing his people on market days – something that happened regularly – invited them to his house. Meanwhile, during the saint's absence, the Roman consul, corrupted by a bribe, had ordered three innocent soldiers to be beheaded. As soon as the holy man heard of this, he asked his guests to accompany him, and they hurried to the spot where the execution was to take place. There he found the condemned men already on their knees, their faces veiled, and the executioner brandishing his sword over their heads. Nicholas, afire with zeal, threw himself upon the headsman, snatched his sword from his hand, unbound the innocent men, and led them away safe and sound.

The saint then hastened to the consul's headquarters and forced the door, which was locked. The consul came hurriedly to greet him, but Nicholas spurned him and said: "You enemy of God, you perverter of the law, how dare you look us in the eye with so great a crime on your conscience?" And he heaped reproaches upon him, but the princes pleaded for him, and the saint, seeing the man repentant, forgave him kindly. Thereupon the imperial emissaries, having received the bishop's blessing, continued their journey and put down the rebels without bloodshed; and when they returned to the emperor, he gave them a splendid reception.

Some other courtiers, however, envying their good fortune, bribed the imperial prefect to go to the emperor and accuse the princes of lese majesty. The emperor was beside himself with anger at the charge, and ordered the accused to be thrown into jail immediately and to be put to death without trial that very night. When the three heard this from their jailer, they tore their garments and wept bitterly. Then one of them, Nepotian, recalled that the blessed Nicholas had lately, in their presence, saved three innocent men from death, and exhorted his companions to invoke the holy man's aid. The result of their prayer was that Saint Nicholas appeared that night to Emperor Constantine and said: "Why have you had these princes arrested unjustly and condemned them to death when they are innocent? Hurry, get up and order them to be set free at once! Otherwise I shall pray God to stir up a war in which you will go down to defeat and be fed to the beasts." "Who are you," the emperor asked, "to come into my palace at night and talk to me this way?" Nicholas answered: "I am Nicholas, bishop of the city of Myra." The saint also appeared that night to the prefect, whom he terrified by saying: "Mindless and senseless man, why did you agree to the killing of innocent men? Go at once and see that they are set free. If you don't, your body will be devoured by worms and your house swiftly destroyed." The prefect retorted: "Who are you, to face us with such threats?" "Know," the holy man replied, "that I am Nicholas, bishop of the city of Myra."

The emperor and the prefect rose from sleep, told each other their dreams, and lost no time summoning the three princes. "Are you sorcerers," the emperor demanded, "to delude us with such visions?" They replied that they were not sorcerers, and that they had done nothing to deserve the sentence of death. Then said the emperor: "Do you know a man named Nicholas?" At the mention of the name they raised their hands to heaven and prayed God to save them, by the merits of Saint Nicholas, from the peril in which they found themselves. And when the emperor had heard from them about the life and miracles of the saint, he said: "Go, and thank God, who has saved you at the prayer of this Nicholas. But also bring gifts to Nicholas in my name and ask him not to threaten us anymore, but to pray the Lord for me and my reign."

Some days later the princes went to visit the servant of God. They threw themselves at his feet saying: "Truly you are a servant of God, truly you love and worship Christ." Then they told him everything that had happened; and he, raising his hands to heaven, offered heartfelt praise to God and sent the princes home after instructing them thoroughly in the truths of the faith.

When the Lord wished to call Nicholas to himself, the saint prayed that he would send his angels. And when he saw them coming, he bowed his head and recited the Psalm *In te Domine speravi* [Ps. 30]; and coming to the words *In manus tuas Domine commendo spiritum meum*, which mean "Into your hands, O Lord, I commend my spirit," he breathed forth his soul to the sound of heavenly music. This was in the year 343. He was buried in a marble tomb, and a fountain of oil began to flow from his head and a fountain of water from his feet. Even today a holy oil issues from his members and brings health to many.

One day this oil stopped flowing. This happened when the successor of Saint Nicholas, a worthy man, was driven from his see by jealous rivals. As soon as the bishop was restored, however, the oil flowed again. Long afterward, the Turks razed the city of Myra. Forty-seven soldiers from the town of Bari happened to be passing through, and four monks opened the tomb of Saint Nicholas to them: they removed his bones, which were immersed in oil, and carried them to Bari, in the year of the Lord 1087.

A man had borrowed some money from a Jew, giving him his oath on the altar of Saint Nicholas that he would repay it as soon as possible. As he was slow in paying, the Jew demanded his money, but the man declared that he had repaid it. He was summoned before the judge, who ordered him to swear that he had paid his debt. However, the man had put the money in a hollow staff, and before giving his oath he asked the Jew to hold the staff for him. He then swore that he had returned the money and more besides, and took back his staff; the Jew handed it over all unaware of the ruse. On his way home the dishonest fellow fell asleep by the roadside, and a coach, coming along at high speed, ran over him and killed him, also breaking open the staff and spilling the money. Being informed of this, the Jew hurried to the spot and saw through the trick; but, though the bystanders urged him to pick up his money, he refused unless the dead man were restored to life by the merits of Saint Nicholas, in which case he himself would become a Christian and accept baptism. At once the dead man was revived, and the Jew was baptized in the name of Jesus Christ.

Another Jew, seeing the miraculous power of Saint Nicholas, ordered a statue of the saint and placed it in his house. Whenever he had to be away for a long time, he addressed the statue in these or similar words: "Nicholas, I leave you in charge of my goods, and if you do not watch over them as I demand, I shall avenge myself by beating you." Then, one time when he was absent, thieves broke in and carried off all they found, leaving only the statue. When the Jew came home and saw that he had been robbed, he said to the statue: "Sir Nicholas, did I not put you in my house to guard my goods? Why then did you not do so and keep the thieves away? Well, then, you will pay the penalty! I shall make up for my loss and cool my anger by smashing you to bits!" And he did indeed beat the statue. But then a wondrous thing happened! The saint appeared to the robbers as they were dividing their spoils and said to them: "See how I have been beaten on your account! My body is still black and blue! Quick! Go and give back what you have taken, or the anger of God will fall upon you, your crime will become common knowledge, and you will every one of you be hanged." "And who are you," the thieves answered, "to talk this way to us?" "I am Nicholas, the servant of Jesus Christ," he replied, "and the Jew whom you robbed has beaten me in revenge!" Terrified, they ran to the Jew's house, told him of their vision, learned from him what he had done to the statue, restored all his property, and returned the to path of righteousness. The Jew, for his part, embraced the faith of the Savior.

A certain man, for love of his son who was learning his letters at school, annually celebrated the feast of Saint Nicholas in solemn fashion. On one particular occasion the boy's father laid on a sumptuous feast, to which he invited many clerks. During the meal the devil, dressed as a pilgrim, knocked at the door and asked for alms. The father ordered his son to take alms to the pilgrim, and the youth, not finding him at the door, pursued him to a crossroad, where the demon waylaid and strangled him. Hearing this, the father moaned with grief, carried the body back to the house and laid it on a bed, and cried: "O dearest son, how could this have happened to you? And, Saint Nicholas, is this my reward for the honor I have paid you all this time?" And while he was saying these things, the lad opened his eyes as if he were just waking up, and rose from the bed.

A nobleman had asked Saint Nicholas to pray the Lord to grant him a son, and promised that he would go with his son to the saint's tomb and would offer him a gold cup. His prayer was answered and he ordered the cup to be made, but he was so pleased with it that he kept it for himself and ordered another of like value. Then he took ship with the boy, to travel to the saint's tomb. On the way the father told his son to fetch him some water in the first cup. The boy tried to fill the cup with water, but fell into the sea and disappeared. Though stricken with grief, the father pursued his journey in order to fulfill his vow. He came to the church of Saint Nicholas and placed the second cup on the altar, whereupon an unseen hand thrust him back with the cup and threw him to the ground. He picked himself up, returned to the altar, and again was thrown down. And then, to the astonishment of all, the boy arrived whole and unharmed, carrying the first cup in his hands. He told how, the minute he had fallen into the water, Saint Nicholas had plucked him out and kept him hale and hearty. At this the father rejoiced and offered both cups to the blessed Nicholas.

A rich man had obtained a son through the intercession of Saint Nicholas and called him Adeodatus [given by God]. He also built a chapel in his house in honor of the saint and there solemnly celebrated his feast every year. The place was close to the territory of the Agarenes, and it happened that Adeodatus was captured by the Agarenes and carried off to serve their king as a slave. The following year, while the father was devoutly celebrating the feast of Saint Nicholas, the boy, serving the king with a precious cup in his hands, thought of his capture, his parents' grief, and the joy that used to be theirs on the feast day, and began to sigh and weep. The king demanded the reason for his tears and said: "Your Nicholas can do as he likes, but you are going to stay right here." Suddenly a mighty wind blew up, demolished the king's palace, snatched up the boy and the cup, and carried him to the threshold of the chapel where the parents were celebrating, to the great joy of all. Other sources would have it, however, that the aforesaid youth was of Norman origin and was on his way to the Holy Land when he was captured by the sultan, who had him whipped on the feast of Saint Nicholas and threw him into prison. There the boy fell asleep and woke to find himself in the chapel his father had built.

What aspects of these lives would have popular appeal? What model of Christian living do they offer to lay people?

33. A PILGRIM'S GUIDE TO THE CHURCH OF THE HOLY SEPULCHER (c. 1350)

This excerpt describing the shrines in Jerusalem's Church of the Holy Sepulcher comes from an anonymous pilgrim's guidebook to the Holy Land written around the middle of the fourteenth century and based on an earlier travelogue by the Franciscan Filippo Brusserio of Savona. The emperor Constantine built the first church on the supposed site of Jesus' tomb in Jerusalem and dedicated it in 335. This Church of the Anastasis (the Greek word for resurrection) was destroyed by Persians in 614, rebuilt, destroyed by Muslims in 1009, and again rebuilt on a smaller scale in the mid-eleventh century. After the crusaders captured Jerusalem in 1099, they renovated and expanded the church in the Romanesque style, consecrating it in 1149. This large basilica now enclosed most of the traditional sites medieval Christians associated with the Passion: along its east end was the court where Jesus appeared before Pontius Pilate, the column where he was scourged, the place where he was crowned with thorns, and – at the extreme southeast – Golgotha or the hill of Calvary where he was crucified. At the basilica's west end was Christianity's holiest spot, the literal center of the world for Christians: a domed chapel called the aedicula *("little house") over the tomb where Jesus was buried and rose from the dead. By the time this anonymous pilgrim wrote his travelogue, Jerusalem had been under Muslim control since 1188 when Saladin reconquered it. Entrance to the Church of the Holy Sepulcher was by a door on its south wall, the keys to which were kept since 1246, when it was re-opened to Christian pilgrims, by two Muslim families (as they still are today). These guards admitted pilgrims to the church usually in the middle of one day and allowed them to stay overnight visiting its many shrines until they were evicted, usually the next morning. The guidebook also describes some of the rival Christian sects who controlled other shrines in and around Jerusalem. Western Christians had to be cautioned not to drop coins inadvertently in the alms-boxes of what were considered to be heretical Christian sects.*

Source: J.H. Bernard (trans.), *Guide-Book to Palestine*, Palestine Pilgrims' Text Society (London, 1894), v. 6, pp. 1-10. Latin.

First, when you have entered the church, you shall find a black marble stone upon which Joseph of Arimathea and Nicodemus washed the body of Christ, and sprinkled it with spices, when they took it down from the cross [John 19:38-41]. And there is [plenary] absolution from pain and guilt [i.e., an indulgence gained from visiting this site].

Thence you shall come to Mount Calvary, where Jesus was crucified, where the blood issuing from his side penetrated through that dense and hard rock, and left the color of blood there to this day. And there is [plenary] absolution from pain and guilt.

For the blood sank in under Mount Calvary, in that part which is called Golgotha, where was found the head of Adam the first man; even up to the mouth of the aforesaid head did it penetrate through the rock. There is absolution for seven years and seven Lenten seasons.

Thence you shall come to the glorious sepulcher of the Lord, which up to the time of the Emperor Aelius Hadrian was outside the [city] gate. This emperor enlarged the city so much that he enclosed the place of the Lord's sepulcher within the circuit of the [city] walls, in which place afterwards the Christians, for the reverence they had to the Lord's sepulcher, built the glorious church of the Lord's Resurrection within the city, with elaborate workmanship, of suitable shape, and round in form, with one window opened in the roof. This not undeservedly holds the chief place among the holy and memorable sites. In this place the precious body of the Lord was honorably buried with spices, and here he rested until the third day; but on the third day he rose again as he had said, "On the third day I shall rise again." And there is [plenary] absolution from pain and guilt.

Thence you shall come to the place [on the northwest wall] where our Lord rising from the dead appeared first to Mary Magdalene when she thought that he was the gardener, and said, "Sir, if thou have borne him hence, tell me where thou hast laid him," etc. [John 20:15]. In which place is a holy altar in honor of that appearance, which is before the door of the chapel of the Blessed Virgin. And there is [plenary] absolution from pain and guilt.

Thence you shall enter the chapel of blessed Mary, and there you shall find a portion, four feet long, of the pillar to which Jesus was bound, and where he was scourged; it is placed as it were in the partition wall on the right-hand side as you go into the chapel. And there is [plenary] absolution from pain and guilt.

Also in the same chapel is the place in front of the altar where a certain dead man was revived by virtue of the holy cross immediately after its glorious discovery in the presence of Helena, the mother of the Emperor Constantine. And there is absolution for seven years and seven Lenten seasons.

There is also the place near the altar where the holy cross stood for a long time, and was most devoutly adored by faithful Christians. And there is absolution for seven years and seven Lenten seasons.

Thence you shall come to the place where Christ was for us imprisoned, bound, and beaten; there is now a small chapel there. And there is [plenary] absolution from pain and guilt.

Thence when you have gone out of the door of that chapel in front of a certain altar, you shall find a certain stone to which Jesus was chained while his cross was being erected. And there is absolution for seven years and seven Lenten seasons.

Thence you shall go to the place where soldiers cast lots for the garments of Christ, as it is written, "And for my vesture did they cast lots." And there is absolution for seven years and seven Lenten seasons.

Thence you shall go to a place where you descend to a certain chapel built at a depth of twenty-eight steps; there are buried the bodies of Mary the mother of James, and Mary Salome, under a certain altar. And there is absolution for seven years and seven Lenten seasons.

Near the altar on the south side is a stone chair on which St. Helena sat when she caused search to be made for the holy cross of the Lord. And there is absolution for seven years and seven Lenten seasons.

Also there is a certain window in the wall at the north side, through which it is said are heard the shrieks of the souls in purgatory.

Also in the same chapel are four stone pillars, which, it is said, sweat water night and day on account of Christ's passion.

Thence you shall descend twelve steps to another yet lower chapel [built off from the church at its southeast], in which was found in a very deep place the holy cross. The place is still visible where the cross of the Lord lay. And there is [plenary] absolution from pain and guilt.

Thence you shall go up to the first gate by which you entered, and on the left side you shall find a marble pillar under a certain altar, near which it is said that Jesus was crowned with the crown of thorns before he was placed upon the cross. And there is an indulgence for seven years and seven Lenten seasons.

Thence you come to Golgotha, which is called The Pavement, where Pilate sat before the tribunal when he led Jesus outside the city. "It was the Passover about the sixth hour," according to John [19:14]. Golgotha is a place under Mount Calvary, as it were concave; and there the blood is visible as above related.

Thence you come to the doors, and in the midst of the choir is the place called the Center of the World, where our Lord Jesus Christ laid his finger, saying, "This is the center of the world." And there is an indulgence for seven years and seven Lenten seasons. It should also be known that at the great altar is an indulgence for seven years and seven Lenten seasons, and at all the altars constructed within the church.

Thence you come to a pillar near the chamber of the holy sepulcher, above which is painted the image of St. Pantaleon, at which it is said that the following miracle once took place. A certain Saracen entered the Church of the Holy Sepulcher, and looking round saw the aforesaid image painted above the pillar. Then he tore out the eyes of the image, and straightway his own eyes fell out on the ground.

Thence you come to the gate by which blessed [hermit] Mary of Egypt was not able to enter, although the other Christians did, until she promised that she would do penance [for her prostitution]; where she heard a voice, "If thou crossest the Jordan, thou shalt be whole." And that gate is placed on the north side of the holy sepulcher in a secret place, and there is the chapel of the aforesaid St. Mary of Egypt. And there is an indulgence for seven years and seven Lenten seasons.

Thence you shall go out of the Church of the Holy Sepulcher, and on the left hand you shall find a little chapel of the Blessed Virgin Mary, under Mount Calvary, where she stood gazing upon her Son hanging on the cross. And there the Nubians [i.e., Nubian Christians] minister. And there is an indulgence for seven years and seven Lenten seasons.

Thence you shall come to the chapel of St. John the Evangelist, joined on to the chapel of blessed Mary, where our Savior commended the Virgin Mother to him, who was a virgin [John 19:26-27]. And there the Jacobites [i.e., Syrian Christians] minister. And there is an indulgence for seven years and seven Lenten seasons.

Thence you come to a chapel hard by, built in honor of St. John the Baptist. Indulgence for seven years and seven Lenten seasons.

Then you shall have opposite you a chapel built in honor of St. Mary

Magdalene, where along with the other women she wept and bewailed the Lord as he hung on the cross. And there the cinctured Christians [i.e., Georgian Christians] minister. And there is an indulgence for seven years and seven Lenten seasons.

Thence you come to a rock in front of the gates of the church, upon which our Lord rested when he came bearing his cross to Mount Calvary. And there is an indulgence for seven years and seven Lenten seasons.

All the aforesaid most holy places are within or hard by the sacred and holy church of the Passion and Sepulcher of the Lord.

What specific sites most attract this pilgrim? Why? Do the sites he describes lend insight into the specifics of his own devotional life? What level of enthusiasm does he convey about Jerusalem in this travelogue?

34. MARGERY KEMPE VISITS JERUSALEM (1414)

The well-born daughter of the mayor of King's Lynn in England, the mother of fourteen children, and a mystic prone to vividly intimate visions of Jesus and Mary accompanied by hysterical sobbing, Margery Kempe (c. 1373–c. 1440) was one of the most eccentric religious figures of the later Middle Ages. She dictated her remarkable autobiography, the first such work in English, to the priest who served as her spiritual advisor. (Throughout the book, he refers to her as "this creature," probably to emphasize her humility.) Chaucerian in her enthusiasm for pilgrimage, she traveled to Assisi, Rome, Santiago Compostela, several shrines in Germany (including Aachen and Wilsnak), the major shrines of England (such as Canterbury and Walsingham), and, of course, the Holy Land. On that trip, her fellow pilgrims quickly tired of her overcharged displays of piety – she was constantly talking about God and breaking into tears – and played mean tricks on her all the way across Europe to the Holy Land. After two months' travel to Venice, their point of embarkation to Jerusalem, they were so weary of her outbursts that they even refused to eat with her. This excerpt from her autobiography begins at that point and gives a good picture of some of the attractions available to pious sightseers in the Holy Land and the responses they could evoke.

Source: modernized by J. Shinners from *The Book of Margery Kempe*, Sanford Brown Meech and Hope Emily Allen (eds.), Early English Text Society 212 (Oxford, 1940), pp. 66–75. Middle English.

[Chapter 28] Also this company [of pilgrims], which had forbidden the aforesaid creature to eat at the same table with them, hired a ship for them to sail in [to Jerusalem]. They bought containers for their wine and ordered bedding for themselves but nothing for her. Seeing their unkindness, she went to the same man they did and purchased bedding as they had done. She went to where they were and showed them what she had done, proposing that she sail with them in the ship they had hired. Then, while this creature was in contemplation, our Lord warned her mentally that she should not sail in that ship; he assigned her another ship, a galley, to sail in. She told this to some of the company and they told it to the rest of the band, who then dared not sail in the ship they had hired. So they sold the vessels they had bought for their wine and wanted to travel in the galley where she was. Though it was against her will, she departed accompanied by them, for they dared not do otherwise.

When it was time to make her bed, they had locked up her bed linens and a priest in their company took a sheet from the creature, saying it was his. She took God as her witness that it was her sheet. Then the priest swore a great oath by the book in his hand that she was as false as she could be, and scorned her, and thoroughly rebuked her. So she suffered very much tribulation until she came to Jerusalem. Before she arrived there, she said to them that she supposed they were annoyed with her: "I pray you, sirs, be in charity with me, for I am in charity with you, and forgive me that I have annoyed you along the way. And if any of you has trespassed against me in any way, may God forgive you as I do." And so they went forth into the Holy Land until they could see Jerusalem [in the summer of 1414].

And when, riding on an ass, this creature saw Jerusalem, she thanked God with all her heart, praying to him for his mercy that, as he had brought her to see this earthly Jerusalem, he would grant her the grace to see the blissful city of Jerusalem above, the City of Heaven. Our Lord Jesus Christ, answering her thought, granted her desire. Then, out of the joy she had and the sweetness she felt from her conversation with our Lord, she was on the point of falling off her ass, for she could not bear the sweetness and the grace God wrought in her soul. Then two German pilgrims, one of them a priest, went up to her and kept her from falling off. The priest put spices in her mouth to comfort her, thinking that she was sick. And so they helped her on the way to Jerusalem.

When she arrived there she said, "Sirs, I ask you not to be displeased if I weep terribly in this holy place where our Lord Jesus Christ lived and died." Then they went to the Temple [the Church of Holy Sepulcher] in Jerusalem and were let in late in the day at evensong and stayed there until the next day at evensong. Then the [custodian Franciscan] friars lifted up a cross and led the pilgrims around from one place to another where our Lord had suffered his pains and his passion, all the men and women carrying candles in their hands. As they went about, the friars always told them what our Lord had suffered in each place. The aforesaid creature wept and sobbed copiously as though she was seeing our Lord with her own eyes suffering his passion right there. Through contemplation, in her soul she truly saw him, which caused her to suffer with him.

When they came to Mount Calvary, she fell down unable to stand or kneel, but she wallowed and writhed with her body, spreading her arms wide and crying with a loud voice as though her heart would burst asunder – for in the city of her soul she saw truly and freshly how our Lord was crucified. Before her face she heard and saw with her spiritual vision the mourning of Our Lady, Saint John, Mary Magdalene, and many others who loved our Lord. She had such great compassion and such great pain to see our Lord's pain that she could not keep herself from crying and howling even if it killed her.

This was the first time that she ever cried during contemplation, and this kind of crying lasted many years afterwards no matter what anyone might do. Thus, she suffered much scorn and reproof. Her crying was so loud and so awful that it astonished people unless they had heard it before or else knew its cause. She had [these crying spells] so often that they left her quite weak physically, especially if she heard [stories] of our Lord's Passion. Sometimes, when she saw the crucifix, or if she saw a wounded man or beast, or if a man beat a child in front of her or hit a horse or other animal with a whip – whether in the field or in town, alone or among people – when she saw or heard it, she thought she saw our Lord being beaten or wounded like the man or the animal. When she first had her crying spells in Jerusalem she had them often, and in Rome too. After she came home to England, when she first arrived they seldom happened – once a month as it were; then, once a week; later, daily; and once she had fourteen in one day, and another day she had seven. And so God would visit her, sometimes in the church, sometimes in the street, sometimes in her room, sometimes in the field God would send them. For she never knew the time or hour when they would come....

She had such intense contemplation in her mind's eye [on Mount Calvary], it was as if Christ were hanging before her eyes in his manhood. When, through the dispensation of the high mercy of our sovereign Savior Christ Jesus, it was granted this creature to behold so realistically his precious, tender body altogether rent and torn with scourges, more full of wounds than ever was a dovecote full of holes, hanging upon the cross with the crown of thorns upon his head, his blessed hands, his tender feet nailed to the hard tree, the rivers of blood flowing copiously out of every member, the grisly and grievous wound in his precious side shedding out blood and water for her love and salvation, then she fell down and cried with loud voice, wondrously turning and twisting her body on every side, spreading her arms wide as if she would have died, and could not keep from crying – these physical movements done for the fire of love that burned so fervently in her soul with pure pity and compassion.

It is no marvel if this creature cried and showed an astonishing demeanor and expression when we may see each day men and women – some through loss of their worldly goods, some for affection for their kinfolk or for worldly friendships, through too much study or earthly affection, and most of all through inordinate love and physical affection – if their friends are parted from them, they will cry and howl and wring their hands as if they had lost their wits and minds, yet they know well enough that they displease God. And if someone counsels them to cease and desist their weeping or crying, they will say that they cannot: they loved their friend so much, and he was so gentle and kind to them that they cannot forget him. How much more would they weep, cry, and howl if their most beloved friends were taken with violence before their eyes, and with all kinds of reproof brought before a judge, wrongfully condemned to death – namely, so vicious a death as our merciful Lord suffered for our sake? How would they endure it? No doubt they would both cry and howl and avenge him if they could, or else men would say they were no friends. Alas, alas, how sad that the death of a creature which has often sinned and trespassed against its Maker should be so disproportionately mourned and grieved over. It is an offense to God and a hindrance to the souls on either side [of this and the next world]. The piteous death of our Savior, by which we are all restored to life, is not kept in the mind of us unworthy and unkind wretches, nor will we support our Lord's own confidants whom he has endowed with love. Instead, we detract them and hinder them as much as we can.

[Chapter 29] When this creature with her companions came to the grave where our Lord was buried, as soon as she entered that holy place she fell down with her candle in her hand as though she would die from grief. Afterwards she got up again with great weeping and sobbing, as though she had seen our Lord buried right before her. Then she thought she saw Our Lady in her soul – how she mourned and wept over her son's death – and Our Lady's sorrow became *her* sorrow.

So, overall, wherever the friars led them in that holy place, she always wept and sobbed wondrously, especially when she came to where our Lord was nailed to the cross. There she cried and wept without measure so that she could not restrain herself. Also, when they came to the marble stone on which our Lord was laid when he was taken down from the cross, she wept there with great compassion, mindful of our Lord's Passion. Afterwards, she received communion on Mount Calvary, and then she wept, she sobbed, she cried so loudly that it was a wonder to hear it. She was so full of holy thoughts, meditations, and holy contemplations on the Passion of our Lord Jesus Christ and the holy words that our Lord Jesus Christ spoke to her soul that she could never afterwards express them, so exalted and holy were they. Our Lord showed this creature much grace during the three weeks she was in Jerusalem.

Another day, early in the morning, they went to the great hills [around Jerusalem], and the guides described where our Lord bore the cross on his back, and where his mother met with him and how she swooned, how she fell down and he fell down too. So they went around all morning before noon until they came to Mount Zion. All the while this creature wept abundantly everywhere she went out of compassion for our Lord's Passion.

At Mount Zion is the place where our Lord washed his disciples' feet a little before he gave his Commandment to his disciples [John 13:5, 34]. Therefore, this creature had a great desire to receive communion in that holy place where our merciful Lord Jesus Christ first sacrificed his precious body in the form of bread and gave it to his disciples. And she did, with great devotion, with copious tears, and with noisy sobbing, for in this place plenary remission [of sins] is granted, as it is in four other places in the Temple. One is Mount Calvary; another, the grave where our Lord was buried; the third is the marble stone on which his precious body was laid when it was taken off the cross; the fourth is where the holy cross was buried – and in many other places in Jerusalem.

When this creature went inside the place where the apostles received the Holy Ghost [Acts 2], our Lord gave her great devotion. Afterwards she went to the place where our Lord was buried. As she kneeled on her knees while hearing two masses, our Lord Jesus Christ said to her: "You do not come here, daughter, out of need but for merit and reward; for your sins were forgiven you before you came here, and therefore you come here to increase your reward and your merit. I am well pleased with you, daughter, for you stand in obedience to Holy Church and you obey your confessor and follow his counsel, which, through the authority of Holy Church, has cleansed you of your sins and dispensed you from going to Rome or to Saint James [at Compostela] unless you yourself wish it. Nevertheless, I command you in the name of Jesus, daughter, to go visit these holy places and do as I ask you, for I am above Holy Church and I shall go with you and keep you well."

Then Our Lady spoke to her soul in this manner, saying: "Daughter, you are well blessed, for my son Jesus shall pour so much grace into you that the whole world shall be in wonder of you. Do not be ashamed, my dear, worthy daughter, to receive the gifts that my son will give you, for I tell you truthfully that they will be great gifts that he will give you. Therefore, dear, worthy daughter, do not be ashamed of him who is your God, your Lord, and your love any more than I was when I saw him hanging on the cross, my sweet son Jesus, to cry and weep for the pain of my son Jesus Christ. Nor was Mary Magdalene ashamed to cry and weep for my son's love. Therefore, daughter, if you partake in our joy you must partake in our sorrow." This creature heard these sweet words and conversations at Our Lady's grave, and much more than she could ever recount.

Afterwards she rode on an ass to Bethlehem, and when she came to the church and to the crib where our Lord was born, she had much devotion and many words and conversations in her soul, and lofty spiritual comfort with much weeping and sobbing so that her companions would not let her eat with them and she ate her meal alone by herself. But then the Gray Friars [Franciscans] who led her from place to place took her in and had her sit with them at dinner so that she would not eat alone. One of the friars asked one of her companions if she was the Englishwoman who, they had heard it said, spoke with God. When she found out about this, she knew well that what our Lord had said to her before she left England was true: "Daughter, I shall make all the world wonder at you, and many men and many women shall speak of me out of love of you and honor (*worshepyn*) me in you."

[Chapter 30] Another time this creature's companions wanted to go to the River Jordan and would not let her go with them. Then this creature prayed to our Lord Jesus Christ that she could go with them, and he ordered that she go with them whether they wanted her to or not. And then she set out by the grace of God and did not ask their permission. When she came to the River Jordan, the weather was so hot that she thought she would burn her feet due to the heat she felt. Later she went with her companions to Mount "Quarentine," where our Lord fasted for forty days. There she asked her companions to help her up the mount, but they said no, for they could barely help themselves. Then she was very sad since she couldn't go up the hill. Soon a Saracen, a handsome man, happened to come by, and she put a groat [a silver coin worth four pennies] in his hands, making a sign to him to help her up the mount. The Saracen quickly took her under his arm and led her up onto the high mountain where our Lord fasted for forty days. Then she was very thirsty but got no comfort from her companions. But God, through his infinite goodness, moved the Gray Friars to compassion and they comforted her when her countrymen would not acknowledge her....

Later, when this creature came down the mount, as God willed, she went to the place where Saint John the Baptist was born. Afterwards she went to Bethany where Mary and Martha lived and to the grave where Lazarus was buried and raised to life. She also went to the chapel where our blessed Lord appeared to his blessed mother before anyone else on Easter Day at morning. She stood in the same place where Mary Magdalene stood when Christ said to her, "Mary, why do you weep?" [John 20:15]. She was in many more places than are written here because she was in Jerusalem and the country thereabout for three weeks; and she had great devotion for as long as she was in that country.

The friars of the Temple gave her great cheer and gave her many great relics, desiring her to stay among them longer, if she wished, due to the faith they had in her. The Saracens, also, made much of her, and conveyed her and led her around the country wherever she wanted to go. She found all the people good and gracious to her, except her own countrymen.

After she left Jerusalem and went to Ramleh [thirty miles from Jerusalem], she wished she had turned back to Jerusalem because of the great spiritual comfort she felt when she was there and in order to acquire more pardon for herself. Then our Lord commanded her to go to Rome and then home to England. He said to her: "Daughter, as often as you say or think 'Worshiped be all the holy places in Jerusalem that Christ suffered bitter pain and passion in' you shall have the same pardon as if you were there physically, both for yourself and for all those that you wish to give it to."

Compare the tone between Margery's account of her pilgrimage and that of the anonymous pilgrim above (Doc. 33). Are Margery's emotional reactions at various sites in and around Jerusalem out of the ordinary? What sites have the deepest impact on her? Why? To the extent Margery is representative of trends in fifteenth-century piety, what would you say those trends were?

35. AN INVENTORY OF RELICS AT DURHAM CATHEDRAL (1383)

Every church had at least one saint's relic embedded in its altar stone; but larger churches, especially cathedrals, amassed collections of dozens, sometimes hundreds, of relics. Where a church boasted the relics of a particularly famous or powerful saint, pilgrims were sure to throng (though typically the spiritual and material fortunes of even famed shrines waxed and waned). The monastic cathedral at Durham housed the body of the tireless Northumbrian missionary and bishop St. Cuthbert (d. 687). Venerated in the Chapel of the Nine Altars built to display it along with the cathedral's other treasured relics, it became the focus of one of the major pilgrim shrines of England, though never as popular as Canterbury or Walsingham. The abundance and variety of relics at Durham suggest how much grander these two more famous shrines must have been, but even Durham's shrine attracted enough pilgrims to require stewards standing guard for crowd control. This excerpt from a late fourteenth-century inventory (with additions from the early 1400s) conveys a fairly vivid picture of a medieval shrine with dozens of reliquaries arrayed around the steps to the saint's tomb. Its mix of local saints (in this case figures from Anglo-Saxon Northumbria), early Christian saints, and biblical notables is typical of the kinds of relics found in larger churches throughout Europe. The excerpt from the account book of the shrine's monk custodian both indicates the kinds of pious offerings left by pilgrims seeking favors or offering thanks for ones granted, and suggests the wealth that could accumulate at popular shrines. By the later Middle Ages most relics had indulgences attached to them which increased their allure even more. Though the cult of relics may seem a quintessentially medieval preoccupation, it is worth remembering its enduring appeal. Martin Luther's staunch patron Elector Frederick the Wise of Saxony kept a treasure trove of relics in his castle at Wittenberg. Three years into the German Reformation, a 1520 inventory of his collection listed 19,013 relics – including a wisp of Jesus' beard and bread from the Last Supper – with a total of 1,902,202 years and 270 days of indulgences attached to them! Modern readers bothered by some of the obviously spurious objects in Durham's collection might consider the degree to which medieval piety was driven by a different standard of what was genuine.

Source: trans. J. Shinners from *Extracts from the Account Rolls of the Abbey of Durham*, ed. J.T. Fowler, Surtees Society v. 100 (Durham: Andrews & Co, 1898), v. II, pp. 425-35. Latin.

A.D. 1383. This book is an account of the relics at the shrine of St. Cuthbert, compiled by Dom Richard de Segbruck, then custodian of the shrine, to describe what kind of relics there are and on what step of the shrine they are kept.

To begin, on the first or highest step at the south there is a gilded silver statue of the Blessed Virgin Mary. Next, a gilded silver statue of St. Oswald [king of Northumbria, d. 642] with one of his ribs contained in the statue's breast. Next there is one black cross called the Black Rood of Scotland [which contained a piece of the True Cross]. Next, another crystal cross (in the custody of the sacrist). Next there is a gold cross with jewels and gilded silver feet. Next there is another cross called the cross of St. Margaret, Queen of Scots [1046-93]. Next, one gilded silver cup donated by the Countess of Kent, with the banner of St. Cuthbert. Next, one silver arm-shaped reliquary containing a bone of St. Lucy the virgin. Next, a silver statue of St. Cuthbert donated by the Lord Bishop William. Next, one cross with a stand donated by Thomas Langley, bishop of Durham [1406-37].

Next, on the step below the first there is one Gospel book decorated with gold and silver with an image of the Trinity on one side of it. Next, one gilded silver stag with a garment of St. John the Baptist enclosed in it. Next, another crystal cross of St. John the Baptist with an image of Christ crucified. Next, an indigo and grey box in a small green chest which sat on the coffin of St. Cuthbert inside his tomb for two hundred years or more.

Next, on the third step, in a small enameled chest, the cope of St. Cuthbert in which he laid in the earth for eleven years. Next, an ivory box with a garment of St. John the Baptist. Next, a book of St. Boisil [d. c. 661], St. Cuthbert's teacher. Next, a small ivory chest with a fringed garment of St. Cuthbert. Next, St. Cuthbert's ivory scepter. Next, two griffin's claws. Next, five handkerchiefs for carrying the relics.

Next, one [blank space] decorated with gold and silver with bones and other relics of the apostles. Next, one crystal vial containing blood of the blessed man St. Thomas, the martyr of Canterbury.

Next, one silver reliquary with a silver chain containing various relics of the blessed Mary Magdalene. Next, one crystal vial with the hair and veil of St. Mary Magdalene. Next, one crystal vial with the rib and scorched bones of St. Lawrence. Next, one purse of cloth-of-gold with a crystal lens and various unlabeled fragments of relics. Next, one white cameo head with a crucifix carved on the back. Next, a tooth of St. Margaret, Queen of Scots, and one eagle-stone and some hair of St. Mary Magdalene, and one piece of the rod of Moses, and one pair of beads of St. Thomas, Earl of Lancaster [1278-1322], contained in two purses of patterned white velvet.

Next, one crystal vial decorated with gilded silver containing a garment of St. John the Baptist and a piece of his salver, a piece from the head of the blessed John Chrysostom, and a piece from the rib of the martyr St. Margaret. Next, one silk purse with a coat of arms containing the garment, some of the hair-shirt, and fingernails of St. Malachy the bishop [d. 1148], and some dust from St. Amphibalus the martyr, and a bone of St. Petronilla the virgin. Next, a bone of St. Martin the virgin [sic] and martyr, and a piece of St. Edward the Confessor's cape, and a bone of St. Andrew, and a piece of cloth from St. Barbara the virgin, and from the hair of the abbot St. Bernard in a purse with a shield in various colors as above. Next, a small silver enameled chest with a skull bone of St. Benedict, and one tooth and an arm bone of St. Giles.

Next, one red purse with relics of St. Peter. Next, a bone of St. Caesarius [of Arles?], confessor. Next, one bone of St. Giles in a silver reliquary. Next, from the garment of and dust from St. Denis, and hair from St. Bartholomew, the hermit of Farne and monk of Durham [d. 1193], in a crystal vial. Next, in a framework housing, a piece of the cloth that St. Ebbe [d. 683] gave to St. Cuthbert on which he lay for 418 years and five months, and part of the chasuble in which he lay for eleven years.

Next, three griffin's [i.e., ostrich] eggs. Next, a red velvet purse embroidered with the Lamb of God. Next, two boxes with the hair and hair-shirt of the venerable Robert de Stanhope, and some bones of St. Columba the abbot [d. 597] with other relics. Next, one red box with the banner of St. Oswald, some bones of St. Patrick, relics of St. Julian the martyr, of Sebastian the martyr, of Eugenia the virgin, and some of St. Godric's [d. 1170] beard.

Next, one small gilded and jeweled silver cross containing a piece of the Lord's Cross. Next, a piece from the Lord's manger in a blue silk purse. Next, four saints' bones in a small silver cross. Next, a piece of St. Godric's beard. Next, a little wooden box with some of the wood with which St. Lawrence was beaten [sic, possibly "burned" is meant] and some tiny bones from the martyr St. Concordius, and pieces from St. Bernard the abbot's rib and from his hair, and a joint of St. Lawrence, partly burned by fire, in a crystal vial decorated with silver. Also bones from the holy martyrs Nereus and Achilleus and a bone of St. Felix the martyr, and one bone of St. Germanus the bishop, and a piece of the bishop St. Acca's chasuble, and one bone of St. Balbina in a silk purse with four pockets with white castles on it.

Next, a crystal pyx containing milk of the Blessed Virgin Mary. Next, a piece from the Blessed Virgin Mary's tomb and from her dress, and from the tomb and wimple of her mother Anne in a crystal vial with silver feet. Next, a black vial with the tooth of St. Stephen and pieces of his skull and bones. Next, in a purse with red piping, a stone from the Lord's sepulcher, a stone from the church of Bethlehem, a stone from the sepulcher on Mount Sinai, and from the rock on which St. Mary, Mother of God spilled her milk [while nursing Jesus], and some of the oil of St. Mary of Sardinia.

Next, a small ivory box decorated with gold and silver containing St. Cuthbert's glove donated by Dom Richard de Kirtly, monk of Durham. Next, a cruet of treacle donated by John de Kellawe. Next, a crystal vial with gilded copper feet containing the bones of St. James and a piece of St. James Zebedee's vestment. Next, a stone from the Lord's birthplace and one from his sepulcher, and relics of St. Helena [mother of Emperor Constantine] in a white purse.

Next, a piece from St. John the Evangelist's vestment in a crystal vial, and a piece from the rib of St. Edward the king and martyr [d. 979]. Next, a piece from St. Nicholas's jawbone, and from his hair shirt, garment, bone, and tomb, and a piece of bone of St. Exuperius in a multicolored silk purse. Next, a crystal vial with a small cross inside it. Next, a piece of St. John the Evangelist's vestment inside a tablet gilded with an eagle.

Next, an ivory statue of the Virgin Mary. Next, a piece of a bone of St. Sebastian, and of a bone of St. Fabian, and the tooth of St. Cecilia the virgin, and relics of the apostles Philip and Andrew, and a piece of St. Christina's garment in a white purse decorated with red tassels. Next, a crystal vial decorated with gilded silver containing manna from St. Mary's tomb and some bone of St. Christopher, the finger joint of St. Stephen, some of the bread that the Lord blessed, some of St. Peter's skull bone, some of St. Helena's and St. Lawrence's bones, and from the tunic of St. Gregory, and from the Lord's Cross, and a bone from St. Giles. Next, a small gilded silver reliquary with the finger bone of St. Firmin the martyr.

Next, a crystal vial with a vestment of St. John the Evangelist and a rib of St. Edward the king. Next, teeth and bones from the martyr St. Cyriac in a white samite purse. Next, one pyx embellished with crystal stones containing flesh and fat from St. Thomas [of Canterbury] the martyr, and some of the clothes in which he was buried.

Next, the hauberk of St. Oswald the king ... [*gap in the manuscript*] and from the cross that he erected in battle in one reliquary. Next, one black crystal pyx containing the sponge [dipped in gall and vinegar offered to Jesus on the cross] from Good Friday and some of the Lord's sepulcher, and a piece of the stone on which Jesus sat in Herod's palace. Next, some of the tree under which the three angels sat with Abraham [see Gen. 18]. Next, a marvelously big, white, carved pearl.

Next, a silver cross with wood from the Cross inside. Next, some of St. Barbara the virgin's skirt in an ivory pyx. Next, three of St. Aidan the bishop's teeth with some other relics in a red muslin purse. Next, some of St. Nicholas's jawbone, hair shirt, and vestment, and some of his oil, bones, and tomb in a small silver enameled box.

Next, one finger joint of St. Maurice the martyr, one tooth from St. Margaret the martyr, and a rib of St. Remigius the bishop [d. 533] on a square silver platter. Next, a rib from St. Maurice the martyr, and some of St. Bede [d. 735] the teacher's tunic, and some of St. Agatha the virgin's veil, and some bones from St. Blaise, St. Silvester, and the Holy Innocents in a crystal vial with gilded silver feet. Next, some bones from St. Brigid the virgin and from her girdle, and bones from St. Colmcille the abbot [i.e., Columba, d. 597], and bones of the Holy Innocents in a red muslin purse. Next, a silver cross with a gilded Christ.

Next, one crystal vial with garments of St. Hippolytus and St. Catherine. Next, in a crystal vial with gilded silver feet and an image of the cross etched and gilded on the back of it, some bones of St. Theobald, and a piece of St. Theobald's vestment.

Next, a swatch of cloth dipped in the blood of St. Theobald, the archbishop of York. Next, [*gap*] a small silver enameled box with pictures [*gap*]. Next, relics of the holy confessors [Popes] Gregory, Silvester, and Leo, and some cloth and hair from St. Boisil the priest in one small ivory chest.

Next, a piece from the rock on which Christ stood when he ascended into heaven, and pieces from his manger and crib, and from Mount Calvary, from the rock on which Christ was born, from the place where he was crucified, and from the Lord's manger, and from his tunic, and from rocks from across the Jordan, and from his handkerchief [i.e., Veronica's veil imprinted with Jesus' face], with other relics of our Lord Jesus Christ in a crystal vial with four feet trimmed with copper. Next, the same sort of relics in a small red purse with a large label. Next, St. Dunstan's ivory comb in a multicolored silk purse.

Next, pieces from St. Godric's beard and hauberk, and from the bones of Saints Paula and Eustochium, her daughter, in a gilded silver reliquary. Next, one gilded silver cross with a crystal between the cross and its stand and with other precious stones of various colors. Next, some of the wood from the Lord's Cross and from his sepulcher, and from the stone that lay at the Lord's head in the sepulcher, and some wood from the tree in the Garden of Paradise, and from Mount Calvary in a crystal pyx. Next, one thorn from the crown of our Lord Jesus Christ donated by Lord Thomas Hatfield, Bishop of Durham [1345-81], in a golden vial encased in a leather cover.

Next, one ivory pyx with unlabeled relics. Next, some of St. Oswin the king and martyr's flesh in a crystal vial with gilded feet. [*Added in another hand:*] Strike that. Whoever wrote this was a liar because St. Oswin rests uncorrupted....

Dom Thomas de Lythe took up his duties as feretrarius, *or custodian of the shrine, in 1398. The account below records the items that pilgrims left at the shrine over the course of his three-year term as custodian, items worth altogether £3,989 16s. Pilgrims also left money offerings of about £30 a year in a collection box near the shrine. To put these numbers in perspective, a Durham unskilled laborer in this period received around three pence (pennies) a day in wages. One pound (£) equaled 20 shillings (s.) or 240 pence (p.); a mark was worth 13s. 4p. The English gold coin called the "noble" equaled 6s. 8p.*

Account of the custodian of the shrine rendered by Dom Thomas de Lythe on the feast of St. Edmund the Archbishop [Nov. 16] A.D. 1401.

.... First, on the western gable of the shrine is attached that precious stone called "le Emeraud" [emerald], which the custodian had previously kept among the relics, estimated value: £3,000. Next, two good brooches donated by the reigning King Henry [IV], estimated value: [*blank space*]. Next, two good brooches donated by the Duke [of Norfolk, Thomas?] Mowbray, estimated value: [*blank space*]. Next, one good brooch donated by the Earl of Rutland, value: [*blank space*]. Next one good brooch donated by Lord Neville and another good brooch donated by his wife, the Countess Neville, estimated value: 20 marks. Next, one good brooch donated by Lord Henry Percy, estimated value: £10. Next, one good brooch donated by the Countess of Kent, estimated value: [blank space] marks. Next, one good brooch donated by the Earl of Salisbury, estimated value: 100s. Next, one brooch donated by Dom John of Charteron, monk, value: 20s. Next, one brooch donated by one of the squires of Bishop [of Durham] John Fordham, value: 40s. Next, five brooches and six gilded silver buttons bought by the said Thomas de Lythe, value: 40s. Next, one gold pair of beads with a gold pendant donated by the wife of John de Killingall, value: 100s. Next, two good gold rings with diamonds donated by the knight, Sir Ralph Ferrers, estimated value: 40s. Next, two old lockets with two rings donated by Richard Redworth, value: 20s. Next, one old pendant donated by some woman, value: 6s. 8p. Next, hanging there is a silver [model] boat which was gilded in the time of Thomas, value: 13s. 4p. Next, hanging there are various rings offered by anonymous pilgrims, value: 40s. Next, one small pendant purchased by Thomas from William Cawood, value: 6s. 8p. Next, one small gilded cross, value: 6s. 8p. Next, hanging there are five small gold rings with gemstones and silver chains which were previously in the keeping of the shrine's custodian, value: 5 marks. Next, one gold cross with various gemstones, value: 40s.

Sum of the estimated value of the offerings attached to the shrine's west gable during the term of office of Thomas de Lythe, custodian: £3,463 10s.

Next on the south side there is a gold statue of the Blessed Virgin with the coat of arms of the Bishop of Durham which the bishop acquired through the mediation of Thomas de Lythe in exchange for a precious jewel offered at the shrine of St. Cuthbert during the term of office of the said Thomas by the knight William Scrope [d. 1399] for a certain transgression he made against the liberty of Durham, estimated value: £500. Next, on the same side of the shrine, one leg bone of the Earl Warenne which was gilded during the term of office of the same Thomas, value: 13s. 4p. Next, attached there is one jewel shaped like a [surgical] lancet donated by the smithy William Prentice, value: 10s. Next, two pendants with two rings donated by two pilgrims, value: 13s. 4p. Next, one pendant donated by William Pencher, value: 6s. 8p. Next, one pendant donated by the sister of John Todd, value: 10s. Next, two pendants donated by two women pilgrims, value: 10s.

Sum of the estimated value of offerings attached to the shrine's south side during the term of office of Thomas de Lythe, custodian: £503 3s. 4p.

Next during the term of office of the aforesaid Thomas there were attached to the north side of the shrine on the left side one gold noble donated by the wife of Henry Hastiler. And one gold noble with a gold halfpenny donated by a certain citizen of Berwick. Next, one quarter of a gold noble donated by Lord Henry Percy [Earl of Northumberland, d. 1408]. Next on the same northern side two rings donated by the chaplain Thomas de Lomley, value: 10s. Next, one gilded silver tabernacle with a picture of the Blessed Virgin donated by the Lady of Ross, value: 5 marks. Next, one gilded silver statue donated by the Countess Douglas, value: 5 marks. Next, one scallop shell [the symbol of pilgrimage to St. James at Compostela] and one gilded silver boat donated by some pilgrim, value: 5s. Next, one gold halfpenny donated by the knight Robert Conyers. Next, one gold halfpenny donated by some pilgrim. Next, one pair of white beads with a silver locket donated by the wife of Henry Hastiler, value: 10s. Next, one pair of amber beads donated by an anonymous woman, value: 6s. 8p. Excluding these things, various other things were offered and attached to the shrine during the term of office of Dom Thomas, which do not come to memory at the moment. Moreover, the ironwork with lights around the shrine along with constructing and painting a room for the custodian, and the work on the pavement, doors, and other things around the shrine beyond the value of 20 marks, were done at the urging and the personal expense of the said Dom Thomas.

Sum of the estimated value of the offerings made and attached to the north side of the shrine during the term of office of Thomas de Lythe, custodian: £23 20p.

What does the range of items on display at Durham tell us about medieval religion? To what extent can this document be used to reconstruct the mind-set of medieval religion? What purpose do you think this inventory served for the monks of Durham? Do you think the monks believed all these relics were authentic? If so, what was their standard of proof?

36. THOMAS MORE'S DIALOGUE ON SAINTS AND THEIR SHRINES (1529)

Though he perched on the cusp of the English Reformation and was imbued with the ideals of the Northern Renaissance humanists, Thomas More's (1478-1535) basic religious instincts were still deeply embedded in the late medieval world. As chancellor of England, for instance, he was a tireless prosecutor of heretics; and the last works he wrote while imprisoned in the Tower of London before his execution – including his treatises on Christ's sadness and passion, several prayers, and his famous Dialogue on Comfort – *were essentially medieval in thought and tone. In his* Dialogue Concerning Heresies *(1529), undertaken at the request of the bishop of London to combat the rising tide of Lutheranism in England, More holds a fictional conversation with a young schoolmaster of protestant sympathies called "the Messenger," grappling with him over a range of issues at the heart of the Reformation. Justification by faith, the nature of the church, translating the Bible, and saints and their shrines are some of the major subjects covered in the four-book treatise, written in English to make it more accessible. Though late in date, it is an excellent summary of the salient features of medieval devotion to saints. In its critique of the abuses surrounding popular venera-tion of saints, it mirrors More's good friend Erasmus's lampooning colloquy called "A Pilgrimage for Religion's Sake." Yet despite the devotional excesses to which the cult of saints was prone, More effectively argued that the abuse of it did not mean it was itself evil.*

Source: modernized by J. Shinners from *A Dialogue Concerning Heresies* in *The Complete Works of St. Thomas More*, ed. T.N.C. Lawler, G. Marc'hadour, and R.C. Marius (New Haven, CT: Yale University Press, 1981), v. 6, pt. 1, pp. 226-34. English.

Book II, Chapter 10

The Messenger raises many objections against pilgrimages, relics, and the worshiping of saints because of many superstitious practices they use, unlawful petitions asked of them, and the harm growing therefrom.

"Sir," [the Messenger] said, "to my mind you have very nicely treated the matter that it is not in vain to pray to saints or to worship them and hold their relics in some reverence. But sir, all this misses the main abuse, for though saints may hear us and help us too, and are glad and willing to do so, and God is contented also that they and their relics and images are held in honor, yet neither he nor they can be content with the manner of the worship. First, because it takes away worship from him since we offer them the same worship in every detail that we do to God. And secondly, because it also takes away worship from them in that we offer their images the same worship that we offer them, mistaking their images for themselves. Thus, we not only make them but also their images the equals and matches of God, for which neither God, nor the good saint, nor the good man ought to be content and pleased."

"In faith," I said, "if this is so, you speak the very truth."

"What do we say then," he said, "about the harm that comes from going on pilgrimages, gadding about idly with no control, with reveling and rib-aldry, gluttony, wantonness, waste, and lechery? Don't you believe that God and his holy saints would rather that they sit still at home than to go seek them this way with such worshipful service?"

"Yes surely," I said.

"What do we say then," he said, "about what I haven't yet mentioned when we do them little worship as we set every saint to his duty and as-

Fig. 4.3. Pilgrims at a shrine

Three pilgrims seek cures at St. Edward the Confessor's shrine in Westminster abbey. Two have squeezed into the niches often cut into the sides of shrines to allow
pilgrims to get closer to the relics. On the floor are two "trindles" – thin wax tapers
measured to the length of the petitioners' bodies, rolled into a coil, and offered to
the saint in exchange for a miracle. A custodian monk rests before a book, perhaps
a record of miracles wrought at the tomb. A nineteenth-century copy of Matthew
Paris's thirteenth-century drawing from a French translation of Aelred of Rievaulx's
Life of St. Edward; reproduced in Daniel Rock's *Church of Our Fathers* (London: C.
Dolman, 1852), v. 3, pt. 1, p. 418 after University of Cambridge Library MS Ee. iii,
59, fol. 65r.

sign him the craft that pleases us? Saint Eligius [a former blacksmith] we
make a horse-doctor, and must let our horse run unshod and injure his hoof
rather than shoe him on his feast day, which in that respect we must more
religiously keep high and holy than Easter day. And because one smith is too
few at a forge, we set St. Hippolytus [martyred by horses] to help him [at
the bellows]. And on St. Stephen's day we must bleed all our horses with a
knife because St. Stephen [by legend a horse-groom] was killed with stones.
St. Apollonia [whose teeth were knocked out during her martyrdom] we
make a dentist and may speak to her of nothing but sore teeth. St. Sitha [a

housemaid] women appoint to find their keys. St. Roch we appoint to attend to the plague because he had a bubo [on his thigh]. And with him they join St. Sebastian because he was martyred with arrows [symbolic of plague]. Some [e.g., St. Lucy, whose eyes were torn out at her martyrdom] serve for the eyes only. And some [e.g., St. Agatha, whose breasts were cut off] for a sore breast. St. Germain serves only for children, yet he will not once look at them unless the mothers bring with them a white loaf and a pot of good ale [as an offering]. But he is wiser than St. Wilgefortis [reputed to rid wives of bad husbands], for she, the good soul, is served and content with oats, as they say. I cannot see why this should be so unless because she has to feed the horse for an evil husband to ride to the devil on. For that is the thing for which she is so sought – so much so that women have therefore changed her name, and instead of St. Wilgefortis, they call her St. Uncumber since they reckon that for a peck of oats she will not fail to unencumber them of their husbands.

"It would be long work to rehearse for you the various ways of many prating pilgrims, but I'll tell you one or two. [Giovanni] Pontano [1426-1503] in one of his dialogues speaks about how St. Martin is worshiped. I've forgotten the town, but the method I cannot forget, it is so strange. His image is borne in procession about all the streets on his feast day. If it is a fair day as he passes by, then they cast rose water and pleasant-scented things upon his image. But if it happens to rain, they pour out pisspots upon his head at every door and every window. Is this not a sweet service and a worshipful devotion? And this, as I say, Pontano describes and says where it happens.

"But what I shall now tell you I dare as boldly make you sure of as if I had seen it myself. At St. Walaric's [or Valery] here in Picardy there is a fair abbey where St. Walaric [d.c. 620] was a monk. About a furlong or two up in the woods there is a chapel in which the saint is especially sought [to cure] the [kidney] stone, not only [by people from] those parts but also from England.

"Now there was a young gentleman who had married a merchant's widow. Having a little luxury money, which he thought was burning out the bottom of his purse, in the first year of his wedding he took his wife with him and went overseas for no other purpose than to see Flanders and France and ride about for a summer in those countries. There was someone in his company who told him in passing many strange things about that pilgrimage spot. So he thought he would go somewhat out of his way either to see if it were true or to laugh at this man if he found it false, as he truly indeed thought he would. But when they came into the chapel, they found it all to be true. They found it even more foolish to behold than he had said. For just as you see wax legs or arms or other [body] parts hanging up at other pilgrimage shrines [offered in thanks for cures of those parts], in that chapel all the pilgrims' offerings hung about the walls, and they were all men's and women's private gear made out of wax. Besides these at the end of the altar there were two round rings of silver, one much larger than the other, through which every man put his privy member, not every man through both but some through the one, some through the other. For they were not of the same size, but one larger than the other. There was also a monk standing at the altar who blessed certain threads of Venetian gold. These he gave to the pilgrims, teaching them in what way they or their friends should use the threads against the stone: they should tie it about their gear and say I cannot tell you what prayers. After the monk had described the method, the gentleman had a servant who was a married man and a merry fellow. He thanked the monk for the thread and desired him to teach him how he should tie it about his wife's gear, which — unless the monk had some special skill in knotting — he thought would be cumbersome because her gear was somewhat short. I need not tell you that every man laughed then except the monk who gathered up his rings and threads in great anger and went his way.

"Wait a moment, I almost forgot one thing that I would not leave out for a fourpence. As this gentleman and his wife were kneeling in the chapel there came a good sober woman to him and showed him one special point used at that shrine, the surest [cure] against the stone, which she didn't know whether he had yet been told about. If it were done, she dared bet her life that he would never have the stone in his life. It was that he should tell her the length of his gear and she would make a candle of that measurement which should then be burned in the chapel while certain prayers were said there. Against the stone this was the very last resort. When he had heard her (and he was someone who feared the stone in earnest) he went and asked his wife's advice. But she, like a good, faithful, Christian woman, had no love for such superstitions. She could put up with the other things well enough, but once she heard about burning up the candle, she knit up her brows and blessed herself: 'Beware in God's virtue what you do,' she said, 'Burn it up? Marry, God forbid! It would waste up your gear on pain of my life. I pray you beware of such witchcraft.'

"Is this kind of service and worship acceptable and pleasing to God and his saints? For people worship saints in such a way that they make them equal to God, and they worship images in such a way that they mistake them for the saints themselves. Then again, on the other hand they honor them with such superstitious ways that the pagan gods were worshiped with none worse. Finally, the worst of all is that they pray to them for unlawful things, as thieves pray to the thief that hung on the right side of Christ to speed them along in their robbery. And they have even found him a name, calling him Dismas, I think, and his companion Gysmas to rhyme with it. Do you not think that the people's dealing in this business is likely to provoke God and his saints to be displeased that the devil should have license and liberty thus to work his wonders to the delusion of our superstitious idolatry? Should these things please and content our Lord so that he should show miracles in approval of that manner of worship which we can clearly see all reason, religion, and virtue reproves?"

Chapter 11

The author answers the objections proposed by the Messenger in the tenth chapter and some of those touched on by the Messenger at greater length in earlier parts.

"Your whole argument in effect," I said, "contains three points. One is that the people worship the saints and also their images with the same honor as they do God himself. Another is that they mistake the images for the saints themselves; these points seem to mean [they commit] idolatry. The third is the superstitious fashion of worship and their desire for unlawful things. And since the worship that the people give to the saints and their images is such, you conclude that this thing displeases God and all the saints, and that it may therefore well appear that their miracles are not the works of God but the delusions of the devil. The first point, which you have now twice touched on, is at once soon and shortly answered, for it is not true. For though men kneel to saints and images, and also cense them, it is not true that therefore they worship them in every point like God."

"What point do they lack?" he asked.

"Why, the chief one of all," I said. "This is that they worship God with the intention that he is God, which is the only thing that makes it *latria* [worship, derived from the Greek], not any gesture or physical observance. We would not lie upon the ground to Christ with the intention that he was the best man we could conceive, not thinking he was God. For if the lowly manner of physical observance were the thing that made it *latria*, then we would be greatly in peril of idolatry in the curtsy we give to princes, prelates, and popes to whom we kneel as low as to God Almighty. And we kiss the hands of some of them as some kiss ours before we ever presume to touch them; we even kiss the pope's foot. As for censing them, the poor priests in every choir stall are as well censed as the [eucharistic] Sacrament. So if *latria*, which is the special honor due to God, consisted in doing such things, then we are great idolaters not only in the worship we give to saints and their images but also to men one to another among ourselves. But though God is duly owed the most humble and lowly bodily reverence that we can possibly devise, physical worship is not *latria* unless we do it so that in our mind we consider and acknowledge him as God and with that consideration and intent worship him. I think that no Christian man does this either to an image or a saint, and so the peril of idolatry is avoided, which is the first point you spoke of.

"Now as to the second point, that people mistake the images for the saints themselves, I trust that there is no man so mad, or woman either, that they do not know living men from dead stones and tree from flesh and bone. And when they prefer – as you mentioned – Our Lady at one shrine to Our Lady at another, or one rood to another, or make their invocations and vows some to one saint, some to another, I think it is easy to see that they mean nothing else but that our Lord and Our Lady (or our Lord on behalf of Our Lady) perform more miracles at one shrine than at another. And in their pilgrimage some of them intend to visit one place, some of them another as their devotion leads them, and sometimes partly due to the shrine's proximity. But it is not because of the place itself but because our Lord likes to provoke men by manifest miracles to seek him, his Blessed Mother, or another of his holy saints in those places more especially than in some others.

"That they prefer one shrine to another itself shows that they do not take the images to be Our Lady herself. For if they did, how could they in any possible manner pay more attention to one than to the other? For they can pay no more attention to one Our Lady than to another Our Lady. Moreover, if they thought that the image at Walsingham were Our Lady herself, then they would have to think that Our Lady herself was the image. Then if they likewise thought that the image at Ipswich were Our Lady herself and (as they would have to think) that Our Lady herself was the image at Ipswich, then they would have to think that all those three things were one thing, and that any two of them were one thing. And thus they must by that reason suppose that the image at Ipswich was the selfsame image that is at Walsingham, which if you ask any of them whom you take for the simplest except for a born fool, I dare wager you she will tell you no. Besides this, take the simplest fool you can choose and she will tell you that Our Lady herself is in heaven. She will also call an image an image and she will tell you the difference between an image of a horse and a real horse. And so it is clear that whatever her words are for her pilgrimage, it is a common figure of speech to call Our Lady's image 'Our Lady' just as men say 'go to the King's Head for wine,' not meaning his head in fact, but the [tavern] sign; thus she means nothing else but that it is Our Lady's image, no matter what she calls it. And if you really wish to prove that she never mistakes Our Lady for the image nor the image for Our Lady (as she must mistake both if she mistakes one), talk with her about Our Lady and she will tell you that Our Lady was saluted by Gabriel, and that Our Lady fled into Egypt with Joseph. Yet in telling you this she will not say that Our Lady of Walsingham or Ipswich was saluted by Gabriel or fled into Egypt. Or if you ask her whether it was Our Lady of Ipswich or Walsingham that stood by the cross at Christ's passion, she will, I guarantee you, answer that it was neither of them. And if you demand of her further which Lady it was, she will not name an image but Our Lady who is in heaven. I have demonstrated this often, as you may when you wish, and you shall find it true except for someone so great a fool that God will give her grace to believe what she wishes. And surely in this respect I think to my mind that all those heretics who act as though they found such a great peril of idolatry among the people who mistake images, only devise that fear to have a cloak to cover their heresy whereby they bark against the saints themselves. When they are discovered, then they say they only mean the misbelief that women have in images.

"Now as to the third point about the superstitious manner of worship or unlawful petitions desired from saints, one example may serve both. What you say is to some extent true that women offer oats to St. Wilgefortis to have her disencumber them of their husbands; and yet not everything should be blamed that you seem to blame. For to pray to St. Apollonia to help our teeth is no witchcraft considering that she had her teeth pulled out for Christ's sake. Nor is there any superstition in other similar things. And perhaps since St. Eligius was a farrier it is no great fault to pray to him for help for our horse."

"Well then," he said, "since St. Crispin and St. Crispinian were shoemakers, it would likewise be good to pray to them to sit down and mend our shoes, and to pray to St. Dorothy for some flowers because she always bears a basketful."

"No," I said, "the two things are nothing alike. For the one thing has nothing pertinent to our need, the other we may do for ourselves or find someone who shall. But as for your [ailing] horse, it is a thing for which (as well as for our own bodies) a very good doctor may fail in his skill and is to many a man a greater loss than he can recover. And although God commanded that we should chiefly resort to heaven, and promised that if we do, all other things that we need shall be cast unto to us [Matt. 6:3], and although he willed that we should not live in anxiety and trouble of mind out of fear of any lack since our Father in heaven provides food for the very birds of the air by whom he sets nothing as much as he does by us, yet he willed that we should labor with our bodies having our hearts all the while in heaven. And he also willed that we should ask it of him without whose help our labor is useless. Therefore, "our daily bread" is one of the petitions of the Our Father, the prayer that he himself taught his disciples. And though he set little store by the horse, rather than see it perish he reckoned it no breech of the

Sabbath day to pull it out of the pit [see Matt. 12:11]. And therefore it seems to me that devotion has gone somewhat too far if smiths will not for any necessity put a shoe on a horse on St. Eligius's day and yet it is lawful enough to pray for the help of a poor man's horse. But as for your teeth, I suppose that if they ached enough you would yourself think it a worthy thing, and not too foolish, to ask St. Apollonia's help and God's too!"

"Yes, marry!" he said, "and the devil's too rather than fail as the Lombard did with his gout. When he had long called on God and Our Lady and all the holy company of heaven and still felt himself no better, he began at last to call as quickly on the devil for help. And when his wife and his friends, completely dismayed and astonished, rebuked him for calling on the devil (which he knew was wrong and if he helped him would be for no good), he cried out as loud as he could again 'hogni aiuto e bono' – 'anything that helps is good!' And so I suppose I would call on the devil and everyone else rather than abide in pain."

"No," I said, "no matter what you say I can't think you would put faith in the devil as that Lombard did. You would fare like another man who when the friar asked him in confession whether he meddled with any witchcraft or necromancy or had any faith in the devil, he answered 'Credere en le dyable my syr no, Io graund fatyge a credere in dio' – 'Believe in the devil? No, no sir, I have work enough myself to believe in God!' And so I would suppose that you were far from believing in the devil since you have so much work to believe in God himself that you are loath, I think, to meddle much with his saints."

When we had laughed awhile at our merry tales, I said: "In good faith, as I was about to tell you, what you said is to some extent true. For that superstitious manner of worship is evil and it is evil to endure it. And as for the story you told about St. Martin, if it is true it is inexcusable, but it has no bearing on our discussion, for it is not worshiping but contemning and dishonoring saints. Concerning the offering of bread and ale to St. Germain, I see nothing much amiss in it. Where you have seen it practiced I cannot tell. But I have myself seen it often and yet I don't remember that I ever saw a priest or a clerk benefit from it or once drink the ale: it is given to children or poor folk to pray for a sick child. And I would suppose it was no offence to offer up a whole ox in such fashion and distribute it among poor people. But now as for our merry matters of St. Walaric, because the place is in France, we shall leave it to the University of Paris to defend. And we will come home here to St. Paul's [cathedral] and give one example of both – that is, the superstitious manner and the unlawful petitions – if women offer oats there to St. Wilgefortis trusting that she shall disencumber them of their husbands. But priests cannot see until they find it there that the foolish women bring oats there, nor is it so often done nor is so much oats brought at any one time that the church may make much money from it beyond feeding the canons' horses."

"No," he said, "a whole year's offering of oats will not feed three geese and a gander together for a week."

"Well then," I said, "the priests don't support the practice out of any great avarice and they can't hear what the foolish women pray for. However, if they pray just to be disencumbered there seems to me no great harm or unlawfulness in that. For they may be disencumbered in more ways than one. They may be disencumbered if their husbands change their cumbersome conditions, or if they themselves perhaps change their cumbersome tongues which are maybe the cause of all their encumbrance. And finally if they can't be disencumbered except by death, it may be by their own death and so their husbands are safe enough."

"No, no," he said, "you'll find them not such fools I guarantee you. They make their contracts with their bitter prayers and, as surely as if they were written, will not give away their oats for nothing."

"Well," I said, "to all these matters there is one evident, easy answer – none of them touch the effect of our matter which consists in this: whether the things we speak of such as praying to saints, going on pilgrimage, and worshiping relics and images may be done for good, not whether they may be done for evil. For if they may be done for good, then although many may misuse them, that does not diminish the goodness of the thing itself. For if from the misuse of a good thing and for the evils that sometimes grow out of its abuse, we should utterly do away with the whole use of something, we should then have to make some marvelous changes in the world. In some countries it is a common custom to go hunting commonly on Good Friday in the morning. Will you break the evil custom or cast away Good Friday? There are cathedral churches into which people from the countryside come in procession on Whitsuntide, the women following the cross with many an unladylike song – such honest wives, who outside of the procession you could not pay to speak one such foul, ribald word, sing whole ribald songs for God's sake as loud as their throat can cry. Will you mend their lewd manner or put away Whitsuntide? You spoke of lewd practices at pilgrim shrines. Do you believe none occur on holy days? And why do you not then advise us to put them clean away, Sundays and all? Some grow drunk during Lent on wheat cakes and biscuits, and yet you would not, I trust, want Lent abolished. If we consider how commonly men abuse Christmas, we may think that they take it for a time of license and all manner of lewdness. Yet is Christmas to be cast away from Christian men, or are men to be admonished to amend their manners and behave more Christianly at Christmas? Let me turn to Christ's own coming and his giving us our faith and his holy Gospel and sacraments. Are there not ten men the worse therefore for every one the better? Are not all the pagans, all the Jews, all the Turks and the Saracens, all the heretics, all the evil-living people in Christendom the worse through their own fault for the coming of Christ? I think they are. And yet would any wise man wish that Christ had not come here? Nor would it be right for God to abandon that occasion of merit and reward which good folk deserve with his help by his coming because of the harm that wretches take from it by their own sloth and malice. Nor likewise would it be at all right that we should abolish and put away all worship of saints, and reverence of holy relics, and honor of saints' images (by which good devout folk do much merit) because some folk abuse them.

"Now concerning the evil petitions, though they that ask them are, I trust, not great in number, there are not yet so many people who ask evil petitions of saints as there are who ask the same also of God himself. For whatever they will ask of any good saint they will ask of God also. And commonly among the wild Irish and some in Wales too, so men say, when they go forth in robbing they bless themselves and pray God send them good fortune that they meet with a good purse and do harm but take none. Shall we therefore find a fault with every man's prayer because thieves pray for fortune in robbery? This, as I say, makes no sense even though there were a great number of people who abused a good thing. And whereas the worst thing that you specify in our discussion is that, as you say, 'the people' commit idolatry in that you say they mistake the images for the saints themselves or the rood for Christ himself – which as I said I think no one does (for some roods have no crucified body on them, and they don't believe that the cross which they see was ever at Jerusalem, or that it was the Holy Cross itself, much less do they think that the image hanging on it is the body of Christ himself) – and although some people think this, they are not, as you put it, 'the people.' For a few foolish dames are not the people.

Furthermore, if it were as you would have it seem, and indeed the whole people were involved, still a good thing should not be put away because bad folk misuse it.

How critical-minded is Thomas More about the popular devotion to saints? Does he actively encourage this devotion or just tolerate it? From a modern frame of mind, who has the better argument: More or the Messenger? What details of popular religious belief emerge from More's dialogue? Would you characterize these practices as "superstitious" or "pious"?

CHAPTER FIVE:
DEVILS, DEMONS, AND SPIRITS

The melting pot of medieval popular religious culture seethed with a brew of demons and spirits randomly mixed from mainstream Christianity, the vestiges of Europe's earlier religions, local folklore, and sometimes even dim memories of classical gods. Besides Lucifer and those rebellious angels who fell with him into hell (the devil proper and his host of minor demons and imps), the earth crawled with all manner of elemental spirits (like fairies, elves, goblins, gnomes, and the Green Man), half-human monsters (like werewolves, vampires, changelings, and the Wild Man of the woods), and ghosts, who were typically souls laboring to be released from purgatory. Encounters with these creatures ranged from vexing to lethal, so most people took pains to avoid or at least restrain them through Christian prayers and charms. Those who willfully conjured them up — witches, necromancers, and anyone else who flirted with black magic — risked their souls and, if discovered by authorities or careless in their spells, their lives.

37. THE ENGLISH PEASANT THURKILL'S VISION OF HELL (1206)

Though heavily embellished by the pen of its credulous monastic editor, this account of the English peasant Thurkill's vision of hell suggests in its broadest strokes how ordinary people absorbed details about the Christian concept of hell. Thurkill's guides here are St. Julian the Hospitaller (a well-known though legendary patron of inns and travelers) and St. Domninus (the patron of Borgo San Donnino – now Fidenza – a small town near Parma on one of the major pilgrim routes to Rome). Both saints were thus associated with journeys and pilgrims. In Thurkill's vision, St. James the Apostle calls him "my pilgrim", suggesting that he may have made a pilgrimage to James' famous shrine at Compostela in Spain. The vision is noteworthy both for its vivid application of contrapasso – *where the punishment fits the crime – a hundred years before Dante's masterful use of it in his* Inferno *and for its theatrical metaphors as demons force sinners to perform their sins. This translation is Roger of Wendover's abbreviated version of Thurkill's vision first recorded in the chronicle of Ralph, the abbot (1207-18) of the Cistercian abbey of Coggeshall just three miles from Thurkill's village of Stisted.*

Source: trans. J. Shinners from Roger of Wendover, *Chronica sive Flores Historiarum*, ed. Henry Coxe (London: English Historical Society, 1841), v. 3, pp. 190-209. Latin.

In this year [1206] there was a certain man in the diocese of London living in the village of Stisted [in Essex]. He was a simple man, raised for farm work, who offered hospitality insofar as his modest means allowed. After evensong on the eve of the feast of the apostles Simon and Jude [October 27] he was draining his field, which he had planted that day, to prevent flooding. Suddenly he looked up and saw in the distance a man coming toward him.

Fig. 5.1. The torments of hell (facing page)

The caption over the woman entwined by a snake in the upper left reads: "The worm of the unholy shall never die, and their fire shall not burn out for eternity." The cauldron in the center left is labeled "Jews," who are depicted wearing pointed hats, a Christian iconic stereotype; the one on the right is marked "Armed Knights." The figure escorted by a demon on the bottom left is captioned "Monk," and on the right sits "Lucifer or Satan." From the *Hortus deliciarum* (*The Garden of Delights*) of Herrad, abbess of Mont Sainte-Odile, Hohenbourg, composed between 1176 and 1196. The manuscript was destroyed when the Strasbourg Library was bombed during the Franco-Prussian War of 1870. This drawing is from Christian M. Engelhardt's 1818 facsimile edition as reproduced in Paul Lacroix, *Military and Religious Life in the Middle Ages and the Period of the Renaissance* (London: Chapman and Hall, 1874), p. 485. See Doc. 37.

When he saw him, he began saying the Lord's Prayer [as protection]. Drawing near, the man urged him to finish his prayer without stopping and he would speak to him when he was done. When he completed the prayer, they greeted each other. The man who had approached then asked him where in the area he could stay that night most comfortably. When the farmer praised the scrupulous hospitality of some of his neighbors, the questioner criticized the hospitality of some them by name. Then the farmer realized that the man knew some of his neighbors so he quickly asked him if he would see fit to stay with him. He replied, "Your wife has just graciously taken in two poor little women, but I will come to your house tonight in order to lead you to your lord, St. James, to whom you have just now devoutly prayed. I am St. Julian the Hospitaller, and I am sent to you to reveal by divine means certain secrets that are hidden from men still living in the flesh. Go quickly to your house and take care to prepare yourself for the journey." Having said this, the man who had been speaking to him disappeared right before his eyes.

Thus Thurkill – for this was the man's name – went straight home, washed his head and feet, and found the two little women lodging there just as the saint had told him. Then, sleeping apart from his wife, he went to sleep on a bed he had made up in a separate part of the house in order to remain chaste.

When the whole household had surrendered their limbs to sleep, St. Julian appeared and, shaking the man from slumber, said, "Here I am just as I promised. It is time for us to go. Let your body rest on the bed – it is only your soul that will travel with me. So that your body won't appear to be dead, I am leaving the breath of life in you." Thus both of them left the house, St. Julian leading and Thurkill following.

How this man, led out of his body, was taken to a great church where there is a congregation of souls.

When they had hastened eastward to the middle of the world – so the man's guide told him it was – they entered a great church (*basilica*) of amazing construction, the base of whose roof rested on only three columns. It was a very vast and spacious church but suspended along a course [of arches] without walls, like a monastery's cloister; still, there was one wall on the north side – not too high, maybe six feet – attached to the church resting on the three columns. In the middle of the church there was something like fire in a baptismal font from which a great flame rose up. It produced no heat but miraculously illuminated the whole church and the area around it like an endless midday sun. Its splendor was caused by the tithes of the just, as St. Julian taught him. When they had entered the church, St. James came up wearing a chasuble. When he saw the pilgrim he had sent for, he told St. Julian and St. Domninus, who were the guardians of the place, that they should show his pilgrim both the places of punishment for the wicked and the mansions of the just [see John 14:2]. Having said this, he moved on. Then St. Julian revealed to the one he guided that this church was a place for all souls newly-departed from the body: here the divinely-determined mansions and other places were assigned to them according to their merits, and some were to be damned and others saved through the pains of purgatory. For the Lord Savior mercifully built this place through the intercession of the glorious Virgin Mary so that, as soon as they left the body, all souls born again in Christ gathered here without any harassment from demons and received judgment according to their works. Thus, in this church of Holy Mary, which is called "the Congregation of Souls," I [sic] saw many souls of the just, totally white and with youthful faces. Led beyond the north wall, I saw standing nearer to the wall many souls speckled both white and black; some of them appeared more white than black, others the opposite. Those who were whiter stayed closer to the wall; those more distant from the wall had no white at all and looked deformed all over.

Of unjust tithers

Next to the wall was the entrance to the pit of hell, which ceaselessly blew the most horribly stinking smoke around through those caverns into the faces of those standing by. This smoke came from tithes unjustly held back and from crops unjustly tithed. The stench encircled the chests of those guilty of this sin, heaping unrivaled pain on them. And he who was being guided twice smelled its stink, causing him such discomfort that he twice had to cough quite severely. (As those standing by his body [later] affirmed, his body had similarly coughed at that very moment.) St. Julian said to him: "It seems you have not properly tithed your harvest, and so you have smelled this stench." When he pleaded poverty, the saint said that the crops from his fields would be more fruitful if he paid his tithes properly, and he ordered him to confess this sin publicly before everyone in church and to seek absolution from his priest....

[St. Julian next shows Thurkill purgatory — an area on the east side of the great church presided over by St. Nicholas — where souls first pass through fire, then a cold salt lake, and finally over a thorny, spiked bridge to atone for lesser sins and unfinished penance. St. Julian then leads Thurkill back to the church where they see St. Michael the Archangel and the apostles Peter and Paul preparing to judge souls.]

Of the weighing of the good and evil [souls]

The blessed apostle Paul also sat inside the church at the end of its north wall. Outside the wall, opposite the apostle, sat the devil and his minions. A pit vomiting flames – the mouth of the pit of hell – gaped near the feet of the devil. Above the wall between the apostle and devil there were affixed scales suspended balanced on a post. The middle part hung outside in the devil's sight. The apostle had two weights – one large, one small – totally gleaming like gold; the devil likewise had two weights, but dark and sooty. The souls that were totally black approached with great fear and trembling one after the other, each to see there the weight of their works, good and bad; for those scales weighed the works of each of the souls according to the good or bad things it had done. When the scales leaned toward the apostle from the weight of the measure, the apostle took that soul and led it to the eastern door joined to the church, to the fire of purgatory where it could atone for its sins there. But when the other side of the scales weighed more and leaned toward the devil, he along with his minions with great cackling immediately snatched that wretched soul – wailing and cursing its father and mother who bore it only to suffer eternal torment – and threw it headfirst into that deep pit belching flames nearby the feet of the devil with the scales. The writings of the church fathers often mention this weighing of the good and evil souls.

Of a certain soul that the devil had transformed into the shape of a horse

On Saturday, near the hour of evensong, while St. Domninus and St. Julian were in that church, suddenly there came a demon from the northern side [the direction associated with the devil] riding the blackest horse at full gallop and urging it on through the many courses there with a great mocking cry. Many of the wicked souls followed after its course, dancing and cackling to one another over the prey brought to them. But St. Domninus ordered the demon rider to come over to him and tell him at once whose soul it was he was leading. When the devil hedged for a bit, taking immense pleasure in the misery of that soul, the saint instantly grabbed a whip and severely beat the demon until he followed the saint to the north wall where the scales for souls were. Then the saint asked the demon whose soul it was he was tormenting by riding it. He answered that this one had been one of the nobles of the English realm who had died the night before without receiving confession or the Lord's Body. Among the other crimes he had committed, he had been especially cruel towards his subordinates (*homines*), driving many of them into extreme need, which he had done particularly at the inspiration of his wife, who always goaded him to cruelty. "I have transformed him into the shape of a horse because we are allowed to change the souls of the damned into whatever shape we like. I would have already descended with him into hell and put him to eternal punishment except that Sunday night is approaching when we are obliged to stop our stage plays (*ludis theatralibus*) and increase the tortures of these miserable souls."

When he finished speaking, he cast his gaze intently on the man the saint was guiding and asked, "Who is this yokel standing by you?" The saint said, "Do you not know him?" The demon replied: "I've seen this man in Essex in the church of Stisted on the feast of its dedication." The saint said, "In what form did you enter that church?" "In the shape of a woman," he answered, "but when I went up to the baptismal font intending to enter the chancel, I ran into the deacon sprinkling holy water. Being sprinkled with that water drove me off so swiftly that I let out a yelp and made a jump all the way from the church into the field two furlongs away from it." Thurkill and some of the other parishioners [later] affirmed that they had heard this yelp but were completely ignorant of its cause.

Of the demons' stage plays

After this, St. Domninus said to the demon, "We want to go with you and see your shows." The demon answered, "If you want to come with me, careful that you don't bring this yokel along; for when he gets back he will reveal our activities and our secret kinds of punishments to the living and recall many people away from our works." The saint said, "Proceed quickly for I and St. Julian will follow you." And so the demon went forward and the saints followed, bringing the man they guided along with them secretly. They continued on to a northern region as if going up a mountain, and then suddenly, after going down the mountain, there was a very large and gloomy house surrounded by ancient walls. In it were many corridors, as it were, filled on every side with countless, blazing-hot, iron chairs. These chairs were made with hoops of white-hot iron [and] with nails sticking out on all sides above and below, right and left. Amazingly, people of either sex and various statuses sat in them. They were punctured on every side and part by the blazing nails and squeezed by the burning hoops. There was such a number of those chairs and so many people sitting in them that no tongue could count them. The blackest iron walls circled the corridors and there were other seats along the walls in which demons sat all around enjoying the show, as it were, chortling to each other over the tortures of these wretches and recalling their former sins to them.

Near the entrance to this horrific scene, at the foot of the mountain, as we have said, there was a wall about five feet high from which one could see whatever was happening in that place of punishment. The aforesaid saints stood at the outside of this wall, observing what the wretches inside were enduring, and – concealed between them – the man they guided clearly saw everything that was happening within.

Of a proud man and his punishment

While these infernal servants sat watching this abusive scene, the chief of that horrible band said to his minions, "Strong-arm that proud man from his seat and let him play before us." After the demons grabbed him and dressed him in a black garment, he performed before the demons every act of a man proud beyond measure while they applauded each one. He stretched up his neck, lifted his face high, raised his eyes in a disapproving look with his eyebrows arched, arrogantly intoned inflated words, held his shoulders high, and could barely lift his arms from disdain. His eyes glowered, his face was threatening. Standing on his tiptoes with his legs crossed, he thrust out his chest, lifted his neck, made his face blaze, flashed anger in his fiery eyes and, tapping his nose with his finger, put on a terribly menacing expression. So puffed up with blustering pride, he easily gained a laugh from the monstrous spirits.

While he was showing off in his clothes and donning his close-knitted gloves, suddenly the clothes took on a fiery cast and burned this miserable man's whole body. Then the demons, blazing with wrath, tore this wretch apart limb from limb with pitchforks and fiery iron hooks. One of them heated fat with pitch and other greasy drippings in a red-hot skillet and splashed the boiling oil over each limb as it was torn off. With every splash from the demon, the limbs let out a hiss like when cold water is poured on boiling blood. When all the limbs had thus been scorched, they were then joined together again and the proud man restored to his prior state.

But then the hammerers of hell approached the miserable man carrying hammers and three red-hot metal sheets studded with three nails apiece. They pressed two of the sheets to the back of his body – one on the right side, one on the left – and cruelly hammered them on with the white-hot nails. These sheets started at his feet, went up his legs and thighs to his shoulders, and wrapped around his neck; the third sheet started at his genitals, went up his belly, and reached to the top of his head. After this wretched man had been tormented with these tortures for a while, he was fiercely shoved back into his former seat where he then sat cruelly tortured on every side by the protruding white-hot nails each five fingers long. Thus taken from that place of punishment, he was put in his own chair – which he had constructed for himself while alive – to be tortured all over again.

Of a certain priest

These servants of iniquity cruelly snatched a certain priest from his burning chair as their plaything and stood him before some monstrous spirits who right there cut his throat, forcibly pulled out his tongue through the middle of it, and sliced it off at the root. When he had had the chance, he had not repaid the people entrusted to him for the temporal goods he received from them with sermons of holy exhortation, or by the example of pious acts, or with the support of prayers and masses. Afterwards, as we have just described for the proud man, they tore him limb from limb, joined him together again, and sat him back in his torture chair.

Of a certain knight

After him a certain knight was led forward who had spent his life slaughtering the innocent, competing in tournaments, and pillaging. Armed with all his military gear, he sat on a very black horse which, when prodded on with spurs, spewed from its mouth and nose flaming pitch that stank and smoked to the rider's torture. The horse's saddle was studded all over with long, burning nails. The knight's hauberk, his helmet, his shield, and his greaves – all of them on fire – heavily weighed him down with not a little weight and they burned him to his marrow with no less torture. But the knight, in imitation of his past martial deeds, after he had spurred his horse to full gallop and brandished his spear at the demons blocking his way and mocking him, was knocked off his horse by them and torn limb from limb. And his limbs were roasted in the same horrible liquid mentioned before. Cooked and then made whole again, like those mentioned above, he was bridled by three metal sheets and, thus restored, violently shoved back into his own chair.

Of a certain advocate

After the knight, a certain man most learned in secular law was led to the middle, snatched with great pain from his seat which he had constructed for himself over a long course of time by evil living and by subverting justice through taking bribes. Among the magnates he was held to be one of the most famous people through all the ends of England, but in the year this vision occurred, he met a miserable end. He died suddenly without making a last will; so everything he had gotten through his ravenous greed was dragged off and completely consumed by strangers. For he been used to sitting at the royal Exchequer where he frequently accepted gifts from both sides in a lawsuit. He too, when he was led before this horrible band to take part in their abusive pageant, was forced to reenact the acts of his former life. Thus, turning first to the right and then to the left, he explained the case to one side and then instructed the other side about its contradictions. All the while he did not hesitate to take the money in their hands – now from one side, now from the other. He counted the money he took and, having counted it, put it in his pockets. After the demons had watched this miserable man's play-acting for a bit, suddenly the coins seemed to catch fire, cruelly burning the wretch. He was forced to throw them burning into his mouth and then to swallow them. After he swallowed them, two demons came up carrying an iron cart-wheel studded along the rim with spikes and nails. Turning it fiercely against the back of the sinner, they skinned off his whole back by its repeated, fiery revolutions. They forced him to vomit up in even greater agony the coins which he had swallowed in agony with his gaping mouth. When he had vomited them out, a demon ordered him to collect them so that he could feed on them again in the same way. Then, turning in a fury, these servants of Hades spent on him all the tortures mentioned above. But his wife sat pressed in a spiked and burning chair because she had had [people] excommunicated [for theft] in many churches over some ring which she had inadvertently left in a chest but she said had been stolen. She had never been absolved from remedying this sin: a sudden bad death prevented her from this necessity.

Of an adulterer and adulteress

After this, an adulterer and adulteress were brought forward for the entertainment of these raging demons. They were joined together in a filthy embrace, and in front of everyone they repeated their most indecent sexual motions and lewd acts much to their confusion and the reproaches of the demons. Then, as if they had been struck insane, they tore into each other, gnawing at each other back and forth. That superficial love that they appeared to have a moment before they now changed into cruelty and hatred. Afterwards, all their limbs were ripped off by the raging crowd and they shared a similar punishment as those above. All the other fornicators there were tortured with the same torments, which, due to the cruelty of their punishments, impose silence on the writer.

Of slanderers

Also from among the other wretches, two from a group of slanderers were led forth into the middle, whose mouths gaped distorted all the way to their ears as they turned their faces toward each other and gazed with grim eyes.

The points of some sort of double-headed, burning spear were placed in their mouths, which they chewed, twisting their mouths until they quickly gnawed to the middle of the spear and drew closer to each other. Mangling each other like this, chomping away they bloodied their whole faces.

Of thieves and arsonists

Among others, thieves, arsonists, and violators of sacred places were led forth, who were placed by the servants of Hades on burning iron wheels studded with spikes and sharp points which rained a shower of fiery sparks due to their great heat. The wretches spun on these suffered horrific torment.

Of merchants

Present at this entertainment was a merchant with false weights and measures, and also those who so forcibly pull new cloth on cloth racks that they overstretch it in both length and width, breaking the threads and making a hole. Carefully sewing up the hole, they sell that [damaged] fabric in dimly-lit places. These people were fiercely dragged from their seats and forced to repeat the past motions of their sins to their shame and to aggravate their punishment. And then, as we have said about those above, they were tortured by the demons.

Of the pit of hell and its cauldrons of punishment

Besides all this, the man the saints were guiding also saw the entrance of lower hell: four courtyards, so to speak, the first of which had countless furnaces and wide, deep cauldrons filled to the brim with burning pitch and other molten liquids. Souls were packed into each one boiling vigorously; their heads were like black fish in burning liquid and were thrust upwards and then plunged back down due to the force of the boiling. The second courtyard had similar cauldrons, but these were filled with snow and frigid ice in which the souls were tortured with horrible cold and unbearable torment. The cauldrons in the third courtyard were filled with boiling liquid sulphur and other things that stink and emit reeking smoke in which were especially tortured souls ending life in the foulness of lust. And the fourth courtyard had cauldrons filled with the saltiest, blackest water – water so potent due to its saltiness that it would instantly strip [the bark from] any kind of wood immersed in it. There were countless sinners in these cauldrons: murderers, thieves, robbers, sorceresses, and rich men who oppressed men with their unjust exactions – all ceaselessly boiling. The servants of iniquity stood around with red-hot forks and pushed those souls together so that they could not escape the burning liquid.

Those who had been boiling for seven days in the burning liquid were put into that horrible cold in the second courtyard on the eighth. By contrast, those who were tortured by cold were put in the boiling liquid. In a similar way, those who had been boiled in the salt water were tortured in the stinking water. These alternating changes were always observed every eight days.

[*The saints now lead Thurkill to the outskirts of heaven where he sees Adam. They enter a golden, jeweled gate where, in a chapel, they see Saints Catherine, Margaret, and Ositha – a local saint of Essex. But suddenly the archangel Michael tells St. Julian to restore Thurkill to his body: "Unless he is quickly returned, the cold water the people standing over him are forcing down his throat [to revive him] will drown him!" Thurkill wakes to discover that he has been lying unconscious in his bed for two days and nights. At first, he hesitates to tell his story, but then:*]

The following night St. Julian appeared to him and ordered him to reveal everything he had seen since he had been led on this journey in order to make public what he had heard [*sic*]. Obeying the saint's orders, on All Saints' Day [Nov. 1] and from then on he described his vision in English steadily and clearly to everyone. They were amazed at his unaccustomed eloquence since before this, out of his great simplicity, he had always been rough-edged (*rusticus*) and tongue-tied. And he did not stop telling about the vision he had seen until he had moved many people to grief and deep sighs.

Is a hierarchy of punishment evident here; are some sins considered worse than others? Is there a moral lesson to Thurkill's vision? What sort of people does Thurkill put into hell? Do the demographics of his hell support or challenge the medieval social order? Are there details here that seem likely to have come from a peasant's world view? Is the monastic editor's hand in reshaping Thurkill's story evident? What effect would his vision have on its audience? What gives his vision authority? Compare this vision to Walchelin's (Doc. 40) and Owein's (Doc. 78)

38. GERMAN ENCOUNTERS WITH DEMONS
(1280s)

For medieval people the world teemed with spirits, some good, most not. A face-to-face encounter with Satan himself was unusual outside of the vision literature so widespread from the twelfth century on; but brushing with his minions in one form or another was a commonplace experience since they were everywhere, "swarming like flies" said St. Bonaventure. Minor spirits were responsible for most of life's misfortunes large and small: bad weather, bad crops, fire, sickness, insanity, accident, annoyance, even soured milk. Meetings with malevolent demons, as these late thirteenth-century stories from a Rhineland Dominican show (see Doc. 18), were dangerous, frightening, and often deadly.

Source: trans. J. Shinners from Rudolf von Schlettstadt, *Historiae Memorabiles, Zur Dominikanerliteratur und Kulturgeschichte des 13. Jahrhunderts*, ed. Erich Kleinschmidt (Cologne: Böhlau-Verlag, 1972), pp. 82-84, 96-98, 103-05.

1. Concerning a woman whom the devil strangled.

There was a pleasure-loving woman from the diocese of Basel who neither by price nor prayer could get enough of what she wanted. She hastened to an old widow, who was an enchantress or sorceress, believing that through incantations to demons she would more easily get what she desired. When the sorceress heard the woman's requests, she said, "Take some plasterwork and a piece of pedestal from a consecrated altar and the shin bone of an [executed] thief collected after he has been hanging for three nights" (and also many other things better left unsaid here), "make a lump out of such and such, which you will find in such and such a place. Then you will easily get the object of your desire." The woman gathered these and similar things for a price, omitting not a single thing so that she could faithfully mix up this wicked concoction. Since she could not mix this brew in her own home, she humbly asked the help of her godmother. At first she wasn't very willing, but then she acquiesced, saying, "I fear both God and man, so I dare not do such terrible wickedness in my house. But if you want to do it, I won't do much to stop you." The woman gave her a thousand thanks, saying, "What you've said is enough." That night she went to her godmother and said to her, "Look, I've already found everything I need, so I want you to go to your house to help me mix the brew at the proper hour." The godmother said, "My husband is there sleeping, so no one will disturb you at your work." Then, with burning candles, they both went into the house. The woman got out all the things she had gathered together that she considered necessary to complete the work. After she had spent some time working away, the door to the house suddenly blew open. The woman quickly got up and carefully shut it. After a time, the door opened again. Again the woman quickly closed it and went back to completing her wicked business. The door opened a third time and in walked a black man (*ethiops*) tall and thin. He grabbed the woman working the magic by the head, twisted it around to her back, and wretchedly killed her. In the meantime, her godmother, who was sitting near her, fainted ter-ror-stricken. The black man, who was the devil, ignored her. After an hour the godmother came to her senses; she went to her husband who lay sleeping in his room knowing nothing of what went on. She woke him up and told him what had happened. The man gathered up the body of the dead woman, put it in a coffin, and had it solemnly buried in the churchyard, saying that the woman – eating, drinking, and reveling with many people around – had suddenly dropped dead....

2. *Concerning a woman giving birth to monsters.*

In the diocese of Utrecht there was a noble knight, quite rich and prosper-ous, who had three castles and many other possessions. He had a bold spirit, and he accumulated his riches day after day. Demons quite often appeared to him. He called them by their names, and they usually answered his ques-tions. One day he left the castle where he lived. He said good-bye to his wife with loving words. When his wife got into bed that night, it seemed to her that her husband came to her and had relations with her in due manner. From this, so she believed, she became pregnant. The next day her husband returned, which caused his wife to be very much amazed, and she said to him, "Where have you come from?" He answered, "From our other castle." She said, "Surely you were with me last night, and had relations with me contrary to your custom." He answered, "I did not." Terrified and upset al-most to death, the woman learned that she had given birth to three monsters at once. One monster had teeth like a hog's, the second had a startlingly long beard, the third had one eye in its face, so reported someone who saw them. But the mother, after the birth of these children, died. The lord, learning that his wife had given birth, quickly arrived. But upon seeing the monsters, he ordered them to be buried immediately. He made his servant show him his wife's body; but the servant said, "Her body was so swollen, we could hardly shut it within the coffin planks." Then he said, "Show her to me." When they had done so and he had seen her body, he said, "Cover her with the planks, and take the body from my house just as fast as you can." They did not hesitate to do it.

3. *Concerning a possessed man in the city of Zürich.*

In 1286 in the city of Zürich there was a man possessed by a demon who, prior to the feast of Felix and Regula (who are the city's special patrons since their holy bodies rest there), with scurrilous words and deeds made light of their bodies. People said to him, "Why are you so light-hearted?" He said,

"Our band of 666 have come together and by the open permission of the Blessed Virgin Mary; we can do anything to torment your souls." Not long after, the city of Zürich caught on fire and almost a third of it burned down. Afterwards, the demon said of the city: "We have punished the people of Zürich for their pride, and if they don't amend themselves, they will shortly suffer the same." Then the people asked the demon, "Why didn't you harm the monastery of Felix and Regula?" He answered, "They bravely defended themselves and made us flee."

4. Concerning a servant flayed by a demon.

A wandering scholar, a necromancer named Walravius, after traveling through many kingdoms and regions, finally is known to have come to Alsace. When Walravius arrived in Rouffach, he went into a tavern and found there Johann Epfig and his worthless servant named Hoper along with other rascals arguing about everything. Among them, the one named Johann Epfig said this: "Many people have said a lot about demons, but I've never seen one of them." Walravius said, "If you'd like to serve me supper, I'll show you a demon at twilight." Then Johann the taverner said, "I'll give you money for supper, Walravius." After supper as night fell, Walravius the necromancer took Johann, brought him to a deserted place, and showed him the terrible shape of a demon. At the sight of the demon, Johann, though he was a bold and daring man, was so terrified that he could scarcely make it back home. He kept to his house and lay desperately ill for many days. Finally he recovered and was restored to his former health. But the nasty servant Hoper harshly abused Walravius with insulting words. Walravius said to him, "Know that when the time is ripe, I'll get my revenge on you." These words didn't bother Hoper a bit, so he carried on serving many lords. But in the year 1285, on Friday, March 9 before Laetare Sunday Hoper was a servant in the town of Gundolsheim where he gladly and faithfully was serving wine to the town's knights and other more respectable people. These noble people were drinking in some house that had not yet been completely finished. When the feasting was over and the lords returned to their own homes, they left a large fire burning with a lot of charcoal. The servant Hoper and two others remained behind and warmed themselves fearing no one. When they were well warmed, two of the servants settled down in the stable. Then Hoper stripped off all his clothes and warmed his naked body all over. While he lay there completely relaxed from the heat, a devil came in the shape of a large man with hands clawed like a bear's and embraced the upper part of his body; Hoper couldn't shout out loud, but he heavily heaved out a weeping sound. One of his companions raised his head and, seeing the demon, dropped down his frightened head and defended himself with a little sign of the cross. After this, the demon flayed Hoper's skin from his navel down to his shins, stripping it away with his claws. Then Hoper let out a horrible scream, begging his friends' help. Hearing his voice, his friends ran together to their lords and told them about this marvelous and terrible thing. The lords, once they heard it, faithfully ran to his aid insofar as they could. His flayed flesh first looked white and then later turned black; finally the flesh peeled off his bones, followed by an unbearable stench. He lay there flayed for three days and then finally his spirit left his body. Boys carried his flayed skin around the town on a stick. Some people said that the demon had said, "Raise your cup to Walravius for this gift."

39. DEMONS VEX SOME ENGLISH VILLAGERS
(c. 1400)

The great Benedictine monastery of St. Albans, just north of London, was a crucible of historians in the high Middle Ages, numbering among its monks both Matthew Paris and Thomas Walsingham. These two stories come from the continuation of Walsingham's chronicle, probably written by William Wyntershylle (d.c. 1424), a contemporary of the events he records here. In the first, a spirit becomes almost a family pet; in the second, a woman's mental illness is ascribed to demonic possession.

Source: trans. J. Shinners from H.T. Riley, *The Chronica Monasterii S. Albani*, Rolls Series 28, pt. 3 (London: Longmans, 1866), pp. 196-99. Latin.

1. [*1397 CE*] Around Lent near the village of Bedford, nearly every day at sunset a spirit roamed invisibly about the village of [*blank*]. It visited the house of a widow and told her that it was her daughter, blaming her that, because of the widow's carelessness, she had been stillborn and then buried by her under a tree in her garden. Then it added that this woman, whom it claimed was its mother, would be damned for her deed.

But the mother, though she was just an uneducated countrywoman, replied that this would not happen since she had confessed this sin and performed a suitable penance according to the discretion and decision of a priest. The spirit objected that she was lying and repeated that she would be damned for her sin. The mother replied that the spirit was an utterly deceitful liar and falsely wanted to make her despair. The two of them often wrangled over this issue.

Now the widow had a son who was a priest, though he spent as much time as he could hunting. With utter disdain the spirit reproached him for his frivolous pastime, warning him that he should spend more time at divine services, and pointing out that he said his matins very badly and his mass even worse. Their conversations were so frequent and friendly that neither the mother nor her son feared speaking with this spirit. During one of many such conversations, the spirit said to the priest, "You went hunting one day with John Hervey, but you didn't catch a thing. Why do you keep hounds that you can't support on your income? With your bare cupboard, you're practically killing them from hunger. They're so weak that they can barely run. Trust me, one day I killed one of your dogs since it was so rickety and skinny and looked so wretched." In fact the priest and John Hervey clearly recalled a dog that had been killed while they were hunting, though they had no idea who had done it.

The family grew so familiar with this spirit from their frequent conversations that they had no fear of it at all, and they asked whether it wished to repeat the Lord's Prayer, the Hail Mary, the Creed, and John's Gospel "In the beginning," after them. It said all these clearly and without fault. But when they told it to say "Jesus of Nazareth" in English, it stammered and either could not or would not say that phrase distinctly. After a while, however, it would say the phrase clearly or any other they wished it to; for it lived with them for three years, occasionally making mischief, knocking over jugs of ale and other pots, and now and then causing other nuisances.

2. Another very great wonder happened in the parish of Tuttington that year, almost at the same time that the first spirit appeared that we have just described.

A certain woman from that village, vexed by an evil spirit, hanged herself. But while life still lingered in her body the woman's husband arrived. Seeing this calamity, he cut the rope from which his wife hung, cradled her in his arms, and revived her until life returned to her. Comforting her, he told her to be strong, and to bear her responsibility as mistress of the house, as was her habit – and this she did for a time. But after Easter, overcome by the same demon, she wanted to hang herself; but the rope broke and she fell down half-alive. When she had recovered her breath, she rushed to an orchard where there was a deep pond filled with muddy water six or seven feet deep. With one leap she jumped headfirst into it trying to drown herself. But though her head went under three times, she wasn't able to sink herself, so she got out of the pond and went to her sister's house. Her sister pitied her terrible misfortune and urged her to go to confession and to drive away such madness from her mind. She prepared a bed for her and made her undress and get into it since she was almost dead from cold. Tucking her in the bed, she warned her not to get up until she had gone to the woman's house and gotten her some fresh, dry clothes from her things.

When her sister had left to get the clothes from her house, she saw that she was alone, got up, and looked all around the room. She happened to see a dagger – called a *baselard* in the vernacular – hanging on the wall. She took it, bent over it, and stabbed herself through the stomach all the way to her back three times. But when she realized that she could not kill herself this way, she tried to yank out her heart, thinking that if she removed it, she would live no more. But the wound was too narrow for her to reach her hand to her heart, so she took the blade of the dagger with which she had stabbed herself and widened the original wound so that it was half a foot long. She inserted her hand, pulled out her intestines which the knife had severed, dashed them onto a footstool, and strewed the rest of them on the floor.

Then her sister came back along with some others and the parish priest. Of course at first stunned and dumbfounded seeing such a dreadful thing, they were horror-struck. Indeed, there she was in the center of this ghastly scene, her wits driven wild and rolling her eyes, which seemed to flash like lightning, in a such a terrible way that for a while they didn't know what to do. Finally after a long pause the priest went in when she had almost given up the ghost. He told her to think of God and to cast away her despair, and he encouraged her to make her confession, promising her absolute forgiveness of her sins if she would now turn herself over to him who hung on the cross for her and for the Jews; and he prayed, arguing that God had resolved to save her since he had preserved her so many times from such a terrible death. Then, gaining confidence, she confessed and was given suitable penance, received the viaticum in good faith, and lived for three more hours. At last she died, forsaking great hope in earthly things and choosing God's mercy which is always at hand for those who seek it.

What images of demons emerge from these German and English stories? What sorts of people meddle with demons? Can these demons be controlled? Is the purpose of these stories to instill fear or inspire faith in their audience? Does our culture tell similar stories?

40. THE YOUNG PRIEST WALCHELIN'S PURGATORIAL VISION (c. 1131)

Encountering the ghosts of Christian souls was no less unnerving than crossing paths with demons. Oderic Vitalis (1075-1143?) was born in England but spent most of his life in the monastery of St. Evroul in Normandy. From this post he assembled his

Ecclesiastical History of Norman England and France. Oderic wrote this famous account around 1131, saying that Walchelin himself told him of his terrible vision of the souls in purgatory.

Source: trans. Marjorie Chibnall, *The Ecclesiastical History of Odericus Vitalis* (Oxford: Clarendon Press, 1973), v. 4, pp. 237-51. Latin.

I am sure that I should not pass over in silence or consign to oblivion something that happened to a priest in the diocese of Lisieux on 1 January. There was a priest called Walchelin, who served the church of St. Aubin the confessor, bishop of Angers and previously monk, in the village of Bonneval. On 1 January 1091, this man was sent for by night, as his office required, to visit a sick man on the fringes of his parish. As he was returning alone, in a spot far from human habitation, he heard a sound like the movement of a great army, and took it to be the household troops of Robert of Bellême, hurrying to the siege of Courcy. The eighth moon was shining brightly in the sign of the Ram, and showed the road clearly to travelers. This priest was a young man, strong and brave, well-built and active. But on hearing the sound of men in disorderly haste he trembled and hesitated between several courses of action, undecided whether to take to his heels to avoid being attacked by low minions and shamefully robbed, or whether to stand his ground and defend himself if anyone accosted him. As he noticed four medlar trees in a field far from the path he made up his mind to hurry there and hide until the troop of horse had passed by. But a man of huge stature, carrying a great mace, barred the priest's way as he ran and, brandishing the weapon over his head, cried out, "Stand; go no further." The priest obeyed at once and stood motionless, leaning on the staff he was carrying. The stern mace-bearer stood beside him without harming him, waiting for the army to pass by. A great crowd on foot appeared, carrying across their necks and shoulders animals and clothes and every kind of furnishing and household goods that raiders usually seize as plunder. But all lamented bitterly and urged each other to hurry. The priest recognized among them many of his neighbors who had recently died, and heard them bewailing the torments they suffered because of their sins. Next came a crowd of bearers, and the giant suddenly fell in with them. They were carrying about five hundred biers, two men to each bier. On the biers sat men as small as dwarfs, but with huge heads like barrels. One enormous tree-trunk was borne by two Ethiopians, and on the trunk some wretch, tightly trussed, was suffering tortures, screaming aloud in his dreadful agony. A fearful demon sitting on the same trunk was mercilessly goading his back and loins with red-hot spurs while he streamed with blood. Walchelin at once recognized him as the slayer of the priest Stephen, and realized that he was suffering unbearable torments for his guilt in shedding innocent blood not two years earlier, for he had died without completing his penance for the terrible crime.

Next came a troop of women, who seemed to the priest to be without number, riding in women's fashion on side-saddles which were studded with burning nails. Caught by gusts of wind they would rise as much as a cubit from the saddle, and then fall back on the sharp points. So their buttocks were wounded by the red-hot nails, and as they suffered torments from the stabs and burning they cried out, "Woe, woe," loudly bewailing the sins for which they endured such punishment. Indeed it was for the seductions and obscene delights in which they had wallowed without restraint on earth that they now endured the fire and stench and other agonies too many to enumerate, and gave voice to their sufferings with loud wailing. The priest recognized a number of noble women in this troop, and also saw the horses and mules with empty women's litters belonging to many who were still alive.

The priest stood shaking from head to foot at these terrible apparitions and began to reflect on their meaning. Not far behind he saw a great troop of clergy and monks, and noticed their rulers, both bishops and abbots, with pastoral staffs. The clergy and bishops wore black caps; the monks and ab-bots too were attired in black cowls. They groaned and lamented, and some greeted Walchelin and asked him for the sake of past acquaintance to pray for them. The priest related that he had seen there many of high repute, who in human estimation are believed to have joined the saints in heaven. Indeed he saw Hugh bishop of Lisieux, and the notable abbots, Mainer of Saint-Évroul and Gerbert of Saint-Wandrille, and many others whose names I cannot re-call and will not attempt to commit to writing. Human judgment is often in error, but nothing is hidden from God's sight. For men judge from outward appearances; God looks into the heart. In the kingdom of eternal blessed-ness light eternal illumines all things; there true sanctity is won and every delight brings joy to the heirs of the kingdom. Nothing there is disorderly, no trace of guilt enters in, nothing evil or wrong can be found there. So all unseemliness of which base humanity is guilty is burned away in purgatorial fire and the soul is purified by every kind of purgation that the eternal judge deems right. And just as a vessel, cleansed from rust and well-polished, is placed in the treasury, so the soul, purified from the stain of every sin is led into paradise, where it enters into perfect blessedness and the joy that knows no fear or shadow.

The priest, trembling at the fearful sights he had seen, stood leaning on his staff and waiting for still worse. Behold, next followed a great army of knights, in which no color was visible save blackness and flickering fire. All rode upon huge horses, fully armed as if they were galloping to battle and carrying jet black standards. Among them appeared the sons of Count Gilbert, Richard, and Baldwin, who had recently died, as well as many others whom I cannot enumerate. Among them Landry of Orbec, who had died within the year, began to speak to the priest, shouting out his messages in a terrible voice, and peremptorily bidding him take his commands to his wife. But the troops in front and behind interrupted, shouting him down and saying to the priest, "Don't believe Landry; he is a liar." He had been vicomte and advocate of Orbec and had risen far above his low origin through his intelligence and merit. But in suits and pleas he determined the case as he chose, and perverted justice by taking bribes, showing greater devotion to greed and dishonesty than to right. Consequently he deserved to be shamed in his torments, and openly called a liar by his fellow sufferers. In that judgment there was no one to flatter him or beg for the help of his ingenious pleading; indeed, because he had stopped his ears to the cries of the poor as long as he was able, now in his torments he was judged beneath contempt, not even worthy of a hearing. Walchelin, after the great army of many thousands had passed by, began to say to himself, "This is most certainly Hellequin's rabble [a company of spirits that forced souls to accompany them on their hunts]. I have heard many who claimed to have seen them, but have ridiculed the tale-tellers and not believed them because I never saw any solid proof of such things. Now I do indeed see the shades of the dead with my own eyes, but no one will believe me when I describe my vision unless I can show some sure token to living men. I will catch one of the riderless horses following the host, quickly mount it, and take it home, to compel the belief of my neighbors when I show it to them." At once he seized the reins of a coalblack steed, but it proudly shook off his detaining hand and galloped after the dark host as if it were winged. The priest regretted his failure to carry out his resolution; but he was young in years, bold and nimble, and physically swift and strong. He placed himself therefore in the middle of the road, holding out his hand to a horse that approached and seemed ready to be taken. The horse stopped for the priest to mount, breathing from its nostrils a great cloud of steam in the shape of a tall oak-tree. The priest put his left foot in the stirrup and, seizing the reins, placed his hand on the saddle; immediately he felt an intense burning like raging fire under his foot, and an indescribable cold struck into his heart from the hand that held the reins.

While this was happening four fearsome knights came up and said, in voices of thunder, "Why are you molesting our horses? Come with us. None of our people has harmed you, yet you try to take what is ours." Terrified he let go of the horse, and as three of the knights were on the point of seizing him the fourth said, "Let him be, and allow him to talk to me, so that I may send messages to my wife and sons through him." Then he said to the priest, who stood aghast, "Hear me, I beg, and take my message to my wife." The priest answered, "I neither recognize you nor know your wife." The knight said, "I am William of Glos, the son of Barnon, who was the renowned steward of William of Breteuil and his father William, earl of Hereford, before him. I have been guilty of unjust judgments and annexations in the world, and have committed more sins than I can tell. But most of all usury torments me. For I lent my money to a poor man, receiving a mill of his as a pledge, and because he was unable to repay the loan I retained the pledge all my life and disinherited the legitimate heir by leaving it to my heirs. See, I carry a burning mill-shaft in my mouth which, believe me, seems heavier than the castle of Rouen. Therefore tell my wife Beatrice and my son Roger that they must help me by quickly restoring to the heir the pledge, from which they have received far more than I ever gave." The priest answered, "William of Glos died long ago and no true believer can carry a message of this kind. I do not know who you are, or who are your heirs. If I presume to tell such things to Roger of Glos and his brothers or their mother they will deride me as a madman." William persisted in his demands, resolutely pressing many visible proofs on him; but the priest, though understanding what he heard, pretended that he knew nothing of all this. Finally, worn down by repeated prayers, he consented and promised to attend to what was asked. Then William repeated everything, and in a long discourse unfolded many things to him. Meanwhile the priest began to turn over in his mind that he would never dare to transmit the messages of the accursed reprobate to anyone. "It is not right," he said, "to declare such things. In no circumstances will I carry your orders to anyone." The knight in a terrible rage then put out his hand and seized the priest by the throat, dragging him along the ground and threatening him. His victim felt the hand that held him burning like fire, and in his great anguish cried out suddenly, "Blessed Mary, glorious Mother of Christ help me." No sooner had he invoked the compassionate Mother of the Son of God than help was at hand, of a kind that the Omnipotent's law ordained. A knight appeared, carrying only a sword in his right hand; brandishing the naked blade as though about to strike, he said, "Wretches, why are you murdering my brother? Leave him and be gone." At once the knights sped on, following the dark host.

When the rest had gone the knight remained alone in the path with Walchelin and inquired of him, "Do you not recognize me?" The priest answered, "No." Then the knight said, "I am Robert, son of Ralph the Fair, and your brother." And as the priest stood thunderstruck at such an unexpected thing, greatly tormented by all that he had seen and felt, as I have described, the knight began to recall many things that had happened when they were boys, and to reveal many proofs to him. The priest had a clear recollection of all he heard, but dared not confess it and denied everything. At last the knight said, "I am amazed by your hardness and obstinacy. I brought you up after both our parents died, and loved you more than any living person. I sent you to the schools of France, kept you well-provided with clothes and money, and in many other ways furthered your progress. Now you have forgotten all this and disdain even to recognize me." When so many true words had been spoken the positive proofs at last convinced the priest, and with tears he admitted his brother's assertions. The knight said to him, "You deserved by right to die and be carried along with us to share in our punishment, for you rashly tried to seize things that are ours. No other man has ever dared to attempt this; but the mass which you sang today has saved you from death. Also I have now been permitted to show myself to you, and to reveal my wretched condition to you. After I last spoke to you in Normandy I left for England with your blessing; there I reached my life's end when my Creator willed, and I have endured severe punishment for the great sins with which I am heavily burdened. The arms which we bear are red-hot, and offend us with an appalling stench, weighing us down with intolerable weight, and burning with everlasting fire. Up to now I have suffered unspeakable torture from these punishments. But when you were ordained in England and sang your first mass for the faithful departed your father Ralph escaped from his punishments, and my shield, which caused me great pain, fell from me. As you see I still carry this sword, but I look in faith for release from this burden within the year."

When the knight had said this and more to the same purpose the priest, who was gazing intently at him, noticed what seemed to be a mass of blood like a human head at his heels around his spurs. Horrified he asked, "How do you come to have that great clot of blood around your heels?" His brother replied, "It is not blood, but fire, and it weighs more heavily on me than if I were carrying the Mont Saint-Michel. Because I used bright, sharp spurs in my eager haste to shed blood I am justly condemned to carry this enormous load on my heels, which is such an intolerable burden that I cannot convey to anyone the extent of my sufferings. Living men should constantly have these things in mind and should tremble and take heed not to incur such dire penalties for their sins. I cannot speak longer with you, my brother, for I am compelled to hasten after this wretched host. Remember me, I beg: help me with your prayers and compassionate alms. In one year from Palm Sunday I hope to be saved and released from all torments by the mercy of my Creator. Take thought for your own welfare: correct your life wisely, for it is stained by many vices, and you must know that it will not be long enduring. For the present, do not speak. Keep silent about all that you have inadvertently seen and heard, and do not venture to reveal it to anyone for three days."

When he had finished speaking the knight galloped away. The priest was seriously ill for a whole week. Then, when he began to recover, he went to Lisieux, related everything to bishop Gilbert just as it had happened, and received from him the remedies he needed. He lived in good health for about fifteen years afterwards; I heard from his own mouth all that I have written and much more which I have now forgotten, and saw the scar on his face caused by the touch of the terrible knight. I have recorded these things for the edification of my readers, so that just men may be encouraged in good, and vicious men may repent of evil.

What kinds of repenting sinners from what social classes does Walchelin encounter and what do they reveal about the moral code of his society? Can you discern differences between the punishments of the damned in Thurkill's account of hell (Doc. 37) and Walchelin's vision of souls suffering in purgatory? What does the account reveal about Walchelin?

41. GHOST STORIES (c. 1400)

As these next stories suggest, demons and ghosts could take on a dizzying number of shapes, both animal and human. Here they typically appear as grotesque humans, or spectral horses, dogs, goats, ravens, fire, and even a bale of hay. Though demons were powerful and malevolent, Christians did not feel totally helpless when faced with them. With the proper blessings, charms, invocations, and sacramentals such as holy water and the sign of the cross, they could be warded off or at least controlled. In fact, fearsome though they were, spirits were often easily fooled. Popular stories of tricks played on the devil and the stage buffoonery of demons in pageant plays helped reassure people that the forces of evil were not invincible. Still, encountering a demon or a ghost was usually a fearsome and dangerous thing; those who crossed paths with them often fell gravely ill for days afterwards. Shortly after 1400, a monk from the Cistercian abbey of Byland in North Yorkshire (who seems as much intent on scaring himself as his readers) recorded these ghost stories, all set in places near his abbey, on several blank folios of a manuscript of Cicero. Both the details and the grammar of several of the stories are often confusing and some words are omitted or worn away. But the stories show how medieval people usually understood ghosts to be the pitiful souls of the dead begging earthly prayers to allay their suffering in purgatory. In these tales humans "conjure" or command the spirits to identify themselves by invoking the name of God, not by using magic spells.

Source: trans. J. Shinners from M.R. James, "Twelve Medieval Ghost Stories," *English Historical Review* 37 (1922): 413-22. Story 13 from H.E.D. Blakiston, "Two More Medieval Ghost Stories," *English Historical Review* 38 (1923): 85-86. Latin.

1. Concerning the ghost of a certain wage laborer from Rievaulx who helped a man to carry beans.

There was a certain man riding on his horse carrying with him a measure of beans. His horse stumbled and broke its leg. Seeing this, the man heaved the beans onto his own back. As he walked along the road, he saw what appeared to be a horse standing on its hind legs with its forelegs outstretched. Terrified, the man ordered the horse in the name of Jesus Christ not to harm him. When he had done this, he walked along with it still in the shape of a horse; but after a little while it changed into the shape of a rolling pile of hay with a light in the middle. The man said to it, "Begone, for you bring me evil!" Upon these words, it appeared in the shape of a man, and the man conjured it [to speak]. Then the ghost told him his name, why he was wandering, and how he could be helped, adding, "Permit me to carry the beans and help you." And so he did as far as a rushing stream, but he did not wish to go further. The living man did not know how he had put the sack of beans on his back again. Afterwards, he had the ghost absolved, and had masses sung for him which helped him.

2. Concerning a marvelous contest between a ghost and a living man during the reign of King Richard II.

It is said that there was a certain tailor named [*blank*] Snowball returning from Gilling on horse one night to his house in Ampleforth, and on the road he heard what sounded like ducks washing themselves in a stream. A little later he spied what looked liked a raven flying around his head and then landing on the ground, its wings barely fluttering as if it were dying. The tailor got off his horse to get the raven but he saw sparks of fire shooting from the raven's sides. He made the sign of the cross and forbade it for God's sake from doing him any kind of harm. Then with a great shriek it flew a stone's throw away. He got back on his horse, but a little later the same raven blocked his path and, diving at him, struck the tailor in the side wounding him and knocking him off his horse to the ground. He lay flat on the ground like this, as if in a trance, with the wind knocked out of him, absolutely terrified. Finally, getting up and staying constant in faith, he fought the raven with his sword until he was exhausted. His blade looked to him as if he had stabbed a stack of peat, and he forbade the raven for God's sake, saying "God forbid that you have power to harm me here. Begone!" Once again with a great shriek it flew away the distance of an arrow shot. The third time it appeared to him, the tailor held the hilt of his sword like a cross over his breast out of fear. Now in the shape of a dog with a chain about its neck, it blocked his path. When the tailor saw this, stirred up in faith he thought to himself, "What's going to become of me? I will command it in the name of the Trinity and through the power of the blood of the five wounds of Jesus Christ that it should speak with me, and do me no harm but stand still, answer my questions, and tell me its name, the cause of its pain, and some suitable remedy for it." He did this, and when he commanded it, it let out a terrible sigh and groaned: "I have done such and such, and I was excommunicated for these deeds. Go therefore to So-and-so the priest and seek absolution for me. I need to have nine times twenty masses said for me. You have one of two choices: either return to me alone on such and such a night with a response to what I have told you and I will tell you how you can be healed [from the wound inflicted by the raven]; in the meantime, do not fear the sight of man-made fire. But if you refuse to do this, your flesh will rot and your skin will wither and peel from you in a short time. Know, therefore, that I was able to block your path just now because today you have not heard mass or John's Gospel "In the beginning," nor have you seen the consecration of the Lord's body and blood; otherwise I would not have had the power to appear to you fully." As he spoke to him, he looked like a flame, and the tailor could see his internal organs through his mouth; he did not speak with his tongue but formed his words in his gut. The tailor sought the ghost's permission to bring a companion with him on his return. But the ghost said, "No. But you should carry the four Gospels with you and the triumphal name, 'Jesus of Nazareth' because of two other spirits lingering here. One of them cannot speak when conjured and appears in the shape of fire or a thornbush; the other appears as a hunter. Both are very dangerous to encounter. You must swear on this stone that you will not defame my bones except to the priests celebrating masses for me and to others that you consult on my behalf who can aid me." The tailor swore on the stone that he would not reveal his secret except as noted above. Finally, the tailor commanded him to go up to Hodge Beck [*hoggebek*, a nearby brook] until his return. Wailing, the ghost said "No! No! No!" Then the tailor said, "Well at least go to Byland Brink Hill [*bilandbanke*, near Byland Abbey]," and he willingly did this.

Afterwards the tailor was sick for several days, but as soon as he was better he went to York to the priest who had excommunicated the ghost in order to seek absolution for him. The priest refused to absolve him and called one of his chaplains to confer with him. The chaplain called another chaplain and that one called still a third chaplain, and all of them pondered together over the absolution. The tailor said to the first priest, "Sir, do you understand the proof I have offered for your hearing?" He said, "Yes, my son." Finally, after much discussion between the tailor and the priests, he satisfied them, paid them five shillings [for masses], and received an absolution written on a certificate. They swore him not to defame the dead man with this [by publicly revealing the ghost's sin], but to bury it secretly in his grave resting near his head. He took the absolution with him and went to a certain Friar Richard de Pickering, a renowned confessor, asking him if it would be sufficient and legitimate. He said yes. Then the tailor went to all the orders of friars in York and had nearly all the aforesaid masses celebrated over the space of two or three days. Returning to the religious house, he buried the absolution in the grave as he had been ordered. When all these things had been duly carried out, he went home. One of his neighbors, a presumptuous man, heard that he was supposed to report everything he had done in York to the ghost on some night or other. He implored him, saying, "God forbid you should visit this ghost without giving me advance warning about the day and hour you are going." The tailor felt duty bound not to displease God, so on the assigned night he went to his neighbor and, shaking him out of sleep, said to him, "I am going now. If you want to come with me, let's go and I'll give you some of the inscribed amulets (*scriptes*) I'm carrying to ward off the terrors of the night." The neighbor asked, "You want me to go with you?" "If you want to," said the tailor, "I don't want to force you." After a pause, the neighbor said, "Go in the name of God, and may God aid you in all you do."

After speaking with his neighbor, the tailor went to the designated place, drew a large circle on the ground, and inscribed a cross inside it. He carried on him the four Gospels and other sacred writings, and as he stood in the middle of the circle, he put four small medallions (*monilia*) at the borders of the circle to form the shape of a cross. On each medallion were written saving words, like "Jesus of Nazareth," and so forth. Then he awaited the arrival of the ghost. Finally the ghost arrived in the shape of a she-goat and it walked around the circle three times saying, "Ah, ah, ah." When the tailor conjured it, it fell flat on the ground and then rose up in the shape of a tall man, horrible and gaunt, who resembled a picture of one of the [Three] Dead Kings. The tailor asked him if his efforts had been of some use to him, and he said, "God be praised, yes! I stood behind you that afternoon when you buried my absolution in my grave and were so afraid. That is not surprising for there were three devils present there who had punished me with every conceivable torture from the first time you had conjured me until my absolution. They suspected that they would be able to imprison and punish me for just a little longer. Know, therefore, that on this coming Monday I will enter into everlasting joy along with thirty other souls. Now go to this certain stream and you will find there a flat rock. Lift it up and take the sandstone underneath it. Wash your whole body and rub it with the sandstone and you will be healed within a few days." The tailor asked him about the names of the other two spirits, but he said, "I cannot tell you their names." When he asked him about their social status, he said, "One of them is secular, a belligerent man not from this country. He killed a pregnant woman and will have no relief before Judgment Day. You will see him in the shape of a little ox that has no mouth, eyes, or ears, and he can never speak no matter how much you conjure him. The other was a religious, and he appears as a hunter blowing his horn. He will have relief and can be conjured through a certain little boy not yet mature, if the Lord so disposes." Afterwards [the tailor] asked him about his own condition, and he said, "You unjustly hold the hood and gown of one of your friends and colleagues [away] on the war across the sea [i.e., a crusade]; give them back to him or you will pay dearly." The tailor said, "I don't know where he is." The ghost said, "He lives in such and such a village near the castle of Alnwick." Finally the tailor asked him, "What is my worst sin?" He responded, "Your worst sin is due to me." The living man asked him how and why. He said, "People are sinning by lying about you, and by defaming other dead souls, saying 'The identity of the dead man he conjured up was So-and-so, or maybe it was this man, or that man.'" He asked the spirit, "What is to be done? I will have to reveal who you are." "No," said the spirit, "but if you will move to such and such a place, you will be rich; and if you remain in the other place, you will be poor. You have some enemies where you are now." Then the ghost said, "I can stay and talk with you no longer." After they had departed from one another, a little deaf, dumb, and blind ox followed the living man all the way to the village of Ampleforth. He conjured it every way he knew how, but it was completely unable to respond. But the other spirit he had helped advised him to put his most powerful amulet (*optima sua scripta*) on his head when he slept, and said, "You should say nothing more or less than what I order you. Keep your eyes toward the ground and do not look at a man-made fire for the rest of the night at least." When the tailor returned home, he was gravely ill for several days.

3. Concerning the ghost of Robert, son of Robert Botleby of Kilburn, seized in a graveyard.

Remember that the said Robert the younger died and was buried in the grave-yard. But it was his custom to go forth from his grave at night and disturb and frighten the villagers; the dogs in the village followed behind him barking ferociously. Finally, the young men of the village were talking together and they proposed to capture him any way they could. They met at the graveyard, but at the sight of him, they all fled except for two of them. Of these, Robert Foxton, grabbed him as he was going out of the graveyard and put him on the church-stile. His friend shouted bravely, "Hold him tight till I get there." Robert yelled back, "Run to the parish priest who can conjure him. For God willing, what I've got, I'll hold till the priest gets here." His friend hurried swiftly to the parish priest and he came and conjured the ghost in the name of the holy Trinity and by the power of Jesus Christ to tell them what they asked. So conjured, the ghost started speaking not with his tongue but from deep within his innards, echoing like an empty barrel. He confessed his various sins. After the priest heard these, he gave him absolution. But he cautioned the two young men who had captured the ghost not to reveal any part of his confession. Afterwards, he left the ghost to rest in peace, God willing.

But it is said that before his absolution, he would stand at the doors and windows of houses, and beneath their walls and partitions as if listening, perhaps waiting for someone to come out and conjure him to help him in his need. Others say that he had aided and plotted the murder a certain man, and that he had done other evil things the particulars of which should not be mentioned at present.

4. Again, old folk pass down the story of a certain man named James Tanker-ley who was once the rector of the church of Kirby and was buried before the chapter house at Byland [Abbey]. It was his [spirit's] custom to go forth at night all the way to Kirby, and one night he blew out the eye (*exsufflavit oculum*) of his concubine there. It is said that the abbot and convent had his body in its coffin exhumed from its tomb, and they made Roger Wayneman cart it to Gormire [Lake]. While he was throwing the coffin into the water, his oxen almost sank into the marsh out of fear. But God forbid that in writing such things I should be placed in any danger, for I have written it down just as I heard it from my elders. May God have mercy on him if in fact he was numbered among the saved.

5. Next I will write about a marvelous thing. It is said that there was a certain woman who took a certain ghost and carried it on her back into her home in the presence of some people, one of whom reported that he saw the woman's hand sunk deep within the ghost's flesh, as if its flesh were rotten, not solid, but an apparition.

6. Concerning a certain canon of Newburg whom [*blank*] seized after his death.

It happened that this man and the head plowman were talking together as they walked in the field. Suddenly, the plowman fled in absolute terror and the other man was left wrestling with some ghost who shamefully tore his clothes to shreds. But at last he gained the victory and subdued the ghost. When he was conjured, the ghost confessed that he had been some canon of Newburg and had been excommunicated because of some silver spoons that he had hidden in a certain spot. He begged the living man to go there, retrieve the spoons, take them back to his prior, and seek absolution for him. When he went there, he found the silver spoons in the place the ghost said. The ghost was absolved and rested in peace from then on. Nevertheless, the man who wrestled with the ghost was sick and incapacitated for many days; and he affirmed that the ghost had appeared to him dressed in the habit of the canons.

7. Concerning a certain ghost conjured elsewhere who confessed that he had been grievously punished because he was a wage laborer for a certain franklin and he had stolen some of his sheaves which he fed to his oxen to make them look fat. Something that burdened him more was that he had not plowed his land deeply but shallowly, hoping to keep his oxen fat. He said that there were fifteen spirits in one spot, being severely punished for the sins they had committed. He begged that he apply to his lord for an indulgence and absolution so that he could get proper relief.

8. Next, concerning another spirit following after William de Bradeforth and shouting "how, how, how," three times over three nights. It happened that on the fourth night, about midnight William returned to the new place [sic] from the village of Ampleforth. And while he was going back along the road he heard a terrifying voice yelling far behind him, as if it were on a mountain. A moment later it yelled again but this time nearer. A third time he heard the voice shouting at the crossroads ahead of him, and then he saw a pale horse. His dog barked meekly, but then hid itself between William's legs utterly terrified. When this happened, William charged the spirit in the name of the Lord and by the power of the blood of Jesus Christ to depart and not block his path. When the spirit heard this, it withdrew, looking like a canvas sail unfurling its four corners and billowing away. From this it can be gathered that this was a spirit greatly wanting to be conjured and given effective aid.

9. Concerning the ghost of a man from Ayton in Cleveland. It is reported that he followed a man for twenty-four miles asking that he conjure him and give him aid. When he was conjured, he confessed that he had been excom-

municated for stealing something worth six pence; but after he received absolution and made satisfaction, he rested in peace. In each of these cases, God
showed himself to be a just remunerator since no bad deed goes unpunished
and no good one goes unrewarded.

It is said that before this spirit had been conjured, he used to toss living
people over a hedge then catch them on the other side as they landed. When
he was conjured he said, "If you had done so in the first place I wouldn't
have harmed you; you were [frequently] terrified in places like this, and I
caused it."

10. How a penitent thief vanished from the sight of a demon after he had
made confession.

Once upon a time in Exeter, there was a certain ditch digger, a hard worker
and big eater, who was staying in a small room inside a large house subdi-
vided by walls into many smaller rooms. The house also had a small upper
chamber. It was the ditch digger's regular habit when he was hungry to climb
up the ladder to this chamber, slice a piece from the meat hanging there,
cook it, and eat it – even during Lent. When the lord of the house saw slices
missing from his meat, he asked his servants about it. After all of them denied
knowing anything and purged themselves with an oath, the lord threatened
to go to a certain wicked necromancer (*nigromanticus*) and consult him about
this odd occurrence. When the ditch digger heard this, he was quite afraid
so he went to the friars, confessed his sin in secret, and received sacramental
absolution. Meanwhile, the lord of the house did indeed go the necromancer
as he had threatened. The necromancer anointed the fingernail of a small boy
[see Doc. 62, No. 29] and, making some incantations, asked him what he saw.
The boy said, "I see a groom with a shaved head." The conjurer then told the
boy, "Let him appear to you in as beautiful form as he can." And so he did.
And the little boy said, "Look! I see a very beautiful horse." Then he saw
a man who looked like the ditch digger going up the ladder and slicing the
meat while the horse followed behind. The cleric [*sic*] asked, "What are the
man and horse doing now?" The child said, "Look! He is cooking and eating
the meat." He asked again, "And what is he doing now?" The little boy said,
"Both of them are going to the friars' church, but the horse is waiting outside
the doors while the man goes in, kneels down, and speaks to some friar, who
is placing his hand over the man's head." Again the cleric asked, "What are
they doing now?" The boy answered, "Both have vanished from my sight
and I can't see them anymore. I have no idea where they are."

11. Concerning the marvelous work of God, who summons things that exist

and things that do not, and who can do whatever he wishes whenever he wishes it, and concerning a certain wonder.

It is worth remembering that there was a man from Cleveland named Richard Roundtree who, leaving his pregnant wife behind, went on pilgrimage to St. James at Compostela with a number of other people. One night they spent the night in the woods near the royal road. Here one of them kept watch for part of the evening for fear of the night while the others slept securely. It happened that during this man's turn at watch he heard a great noise of people passing by along the royal road. Some of them were seated riding on horses, sheep, and oxen; others rode on other animals. Each of these animals had been their mortuaries when they died. Finally he saw a little boy tumbling over the ground in a stocking. He conjured this child to tell him who he was and why he was rolling about like this. The little boy responded, "It is unfitting for you to conjure me, for you were my father and I was your son, stillborn (*abortivus*), unbaptized, and buried without a name." When he heard this, the pilgrim took off his shirt and dressed the little boy in it, and he gave him a name in the name of the holy Trinity. Then he took the old stocking with him as proof. When the baby boy had thus been named, he greatly rejoiced and thereafter walked upright on his own two feet where before he had rolled. When his pilgrimage was over, the man held a feast with his neighbors, and then he asked his wife where her stockings were. She gave him one of them, but could not find the other. Then her husband showed her the other stocking which the boy had rolled about in, and she was amazed. When the midwives confessed the truth about the death of the child and its burial in the stocking, the husband and his wife were separated (*divorcium*) since he was the godfather of his own stillborn child [by virtue of having baptized him]. But I think that this divorce greatly displeased God.

A mortuary was a customary death duty – usually one's second-best farm animal – given to the parish rector in lieu of any tithes inadvertently unpaid. Here the spirits ride on their mortuary animals. The separation of the couple is odd since canon law stressed that parents could baptize their children in an emergency without creating an impediment to their marriage through spiritual affinity. See Doc. 3.1.

12. Concerning the sister of Adam de Lond the elder, seized after death according to the reports of the old folk.

It should be remembered that this woman was buried in the graveyard at Ampleforth and shortly after her death William Trower the elder seized her ghost and conjured it. She confessed that she wandered her way in the night because of some property deeds that she had unjustly handed over to her brother Adam. This happened after a disagreement occurred between her husband and herself. To the harm of her husband and his sons she gave these deeds to her brother, which after her death allowed her brother to evict her husband with violence from his property – namely a toft and croft with appurtenances in Ampleforth, and in Heslerton one bovate of land with appurtenances. So she begged William to suggest to her brother that he return the deeds to her husband and sons and restore her land to them, otherwise, she would have no rest at all until Judgment Day. Obeying her behest, William proposed this to Adam, but he refused to return the deeds, saying, "I do not believe what you've told me." William said, "Every word I've told you is true. God willing, you will hear your sister speaking to you about this in a short while." The next night, he again caught the ghost and took her to Adam's room where she spoke to him. According to one person, her hard-hearted brother said, "Even if you have to wander for eternity, I still won't return the deeds." Groaning, she said to him, "May God judge between you and me over this matter. But know that I will have little rest until your death; but after your death you will wander in my place." It is further said that her right hand hung limp and was very black. Asked why, she said it was because she so often extended it in quarreling and swearing false oaths. Finally, she was conjured to go to another place because of the terrors of the night and the fear of the people of the village. But I beg your pardon if I have given offense by writing anything contrary to truth. For it is said that Adam de Lond the younger, made partial restitution to the rightful heirs after the death of Adam the elder.

13. By Master Richard de Puttes, etc. A story about the celebration of mass. 1373 A.D.

A certain man from Haydock in the county of Lancaster had a concubine with whom he had children. This woman died and he took another woman as his wife. Later, it happened one day that this man went to a blacksmith to repair and sharpen the iron coulter and plowshare of his plow. This blacksmith lived in another village called Hulme, about two miles from Haydock. As he was returning at night he came to a standing cross on the road which is called Newton Cross and there he was seized with a terrible horror. Thoroughly terrified, he looked about and saw what appeared to be a dark shadow which he conjured not to hurt him but to tell him what it was. A voice answered from the shadow and said to him, "Don't be afraid. I am the woman who was once your lover, and I am permitted to come to you to seek your help." The man asked her how she was doing. She said, "Badly, but you can help me if you wish." The man answered, "I'll willingly do whatever I can if you tell me how." She said, "Through masses celebrated by good priests I can be freed from the great pain I'm suffering." He told her, "I will have masses said for you even if I have to spend everything I own down to my last penny." And then she said, "Don't be afraid, but put your hand on my head and take what you find there." He put his hand on her head and took from it just about half a handful of very black hair; yet the woman, when she was alive, had very beautiful, saffron-colored hair. Then the woman said, "If you have as many masses said for me as there are strands of hair here, I will be freed from pain." He agreed, and then she said, "Come to this place at the appointed hour and you will know my fate." And then she vanished. He took these hairs and attached them to a hole in a post with a peg. He sold some of his goods, raised the money, set out near and far in search of priests, and had the masses celebrated. When he had done this, he looked again at the strands of hair and found that as many of them had changed to the color of saffron as he had had masses celebrated. And so he had more and more masses said until all the hairs had changed to the color of saffron. Afterwards, at the appointed time he returned to the cross. He waited there for a little while and saw a light in the distance quickly moving toward him. When it reached him, a voice from within it spoke to him thanking him. It said, "You are blessed among all men because you have liberated me from the greatest pain, and now I head for joy." After this brief conversation, the light receded from him at great speed. Supply [a conclusion about] the power of the mass, etc. [*This last sentence is for a preacher using this story in a sermon.*]

What motives might the author have had in recording these tales? How dangerous or frightening are these spirits? To what extent can they be controlled? What keeps them from finding rest? Do the images they assume when they appear seem to have symbolic value for the storyteller? Do we conceive of ghosts in a similar way and tell similar tales?

42. THE SORCERY TRIAL OF LADY ALICE KYTELER (1324)

Despite the stereotype, the Middle Ages was not an era preoccupied with witches and witch-hunting; these were paranoias of the sixteenth and seventeenth centuries. Still, medieval people did believe that some people – usually women – trafficked with demons and became their servants. When authorities discovered these traitors to Christianity, they were arrested and frequently capitally punished. Pope Gregory IX originally established the papal inquisition in 1231 to investigate and prosecute heretics. Staffed typically by Dominicans and vested with jurisdiction that superseded local episcopal courts, its investigative protocols (including the gathering of evidence through anonymous informants and torture of defendants when necessary) overrode many of the legal safeguards that canon law traditionally offered the accused. Though inquisitors received papal permission in 1258 to extend their jurisdiction to suspected witches if they were also heretics, it was Pope John XXII, himself obsessed with uncovering supernatural plots, who first permitted inquisitors to investigate cases of witchcraft per se in 1320. Nevertheless, mass waves of witch-hunting did not follow in the wake of this permission. In fact, the trial in 1324 of Alice Kyteler of Kilkenny in Ireland, her son William Outlaw, and ten associates (three men and seven women) marks the earliest case on record of an organized group of medieval people accused of practicing black magic, though throughout the account they are described as heretics and sorcerers rather than witches. The claim that Alice had sexual intercourse with her demon familiar is the first recorded instance of what would become a stock charge in the witch-hunts of later centuries. In fact, all the allegations against Alice and her company bear hallmarks of the later persecutions. But the charges against Alice and her company seem born as much out of social malice as fear of witchcraft. Alice, who came from a wellborn Kilkenny family, married a wealthy banker, William Outlaw, Sr. After his death she remarried three more times. Legal records reveal that a number of local knights and gentry were bound to Alice and her eldest son, William Outlaw, Jr., for large loans, and evidently the two had gained a reputation in Kilkenny as money grubbers. (At his trial, William was also accused of usury.) Fueling this local notoriety, her stepchildren from her three later marriages felt cheated from the due share of their inheritances, which seems to have passed largely to Alice and, by default, William. These financial grudges, harbored by the stepchildren who first denounced Alice and William to the bishop and eagerly supported by their debtors, lay at the heart of the charges of sorcery against them and their friends. Igniting this situation was the militant Franciscan bishop of Ossory, Richard Ledrede, who, as a protégé of John XXII, showed a zeal for sniffing out suspected heretics and sorcerers in his diocese rare for the time. Indeed, most of the summary of the trial and its surrounding events (omitted here) recounts his relentless efforts to arrest and try William Outlaw despite opposition from most of Kilkenny's secular officials. After legal maneuvering, threats veiled and otherwise, and a stint in prison, William finally admitted his crimes and did penance, which included a promise to make a pilgrimage to the Holy Land and to put a new lead roof on Ledrede's cathedral church. Alice herself avoided trial by fleeing the city and was excommunicated. Several of her companions, including her servant, Petronilla of Meath, paid for the accusations against them with their lives.

Source: trans. J. Shinners from Thomas Wright (ed.), *A Contemporary Narrative of the Proceedings Against Dame Alice Kyteler, Prosecuted for Sorcery in 1324* (London: John Bowyer Nichols, 1843), pp. 1-4, 25-26, 31-33, 40. Latin.

The events that follow happened in Ireland during the time of Pope John [XXII]. Upon making a visitation of his diocese, the venerable father, Brother Richard, bishop of Ossory, accompanied by five knights and a large number of noblemen, discovered through formal inquiry that in the city of Kilkenny there were for a long time past and still were many heretic sorcerers employing various kinds of sorcery that had the whiff of assorted heresies about them. Undertaking to investigate these things, as he was duty-bound to do, he discovered that a certain wealthy lady called Lady Alice Kyteler (the mother of William Outlaw) along with many of her companions was ensnared in various heresies.

To wit: first, intent on getting things through their wicked sorcery, they would completely reject faith in Christ and the church either for a year or for a month (depending on whether what they wanted to get through sorcery was a large or small matter) so that during this whole period they believed nothing that the church believes: they would not adore the Body of Christ, or go into a church, or hear mass, or eat blessed bread or [use] holy water.

Second, that to make sacrifice to demons they used live animals that they cut up limb from limb and, placing them at the crossroads, they offered them to a certain demon – from among hell's poorer ones – who wanted to be called the Son of the Art (*Artis Filium*).

Third, that through their sorcery they sought counsel and answers from demons.

Fourth, that in their assemblies (*conventiculi*) at night they usurped the church's jurisdiction and the power of its keys by fulminating sentences of excommunication with burning candles even against their own husbands, expressly naming and specifying every member of the [excommunicate's] body from the sole of the foot to the top of the head, and, extinguishing the candles at the end, saying "Fi, fi, fi. Amen."

Fifth, that taking the intestines and entrails of the cocks they sacrificed to demons along with certain disgusting worms, assorted herbs, fingernails taken from dead people and hairs from their backsides, the brains and swaddling clothes (*panni*) of babies dying without baptism, and also many other disgusting things boiled together over an oak fire in the skull of a beheaded thief, they employed these various powders, ointments, and pastes, as well as candles made from the fat rendered from the boiling in the said skull, along with their various spells, in order to stir up people to love or hate, to kill or afflict the bodies of faithful Christians, and to get countless other things.

Sixth, that four of the sons and daughters of the said lady's husbands raised public complaints to the bishop, seeking remedy and aid against her and openly alleging before the people that through various kinds of sorcery she had herself killed some of their fathers and had infatuated the others, so befuddling their good sense that they had turned over all their goods to her and her son, to the everlasting impoverishment of their children and heirs. Thus, her current husband, the knight John le Poer, had been put into such a state through powders and pastes like this and also through sorceries that he was totally wasted away, his fingernails fallen off and all the hair on his body gone. But alerted by one of the lady's maidservants, he forcefully grabbed from the lady's hands the keys to some chests belonging to her, opened the chests, and in them the knight found a bag filled with horrible and revolting things of the sort mentioned above. After he found these, he gave them to two pious priests to turn over to the above-mentioned bishop.

Seventh, that the said lady had a certain demon as her incubus which she allowed to know her carnally. It wanted to be called Son of the Art or, occasionally, Robin, Son of the Art. Sometimes it appeared to her in the shape of a cat, sometimes as a furry black dog, sometimes as a black man (*Ethiops*) accompanied by two larger and taller companions one of whom carried some kind of iron rod in his hands. She entrusted herself and all her of things to him and also acknowledged that she had gotten all her riches and everything she owned from him....

[*After Alice fled the bishop's justice, he tried her* in absentia *and found her guilty of being a "sorceress, a magician, and a relapsed heretic." He also dealt with the charms allegedly confiscated from her:*]

Therefore, on that same day [of her judgment] the bishop had a large fire built in the middle of the town of Kilkenny, and in it he ordered burned publicly in everyone's presence the bag filled with the ointments, powders, unguents, fingernails, hair, herbs, worms, and the countless other horrible things with which she had perpetrated her sorcery and sacrilege....

[*Ledrede then turned his attention to prosecuting her son William, who eventually confessed to aiding and abetting heretics. He also executed justice against one of Alice's alleged followers:*]

This same day [of William's arrest], the heretic Petronilla of Meath, one of the said Lady Alice's accomplices, was burned, who, after being whipped [as penance] six times by the bishop for her sorceries, was ultimately arrested because she was a heretic. She publicly confessed before the clergy and people that, with the instruction of the said Lady Alice, she had completely rejected faith in Christ and the church, and had sacrificed three times to demons on her lady's behalf. Each of these times she had offered three cocks at the crossroads outside the city to a certain demon who wanted to be called Robert, Son of the Art – one of hell's poorer ones – by spilling their blood and cutting them up limb from limb. At the said lady's instruction, in the skull of some beheaded thief she made many potions, pastes, and powders out of the cocks' entrails along with spiders and other black worms similar to scorpions, a certain herb called yarrow (*millefolium*), other herbs and detestable worms, and the brains and swaddling clothes of an infant dying unbaptized. [These were used] to afflict the bodies of the faithful and to stir up love or hate, and, by casting certain spells, to make the faces of certain women appear to some people to be horned like a goat.

She also confessed that many times at the said Alice's goading and in her presence she had consulted demons and received answers from them, and she had made a pact with her that she would be the go-between for her and her friend, the said demon Robert. She also confessed publicly that with her own eyes she had seen the spot where the said infernal demon in the shape of three black men carrying three irons rods in their hands had appeared in broad daylight to the same lady. With her looking on, he had carnal relations with [Alice]. When this enormously evil deed was done, she had cleaned this foul spot with her own hands using her canvas bedspread. She said, among other things, that she herself, along with the said lady, often pronounced a sentence of excommunication against her own husband using a burning wax candle and various sorts of spitting as their ritual required. And though she was highly skilled in their wicked arts, she said that she was nothing compared to her mistress from whom she had learned all these things and many others; in the whole realm of the king of England there was no one wiser than she, and no one in the world was reputed her equal in her craft.

When the sacrament of penance was offered to her, before all the people she bluntly refused it, and, her detestable crimes uncovered, she was burned with due solemnity before an infinite multitude of the people. She was the first sorceress-heretic among the so many who were ever burned in Ireland....

Concerning the fate of the other heretics and sorcerers of the above-mentioned baleful society of the aforesaid Robin, Son of the Art: following the due course of the law, some of them were publicly burned; others, when they had openly admitted their crimes before all the people and had abjured their heresy, were signed with the cross on the front and back of their outer garments as is customary; others were solemnly whipped through the city and marketplace; others were banished from the city and diocese; others, who evaded the jurisdiction of the church, were publicly excommunicated; still others fleeing in fear and lying low have not yet been found. And so this most foul nest was dispersed and destroyed by the authority and special grace of Holy Mother Church with the Lord's aid and – truth be told – with God's special grace....

Was Lady Alice a witch? What is the evidence against her? What kinds of power are imputed to her? To what extent is the accusation of witchcraft a way to exert social control over Alice? Does the fact that she is a woman have any bearing on the charge against her and its details?

43. BERNARDINO OF SIENA ON WITCHCRAFT AND SUPERSTITION (1427)

Bernardino of Siena (1380-1444) joined the Franciscan order in 1402 and spent the next forty years preaching up and down Italy. Since he was such a skilled and popular preacher – one of the greatest of the Middle Ages – clerics commonly transcribed his sermons verbatim as he delivered them, and the scores of them that survive make us particularly well informed about what he preached and how. This excerpt, from a much longer sermon on pride, lechery, and avarice preached at Siena's Campo in August 1427, discusses blasphemy, superstition, and witchcraft as subdivisions of pride.

Source: trans. Helen J. Robins in Nazareno Orlandi (ed.), *Bernardine of Siena, Sermons* (Siena: Tipografia Sociale, 1920), pp. 163-76; revised by J. Shinners from Bernardino da Siena, *Prediche volgari sul Campo di Siena, 1427*, ed. Carlo Delcorno (Milan: Rusconi, 1989), v. 2, pp. 1002-40. Italian.

.... God forbid that a fearful judgment should overtake you because of your sin, for I know well that you have blasphemed and that daily you do blaspheme God and the saints. Your land will be laid waste and fire will light upon your city, Siena, and your country will fall under the rule of the enemy and be sacked of all the good things found in it. Then it will be desolate of those who dwelled there, and abandoned by those who used to till it, and the soldiers will possess it, and the daughter of Zion will be like an empty shadow, like the vine when it is stripped of its fruit. God will say, "Until now I have used oil, I have allured you with sweet promises to make you return to me. Now you will be in greater peril than you ever have been, for now you will become like the shadow of a vine." Did you not know that after the vintage, only the phantom of the vine remains? So will it be with your vines: they will be like shadows, since, because of the wars, it will be impossible to till the vineyards, and even if they were tilled, their fruit will be plundered. The soldiers will leave your houses without floor or windows or doors. Here will lie a house half in ruins; the beams of another's ceiling will have fallen to the ground. O how then shall [Siena] be called when she is so devastated? She shall be called a shadow. Mark me! Have you noticed that when they build the little hut for the man who guards the melons, it is always a habitable shelter while there are melons? But when these are gone, then it stands there like a hovel. Ah, citizens, give heed to him who has seen such things with his own eyes! I have come upon a place which, because of the wars raged there, had been abandoned, so that only three or four friars were left there. Wild beasts dwelled there as if there had always been a forest there. Where once lived so many men of high estate, now there lived wild beasts. Alas, woe is me! City of Siena, beware! You had better beware! When the house of your neighbor is on fire, have you never heard these words: "Hasten with water to your own house?" O my fellow citizens, have you not eyes? If you have them, open them a little! O city of Siena, open your eyes and amend yourself now so far as you can, so that you won't become a hovel or a shadow. Enough! I want this to suffice now regarding the sin of blasphemy. What is this sermon called, O women? This is a sermon about truth.

Another sin which derives from pride is the sin concerning charms and divinations, because of which God many times sends his scourges into cities. I realize that I spoke about this once before, and I said so much about it that he who heard me and understood what I was talking about must have been struck with fear. For I spoke so plainly and clearly about it that I thought nothing more needed to be said. Here is someone who [for health] measures by a span of the palm, another with parchment talismans (*brevi*), another with charms, another with sorceries, another with divinations. Some have visited the enchanter or diviner if they have been robbed of five cents. Do you know what you have done? You have caused men to renounce God, and you have caused the devil to be adored. O me, O me! The Lord of Heaven and Earth has been debased, and to think that the devil is adored through such a great iniquity. And this man says, "Really, I don't know what the matter is; I find that I've been told the truth." And I say to you that you do not perceive how you have been deceived, and that you were shown one thing for another. Alas! you who are so blinded, have you never comprehended his snares and deceits, how he has always deceived us, and has struggled to do so? Go look at the beginning of the book of Genesis, when he began to tempt Eve and Adam; how, persuading them to break God's commandment, he said, *Eritis sicut dii, scientes bonum et malum* – "You shall be as gods, knowing good and evil" [Gen. 3:5] if you eat the fruit. And so he caused them to fall. O you who have cast lots, what a great evil you do, and how many people have trusted in them and followed them! How well they teach you the truth! And have they never told you nothing that would make you see that they lie? And despite this have you been willing to forsake them? Woe unto you! O you who have used the charm of the three good brothers [against wounds], what a great evil you do. O you who have used the charm for broken bones, to you, and to him or her who says that she is bewitched, and who makes you believe she is – to all these I say, take heed! For the first to feel the strokes from God's scourges will be those who have trusted in these enchantments and followed them; and next vengeance will overtake those who have not brought them to justice. Have you never noticed in the Old Testament how God condemned this? Solely because it was displeasing to God, and he made this plain and clear. Know that she or he who claims to have the power to break a charm knows as well, be assured, how to work one. When such people say that they wish to cure anyone, do you know what you should do? There is nothing better to do than cry "To the fire! To the fire! To the fire!" Woe is me! Don't you know what happened at Rome while I was preaching there? I wish I could make it happen here too! Come, let us offer a little incense here at Siena to the Lord God. I want to tell you what happened at Rome.

I had preached about these charms and about witches and sorceries to them, but they seemed to think that I had dreamed it all up. Finally it occurred to me to say that whoever knew of a man or woman doing such things and did not accuse them would be guilty of the selfsame sin.... And after I had preached, a multitude of witches and enchanters were accused. And due to the very great number of those accused, a guardian of the monastery came to me and said, "Are you aware that one and all of them are going to the flames?" I asked him, "What then? What is this? What is this? A great number of men and women have been accused." Finally, seeing how the matter stood, he took counsel with the pope, and it was determined that the most important of these women – that is, those who had done the worst – would be taken into custody. One of them told and confessed, without being put to torture, that she had killed thirty children by sucking their blood; she also said that she had let sixty go free. She said that every time she let one of them go free, she had to sacrifice a limb to the devil, and she used to offer the limb of an animal. She had done this for a long time. Yet she confessed more, saying that she had killed her own little son, and had made a powder out of him, which she gave people to eat in these practices of hers. And because it seemed beyond belief that any creature could have done so many wicked things, they wished to prove whether this was indeed true. Finally she was asked whom she had killed. She said who they were, and whose children they were, and in what way and when she had killed them. Going there, they sought proof from the father of the children who had been killed: "Did you ever have a little son who at such and such a time began to pine away and then die?" Finally, since he replied this was so, and since the day and the hour and the manner in which this had happened all agreed, it was proved to be no more or less than what she had said. And she told how she used to go before dawn up to the piazza of St. Peter's, and there she had certain jars or unguents made of herbs which were gathered on the feasts of St. John and on the feast of the Ascension. (Do you know this, witch? Do you understand me? Are you present here? Are there here as well perhaps even some of those accursed ones who are in league with the devil?) Finally I got hold of these unguents, and when I put them to my nose, they stank with so foul a stench that they seemed in truth to be of the devil, as they were. And they said that they anointed themselves with these, and when they were anointed, they seemed to be cats (though this was not so, for their bodies did not change form – but it seemed to them that they did).... At length she was condemned to be burned at the stake. And she was burned so that nothing remained but her ashes.

There was also another woman taken who confessed that she had done like deeds, and she was as well condemned to be burned, but she died in another manner: for she was not strangled before she was put upon the pyre, and the fire was kindled there while she was alive, and nothing more was seen of her but her ashes. What was done to them should be done wherever one of them is found. And therefore I would give you this caution and warn you that wherever one may be, and whoever may know him or her, in any place whatsoever inside or outside the city, straightaway accuse her before the Inquisitor. Whether within the city or outside its walls, accuse her – every witch, every wizard, every sorcerer or sorceress, or worker of charms and spells. Do what I tell you in order that you will not be called upon to answer for it on the Day of Judgment, having been able to prevent so great an evil which might have been prevented if you had accused her. And I tell you another thing: if any man or woman shall be accused of such things and if any person shall go to their aid, the curse of God will light upon his house and he will suffer for it in his goods and in his body, and afterwards also in his soul. Oh! Answer me: does it really seem to you that someone who has killed twenty or thirty little children in such a way has done so well that when finally they are accused before the *Signoria* you should go to their aid and beg mercy for them? If it had happened that she killed one of your little children, what would you think about the matter then? From your own feelings take thought for another. Think of another and greater fact: has it not occurred to you that such enchanters, every time they have worked any charms or spells have denied God by doing so? How great a sin does it seem to you to deny God, eh?....

Does Bernard really believe in witches or is this preacher's rhetoric? What kinds of evidence does he offer for the existence of witches? Why does he choose this topic as part of his sermon on pride?

44. THE *MALLEUS MALEFICARUM* ON SUPERSTITIOUS PRACTICES (c. 1486)

The Malleus Maleficarum *(Hammer of Witches) was compiled around 1486 by the German Dominican inquisitors Heinrich Kraemer and Johann Sprenger working under the authorization of Pope Innocent VIII, who wished to root out what he saw to be a growing epidemic of witchcraft in Germany. It became the chief handbook for witch-hunters – both Catholic and Protestant – for the next two centuries. Though a document of the late Middle Ages, here it draws on church authorities from across the centuries as it makes the distinction between lawful and unlawful magic and, in so doing, offers revealing details about the popular use of Christian folk magic.*

Source: *The Malleus Maleficarum of Heinrich Kramer and James [sic] Sprenger*, trans. Montague Summers (New York: Dover Publications, 1971; reprint of the 1928 edition [London: John Rodker]), pp. 188–92. Latin.

(Part II, question 2, chapter 7) Remedies prescribed against hailstorms, and for animals that are bewitched.

With regard to the remedies for bewitched animals, and charms against tempests, we must first note some unlawful remedies which are practiced by certain people. For these are done by means of superstitious words or actions; as when men cure the worms in the fingers or limbs by means of certain words or charms, the method of deciding the legality of which has been explained in the preceding chapter. There are others who do not sprinkle holy water over bewitched cattle, but pour it into their mouths.

Beside the proofs we have already given that the remedy of words is unlawful, William of Paris, whom we have often quoted, gives the following reason. If there were any virtue in words as words, then it would be due to one of three things: either their material, which is air; or their form, which is sound; or their meaning; or else to all three together. Now it cannot be due to air, which has no power to kill unless it be poisonous; neither can it be due to sound, the power of which is broken by a more solid object; neither can it be due to the meaning, for in that case the words *devil* or *death* or *hell* would always be harmful, and the words *health* and *goodness* always beneficial. Also it cannot be due to all these three together; for when the parts of a whole are invalid, the whole itself is also invalid.

And it cannot validly be objected that God gave virtue to words just as he did to herbs and [gem]stones. For whatever virtue there is in certain sacramental words and benedictions and lawful incantations belongs to them, not as words, but by divine institution and ordinance according to God's promise. It is, as it were, a promise from God that whoever does such and such a thing will receive such and such a grace. And so the words of the sacraments are effective because of their meaning; although some hold that they have an intrinsic virtue; but these two opinions are not mutually inconsistent. But the case of other words and incantations is clear from what has already been said; for the mere composing or uttering or writing of words, as such, can have no effect; but the invocation of the divine name, and public prayer, which is a sacred protestation committing the effect to the divine will, are beneficial.

We have treated above of remedies performed by actions which seem to be unlawful. The following is a common practice in parts of Swabia. On the first of May before sunrise the women of the village go out and gather from the woods leaves and branches from willow trees, and weave them into a wreath which they hang over the stable door, affirming that all the cattle will then remain unhurt and safe from witchcraft for a whole year. And in the opinion of those who hold that vanity may be opposed by vanity, this remedy would not be unlawful; and neither would be the driving away of diseases by unknown cantrips [spells] and incantations. But without meaning any offence, we say that a woman or anyone else may go out on the first or any other day of the month, without considering the rising or the setting of the sun, and collect herbs or leaves and branches, saying the Lord's Prayer or the Creed, and hang them over the stable door in good faith, trusting to the will of God for their protective efficacy; yet even so the practice is not above reproach, as was shown in the preceding chapter in the words of St. Jerome; for even if he is not invoked, the devil has some part in the efficacy of herbs and stones.

It is the same with those who make the sign of the cross with leaves and consecrated flowers on Palm Sunday, and set it up among their vines or crops; asserting that, although the crops all round should be destroyed by hail, yet they will remain unharmed in their own fields. Such matters should be decided upon according to the distinction of which we have already treated.

Similarly there are women who, for the preservation of milk and that cows should not be deprived of their milk by witchcraft, give freely to the poor in God's name the whole of a Sunday's yield of milk; and say that, by this sort of alms, the cows yield even more milk and are preserved from witchcraft. This need not be regarded as superstitious, provided that it is done out of pity for the poor, and that they implore the divine mercy for the protection of their cattle, leaving the effect to the good pleasure of divine providence.

Again, [the Dominican Johannes] Nider in the first chapter of his *Prae-ceptorium* says that it is lawful to bless cattle, in the same way as sick men, by means of written charms and sacred words, even if they have the appearance of incantations, as long as the seven conditions [among which are that there is no invocation of demons, use of unknown names, or emphasis on the manner of writing or placement of the charm] we have mentioned are observed. For he says that devout persons and virgins have been known to sign a cow with the sign of the cross, together with the Lord's Prayer and the Angelic Salutation [Hail Mary], upon which the devil's work has been driven off, if it is due to witchcraft.

And in his *Formicarius* he tells that witches confess that their witchcraft is obstructed by the reverent observation of the ceremonies of the church; as by the aspersion of holy water, or the consumption of consecrated salt, by the lawful use of candles on the Day of Purification [Feb. 2] and of blessed palms, and such things. For this reason the church uses these in her exorcisms, that they may lessen the power of the devil.

Also, because when witches wish to deprive a cow of milk they are in the habit of begging a little of the milk or butter which comes from that cow, so that they may afterwards by their art bewitch the cow; therefore women should take care, when they are asked by persons suspected of this crime, not to give away the least thing to them.

Again, there are women who, when they have been turning a churn for a long while to no purpose, and if they suspect that this is due to some witch, procure if possible a little butter from the house of that witch. Then they make that butter into three pieces and throw them into the churn, invoking the Holy Trinity, the Father, the Son, and the Holy Ghost; and so all witchcraft is put to flight. Here again it is a case of opposing vanity to vanity, for the simple reason that the butter must be borrowed from the suspected witch. But if it were done without this; if with the invocation of the Holy Trinity and the Lord's Prayer the woman were to throw in three pieces of her own butter, or of that belonging to someone else if she has none of her own, and were to commit the effect to the divine will, she would remain beyond reproach. Nevertheless it is not a commendable practice to throw in the three pieces of butter; for it would be better to banish the witchcraft by means of sprinkling holy water or putting in some exorcized salt, always with the prayers we have mentioned.

Again, since often the whole of a person's cattle are destroyed by witchcraft, those who have suffered in this way ought to take care to remove the soil under the threshold of the stable or stall, and where the cattle go to water, and replace it with fresh soil sprinkled with holy water. For witches have often confessed that they have placed some instrument of witchcraft in such places; and that sometimes, at the instance of devils, they have only had to make a hole in which the devil has placed the instrument of witchcraft; and that this was a visible object, such as a stone or a piece of wood or a mouse or some serpent. For it is agreed that the devil can perform such things by himself without the need of any partner; but usually, for the perdition of her soul, he compels a witch to cooperate with him.

In addition to the setting up of the sign of the cross which we have mentioned, the following procedure is practiced against hailstorms and tempests. Three of the hailstones are thrown into the fire with an invocation of the most Holy Trinity, and the Lord's Prayer and the Angelic Salutation are repeated twice or three times, together with the Gospel of St. John, *In the beginning was the Word*. And the sign of the cross is made in every direction towards each quarter of the world. Finally, *The Word was made flesh* [John 1:14] is repeated three times, and three times, "By the words of this Gospel may this tempest be dispersed." And suddenly, if the tempest is due to witchcraft, it will cease. This is most true and need not be regarded with any suspicion. For if the hailstones were thrown into the fire without the invocation of the divine name, then it would be considered superstitious.

But it may be asked whether the tempest could not be stilled without the use of those hailstones. We answer that it is the other sacred words that are chiefly effective; but by throwing in the hailstones a man means to torment the devil, and tries to destroy his works by the invocation of the Holy Trinity. And he throws them into the fire rather than into water, because the more quickly they are dissolved the sooner is the devil's work destroyed. But he must commit to the divine will the effect which is hoped for.

Relevant to this is the reply given by a witch to a judge who asked her if there were any means of stilling a tempest raised by witchcraft. She answered: "Yes, by this means. 'I adjure you, hail storms and winds, by the five wounds of Christ, and by the three nails which pierced his hands and feet, and by the four Holy Evangelists, Matthew, Mark, Luke and John, that you be dissolved and fall as rain.'"

Many also confess, some freely and some under stress of torture, that there are five things by which they are much hindered, sometimes entirely, sometimes in part, sometimes so that they cannot harm a certain man himself, and sometimes so that they cannot harm his friends. And these are, that a man should have a pure faith and keep the commandments of God; that he should protect himself with the sign of the cross and with prayer; that he should reverence the rites and ceremonies of the church; that he should be diligent in the performance of public justice; and that he should meditate aloud or in his heart on the Passion of Christ. And of these things Nider also speaks. And for this reason it is a general practice of the church to ring bells as a protection against storms, both that the devils may flee from them as being consecrated to God and refrain from their wickedness, and also that the people may be roused up to invoke God against tempests. And for the same reason it is common to proceed against tempests with the Sacrament of the Altar and sacred words, following the very ancient custom of the church in France and Germany.

But since this method of carrying out the Sacrament to still a storm seems to many a little superstitious, because they do not understand the rules by which it is possible to distinguish between that which is superstitious and that which is not; therefore it must be considered that five rules are given by which anyone may know whether an action is superstitious, that is, outside the observances of the Christian religion, or whether it is in accordance with the due and proper worship and honor of God, proceeding from the true virtue of religion both in the thoughts of the heart and in the actions of the body. For these are explained in the gloss on Colossians ii[:23], where St. Paul says: "Which things have a show of wisdom in superstition"; and the [standard] gloss [on the passage] says: Superstition is religion observed without due discipline; as was said before.

The first of these [five rules] is, that in all our works the glory of God ought to be our chief aim; as it is said: "Whether ye eat or drink, or whatsoever else ye do, do all in the glory of God" [I Cor. 10:31]. Therefore in every work relating to the Christian religion let care be taken that it is to the glory of God, and that in it man should give the glory chiefly to God, so that by that very work the mind of man may be put in subjection to God. And although, according to this rule, the ceremonies and legal procedures of the Old Testament are not now observed, since they are to be understood figuratively, whereas the truth is made known in the New Testament, yet the carrying out of the Sacrament or of relics to still a storm does not seem to militate against this rule.

The second rule is that care should be taken that the work is a discipline to restrain concupiscence, or a bodily abstinence, but in the way that is owed to virtue, that is, according to the rites of the church and moral doctrine. For St. Paul says, Romans xii[:1]: "Let your service be reasonable." And because of this rule, they are foolish who make a vow not to comb their hair on the Sabbath, or who fast on Sunday, saying, "the better the day the better the deed," and such like. But again it does not seem that it is superstitious to carry out the Sacrament, etc.

The third rule is to be sure that what is done is in accordance with the statutes of the Catholic Church, or with the witness of Holy Scripture, or according at least to the rites of some particular church, or in accordance with universal use, which St. Augustine says may be taken as a law. Accordingly when the bishops of the English were in doubt because the mass was celebrated in different manners in different churches, St. Gregory wrote to them that they might use whatever methods they found most pleasing to God, whether they followed the rites of the Roman or of the Gallican or of any other church. For the fact that different churches have different methods in divine worship does not militate against the truth, and therefore such customs are to be preserved, and it is unlawful to neglect them. And so, as we said in the beginning, it is a very ancient custom in the churches of France and some parts of Germany, after the consecration of the Eucharist to carry it out into the open; and this cannot be unlawful, provided that it is not carried exposed to the air, but enclosed and contained in a pyx.

The fourth rule is to take care that what is done bears some natural relation to the effect which is expected; for if it does not, it is judged to be superstitious. On this account unknown characters and suspected names, and the images or charts of necromancers and astronomers, are altogether to be condemned as suspect. But we cannot say that on this account it is superstitious to carry out holy relics or the Eucharist as a protection against the plagues of the devil; for it is rather a most religious and salutary practice, since in that Sacrament lies all our help against the Adversary.

The fifth rule is to be careful that what is done should give no occasion for scandal or stumbling; for in that case, although it be not superstitious, yet because of the scandal it should be forgone or postponed, or done secretly without scandal. Therefore if this carrying of the Sacrament can be done without scandal, or even secretly, then it should not be neglected. For by this rule many secular priests neglect the use of benedictions by means of devout words either uttered over the sick or bound round their necks. I say that nothing should be done, at least publicly; if it can give any occasion of stumbling to other simple folk.

Let this be enough on the subject of the remedies against hailstorms, either by words or lawful actions.

How useful is this advice for distinguishing between good magic and bad magic? Is the tolerance for magic here surprising? What kinds of problems do ordinary people employ magic against? Are their concerns reasonable? What kinds of talismans do Kraemer and Sprenger consider to be most effective against trouble?

45. A NECROMANCER'S LOVE SPELL (FIFTEENTH CENTURY)

Beyond folk magic, there was also a long tradition of learned magic which tapped into medieval Jewish and Arabic magical lore and even the vestiges of magic from the pre-Christian era. These traditions later fascinated Renaissance humanists like Marsilius Ficino and Pico della Mirandola. Though natural magic was not itself outlawed, when its rituals explicitly summoned demons for magical aid, they were considered necromancy, the most dangerous and damning kind of magic. As early as the twelfth century there is evidence of a subculture of Christian clergy interested in these dark arts. But church officials regarded books of necromancy with such fear and disgust that whenever they confiscated them, they usually had them burned. This love spell comes from a fifteenth-century necromancer's manual compiled by an anonymous cleric, probably in Germany. In addition to several other love charms, it contains Latin incantations for such tasks as recovering stolen goods, becoming invisible, using a mirror to see into the past, present or future, conjuring up a boat, a feast, a castle, or a horse that can travel anywhere, or gaining total knowledge of the liberal arts in just thirty days from a demonic professor. Note how this spell invokes both demons, the Trinity, the Virgin Mary, and saints. Examples of the wax effigy pierced with needles described here date back to ancient Egypt and Greece.

Source: Richard Kieckhefer, *Forbidden Rites: A Necromancer's Manual of the Fifteenth Century* (University Park: Pennsylvania University Press, 1997), pp. 87-88; with some additional passages trans. J. Shinners, pp. 227-28. Latin.

Take virgin wax, rendered virginal by art [*ceram virgineam, arte virginizatam*], and do this on a Thursday or Sunday, at the hour of Venus or the hour of Jove; and from this wax make an image over burning coals placed in a pot, without smoke. And the master should have some of the hairs of the woman for whom he wishes to act, and three bristles of red hair, and you should have with you a knife with a white handle made for this purpose. And go to the place where a craftsman makes needles, and have the same craftsman make them, from the hour of the Sun until the hour of Saturn. Then the master should take two faithful companions and go to a fruit-bearing tree, and the master should make a circle. And the master should begin this operation, making an image of the woman for whom you perform it, murmuring constantly in your heart, "Thou, Belial, and thou Astaroth, and thou, Paymon, be my helpers in this undertaking." Likewise, you should murmur the words, "I, N[omen or Name], form this image for the love of so-and-so, that it may accomplish that for which it is made. And may thou, Belial, principal prince [of demons], be my helper in this undertaking." Then the master should make the image of this wax, beginning at the hour of Jove, and proceeding until the hour of Saturn. And when the image has thus been made, the master should have nine needles made by an experienced craftsman, who should be bathed and dressed in sparkling clean [*nitidis*] garments when he makes them; he should make the needles from the hour of the Sun until the hour of Saturn. Then the master should fix the needles in the image, placing one in the head, another in the right shoulder, the third in the left, the fourth where people are accustomed to locate the heart, saying, "Just as this needle is fixed in the heart of this image, so may the love of N. be fixed to the love of N., so that she cannot sleep, wake, lie down, [sit], [or] walk until she burns with love of me." He should fix the fifth in the navel, the sixth in the thigh, the seventh in the right side, the eighth in the left, the ninth in the anus. When the image has thus been made, you should baptize [*christianizes*] it, giving it the name [of the woman] for whom you perform the operation, immersing it three times and saying, "How shall it be called?," with the response, "N." And you should say, "I baptize thee, N., in the name of the Father, and of the Son, and of the Holy Spirit. Amen." And then place the image in a new and clean cloth, leaving it aside from the hour of the Sun until the hour of Mars. Then make this conjuration under the fruit-bearing tree, with the burning coals; turning toward the east, say, "O so-and-so, N., I conjure your head, your hair, your eyes, your ears, [your cheeks; O so-and-so, I conjure your brain; I conjure, N., your brain's membrane, both the outer and inner; I conjure, N., your eyes; I conjure, N., your eyelids; I conjure, N., your forehead; I conjure, N., your teeth; I conjure, N., your mouth; I conjure, N., your chin; I conjure, N., your nose; I conjure, N., your nostrils; I conjure, N., your palate; I conjure, N., your gums; I conjure, N., your throat; I conjure, N., your shoulders; I conjure, N., your shoulder-blades; I conjure, N., your chest; I conjure, N., your breasts; I conjure, N., your torso; I conjure, N., your navel; I conjure, N., your thigh; I conjure, N., your kidneys; I conjure, N., your sides; I conjure, N., your anus; I conjure, N., your ribs; I conjure, N., your vulva; I conjure, N., your knees; I conjure, N., your shins; I conjure, N., your toenails; I conjure, N., your arms; I conjure, N., your fingers; I conjure, N., your hands; I conjure, N., your fingernails; I conjure, N., your heart; I conjure, N., your lungs; I conjure, N., your morsels (*bucellas*); I conjure, N., your stomach; I conjure, N., your whole person;] O, N., I conjure your entire substance, that you may not sleep or sit or lie down or perform any work of craft until you have satisfied my libidinous desire. I conjure you by the Father and the Son and the Holy Spirit, [by the Master of the Art, by his power, by the wisdom of Solomon, by the true Sabaoth, by the true seraphim, by the true Emmanuel, by all the bodies of the saints that lie in Rome, by the sun, moon, and greater lord, and by the milk of the Virgin, by

Holy Mary, the mother of our Lord Jesus Christ, by the holy Eucharist, and by the Body and Blood of Jesus Christ,] I conjure you and exorcize you and command you, that as the deer yearns for a fountain of water [Ps. 41:2], so you, N., should desire my love. And as the raven desires the cadavers of dead men, so should you desire me. And as this wax melts before the face of the fire, so should N. [melt in] desire for my love, so that she cannot, etc."

The signs [to be sought in] the woman are these: solitude, dizziness [*inuolucio*] of the head, lamenting, sighing, beating [of the breast], wakefulness [and] wailing. Then the master or the one who is taking action [viz., for whom it is performed?] should go to her, and if he sees her standing or sitting alone then the master should continue the conjuration unto the fifth day. And if she is anywhere in the countryside, she will be consumed; but if she is in a town or passing through another city, the master should perform the conjuration until she can come.

And in this all the Spanish, Arabic, Hebrew, Chaldaean, Greek and Latin astrological necromancers [*nigromantici omnes astroloyci*] are in accord. And this experiment was taken [from the book] *On the Secret Arts of the Imaginary Art*, [from the book] *On the Flowers of All Experiments*, etc.

What assumptions about reality lay behind this spell? How far is this ritual removed from the sorts of Christian charms in Doc. 53? Would the practitioner of this spell consider himself a Christian?

CHAPTER SIX: RITUALS

Religion strives to bridge the gap between the sacred and the profane. Crossing that boundary involves ritual words and actions, which are always at the heart of both the prayers and ceremonies of institutional religion and the practices of popular belief. In the Middle Ages the convergence of Christian liturgy, pastoral theology, and the needs and inclinations of popular piety wove a fabric of faith in which the church's sacraments and rituals threaded through every aspect of medieval life: every day was ideally interspersed with public and private prayer, every Sunday and major feast day parishioners gathered for mass, every important rite of passage was blessed by the church. Christianity's holy days even set the rhythm for the year, the days of which were themselves reckoned and named after the dozens of feasts of God, Mary, and the saints that constantly inter-rupted secular time with sacred time.

Soe wie ons here wapenen aen hiet Daer hi int doghede sijn
vdriet Eu iammerlijc waert getormeut Vanden wde oubeket
Eu dan spreet op sine knien Drie pr nr eu ·iij· aue marien
Eu rouwe heeft van sinen sonden Du waer wilhc dat
ouconden Dat die ·xiiij· iaer aklaets heeft Die hem die paus
gregorius geeft Eu noch ·ij· pause dats waerhede Die daer
gauen aklaet mede Eu xl bisscopen des gelike Dit mach
verdieueu aun eu rike Stb verdient al oetmoedehke

46. ADVICE TO A YOUNG WIFE ON MASS AND CONFESSION (c. 1393)

Two key rituals of medieval Christianity were the mass and confession. The book traditionally called Le Ménagier de Paris *(The Householder of Paris) offers insight into how lay people understood these crucial Christian sacraments. The book survives in three fifteenth-century copies based on the original written about 1393. Its author was a wealthy, well-educated, and well-placed Paris burgher in his sixties who composed it for the domestic and moral education of his inexperienced, fifteen-year-old, orphaned wife (whom he addresses here as "sister"). The ménagier's book is an omnium-gatherum of household management, including recipes, gardening tips, veterinary advice, instructions for hiring servants, and even a treatise on falconry. But in the first part of the three-part work, from which the following synopsis of the mass and confession is taken, her solicitous husband assembled basic prayers and other instructions for his young wife's religious and moral guidance. The ménagier's account is not original; his description of the mass can be found in several devotional Books of Hours – a likely source for him to copy – and his summary of confession draws on a popular moral treatise called the* Somme le Roi *written by a thirteenth-century Dominican. Like its close contemporary,* The Book of the Knight of La Tour-Landry *(see Doc. 59), this section from the ménagier's book includes a number of traditional stories plucked from the Bible, ancient history, and oral tradition, many of them stressing a wife's duty*

Fig. 6.1. The Mass of Saint Gregory (facing page)

Devotion to Christ's passion grew popular in the later Middle Ages. This woodcut (c. 1460) depicts a vision granted, according to legend, to Pope Gregory the Great who kneels before the crucified Christ while a cardinal holds the papal tiara over him. Around the cross are items from the Passion: the pillar and scourge, the pliers for removing the nails, a cock crowing Peter's betrayal, three nails, the crown of thorns on the cross beam, the ladder used to remove the body, a man spitting, the dice cast for Jesus' garment, a blindfold, the spear that pierced Christ's side, the wine and gall-soaked sponge on a pole, Judas's thirty pieces of silver, St. Peter, the lantern Judas took to the garden of Gethsemane, Christ's seamless garment on the cross beam, a high priest (wearing a bishop's miter), King Herod or Pilate, the face of Jesus on Veronica's veil, the bundle of reeds and hand that struck him, the bucket of wine and gall, the hand that hammered the nails, and the spice pots carried by the three Marys resting on the empty tomb. The Dutch caption points to "our Lord's weapons" (or emblems) with which he was "miserably tormented by the unknowing Jews," and promises that anyone who says "three Our Fathers and three Hail Marys, and repents of his sins" will gain an indulgence – available to "poor and rich alike" – of 14,000 years granted "by Pope Gregory, as well as by two other popes ... and by forty bishops." From a nineteenth-century facsimile reproduced in F.X. Kraus, *Geschichte der Christlichen Kunst* (Freiburg im Breisgau: Herder, 1897), v. 2, p. 304.

to be obedient. His advice about confession can be compared to the rules contained in Doc. 4.

Source: trans. W.P. Barret in Eileen Power, *The Goodman of Paris, A Treatise on Moral and Domestic Economy by a Citizen of Paris* (New York: Harcourt, Brace and Co., 1928), pp. 54-65; revised here from Georgine Brereton and Janet Ferrier (eds.), *Le Ménagier de Paris* (Oxford: Clarendon Press, 1981), pp. 12-21. Middle French.

The third article says that you should love God and keep yourself in his grace. So I counsel you that, straightaway, and putting aside all tasks, you give up eating and drinking even a little at night, or vespers, and that you take your mind from all earthly and worldly thoughts, and stay in a private place, far from other folk; that you think of nothing but hearing mass at an early hour in the morning, and after this, of accounting to your confessor for your sins in a good, thoughtful, and modest confession. And as these two things – hearing mass and confession – are separate, we will speak first of mass and then of confession.

And as for mass, dear sister, you must learn that mass has several dignities, in three estates or degrees, which it is proper to describe and explain to you. And first, when the priest is robed and has said his *Confiteor* and is ready, he begins his mass: and this is called the *Introit* of the mass; it is the beginning or the entry of the mass, at which point every man and every woman should restrain their thoughts and think of no worldly thing they may previously have seen or heard. For when men and women are in church to hear the divine service, their hearts should not be at home or in their fields, nor with any other things of this world; and they should not think of temporal things, but of God purely, singly, and sincerely, and should pray devoutly to him. After the *Introit* is sung or said, is said nine times *Kyrie eleison, Christe eleison* [Lord have mercy, Christ have mercy], to signify that there are nine hosts of angels called hierarchies, and of each host or hierarchy some come to the mass, not all the order, but of each order a few. Then should everyone pray to these blessed angels that they should pray for us to our Lord, and say: "O you holy angels, who descend from glory to our Lord to minister for him and serve him on earth, pray him to pardon our transgressions and send us his grace."

After this is said *Gloria in excelsis Deo* [Glory to God in the highest]; then should we praise our Savior in these pleasant words: "Most gentle Lord, glory and honor be to you, and to you praise, and blessing, and worship, etc." Then come the orisons to the saints and to Our Lady; we ought to beseech the most gentle Mother of God and the saints to pray for us, saying: "Most glorious Mother of God, you who are a way between thy gentle Son and penitent sinners, pray to your child for us; and you, blessed saints, whom we commemorate, help us and pray with the Queen of the angels that God in his mercy shall pardon my sins and light my heart with his grace." After this is said the *Epistle*, which is as if to remind us that a messenger has come bringing letters that report that the Savior of the world is soon to come. After this is sung the *Gradual* or the *Alleluia* or *Tract* in Lent, and the *Sequence* is said: this shows that there are heralds who come before and declare that the Savior is already on his way, and who sound their trumpets to gladden the hearts of those who wait and believe in the coming of the sovereign Lord. After that is read the *Gospel*, which is the truest and nearest message. For here are the banners, the pennants, and the standard to show beyond doubt that now the Lord is near; and now should everyone be silent and stand upright, and set his heart to hear and mark what the Gospel says, for these are the very words that our Lord spoke with his lips, these are the words that teach us how to live, if we wish to be of the household of the sovereign Lord. Therefore all men ought to be eager and attentive to hear the words of the Gospel, and to remember them. After this the *Offertory* is made, when we ought to offer into the priest's hands something to signify that we offer our hearts to God, saying: "Holy Trinity, receive my heart that I bring as an offering; enrich it with thy grace." And while saying this we should make our offering. After this, when the priest has come again to the altar, he asks us to pray for him; and we ought diligently to pray, for he enters into our needs and makes prayers for us.

Then the priest says *Per omnia saecula saeculorum* [Forever and ever], and then *Sursum corda*. That is to say: Lift up your hearts to God; and the clerics and others reply: *Habemus ad Dominum*: We lift them up to the Lord. Then we ought to prepare ourselves and have our eyes on the priest. After this are sung the praises of the angels, namely *Sanctus, Sanctus, Sanctus* [Holy, Holy, Holy], at which the angels come down and make ready and surround and defend the table where God will descend and by his look alone feed his friends. And then we hope to see his coming, and we ought to prepare ourselves as good loving subjects when the king enters his city. We ought lovingly and with great joy of heart to look upon him and receive him, and looking upon him, to be grateful for his coming, and give praise and blessing, and in our hearts and with a low voice beseech him to grant us remission and pardon for our past errors. For he comes on earth for three things: the first is the forgiveness of our sins, if we are worthy; the second is the gift of his grace, if we know how to ask it; and the third is our salvation from the path of hell.

After this is the *Paternoster* [Our Father] which teaches us to call him Father and to pray to him to forgive us our trespasses as we forgive them that trespass against us, and to lead us not into temptation, but deliver us from evil, Amen. Then is said thrice the *Agnus dei* [Lamb of God], praying God to have mercy on us and give us peace, which may be taken as peace between body and soul, that the body may be obedient to the soul, or peace between us and our enemies, in whatever sense peace is understood.

Next is sung the *Post-communion* and then we ought to beseech our Lord not to withdraw from us, nor to leave us orphans or fatherless. Afterwards are said the last orisons and then we ought to withdraw and commend ourselves to the Blessed Virgin Mary and beseech her to pray her Blessed Child to dwell with us. And when all is said and finished, and the priest has taken off his robes, then we should thank our Lord that he has given us sense and understanding to hear mass and to behold his Blessed Sacrament, thus keeping us in remembrance of his blessed birth and of his blessed passion and blessed resurrection; and we should also pray to him that, as we persevere, he may grant us true and perfect absolution. And then, dear sister, be all alone, with your eyes inclined to the ground and your heart to heaven, and think earnestly and sincerely with your whole heart of all your sins so that you may rid and deliver yourself of them at this hour. But to advise you now how this should be done, I will here treat of it a little according to what I know and believe.

Dear sister, believe me in this that whoever, man or woman, desires faithfully to confess their sins for the salvation of his or her soul, must know that three things are necessary: to wit, contrition, confession, and penance. And he or she must know that contrition demands sorrow of heart in deep agony and repentance, and that it is proper for the sinner with a most humble and contrite heart to ask pardon and mercy and to beseech most earnestly our Creator and sovereign Lord for forgiveness for that which has angered and offended him. The sinner must know that without contrition his prayer is unavailing, since he has his mind and heart elsewhere. And, dear sister, remember the example of the man to whom a horse had been promised if he said an Our Father and kept his thoughts on that alone, but who while praying wondered whether the giver of the horse would leave him the saddle also, and so miserably lost both. So it is with him who prays to our Lord without thinking of his prayer nor of him to whom he prays: who, if he has, by chance, committed some sin for which he merits hanging on the gallows of hell, yet sleeps in this sin, and heeds it not. Yet how would the same man, condemned in this mean world by a petty provost to be hanged on a gallows of wood or stone, or even less, to pay a large fine, if he thought he might escape by contrition, by weeping and imploring the provost or judge, how he would implore him with his whole being in sincerity and tearfulness, with groans and promises of great penance, though now he cannot weep nor earnestly pray the great Lord his sovereign and maker, who from the lofty windows of his providence, where he reigns above, sees all the passions of the sinner's heart! And the sinner knows that his Lord is so piteous and merciful that for the smallest prayer, if it comes from a humble and contrite heart, he would have forgiven all. Even if the sentence against the sinner had already been pronounced, or the sinner was but lately condemned to death, yet can this sovereign repeal and cancel everything, though there is neither provost nor judge except him alone, who for the weeping or prayers that a guilty prisoner may make can cancel the judgment he has given against him. See then, dear sister, what a comparison this is. Yet there is worse to come, for when a man is sentenced to death by the sovereign Judge, if he does not repeal his sentence, it means that the punishment of death is eternal and everlasting; but when he is condemned by a provost the punishment of death is but for a moment. So, fair sister, there is no comparison of the power of the judges nor of the penalties they are able to inflict. Therefore it is wiser, fair sister, to weep and be contrite and address our prayers to him who has sovereign and absolute power, rather than to him who has no power except what is lent and conditional and may not be exceeded. For the sovereign Judge is he who will finally examine and judge us. Therefore, fair sister, what account shall we render to him of the riches of fortune and nature he has lent to us that we have with folly expended for our own use and pleasure, having made no loan or gift of alms to him or to the wretched and patient sufferers, who for love's sake and in his name have asked it of us? If he accuses us of robbing him, as in this theft, what shall we reply? The same is true of our soul, which is his daughter that he loaned to us clean and healthy without stain or blemish, but which we have poisoned with the drafts of mortal sin. If he accuses of us of murder saying that we have slain his daughter that he put in our care, what defense shall we have? The same is true of our heart, our body which is the castle that he gave us to defend, but we have delivered it to his enemy, the devil of hell. What excuse shall we have? Surely, fair sister, unless the Blessed Virgin Mary his mother pleads for us as an advocate, I cannot see how we may escape being, by the good judgment of that sovereign Judge, punished and chained to the gibbet of hell forever as thieves and murderers and traitors, unless the hot tears of our heart's contrition drive the enemy from within us during our life; but that may be done as easily as hot water drives the dog out of the kitchen.

After contrition comes confession, which has six conditions, or it is worth nothing. The first condition of confession is that it be wisely made. First the sinner should choose a wise and worthy confessor. The sinner ought thus to take as an example and mark how every sick creature desires health, and to have and recover health, desires to find the better rather than the worse physician. And the sinner ought also to mark how, since every creature desires bodily health which is a fleeting pleasure that time devours, by greater reason should he care for his noble soul, which it is ordained shall be visited either with eternal good or evil without end. And therefore, he ought to choose a most skillful, wise, and excellent physician so that he may soon regain the health of his sick and wounded soul. For if by chance he takes for his physician one who does not know the remedy to his sickness, he will die. This you see for example when the blind lead the blind; for it is no wonder that they both fall into the ditch. Therefore, a sinner should seek out a most wise and far-seeing counselor who shall be able to cure him of his sins and advise him, who can distinguish one sin from another and so cure them. The confessor should set his whole thought and mind to hear and receive what the sinner shall tell him, and he should as well have the power to absolve him. Then the sinner ought to be aware of and have thought of all his sins long and earnestly beforehand, as I have said before, so that he may be able to tell them, recount them in order, and describe their circumstances to his confessor and counselor. He should have sorrow in his heart that he has committed the sins, and great fear of the vengeance of our Lord, great shame and repentance for the sins, firm hope and sure intent of amending his ways and of never falling back into his errors, but rather hating them like poison, and desiring gladly to receive and joyfully to perform whatever penance his confessor shall prescribe for him to the end that he may be cured and recover his health.

The second condition of confession is that as soon as we have fallen into sin we ought to make confession with haste and speed. For you do not know when God will take speech and health from you; therefore, it is good to make frequent confession. Beggars prove this abundantly who from day to day and hour to hour display their injuries to kind folk to get alms anew. Wounded men from day to day show their sores to the surgeon to gain speedy and fresh healing; in the same way the sinner ought immediately to show and reveal his sin to gain anew healing and a fuller mercy.

The third condition of confession is that we ought to confess and reveal everything at one and the same time, to display and open to the surgeon the whole wound. It is proper to tell everything in the greatest humility and repentance and to forget nothing or leave anything unsaid; however large the mouthful is, it is necessary for it to come forth from your throat. And if the proud heart of the sinner cannot endure this, let him make the sign of the cross before his lips so that the enemy who is stopping up the passage of his words shall depart from him. Then the sinner should constrain himself to tell the heavy sin that is killing his soul. For if he delays any longer, he will forget it in his delay, and so will never confess it; he will thus dwell in such peril that by reason of the sin in which he has remained but has not remembered, there shall be no good deed of his that shall not be blotted out, except by the grace of God. So consider – what pardon shall he ever gain by fasting, or by alms, or by toil of pilgrimage that he undertakes if he has not fully confessed? How shall he who has not truly confessed dare to receive his Creator? And if he does not receive him, how he deceives himself and in what peril he runs. Perhaps on this occasion he hides his sin, thinking to confess it on another near occasion, but not remembering that he is in God's power, who may at will snatch from him his speech or cause him to die suddenly at his desire. If this happens he will be damned for his omission, and on the Day of Judgment he will not know what to reply.

The fourth condition of confession is that we must make an orderly confession and tell our sins in order and according to how theology arranges them. They should be put one after another without interference or dissimulation, nor should the first be put last, nor anything diminished. And we should not excuse ourselves nor accuse others. The sinner must tell the circumstances of the sin, how he thought of it, the cause and motive of his thought, how he has since pursued and committed it, spoken of it, and caused it to be committed. He should tell the time, the place, why and how he performed it, if the sin is natural or against nature, if he did it wittingly or in ignorance, and he should tell everything concerning it – its circumstances and conditions – that may burden his soul.

The fifth condition is that we should confess all our sins at the same time, and to one confessor, not to several. We ought not to divide our sins into two parts and tell half to one confessor and half to another. For confession made in this vicious manner would be unavailing, and would make us even greater sinners inasmuch as we were attempting to deceive our confessor, who represents the person of our Lord Jesus Christ.

The sixth condition is that we ought to confess devoutly and with great meekness, with our eyes turned earthward to signify our shame and abasement for our sin, and our thoughts and mind in heaven. For we ought to remember that we are speaking with God and should address our heart and words to him, and pray him for forgiveness and mercy. For he sees the whole depth of your heart's wile; the priest only understands what he hears.

Now you have heard, dear sister, how we ought to confess; but know that there are [four] things that prevent confession, namely: shame of confessing the sin, an evil fear of having great penance to do, hope of long life, and despair that we take such great delight in our sin that we cannot eschew it or repent of it, and think therefore that confession would be worthless, since we will presently fall again: and for this there is death.

After confession comes penance. This we must do according to the decision and counsel of the wise confessor, and it is performed in three ways, namely by fasting, by alms, or by prayer, as you will hereafter learn....

Now I will show you how to know in what you have erred. We will take first the names and conditions of the seven deadly sins that are so evil that all sins derive from them. They are named deadly by reason of the death that comes to the soul when the Adversary can command the heart to commit them. And also, to keep you henceforth from these sins, I will show and teach you the names and the power of the seven virtues that are contraries of the seven aforesaid sins, and are fit medicine and remedy against them when they are committed. They are so hostile to the sins that as soon as the virtue comes, the sin flies away.

First here are the names of the failings you may confess when you have erred, and after them the virtues in which you should henceforth continue.

> Pride is the sin, the opposite virtue is Humility.
> Envy is the sin, the opposite virtue is Affection.
> Wrath is the sin, the opposite virtue is Gentleness.
> Sloth is the sin, the opposite virtue is Diligence.
> Avarice is the sin, the opposite virtue is Generosity.
> Gluttony is the sin, the opposite virtue is Temperance.
> Lechery is the sin, the opposite virtue is Chastity.

How well conceived is this symbolic explanation of the mass? Would this explanation suffice for lay people who by and large would not understand any of the words of the mass ritual? How psychologically sensitive and discerning is the ménagier's advice for confession? Would it be spiritually comforting or just intimidating?

47. BISHOP GUILLAUME DURANDUS'S LIST OF BLESSINGS (c. 1295)

Ideally, ordinary Christians received six of the church's seven sacraments during their lives. Baptism and confirmation could be received only once; confession, the eucharist, matrimony, and extreme unction were repeatable – the first two regularly, the latter two, hopefully not. (Only clergymen, of course, could receive the seventh sacrament, holy orders.) But beyond the sacraments, the church's rituals constantly touched the lives of medieval Christians. There were few important events for which ritual did not seek divine ratification. This excerpt from the pontifical of Bishop Guillaume Durandus (c. 1230-96; see Doc. 7) suggests the range of medieval ritual life. A pontifical was a service book containing instructions for all the rites, blessings, and ceremonies that a bishop needed to carry out his office, though many of the more familiar rites and blessings could be performed by ordinary parish priests as well. Durandus compiled this most widely used medieval pontifical around 1293-95. Though meant for use in his own diocese and based on an earlier papal pontifical, it soon spread across Europe.

Source: trans. J. Shinners from Michel Andrieu, *Le Pontifical Romain au Moyen-Age: Le Pontifical de Guillaume Durand* (Vatican City: Biblioteca Apostolica Vaticana, 1940), v. 3, pp. 327-33.

The second part of the book concerns the consecration and blessings of things both sacred and profane, namely:

The blessing and laying of the first stone in building a church.

The dedication of a church.

The dedication of an altar done without the consecration of the church.

The consecration of a portable altar.

The blessing of a cemetery.

The reconciliation of a church and graveyard [after some defilement, usually bloodshed].

The reconciliation of a graveyard per se, done without the reconciliation of a church.

The consecration of a paten and chalice.

The blessing of priestly vestments.

The blessing of altar-cloths and linens.

The blessing of a corporal [a square cloth on which the consecrated bread and wine rest].

The blessing of a new cross or a panel on which a cross is painted.

The blessing of an image of the Blessed Mary.

The blessing of images of the saints.

The blessing of a thurible [a vessel for burning incense].

The blessing of sacred vessels and other ornaments in general.

The blessing of a vessel made for conserving the eucharist.

The blessing of reliquaries for storing and conserving relics and other holy objects.

The blessing of a canopy or baldachino (*umbraculum*) over the altar.

The blessing of a panel put in front of or behind the altar.

The blessing of a baptistery or stones of the baptismal font.

The blessing of a signal or bell.

The blessing of a gift offered to the church.

The blessing of the bread given to the people in church after mass or distributed to the poor on the feast of the Ascension.

The blessing of a lamb or other meat, of cheese, milk, and honey at Easter.

The blessing of grapes.

The blessing and investing of a hair-shirt [worn as penance].

The blessing of the first fruits [of the harvest].

The blessing and investing of the cross on those departing in aid of the Holy Land.

The blessing of the staff and pouch or shoulder-bag of pilgrims.

The office performed for those returning from pilgrimage.

The blessing of a new house.

The blessing of a boat.

The blessing of a new well.

The blessing of a new field.

The blessing against animal diseases.

The blessing of weapons and military banners.

A general blessing for anything you wish.

48. VARIOUS BLESSINGS (EARLY ELEVENTH TO THIRTEENTH CENTURIES)

These blessings collected from German service books of the eleventh to thirteenth centuries convey an idea of the sorts of solemn formulas and gestures that accompanied several popular blessings.

Sources: trans. J. Shinners from Adolf Franz, *Die Kirchlichen Benediktionen im Mittelalter* (Freiburg im Breisgau: Herder, 1909; rpt. 1960), II, pp. 77-78, 198-99, 224, 391-92; Blessing for a New Knight: trans. J. Shinners from *Le Pontifical Romain au Moyen-Age*, v. 3, pp. 447-450. Latin.

1. A ritual against intemperate weather from an early eleventh-century manuscript from Freising

Prayers against hails and storms. First, say a litany (see Doc. 50) where the following is inserted: "From harmful storms, deliver us Lord. From the ravages of hail, deliver us Lord. From the provocation of your lightning, deliver us Lord. From the flails of your vengeance, deliver us Lord." "Our Father, who art in heaven, etc." Then let this prayer follow:

1. We beseech you, O Lord, that by your most powerful majesty you repel the devil and all his angels from our borders and fields and all our dwellings, and by your most bounteous mercy you defend us from imminent dangers.

2. Remember us, O Lord, so that, just as you promised our fathers Abraham, Isaac, and Jacob, you spare your wrath from our borders and fields, and defend

our crops so that they may come into your church freed from infestations by their enemies, and may be stored away in our barns so that wayfarers and the poor refreshed by them together with us may bless the Father, the Son, and the Holy Spirit, who live in perfect trinity, etc....

2. A blessing for childbirth from a twelfth-century manuscript from Prüm

1. When a woman has run into danger while delivering, these things should be said. First, touch her stomach at the navel and say: "Uncreated Father, etc." And then on her right side: "Infinite Father, etc." And then on her left side: "Eternal Father, etc." Do this three times and then say: "Anna bore Samuel, Elizabeth bore John, Ann bore Mary, Mary bore Christ. Infant, boy or girl, living or dead, come out; the Savior calls you to the light."

Do this three times and then, with your hand placed over her head, read the Gospel, "In the beginning was the Word [John 1:1]," and swear her to fast on the vigil of St. Margaret [the patroness of childbirth]; take a candle-wick long enough to circle around her stomach, and have her make a vow that she will make a candle from the wick and offer it in honor of St. Margaret the virgin.

2. Another approach: "Little innocent, come out; your brothers call you to the light. Anna bore Samuel, Elizabeth [bore] the one who went before [i.e., John the Baptist]; Mary bore Christ; Elizabeth bore John, holy Mary bore the Savior. In the name of Jesus, break forth ..." [*manuscript ends*].

3. Ritual for a woman's purification from a late-eleventh to early twelfth-century manuscript from Salzburg

Ceremony for the purification of a woman after [childbirth]. After forty days, let the woman come to the church if she has borne a son (but if a daughter, forty-six days); standing at the front of the church let the priest say the psalms "Praise the Lord, ye children" [Ps. 112 (113)] and "Blessed are all they that fear" [Ps. 127 (128)]. Prayers:

1. "Holy Lord, Almighty Father, Eternal God, who pouring forth the grace of your blessing on the sick, etc."

Gospel: "In the beginning was the Word." Then taking her by the right hand, let him lead her into the church saying:

2. "Remove our iniquities from us, we beseech you, O Lord, that we may

merit to enter the holy of holies with pure hearts."

While she lies prostrate, let him say this antiphon: "Pure heart." Psalm: "Have mercy on me" [Ps. 50 (51)]. Our Father. "May the Lord bless you from Zion," etc.

3. "Almighty and sempiternal God, as suppliants we beseech your majesty, that, as your only-begotten Son was made present in the temple in the substance of our flesh, so you make your servant be present to you with a pure heart."

Let her be sprinkled with holy water three times and let the priest say:

4. "O Lord, through the sprinkling of this water give your servant soundness of mind, wholeness of body, preservation of health, firmness of hope, strength of faith here and in eternity world without end."

Let him offer her incense, saying: "May the Lord kindle you by the odor of this heavenly inspiration and fill your heart with the love of his Holy Spirit. Amen."

4. *Ritual of judicial proof from a twelfth-century manuscript probably from Prüm*

To reach a judgment using a psalter [the book of Psalms]. Take a wooden stick with a tip on it and put it in a psalter on the verse, "Thou art just, O Lord, and thy judgment is right" [Ps. 118 (119):137]. Close the psalter with the tip of the stick showing, and tightly tie it shut. Fasten another stick with a hole in it middle and let the tip of the first one be put through it so that the psalter hangs from it and is able to revolve. Let them hold the second stick with the psalter hanging in the middle, and let the suspect person be stood before them. Let one of those holding the psalter say three times to the other: "This man has done this thing." Let the other respond: "He has not." Then let the priest say: "See fit to reveal the truth to us, you by whose judgment the affairs of heaven and earth are governed. "Thou art just, O Lord, and thy judgment is right." "Turn back the evils upon my enemies; and cut them off in thy truth" [Ps. 53 (54):7].

1. Prayer: Almighty and sempiternal God, who created everything from nothing and who formed man from the mud of the earth, we, your supplicants, beseech you through the intercession of Mary, the most holy mother of God, and through the intercession of St. Chrysanthus and St. Daria, and through the intercession of your confessor St. Brandanus, and through all the saints, that you give us the proof of this thing about which we are unsure,

so that if this man here is innocent, this book that we bear in our hands will turn following the true course of the sun; but if he is guilty, this book will turn in the opposite direction. Through the virtue of our Lord Jesus Christ, who lives and reigns, etc.

2. "In the beginning was the Word." Through these words of the holy Gospel of his son, may the Lord be lenient toward all our faults.

3. "We seek that our actions, etc." "Thou art just, O Lord, and thy judgment is right."

5. An episcopal blessing for a new knight (c. 1295)

Blessing for a New Knight

1. In the blessing of a new knight, proceed in this manner: Before the epistle is read the bishop blesses the knight's sword, saying:

2. (Blessing of the sword): "We beseech thee, Lord, hear our prayers and, by the majesty of your right hand, deign to bless this sword, which your servant wishes to gird on him, so that it can be a defender of churches, widows, orphans, and all God's servants against the rage of heathens, and a terror and dread to others lying in wait for them, and make it helpful for fair pursuit and just defense. Through Christ, etc." Response: "Amen."

3. (Another blessing): "Holy Lord, Almighty Father, Eternal God, through the invocation of your holy name, and the coming of Christ, your Son our Lord, and through the gift of the Holy Spirit, the Paraclete, bless this sword so that he your servant who this very day is girded with it may, your mercy granting, trample invisible enemies underfoot and, every victory falling to his hands, may always endure unharmed. Through Christ, etc." Response: "Amen."

4. (Other blessings for arms may be said here, for which see below under "The Blessing of Arms.") Once the arms are blessed, before he belts the sword on him the bishop says:

5. "Blessed be the Lord my God, who teaches my hands to fight" [Ps. 143 (144):1]. Having said this three times with the *Gloria patri* [Glory to the Father], he says: Versicle: "Save your servant. Be for him, Lord, a tower. Lord hear my prayer. The Lord be with you. Let us pray."

6. Prayer: "Holy Lord, Almighty Father, Eternal God, you who alone orders and rightly disposes all things, who by your benevolent arrangement allowed men on earth the use of the sword to restrain the malice of the reprobate and to teach justice, and wished to institute the knightly order to protect the people, and who made Blessed John say to the soldiers coming to him in the desert that they should plunder no one but be content with their pay [see Luke 3:14] – we humbly implore your mercy, Lord, that, just as you bestowed the power on your servant David to conquer Goliath, and as you made Judas Machabeus triumph over the ferocity of those nations not invoking your name, so also with heavenly mercy may you offer to this your servant, who newly puts the yoke of knighthood on his neck, the strength and daring to defend the Faith and justice; and may you rightly dispose him as a guardian for the equal increase of faith, hope, charity, and the fear of God, and for love, humility, perseverance, obedience, and good patience all together, so that he wounds no one unjustly with this or any other sword and defends all things just and right with it; and, as he himself is conveyed from a lesser state to the new honor of knighthood, in the same way, putting off the old man with his acts, he may put on the new man [see Eph. 4:22-24] so that he may fear and rightly worship you, shun the company of the wicked, bestow charity on his neighbor, by his intention be rightfully obedient in all things, and justly carry out his office in all things. Through Christ, etc." Response: "Amen."

7. After this the bishop lifts the unsheathed sword from the altar and puts it in the knight's right hand, saying: "Accept this sword in the name of the Father, and of the Son, and of the Holy Spirit, and use it for your defense and that of God's holy church, and for the confounding of the enemies of the Cross of Christ, the Christian faith, and the crown of the king of France, or others such as these, and, as far as human frailty shall allow you, harm no one unjustly with it. And may he deign to aid you who lives and reigns with the Father and the Holy Spirit world without end." Response: "Amen."

8. Resheathing the sword, the bishop belts the sword and its scabbard onto the knight and while doing this says: "Gird thy sword onto thy thigh, O thou most mighty, in the name of our Lord Jesus Christ, and bear in mind that holy men have conquered kingdoms not by the sword but through faith."

9. When the sword has been belted on, the new knight draws it from the scabbard and boldly brandishes the unsheathed sword three times in his hand and, after wiping it on his arm, he immediately returns it to the scabbard.

10. When this is done, marking him with military status the bishop gives him the kiss of peace, saying: "Be a knight peaceful, vigorous, faithful, and devoted to God."

11. Immediately he gives him a light slap, saying: "Awake from your evil dream and be vigilant in the faith of Christ and of praiseworthy repute. Amen."

12. Then the nobles standing nearby put his spurs on him (where this is the custom) and this antiphon is sung: "Thou art beautiful above the sons of men.... Gird thy sword onto thy thigh, O thou most mighty" [Ps. 44 (45):3-4].

13. Prayer. "Almighty and ever-eternal God, pour forth the grace of your blessing upon this your servant .N. who longs to be girded with this eminent blade, and by the power of your right hand make him confident that he is armed against all adversity by heavenly guardians, so that he should be vexed by no times of wars in this world. Through Christ, etc."

14. Finally he gives him a war banner where this is the custom. (For the blessing of the banner see below under "The Blessing of Arms.")

What is the purpose of a blessing? What are the ritual aspects of a blessing that give it authority? What assumptions about reality does the act of blessing make? To what extent are these blessings ways to exert social control?

49. JACOB OF VORAGINE ON THE GREATER AND LESSER ROGATIONS (c. 1260)

By the sixth century the western church set aside two periods during the spring for public processions and prayers. The Greater Rogation (or Litany) was celebrated on April 25 (later called Saint Mark's Day) and was essentially a Christian adaptation of the ancient Roman Robigalia *in which the agricultural numen,* Robigus, *who both protected wheat from red mildew or rust and gave his name to the disease, was propitiated on April 25 by the sacrifice of a rust-colored dog and a sheep. The Lesser Rogation was celebrated on the Monday, Tuesday, and Wednesday before the feast of the Ascension, from the inspiration, apparently, of Bishop Mamertus of Vienne (d.c. 475) who ordered processions to prevent volcanoes and earthquakes in his diocese. In this excerpt, Jacob de Voragine (see Doc. 32) offers a partly legendary explanation for the origins of these two litanies and describes the ceremonies surrounding them. In many parishes, during Rogation Days parishioners "beat the bounds of the parish" by leading their procession around the boundaries of the parish, making sure it had not been encroached by neighbors, blessing it against the invasion of evil, and praying for a good harvest.*

Source: trans. William G. Ryan, *Jacobus de Voragine's Golden Legend, Readings on the Saints* (Princeton, NJ: Princeton University Press, 1993), v. 1, pp. 285-89. Latin.

The litanies [or rogations] occur twice in the year. The first time is on the feast of Saint Mark [April 25], and this is called the Greater Litany. The second, or Lesser Litany, falls on the three days before the feast of the Lord's ascension into heaven. The word "litany" means prayer, supplication, rogation.

The first litany has three names: Greater Litany, Septiform Procession, and Black Crosses. It is called the Greater Litany for three reasons: the first, the one who instituted it, namely Pope Gregory the Great [590-604]; second, the place where it was instituted, namely Rome, mistress and head of the world due to the presence there of the body of the chief of the apostles and of the apostolic see; the third, the occasion for its institution, which was a widespread and deadly pestilence. The Romans, having lived a continent and abstemious life throughout Lent and having received the Body of the Lord at Easter, afterwards threw off all restraints in feasting, in games, and in voluptuous living. Therefore God, offended by these excesses, sent a devastating plague upon them – a malady called *inguinaria* because it caused a swelling or abscess in the groin [*inguen*]. The plague was so virulent that people died suddenly while walking in the street or at table or at play or just talking to each other. It frequently happened that someone sneezed, as they say, and expired in the very act of sneezing so, if one heard a person sneeze, one quickly said, "God bless you!" This is said to be the origin of the custom that still prevails, of saying "God bless you" when we hear anyone sneeze. Moreover, it is said, when anyone yawned, it was often that person's last breath; so if anyone felt a yawn coming on, one quickly made the sign of the cross – another custom still common among us. A full account of this plague is included in the life of Saint Gregory.

Secondly, the Greater Litany is called the Septiform Procession because Saint Gregory arranged the processions associated with the litany according to seven orders or classes: first, the clergy; second, all the monks and religious men; third, the women religious; fourth, all the children; fifth, all the laymen; sixth, all widows and unmarried women; seventh, married women. In our day we cannot count on that many people, so we supply by providing seven litanies to be recited before the insignia are lowered.

Fig. 6.2. Three Sacraments

The sacraments of baptism, confirmation, and, at the rear, confession. The confirming bishop is Jean Chevot, bishop of Tournai, who commissioned the triptych. Engraving by Huyot of the left panel of Roger van der Weyden's *Seven Sacraments Triptych* (1445-50; oil on wood panel) reproduced in Paul Lacroix's *Military and Religious Life in the Middle Ages and the Period of the Renaissance* (London: Chapman and Hall, 1874), p. 231.

Thirdly, the Greater Litany is called the Black Crosses because, as a sign of their grief over the death toll of the plague, people put on black clothing, and, probably for the same reason, crosses and altars were shrouded in sackcloth. In these days of penance likewise, penitential clothing should be worn.

The other litany, which occurs on the three days before Ascension Thursday, was instituted by Saint Mamertus, bishop of Vienne, in the time of the emperor Leo [the Great], who began to reign in 458 [correctly, 457]. It began earlier, therefore, than the institution of the Greater Litany and has three names: Lesser Litany, Rogations, and Processions. It is called Lesser to differentiate it from the Greater, because it was inaugurated by a lesser bishop, in a less distinguished place, and on account of a less grave situation than the above-described plague.

The reason for the institution was the following. At that time Vienne suffered frequent earthquakes, so violent that they leveled many houses and churches, and rumblings and crashes were often heard at night. Then something more terrible happened: on Easter Sunday fire fell from heaven and reduced the king's palace to ashes. And, yet more dreadful: as in the past God had allowed demons to enter into swine, now, the Lord permitting because of the sins of men, evil spirits entered wolves and other wild beasts, and these, fearing no man, came running openly over the roads and into the city itself, and at times devoured children and old men and women. The bishop, faced daily with such woeful calamities, proclaimed a three-day fast and instituted litanies, and so brought these tribulations to an end. At a later time the church established and confirmed this litany for universal observance.

The Lesser Litany is called Rogations [from Latin *rogare*, to ask or beg] because in these three days we implore the help of the saints. This practice should certainly be maintained, and the prayers to the saints and the fasts insisted upon, for several reasons. First, we ask God to end the wars that so often erupt in springtime. Second, we ask him to preserve and multiply the still-tender young fruits of the earth. Third, we seek his help so that everyone may be able to control the impulses of the flesh, which at this season are stronger than usual; for in the spring the blood is hotter and temptations to wrongdoing abound. Fourth, we pray for help in preparing to receive the Holy Spirit: fasting is an excellent preparation and our supplications increase our worthiness....

The Lesser Litany is called the Procession, because on this occasion the church holds a great procession at which the cross is borne aloft, the bells are rung, the standard is carried. In some churches men carry a dragon with a huge tail. All the saints are besought one by one for their protection. In this procession we carry the cross and ring the bells to make the devils flee in terror; for just as a king in the midst of his army has the royal insignias, namely trumpets and standards or banners, so Christ the eternal King in the midst of his church militant has bells for trumpets and crosses for standards. Any tyrant would be terrified if he heard in his land the trumpets and saw the banners of some powerful king, his enemy; and so the demons who are in that murky air are sore afraid when they hear Christ's trumpets – the bells – and catch sight of his standards – the crosses. It is said that this was the reason for ringing the church bells when storms were brewing, namely that the demons who stir up the storms should hear the trumpets of the eternal King and flee aghast, letting the storms die down. Of course, there was another reason, which was that the bells would warn the faithful and incite them to pray hard in view of the impending danger.

The cross itself is the banner of the eternal King, as a hymn for Passiontide has it:

> The standards of the King advance;
> The mystery of the cross shines out;
> The cross on which life suffered death
> And by death brought forth life.

The demons are afraid of this standard, according to what [St. John] Chrysostom says: "Wherever the demons see the Lord's sign, they take flight fearing the rod that scourged them." Moreover, this is why, in certain churches, when storms come up, the cross is brought out of the church and held up against the tempest, precisely so that the evil spirits may see the standard of the King and flee in terror. There, to sum up, is why the cross is held aloft in the procession and the bells are rung – that the demons who are in the air may flee in fright and desist from harassing us.

Another reason for carrying the standard in the procession is to represent the victory of Christ's resurrection and the victory of his ascension. He ascended to heaven with much booty; thus the banner advancing through the air is Christ ascending to heaven, and as a multitude of the faithful follows the standard carried in the procession, so a great assemblage of saints accompanies Christ ascending.

The chants sung in the procession stand for the chants and praises of the angels who met the ascending Christ and led him with his company into the heavens with choruses of praise. In some churches, and especially in France, the custom obtains of carrying a dragon with a long tail stuffed with straw or some such material: the first two days it is carried in front of the cross, and the third day, with the tail empty, behind the cross. The significance of this is that on the first day, before the Law, and on the second, under the Law, the devil reigned in this world, but on the third, the day of grace, he was expelled from his realm by the passion of Christ.

Again, in that procession we ask for the protection of all the saints. Several reasons for this have already been noted, but there are other general reasons for which God has commanded us to pray to the saints: our neediness, the saints' glory, and the reverence due to God. The saints can know about the prayers of their supplicants, because in that eternal mirror they perceive whatever pertains to their joy or to our aid. Therefore, the first reason is our neediness, which may be due to a lack of merit, in which case, our merits not sufficing, we pray that others may supply for us. Or we may be deficient in contemplation, and since we cannot look upon the supreme light in itself, we pray to be able at least to see it in the saints. Our shortcomings may be in our loving, because it is not uncommon for imperfect man to feel himself more drawn to one particular saint than even to God. The second reason is the glory of the saints, for God wills that we invoke the saints in order that, obtaining what we ask for through their intercession, we may enhance their greatness and by glorifying them join in praising them. The third reason is the reverence due to God, in that we sinners, because we offend God, do not dare, so to speak, to approach him in his own person, but can implore the support of his friends.

In these litanies the angelic canticle *Sancte Deus, sancte fortis, sancte et immortalis, miserere nobis* [O holy God, holy and strong, holy and immortal, have mercy on us] would frequently be sung. John of Damascus tells us in Book III that on one occasion, when, on account of some public tribulation, the litanies were being celebrated, a boy was caught up from the midst of the people and carried to heaven. There he learned this canticle, then returned to the congregation and, in full view of the people, sang the canticle and the tribulation was ended. At the Council of Chalcedon [in 451] the canticle was approved. Damascenus concludes as follows: "We say also that through this canticle the demons go away." The praiseworthiness and authority of the canticle are assured in four ways: first, from the fact that an angel taught it; second, because when it was sung publicly the said tribulation ceased; third, that the Council of Chalcedon approved it; fourth, that the demons fear it.

50. A LITANY OF THE SAINTS (c. 1420-30)

Another kind of litany was the formal ritual supplication of God and the saints. A priest sang each petition aloud followed by a response – italicized here – from the people ("Have mercy on us," "Pray for us," etc.). The litany of the saints, which invokes God, the Virgin Mary, and all the angels and saints, in its earliest form dates back to the third century. In the Middle Ages each region adapted the litany to incorporate local saints. This English version, dating from around 1420, is typical.

Source: modernized by J. Shinners from Henry Littlehales, *The Prymer or Lay Folk's Prayer Book*, Early English Text Society, Original Series 105 (London: Kegan Paul, 1895), pp. 47-51. Middle English.

Lord, be not mindful of our guilt nor of our kindred; and take no vengeance on our sins, for your name, Lord! Spare, Lord, spare the people, you who ransomed the world again with your precious blood. Be not wroth with us without end!

Lord have mercy on us.
Christ have mercy on us.
Lord have mercy on us.
Christ hear us.
God, Father of Heaven; *have mercy on us.*
God the Son, who ransomed the world; *have mercy on us.*
God the Holy Ghost; *have mercy on us.*
Holy Trinity, One God; *have mercy on us.*
Saint Mary; *pray for us.*
Holy Mother of God; *pray for us.*
Holy Virgin of virgins; *pray for us.*
St. Michael; *pray for us.*
St. Gabriel; *pray for us.*
St. Raphael; *pray for us.*
All holy angels and archangels; *pray for us.*
All orders of holy spirits; *pray for us.*
St. John the Baptist; *pray for us.*
All holy patriarchs and prophets; *pray for us.*
St. Peter; *pray for us.*
St. Paul; *pray for us.*
St. Andrew; *pray for us.*
St. John; *pray for us.*
St. Philip; *pray for us.*

St. James; *pray for us.*

St. Bartholomew; *pray for us.*

St. Matthew; *pray for us.*

St. Simon; *pray for us.*

St. Jude; *pray for us.*

St. Matthias; *pray for us.*

St. Thomas; *pray for us.*

St. Bernard; *pray for us.*

St. Thaddeus; *pray for us.*

St. Luke; *pray for us.*

St. Mark; *pray for us.*

All holy Apostles and Evangelists; *pray for us.*

All holy disciples of our Lord; *pray for us.*

All Holy Innocents of our Lord; *pray for us.*

St. Stephen; *pray for us.*

St. Linus; *pray for us.*

St. Cletus; *pray for us.*

St. Clement; *pray for us.*

St. Cyprian; *pray for us.*

St. Lawrence; *pray for us.*

St. Vincent; *pray for us.*

St. George; *pray for us.*

St. Fabian; *pray for us.*

St. Sebastian; *pray for us.*

St. Cosmas; *pray for us.*

St. Damian; *pray for us.*

St. Denis; *pray for us.*

St. Eustace and your companions; *pray for us.*

St. Thomas; *pray for us.*

St. Christopher; *pray for us.*

All holy martyrs; *pray for us.*

St. Silvester; *pray for us.*

St. Hilary; *pray for us.*

St. Martin; *pray for us.*

St. Ambrose; *pray for us.*

St. Augustine; *pray for us.*

St. Jerome; *pray for us.*

St. Gregory; *pray for us.*

St. Nicholas; *pray for us.*

St. Cuthbert; *pray for us.*

St. Swithin; *pray for us.*

St. Benedict; *pray for us.*

St. Leonard; *pray for us.*

St. Giles; *pray for us.*

St. Dunstan; *pray for us.*

All holy confessors; *pray for us.*

St. Mary Magdalene; *pray for us.*

St. Mary of Egypt; *pray for us.*

St. Agatha; *pray for us.*

St. Agnes; *pray for us.*

St. Lucy; *pray for us.*

St. Catherine; *pray for us.*

St. Margaret; *pray for us.*

St. Juliana; *pray for us.*

St. Christine; *pray for us.*

St. Petronilla; *pray for us.*

St. Radegunde; *pray for us.*

St. Frideswide; *pray for us.*

All holy virgins; *pray for us.*

All manner of saints; *pray for us.*

Lord, be merciful and spare us.

From all evils; *Lord deliver us.*

From all temptations of the devil; *Lord deliver us.*

From endless damnation; *Lord deliver us.*

From uncleanness of body and soul; *Lord deliver us.*

From the spirit of lechery; *Lord deliver us.*

From wrath and hate and all evil will; *Lord deliver us.*

From unclean thoughts; *Lord deliver us.*

By your Incarnation; *Lord deliver us.*

By your Passion; *Lord deliver us.*

By your Resurrection; *Lord deliver us.*

By your Ascension; *Lord deliver us.*

By the grace of the Holy Ghost; *Lord deliver us.*

In the Day of Doom; *Lord deliver us.*

We sinful people pray you to hear us.

That you give us peace; *we pray you to hear us.*

That your mercy and you pity keep us; *we pray you to hear us.*

That you govern and keep your church; *we pray you to hear us.*

That you give peace to our kings and princes; *we pray you to hear us.*

That you keep our bishops in holy religion; *we pray you to hear us.*

That you keep all Christian souls from eternal damnation; *we pray you to hear us.*

> That you vouchsafe to give us the fruits of the earth; *we pray you to hear us.*
>
> Lamb of God who takes away the sins of the world; have mercy on us and give us peace.
>
> Christ hear us.
>
> Lord have mercy on us.
>
> Christ have mercy on us.
>
> Lord have mercy on us.
>
> *Our Father who art in heaven, etc.*
>
> *And lead us not into temptation,*
>
> *But deliver us from evil. Amen.*
>
> And your mercy come upon us, Lord;
>
> Your health according to your word.
>
> Be to us, Lord, a tower of strength
>
> From the face of our enemy.
>
> Peace be made in your virtue.
>
> And plenty in your towers.
>
> Lord God of Virtues, convert us,
>
> And show us your face, and we shall be safe.

God, to whom it is proper always to be merciful and to spare, hear our prayer and let your mercy and pity pardon those who have been bound with the chains of sins, through Christ, our Lord. *Amen.*

Lord, be pleased with the prayers of your church, and grant that all errors and adversities be destroyed, through Christ our Lord. *Amen.*

Lord, we beseech you that you burn our lands and our heart with the fire of the Holy Ghost, that we might serve you with chaste body and be pleasing to you with a clean heart, through Christ, our Lord. *Amen.*

Almighty God without end, who are the endless help of all who believe in you, hear our prayer for all men and women, for which we beseech your goodness; and grant them health in body and soul, so that when they are whole, they may give thanks to you in your church, through Christ, our Lord. *Amen.*

For your pity, Lord, we beseech you unbind the bonds of all our sins; and through the prayer of the glorious everlasting maid Mary, with all your saints, keep us your servants, and our king, and all Christian people in all holiness; and all who are related to us by blood or homeland or prayer, be joined with us, cleanse them of all vices, and lighten them with virtues; peace and help give to us, and remove us from our enemies, both those we see and those we cannot. Give your charity to our friends and to our enemies; and help all the sick; and to all Christians living and dead, grant life and endless rest, through Christ, our Lord. *Amen.*

51. LITURGICAL DRAMA (THIRTEENTH AND FOURTEENTH CENTURIES)

Western drama made its medieval revival through liturgical dramatizations of episodes from the Gospels. The troped liturgical sequence Quem quaeritis, *in which the angel asks the three Marys visiting Jesus' empty tomb "Whom do you seek?," was first acted out in a rudimentary drama during Easter mass in the tenth century. As it evolved it became the most popularly performed piece of liturgical drama. But other events in the life of Jesus also lent themselves to increasingly elaborate performance inside and outside the church (see Doc. 57). Seeing the events of sacred history acted out must have always impressed lay congregations who normally would not have understood liturgies conducted in Latin; they almost could not help being struck by these dramatic interruptions in the normally predictable ritual flow of the mass. As the traditions developed, they even assumed roles in the action, if only indirectly. For instance, in the "Visitation of the Sepulcher" from Essen below, they are prompted to sing "a hymn in German about the Resurrection," thus adding their own voice to formal ceremonies typically reserved to clergy. Both excerpts below come from service books of the thirteenth and fourteenth centuries.*

Source: trans. J. Shinners from Karl Young, *The Drama of the Medieval Church* (Oxford: Clarendon Press, 1933), v. I, pp. 333-35; v. II, pp. 99-100. Latin.

1. *During Eastertide the custom arose of depositing a consecrated host on Good Friday in a specially prepared "Easter sepulcher" away from the main altar and meant to represent Jesus' tomb. This interlude, which incorporates and expands upon the early* Quem quaeritis *trope, is from a fourteenth-century manuscript of the collegiate church of canons and canonesses at Essen in Germany.*

The Visitation of the Sepulcher

When the third responsory is over, before the singing of the *Te Deum laudamus* [We praise you, God], the convent, canons, and choristers should again take their places together in the middle of the monastery [church] before the candelabra in the choir stalls. Note that whenever there is a general assembly in this place, as on this day, the convent [the women] shall always remain on the north side, the canons and choristers [the men] on the south. At this assembly all the canons shall be dressed in copes, except for the two who are the Angels. These shall wear white dalmatics over their surplices; also these two shall not take their places with the others until the end, as described below. When they have taken their places together, the two Angels shall go to the sepulcher, passing along the women novices' choir, the small throne, and the raised gallery on the north side. Entering the tent [over the Easter sepulcher], they should sit on the sepulcher (that is, the aforesaid chest [archa]); they may carry the book that contains the chants they will sing if they do not know them by heart and a candle in order to see. They shall await the three Marys coming to the sepulcher. The Marys (that is, three canonesses) shall come along the other raised gallery on the west. Meanwhile, as the Marys go to the sepulcher, the convent shall sing this antiphon in their places:

The Visitation of the Sepulcher

Convent [singing]: *At dawn Mary Magdalene and the other Mary were carrying spices seeking the Lord in his tomb* [see Mk. 16, Lk. 24].

When all three Marys have arrived, they shall stand a little distance from the sepulcher, singing on the way this antiphon – Marys: *Who will roll away for us the stone which we see covering the entrance of the holy sepulcher?*

Then the Angels responding from the sepulcher shall sing this antiphon – Angels: *Whom do you seek, O trembling women, weeping at this tomb?*

Then the Marys shall again sing this antiphon – Marys: *We seek Jesus of Nazareth, crucified.*

Then the Angels again sing in response – Angels: *He whom you seek is not here, but go quickly and tell his disciples and Peter that Jesus has risen.*

Then each of the Marys shall go singly to the tent, peering into it one after the other and saying this to the Angels: *Where is Jesus?* or similar words. The Angels shall answer in this way: *He has risen, he is not here* or similar words also. When this is done, the three Marys shall go up the way to the organ singing this antiphon – Marys: *We go trembling to the tomb and see the angel of the Lord sitting there and saying that Jesus has risen.*

Then immediately two other canons – one older, one younger – in the roles of the Apostles Peter and John shall go quickly from their places to the sepulcher, passing along the women novices' choir and the raised gallery through which the Angels went; but let the younger man go more quickly than the older and arrive at the tomb first. Meanwhile, as these Apostles go thus along their way, the clerics in their places shall sing this antiphon – Clerics: *The two were going together, and that other disciple dashed along faster than Peter and got to the tomb first.*

But when the older man meets the younger at the sepulcher, then they both shall go into the tent, and the elder man shall enter first even though he has arrived last. Then the Angels, holding a cloth or shroud and raising it up a little, shall sing this antiphon – Angels: *Look, O fellows, behold the cloth and the shroud, and the body is not to be found.*

Then one of the Apostles shall go up to the organ and back to his place and shall shout this – Apostle: *Christ the Lord is risen!*

The convent shall respond *Thanks be to God!* The Apostle shall sing this three times: first in a low voice, next in a higher voice, and finally in his highest voice, and the convent shall answer him likewise using similar tones. When this is done, let the people [in the congregation] sing a hymn in German about the Resurrection. Then, when this hymn is concluded, let the leader of the women's choir begin the *Te Deum laudamus*; the convent shall complete the first verse, the male clergy the second, and so on until the end, or (something I have not hitherto seen) let the organ begin and play the first verse, the convent the second, and the clerics the third, and so on with the other verses.

How the Apostles and Angels shall return. Meanwhile the Apostles with the Angels shall return to their places going along the other raised gallery on the west side through which the Marys had come, the Apostles leading, the Angels following. But the Marys shall go back along the other gallery on the north side through which the Angels and Apostles had come. When the Angels and Apostles are back in their places, they shall go to the middle between the convent and clerics, standing in line one after the other, facing towards the east so that the Apostles should be on either end and the Angels in the middle; and thus they should jointly bow to the east and then return to their places among the clerics.

2. *From a thirteenth-century ordinal used at the cathedral of Padua in Italy, this scene represents Herod's fury on learning from the Three Kings of the birth of Jesus (Matt. 2: 1-17). It was performed on the feast of the Epiphany (January 6), celebrating the arrival of the Three Kings before the infant Jesus. Herod's boisterous antics are completely at odds with the solemnity of the mass, but the Christmas season often allowed a spirit of misrule into church ritual, the most notable example being the brief reign of the "boy bishop" in many cathedrals across Europe. Church leaders rued these outbreaks of folly, but they were seldom successful at suppressing them.*

The Representation of Herod on the Night of the Epiphany

When the eighth lesson is ended, Herod comes out of the upper sacristy with his acolyte; they are dressed in the shabbiest tight chasubles. He holds a wooden spear in his hand and, with the greatest fury, he hurls it at the choir and in anger ascends the pulpit, with two choristers carrying candles before him. In great anger, he begins the ninth lesson. Meanwhile his attendants, with great furor, roam around the choir striking the bishop, the canons, the choristers, and also the men and women inside the church with inflated [animal] bladders. At one point they carry around the church the spear that Herod hurled. When the lesson ends, Herod comes down from the platform with his attendants; with the same fury as above, they again wander through the choir striking people. When the responsory ends, a deacon dressed in a dalmatic ascends the platform with Herod and his acolyte who carries a thurible and is preceded by two choristers with candles. In the meantime, the bishop begins saying the antiphon *In Bethlehem Jude.* Then the deacon reads the gospel, namely *Genealogia Domini* [Matt. 1:1]. When this has ended, the bishop recites the *Te Deum laudamus.* Herod carries the Gospel book, and his acolyte with the thurible censes the bishop and the canons who kiss the Gospel book as Herod carries it to them; then the choristers are censed without the book. The choir starts the antiphon for Lauds, *Caput,* as above. Then one of the choristers above the altar of St. Michael sings the first verse of the hymn *Nuntium vobis.* When he has finished, he holds out a burning candle in the shape of the Star of the East which he tosses toward the choir who continue the hymn.

Imagine yourself in the audience of these performances. What impression would they make? Would their spiritual message be clear? How effective would they be as methods of religious instruction?

52. CEREMONY FOR THE EXCLUSION OF A LEPER (c. 1360s)

Rituals provided for every contingency. This ceremony for removing a leper from the community underscores quite clearly how the church's rituals typically blended spiritual and social concerns. The medieval diagnosis of leprosy included other kinds of chronic skin inflammations besides Hansen's disease. The physical disfigurement accompanying these maladies made it easy to single out the afflicted, and by the twelfth century leprosy was commonly considered to be the outcome of sin, a disease brought on by some moral rather than physical illness. Lepers — like Jews, heretics, prostitutes, and homosexuals — became social outcasts whose presence threatened to poison society. So while this ritual for banishing a leper suggests that the sick person has gained a closer relationship to God by suffering in life what others will suffer in death, it still leaves no doubt that the leper, symbolically dead to the world, is to be thoroughly cut off from healthy society. The Sarum (or Salisbury) liturgical manual used widely in England probably copied this ritual verbatim from one in use in the French dioceses of St. Flour and Clermont Ferrand in the late fourteenth century and printed in 1490. Such rituals seem to have grown more popular after the Black Death. Its inclusion in fifteenth century editions of the Sarum manual was purely of morbid historical interest since leprosy was rare in England by this era.

Source: trans. Rotha Mary Clay, *The Medieval Hospitals of England* (London: Frank Cass, 1909), Appendix A, pp. 273-76, revised by J. Shinners from A. Jefferies Collins, *Manuale ad Usum Percelebris Ecclesiae Sarisburiensis* (Chichester: Henry Bradshaw Society, 1960), v. 91, pp. 182-85. Latin.

The Method for Separating Lepers

Method for casting out or separating those who are sick with leprosy from the healthy.

First of all the sick man or leper clad in a cloak and in his usual dress, being in his house, ought to have notice of the coming of the priest who is on his way to the house to lead him to the church, and must in that guise wait for him. For the priest vested in surplice and stole, with the cross preceding him, makes his way to the sick man's house and addresses him with comforting words, pointing out and proving that if he blesses and praises God, and bears his sickness patiently, he may have a sure hope that though he be sick in body he may be whole in his soul, and may obtain the gift of everlasting health. And let him offer other words suitable to the occasion. When he has sprinkled him with holy water, let the priest lead the leper to the church, the cross leading the procession, the priest following, and then the leper. Within the church let a black cloth, if it is available, be set upon two trestles at some distance apart before the altar, and let the sick man take his place on bended knees beneath it between the trestles, after the manner of a dead man, although by the grace of God he yet lives in body and spirit, and in this posture let him devoutly hear mass. When this is finished, and he has been sprinkled with holy water, he must be led by the priest with the cross to the place where he will live. When they have arrived there, the priest shall counsel him with the words of holy scripture: "Remember thy last end, and thou shalt never sin" [Ecclus. 7:40]. Whence Augustine says, "He readily rejects

311

all things, who ever bears in mind that he will die." Then the priest with a spade (*palla*) casts earth on both of his feet, saying "Be dead to the world, but live again with God." And he comforts him and strengthens his patience with the words of Isaiah spoken concerning our Lord Jesus Christ: "Truly he hath borne our infirmities and carried our sorrows, and we have thought him as it were a leper, and as one struck by God and afflicted" [Isa. 53:4]. Let him say also: "If in bodily weakness by means of suffering you become like Christ, you may surely hope that you will rejoice in spirit with God. May the Most High grant this to you, numbering you among his faithful ones in the book of life. Amen."

It is to be noted that the priest must lead him to the church and from the church to his house as a dead man, chanting the Responsory [from the Office of the Dead] *Libera me domine*. Thus, the sick man should be covered with a black cloth. And the mass celebrated at his exclusion may be chosen either by the priest or by the sick man, but it is customary to say the following:

Introit: "They have surrounded me" [Ps. 16 (17):11]. See Septuagesima Sunday. *Collect*: "Almighty and ever-eternal God, give everlasting salvation to those believing in you." *Epistle*: "Beloved, is any one of you sad?" [James 5:13]. *Response*: "Have mercy on me." *Verse*: "For my bones are troubled." Alleluia [Ps. 6:3]. *Verse*: "He who heals." If during Lent, *Tract*: "Thou hast moved the earth" [Ps. 59 (60):4]. *Gospel*: "Jesus entered Capharnaum" [Luke 7:1]. *Offertory*: "Lord, hear me" [Ps. 16 (17):1]. *Secret and Post-communion*: "Deliver Israel, O God, from all his tribulations" [Ps. 24 (25):22].

When leaving the church after mass the priest ought to stand at the door and sprinkle him with holy water. And he ought to commend him to the care of the people. Before mass the sick man ought to make his confession in the church but never again there. In leading him forth the priest again begins the Responsory *Libera me domine* with the other versicles. Then when he has come into the open fields he does as is aforesaid; and he ends by imposing prohibitions upon him in the following manner:

"I forbid you ever again to enter churches, or to go to a market, a mill, a bakehouse, or gatherings of people.

Also I forbid you ever to wash your hands or even any of your belongings in a spring or stream of water of any kind; and if you are thirsty you must drink water from your pot or some other vessel.

Also I forbid you ever henceforth to go out without your leper's dress, that you may be recognized by others; and you must not go outside your house unshod.

Also I forbid you, wherever you may be, to touch anything which you wish to buy other than with a rod or staff to show what you want.

Also I forbid you ever henceforth to enter taverns or other houses if you wish to buy wine; and have what they give you put into your cask.

Also I forbid you to have intercourse with any woman except your wife.

Also I command you when you are on a journey not to answer anyone who questions you until you have moved to the side of the road downwind from him so that he may not be harmed by you; and that you never go down a narrow lane lest you should meet someone.

Also I charge you that if you need to pass across some toll bridge over water or elsewhere you touch no posts or structures on the path where you cross until you have first put on your gloves.

Also I forbid you to touch infants or young folk, whoever they might be, or to give to them or to any others any of your possessions.

Also I forbid you henceforth to eat or drink in any company except that of lepers. And know that when you die you will be buried in your own house, unless you received permission beforehand to be buried in a church."

And note that before he enters his house, he ought to have a coat and shoes of fur (*griseum*), his own plain shoes, a clapper as his signal, a hood and a cloak, two pairs of sheets, a pot, a funnel, a belt, a small knife, and a bowl. His house ought to be small, with a cistern, a bed furnished with sheets, a pillow, a chest, a table and chair, a lamp, a shovel, a cup, and other necessities.

When all is complete the priest must point out to him the ten rules which he has made for him; and let him live on earth in peace with his neighbor. Next, in the presence of the people the priest must point out to him the Ten Commandments of God, that he may live in heaven with the blessed. And let the priest also point out to him that every day each faithful Christian is bound to say devoutly the Our Father, Hail Mary, and the Creed, and to protect himself with the sign of the cross, saying often *Benedicite*. The priest departs from him saying: "Worship God and give thanks to God. Have patience and the Lord will be with you. Amen."

53. CHRISTIAN CHARMS (ELEVENTH TO FIFTEENTH CENTURIES)

Like any other society, people of the Middle Ages sought relief from illness or accident through a blend of medical expertise and divine intervention. Though the following remedies come from British manuscripts, all of them either had continental counterparts or were themselves based on continental practices. They reflect an expedient blend of Christian, extra-Christian, and folk belief.

1. Anglo-Saxon charms

Source: trans. Felix Grendon, "The Anglo-Saxon Charms," in *The Journal of American Folklore* 22 (1909) (rpt. 1930): pp. 173-77, 205, 207-09. Anglo-Saxon.

For diarrhoea (from the late eleventh century).

The angel brought this epistle to Rome when they were severely scourged with diarrhoea. Write this on a parchment so long that it can envelop the head outside, and hang it on the neck of the person who is in distress. He will soon be well:

"Ranmigan adonai eltheos mur. O ineffabile Omiginan mid anmian misane dimas mode mida memagarten Orta min sigmone beronice irritas venas quasi dulap feruor fruxantis sanguinis siccatur fla fracta frigula mirgui etsihdon segulta frautantur in arno midoninis abar uetho sydone multo saecula pp perperperper sother sother miserere mei deus deus mini deus mi. Alleluia. Alleluia."

[*The formula is a macaronic gibberish of garbled Latin and Anglo-Saxon.*]

For delayed birth (from the late eleventh century).

Let the woman who cannot bring forth her child go to the grave of a wise man, and step three times over the grave, and then say these words three times:

> "This be my cure for the loathsome late birth,
> This be my cure for the grievous swart [dark]-birth,
> This be my cure for the loathsome lame birth."

And when the woman is with child and she goes to bed to her husband, then let her say:

> "Up I go, over you I step,
> With a live child, not with a dying one,
> With a full-born child, not with a dead one."

And when the mother feels that the child is quick, let her then go to church, and when she comes before the altar, let her then say:

> "By Christ, I said, this [miracle] has been manifested."

Let the woman who cannot bring forth her child, herself take some [earth] from the grave of one of her own children, wrap it up afterwards in black wool, sell it to merchants, and then say:

> "I sell it or have sold it,
>   This evil wool and the grains of this woe."

Let the woman who cannot bring forth her child take, in her palm, the milk of a cow of one color and sop it up with her mouth, and then go to running water and spit the milk therein; and with the same hand let her scoop up a mouthful of water and swallow it. Let her then say these words:

> "Always have I carried with me this great strong hero,
>   Through this famous food, a hero.
>   Then I wish to have it and go home."

When she goes to the brook, then let her not look around, nor yet when she goes thence; and let her thereafter go into a house other than the one from which she set out, and there let her take food.

A remedy for barren land (from the early eleventh century). This Anglo-Saxon charm had many Germanic antecedents.

Here is the remedy with which you can amend your fields, if they are not sufficiently fruitful, or if, through sorcery or witchcraft, they suffer any harm.

At night, before daybreak, take four sods from four sides of the land, and note how they previously stood. Then take oil and honey and barm [yeast], and milk of all the cattle on the land, and part of every kind of tree growing on the land, except hard trees, and part of every known herb except burdock alone; and put holy water thereon, and then sprinkle [holy water] thrice on the bottom of the sods, and then say these words: "*Crescite*, grow, *et multiplicamini*, and multiply, *et replete*, and replenish, *terram*, the earth. *In nomine patris et filii et spiritus sancti sitis benedicti*" [In the name of the Father, and of the Son, and of the Holy Spirit, may you be blessed]. And [say the] *Paternoster* as often as the other.

And then take the sods to church, and have a mass-priest sing four masses over the sods, and have the green part turned toward the altar; and thereafter, before sunset, take the sods where they were at first. And let [the land-owner] have made for him four crosses of aspen-wood, and write on each end, *Matthew* and *Mark, Luke* and *John*. Lay the cross on the bottom of the hole, then say: "*Crux Mattheus, crux Marcus, crux Lucas, crux sanctus Joannes*."

Next take the sods and put them down upon [the crosses], and then say these words nine times: "*Crescite* [grow]," and as often a *Paternoster*; and thereupon turn to the east and bow reverently nine times, and then say these words:

> "Eastward I stand, for blessings I pray,
> I pray the mighty Lord, I pray the potent prince,
> I pray the holy guardian of the celestial realm,
> Earth I pray and heaven above,
> And the just and saintly Mary,
> And heaven's power and temple high,
> That I, by grace of God, this spell
> May with my teeth dissolve; with steadfast will
> [May] raise up harvests for our earthly need,
> Fill these meadows by a constant faith,
> Beautify these farm-turfs; as the prophet said
> That he on earth had favor who his alms
> Apportioned wisely, obedient to God's will.

Then turn thrice with the course of the sun, prostrate yourself completely, and say then the litanies; and thereafter say, "*Sanctus, sanctus, sanctus*," to the end. With arms outstretched then sing the *Benedicite* and *Magnificat* and *Paternoster* thrice, and commend it [the prayer] to the praise and glory of Christ and Saint Mary and the Holy Rood, and to the benefit of him who owns the land, and of all those who are under him. When all this is done, let unknown seed be taken from beggars, and let twice as much be given to these as was taken from them. And let [the land-owner] gather all his plowing implements together, then bore a hole in the beam, [and place therein] incense and fennel and hallowed soap and hallowed salt. Next, take the seed, put it on the body of the plough, then say,

> "Erce, Erce, Erce, mother of Earth,
> May the almighty, the eternal Lord, grant you
> Fields flourishing and bountiful,
> Fruitful and sustaining,
> Abundance of bright millet-harvests,
> And of broad barley-harvests,
> And of white wheat-harvests,
> And all the harvests of the earth!
> Grant him, O eternal Lord,
> And his saints in heaven that be,
> That his farm be kept from every foe,

And guarded from each harmful thing
Of witchcrafts sown throughout the land.
Now I pray the prince who shaped this world,
That no witch so artful, nor seer so cunning be
[That e'er] may overturn the words hereto pronounced!"

Then drive forth the plough and make the first furrow. Then say,

"All hail, Earth, mother of men!
Be fruitful in God's embracing arm,
Filled with food for the needs of men."

Then take meal of every kind, and have a loaf baked as big as will lie in the hand, and knead it with milk and with holy water, and lay it under the first furrow. Say then,

"Full field of food for the race of man,
Brightly blooming, be you blessed
In the holy name of him who shaped
Heaven, and earth whereon we dwell.
May God, who made these grounds, grant growing gifts,
That all our grain may come to use!"

Then say thrice, "*Crescite, in nomine patris, sitis benedicti. Amen,*" and *Paternoster* thrice.

2. From John of Gaddesden's *Rosa medicinae* (c. 1305–17)

Trained both as a physician and a theologian at Merton College, Oxford, John was court physician to Edward II. Along with cures and procedures derived from advanced Arabic practice, his treatise also includes medicinal folklore.

Source: trans. J. Shinners from Tony Hunt, *Popular Medicine in Thirteenth-Century England: Introduction and Texts* (Cambridge: D.S. Brewer, 1990), pp. 27–28. Latin.

[For a nosebleed] let us now consider an empirical approach: Go to a place where the *sanguinaria* (that is, shepherd's purse) grows and kneeling say Our Father and Hail Mary, etc. Then [say] this versicle: "You, who have redeemed us by your precious blood, we ask you to come to the aid of your servants." And then collect one or two plants. But if you collect more plants, it would be fitting to repeat these prayers. And then hang this plant about the neck of the patient from whom the blood flows, and instantly it will stop and surely constrict.

A procedure of [the physician] Gilbert [Anglicus] to stop any flow of blood, which he puts third in his practice. He says "In the name of the Father, etc." [You should repeat] nine times "With this precious cup strengthen the blood of the Israelite" and straining water through the sick person's shirt, you should offer it to the patient or speak the sick person's name.... Also, write the name "Veronica" [who according to legend wiped Jesus' bloody face on the way to his crucifixion] on the patient's forehead with his blood and say this prayer: "God, you who deigned to cure the woman with the bloody flux with just the touch of the hem of your garment [Luke 8:43-48], we humbly implore you Lord Jesus Christ, who alone cures the sick, to lift the right hand of your power and holiness and restrict and stop the flow of blood of this person for whom we pour forth prayers: In the name of the Father, the Son, and the Holy Spirit. Amen." Our Father and Hail Mary.

For toothache ... charm for teeth: Write these words on the patient's jaw: "†
In the name of the Father, the Son, and the Holy Spirit, Amen. † rex † pax
† nax † in Christ the Son." And [the toothache] will instantly cease, as has often been observed.

Also, whoever shall say the prayer in honor of St. Apollonia the virgin [whose teeth were knocked out during her martyrdom], on that day he will not have a toothache if it is said three times for the martyr St. Nicasius [a bishop of Reims beheaded in the fifth century].

Also, on any day while the Gospel is being read at mass, as someone listens to the mass he should sign the [sore] tooth and his head with the sign of the cross. And let him say an Our Father and a Hail Mary for the souls of the father and mother of St. Philip. [If he prays] this continuously [as the Gospel is read] it preserves him from future toothache and cures the current one according to trustworthy men.

3. From a medical compendium of Friar John of Greenborough (late fourteenth century)

John of Greenborough was the infirmarer of a Franciscan house in Coventry for over thirty years. In the prologue to his work, he explained that the treatments he described came from "the practice of English, Irish, Jewish, Saracen, Lombard, and Salernese physicians" as well as his own experience. Included in the treatise were a number of charms in Latin, Anglo-Norman, and Middle English, often mixing Latin and the

vernacular in the same charm. Like the modern magician's pseudo-Latin "hocus pocus"
– perhaps a corruption of the words of consecration, "hoc est corpus meum," or "this is
my body" – medieval charms such as this one often included nonsense Latin, garbled
Greek, and even Hebrew in the belief that arcane words – in this case, various titles of
God – carried magical power.

Source: trans. J. Shinners from Tony Hunt, *Popular Medicine in Thirteenth-Century England*, pp. 359-60, 86.

[*Latin*] Against toothache: Lord Jesus Christ, Son of God, come spare your servant .N. today and every day, night, and forever from the persecution of toothache. May God liberate us from all persecutions: Messiah [anointed], Soter [savior], Emmanuel [God is with us], Sabaoth [of hosts], Adonai [my Lord], Panton, Craton [for *pantokrator*, almighty], Permocraten [for *perikratos,* controller], Iskiros [for *ischiros*, mighty], Agios [for *hagios*, holy], Ymas [(He died) "for us"], Eleison [have mercy], Otheos [for *o theos*, the God], Athanatos [eternal], Alpha and Omega, lion, worm [see Ps. 21(22):7], hart, lamb, man, ram, ousion [for *(homo)ousios,* (same) substance], serpent [see John 3:14], first and last, the end, Father, and Son, and Holy Spirit, amen. "Good cross, worthy cross, wood above all wood, seal me to you, redeeming me from an evil death." "The cross vanquishes every evil, the cross restores all things; through this sign of the cross let every evil flee." Peter, Paul, Andrew, John, James, Philip, Bartholomew, Simon, Thaddeus, Matthew, Mark, Luke, Mathias. May the holy cross and Christ's passion be your remedy. Amen.

[*Latin and Anglo-Norman*] Also another charm: Let the patient say: "I, N[omen or Name], seek remedy for the love of God. Just as surely as God suffered pain on the holy cross to redeem sinners from death to life, truly guard this Christian from toothache if it please God."

[*Anglo-Norman*] To stanch blood: [Say] "Stanch blood, stanch in honor of the Father, the Son, the Holy Spirit, and the holy cross. Just as our Lord Jesus Christ truly suffered death on the cross on Good Friday for us and for our sins, and just as he rose from the dead to life on the third day, and just as Longinus pierced our Savior Jesus Christ's heart and side and took blood from his precious heart and side, in honor and by virtue of this precious blood, stanch, blood, stanch! Amen."

[*Latin and Middle English*] Another charm: First ask the name of the man and say five Our Fathers and Hail Marys and then say: "For the wounds that God suffered on the cross to ransom us from the world, stanch blood; in worship of the five bloody tears that Our Lady shed for love of Christ, stanch blood; as surely as Longinus pierced to his heart with his spear, as surely as he died for man's sake and not for his own, stanch blood; for the blood that Christ shed on the cross, in worship of that blood stanch blood." And then say five Our Fathers and Hail Marys.

[*Latin*] Charm against fever: St. Architriclinus [lit., "chief steward," see John 2:8] sat upon a bench holding in his left hand a tufted briar; and he cut it down the middle and had two men take each end and firmly bend them apart. And he blessed it with his right hand and spoke holy words and said "Father and Son and Holy Spirit, relieve this man from this fever hot or cold and the two pieces will join together [again]." And as the two pieces come together say an Our Father and a Hail Mary. Then split apart the middle of the rejoined pieces as wide as you can put your hand, but they should not touch the ground. And hang that section split in the middle around the neck of the sick person for seven days.

4. To cure muscular cramps (early fifteenth century)

Source: trans. J.E. Anderson from Marc Bloch, *The Royal Touch: Sacred Monarchy and Scrofula in England and France* (London: Routledge & Kegan Paul, 1973), p. 96.

To cure the cramp, go on Good Friday into five parish churches, and in each of them take the first penny that is given as an offering at the Adoration of the Cross. Then gather them all together, go up to the cross, and there say five Our Fathers in honor of the five wounds and carry them with you for five days, each day saying the same prayer in the same manner. After this, have a ring made out of these coins, without any other alloy; write on the inside *Gaspar, Balthazar, Attapa*, and on the outside *Ihc. Nazarenus*; then go and fetch it from the goldsmith's on a Friday, and say five Our Fathers as before; and then wear it continuously.

5. A Cross Charm

This charm, with Middle English instructions and a Latin prayer, dates from the late fourteenth century, but versions of it in other vernaculars circulated widely throughout medieval Europe from the thirteenth century onward. Printed on long parchment scrolls, such charms were sometimes wrapped around women in labor as a "birth-girdle." The legend of Saints Quiricus and Julitta recounted how the three-year-old Quiricus, as he watched his Christian mother, Julitta, tortured by a pagan prefect, cried out in protest,

"I too am a Christian." Both mother and child were then martyred.

Source: trans. J. Shinners from Curt F. Bühler, "Prayers and Charms in Certain Middle English Scrolls," *Speculum* 39 (1964): pp. 274-75. Middle English and Latin.

This cross [drawn on the parchment], fifteen times multiplied, is the length of our Lord Jesus Christ. And the day that you bear it with you or look upon it, you shall have these great gifts that follow: The first is that you will not die a sudden death. The second is that you will not be hurt or slain by any kind of weapon. The third is that you will have reasonable goods and health until the end of your life. The fourth is that your enemies will never overcome you. The fifth is that no kind of poison or false witness shall ever grieve you. The sixth is that you will not die without the sacraments of the church. The seventh is that you will be defended from all manner of wicked spirits, tribulations, and diseases, and from all infirmities and the sickness of the pestilence. The eighth is that if a women laboring in childbirth lays this on her womb, the child shall be baptized and the mother shall have the service of purification, since St. [Quiricus] and St. Julitta, his mother, desired these gracious gifts of God, which he granted to them, and this is recorded at Rome.

[*Latin*] Hail, O Quiricus, with the blessed Julitta, glory of children, soldier of the king of the angels. Christ and Mary save us at the hour of our death. Amen. The death of his saints is precious in the eyes of God. God, you who allowed your glorious martyrs Quiricus and Julitta to conquer the harsh tortures of a hateful judge, grant me, your servant William, humility by virtue of your glorious height and your venerable cross and your precious body and blood, and through the intercession of your almighty power and virtue and of your saints make me triumph over my enemies so that I may forever remain constant through Christ our Lord, Amen.

6. An All-Purpose Charm

This prayer charm comes from a French psalter, or book of Psalms, from the first half of the fifteenth century.

Source: trans. J. Shinners from Aberdeen University Library MS 25, f. 12r. The Burnet Psalter <http://www.abdn.ac.uk/diss/historic/collects/bps/text/012r.htm>.

Whoever devoutly says this following prayer daily shall have an indulgence for their sins and never die a bad death [without the sacraments] but will obtain good grace anywhere. And if he wishes to go on any journey and has said this prayer he will never have trouble during the trip but will arrive safely (*bene*). Let him take water from a well [*fons*, but perhaps "baptismal font," though this would be illegal] and say this prayer over the water and give it to a woman laboring in childbirth and she will immediately have a good delivery through the grace of God. Have the Mass of the Blessed Mary – namely, [the one that begins] "All the rich among the people, shall entreat thy countenance" [Ps. 44:13] – celebrated over this prayer once. And let him put this prayer over his head before he goes before kings or any nobles (*magnatates*) and he will gain favor and honor and on that day will not be defeated in battle. And if he gives a feast for anyone, let him say this prayer over the food and drink and there will be both a rich abundance for them, and everyone eating and drinking anything there will give him thanks as well as honors because this feast will please them. For this following prayer – namely, "Lord God almighty, Father, Son, and Holy Spirit, give to me, your servant N" [etc.] – is full of power (*virtus*) and the grace of the Holy Spirit. And if anyone is in a storm at sea, let him take a cup of seawater and say this prayer – namely, "Lord God almighty, Father, Son, and Holy Spirit, give me, your servant, N., victory over my enemies" – and other prayers over that water and then toss that water into the sea and the storm will cease. And this prayer is a medicine for any type of distress for anyone who will daily say it devoutly. He will also obtain wisdom and will eternally gain both his inheritance and an angelic mansion in the kingdom of the saints. No one knows the great power of this prayer more so than God alone who said "ask, and it shall be given to you, etc" [Matt. 7:7]. God who lives and reigns with God the Father and the Holy Spirit, world without end. Amen.

What assumptions about reality are implicit in these various charms? Would you class these charms as "religion," "magic," or "superstition"? Would a medieval person agree with you? What is the difference between a charm and a prayer? What conclusions do you draw when you see these charms included in medieval medical manuals? Do we have modern equivalents of these charms?

CHAPTER SEVEN:
DAILY DEVOTIONS AND PRACTICES

The daily devotions and practices of lay people take us to the heart of popular religion, for in them we see the choices people made, both individually and corporately, for expressing their faith. These devotions show how well people understood Christian doctrine, how they shaped it to their own needs, and how they tried day by day to live in their own way as Christians. They had many options. Corporate efforts such as religious fraternities allowed them to feel connected to other people and engaged in a common enterprise, thus creating the sort of communal identity so important to medieval people and magnifying their divine petitions through the strength of numbers. Those lay people who could read – whose numbers were growing by the thirteenth century – now had access to scores of written prayers (such as those in Books of Hours), moral treatises, saints' lives, and other devotional materials. Non-readers could encapsulate Christian precepts in church art, or proverbs and mnemonic verses, or they might perform or watch religious pageants, or learn from the church's oldest form of teaching by listening to sermons. The documents that follow suggest the various and inventive ways medieval people found to bring Christianity intimately into their lives.

Fig. 7.1. The tutelary image of St. Christopher

Painted on church walls, panels and in Books of Hours, and printed on devotional cards, the image of St. Christopher, credited with the power to protect anyone seeing it from sudden death for that day, was a popular medieval devotion. This woodcut (made in 1423 and among the first dateable European wood engravings) is from a book found in a Carthusian convent in Buxheim, Swabia. Here, the giant Christopher, whose name means "Christ-bearer," ferries the Christ-child across a river, a central episode in this saint's legend. He holds the palm tree that blossomed from his staff as he forded the river. On the right the hermit who taught him about Christianity looks on with a lantern; on the left, a man carries a sack of flour from a mill. The text reads: *Christofori faciem die quacumque tueris, illa nempe die morte mala non morieris + Millesimo cccc xx tercio:* "On whatever day you look upon the image of Christopher, on that day you will not die a bad death. 1423." From an engraved reproduction by John Jackson in William A. Chatto, *A Treatise on Wood Engraving* (New York: Bouton, 1861), p. 46.

54. RULE FOR THE FRANCISCAN THIRD ORDER (c. 1221)

Francis of Assisi's (see Doc. 9) rule for lay people intent on holy living reflects the concerns of other penitential companies already popular in early thirteenth-century Italy. Groups called "brothers and sisters of penance" or "brothers and sisters of continence" (because of their acts of self-denial) highlight the growing emphasis on penance in medieval Christianity. Francis and his original band of followers likely initially thought of themselves as members of this wider penitential movement rather than as a new religious order. He probably wrote a simpler version of these regulations at least a decade earlier than 1221, the year Cardinal Ugolino, the Franciscan order's protector, received official approval for them. As Franciscans and the other mendicant orders won fame, lay people, called tertiaries, increasingly associated with them as members of "third orders" (the first and second orders being restricted to men and women taking formal religious vows). Lay women, in particular, found an outlet for their religious energies in such associations. This rule has clear affinities with the regulations of religious guilds organized by the laity (see Docs. 55 and 56).

Source: trans. Benen Fahy, *The Writings of St. Francis of Assisi* (Chicago: Franciscan Herald Press, 1964), pp. 168-75. Latin.

Here begins the Rule of the Continent Brothers and Sisters

In the name of the Father and of the Son and of the Holy Spirit. Amen. The memorial of what is proposed for the Brothers and Sisters of Penance living in their own homes, begun in the year of our Lord 1221, is as follows.

Chapter I: Daily Life

1. The men belonging to this brotherhood shall dress in humble, undyed cloth, the price of which is not to exceed six Ravenna soldi an ell, unless for evident and necessary cause a temporary dispensation be given. And breadth and thinness of the cloth are to be considered in said price.

2. They shall wear their outer garments and furred coats without open throat, sewed shut or uncut but certainly laced up, not open as secular people wear them; and they shall wear their sleeves closed.

3. The sisters in turn shall wear an outer garment and tunic made of cloth of the same price and humble quality; or at least they are to have with the outer garment a white or black underwrap or petticoat, or an ample linen gown without gathers, the price of an ell of which is not to exceed twelve

Pisa denars. As to this price, however, and the fur cloaks they wear a dispensation may be given according to the estate of the woman and the custom of the place. They are not to wear silken or dyed veils and ribbons.

4. And both the brothers and the sisters shall have their fur garments of lamb's wool only. They are permitted to have leather purses and belts sewed in simple fashion without silken thread, and no other kind. Also other vain adornments they shall lay aside at the bidding of the Visitor [a Franciscan clerical official].

5. They are not to go to unseemly parties or to shows or dances. They shall not donate to actors, and shall forbid their household to donate.

Chapter II: Abstinence

6. All are to abstain from meat save on Sundays, Tuesdays, and Thursdays, except on account of illness or weakness, for three days at blood-letting, in traveling, or on account of a specially high feast intervening, namely, the Nativity for three days, New Year's, Epiphany [Jan. 6], the Pasch of the Resurrection for three days, the holy Apostles Peter and Paul [June 29], St. John the Baptist [June 24], the Assumption of the glorious Virgin Mary [Aug. 15], the solemnity of All Saints [Nov. 1], and of St. Martin [Nov. 11]. On the other days, when there is not fasting, they may eat cheese and eggs. But when they are with religious in their convent homes, they have leave to eat what is served to them. And except for the feeble, the ailing, and those traveling, let them be content with dinner and supper. Let the healthy be temperate in eating and drinking.

7. Before their dinner and supper let them say the Lord's prayer once, likewise after their meal, and let them give thanks to God. Otherwise let them say three Our Fathers.

Chapter III: Fasting

8. From the Pasch of the Resurrection to the feast of All Saints they are to fast on Fridays. From the feast of All Saints until Easter they are to fast on Wednesdays and Fridays, but still observing the other fasts enjoined in general by the church.

9. They are to fast daily, except on account of infirmity or any other need, throughout the fast of St. Martin from after said day until Christmas, and throughout the greater fast from Carnival Sunday [preceding Lent] until Easter.

10. Sisters who are pregnant are free to refrain until their purification from the corporal observances except those regarding their dress and prayers.

11. Those engaged in fatiguing work shall be allowed to take food three times a day from the Pasch of the Resurrection until the Dedication feast of St. Michael [Sept. 29]. And when they work for others it will be allowed them to eat everything served to them, except on Fridays and on the fasts enjoined in general by the church.

Chapter IV: Prayer

12. All are daily to say the seven canonical Hours, that is, Matins, Prime, Terce, Sext, None, Vespers, and Compline. The clerics are to say them after the manner of the clergy. Those who know the Psalter are to say the *Deus in nomine tuo* [Ps. 53 (54)] and the *Beati immaculati* [Ps. 118 (119)] up to the *Legem pone* for Prime, and the other psalms of the Hours, with the *Glory be to the Father*; but when they do not attend church, they are to say for Matins the psalms the church says or any eighteen psalms; or at least to say the Our Father as do the unlettered at any of the Hours. The others say twelve Our Fathers for Matins and for every one of those Hours seven Our Fathers with the *Glory be to the Father* after each one. And those who know the Creed and the *Miserere mei Deus* [Ps. 50 (51)] should say it at Prime and Compline. If they do not say that at the Hours indicated, they shall say three Our Fathers.

13. The sick are not to say the Hours unless they wish.

14. All are to go to Matins in the fast of St. Martin and in the great fast, unless inconvenience for persons or affairs should threaten.

Chapter V: The Sacraments, Other Matters

15. They are to make a confession of their sins three times a year and to receive Communion at Christmas, Easter, and Pentecost. They are to be reconciled with their neighbors and to restore what belongs to others. They are to make up for past [unpaid] tithes and pay future tithes.

16. They are not to take up lethal weapons, or bear them about, against anybody.

17. All are to refrain from formal oaths unless where necessity compels, in the cases excepted by the Sovereign Pontiff in his indult, that is, for peace, for the Faith, under calumny, and in bearing witness.

18. Also in their ordinary conversations they will do their best to avoid oaths. And should anyone have sworn thoughtlessly through a slip of the tongue, as happens where there is much talking, he should the evening of the same day, when he is obliged to think over what he has done, say three Our Fathers in amends of such oaths. Let each member fortify his household to serve God.

Chapter VI: Special Mass and Meeting Each Month

19. All the brothers and sisters of every city and place are to foregather every month at the time the ministers see fit, in a church which the ministers will make known, and there assist at divine services.

20. And every member is to give the treasurer one ordinary denar. The treasurer is to collect this money and distribute it on the advice of the ministers among the poor brothers and sisters, especially the sick and those who may have nothing for their funeral services, and thereupon among other poor; and they are to offer something of the money to the aforesaid church.

21. And, if it be convenient at the time, they are to have some religious who is informed in the words of God to exhort them and strengthen them to persevere in their penance and in performing the works of mercy. And except for the officers, they are to remain quiet during the mass and sermon, intent on the [divine] office, on prayer, and on the sermon.

Chapter VII: Visiting the Sick, Burying the Dead

22. Whenever any brother or sister happens to fall ill, the ministers, if the patient let them know of it, shall in person or through others visit the patient once a week, and remind him of penance; and if they find it expedient, they are to supply him from the common fund with what he may need for the body.

23. And if the ailing person departs from this life, it is to be published to the brothers and sisters who may be present in the city or place, so that they may gather for the funeral; and they are not to leave until the mass has been celebrated and the body consigned to burial. Thereupon each member within eight days of the demise shall say for the soul of the deceased: a mass, if he is a priest; fifty psalms, if he understands the Psalter, or if not, then fifty Our Fathers with the *Requiem aeternam* at the end of each.

24. In addition, every year, for the welfare of the brothers and sisters living and dead, each priest is to say three masses, each member knowing the Psalter is to recite it, and the rest shall say one hundred Our Fathers with the *Requiem aeternam* at the end of each.

25. All who have the right are to make their last will and make disposition of their goods within three months after their profession, lest anyone of them die intestate.

26. As regards making peace among the brothers and sisters or non-members at odds, let what the ministers find proper be done; even, if it be expedient, upon consultation with the Lord Bishop.

27. If contrary to their rights and privileges trouble is made for the brothers and sisters by the mayors and governors of the places where they live, the ministers of the place shall do what they shall find expedient on the advice of the Lord Bishop.

28. Let each member accept and faithfully exercise the ministry of other offices imposed on him, although anyone may retire from office after a year.

29. When anybody wishes to enter this brotherhood, the ministers shall carefully inquire into his standing and occupation, and they shall explain to him the obligations of the brotherhood, especially that of restoring what belongs to others. And if he is content with it, let him be vested according to the prescribed way, and he must make satisfaction for his debts, paying money according to what pledged provision is given. They are to reconcile themselves with their neighbors and to pay up their tithes.

30. After these particulars are complied with, when the year is up and he seems suitable to them, let him on the advice of some discreet brothers be received on this condition: that he promise he will all the time of his life observe everything here written, or to be written or abated on the advice of the brothers, unless on occasion there be a valid dispensation by the ministers; and that he will, when called upon by the ministers, render satisfaction as the Visitor shall ordain if he has done anything contrary to this condition. And this promise is to be put in writing then and there by a public notary. Even so nobody is to be received otherwise, unless in consideration of the estate and rank of the person it shall seem advisable to the ministers.

31. No one is to depart from this brotherhood and from what is contained herein, except to enter a religious Order.

32. No heretic or person in bad repute for heresy is to be received. If he is under suspicion of it, he may be admitted if otherwise fit, upon being cleared before the bishop.

33. Married women are not to be received except with the consent and leave of their husbands.

34. Brothers and sisters ejected from the brotherhood as incorrigible are not to be received in it again except it please the senior portion of the brothers.

Chapter VIII: Correction, Dispensation, Officers

35. The ministers of any city or place shall report public faults of the brothers and sisters to the Visitor for punishment. And if anyone proves incorrigible, after consultation with some of the discreet brothers he should be denounced to the Visitor, to be expelled by him from the brotherhood, and thereupon it

should be published in the meeting. Moreover, if it is a brother, he should be denounced to the mayor or the governor.

36. If anyone learns that scandal is occurring relative to brothers and sisters, he shall report it to the ministers and shall have opportunity to report it to the Visitor. He need not be held to report it in the case of husband against wife.

37. The Visitor has the power to dispense all the brothers and sisters in any of these points if he finds it advisable.

38. When the year has passed, the ministers with the counsel of the brothers are to elect two other ministers; and a faithful treasurer, who is to provide for the need of the brothers and sisters and other poor; and messengers who at the command of the ministers are to publish what is said and done by the fraternity.

39. In all the abovementioned points no one is to be obligated under guilt, but under penalty; yet so that if after being admonished twice by the ministers he should fail to discharge the penalty imposed or to be imposed on him by the Visitor, he shall be obligated under guilt as contumacious.

Here ends the Rule of the Continent.

55. THE FRATERNITY OF THE BLESSED VIRGIN AT PERUGIA (1312)

After their parish, the place where Christians met most frequently to share communal religious experience was the religious guild or fraternity. By the later Middle Ages such fraternities had sprung up across Europe's villages, towns, and cities. Though clergy could preside over them and certainly were needed to perform most of their liturgical demands, fraternities were essentially associations of lay people gathered together to pursue common religious ends (though this definition begs fine-tuning). Typically fraternities required members to meet regularly for some kind of communal prayer or devotions, to make provisions for mutual assistance of members in time of need, to arrange the funeral and burial of dead members, and to offer intercessory prayers for them. In an age where the fate of the soul was an obsession, this latter purpose was particularly important for fraternities, so much so that it would not be inaccurate to think of them as "communal chantries." But religious fraternities encompassed everything from a small group of lay people occasionally gathering to pray together, to lay associations that regulated their communal worship so elaborately that their routines were quasi-monastic, to large and powerful corporations of merchants or craftsmen whose mutual attraction was less the service of God than mammon. Membership in most of these fraternities seldom spread beyond the local parish, but in larger towns they could grow big or popular enough to attract members from throughout the town and even beyond. Though professional guilds of trades and crafts existed without religious overtones, in many places what began as associations of fellow professionals joined for pious purposes evolved into the great merchant and craft guilds of the later Middle Ages. In Italy, by the fifteenth century religious fraternities were so widespread, they seem to have eclipsed parishes as the basic unit of lay religious association.

Source: trans. J. Shinners from G.G. Meersseman, *Ordo Fraternitatis: Confraternite e Pietà dei Laici nel Medioevo* (Rome: Herder, 1977), v. II, pp. 1063-66. Latin.

In the name of God. Amen. For the honor and reverence of Almighty God; the glorious Virgin Mary, his mother; the glorious apostles Peter and Paul; the blessed martyrs Lawrence, Herculanus [of Perugia, d.c. 547], and Constantius [of Perugia, d.c. 178]; the Blessed Peter Martyr [1205-52]; the most blessed confessor St. Dominic [1170-1221]; and all God's saints.

These are the ordinances, provisions, and articles of the fraternity of the Blessed Virgin Mary which meets at the house of the Friar Preachers of St. Dominic of the city of Perugia, and was founded, instituted, made, and ordained in 1312, the tenth indiction, in the time of Pope Clement V, July 12.

Chapter 1. Procedure for holding our procession.

First, we say and ordain that all members of our fraternity, men as well as women, are bound and obliged always to meet every Sunday of the month at the church of Blessed Dominic the Confessor at the ringing of the bells, with everyone taking their candles from the chamberlains and paying two denars for each candle. They should listen to the whole sermon and, when it is over, everyone should go in procession with lit candles in their hands through the church, cloister, and town, devoutly singing lauds in response to the chanters at the head of the procession. We wish, however, the women to remain devoutly and quietly in the church with their lit candles. When the procession is over, each man and woman is obliged and bound to return to the chamberlains whatever remains of their candles from the procession. And if any member of the aforesaid fraternity passes from this world [we ordain] that the [fraternity's] officials shall assign one of the friars to preach and recite [prayers] for the congregation, and each person is obliged to say for the soul of the person five Our Fathers and Hail Marys along with a *Requiem aeternam.*

Chapter 2. The subsidy that should be made every month for the souls of all our dead members.

Next, we wish and ordain that always on the first Monday of every month, the chamberlains and officials currently in office are bound and obliged to have one memorial office of the dead with a mass solemnly said for the souls of all the dead members of our own fraternity at the main altar of the Dominican house with wax candles burning throughout the choir. We wish this to be done perpetually and unerringly in aid of their souls.

Chapter 3. The mass said on behalf of all the living and the veneration made on the feasts of the Virgin Mary.

Next, we ordain and wish that always on the first Wednesday of every month, the officials should have a mass of the Blessed Virgin Mary celebrated at the altar dedicated to her in the church of St. Dominic for all the fraternity's living brothers and sisters, all of whom are obliged to offer their gift there so that the glorious Lady will always direct and preserve us all in her service. Also, we wish that each of us, men and women alike, are obliged to celebrate and honor all four feasts of the Blessed Virgin Mary, and to fast on the vigils of these feasts when they can.

Chapter 4. All members should make confession and receive communion.

Next, we ordain and wish that all members of our fraternity be bound and obliged to confess their sins devoutly at least four times a year and to receive devoutly the Body of our Lord Jesus Christ twice, namely on the feasts of his birth and his resurrection.

Chapter 5. The officials and their duties.

Next we wish and ordain that this fraternity should and ought to have two chamberlains and one secretary (*notarius*). The chamberlains should keep and maintain the fraternity's goods and make an inventory of all the fraternity's possessions. Their term of office should be for one year, at the end of which they should render an account at the end of their term of office of everything that passed through their hands to the new officials along with those members of the fraternity it pleases them to have present.

The chamberlains are obliged every evening to have the lauds of the Blessed Virgin sung in the church of Blessed Dominic the Confessor along with other services they think best, with the end in mind of best causing our devotion to the Virgin to grow and increase.

The secretary should record the names of every man or woman wishing to join the fraternity. He should enroll in perpetuity both the living and those who have died. Similarly, he should have a book in which those joining or leaving the fraternity are recorded.

Chapter 6. Our fraternity's almsgiving.

Next, we wish and ordain that when they come to dispose of their soul and property through a testament or last will, each brother and sister of our fraternity should and ought to bequeath something to the fraternity out of love for God and the Blessed Virgin, insofar as he or she is able. This [bequest] should be for almsgiving to the poor, for the cost of [processional] torches, candles, and expenses incurred for other things.

Chapter 7. The gift made on the feast of the Blessed Peter Martyr.

Next, because the glorious St. Peter Martyr of the Order of Preachers was the chief author and founder of these kinds of fraternities that thrive in the secular world, by this present chapter we were led to ordain that every year on the Blessed Peter's feast [April 29] the chamberlains should have a candle made in his honor and reverence as shall appear expedient to them.

Chapter 8. The officials should have the power to acquit everyone.

Next, we wish that our chamberlains, when it seems [necessary] to them, can and ought to give full authority to the friar who shall preach on the aforesaid Sunday to absolve any member of the fraternity delinquent in carrying out these ordinances.

Chapter 9. The torches carried for the dead and who should bear them.

Next, we wish that our chamberlain should and can carry or should make to be carried our fraternity's torches to bury the fraternity's dead members and also the dead who are in our fraternity's hospitals.

56. THE FRATERNITY OF ST. CATHERINE, ALDERSGATE, LONDON (1389)

In the autumn of 1388, Parliament ordered every guild and fraternity in England to submit by February a certificate describing its origin, purpose, rules, and possessions. The returns of 507 of these guilds still survive, about three-quarters of which were founded after 1350. These regulations may be usefully compared to those of the fraternity of Perugia above.

Source: modernized J. Shinners from Toulmin Smith, *English Gilds*, Early English Text Society, original series v. 40 (London: N. Trübner, 1870), pp. 6–8. Middle English.

These are the points and the articles ordained by the brothers of St. Catherine in the city of London, which was founded in the church of St. Botolph, Aldersgate.

The first point is this: when a brother or sister shall be received, they shall swear on a book to the brotherhood to uphold and maintain the points and articles that are hereafter written, each man to his ability and according to his status. And every brother and sister upon entering shall kiss everyone who is there as a token of love, charity, and peace.

Also if it shall happen that any of the brothers falls into poverty or is overcome with age so that he is unable to help himself, or through any other chance, through fire, water, thieves, or sickness, or any other accident – so that he shall not have to bear his wretchedness alone, he shall have 14 pence a week.

Also any man received into the brotherhood shall pay alms upon his entry as the guild-masters and he agree; every quarter he shall pay three pence in order to maintain the [devotional] lights and the alms of the brotherhood.

Also all the brothers and sisters of the aforesaid fraternity shall assemble together in the church of St. Botolph abovesaid on St. Catherine's Day [Nov. 25] and hear a mass there and make an offering in veneration of her. And also on the afternoon of that day or the next Sunday following they shall gather together to choose their masters for the next year following.

Also when a brother or sister dies, the members shall come to the *Dirige* and make an offering for them the next day, on the oath abovesaid unless they have reasonable cause to be excused.

Also if any brother dies who does not have enough to pay for burial, if it may be so done, then he shall be buried with the money from the communal box.

Also if it happens that any of the brothers falls sick and dies within ten miles around London, if that year's wardens are sent for, they shall go and fetch his body home to London. And all the brothers and sisters shall be ready at their warning to meet the body at the city limits and bring it to the place there with reverence. As mentioned above, he shall be carried there at the wardens' expense unless they have a good reason to be excused.

Also all his funeral expenses are to be paid from the communal box if he does not have the ability to pay for them himself; if he has the ability let his executors pay the expenses themselves. Whatever the case, the expenses of the wardens [in bearing the body to London] shall be made good from the communal box.

Also if it happens that any members of the brotherhood have need to borrow a certain sum of money, they should go to the keepers of the box and take what they need, though the sum should be small enough that one may be helped as well as another. They should leave a sufficient pledge or else find sufficient sureties from the brotherhood.

Also five round wax tapers weighing twenty pounds shall be found to be lit on high feast days, all five at all hours of the day, in worship of God, of his mother the maid Mary, and of St. Catherine the glorious virgin and martyr, and all saints. On Sundays and other simple feast days, two of the five tapers shall be lit at high mass. And if it happens that an ordinary brother shall die who cannot afford a light, then the five tapers shall be found anew and set about the body, and the torches also. When any brother dies, they shall have the torches ready to bring with them to church if need be.

Also when a brother or sister dies, the wardens shall alert the Friars Minor to come to the place where he [or she] shall be buried and say a *Dirige* there. And on the next day the friars shall say thirty masses [for his or her soul]; the wardens shall pay them for their labor.

And no brother shall be received on the day of our assembly except by all the company's assent.

Also there shall be four sufficient men to keep [the fraternity's] property well and sufficiently: one to keep the box, the other to keep the key, and the other two to collect the money from the quarterly dues. The four shall give their account truly on St. Catherine's Day before all the brothers, or else before six of the company's wisest men.

Also none of the wardens shall make any new statutes or new ordinances without the assent of all the brotherhood, and this shall be done on the day of their assembly.

This brotherhood has vestments, a chalice, and a missal, together worth 10 marks.

What kind of life do the rule of the Franciscan Third Order and the guild rules of Perugia and St. Catherine envision for their members? What kinds of behavior do they regulate? How do these rules promote Christian living? What benefits, both spiritual and material, do members of these groups enjoy?

57. GUILD SPONSORS OF THE YORK MYSTERY PLAYS (1415)

This most famous cycle of mystery plays recounting sacred history was performed annually on the feast of Corpus Christi by amateur actors from the professional guilds of York. They staged the plays on elaborate pageant wagons that were pulled to twelve sites across the town where each play was repeated. Probably written by clerics in the middle of the fourteenth century, the cycle was regularly performed until 1580. The manuscript translated here (written around 1430) lists 51 plays, but the register of the plays itself contains the scripts of only 48 of them (with over 300 speaking parts). There were several deletions and additions to the list of professions as faltering guilds fell into poverty and could no longer afford to produce their plays and new guilds took them over. Typically, each play was performed by the guild whose occupation was germane to the action of the play. The plays are numbered here consecutively, an order that does not always correspond to their order of performance. Though the plays are based on Genesis, Exodus, and the Gospels, many details of the cycle's episodes concerning the crucifixion come from the fourth-century apocryphal Gospel of Nicodemus, widely popular in the Middle Ages. Likewise, the scenes about Mary's later life – for example, the Linen-weavers' play (No. 48) – draw on legendary material. This cycle was only one of the religious dramas that the citizens of York acted in the later Middle Ages. There was also a play of St. George staged on Midsummer Day, a play of the Lord's Prayer performed apparently by both the men and women of a religious guild created expressly for that purpose, and a Creed play staged once every ten years by the Corpus Christi guild.

Source: trans. J. Shinners from Lucy Toulmin Smith, *York Plays* (1885; rpt. New York: Russel & Russel, 1963), pp. xix–xxvii. Latin.

The Order of the Pageants of the play of Corpus Christi at the time of Mayor William Alne, in the third year of the reign of King Henry, the Fifth after the conquest of England, compiled by Roger Burton, town clerk, in 1415.

[1.] Tanners: God the Father Almighty creating and forming the heavens, the angels and archangels, and Lucifer and the angels who fell with him into hell [Gen. 1:1–9].

[2.] Plasterers: God the Father in his own substance creating the earth and everything in it in the space of five days [Gen. 1:10-31].

[3.] Wool comb-makers: God the Father forming Adam from a lump of earth, and making Eve from Adam's rib, and breathing the spirit of life into them [Gen. 2:7-24].

[4.] Fullers: God forbidding Adam and Eve from eating from the tree of life [Gen. 2:17].

[5.] Coopers: Adam and Eve with the tree between them, the serpent deceiving them with the apples; God speaking to them and cursing the serpent, and the angel casting them out of paradise with a sword [Gen. 3].

[6.] Armorers: Adam and Eve, the angel assigning them to labor with the spade and the distaff [Gen. 2:16-19].

[7.] Glovers: Abel and Cain offering their sacrifices [Gen. 4:1-16].

[8.] Shipwrights: God ordering Noah to make an Ark from timber planks [Gen. 6].

[9.] Fishmongers, Mariners: Noah in the Ark with his wife, his three sons and their wives, and various animals [Gen. 7-8].

[10.] Parchment-makers, Bookbinders: Abraham offering his son Isaac on the altar – the boy with the firewood – and the angel [Gen. 22].

[11.] Hosiers: Moses lifting up the serpent by the tail in the desert [Ex. 4:4]; King Pharaoh, eight Jews marveling and waiting.

[12.] Spicers or Grocers: A learned man announcing the sayings of the prophets about the birth of Christ to come. Mary, the Angel greeting her; Mary greeting Elizabeth [Luke 1:21-56].

[13.] Pewter-makers and Founders: Mary; Joseph wanting to send her away; an angel telling them to go to Bethlehem [Matt. 1:19].

[14.] Roof-thatchers: Mary, Joseph, the midwife; the newborn boy lying in a manger between the ox and the ass; and the angel speaking to the shepherds and the players in the next pageant [Luke 2].

[15.] Chandlers [i.e., candle makers]: Shepherds speaking together; the star in the East; an angel proclaiming the glad tidings of the newborn boy to the shepherds [Luke 2:8-20].

[16.] Goldsmiths, Goldbeaters, Moneymakers: Three kings coming from the East; Herod questioning them about the baby Jesus; and Herod's son, two counselors, and a messenger. Mary with the baby, and the star above; the three kings offering gifts [Matt. 2].

[17.] Formerly the Hospital of St. Leonard's, now the Masons: Mary with the child, Joseph, Anna, a midwife with young doves. Simeon taking the boy in his arms, and Simeon's two sons [Luke 2:21-40].

[18.] Marshalls [i.e., horseshoers and vets]: At the angel's warning, Mary with the child and Joseph fleeing into Egypt [Matt. 2:13-15].

[19.] Girdlers [i.e., makers of small metal items], Nailers, Sawyers: Herod ordering the boys to be killed; four soldiers with lances, two counselors of the king, and four women weeping at the slaughter of their children [Matt. 2:16].

[20.] Spurriers and Lorimers [i.e., spur- and bit-makers]: Learned men, Jesus sitting in the temple in their midst questioning and answering them; four Jews, Mary and Joseph searching for him, and finding him in the temple [Luke 2:41-50].

[21.] Barbers: Jesus, John the Baptist baptizing him as two angels assist [Matt. 3:13-17, Luke 3:21-22].

[22.] Vintners: Jesus, Mary, the bridegroom with his bride [at Cana], the host of the feast and his household, with six urns of water for when the water is turned to wine [John 2:1-11].

[23.] Fewers [i.e., smiths]: Jesus at the pinnacle of the temple, and the devil tempting him with the stones, and two angels ministering to him, etc. [Luke 4:1-13].

[24.] Curriers [of leather]: Peter, James, and John; Jesus going up the mountain and transfiguring himself before them. Moses and Elias appearing, and a voice speaking from a cloud [Matt. 17:1-5].

[25.] Ironmongers: Jesus and the leper Simon asking Jesus to eat with him [Matt. 26:6-13, Mark 14:39]; two disciples, Mary Magdalene washing Jesus' feet with her tears, and wiping them with her hair [Luke 7:36-50].

[26.] Plumbers, Pattenmakers [i.e., patten shoemakers]: Jesus, two disciples, the woman taken in adultery, four Jews accusing her [John 8:1-11].

[27.] Pouchmakers, Bottlers [i.e., makers of leather bottles], Capmakers: Lazarus in the tomb; Mary Magdalene and Martha, and two Jews marveling [John 11:1-44].

[28.] Skinners [and later, Vestment-makers]: Jesus on the ass with its colt, the twelve apostles following Jesus; six rich men and six poor men; eight children with palm leaves singing "Blessed is he, etc." and Zaccheus climbing into the sycamore tree [Matt. 21:1-11, Luke 19:29-38].

[29.] Cutlers, Bladesmiths, Sheathers, Scalers, Bucklermakers, Horners: Pilate, Caiphas, two soldiers, three Jews, Judas selling out Jesus [Matt. 26:4-16].

[30.] Bakers [and later, Water-carriers]: The paschal lamb; the Last Supper, the twelve apostles, Jesus girded with a towel washing their feet; institution of the sacrament of Christ's Body in the New Law, the communion of the apostles. [John 13:4-5, Luke 22:14-20].

[31.] Cordwainers: Pilate, Caiphas, Annas, fourteen armed soldiers, Malchus, Peter, James, John, Jesus, and Judas kissing and betraying him [John 18: 1-11, Matt. 26:47-52, Mark 14:43-50, Luke 22:47-53].

[32.] Bowers [i.e., bow-makers] and Fletchers: Jesus, Annas, Caiphas, and four Jews striking and punching Jesus; Peter, the woman accusing Peter, and Malchus [John 18:12-27, Matt. 26:57-75].

[33.] Tapsters [i.e, tapestry-makers] and Couchers [couch-coverers]: Jesus, Pilate, Annas, Caiphas, two counselors, and four Jews accusing Jesus [John 18: 28-38, Gospel of Nicodemus].

[34.] Littesters [i.e., bedmakers]: Herod, two counselors, four soldiers, Jesus and two Jews [Gospel of Nicodemus].

[35.] Cooks, Water-carriers: Pilate, Annas, Caiphas, two Jews, and Judas returning the thirty pieces of silver [Matt. 27:1-10].

[36.] Tilemakers, Milners, Ropers, Sieve-makers, Turners, Hayresters [i.e., workers in horsehair], Bollers [i.e., bowl-makers]: Jesus, Pilate, Caiphas, Annas, six soldiers carrying spears with banners, and another four leading Jesus from Herod, seeking that Barabas be released and Jesus crucified; and then binding him and scourging him, putting a crown of thorns on his head; three soldiers casting lots for Jesus' garments [Matt. 27:11-30, John 18:28-40, 19:1-16].

[37.] Tunners [i.e., barrel-makers]: Jesus blood-soaked carrying his cross to Calvary. Simon the Cyrene, the Jews forcing him to take the cross [Matt. 27:31-33, Mark 15:20-22]; Jesus' mother Mary, the apostle John just then telling her of his condemnation and his trek to Calvary. Veronica wiping the blood and sweat from Jesus' face with her veil on which is imprinted the image of Jesus; and other women weeping for Jesus [Gospel of Nicodemus].

[38.] Pin and wire-makers, Laten-makers, Painters: The cross, Jesus stretched out on it upon the ground; four Jews scourging and stretching him with ropes, and afterwards raising the cross and Jesus' body nailed to the cross on Mount Calvary [Matt. 27:34-44].

[39.] Butchers, Poulterers: The cross, two thieves crucified, Jesus hanging on the cross between them; Jesus' mother Mary, John, Mary [Magdalene], James, and Salome. Longinus with the lance, the servant with the sponge, Pilate, Annas, Caiphas, the Centurion, Joseph of Arimathaea and Nicodemus, carrying him to the sepulcher [Mark 15:23-47].

[40.] Saddle-makers, Glaziers, Joiners: Jesus harrowing hell; twelve spirits: six good and six bad [Gospel of Nicodemus].

[41.] Carpenters: Jesus rising from the tomb, four armed soldiers and three weeping Marys. Pilate, Caiphas, and Annas. A young man sitting in the sepulcher dressed in white speaking to the women [Matt. 28:1-8, Mark 16:1-8].

[42.] Winedrawers: Jesus, Mary Magdalene with spices [John 20:1-18].

[43.] Brokers, Woolpackers: Jesus, Luke, Cleophas dressed as pilgrims [Matt. 24:13-35].

[44.] Scriveners, Illuminators, Pardoners, Dubbers [i.e., furbishers of cloth]: Jesus, Peter, John, James, Philip, and the other apostles with part of a cooked fish and a honeycomb, and Thomas the apostle feeling Jesus' wound [John 20:19-29].

[45.] Tailors: Mary, John the Evangelist, eleven apostles, two angels, Jesus ascending before them, and four angels carrying the cloud [Mark 16:19-20, Luke 24:50-51].

[46.] Potters: Mary, two angels, eleven apostles, and the Holy Spirit descending on them, and four Jews marveling [Acts 2:1-13].

[47.] Drapers: Jesus, Mary, Gabriel with two angels, two virgins, and three Jews of Mary's lineage, eight apostles, and two devils.

[48.] Linen-weavers: Four apostles carrying Mary's catafalque, and Fergus stuck hanging on it with two other Jews with one angel.

[49.] Wool-weavers: [The Assumption.] Mary ascending with a band of angels, eight apostles, and Thomas the apostle preaching in the desert.

[50.] Hostelers: Mary, Jesus crowning her, with a band of angels singing.

[51.] Mercers: [The Last Judgment.] Jesus, Mary, the twelve apostles, four angels with trumpets, four with a crown, a lance, and two scourges; four good spirits and four bad spirits, and six devils.

What aspects of the Christian story do these plays emphasize? Which guilds are best connected to the theme of the scenes that they sponsor? How effective would these plays be as tools for teaching Christianity?

58. GUILLAUME DE DEGUILEVILLE'S *PILGRIMAGE OF HUMAN LIFE* (1331)

One of the most popular devotional books of the Middle Ages, The Pilgrimage of Human Life *(*Le Pèlerinage de la vie humaine*) was written by the Cistercian monk Guillaume de Deguileville (c. 1295-post 1358) between 1330-31 at his monastery of Chaalis some forty miles northeast of Paris. His allegorical poem met with immediate success, so much so that around 1355 he was compelled to issue a second edition – The Pilgrimage of the Soul (*Le Pèlerinage de l'âme*) – since so many unauthorized copies of the work were already in circulation. A third pilgrimage allegory, Le Pèlerinage de Jhesuchrist, completed his trilogy. The Pilgrimage of Human Life served up an intricate allegorical puzzle of a Christian pilgrim's urgent search for salvation through the sacraments and teachings of the church, engaging its readers through elaborate personifications of the church, the vices, and the virtues etched in vivid strokes. The original French version of* The Pilgrimage of Human Life *survives in at least fifty-three manuscripts, an indication of its popularity. John Lydgate translated it into*

English (1426-30) and Chaucer wrote an English version of its famous "ABC Prayer." It was also translated into German (both in prose and verse), Dutch, Spanish, and Latin, and was printed several times in the later fifteenth century.

Source: trans. Eugene Clasby, *The Pilgrimage of Human Life* (New York: Garland Publishing, 1992), pp. 3-9, 80-83, 147-52. Middle French.

Book I

To those of this country, who have no home here, but are all pilgrims, as St. Paul says – men and women, rich and poor, wise and foolish, kings and queens – I want to recount a vision that came to me the other night as I was sleeping. While I was awake, I had read, studied, and looked closely at the beautiful *Romance of the Rose.* I am sure that this was what moved me most to have the dream I will tell you about in a moment. Now come near, everyone, gather around and listen closely. Do not draw back, ladies and gentlemen. All of you, move forward, sit down and listen. This vision concerns the mighty and the humble, without exception. I have put it all in [French], so that laymen can understand it. Everyone can learn from it which path to take and which to leave and abandon. This is something very necessary to those who are pilgrims in this wild world. Now listen to the vision that came to me as I was in my bed during my religious life at the Abbey of Chaalis.

As I was sleeping, I dreamed I was a pilgrim eager to go to the city of Jerusalem. I saw this city from afar in a mirror that seemed to me large beyond measure. The city was richly decorated both inside and out. The streets and lanes were paved with gold. The foundation was set up high, the masonry was made of living stones, and a high wall enclosed it on all sides. It had many houses, squares, and mansions. Inside, all was gladness and joy without sorrow. To be brief, all those within it had, in general, more of all good things than they could ever think of or ask for. But I was greatly disturbed that people could not enter as they pleased, because the entrance was very strongly guarded. Cherubim was the gate-keeper, and he held a polished sword, double-edged, well-sharpened on both sides, and easily turned this way and that [see Gen. 3:24]. He knew how to wield it well and no one was skillful enough with a shield to pass through without being wounded or killed. Even the Prince of the city, because of his human nature, suffered death at the entrance and was pierced through his side with the blade. He left his blood as payment, although he owed no debt there. His knights, his champions, and his servants did the same. They all drank from his cup and met their death at the entrance. I saw pennants, stained red with blood, hanging on the battlements over the gate – the porter of that gate spares no one. When I had seen all this, I knew for certain that one had to enter here by force if there were no other way in. However, I did not see anyone pass through this way. They were all completely overcome when they saw the Cherubim, and from then on he could put away his fiery sword.

Just as I looked up, I saw a marvelous thing that astonished me greatly. I saw St. Augustine sitting high up on the battlements and he seemed to be a fowler or a bird-keeper. With him there were many other great masters and teachers who were helping to feed and nourish the birds. To get the food they were holding and the seeds they were scattering – their honeyed morsels and their sweet, beautiful words – many people were becoming birds and flying up on high. Indeed, I could see many Dominicans, Canons, and Augustinians, all kinds of people, lay and secular, clergy and religious, beggars and the needy, gathering feathers and making great wings for themselves. Then they began to fly, rising high up into the city. They flew over Cherubim and paid little heed to his power.

As soon as I turned and looked in the other direction, I was even more astonished at what I saw there. Up on the walls of the city I saw other persons of authority helping their companions to get inside by clever means. First, I saw St. Benedict, who had placed against the wall a great ladder made up of the twelve rungs of humility. His companions – many black monks, white monks, and grey monks – climbed quickly up these into the city without hindrance from anyone. Next I saw St. Francis, who proved to be a good friend to those of his order. As I saw in my vision, he had let down over the walls a strongly-braided rope with knots in it and all his true companions were climbing up it. None of them had hands so slippery that they could not climb right to the top if they grasped the knots firmly. I saw many others on top of the wall, but I am not sure I can tell you all their names or how they were helping their companions to climb up on all sides, because I was looking only at the side that faced me. I could not see beyond this, much to my regret. But I can tell you that in the wall facing me I saw a small narrow door [Luke 13:24] that the king of the city had placed under guard for the sake of justice. He had given the key to St. Peter, whom he trusted. That trust was surely well-placed, because he let no one pass through except the poor, for the one who does not lie has said that the rich cannot enter there any more than a camel can pass through the eye of a needle [Matt. 19:24]. Entering was very cleverly arranged, for all the people were taking off their clothes and stripping naked at the entrance [Eccles. 5:14]. Old clothes piled up there quickly. None of the people passed through there clothed, unless they wore the king's robes, but those who did so could always pass through anytime they wanted. This way of entering pleased me very much, because all the people had an advantage in common if they became truly poor. There was no difficulty at all, as long as they would take off their old clothes and leave them outside, in order to have new ones within. This arrangement should be quite agreeable, because there is not much to do. In truth, people cannot be so rich that they may not become poor, if they want. And surely it is good to be so, in order to enter into such a beautiful state. It would be good to fast a little, in order to feast at dinnertime.

Now I have told you briefly how I saw the fair city in a beautiful mirror and how I was inspired to go there as a pilgrim, if I could, by any means. Indeed, in my dream I could see no rest anywhere else. It seemed to me that I would find great peace if I could be within its walls. If I could get there, I would never think of leaving. As I was thinking about this, it occurred to me that I had no scrip [a knapsack] or staff and that I needed them, for these are things most fitting for every wayfaring pilgrim. Then I came out of my house, where I had been for nine months without going out, and I began to look for the staff and the scrip I needed for what I had to do.

As I went looking, worried and concerned about where I might find a merchant who could help me get these things, I saw on my way a lady whose beauty gave me great joy. She seemed to be the daughter of an emperor or a king or some other great lord. She was wearing a gown of beaten gold, bound with a sash of green lamé that was seeded its entire length with rubies. On her breast she had a golden broach with an enamel in the middle, and in the center of the enamel there was shining star that left me in awe. Her head was crowned with a golden crown and encircled by a multitude of shining stars. The one who had given her these things and had dressed her in this way was clearly very powerful. She was courteous, I thought, for she spoke to me first and asked me kindly what I was looking for. I was completely surprised at this, because I had not thought that a lady in such fine array would bother to notice me, but I soon realized, as I learned then and now know well, that the more goodness people have in them, the more humility they have as well. The more apples the tree has, the more it bends down toward the people. Humility is the sign of all good and kind hearts. Those who do not carry this banner do not have complete goodness. Then I answered her and told her how it had happened that I was inspired to go to the city of Jerusalem, and how I was unhappy because I did not have a scrip and a staff, and so I was looking for them, asking for them everywhere.

"Dear friend," she answered, "if you want good news about what you are looking for, come with me. Nothing better ever happened to you than to have met me today. I want to help you right away with whatever you need."

Then I could no longer hold back, no matter what might happen to me.

I wanted to know everything – her name and who she was. "Lady, I said, "I would like very much to know your name, your country and region, and exactly who you are. Tell me, please, and I think I will be the happier for it."

Then she answered me: "Listen and I will tell you. I do not want to be at all puzzling or mysterious to you. I am the daughter of the emperor who is lord over all others. He has sent me into this country to win friends for him, not because he needs them, but because he would be very glad to be friends with all people for their own good. Do you see how I am dressed, elegantly arrayed with rubies and stars? You have never seen any more beautiful. They give light to all those who travel in the night, so that everyone can find me – by day as well as by night, and by night as well as by day – and not do foolish things. I am the one you must seek when you go into a strange land. As long as you have me for a companion, you will have no better friend. If you go into that country without me, you will surely be hated both by my father, the great king, and all who are with him. Without me no one can do good. Everyone needs me. The world would have been lost long ago if I had not taken care of it. Whoever has me lacks nothing, and whoever does not have me lacks everything. I govern all things and I heal all ills. I give sight to the blind and strength to the weak. I raise up those who have fallen and I set right those who have gone astray. I will not turn away anyone, except those who commit mortal sin. But for people like that I have no concern, as long as they are in such filth. I am called God's Grace and I have no other name. You will call me by that name when you need me. That will surely be very often before you reach the city you have seen, because you will find many obstacles and troubles, misfortunes and difficulties that, believe me, you cannot pass through – neither you nor anyone else – without me. And if you could pass through or escape them without me – and that is impossible – I tell you that without me you will not enter or set foot in the realm of Jerusalem. Although you have seen many things – you have seen that some people enter there completely naked, others fly up there, others get in by clever devices, and others go past Cherubim – you can be sure, however, that no one can enter except through me. I make some people undress outside, in order to clothe them better inside. For others I make wings of my virtues so they can fly well and then they fly up, as I wish. You have seen this clearly with your own eyes. Still others I put to the test in various ways, as best I can, so that I have them all pass through and enter. Now you can tell, without doubt, if my friendship is good. If it pleases you, say so now and do not hide your answer any longer."

Right away I replied: "Lady, for the love of God, please be my friend and never leave me. Nothing is more necessary to me for what I have to do. I am very grateful that you have come first to my aid. I needed nothing else. Now lead me where you wish, I ask you, and do not delay."

Then she took me at that very moment and led me straight to a house that belonged to her, she said, and she told me that I would find there everything that I would need. She said she had founded and built it 1330 years ago, as she remembered very well. I was eager to see this house and I was amazed at the sight of it, because it was floating high up in the air, between the earth and the sky as though it had come down from the heavens. It had steeples and fine towers, and these adornments were very beautiful. But I was greatly troubled, because there was water in front of it that I had to cross if I wanted to enter the house. There was no boat, plank or bridge, and it was deep there, as I discovered later when I was plunged into it. Then I began to ask Grace how I could avoid this, why there was such a crossing, whether there was another one elsewhere, and I asked her to tell me clearly what good this water might do me.

Then she replied: "What are you saying? Are you frightened by such a little thing? You want to go to Jerusalem, and to get there you must cross the great sea. The great sea is the world, and it is full of many troubles, tempests and torments, great storms and winds. How will you be able to cross that, when you are so afraid of such a little thing? You must not be afraid of this, because, as you should know, more little children cross over here than adults and old people. This is the first crossing of every good pilgrimage. There is no other path elsewhere except past Cherubim. Some have gone that way and they have been bathed in their own blood. Nevertheless, if you want to take the path by Cherubim, this crossing is not bad for you, but it is indeed quite necessary, for if you consider where you come from and the house full of filth you have been in for nine months, you certainly need to wash yourself. I advise you, therefore, to cross here. You cannot find a safer way. A king once passed over here, and he made the crossing safe. He made the crossing, and he was not unclean and had done no evil. If you want to cross here, say so, and I will send right away for a special servant of mine who is God's minister. He is the guardian of my household and the steward of this crossing. He will help you to cross over and to bathe and wash yourself. He will also make a cross on you, because he will see at once that you want to go over the sea and conquer Jerusalem. So you will fear your enemies less, he will make a cross upon your breast. So you will have little fear of all danger, he will also anoint you on your back and on your head like a champion, and you will think your enemies of little account. Answer me now. What do you think?"

"I want you to send him to me right away," I said.

Then, at her command, the minister I have spoken of before came and took me by the hand and put me into that same water. He washed me, he bathed me, and he plunged me into it three times. Grace had not lied to me about anything. He made the sign of the cross on me and anointed me. Then he led me into the house, where there are very fine and elegant lodgings. There Grace treated me kindly, even more kindly than she had before. There she told me that she would show me and teach me many things, and that I would be very wise to pay attention to them. Just as she was saying this to me, I saw many marvelous things. I will not pass over them in silence, but I will tell you something about them. Later, when I see the right moment, I will tell you about the staff and the scrip I wanted, for then I will have time enough.

After Grace shows the Pilgrim a complex allegorical display of the sacraments and introduces him to Nature, Penance, Charity, and Wisdom, she at last gives him his scrip (Faith, hung with twelve little bells: the twelve articles of faith) and his staff (Hope, "to lean on in all the rough paths"). She arms him with pieces of armor representing the four cardinal virtues – prudence, temperance, fortitude, and justice – and he sets off on his journey. But on the road, the Pilgrim is confused as he feels his will pulled in two directions. He poses a basic question to the personification of Reason:

"Lady," I said, "now I ask you to tell me, who am I? Since I am not my body, then tell me who I am. I will never be at ease unless I know something about this."

"Ha!" she said, "what have you learned? You do not know much, I think. It is much more valuable to know oneself, than to be an emperor, a count, or a king, than to understand all learning and to have all the goods in the world. But since you have not learned this, you are well advised to ask, and so I will tell you very briefly something I know about it.

"Apart from the body – I have spoken about this and set it apart in every way – you are the picture, the image and likeness of God. He made you out of nothing and created and shaped you in his likeness. He could not have given you or impressed upon you a nobler form. He made you beautiful and clear-sighted, lighter than the bird on the wing, immortal, never to die, enduring forever. If you consider yourself well, except for your transgressions, nothing, not the heavens, the earth, the sea, the birds or any other creature, except the angels, can compare to your nobility. God is your father and you are his son. You must not think that you are the son of Thomas de Deguileville, for he never had a son or daughter who was of this kind or of such a noble race. Your body – your enemy – you have from him. It came to you from him, for he begot it, as Nature ordained. It is right that the trees bear such fruit as Nature teaches them. Just as the thorn tree cannot bear or produce figs, so the human body can bear no fruit but what is disgusting and weak, vile filth and corruption, rottenness and foul mud. But you are no such thing, for you were not made by a mortal man, but by God, your father. God made with his hands only two human bodies in the world, and these two he commissioned to make others according to the model. But he reserved the making of the spirit, for a certain purpose. He wanted to make all of them, without interference from anyone else. He made you, for you are a spirit, and he placed you in the body you are in. He put you there to live in it for a while, to prove whether you were truly virtuous and brave, and to see whether you would conquer the body or yield yourself up to it. You are always in battle with it and it with you, if you do not give up. It overthrows you by flattery and deceives you and defeats you. It keeps you under its rule, if you trust it, and you must defeat it by strength. It would never have power over you, except by your will. You are Samson, it is Delilah [see Judg. 16]. You have strength in you, but it has none. It can only flatter you and deliver you to your enemies. It will bind you, if you let it, and shear off all your hair, and when it knows your secrets it will reveal them to the Philistines. This is the friendship it has for you, the loyalty and the fidelity. Now consider whether you will give in to it without striking a blow, whether you will be deceived and made a fool of like Samson."

"Lady," I said, "I am hearing strange things. I think I am dreaming or asleep. Here I am, thrust into my body, and you call me a spirit and you say I am clear-sighted. And yet I see neither more nor less. And you have said that my body, which sees well, is blind, and many other very strange things that are fleas in my ears. So I ask you to teach me and instruct me more plainly, for I do not know what to ask, because I am confused by what I am hearing."

Then Reason began again. "Now understand this," she said. "When the sun is obscured at noontime, hidden behind a cloud, and it cannot be seen, I ask you, for the sake of true love, to tell me where the daylight comes from."

"I think it comes from the sun," I said. "It is hidden and it makes its light pass through the cloud and shine down."

"How can its light be seen through the cloud?" asked Reason.

"Just as it is seen through a glass," I said, "or as a flame can be seen in a lantern."

"Certainly," Reason responded, "if you have understood what you have said, by the sun you will understand the soul you have in this mortal body. The body is a cloud and a smoky lantern, through which, however it may be, the light within can be seen. The soul that lives in the body shines outward and makes foolish people think that everything is illuminated by the poor cloud that obscures the soul. But if there were no cloud, the soul would have such great light that it would see quite plainly from east to west, and it would see and know and love its creator. The eyes of the body are not eyes, but windows through which the soul gives light to the body outside. But you must not think, for that reason, that the soul has any need of these eyes, these windows.

Fig. 7.2. Jangling church-goers

As a tonsured priest begins the consecration of the mass and his acolyte raises a lighted candle, two women – one holding rosary beads – talk or "jangle" while a demon hops on their heads. A man stands reverent and quiet. Paintings of the Annunciation and a small Virgin and Child are behind the altar. From Michael Furter's edition of *Der Ritter vom Turn*, the German translation of the Knight of Tour-Landry's book (see Doc. 59). Evidence suggests that Albrecht Dürer had a hand in some of the woodcuts designed for this edition printed in Basel in 1493.

It sees its spiritual good before it and behind it, without bodily windows. And sometimes it would see it better if the body had no eyes. Tobit once was blind in body but not therefore blind in soul, for he taught his son how to conduct himself and what path to take [Tob. 2:11]. He would never have taught him this if he had not seen it with his soul. The soul saw and knew clearly the things he said to him. So if I say you see clearly, I want to reaffirm this, for it is you who can see, not the body, which is blind both inside and out. It would never see anything, if it were not by your light. And as I have told you about sight, so I tell you about hearing and about all its senses, for they are only instruments by which it receives from you what it has. It sees and hears nothing except through you. And so I tell you plainly that if you were not carrying it and supporting it, it would be like a pile of dung and never move."

How easy is it to understand the allegories here? What is Guillaume's view of human nature? What might account for the widespread popularity of The Pilgrimage?

59. BEHAVING PIOUSLY: A KNIGHT'S ADVICE FOR HIS DAUGHTERS (1373)

The knight Geoffrey de la Tour-Landry, whose family castle "Landry Tower" was in Anjou, composed two books of deportment: one for his two sons, which no longer survives, and the other, which he finished around 1373, for his three daughters. In its introduction he recounts how he sat in his garden at the end of April in 1371 remembering his wife whose death years earlier left his daughters motherless. Worried about their upbringing, he decided to "make a book of examples in the vernacular for [his] daughters teaching them how to conduct themselves and to distinguish good from evil." To this end he had four clerics extract stories from "the Bible, the deeds of kings, and the chronicles of France, England, Greece, and many other foreign lands." His book, filled with dozens of stories meant to instill morals, struck a chord with medieval audiences always eager for authoritative guides to the good life. It survives in at least twelve French manuscripts, was translated into English in the mid-fifteenth century, and was first printed by Caxton in his own translation in 1484. It was especially popular in Germany where it was printed in 1493 as Der Ritter vom Turn *and often reprinted thereafter. The "Hours" he mentions is the Little Office of the Blessed Virgin, or Book of Hours: a collection of psalms, hymns, lessons, readings, and prayers for lay people that resembled the seven daily cycles of prayer – the Divine Office – required of the regular clergy. The morning Hours are called matins.*

Source: trans. J. Shinners from Anatole de Montaiglon (ed.), *Le Livre du Chevalier de la Tour Landry* (Paris: P. Jannet, 1854), pp. 10-16, 63-65. Middle French.

Chapter 5. Concerning what should be done on rising.

Fair daughters, when you get out of your bed, enter into the service of the exalted Lord and begin your Hours. This should be your first deed, the first thing you do. When you say them, say them with a good heart; and as far as you can do not let your mind wander, for you cannot go two ways at once: you will either take one path or the other. This, then, is the service of God. For as the wise man in his wisdom says, "he who listens but does not understand is worth as much as he who hunts and does not gather." Thus he who thinks of earthly things while saying the Our Father and prayers that concern heavenly things has done a worthless deed which does nothing but mock God. This is why Holy Writ says that a brief prayer pierces heaven, which should be taken to mean that a short prayer briefly said devoutly from the heart is worth more than great, long Hours said while thinking of other things, or talking about other things while saying your Hours. For the more devoutly you say all these words, the more value they have and, in the end, more merit. And again, as Holy Writ says, "as the sweet dew of April and May satisfies and tempers the earth, and makes it take seed and be fruitful, so too devotions and prayers are pleasing to God." You will find this in many places in the stories of the holy confessors, virgins, and holy women, who made their beds out of thorny vines and lay on them in order to sleep less and have less rest so that they could more quickly awaken, begin their prayers, and be in God's service day and night, and through their service and effort acquire glory from God. He plainly shows the world that these people are with him in their holy joy, which is why he makes great miracles and signs through them; for in this way God repays the service people do him two hundred times, as I said above. And for this reason, fair daughters, say your prayers with a good heart and devoutly, without thinking of other things; and take care that you do not take breakfast until you have said your devotions with a good heart, for a full stomach may not be humble or devout. Afterwards take care that you hear as many masses as you can, for you will have great good from God; and so it is a good and holy thing, about which I will give you an example.

Chapter 6. Concerning a knight who had two daughters, one devout, the other a gourmand.

There was a knight who had two daughters, one by his first wife, the other by his second. The one by the first wife was wonderfully devout, for she would never eat until she had said all her Hours and heard all the masses she could. But the other daughter was so cherished and so coddled that she was allowed to do whatever she wanted, so that as soon as she had heard a little of the mass and said two or three Our Fathers, she would go to her room and eat breakfast or some other dainties, for she said that fasting made her head hurt. But this was a bad habit. Also, when her father and mother were sleeping, it suited her to eat some tasty bite or delicious supper. This was how she lived until she was married to a wise but bad-tempered knight, who, being her husband, quickly recognized her ways, which were bad for the body and the soul. So he showed her most sweetly several times that she was wrong to live such a life; but each time she did not want to be corrected despite his good words.

Now it happened one time that he had gone to bed and he felt around at his side for her but did not find her. He was angry so he got out of bed, put on a gray-furred mantle, and went into the room where his wife was with the housekeeper and two of his young men. They were eating and laughing so loudly and the men and women playing and raising such a ruckus together that one couldn't have heard God's thunder. The lord took a look at all of this disorder and was enraged. He took his staff to strike one of his men who was holding one of the chambermaids half undressed, and struck the man with the staff, which was dry, so that it shattered and, through this misadventure and accident, a splinter pierced the eye of his wife sitting beside him. As a result, she was so unbecoming with her one eye, and her husband bore her so much hate for the dishonor she did him, that he gave his heart to another; thus, their household fell into utter ruin. This befell them because of the woman's poor self-control, who was accustomed to living a dissolute and disordered life from morning till night. Due to this, such evils befell her as the loss of both her eye and the love of her husband to whom she had been a bad wife. This is why it is good to say all of your prayers, hear all the masses you can while fasting, and accustom yourself to living soberly and decently; because something done by habit and regular use is no burden, as the wise man's proverb says: "put a colt to amble and it will keep to it for as long as it lives."

But here is what happened to her sister. From her youth she had grown used to serving God and the church, to saying her Hours devoutly and hearing all the masses she could while fasting. So it came about that God rewarded her and gave her a good knight, rich and powerful, and they lived together agreeably and honorably. It happened that their father, who was a most prudent man, went to see his two daughters. He found the house of the first daughter greatly respected and wealthy, and he was welcomed there most honorably. At the house of the other, who had lost her eye, he found things in disarray and the house poverty-stricken and badly provided. When he returned to his own house, he reported all this to his wife and upbraided her for causing the ruin of his daughter whom she had so coddled and dearly nurtured, and to whom she had given free rein for so long and allowed her to do whatever she wanted that she had wound up in dire straits. And by this example it is good to serve God, and to hear all the masses you can fasting, and to live an honest life, eating and drinking at the proper hours between prime and terce, and to dine at a suitable hour, according to the time. For the life you have and live in your youth will be the life you have and live in your old age.

Chapter 7. How all women should fast.

Next, my dear daughters, for as long as you are married you ought to fast for three days a week, the better to overcome your flesh – in which you should not take too much delight – in order to keep you chaste and holy in God's service, who will guard and repay you doubly. If you cannot fast three days, at least fast on Friday in honor of the precious blood and the passion of Jesus Christ, which he suffered for us. And if you cannot fast on bread and water, at least eat nothing that has been butchered, for that is a most noble thing, as I heard told about a knight who was in a battle between Christians and Saracens. It happened that there was a Christian whose head, struck by a blow from a scimitar, was completely severed from his body. But the head cried out and requested to be confessed. Thus a priest came who heard his confession and asked by what merit it was that his head could speak without a body. The head answered that God left no good deed unrewarded by his grace, and that he had not eaten meat on Wednesday in honor of the Son of God, who was sold [by Judas] on that day, and on Friday he had not eaten anything that suffered death. So for this service God did not wish him to be damned or to die in a mortal sin that he had not confessed. Here is a good example that you should take care not to eat anything on Friday that suffered death. And after, fair daughters, make a good fast on Saturday in honor of Our Lady and her holy virginity so that she will wish to give you the grace to chastely guard your virginity and purity for the glory of God and the honor of your soul, and so that she will lead you from evil temptation. And so it is a very good and most noble thing to fast on these two days on bread and water, which is a great victory over the flesh and a most holy thing. Truth to tell, if you have the desire to accustom yourself to these fasts, you may endure them; for if you have grown accustomed to it, it is no load to say your devotions, hear the mass and the divine office, fast, and do blessed works like holy women did, according to the stories and the lives of the saints now in paradise....

Chapter 28. Concerning those who jangle in church.

I will tell you another example about those who jabber and jangle in church when they should be listening to the divine service. In the deeds of Athens there is the story of a holy hermit who led a good and saintly life. In his hermitage he had a chapel dedicated to St. John, and knights, ladies, and maidens from that country went there on pilgrimage, as much to celebrate the saint's feast as for the saintliness of the holy man. As the hermit chanted high mass, he turned to the people after he had said the Gospel and saw the ladies, the maidens, and several of the knights and their esquires chattering and jangling and taking counsel among themselves during the mass. He looked at their foolish faces and next to each of their ears saw dark and horrible demons laughing at their jangling and writing down each word they heard. These demons were leaping on their hair done up like horns, on their rich attire, and on their finery like little birds hopping from branch to branch. The holy man crossed himself and was astonished. From the beginning to the end of the canon of the mass he heard them talking and flattering each other, laughing and jesting. He struck the [mass] book in order to make them be quiet, but none of them stopped talking. Then he said, "Good Lord God, make these people be quiet and realize their folly." At that moment those who had been laughing and jangling started to weep and wail, men and women both, like people possessed and suffering such torment that it was a pitiful thing to hear. And when mass was sung, the holy hermit told them how he had seen the demons of hell with their horrible faces laughing at what they were doing at mass. Then he told them how dangerous and what a fault it was to talk and jest, and how sinful it was to laugh, since no one should come to mass or the divine office except to listen to it humbly and devoutly and to adore and pray to God. Then he told them that when he saw demons hopping and dancing on their horned hair and on the gowns of several women, it was on those who were talking and quarreling with their companions and those who thought more about amorous things and earthly delights than about God in order to please and gain the regard of those scatterbrains. On these he saw the demons dancing. But on those who said their prayers and kept to their devotions there was nothing, even though they had plenty of finery and were well-attired, for they held their prayers dearer to their heart.

And then he told them that the devil was greatly amused by those who bedecked themselves to get a better reputation and were more bound to great pleasures than to God's service. Afterwards it happened that the women who had been wailing and tormented in a frenzy abandoned their horned hairstyles, their gowns, and their ornaments; however they made their novena, and at the end of nine days they returned to their senses through the prayers of the holy hermit, and were well chastised for having talked and jangled during the divine service. Thus, this is a good example of how no one ought to talk during or disturb God's divine worship.

If Geoffrey's daughters followed the advice he offers here, what kind of women would they have been? What details about codes of personal behavior emerge here?

60. GEERT GROTE PREACHES THE MODERN DEVOTION (c. 1380-83)

In his mid-thirties Geert Grote (1340-84), the orphaned son of a wealthy Deventer merchant and a graduate of the University of Paris, put aside his long-laid plans to join a monastic order and, after several years of soul searching, took a new tack. Realizing that his spiritual aspirations could not be satisfied by following the traditional avenues of organized religious life, he invested most of his inherited wealth in founding a hospice for poor women, and himself embraced an austere life of penitence. Then, after being ordained a deacon and receiving special permission, he began his mission of preaching religious repentance and conversion throughout the diocese of Utrecht. When he died of plague in 1384 (as had both his parents during the Black Death), he had planted the seeds of the most original movement of late medieval religion: the Brothers and Sisters of the Common Life whose particular brand of piety became known as the devotio moderna, *or Modern Devotion. A generation after Grote's death, the Modern Devotion produced the last great work of medieval devotional writing, the enormously popular and influential* Imitation of Christ, *probably written by Thomas of Kempen (or à Kempis) in the 1420s. What set the Brothers and Sisters of the Common Life apart from most other medieval religious movements was their insistently lay character. Pooling their wealth and living together in a common house, the New Devout, as they were called, took no religious vows, lived by no religious rules, and undertook no particularly rigorous devotional routine. Instead, they devoted their lives to common prayer and meditation — especially meditation on the life of Christ — as they pursued inward spiritual perfection. In this the New Devout resembled the women beguines and men beghards who had spread across the Netherlands and Rhineland at the end of the twelfth century and prospered until outlawed in the early fourteenth. This sermon, which Grote preached in Dutch sometime between 1380 and 1383, offers a thumbnail sketch of many of the chief themes of the Modern Devotion and, in its emphasis on interior transformation over external acts, anticipates a cardinal point of Martin Luther's theology over a century later. It also must have pricked the consciences of the prosperous Lowlands commercial classes.*

Source: trans. John Van Engen in *Devotio Moderna, Basic Writings* (New York: Paulist Press, 1988), pp. 92-97. Middle Dutch.

The holy teacher St. Paul says that God's heavenly kingdom consists of righteousness, peace, and joy in the Holy Spirit [see Gal. 5.32]. Whoever desires to reign eternally with God, or to come to God, or to have God come and dwell in him, must sense these three in himself, or else reach out and study to acquire them with all his strength. In seeking these three, a man should let every external religious exercise go. For all external exercises, whether fasting, scourging, keeping vigil, much psalm-singing, many Our Fathers, manual labor, hard beds, or hair shirts, have only so much good and profit as they bring righteousness, peace, and joy in the Holy Spirit. Men should do such works only in order to acquire those three and measure accordingly whether to do more or less. Any exercise that gets in the way of righteousness, peace, and joy in the Holy Spirit, or any one of the three, is harmful, burdensome, and improper for a man. It comes rather from man's enemy, the devil, and from man's own perverse conceit and self-absorption. The devil sets men to doing many such exercises that look good on the outside – and could also be good if they were done righteously and for the right reasons. But the devil leads men into such an ascetic life that – as he knows well it will – it makes them sick in the head, quick to anger, ill-natured, and arrogant, or he brings a man to think he is doing something good so that his own works become pleasing to him. The devil knows very well that exterior works are in fact more harmful than helpful. The devil drives some persons to such an austere life that they lose the kingdom of heaven by neglecting their interior life and the things that are more needful.

And so it is little wonder that there are many people who are much in prayer and who lead very austere lives, and yet are unrighteous within and covetous still of temporal goods. Goods earned unjustly they have not returned, and indeed cannot, though they may at times want to, because such goods have grown so near their hearts that wickedness, miserly practices, and the devil's pleasures are now closer to their hearts than God himself, his love, and his commandments. Through their religious exercises these people make a good appearance on the outside among simple people, but that is of as little profit to them, in Christ's own words, as the external gleam of sepulchers which on the inside are full of worms and stench – and so it is with these people [see Matt. 23:27]. We should know, as St. Paul said, that though these people could speak with angelic tongues and do all things and understand all mysteries and practice all the arts and do such miracles as move mountains and live so ascetically as to give their bodies to be burned, yet it would be worth nothing if they had not a godly love which outweighed all temporal things [see 1 Cor 13:1-3].

No godly love or power resides in the man who knowingly clings to or desires unjust goods. Justice and judgment must prepare the way in a man before God or love, which is God, will enter into him, as David says in the Psalter: *iusticia et iudicium, praeparatio sedis tuae* [Ps. 88 (89):15]. Which is to say, justice and judgment are a preparation for the throne of God in us, presupposing that we prepare ourselves to become fit places for God to come in and take his seat. This, I repeat, is the first thing: God will have judgment from us according to the justice that is within. We should so judge ourselves that, so far as we can, we render full restitution to our fellow Christians for all misdeeds done to them and for all that we have taken from them unjustly – even if we ourselves must suffer in order to make sure that we do not see them forced to beg for their bread. So much at least the command of God and holy love ought to move us to give.

Love encompasses justice and wants to praise her beyond all speaking. A righteous Christian should not bring his sacrifice to the altar until he has done justice; until then, in fact, his sacrifice, whether interior or exterior, is not pleasing to God. It should be recognized that St. Thomas [Aquinas] spoke truly in the *Secunda Secundae* [of his *Summa theologica*]: A man can, may, and should restore what he has taken unjustly; but if he withholds and increases it, doing nothing else, the withholding and increasing is a mortal sin bringing death to the soul. The love of God cannot dwell in a man during the time that some temporal good so stirs him that he desires unjustly and against God to have or get it, and takes it at any hour that he can, with might or with cunning, in secret or in public. And all confessors and others who keep him in this business are nothing but advocates and helpers of the devil. For so long as a man possesses goods of other people that are pleasing to him, or goods that he has to produce, prepare, or preserve in an underhanded way, or takes of them as it suits him without the people's concurrence, or exchanges them to suit himself, or advises people in a way harmful to them but profitable to himself – for all that time the love of temporal goods possesses a man's heart more than the love of God. This is contrary to God's command and makes a man blind, inclining him toward himself and, still more, toward the devil and the advice of false confessors. And so he is ever finding things he wants, always managing to excuse his covetousness, and thus deceives himself horribly, indeed all the way to hell and death, because all such false pretensions allow a man to remain in his foolishness.

If such men would reflect on their lives and not abandon them at once to gathering and a blindly ascetic life-style, they would discover that their lives actually stand outside love. For they would discover the degree to which little temporal things, no matter how small they might be, move them against God and against justice. A small word, for instance, may easily unsettle their hearts and loosen their mouths. They quickly become wretched over some one little thing that has escaped their grasp. This is entirely contrary to joy in the Holy Spirit which renders men so much less grieved over worldly things as they come to love ever more things that are truly godly. And for that reason such people eventually become quick to anger, quarrelsome, murmurers, gossips, obstinate, and out to please themselves. Nor have they any peace within, as shown by their words and works. But wherever there is no outer peace, not God but the devil is present. For the Prophet says that God's city enjoys peace, and the Lord says that his spirit comes to rest only in restful men.

Peace was the first gift the angels announced to all men of goodwill at Christ's birth. A good will is to be measured by peace: You have much goodwill if you have genuine peace, and you will also have genuine peace if you have goodwill. What then is goodwill except that a man conform his will to God's so that he wills nothing other than what God wills? Now since all things that happen come from the will of God, working and disposing things according to his holy peace, the good man should be at peace with all things that God arranges in pain or difficulty and sends against sin. The just man of goodwill can always make peace within and without, keeping himself from slanderous talk, rebellious action, or anything that might unsettle others. The apostles spoke peace to all the houses they entered, and David said in the Psalter, God spoke peace to his people, and turns around the hearts that are dead within. Christ, in coming and going, spoke peace to his people inwardly and outwardly. Inwardly he spoke of peace that passes all understanding for those who are perfect, and so the more impure a man in heart, the less he has of genuine peace. For purity of heart cannot exist without interiority of heart and interiority and kindness are practically the same. A distraught heart cannot withhold itself from complaint and lashing out, and thence come externally unrest and lack of peace.

External suffering and dissatisfaction come easily especially when a man wants things to be other than the way they have turned out, and cannot and will not accept what has happened, whether pleasure or loss, good or evil, as coming from the hand of God. The just man makes an effort to bear these things equitably, along with all that God sends, and those who cannot do this perfectly, should strive for it more and more. It is much better for a man to suffer through the pain or difficulties that God sends or arranges in his eternal wisdom and goodness than to attempt to deal with these things with his own strength and never know whether they are pleasing to God or not. But a man should know that God wills all that he disposes for a man to suffer, and should know that more surely than if the holy angels themselves had said it with their own mouths. Indeed God speaks it to him with his own mouth, for God's speech is nothing other than his works, and therefore his works are the most authentic testimony on earth to God's will that all things should fit together. And for that reason the just and kindly man represses all evil-speaking and all injustice because for him all is at peace.

All too distant from these men are those who cry out dreadfully within and without over one little unworthy thing, and thus destroy the peace of everyone around them. In truth they ought to know that their tongues and hearts are enflamed with the fires of hell, like those tongues whereof St. James spoke. These men desecrate not only their hearts but also their bodies and set them afire with the flames of hell [see James 3:6]. Oh, poor souls! How many a wife is enflamed with hell-fire over one little word, heard from her maid or husband, which so unsettled her that she set up a great clamor, scolding without ceasing and destroying the peace of all about her. What more can one say than that these are hellish beasts, and yet they do not repent. Yea, in my own mind, they are spiritually burdened in this state with the hellish beast himself.

And so this ends up concerning much more than one little thing. It is much worse than if they simply mistreated someone to whom by God's command they ought to be subject, as a child his father or a wife her husband or a servant his lord, and worse too than if a lord thus mistreated his servant or a father his child or a husband his wife. For God willed and foresaw that they should be subject and also arranged it so, but, contrary to God, they have set themselves above, against his wisdom and law to their own great loss of peace. It frequently happens that elderly folk become ruined in body, goods, or wisdom, or that a husband cannot earn enough or becomes old and lame, and then along comes the evil child or nasty wife to set themselves above their father or husband, wishing them subject instead to child or wife and thus breaking God's law simply to gain a little earthly advantage.

Speak, wife, is that why you have disturbed and broken the ordinances that God has set and no man can trim? Just because your husband or father can no longer earn enough? Because, dear wife, it is God's holy law that you neither can nor should be without a head: Your husband should be your head and Christ should be the head of your husband. You should come to Christ in this way, and in no other than with your husband as your head. That is, he should be above you in all governance and in all things concerning your household and body. You have no power over your own body; indeed if you were to earn anything by your own work, it would come under the power of your husband. On the other hand, if you earn nothing, your husband should still provide for you with tenderness and as best he can. Whatever you earn is your husband's, as if he had earned it with his own hands, and in this way your hands are more your husband's than your own.

A man likewise should look upon his wife, as St. Paul said [Eph. 5:22-23], even as Christ looks upon his holy church, that is, as a communion of marital love. He should love her and protect her with all his strength, while a wife should be subject so that all she brings is held in common. Each should love the other spiritually, and so all that he earns and possesses he should pour out and set afire and offer up in the same love as does God himself. Oh, if only husband and wife would only reflect on the love and ordinances that prevail between Christ and his communion of souls! For married love is an image and sign of that love. Both man and wife should see in the heavenly wedding feast their own mutual belonging to each other and should take their ordinances from it. Meditate on it, all you wives who serve God! Let the heavenly marriage take root within you. Learn from it many wonders and special things which you should do for your husbands. And you husbands, likewise, learn from it what you owe your wives. Out of it should grow unity, peace, and tranquillity so that you love to be together, preferably more in spirit than in the flesh. And you wives too: Out of it you should grow to prefer your husband's rule and instruction to doing your own will. And so you will become very careful not to wreck this peace or to spread abroad your mutual secrets and burdens, but rather quietly to bear together both good and evil and happily to remain together in your home. You, wife, will think you see Christ in your husband, and you, husband, will think you see the loving soul in your wife.

Yea, those who taste of this will care little about going into taverns and clubs, as do so many now who spend much time abroad and little at home. One should not say this of wives, for no good wife goes, nor may go, abroad to eat or out into society without her husband's permission according to the command of God and the saints – just as Christ says to the soul: Without me you may not do anything that depends on our mutual unity. I would rather, says Christ, have a wife who was extraordinarily subject to her husband in peace and tranquillity, but who did not lead a very ascetic life, than a wife who in penance led the most austere life ever known among women but who was not subject to her husband or lacked kindness or chattered useless things ceaselessly. An ascetic life is an extraordinary good and one necessary for us and for all men – if, that is, it is done in righteousness and obedience. For an ascetic life finds all of its goodness in justice and obedience and peace and quietness and joy in the Holy Spirit. Without them an austere life is dead; it is as chaff and dust, and will be without the fruit of eternal life.

What appeal does Grote's message have for lay people? Is he criticizing the lives of members of religious orders? Would women react differently from men to this sermon?

61. A SPIRITUAL REGIMEN FOR A FIFTEENTH-CENTURY GENTLEMAN

More a memory aid than a developed treatise, these instructions for an anonymous married English layman of the early to mid-fifteenth century were written in Latin by his spiritual director. The word "welawey" (or "wellaway") scattered throughout the text, is an expression of sorrow. The reference to St. Godric of Finchale concerns the renowned English hermit (c. 1065-1170) who, according to one legend, was once attacked in bed by the devil before he had a chance to sign himself with the cross.

Source: trans. W.A. Pantin, "Instructions for a Devout and Literate Layman" in *Medieval Learning and Literature, Essays Presented to Richard William Hunt*, ed. J.J.G. Alexander and M.T. Gibson (Oxford: Clarendon, 1976), pp. 398-400. Latin.

Always carry this about in your purse.
Remember to take holy water every day.
You should get up out of bed with all swiftness.

Make the sign of the cross at the head, at the feet, at the hands, and at the side.

"In the name of the Father and of the Son and of the Holy Ghost may we be delivered from pains and sins, Amen."

Concerning Saint Godric, who did not at once sign himself.

Say: "Into thy hands, Lord Jesus Christ"; Our Father; Hail Mary; I believe in God [i.e., the Creed]; immediately afterwards: "Thou who hast made me, have mercy upon us and upon me."

At the door when you go out say: "All the men of this city or town from the greater to the less are pleasing to God, and only I am worthy of hell. Woe is me. Welawey"; let this be said from all your heart so that the tears run; you need not always say it with your mouth; it is sufficient to say it with a groan.

As far as [the walk to] the church, say no other word except: "Thou hast made me [etc.]." Yet sometimes if you meet a dog or other beast, you may say: "Lord, let it bite me, let it kill me; this beast is much better than I; it has never sinned. I after so much grace have provoked you; I have turned my back to you and not my face, and I have done nothing good, but all ill. Woe is me. Welawey."

On entering the church say: "Lord, it is as a dog and not as a man that I presume to enter your sanctuary. Woe is me. Welawey."

Then, plucking up some confidence, with Mary Magdalene throw yourself at the feet of the most sweet Jesus, and wash them with your tears and anoint them and kiss them; and if not with your eyes and mouth, at least do this in your heart. Do not climb up to the cross, but in your heart say with the publican: "Lord, be merciful to me a sinner."

Afterwards say the matins of the Blessed Virgin, reverently and not too fast.

When you hear mass, do not by any means engage in talk with other people; but while the clerks are singing, look at the books of the church; and on every feast day, look at the Gospel and the exposition of it and at the Epistle. There is a certain *Legenda Sanctorum* which is very old; look at that and especially at the Common of Saints at the end of the book.

I do not counsel you to go up to the altars, as we used to do; but be afraid, and say what you have to say in a side chapel with the Lord Jesus.

On weekdays, after the others have gone, say one "fifty" of the Psalter of the Blessed Virgin [five decades of the rosary]; and then going back to your house have nothing else in your heart or your mouth except "Hail Mary full of grace the Lord is with thee"; sometimes the whole of it, sometimes only "Hail Mary." When you sit at table, ruminate in your mind those two words, or as far as the middle, or sometimes to the end. And every time when you drink at table, say in your heart: "In the name of the Father," as above; make the sign [of the cross] with your hand outside the table.

If dinner is not ready when you get home, go to that room and say another fifty of Our Lady.

When you dine, and also after dinner, say grace standing.

And lest the tongue speak vain or hurtful things, let there be reading, now by one, now by another, and by your children as soon as they can read; and think of the wicked Dives, tormented in hell in his tongue more than in any other members [see Luke 16:19-31].

Let the family be silent at table, and always, as far as is possible.

Expound something in the vernacular which may edify your wife and others.

When there is no reading have your meditations; and let there be these three at least this year [?], that is to say: "Hail Mary," "Thou who hast made me, have mercy upon us and upon me," "In the name of the Father and of the Son and of the Holy Ghost may we be delivered, Amen."

You can make a cross on the table out of five bread crumbs [perhaps to contemplate the Five Wounds]; but do not let anyone see this, except your wife; and the more silent and virtuous she is, the more heartily you should love her in Christ.

After grace, said standing, go to that private place, and send for William Bonet or Sir William Trimenel or others as you please, and confer with them there until vespers.

Drink once, or twice at most, and that in summer. By no means let anyone spend anything, not even one farthing, but let all be done for God's sake.

I forbid you forever all spectacles, that is to say, dances, buckler-play [i.e., fencing], dicing, wrestling, and the like.

Look back, like blessed Anselm, and see how your whole life has been barren or wicked.

Let your supper be brief, lest you ingurgitate, and let all be done as above at dinner.

After supper or before, sometimes before as well, go up into your cell and pray.

As the determiners at Oxford do: When you are in bed, go back to the beginning of the day, and look diligently in your heart: if you have done any evil, and there be sorry; if any good, and there give thanks to God, always in fear and trembling, and do not think it certain that you will survive till the morrow.

What virtues do these instructions try to instill in their owner? How would they affect his sense of self and his relations with others? What is the focus of his piety?

62. A FIFTEENTH-CENTURY ENGLISH YEOMAN'S COMMONPLACE BOOK (1470s)

Robert Reynes seems to have been the reeve, or local overseer, of the village and manor of Acle in Norfolk held by Tintern Abbey. Born and raised in the village, he also held other important village offices such as churchwarden, alderman of the local guild, and perhaps village scribe. What little we know of his property holdings suggests that he was a fairly prosperous peasant, what his contemporaries would have called a yeoman. His commonplace book, which he undoubtedly wrote himself mostly between 1470 and 1475, is a random gathering of things that interested him professionally and person-ally. It offers a very rare and invaluable glimpse into the private devotional life of a fairly ordinary, if fairly well-educated, layman. Scattered among the manorial and legal records, financial tallies, notarial contracts, royal edicts, local history, family genealogy, notes on weights and measures, and even travel tips, are dozens of entries in English and Latin touching his religious preoccupations, both orthodox and not so orthodox. He culled almost all of this material from the popular moral writing of his day, though we do not know how he gained access to this literature. Most of the entries touching on religion are included here. Those marked with an ★ he wrote in Latin; the others were in English. In modernizing the verse, I have preserved the rhymes and meters of the Middle English as much as sense allows. Numbers and titles in brackets are modern additions.

Source: trans. J. Shinners from Cameron Louis (ed.), *The Commonplace Book of Robert Reynes of Acle* (New York & London: Garland, 1980), passim. Middle English and Latin.

[15. The drops of Christ's Blood]

> The number of these drops all
> I will rehearse in general:
> 500 thousand for to tell,
> Plus 47,000 as well
> 500 also great and small
> Here is the number of them all.

[*That is, 547,500 drops shed during the Passion.*]

[17.] The Glorious Virgin Mary's Age★

The Virgin Mother Mary lived sixty-three years:
She was fourteen at her blessed conception [of Jesus].
She lived thirty-three years with her Son.
Sixteen more years on earth, and then she went to heaven.

[18. The Ember Days]★

On the Wednesday following the first Sunday in Lent let the Ember Day fasts begin. On the Wednesday during Pentecost week let the Ember Day fasts begin. On the Wednesday following the feast of the Exaltation of the Holy Cross [Sept. 14] let the Ember Day fasts begin. On the Wednesday after St. Lucy's [Dec. 13] let the Ember Day fasts begin.

[*Ember days were the quarterly periods of fasting on Wednesday, Friday, and Saturday.*]

[23. A Mnemonic Verse]★

> [King] David chants 150 psalms in order.
> He sings 2,606 verses.

[27. A Charm for Fever]★

Here begins a charm against fevers, tried and true.

In the name of the Father, and of the Son, and of the Holy Spirit, amen. Almighty and eternal God, you who lent your hand to your apostle the Blessed Peter do this for your servant †, (Name) †. I conjure you fevers which are seven sisters. The first is named Ylia †, the second Zicalia †, the third Valecta †, the fourth Suffocalia †, the fifth Sineya †, the sixth Geneya †, the seventh Emica †. I conjure you fevers from whatever quarter or whatever nation you reside †, through the Father †, through the Son †, and through the Holy Spirit †, through the power †, through the coming of Christ †, through his nativity †, through the holy circumcision †, through his baptism †, through his fasting [in the desert] †, through the cross and the Passion †, through his death and burial †, through his holy resurrection and miraculous ascension †, through the glory of the Holy Spirit, the Paraclete †, through Holy Mary and all God's holy angels and archangels †, through the thrones and dominions †, through the cherubim and seraphim †, through the twenty-four Elders before the throne of God †, through St. John the Baptist †, through the twelve Apostles †, through the four Evangelists †, through the martyrs and confessors †, through all the saints and holy virgins dwelling in heaven †, through the whole earth †, through the sun and moon †, through the stars and everything that God made in heaven and on earth — I conjure you that you have no more power over this your servant †, (Name) †, whether you be a diurnal fever †, biduous †, tertian †, quartan †, quintan †, sextan †, septan †, and all the way up to a duodecan †.

St. Peter lay before the gate of Galilee, and Jesus came up and asked him, "Peter, why are you lying here?" St. Peter answered, "Lord, I am ill with a fever." And the Lord touched him and healed him. Jesus walked on and Peter followed him. Jesus turned round to Peter and asked him, "Peter, what do you want?" "Lord, I ask that whoever shall carry these words with them or shall recite them over the head of a sick person shall not have fevers." And our Lord Jesus Christ said to him, "Peter, it shall be as you ask." St. Peter answered, "Amen."

† Alga †, lauda †, alpha †, and omega †, first and last †, may the Passion of our Lord Jesus Christ be a remedy for you, amen.

[*Employing Latin and Greek words was thought to increase the efficacy of charms. The names of the seven sisters have no obvious meaning.*]

[28.] For Falling Sickness [Epilepsy]★

Jasper bears myrrh, Melchior incense, Balthazar gold. Whoever will carry with him the names of these Three Kings will be freed from falling sickness through the Lord's pity. Come you angel, who, through heavenly pity, guards me.

[29. A Method of Divination: Onychomancy]

[*English*] Take a young child – that is, between 7 and 13 years old – and set him in the sun between your legs. And then wrap a red silk thread around his right thumb three times, and scrape his fingernail well and clean. And then write on the nail these letters with olive oil [to make the nail reflective]: O, N, E, L, I; while writing these letters have the child say the Our Father. And then say this prayer: [*Latin*] "Lord Jesus Christ, King of Glory, send us three angels on your behalf, who may tell us the truth and nothing false about everything we shall ask them." [*English*] And say this prayer three times with good heart and devoutly. And then three angels shall appear in the child's nail. And then have the child say this after you, either in Latin or English: [*Latin*] "Lord Angels, I command you through the Lord Father Almighty who made you and us from nothing, and through the Blessed Virgin Mary, and the blessed John the Evangelist, and through all virgins and the power of all of God's saints, show us the truth and nothing false about everything we shall ask you. [*English*] And then have the child ask what he wishes and they shall show it to him.

[31.] For the Intermittent Fever★

In the name of the Father, and of the Son, and of the Holy Spirit, amen. Peter was lying on a marble stone with a fever. Jesus came up and said to him, "Peter, why are you lying here?" He said to him, "Lord, I lie here from a bad fever." And Jesus said to him, "Get up and let it go." And he rose up from the fiery furnace and let it go. Peter said to him, "Lord, I ask you that whoever carries on himself in writing these words with my name, let no fevers harm him, neither with chills nor heat, neither diurnal, biduous, tertian, quartan, quintan, sextan, septan, octan, nor nonan." And Jesus said to him, "Peter, let it be as you have asked."

"Lord, by your will and power may this your servant, (Name), be defended without end from all evil fevers. In the name of Jesus, I sign myself with the letter *tau* [Greek: T] †. Jesus of Nazareth, King of the Jews, Son of God, have mercy on me, amen." And let five Our Fathers and five Hail Marys and one Creed be said in honor of our Lord Jesus Christ, and an Our Father, Hail Mary, and Creed in honor of Saint Peter the Apostle.

[36. Precepts in Verse]

Serve God truly,
And the world busily.
Eat your food merrily,
If you wish to live.
Thank God highly,
Though he keeps you poorly.
He may amend you lightly,
Without any grief.

[37. A Prayer]

Lord Jesus Christ, God's Son alive,
Have mercy on us for your wounds five.

[38. The Sacraments]★

How many sacraments are there? Seven. What are they? Baptism, confirmation, eucharist, penance, extreme unction, holy orders, and matrimony. Which are repeatable and which not? Four are repeatable: eucharist, penance, extreme unction, matrimony. Three are not repeatable: baptism, confirmation, and holy orders.

[40. Verse]

Law is cast down,
Love is full small,
Charity's left town,
Truth's gone withal.

[41. Three Virtues]

There are three things that are of much price:
One is to be courteous; another, to be wise.
The third is to keep the law as the law is.
Whoever works folly, the folly shall be his.

[44. A Series of Triads]

There are three points of mischief
That cause confusion to many a man,
Which cause the soul great grief.
I shall tell you of them as I can.
Poor men proud, who have little,
That would adorn themselves as rich men go,
If they commit folly and are caught,
They may blame themselves for their own woe.

A rich man thief is another,
Who will not slake his avarice.
If he wrongly cheats his brother,
He shall forsake heaven's bliss.
Before God, it is deemed theft,
All that he wrongly wins so.
But unless he makes amends,
He may blame himself for his own woe.

Old man lecher is the third,
For his complexion waxes cold.
It brings his soul pain in mind,
And offends God many a time.
The three things that I have told
Are pleasing to the Fiend, our foe.
Whoever is bold to use them,
He may blame himself for his own woe.

God may find many defects
In us who should be his servants,
He showed us love; we are unkind.
Surely, we are the more to blame.
Some look hard and cannot see:
Such is the case with many a cleric.
They who do not fear God,
May blame themselves for their own woe.

In three things, I dare well say,
God should be worshiped over all things:

With righteousness and mercy: here are two,
The third is cleanness of living.
To men who have holy church in their care,
This is their charge, and to lords also.
And when they do contrary to God's bidding,
They may blame themselves for their own woe.

Wrong is set where right should be,
Mercy from mankind is put away,
Lechery has made cleanness flee,
Love dares not dwell either night or day.
Thus the devil, I dare well say,
Would make our friend our worst foe.
Man, amend you while you may,
Or blame yourself for your own woe.

It is no wonder that you have woe,
When your own will you would sow;
God's bidding you will not do,
You are false and he is true.
Since he sends you all things new,
But you serve the Fiend and from God go,
Unless you amend, you shall have sorrow,
You shall blame yourself for your own woe.

Among three degrees the Word is kept:
With priesthood, knighthood, and laborer.
There are but few that have not done wrong.
Therefore they shall dearly pay.
By good example the priests should teach
The unlearned what they should do.
And because they do not follow that word and work with fear,
They shall blame themselves for their own woe.

Lords also, both knights and others,
Many of them have consciences light.
They should help their poor sister and brother,
To strengthen them in their rights.
Pride and avarice have caused them to lose their might,
Grace is kept from them because of lechery.

Unless they behold their own sight,
They may blame themselves for their own woe.

The laborer should work for God and man,
Rightfully in word and deed,
According to the estate he holds,
And reasonably take his reward.
Some lead their lives wrongfully,
Among rich and poor it is found so.
The end of life is to be feared:
They shall blame themselves for their own woe.

Man, take heed of what you are:
Just worms' meat, you well know this.
When the earth has claimed its part,
Heaven or hell will have theirs.
If you do well, you go to bliss,
If you do evil, to the foe.
Love the Lord and think on this,
Or blame yourself for your own woe.

Glorious God, for your mercy,
Slake your heavenly wrath
Against us who live here falsely.
Unto your mercy ever take us.

Now, Jesus Christ, our Savior,
From our foe, us defend;
In all our needs, be our succor,
Before we shall hence wend.
And send us grace so to amend,
So that we may come to your bliss,
Here to have so good an end,
That we are not the cause of our own woe. Amen.

[49. The Life of St. Anne and the Virgin Mary]

The parish guild at Acle was dedicated to St. Anne. This 115-stanza poem, recounting the husbands of St. Anne and the early life of her daughter, the Virgin Mary, was probably read at guild meetings, perhaps on her feast day, July 26. The first fifty-three stanzas of the poem, omitted here, relate Anne's complicated family tree: she had two prior husbands before she married Mary's father, Joachim. The couple was childless for twenty years until God intervened and Anne conceived Mary:

After that, when the time came, Anne bore her child,
Who was called Mary, as I said before,
A cheery child and fair, with folly never defiled,
From the time that she was of her mother born.

After this child was three years of age,
It was weaned, as I think, from suckling.
And after common custom and old usage,
They went with this child and made her offering

To the great Temple of Jerusalem,
That comely is set up high, as I think.
And, so men say who have seen it,
There are steps up to it no less than fifteen.

And these are made, so men say, all of marble stone,
Over which pilgrims and other men pass.
And there this child Mary, quite lightly alone,
Went up these steps, as young as she was.

And all folk were amazed who saw that sight,
That such a young child might walk at such a pace.
And every man blessed her, her beauty was so bright,
Fair of feature and face, and full of God's grace.

Joachim and Anne left her still there
In the aforesaid temple, since they had made their vow
That she would serve God when the time came.
And so she did devoutly; I shall tell you how.

She and other children who were maiden-children,
Were taken to the temple at a certain age,
In that place to abide and there the law learn,
And thus be kept in cleanliness from terrible sights.

And this was the right rule that Our Lady kept.
For, as a wise woman, her will was to work.

When it was time, she waked; when it was time, she slept.
But every day in the morning, she went to the church.

And there she made her prayers until late in the morning,
And afterwards she went to do weaving work,
And at afternoon, she went again, as the book says,
To her prayers and her beads, until it was dark.

And every day an angel appeared to her,
Comforted her, and brought her angels' food.
And with that she was fed – she would take no other.
For she would eat no worldly food, no matter how good.

And though every day she had food and drink
From the bishops of the law, as the law required,
(And her companions also, so that they should not toil
Except to God's service, and to that end they were bold),

Yet all the food that she took from the bishops,
She distributed it quite secretly among poor men;
She gave them her drinks to put in their cups,
To drink when they would, and especially to women.

And many diverse times, as the book tells,
Many men and women saw without doubt
What comfort she had of holy angels.
And when they spoke to her, quite low did they bow.

And whatever man had a sickness,
If she would touch him, he would be healed anon.
And this was through the might of her holiness.
Now blessed be this lady there she sits enthroned.

And notwithstanding that she was the fairest woman
Of all that ever were born, still, according to scholars,
If a man had looked on her who was tempted
To the sin of lechery, at once it went away.

It was a great marvel that Mary could do thus,
For she was full of grace, without any fear.
Now Mary and Saint Anne, we pray you, pray for us,

That God may give us grace to succeed well. Amen.

But at the time that Our Lady and other maidens
Had come to their full age of fourteen years,
As the law required, the bishops bade them go
To be married to men and dwell no longer there.

And all these maidens went, as the bishops bade them,
Home to their friends, save Mary alone.
And she said for sure that she had a great cause,
And therefore she would not go from the temple.

They asked her the cause and the reason why
She would not do as the other maidens did.
And she answered again and said surely,
"For two causes and reasons, that might not be seen.

"For my father and my mother made this vow,
That I should serve God for the course of my life,
And I have made a vow to keep myself chaste, if I may.
Sirs, answer to reason, and let us not have strife."

The bishops were astonished and stood stone-still.
They could not answer her with any reason,
For both the old law and the new in this matter bade
That a good vow be kept with good devotion.

Thus, because of the vow that Our Lady made,
And because of the custom that needs must be kept,
The bishops of the law were not glad,
And therefore, they took counsel together

With all the wise men who were in that land
To know what was best in this aforesaid case;
And all said together that it was good to find
If good God would help them through his great grace.

Then these bishops and these men by common assent,
Every man prayed to God in his best manner
That some true sign among them might be sent
Before they should rise up from their prayer.

And so they stayed at their prayers for as long as it takes to walk
    a mile,
And at once they heard a voice among them all,
That bade them make their prayers, for within a little while
They should see without fail what should befall.

And then said the angel, so that everyone could hear,
"Almighty God bids you and charges you therewith,
That all men, old and young, in this place appear
Who are not wedded from the house of David.

"And that every man shall bear in his hand a long dry branch,
In his hand openly, that all men may see it.
For that man shall be wedded to maid Mary
Whose branch will flourish with leaves that are green.

"And on the same rod the Holy Ghost shall light
In the likeness of a dove, that all men may see.
And so shall you know, by that comely sight,
To whom maid Mary wedded shall be."

And then it was commanded by common cry
That those who were not wedded, whether old or young,
From the highest to the least, excepting children only,
Who were dwelling in the court with David the king,

That every man should have a long rod in his hand,
And in the great temple stand all together.
And this indeed was done, as I understand.
But Joseph brought no rod when he came there.

For Joseph was a feeble man, and of great age;
For him to be wedded, he had no great desire.
And therefore, that he should make no marriage,
He left at home the rod that he should bear.

So when these men were gathered and together stood,
And every man save one held up his rod,
There was no sign showed, bad or good,
And the people knelt down and prayed to good God,

That he would show and tell his mercy
Why and wherefore they could no sign see.
And they were answered again, fair and honestly,
And these were the words in truth, as I understand:

"Every man has brought a rod, save only that man
Who shall be wedded to maid Mary.
And therefore, look about, as well as you can,
If there be any such man in this company."

Then they saw and found no one but one
Who left his rod at home: Joseph was his name.
And then the bishop bade him that he should go,
And bring a rod with him, or else he would be blamed.

Joseph went forth, as he was ordered,
And brought with him a long branch that was barren and bare,
And came again at once into that same place,
And stood with his fellows, and took much care.

And then the bishops bade them all that they should each one
Hold up their rods, so that they could be seen.
And so they did indeed, and after that anon,
The branch that Joseph bore suddenly waxed all green,

And flourished full fair with leaves and with flowers,
And the Holy Ghost in the likeness of a dove,
Came down from heaven with full great honor.
And that all men might see it, he sat all above.

Then said all the people, both learned and simple,
After they had seen that glorious sight,
"Now it is well known and surely shown
That Joseph shall wed Mary of beauty so bright."

But many folk marveled over that marriage,
And about why God would ordain such a wedding
Of so young a maiden and a man of great age,
And what was the cause, was their talk.

And there are some who yet will ask the same question:
Why would God himself be born in wedlock
Rather than outside it? This is their question,
And about this matter many men muse.

But the scholars answer, as I understand,
And tell the cause why Christ would be bred
and born of a maiden that had a husband,
And not of a maiden who was never wed:

For God himself willed that she should him bear
In the law of wedlock, that he himself ordained,
And so that no man should desire her or dare,
Under the same law, he made his mother stand.

For if she had been married to no man
And been with child in the manner that she was,
She would have been slandered by many, certainly,
And had sorrow and shame for no fault.

And therefore, Christ had rather that some folk were in doubt
In what way and how he might be born,
Than that she should be put to slander by all folk about,
And her name and her fame for that reason lost.

And for another reason she had a husband
Joseph, who was noble, so that he could take care,
And go with her and be with her on water and on land,
And be a true witness to her maidenhood.

And Our Lady bore Christ, for another reason,
A maiden, a married maiden, and a wife,
Since God will work wonders at his own will,
So that the devil shall not know, that stirrer of strife.

For the fiend supposed, since she was wedded,
That the child had been begotten and brought forth by the two
    of them.
But he did not know about the matter of her maidenhood,
So that he was deceived, and many a Jew also.

For if the devil had known that he was God's son,
He would not have dared to tempt him, without fail.
But Christ, knowing best what should be done,
Allowed him to tempt him, and him to assail.

And also, he suffered him to tempt other men
To betray Jesus Christ through some false treason,
As Judas and others, more than nine or ten,
Who put him full piteously to his Passion,

And other masters of the law, less and more,
Pilate and Herod, with all their company,
Who battered and beat him, full sad and full sore,
And all this he suffered meekly, blessed must he be. Amen.

Now have you heard of the marriage of mild Mary,
In what way it was done, and for what reason.
Now shall you hear a short word of the story
How Christ was conceived through his own will.

Anon, after the marriage of Mary was made,
God sent to her his angel Gabriel,
To greet her, and comfort her, and gladden her,
And tidings that were true to her tell.

And thus he said to her with a mild voice:
"Hail Mary, full of grace, our Lord is with thee.
Thou shall conceive and bear God's Son of heaven,
And passing all women, blessed shall thou be."

Mary was astonished at his tale-telling,
And asked him in what way this would be so.
And he answered and said, "Through the Holy Ghost's
    working."
And many good words they had between the two.

But at last, Our Lady in this manner said
To the angel that greeted her called Gabriel:
"Thy word be wrought in me as God pleases."
And at once she conceived Christ, as our books tell.

Not in the manner as other women have done:
Such women conceive by men, as God ordained,
And many days go by, be it daughter or son,
Before it waxes and quickens, as I understand.

But in that same time and in that same hour, anon,
When Christ was conceived, this miracle befell:
Christ was a perfect child of flesh, blood, and bone,
With all his features fully, without any fail,

And was as wise and intelligent on the same day
That he was conceived of his mother dear,
As he was afterward, as scholars say,
When he had reached thirty years of age.

Now blessed be this baby that was born of a maid,
And blessed be this maiden that brought forth this birth,
And blessed be Saint Anne, her mother, as men say,
In the worship of whom we make all our mirth.

And Mary and her mother maintain this guild,
To the worship of God, and for his pleasure,
And all who maintain it, whether man or child,
God of his high grace give him good fortune.

Good end and good life might they all have,
And Christian folk, our foe and friend,
And God save us all who all things saves,
And bring us to the bliss that lasts without end. Amen.

[50. Two Miracles of the Virgin]

Sirs, a miracle or two I shall you tell,
That for Our Lady's love once befell,
Two gentlemen who were known as knights,
And their doings, and what happened to them.
One of them was no clerk, but an unlettered man,
But he was sent to school to learn, for certain;
He was put to the books to learn to spell and read
His ABCs, Our Father, Hail Mary, and his Creed.

But when Hail Mary was his lesson,
He would learn nothing else for any reason.
But Hail Mary always in his mind he kept,
And said it with his mouth, except when he slept.
And so these words "Hail Mary" he never forgot,
No matter where he went, no matter what he wrought.
So befell afterwards as God's will was,
This knight should die and from this world pass.
His body was buried in a churchyard,
Among the common people, simple and learned.
But within a few days, as all men had seen
There grew a lily on his grave, full gay and green.
And five full fair leaves had that lily,
And on every leaf was written "Hail Mary."
And many folk went to see the seemly sight
Of that lovely lily that was so fair and bright.
Some men said that it had not sprung up naturally,
But was planted there by some man's hand.
And therefore with a spade they dug into the ground,
Until the lily's root could be found.
They dug so deeply into that bed,
They finally reached the dead man's head.
And there they sought the root as best they could,
And saw that the root stood in the dead man's mouth.
And then all the people said thus certainly,
That it was a miracle of God and of Our Lady.
And the people afterwards for that reason,
Said their Hail Mary with good devotion.
And God give us grace to say our Hail Mary,
That it be pleasing to him, also to Our Lady. Amen.

The other knight was keeper of a castle,
And there he robbed many men, as our books tell.
And there he lived as a thief many days and years.
And maintained many false folk, who were his companions.
But it was his custom, in truth, to say
Once at the least five Hail Marys every day.
And whatever business might befall,
He never forgot to say them all.
And all day after that, he did no good deed.
But Our Lady at the last paid him his reward.

For, as you shall here understand,
There came a good man through the land,
St. Bernard, a man of religion,
Who went by that castle to another town.
Anon, this man was taken and foully mistreated,
And robbed and despoiled of all that he had.
And afterward they brought him to a prison,
Where other man were without good reason.
And then he began to pray to the men who took him,
"Sirs, I pray you all for Our Lady's sake,
That I may speak with the lord of this castle,
For a private counsel I shall tell him."
And so the men who seized him came to accord,
And bound him and brought him before their lord.
And before the lord they kneeled him down,
To give him worship, reverence, and renown.
And he prayed the lord to grant him a boon,
And the lord answered, saying, "What do you want done?"
"Lord, give me leave for our Lady's sake,
In worship of Our Lady, a sermon to make."
And at once the knight consented thereto,
And whatever he bade, they had to do.
Then he asked the knight at the beginning
That all his men might come hear his preaching.
And anon they were bidden and charged
That they should come there to a man.
And all his men gladly, and with good cheer,
Before this holy man soon started to appear.
Then said this holy man, "Has everyone come?"
They said, "Yes," but he said "No! One is missing."
And these men answered and said all in fear,
"All the men of the place stand before you here."
Then this holy man said to them again,
"Where is my lord's chamberlain?"
Then every man looked closely all about,
But he was not there, without any doubt.
And then, with the lord's will and assent,
Seeking the chamberlain to his chamber they went.
And when he was brought back to that place,
He had a foul semblance and a foul face,
And he was commanded by that holy man,

379

By the virtue of Christ's Passion,
To tell all the men there what he was,
And why he had come, and what he had done.
Then said this man, "No more can I say,
I must do as you bid, I cannot say nay.
I confess to all men in this castle,
That I am no man, but a fiend from hell.
And why and wherefore I've come here,
I shall tell you now all together.
I have dwelled with this knight for thirteen years,
And been his chamberlain, and made him good cheer
For his false living and his wickedness,
And for keeping false men in their falseness.
And till now I have tempted him many a day, and long,
And I have lain in wait for a long time among,
For him to fail once in a day
One Hail Mary at the least to say.
And because he said his Hail Mary every day,
I have had over him no mastery.
For if one day he had failed to pray,
Suddenly, in truth, he would been my prey,
And suddenly died and gone to hell.
Take this tale as true as any Gospel.
But Mary, mother and maid,
She is our enemy both night and day.
For all the folk that do her please,
We may in no way do them disease."
And then this knight kneeled down anon,
Cried, "God, mercy!" and made a mighty moan.
And all his fellows there in fright,
They cried to God with doleful spirit,
And made a vow to God and Our Lady
That they never after would use such folly,
And prayed this holy man of religion,
To give them penance and absolution.
And he gave them a penance especially,
That they should evermore worship Our Lady.
And this holy man conjured the fiend,
And by God's name he bade him depart:
"And off to the wilderness take you away,

And never tempt man by night or by day."
The fiend went away, as he had been bade,
And when he was gone, the men were all glad.
And on their knees they went down all,
And from this holy man "Mercy!" did they call,
And he forgave them their trespass for Christ's sake,
And they gave him back all they had taken,
And were true men afterwards, as I believe,
Through help of Our Lady, blessed must she be,
And lived a good life and made a good end.
And for their good living, to heaven did they wend.
To that place bring us Christ, God and man,
Through the prayer of Our Lady and of St. Anne. Amen.

[54. Notes on London Churches]

Here is the length of the shaft of the cross on St. Paul's steeple at London: from the ball to the eagle is 12 feet, and the length of the cross at the weathercock is 7 feet. The ball from side to side is over 3 feet: that is three yards around.

Paul's church is 142 paces in length from the west door to the door of the choir; and from the choir door to the east end is 90 paces. The sum of the whole length from one end to the other is 232 paces. Also the transept crossing from the north to the south door is 130 paces.

Westminster Hall is 112 paces long. Therein is the King's Bench, the Chancery, the Court of Common Pleas, the King's Council Chamber, and the King's Chapel.

Westminster church [Abbey] is dedicated to St. Peter. Behind the high altar lie many kings and queens. And in the middle of the chapel lies the shrine of St. Edward [the Confessor] the King. And on the south side beside the high altar is the lily fountain with 6 branches running fair, clean water both night and day.

And in the great belfry at Westminster are 6 great bells. Also in the great belfry at St. Paul's are 7 great bells. From Paul's to Westminster is a long mile or more.

[58. Notes on the Zodiac]

Winter lasts through three signs: Sagittarius, Capricorn, and
Aquarius.

Spring lasts through another three signs: Pisces, Aries, and Taurus.

Summer lasts through another three signs: Gemini, Cancer, and Leo.

Autumn lasts through the other three signs: Virgo, Libra, and Scorpio.

Winter begins on St. Clement's Day [Nov. 23] in November.

Spring begins on the feast of St. Peter's Chair [Feb. 23] in February.

Summer begins on St. Urban's day [May 25] in May, the 8th kalends of June.

Autumn begins on St. Symphorian's day [Aug. 22] in August, the 11th kalends of September.

Whoever is born under the sign of Taurus shall have much grace in all his beasts and all other things, except his wife: she shall be master.

Whoever is born in Aries shall be fearful and considered gracious.

Whoever is born in Gemini shall be poor and weak, and live in much disease.

Cancer: he shall be poor and weak, and thought gracious.

Leo: he shall be bold and a strong thief.

Virgo: he shall be wise and lettered, and he shall be blameless.

Libra: he shall be a [shrew] in boastfulness and a thief, and die in wicked deed.

Scorpio: he shall be a great goer in the world.

Sagittarius: he shall be hardy and a great lecher.

Capricorn: he shall be rich and loved.

Aquarius: he shall be reckless and able to lose his men.

Pisces: he shall be gracious in all manner of works.

[61. Biblical names]*

Twenty-four: Adam, Abel, Enoch, Samuel, David, Nathan, Noah, Abraham, Isaac, Eliseus, Elias, Ezechiel, Jacob, Joseph, Moses, Isaiah, Jeremiah, Daniel, Aaron, Joshua, Sampson, Zacharias, Joel, John the Baptist.

Twelve Apostles: Peter, Paul, Andrew, James, John, Thomas, Bartholomew, Matthew, James, Philip, Simon, Jude.

[Images of?] the martyrs, confessors, monks, virgins, widows, and both [widows and virgins?]. Cherubim and seraphim.

[*Perhaps a description of figures in a wall-painting or stained glass.*]

[62. Religious Knowledge]

The Ten Commandments

The first is: Worship God above all things.
The second is: Take not his name in idleness.
The third is: Truly hallow your holy day.
The fourth is: Worship your father and mother, both physical and spiritual.
The fifth is: Slay no man with your tongue.
The seventh is: Do no lechery out of wedlock.
The eighth is: Steal nothing.
The ninth is: Bear no false witness.
The tenth is: You shall not covet your neighbor's house, his wife, nor his servant, etc. Ten Commandments.

[*The sixth commandment is missing and those following are misnumbered. The tenth commandment here combines the ninth and tenth commandments.*]

Seven Mortal Sins

Pride, envy, wrath, covetousness, gluttony, lechery, and sloth: these are the VII Deadly Sins.

Seven Works of Mercy

You shall feed the hungry, give drink to the thirsty, visit those who are sick, harbor those that have need, clothe the naked, comfort those in prison, bury Christian bodies that are dead: these are the VII Works of Mercy.

Seven Principal Virtues

Fides, spes, caritas, prudencia, iusticia, fortitudo, temperancia. Trust, faith, hope, charity, prudence, righteousness, strength, sobriety: these are the VII Virtues.

Seven Sacraments of the Church

Baptismus, confirmatio, penitencia, eucharistia, extrema unctio, ordo, sponsalia. Christening, confirmation, shrift and penance, housling, anointing, holy order, spousing: these are the VII sacraments of holy church.

[63. The Signs of Death]

When your head quakes, Remember.
When your lips blacken, Confess.
When your nose grows thin, Be contrite.
When your limbs stiffen, Make satisfaction.
When your breast heaves, Know thyself.
When your breath grows short, Seek mercy.
When your eyes film, Free me Lord.
When death follows, Go forth to Judgment.

[64. Verse]

For love of God and dread of pain,
From deadly sin yourself restrain.
A man shall have mercy who merciful is,
And he without mercy, mercy shall miss.

[65. A Charm from the Popes]

[*English*] St. Gregory, St. Sylvester, and St. Leo, who were Roman popes, received this writing and said, "Whoever bears this writing on his person, shall have no dread of any enemy, or sudden death, or fire, or water, or poison, or prison, or thunder, or lightning, or fevers, or any other wicked evil. And he shall be loved by his sovereign. And if he is out of his way, he shall find his way again." And an angel took this writing to King Charles [Charlemagne] in battle and said, "Whoever bears this writing on his person, shall overcome his enemies without fail. Also, when a woman is giving birth, read this writing over her or put it on her and she shall soon be delivered by the grace of God without peril. And whoever bears this writing on his person shall not depart this world in misfortune, but shall have the sacraments of holy church by the grace of God. Nor shall he be robbed by thieves by day or night; nor shall he be overcome by any spirits by the grace of God and the virtue of these names."

[*Latin*] In the name of the Father, and of the Son, and of the Holy Spirit, amen. Tetragrammaton, Adonatos, Ananapta, Anazapta. Jesus of Nazareth, King of the Jews, Son of God, have mercy on me, amen. Messias, Soter, Emmanuel, Sabaoth, Adonai, have mercy. Jesus of Nazareth, etc. Lamb of God, who takes away the sins of the world, have mercy on us, amen. Christ conquers, Christ rules, Christ overcomes. Adonai, El, Agla, Jesus of Nazareth, etc. Behold the Cross of the Lord. Flee, hostile factions. Leo triumphed over the tribe of Juda, the root of David, Alleluia. Adonai, have mercy. I, the distributor of this letter, go forth, and you, through these holy names of God the Almighty Father, and through the humanity of Christ and the Virgin Mary, through the faith and passion of St. Paul the apostle, and through the names of the Three Kings: Jasper, Melchior, and Balthasar, and the virginity of John the Baptist and through the nine orders of angels, through the Passion, through the merits and prayers of all the saints and elect of God. Save the bearer of this charm from every evil present, past, and to come, and afterwards may the bearer have life and eternal glory, amen. ††††††††

[66. The Christian Life]

Fear God and all things shall fear you.
Love the Lord and nothing shall you need.
Flee sin and all things shall speed you.
Remember your death, and think on Christ's Passion,
And then you shall conquer the devil's temptation.

[67. A Popular Epitaph]

He who has thought
Full inward and oft
How bad it is to flit
From bed into [grave]-pit,
From pit into pain,
Which never shall end,
For all this world to win,
Would not do a sin.

[72. What World is This. Verse]

O Jesus, mercy! What world is this?
Friends be afraid and faint in need.
Woe is him who's done amiss,
And lies in pain, and may not succeed.
What Fortune shall have, it shall be had,
Whosoever will say nay.
Therefore, let it pass, and be not sad.
And think on Him who all amend may.

[74. Notes on Adam]

Adam lived 930 years and had 30 sons and 30 daughters.
They died and were both buried together, Adam and Eve.

[75. Rome. A fragment]

From the beginning of the world until the founding of Rome was 4,149 years. And from the founding of Rome until the Nativity of our Lord Jesus Christ, 750 years.

In the city of Rome there are this many churches: 400, in which mass is said daily. But there are 7 churches privileged above all others ... as is hereafter shown. The first is called St. Peter's church, the Apostle. There [a pilgrim] is released of the seventh part of penance enjoined, granted by Pope Alexander. The second altar is St. Andrew's. [*Marginal note:*] More to follow.

[*The author has apparently confused seven churches with seven altars in St. Peter's.*]

[77. Septuagesima]

Septuagesima Sunday: [derived] from the number 70. Septuagesima begins on that same Sunday and ends on the Sunday [correctly, Saturday] after Easter.

[78.] The 4 Knights that Watched the Sepulcher

Sir Iheraunt, Sir Cosdran, Sir Ameraunt, Sir Arfaxat

[*These names of the four knights guarding Jesus' tomb come from the Passion Play of the East Anglian "N-Town" cycle.*]

[84. The Wounds of Jesus]

A woman anchoress and recluse desiring to know the number of the wounds of our Lord Jesus Christ often prayed to God for the special grace that he would vouchsafe to show them to her. And finally our Lord Jesus Christ spoke to her and said, "Say every day for a whole year fifteen Our Fathers and fifteen Hail Marys, and at the year's end you shall have worshiped every wound and fulfilled the number of the same [i.e., 5,475]."

And our Lord Jesus Christ also said, "For every man that says these Our Fathers and these Hail Marys, and prays them for a whole year, the souls of fifteen of his family shall be delivered out of the pains of purgatory, and fifteen righteous men from his family shall be kept in good life. And he who first says the prayers written below shall have the grace of perfect knowledge of and bitter contrition for all his old sins."

And our Lord Jesus Christ also said, "He who says these prayers in the prescribed form, fifteen days before his death shall see my holy body and receive it, and thereby be delivered from everlasting hunger. I shall give him my blood to drink so that he shall never have thirst. And I shall set before him the sign of my victorious Passion as a subsidy and defense against all his enemies. And before his death, I shall come with my own dear mother and take his soul and lead it into everlasting joy. And when I have brought it there, I shall give him a sip from the chalice of my godhead.

"And if a man has lain in sin for twenty years, and he will say these prayers, I will forgive him all his sins, and keep him from all temptations, and maintain his five senses, and defend him from a sudden death, and moreover keep him from everlasting pain. And I will forgive him all the sins that he has committed from his childhood until this day, and by my grace he shall be better than he was before. And whatsoever he rightly asks of me or my mother, it shall not be denied. And I shall keep him perfectly in virtue and confirm him in good life, as though he had ever after lived and done my will. And if he were meant to die tomorrow, his life shall be lengthened. And so often as he says these prayers, he shall have forty days of pardon. And he that teaches other men these prayers, his joy shall never decrease but dwell without end. And wherever he is that says them, I am present, as St. Paul preaches, and I shall defend him from his enemies. Therefore, let every lettered man and woman read every day these prayers of my bitter Passion for his or her own medicine."

Next to this woman dwelled a holy man to whom she showed this revelation, and he showed it to an abbess. And she showed it to her sisters and bade them say these prayers. Some said them with great devotion, some said them in order not to disobey her command, and some fulfilled her command not willingly but under constraint. Afterwards, one day when the same holy man rested, he was ravished by a vision into a fair field. In it was a delectable well. And it seemed to him as if the well were full of precious stones. And at the well were the same sisters who said these prayers. Some of them washed [the stones] with great vigor, some with less, and some barely touched a little drop to them, for they washed according to the devotion with which they said the prayers. This was showed to the holy man. And he showed it to the abbess, and she told the same to her sisters, for which they were mighty glad. And those who before had said the prayers without devotion now amended themselves and said them better, with greater devotion and desire.

One night afterwards this holy man heard a great noise and a hideous cry, as if everything in the woods had been overthrown and torn up by the roots. He went out of his cell, and conjured one of the fiends that he had heard, and bade him to tell him what that noise meant. The fiend said, "In these woods dwells an old woman full of many holy words, and she says a prayer so pleasing to the God of Heaven that through it we often suffer great harm. For with that prayer she gets full many souls to God that were fast in our power before. And it pleases Almighty God so much that it is granted to him who says these prayers that if he were about to die and go the way of everlasting damnation, our Lord God would change everlasting pain into the pain of purgatory. And if he were in the state of the greatest pain of purgatory, our Lord would change it into the pain of this world and bring his soul to heaven. It is said that this woman's name is St. Bride [St. Bridget (1303-73)], the Queen [*sic*] of Sweden, who had many revelations and great grace from God.

[*This legend is frequently found in fifteenth-century Books of Hours, underscoring the popularity of the devotion to the wounds of Jesus, to which huge indulgences were attached. It often prefaced the "Fifteen Oes of St. Bridget," a popular Passion prayer.*]

[86. Epilogue to a Church Play]

Now worshipful sovereigns that sit here in sight,
Lords, and ladies, and franklins, in faith,
With all manner of obeisance we recommend ourselves right
Pleasantly to your persons, we who have just been in the play.
And for your patient silence that you have kept this day,
While we played our play without any resistance,
Dearly we thank you mightily, as we may,
And for your laudable listening in good audience,
That we have had this day.
For truly our intent was well to do,
And if any fault be found there, it is our negligence,
And short time rehearsing caused it also.
For little time to learn it we have had, surely,
And every man is not an expert in eloquence
To utter his lines gaily unto your audience.
Wherefore, we beseech you of your great gentry,
To report the best of us in our absence,
In any such place.

Sovereigns, all the same,
You that have come to see our game,
We pray you all in God's name,
To drink before you leave.
For an ale is here ordained by a pleasing assent
For all manner of people that appear here today,
To be of profit to holy church,
All that exceeds the costs of our play.

[*The actors here call for a church-ale, where profits from the sale of ale went to buy furnishings for the parish church.*]

[90. Prayer with the Rosary]

Man, in church do not idle stand,
But take your beads in your hand.
And if you have here none of thine,
I pray you, take these for the time,
And say a psalter with glad cheer
In worship of Our Lady dear.
She will give you what you're due,
And intercede with her Son for you.
And you shall have for one rosary
Pardon for twenty-four years,
Two hundred and thirty-four days,
Granted altogether by two popes,
In release of your sin,
For which your soul should flame and burn.
So therefore pray with heart and mind,
And make the Queen of Heaven your friend,
That you may so stand in her grace,
That she will be your shield when you pass.
And when you leave the church,
Leave the beads where you found them.

[*The "psalter" here is a series of 150 Hail Marys said presumably on rosary beads kept in the church for public use.*]

[91.] The [Three] Kings [or Magi in the famous pilgrim shrine] at Cologne

Jasper, King of Sabaea; Melchior, King of Araby; Balthazar, King of Tarsus.

[93. An amulet: The nails of Christ]

Pope Innocent [VIII?] has granted seven gifts to every man who carries with him the length of the three nails of our Lord Jesus Christ and worships them daily with five Our Fathers and five Hail Marys and the Creed: the first, he shall not die a sudden death; the second, he shall not be slain by a sword or knife; the third, his enemies shall not overcome him; the fourth, he shall have sufficient goods and an honest living; the fifth, poison or false witness will never harm him; the sixth, he shall not die without the sacraments of the church; the seventh, he shall be defended from all wicked spirits, fevers, pestilences, and all evil things.

[*Below this is a drawing of a nail 5¾" long.*]

[94. Major Events in World History]*

From the creation of the world to the time when the brothers Romulus and Remus built Rome and encircled it with a 42 mile-long wall that had 360 towers: 4,447 years.

From the creation of the world to the time of the Flood when Noah's ark was built (which now rests on Mount Ararat in Armenia): 2,000 years.

From the creation of the world to the time of the Trojan War when Priam ruled Troy, and during the siege of which the game of chess was invented: 4,059 years.

From the creation of the world to when the Trojan Duke Brutus came by ship to this island England, and built the city of New Troy (namely London), and called the island Britain, which had until that time been inhabited by giants: 3,099 years.

From the creation of the world to when Lud, king of the Britons, built a wall around the city of New Troy and named it London (and King Lud is buried at Ludgate): 5,129 years.

The year of the reign of Emperor Octavian during which the King of Peace, Christ, was born and gave peace to the angels and to men of goodwill: 42.

The Year of the Lord that King Cnut of Dacia conquered England and ruled it for 20 years (and who is buried at Winchester): 1020 AD.

The Year of the Lord during which Anselm Archbishop of Canterbury [1093-1109] flourished, in whose time William Rufus, the king of England, built the Great Hall at Westminster: 1080.

The Year of the Lord that a certain [boy], called St. William, was crucified [falsely blamed on Jews] at Norwich, and he is buried among the monks there: 1144.

The Year of the Lord that the Sign of the Cross appeared on the moon: 1146.

The Year of the Lord that a certain boy was crucified at Gloucester: 1146.

The Year of the Lord that St. Thomas [Becket] was martyred at Canterbury during the reign of Henry II, king of England: 1170.

Years from the creation of the world until Christ: 5,199.

The Year of the Lord that there was an earthquake during the Wednesday of Pentecost: 1381.

[96. Satiric verse]

A friar, a hayward, a fox, and a polecat sitting in a row,
A tapster sitting by them to complete the company. The best is a wretch.

[*Haywards typically supervised boon-work owed to the manor's lord and collected his grain from tenants' fields. Tapsters had a reputation for dishonesty.*]

[97. An off-color ditty]

Carmelite friars sailed in a boat near Ely.
[They were not in heaven since they fucked the wives of hell.]
They all got drenched because they had no helmsman.
[The friars with knives go about and swive men's wives.]

[*Latin and English. Bracketed stanzas are supplied from another manuscript where the vulgar words were written in a simple code.*]

[98. Verse]

Man unkind,
Keep in mind,
My Passion's pain smart.

And me you shall find,
To the righteous kind,
Lo, here is my heart.

[*The word "heart" is depicted by a small hand-drawn heart.*]

[99.]★

Go not this way unless you say Hail Mary.
Far from woe (*a ve*) you will be if you say to me Hail Mary (*Ave*).

[104.] Toothache★

St. Apollonia [d. 249] was a famous virgin whose teeth, for the love of our Lord Jesus Christ, were pulled out [during her martyrdom]. She implored God that whoever will say her name or carry it upon them would overcome vermin, gout, and toothache, and this was granted to her. In the name of the Father †, and of the Son †, and of the Holy Spirit †, amen. Medicine for toothache.

[106. Prognostications According to the Dominical Letter]

[*Dominical letters were the letters A to G assigned consecutively to the first Sunday (Dies Dominica) in each new year, so that if Sunday fell on the first day of the year, that year's Dominical letter was "A"; if it fell on the second day, its Dominical letter was "B," etc. Knowing the year's Dominical letter allowed one to calculate on what day of the week the first day of the year would fall and thus plot the days of the rest of the year.*]

A: When the Dominical letter falls on the A, then there shall be a warm winter and a stormy summer, grain in the field, but just a reasonable amount of fruit; in the same way there shall be pestilence among young people and death of beasts, especially of cattle; great conflict and fighting among robbers, and new tidings of kings, etc.

B: When the Dominical letter falls on the B, then there shall be a warm beginning of winter and drizzling and thick weather in the back winter, and a wet summer, a terribly small amount of grain in the field, great lightning storms, great plenty of oil, and much grief among the people; kings and beans shall die, great battles among people, and there shall be many widows that year, etc.

C: When the Dominical letter falls on the C, then there shall be a long winter and a stormy summer, a dry harvest, reasonable plenty of grain and fruit, but small harvests of beans; but young people shall die, death of swine, tempests for ships in the sea, and dearth of wines that year, etc.

D: When the Dominical letter falls on the D, then there shall be a warm winter, a good summer, and a good harvest, and plenty of grain and fruit, but average oil; great plenty of beans, though average; women with child shall die, great loss of hay, new tidings of kings, etc.

E: When the Dominical letter falls on the E, then there shall be a stout winter of winds, a good summer, a good harvest and plenty of grain, a great measure of fruit but it will soon rot, a dearth of meat, great plenty of beans, death of beasts, a good year after, and peace among the people, and great floods of fresh water, etc.

F: When the Dominical letter falls on the F, then there shall be a black winter, sharp and cold; a dry summer, plenty of oil, great sickness of the eyes; there will be but average death among young people, great war in diverse places, and earthquakes, etc.

G: When the Dominical letter falls on the G, then there shall be a warm winter and a various summer, great plenty of grain, great storms of house fires, great sickness from intermittent fevers, plenty of beans, great fellings of timber, death of old people, and great plenty of hay.

[107. Prognostications according to thunder]*

When thunder is first heard in January, it means strong winds, an abundance of fruits and vegetables; one should see to it that his blood is let.

When there is thunder in February, it means the death of many men, especially the wealthy.

When there is thunder in March, it means strong winds, an abundance of fruits, and strife among the people.

When there is thunder in April, it means a delightful year, fruitful death among wicked men (namely thieves) and of men generally.

When there is thunder in May, it means a scarcity of fruits and famine in many places.

When there is thunder in June, it means an abundance of fruits; it means that there will be many illnesses during the year.

When there is thunder in July, it means an abundance of fruits; it means that there will be good food during the year; this will be a good year, etc.

[113. Religious significance of numbers]*

One is Christ who reigns in heaven.

Tell me what two is: Two is the tablets of Moses. One is Christ, etc.

Tell me what three is: Three is the Patriarchs: Abraham, Isaac, and Jacob.

Tell me what four is: the four Evangelists.

Tell me what five is: the five books of Moses.

Tell me what six is: the six wine jars located at Cana in Galilee [see John 2:1-11].

Tell me what seven is: there are seven candles burning before God [see Rev. 1:12-13, 20].

Tell me what eight is: the eight beatitudes.

Tell me what nine is: the nine orders of angels.

Tell me what ten is: the Ten Commandments.

Tell me what eleven is: the eleven [faithful] Disciples.

Tell me what twelve is: the twelve Apostles.

[*A version of this list endures in the folk song "Oh, Green Grow the Rushes" or the "Dilly Song."*]

[115.] The Nine Orders [of Angels]

Seraphim, Cherubim, Thrones
Dominions, Principalities, Powers
Virtues, Archangels, Angels

[116. A description of the Our Lady's shrine at] Walsingham

[English and Latin.]

[*Latin*] In the year of our Lord 1061 this chapel of Walsingham was miraculously founded in honor of the Annunciation of the Blessed Mary.

[*English*] A knight called Sir Ralph Boutetort in full armor [pursued by his enemies] rode through this little postern gate door after his horse bolted, but he was unharmed by a miracle of Our Blessed Lady, the year of our Lord 1314. The postern gate door is not more than an ell [about 45 inches] high nor three-quarters wide.

[*Images in the shrine:*] Gabriel greeting Our Lady; in the middle of the table at the altar stands Our Lady, on each side of her stands an angel; St. Edward, St. Catherine on the right hand; St. Edmund, St. Margaret on the left hand: all pure gold.

[120. A *Cisio-Janus*]★

So called from its opening words, the Cisio-Janus *was a calendar of liturgical feasts written in highly abbreviated Latin that was meant as a mnemonic. The translation here (largely drawn, with some revisions, on the editor Cameron Louis's, pp. 510-15) is a large expansion on otherwise minimal information since the calendar typically records only the first one or two syllables of each feast. The bracketed number after each name is the date of the month on which the feast falls, not indicated in the original. Feast days usually recollect the day on which a saint died, and so was born again in Christ. To suggest the condensed character of the* Cisio-Janus *calendar, here is the complete Latin text for the month of January: "Januarii. Cisio Janus Epi Lucianus et Hil Fe Mau Mar Sulp Pris Wol Fab Ag Vin Pete Paulum Iul Agque Batil."*

January

The Circumcision [1], the Epiphany [6], St. Lucian [8], St. Hilary [13], St. Felix [14], St. Macarius [15], St. Marcellus [16], St. Sulpicius [17], St. Prisca [18], St. Wulfstan [19], St. Fabian [20], St. Agnes [21], St. Vincent [22], St. Peter [?], St. Paul's Conversion [25], St. Julian [27], St. Agnes's nativity [28], St. Batilda [30].

February

St. Brigida [1], the Blessed Virgin's Purification [2], St. Blaise [3], St. Agatha [5] St. Vedast [6], St. Scholastica [10], St. Valentine [14], St. Juliana [16], St. Peter's Chair at Antioch [22], St. Matthias [24].

March

St. David [1], St. Chad [2], St. Gregory the Great [12], St. Edward the Martyr [18], St. Cuthbert [20], St. Benedict [21], the Annunciation [25].

April

St. Richard of Chichester [3], St. Ambrose [4], St. Eustace [14], Sts. Tiburtius and Valerian [14], St. Alphege [19], St. George [23], translation of St. Wilfrid [24], St. Vitalis [28], translation of St. Edmund, king and martyr [29].

May

Sts. Philip and James [1], Invention of the Holy Cross [3], St. John before the Latin Gate [6], Sts. Gordian and Epimachus [10], Sts. Nereus and Achilleus [12], St. Dunstan [19], St. Aldhelm [25], St. Augustine of Canterbury [26], St. Germain of Paris [28], St. Petronilla [31].

June

St. Nicomedes [1], Sts. Marcellinus and Peter [2], St. Boniface of Crediton [5], Sts. Medard and Gildard [8], translation of St. Edmund the Archbishop [9], St. Barnabus [11], Sts. Basilides, Curinus, Nabor, and Felix [12], St. Basil [14], Sts. Vitus and Modestus [15], translation of St. Richard of Chichester [16], Sts. Mark and Marcellian [18], Sts. Gervase and Protase [19], St. Edward the Martyr's second translation [20], St. Alban [22], St. Etheldreda [23], nativity of St. John the Baptist [24, Midsummer Day], St. Zoilus [27], St. Leo II [28], Sts. Peter and Paul [29].

July

Sts. Processus and Martinianus [2], translation of the apostle St. Thomas [3], the Seven Brothers [martyred sons of St. Felicity: Alexander, Felix, Januarius, Martial, Philip, Silvanus, Vitalis; 10], translation of St. Benedict [11], translation of St. Swithin [15], St. Kenelm [17], St. Arnulf [18], St. Margaret [20], St. Praxedes [21], St. Mary Magdalene [22], St. Apollinaris [23], St. Christina [24], St. James the Greater [25], St. Anne [26], the Seven Sleepers of Ephesus [Constantine, Dionysius, John, Malchus, Martinaus, Maximian, and Serapion; 27], St. Samson [28], St. Felix [29], Sts. Abdon and Sennen [30], St. Germain of Auxerre [31].

August

St. Peter in Chains [1], St. Stephen the Pope [2], Invention of St. Stephen the proto-martyr [3], St. Oswald [5], St. Sixtus [6], St. Donatus [7], St. Cyriacus and his Companions [8], St. Romanus [9], St. Lawrence [10], St. Tiburtius [11], St. Hippolytus [13], St. Eusebius of Rome [14], the Assumption [15], St. Oswyn [20], Sts. Timothy and Symphorian [22], St. Bartholomew [24], St. Rufus [27], St. Augustine of Hippo [28], the Decollation of St. John the Baptist [29], Sts. Felix and Adauctus [30], St. Cuthberga [31].

September

St. Giles [1], translation of St. Cuthbert [4], St. Bertin [5], Nativity of the Blessed Virgin [8], Sts. Gorgonius and Dorotheus [8], Sts. Protus and Hyacinth [11], Exaltation of the Holy Cross [14], St. Mirin [15], St. Edith of Wilton [16], St. Lambert of Maastricht [17], St. Matthew [21], St. Maurice and his Companions [22], St. Thecla of Iconium [23], St. Firmin [25], Sts. Cyprian and Justina [26], Sts. Cosmas and Damian [27], St. Michael the Archangel [29, Michaelmas], St. Jerome [30].

October

St. Remi [1], St. Thomas Cantelupe of Hereford [2], St. Francis of Assisi [4], St. Osyth [7], St. Margaret Pelagius [8], Sts. Denis, Rusticus, and Eleutherius [9], St. Gereon [10], St. Nigas [11], St. Edward the Confessor [13], St. Calixtus [14], St. Wulfran [15], St. Michael on the Mount [16], St. Luke [18], Eleven Thousand Virgins [21], St. Romanus [23], Sts. Crispin and Crispian [25], Sts. Simon and Jude [28], St. Quentin [31].

November

All Saints [1], Sts. Zachary and Elizabeth [5], St. Leonard [6], The Four Crowned Martyrs [Severus, Severianus, Carpophorus, Victorinus; 8], St. Theodore [9], St. Martin of Tours [11], St. Brice [13], St. Machute [15], St. Edmund of Canterbury, archbishop [16], St. Hugh of Lincoln [17], St. Edmund, king and martyr [20], St. Cecilia [22], St. Clement [23], St. Chrysogonus [24], St. Catherine of Alexandria [25], St. Linus [26], St. Saturninus [29], St. Andrew [30].

December

St. Sabas [1], St. Nicholas [6], the Immaculate Conception [8], St. Lucy [13], *O sapientia* [the Advent antiphon, 16], St. Thomas the Doubter [21], the Nativity of the Lord [25], St. Stephen [26], St. John the Evangelist [27], The Holy Innocents [28], St. Thomas of Canterbury [29], St. Silvester [31].

What are Robert Reynes' religious preoccupations? What are the focal points of his daily exercise of his faith? How deeply and sincerely does he understand and embrace Christianity? Does his commonplace book offer good advice for living virtuously? If this were the only document available to you for evaluating medieval popular religion, what conclusions would you draw?

63. POPULAR PROVERBS (c. 1480)

People who cannot read typically preserve their common wisdom in short proverbs that stick in the memory. While a written collection of proverbs cannot tell us how widely any particular saying circulated in a society, it can imply some of the ways the knowledge of Christianity permeated popular culture. The Proverbia Communia *was a Dutch collection of 803 proverbs assembled in manuscript perhaps a decade before 1480 when it was first printed. The work proved popular: it was printed at least twelve times by 1497, so it at least struck a chord with its reading audience. Though they were collected in the late fifteenth century, most of the proverbs trace back to Greek, Roman, and Judeo-Christian antiquity; about one eighth of them come from the Bible (and at least ten come from the Talmud). The origin of roughly a third of them is unknown, and about ten per cent come from popular sayings in medieval French, German, Dutch, and English. Though almost all the proverbs have some bearing on personal or community morality and so could be broadly construed as relevant to religion, the sample here – just shy of one-tenth of the whole – consists only of proverbs that explicitly mention Christianity or humanity's relation with the divine, or that derive from more familiar biblical proverbs. They suggest how popular culture both used and adapted ideas absorbed from literate Christian culture.*

Source: trans. Richard Jente, *Proverbia Communia, A Fifteenth-Century Collection of Dutch Proverbs*, Indiana University Publications Folklore Series No. 4 (Bloomington: Indiana University, 1947), pp. 110-304, passim.

17. If luck wills it, a man is happy.
19. If we leave it to God, it is already half lost.
35. When it vexes the whole world, it vexes God.
40. When the shepherd goes astray, the flock goes astray. [See Ezek.

34:5]

44. They cry Easter, till Easter finally comes.

51. All rivers run into the sea. [Eccl. 1:7]

93. The tree is known by its fruit. [Matt. 12:33]

94. Be the church ever so large, the priest sings what he knows.

98. When I die, the world dies with me.

101. Where the abbot carries dice, the monks will gamble.

107. The poor man is rejected everywhere. [See Prov. 19:7]

111. Both are good, God and his mother.

153. Copper money, copper soul-mass [said for a departed soul].

161. Where the devil cannot go, he sends his messenger.

167. What a priest doesn't want, the sexton is glad to take.

169. What is withheld from God, the devil often takes.

189. Many prayers go in a bag [i.e., More prayers are spoken than heard].

191. The bride wants to become known and sprinkled [with holy water] in the church.

209. The evil man shuns the light as the devil the cross.

212. He who takes the devil into his boat must carry him over the sound.

236. He who dies of threats should be tolled to his grave with farts.

252. He who is afraid, let him run to the church.

254. He that touches pitch shall be defiled. [Ecclus. 13:1]

266. Who loves God loves his servant.

267. He who lives longer than Christ [33 years] and is not blessed with a cow then, will never be rich.

284. He who made the moon knows how old it is.

288. The greatest clerics are not the wisest men.

320. One convent, one menu.

333. Honor is better than riches. [See Prov. 22:1]

350. Everyone prays that God may help him.

352. God is above all.

353. God gave, God has taken away. [See Job 1:21]

354. "God willing" is the mother of all prayers.

355. With God all things are possible. [Matt. 19:26]

356. God never struck a stroke but that he salved it again. [see Job 5:18]

357. God visits his own [friends].

358. God punishes, even though it take long.

392. Herod and Pilate are reconciled. [See Luke 23:12]

393. Why did Pilate get into the Creed?

397. Dog's prayers never reach heaven.

403. He must act terrible who would frighten the devil.

404. He is not free who is the devil's own.

405. He is long dead who died a year ago.

419. He is like the priest; he blesses himself first.

481. All the farts that the Beguines make cannot be weighed in scales.

491. On the Last Day it will be seen who has the broadest buttocks.

491a. On the Last Day it will be seen who has been a good pilgrim.

493. A man must sometimes set a candle before the devil [i.e., venerate him].

494. Thou shalt not believe all spirits.

495. Do not sing two masses to a deaf man.

537. No confession should be betrayed.

539. God provides according to the host.

551. After the carnival comes the fast.

552. After Lent comes Easter.

558. As you sow the field so it shall bear fruit. [See Gal. 6:8]

559. Now the devil will shame the devil.

582. Old sin makes new shame.

584. Unhappy [or unfortunate] people make rich saints.

593. Priests' wives and soup are ordinary fare.

596. Don't come too near God for he is indulgent.

608. He touches the hills and they smoke. [Ps. 103 (104):32]

625. All are not priests who wear the tonsure.

626. There is no chapel so small but has kermis [the fair held on a church's dedication day] once a year.

629. No monk goes [travels] alone. [An exhortation to have a second drink.]

635. No prophet is accepted in his own country. [Luke 4:24]

684. There is a time to speak and a time to be silent. [Eccles. 3:7]

690. God helps them that help themselves.

701. All goes ill that God hates.

702. What you spin on Sunday will come to grief.

727. It is bad to jest with God, for he may be indulgent.

737. If the sky falls, no pots will remain whole.

738. If the sky falls, no chair will be left standing.

739. If the sky falls, we shall all die.

740. If the sky falls, all is lost.

751. Where the Pope is there is Rome.

756. A benefit lives beyond death.

762. Woe to the kingdom whose king is a child. [Eccles. 10:16]

778. When Adam delved and Eve span, Who was then the gentleman?

792. All are not saints that go to church.

798. The nearer the Pope, the worse the Christian.

64. INDULGENCES (1216-1520)

An indulgence was a remission of the temporal punishment, or penance, imposed on a confessed sinner that had to be performed either in this world or in purgatory; it did not cancel either the sinner's duty to confess the sin or the guilt, or contrition, caused by it. The first significant and widely regarded indulgence was the plenary indulgence that Urban II offered at the Council of Clermont in 1095 to all Christians who joined the First Crusade to recapture the Holy Land. But plenary indulgences, which deleted all the punishment earned for sins, were rare. The more common partial indulgence erased some shorter term of punishment, typically the "quarantine" of 40 days. Certificates of indulgence almost always demanded that those wishing to receive it first had to be contrite and confessed before the indulgence took effect. But people frequently misunderstood or ignored this proviso, and the popular conception tended to be that indulgences could substitute for confession, a misconception churchmen worked to undo fairly fruitlessly. Indulgences could be granted for almost any pious act, large or small: for building or repairing churches, monasteries, hospitals, public roads or bridges, for giving alms to the poor, for visiting holy sites like Jerusalem, Rome, saints' shrines or important churches, for praying certain cycles of prayers or saying special devotions, and for crusading against enemies of the church. As grants of indulgences increased beginning in the thirteenth century, an inflationary spiral set in; people collected more and more indulgences for ever-growing terms of remission so that by the fifteenth century indulgences were typically measured in thousands of years instead of days.

1. The jubilee indulgence of 1300

The indulgence that Boniface VIII issued for the jubilee year of 1300 was the first widely recognized plenary indulgence granted for purposes other than a crusade. Though Boniface could find no written proof in the papal archives either of past jubilee years or of plenary indulgences issued during them, one chronicler reports the story of a 107-year-old man whose father had impressed upon him the rewards granted in the last jubilee a century earlier. Carried to the pope by two of his sons, this centenarian keeper of the oral tradition helped convince him to issue the indulgence. Or so the story says. Boniface's jubilee was, by all contemporary accounts, an unqualified success. Several hundred thousand pilgrims poured into Rome during the year. In fact, the indulgence caused such excitement that in 1342 a Roman delegation traveled to Avignon imploring Clement VI to cut the interval between jubilees in half since human life was brief.

Convinced by their pleas — or perhaps by a sonnet Petrarch addressed to him on the same subject — Clement set the next jubilee for 1350. His bull of 1343, Unigenitus dei filius, *officially declared the theory of Christ's "treasury of merits" as the foundation for indulgences. It argued that one drop of the sacred blood was enough to redeem the world; thus, the great effusion Jesus shed on the cross plus the merits of Mary and the saints served as a reservoir on which the church could draw to wash away the penance due for confessed sins.*

Source: trans. J. Shinners from Pope John XXII's *Extravagantes* 5.9.1. in E. Friedberg (ed.), *Corpus Juris Canonici* (Leipzig: Tauchnitz, 1881), cc. 1303-04. Latin.

The faithful account of our ancestors holds that great remissions of sins and indulgences are granted to those going to the honorable basilica of [Peter], the Prince of the Apostles in the city [of Rome]. We, therefore, who by virtue of the duty of our office most willingly strive for and attend to the salvation of everyone, by apostolic authority confirm, approve, and also renew and, by this present document, fortify with our patronage these kinds of remissions and indulgences, holding them each and every one valid and pleasing. But, for the most blessed apostles Peter and Paul to be more fully honored as the faithful visit their basilicas in the city more devoutly, and for the faithful to consider themselves even more sated with the largess of spiritual favors through frequent visits of this kind, we — through the mercy of Almighty God, the merits of his same apostles, the authority granted by the counsel of our brothers, and the plenitude of apostolic power — in the current year 1300 (dating from last Christmas) and each centennial to follow do grant and will grant not just full and generous but the fullest possible pardon of all their sins to all who, truly contrite and confessed, reverently visit and will visit these basilicas in this present year and in each centennial to follow. We order that whoever wishes to share in this indulgence granted by us must go to these basilicas at least once a day for at least thirty days successively or at intervals if they are Romans; if they are pilgrims or outsiders, for fifteen days in a similar way. A more effective indulgence will result and someone will be more rewarded who will visit these basilicas more frequently and devoutly. May no act of men in general infringe on this record of our confirmation, approval, renewal, concession, and decree, etc. Given at Rome at Saint Peter's, February 22 in the sixth year of our pontificate [1300].

2. A model indulgence (1300)

Bishops as well as popes could grant indulgences, though the Fourth Lateran Council limited their length to between 40 days to a year (a limit often later ignored). This exemplar from a legal formulary of 1300 is unusual in that it grants an indulgence for prayers on behalf of the members of an apparently ordinary private family as opposed to members of a royal or noble house. The see of Nicastro was in Calabria.

Source: trans. J. Shinners from J.E. Thorold Rogers, "Roll of the Thirteenth Century Containing Various Legal Forms," *Archaeological Journal* 22 (1865): 62. Latin.

To all the faithful of Christ who shall examine these present letters, we, A., B., and C., by divine mercy bishops of Nicastro, etc., give greetings in the everlasting Lord. Because it is pious to pray on behalf of the living and the dead that they may be absolved from the bonds of their sins, we think that grateful and pious service is paid to God as often as we stir the minds of the faithful to works of piety and charity. For this reason, to all those who are truly contrite and confessed who shall say an Our Father and a Hail Mary with devout mind for the souls of R., H., and H., the children of [J. and his wife, A.], whose bodies rest in the cemetery of Blessed Mary of T. in the diocese of Chichester, and Nicholas whose body is buried in the church of T., and however many times or whenever they shall pray for the state of the health of J. and his wife A., and for H., the mother of J. while they are alive and for their souls after they have died, from the mercy of Almighty God and by the authority conceded to his apostles Peter and Paul, each of us mercifully grants in the Lord to each of them indulgences of forty days from the penance enjoined on them, provided it is the local bishop's wish to agree and consent to this. In witness of this matter we have ordered our seals to be attached to this document. Given at Rome in the year of the Lord 1300, thirteenth indiction, in the sixth year of the pontificate of the Lord Pope Boniface VIII.

Sum of the days [of indulgences]: *blank*

The lord G[ilbert of St. Leofard], bishop of Chichester has approved these indulgences and has ratified them as authentic fortified by his seal.

3. The Portiuncula indulgence (1216?)

The plenary indulgence attached to the tiny church of Santa Maria Portiuncula, which St. Francis of Assisi had rebuilt with his own hands (see Doc. 9), made it one of the most popular pilgrim centers of the later Middle Ages. But the indulgence caused controversy almost from the moment it appeared, for there is no official document demonstrating that it was ever formally issued. Bishop Teobald of Assisi wrote the following account in 1310, almost a century after the event it purports to record, to certify the legitimacy of the indulgence. According to him, in 1216 Pope Honorius III granted Francis a plenary indulgence to anyone visiting the church at Portiuncula; but it was valid only once a year from early evening August 1 to sunset (later midnight) August 2. Teobald reports that Honorius's cardinals feared that the Portiuncula indulgence, granted for a comparatively minor pilgrimage, would undermine the only other plenary indulgence then available: the one granted for crusaders fighting in the Holy Land.

Source: trans. E Guerney Salter in Raphael M. Huber, *The Portiuncula Indulgence, Franciscan Studies* XIX (New York: Joseph W. Wagner, 1938), pp. 6-7; revised and corrected. Latin.

When the blessed Francis was staying at Santa Maria Portiuncula, it was revealed to him one night by the Lord that he should go to Pope Honorius, who then was at Perugia, to seek an indulgence for the church of Santa Maria Portiuncula, then being repaired by him. Rising at early morning, he called for Brother Masseo of Marignano as his companion, and going with him to the Lord Pope Honorius, said to him, "Holy Father, lately I repaired a church to the honor of the glorious Virgin. I beseech Your Holiness to give it an indulgence to be granted without any obligations." He answered, "This may not be conveniently done, for whoever seeks an indulgence should rightly offer a helping hand to deserve it. But show me for how many years you desire it, and how large an indulgence I should grant it." St. Francis said, "Holy Father, may it please your Holiness to give me not years, but souls." The lord pope said, "What do you mean by souls?" Blessed Francis said, "Holy Father, if it please your Holiness, I wish that all those who come to that church contrite and confessed, and duly absolved by a priest, shall be absolved from punishment and blame in heaven and on earth, from the day of their baptism to the day and hour of their entrance into the aforesaid church." The lord pope answered, "This is a considerable thing you seek, Francis, for it is not the Roman Curia's custom to grant such an indulgence." The Blessed Francis said, "My lord, what I seek, I seek not on my own behalf, but on behalf of him who sent me, the Lord Jesus Christ." The lord pope instantly conferred the same, saying three times, "It is my pleasure that you should have it." Then the lords cardinal that were present said, "Consider, lord, that if you grant this man such an indulgence, you are ruining the one granted to them who go across the seas [on crusade] and reducing the indulgence of the apostles Peter and Paul to nothing so that it will be reckoned worthless." The lord pope answered, "We have given and granted it to him, and we cannot and should not undo what we have done. But let us restrict it so that it shall last for one natural day." Then calling Brother Francis, he said to him, "Look, from now on we grant that any who shall come and enter the said church truly contrite and confessed, shall be absolved from punishment and blame. And we wish that this shall be valid each year forever, but for one day only; namely, from the first vespers through the night to vespers the following day." The Blessed Francis, bowing his head, started to leave the palace. The lord pope, seeing him go out, called him, saying, "O simpleton, where are you going? What proof do you carry away with you concerning this indulgence?" The Blessed Francis answered, "Your word alone suffices. If it is God's work, it is for him to manifest his own work. Concerning this I desire no other document, but let the Blessed Virgin Mary alone be my charter, Christ my notary, and the angels my witnesses."

4. Indulgences for the Virgin's fraternity at Perugia (1337)

Religious fraternities were particularly eager to collect grants of indulgence, which were not only a boon to their members but also attracted new members and money. The more popular fraternities had long rosters of non-participating, honorary members recruited from far away by virtue of indulgences granted to the association. For the fraternity of Perugia's statutes, see Doc. 55.

Source: trans. J. Shinners from G.G. Meersseman, *Ordo Fraternitatis: Confraternite e Pietà dei Laici nel Medioevo* (Rome: Herder, 1977), v. II, pp. 1070-71. Latin.

These are the indulgences conceded to the fraternity of the Blessed Virgin Mary by the bishops named below, as is explained in their privileges and seals. The tenor of these is here described below.

1. Lord Oddo, canon of Perugia and prior of the church of St. Savinus, vicar spiritual of the chapter and church of Perugia *sede vacante*, has relaxed by indulgence forty days [of penance] to any of the same fraternity who, truly contrite and confessed, enter the fraternity of the Blessed Mary Glorious Virgin and gather together in the church or the house of the Friars Preachers.

   2. Each time they do so, Lord Albicus de Brancalo, vicar general of the venerable father, the lord Friar Francis, by the grace of God bishop of Perugia, has mercifully relaxed forty days from the penance enjoined on them

to each and every member of the fraternity of the Blessed Virgin Mary who gathers at the house of the Friars Preachers of Perugia, to all who, truly contrite and confessed, assemble in the said house or the church of St. Dominic, or who offer helping hands to the same fraternity, and also to all those who offer charity to the said fraternity from the goods given them by God.

3. The lord Friar [Bel]tramus, by the grace of God bishop of Orvieto has mercifully relaxed forty days to each and every member of the fraternity of the Blessed Virgin Mary who, truly contrite and confessed, gathers at the church of St. Dominic the Confessor, and to each and every member of the aforesaid fraternity and to others entering that church coming to mass and gathering to hear the divine office celebrated there, and [who] offer alms whenever they visit poor people who are sick, and when they meet any member of the fraternity along the way, say "Blessed be our Lord Jesus Christ and his Mother," and whenever they devoutly pray for the happy state of all Christian people, the pope, the city of Perugia, and all those benefactors who offer helping hands to the said fraternity.

4. The lord Friar Angelus, by the grace of God bishop of Grosseto has likewise mercifully relaxed forty days to each and every member of the fraternity of the Blessed Virgin Mary in the same manner as above.

5. The lord Alexander, by the grace of God bishop of Nocera, has mercifully relaxed forty days to each and every member of the fraternity of the Blessed Virgin Mary in the same manner as above, that is to all those truly contrite and confessed.

6. The lord Ugolino, by the grace of God bishop of Perugia, has mercifully relaxed forty days to each and every member of the said fraternity in the same manner of the above, to all those truly contrite and confessed.

5. A Spanish indulgence for the dead (1488)

In 1476 Pope Sixtus IV took the last step in the evolution of indulgences when he officially sanctioned the application of indulgences to the souls in purgatory, a practice which had stirred controversy since first introduced in the thirteenth century. This printed indulgence for the dead, dated just twelve years after Sixtus's bull, is from Spain, where such indulgences were particularly popular. In fact, they were often buried with the dead as a sort of first-class ticket through purgatory.

Source: trans. J. Shinners from Kenneth W. Cameron, *The Pardoner and His Pardons, Indulgences Circulating in England on the Eve of the Reformation* (Hartford: Transcendental Books, 1965), p. 19. Latin.

In the name of God, Amen. May all Christ's faithful know how our most

holy lord of happy memory Pope Innocent VIII [1484-92] granted by special privilege and grace that the salvation of the souls of those who have
departed this life in charity may be procured if, stirred by charity, their
parents, friends, or others of Christ's faithful of any nation or province no
matter where they might be shall give or send the twentieth part of a ducat
for the soul of each of these dead in order to rebuild the great hospital at St.
James Compostela and also for hiring two chaplains for the hospital, one for
the men, the other for the women. Both those making a donation and the
aforesaid dead are made to share in all the suffrages, intercessions, alms, fasts,
prayers, disciplines, and other pious works and spiritual benefits currently
pertaining to the said hospital and chapel according to the tenor of other
letters from our most holy lord Pope Alexander VI [1492-1503]. And because
you, [*blank space for name of donor*] have paid the aforementioned sum for the
soul of [*blank space for name of deceased*], the Treasurer or his deputy grant you
[this] testimonial letter. Sealed by the Treasurer's seal and signed by Alfunso
de Lola, apostolic notary. A.D. 1488.

*Printed on the certificate is a woodcut seal depicting a pilgrim with his pilgrim's staff,
scrip, and pilgrim badge – St. James's cockle shell – pinned on his hat. The legend surrounding the seal reads: "Thy rod and thy staff have comforted me [Ps. 22 (23):4]."*

6. A spurious printed indulgence (c. 1520)

*The invention of printing in Europe in the mid-fifteenth century made the sale and
circulation of indulgences even more widespread. In fact, it is noteworthy that the first
dated piece of western printing in moveable type is an indulgence from 1454 for a crusade against the Turks. The fake indulgence below may have come from the workshop
of the famous English printer Wynken de Worde; he at least made the small woodcut
of the crucifixion that accompanies the text. Printed in red ink to increase its allure, the
certificate offers enticing material and spiritual blessings in exchange for donations for a
hospital that apparently never existed. Thus the sole beneficiary of the purchaser's charity was whoever sold the indulgence. It was the sort of pious scam Chaucer lampooned
in the figure of his Pardoner. The preface to the list of names is in English; the list
itself – an impressive, if garbled, grab bag of Latin, Greek, and Hebrew – is typical
of medieval prayer charms. Compare, for instance, Doc. 53.3. For Sts. Quiricus and
Julitta mentioned below, see Doc. 53.5.*

Source: trans. J. Shinners from Kenneth W. Cameron, *The Pardoner and His Pardons*, pp. 24, 44.
Middle English and Latin.

A devout invocation of all the blessed names of our Lord Jesus Christ that lately through a revelation was found upon the holy rood in the sea, which is within the diocese of Norwich in the county of Suffolk and in the parish of Newton standing upon the sea bank named the Hospital of Pity. Every man, woman, and child giving or sending any part of their goods for the maintenance of the said hospital shall enjoy great gifts of grace. Whatever day you look upon [this list of names] or bless yourself with it, or wear it with good devotion, no wicked spirit or enemy shall have the power to hurt you sleeping or waking, nor shall thunder, lightning, winds or weather on land or water. He shall also not die without confession. And if a woman laboring in childbirth has it on her, the child and she shall be parted without peril of death, and shall never be vexed by the sickness called the access or [intermittent] fevers, nor with the plague of pestilence, by virtue of these holy names that hereafter follow. St. Quiricus and Julitta his mother obtained these special petitions from God as is recorded in Rome at St. John Lateran: Omnipotent † God † Christ † Messiah † Soter † Emanuel † Sabaoth † Adonai † Only-begotten † the Way † the Life † Hand [of God] † Homousion [same substance] † Savior † Alpha † and Omega † Font † Origin † Hope † Faith † Charity † Oza [Hosanna?] † Lamb † Sheep † Calf † Serpent [John 3:14] † Ram † Lion † Worm [Ps. 21 (22):7] † First † Last † King † Father † Son † Holy Spirit † I am † Who am [Exod. 3:14] † Creator † Eternal † Redeemer † Trinity † Unity † Clement † Principal † Otheotecos [probably for *o theotokos*, the God-bearer − a title of Mary] † Tetragrammaton † May these written names protect, defend, and completely free you from all misfortune, disease, and sickness of body or spirit, and may they assist me with aid. These are the names of the [three] kings, namely Jaspar, Melchior, and Balthazar. And these are the names of the twelve apostles of our Lord Jesus Christ: Peter, Andrew, John, James, Thomas, James, Philip, Bartholomew, Matthew, Simon, Thaddeus, Mathias. And the names of the four Evangelists are these: Mark, Matthew, Luke, John. May these assist me in all my needs and defend and free me from all dangers, temptations, and distress of body and soul; and may they guard me now and forever from all evil, past, present, and future. Amen.

What would be the appeal of indulgences for medieval Christians? How easy was it to obtain an indulgence? Do these examples suggest why they were prone to abuse?

CHAPTER EIGHT: ENTHUSIASM

Like most societies, the people of the Middle Ages now and then focused their energy into almost inexplicable popular outbursts of religious enthusiasm. Recall, for example, that the first Christians to answer Pope Urban II's call in 1095 to defend the Holy Land were ragtag bands of the poor, peasants, and minor nobility led by Peter the Hermit, Walter Sansavoir, and other magnetic leaders. Randomly gathering from across northwestern Europe, this People's Crusade set out almost half a year before the organized knightly armies. As these various bands foraged their way towards Constantinople, they released some of their religious zeal against the Jewish communities they stumbled upon, massacring them in the earliest large-scale pogroms of the Middle Ages. When they crossed into Anatolia, most were quickly wiped out by Turkish armies; the rest were sold into slavery. Not all popular movements, however, took such a sour turn. The Children's Crusade (Doc. 66), for instance, seems to have been born from a genuine pious urge, however misbegotten, to do something to free the Holy Land from infidels. The Great Halleluia channeled popular pious zeal through the officially approved methods of Franciscan spirituality. Beyond the impetus of religious belief, other causes – social, economic, political, and psychological – collided to help spark these spontaneous outpourings. Although most of those who joined them did so out of a sincere need to act decisively on their beliefs, it was precisely the self-expressive and volatile character of these lay movements that so often worried church leaders; for while usually short-lived, they were driven by a religious fervor that was hard to control, prone to slip into error, and often took an anti-clerical turn.

Fig. 8.1. A flagellant procession

A nineteenth-century reproduction (from De-Smet's edition) based on an illustration in Gilles le Muisis's chronicle of the Black Death. The drawing shows a flagellant band hooded, stripped to the waist in their penitential shifts, and scourging themselves as they walk behind a crucifix and banner on which are painted two flagellums. The original is in Brussels, Bibliothèque royale du Belgique ms 13076-7, f. 16v. (See Doc. 69.)

65. PIOUS CHURCH-BUILDERS AT CHARTRES CATHEDRAL (1145)

Haimon, the abbot of St. Pierre-sur-Dives in Normandy, wrote this letter to the prior of Tutbury, Staffordshire, a dependent cell of St. Pierre, describing the remarkable movement of lay people hauling stones from the quarries of Berchères-l'Evêque to the building-site of Chartres cathedral five miles away. Reports of this pious impulse to lend a hand in constructing churches occur elsewhere in France in this period, and the Franciscan chronicler Salimbene reports the same phenomenon in early thirteenth-century Italy (Doc. 68).

Source: trans. G.G. Coulton, *Life in the Middle Ages* (Cambridge: Cambridge University Press, 1910; rpt. 1967), v. II, pp. 18-22; revised. Latin.

Brother Haimon, the humble servant of the servants of the Blessed Mother of God at the monastery of Dives, desires to his most sweet brethren and fellow-servants in Christ that dwell at Tutbury that consolation which is promised to those who love God. Rejoice with us, brethren, rejoice and exalt in the Lord; for the day-spring from on high [Luke 1:78] has visited us, not indeed by our own merits, but by his abundance of grace and wonted compassion; he has poured forth upon us the depths of his mercy, nor withheld in wrath the gifts of his loving kindness. Oh, how great is the superfluity of his sweetness that has been shown in our times to a world sick with sin, wounded with crimes, desperate with the enormity of its wickedness; to a world in short which was already almost godless, because by sin it had become estranged from God: for the wickedness of man had come to such a pitch that, unless that loving day-spring from on high had quickly visited the world, unless it had merci-fully succored our falling race, he would by no means have found faith when he came to the earth. But, where sin abounded, grace also did much more abound [Rom. 5:20]. The loving Lord has looked down from heaven upon the children of men, because there was none who understood and sought God; almost all were gone aside from him and had become abominable in their iniquities; and there was none who thought in his heart and said, "What have I done?" Then he drew to himself those that started away from him, and recalled the wandering, and taught them a new manner of seeking him, a manner new, I say, and unheard-of in all ages. For who ever saw, who ever heard, in all the generations past, that kings, princes, mighty men of this world, puffed up with honors and riches, men and women of noble birth, should bind bridles upon their proud and swollen necks and submit them to wagons which, after the fashion of brute beasts, they dragged with their loads of wine, corn, oil, lime, stones, beams, and other things necessary to sustain life or to build churches, even to Christ's abode? Moreover, as they draw the wagons we may see this miracle that, although sometimes a thousand men and women, or even more, are bound in the traces (so vast indeed is the mass, so great is the engine, and so heavy the load laid upon it), yet they go forward in such silence that no voice, no murmur, is heard; and, unless we saw it with our eyes, no man would dream that so great a multitude is there. When, again, they pause on the way, then no other voice is heard but confession of guilt, with supplication and pure prayer to God that he may vouchsafe pardon for their sins; and, while the priests there preach peace, hatred is soothed, discord is driven away, debts are forgiven, and unity is restored between man and man. If, however, anyone be so sunk in evil that he will not forgive those who have sinned against him, nor obey the pious admonition of the priests, then is his offering forthwith cast down from the wagon as an unclean thing; and he himself, with much shame and ignominy, is separated from the unity of the sacred people. There at the prayers of the faithful you may see the sick, and those that are vexed with diverse diseases, arise whole from the wagons on which they had been laid; you may see the dumb open their mouths to God's praise, and those who are vexed by demons come to a sounder mind; you may see the priests of Christ set each above his own wagon and exhorting all men to confession, to lamentation, to the resolution of better life, while the people fall to the ground, where they lie outstretched and kiss the earth again and again; old men and young men, with children of the tenderest age, cry unto the Mother of God, to whom especially they uplift their sobs and sighs from the inmost recesses of their heart with the voice of confession and praise: for this work is known to be specially hers next to her gentle Son. She more especially commended herself in this work after him; she adorned first the cathedral of Chartres and then our church dedicated to her with so many and so great signs and wonders that, if I would express all that it has been vouchsafed to me to see, even in a single night, my memory and tongue would utterly fail me. For these miracles would seem to exceed both number and faith, yet I will tell of them below as truly as I may, so far as the strength which God has given me will permit.

When, therefore, the faithful people (to return to my purpose) set on their way again with bray of trumpets and waving of banners borne before, then, marvelous to relate, the work went on so easily that nothing hindered them on their way, neither steep mountains nor deep waters rolling between, but (as we read of the ancient Hebrews that they entered Jordan in their bands), so one by one, when they came to cross the river, these suddenly entered without delay into the waters that stood over against them, under the Lord's guidance, so that even the waves of the sea at the place called St. Marie du Port, while the whole company were crossing on their way to us, are credibly said to have stood away from them on their passage. Nor can we wonder that the older and more aged undertook this burdensome labor for the multitude of their sins; but what urged boys and children to this work? Who brought them to that good Teacher who has perfected his praise in the mouths and works of children? Has perfected, I say, that by all means the work begun among the elders may be proved to have been completed by the children; for you might see them, with their own little kings and leaders, bound to their laden wagons, and not dragging with bowed backs like their elders but walking erect as though they bore no burden, and (more wonderful still) surpassing them in nimbleness and speed. Thus went they in a fashion far more glorious, holy, and religious, than any words of ours could express.

When they had come to the church, then the wagons were arrayed around like a spiritual camp; and all that following night this army of the Lord kept their watches with psalms and hymns; then waxen tapers and lights were kindled in each wagon, then the sick and infirm were set apart, then the relics of the saints were brought to their relief, then mystical processions were made by priests and clergy, and followed with all devotion by the people, who earnestly implored the Lord's mercy and that of his blessed Mother for their restoration to health. If, however, the healing were but a little delayed, or did not follow forthwith after their vows, then all might have been seen putting off their clothes – men and women alike, naked from the loins upward, casting away all confusion and lying upon the earth. Moreover, their example was followed even more devoutly by the children and infants who, groveling on the ground, not so much crept from the church porch upon their hands and knees, but rather dragged themselves flat upon their bodies first to the high altar and then to all the others, calling upon the Mother of Mercy in this new fashion of prayer, and there extorting from her surely and forthwith the pious desires of their petitions; for what – I will not say could they not *obtain*, but – could they not *extort* by this fashion of prayer, this affection of piety shown in their groans, their sighs, their tears, and therefore ascending even to the divine ears of the Mother of all Pity? Who indeed would not be moved, nay rather, whose stony heart would not be softened as he watched that pious humility of the innocent children dragging their naked ribs on the bare ground? Who would not be pricked to tears by those lamentable voices crying aloud to heaven? Who, I ask, would not be bent by those tender hands and arms stretched out to be beaten with rods? For it did not suffice them (though that surely was admirable at so tender an age!) to cry so long with the voice of weeping; it did not suffice that so many tears should be shed, but of their own accord they needed to add bodily affliction also, to obtain the healing of these sick folk. The priests stood over them, shedding tears while they beat with their scourges upon the tender limbs thus exposed, while the children urged them not to spare their stripes nor with-hold their hand in too great mercy. All voices echoed the same cry, "Smite, scourge, lash, and spare not." There might be seen more than a thousand hands outstretched to the scourge; nay, they exposed their very ears and eyes and tongues, saying, "Let these hands be smitten which have wrought iniquity; let these ears be lashed which have listened to vanity, these eyes which have seen it; this tongue and these lips which have uttered idle and lying words!" Here I ask with assurance, who is so hardhearted that he is not moved to tears? Who is so fierce and merciless that he is not moved forthwith to pity at this pious sight? Truly the Mother of Mercy is moved without delay to pious compassion on those who afflict themselves before her, and shows by the immediate efficacy of her healing hand how nearly she is touched and how truly she has heard their cries; for soon all the sick and infirm leap forth healed from wagon after wagon, casting away the staff on which they had hitherto leaned their crippled limbs, and hastening without support to render thanks at her altar. Blind men see, and thread their way with ease; the dropsical are relieved of their grievous load and lose their fatal thirst. What shall I say? Why should I enumerate one healing after another, when they are innumerable and more than man can tell? After each miracle a solemn procession is held to the high altar, the bells are rung, praise and thanks are rendered to the Mother of Mercy. This is the manner of their vigils, these are their divine nightwatches, this is the order of the Lord's camp, these are the forms of new religion, these the rites, the heaven-taught rites, in their secret watches. For here nothing carnal is seen; nothing earthly of any kind; all is divine, all is done as in heaven; heavenly altogether are such vigils, wherein nothing is heard but hymns, lauds, and thanks!

How credible is Haimon's account? What does he think motivates people to undertake this task? How does he characterize the mood of these pious crowds?

66. THE CHILDREN'S CRUSADE (1212)

The Children's Crusade was actually two simultaneous mass gatherings. The so-called "French phase," led by Stephen of Cloyes, was never a crusade in any formal sense. More an unfocused burst of popular piety, it is linked to the "German phase" led by the boy Nicholas of Cologne only insofar as it reflected the same brand of mass enthusiasm. The German children and others whom Nicholas led down the Rhine Valley into Italy were more purposeful about their desire to recapture the Holy Land; in fact, many of them were later sworn to abide by their crusader oaths. The specific religious and social elements that spurred these young crusaders on their mission are difficult to pinpoint;

*but the nine accounts below – all written roughly contemporary to the Crusade and sometimes by eyewitnesses – offer some insight into how different chroniclers reported and interpreted the event. Alberic of Trois-Fontaines's description is usually presented as the classic account, but its details are not reliable. In the last twenty-five years, some historians have argued that the participants in both movements were not children (*pueri*) but rather groups of dispossessed poor, since "pueri" could be used to designate inferior social status as well as age. But the general opinion remains that young people, if not small children per se, probably made up the bulk of these crusaders.*

The French Phase

1. From the chronicle of an anonymous canon of Laon (d.c. 1219).

Source: "Child-Pilgrimages" trans. Robert H. Cooke in J.F.C. Hecker, *The Epidemics of the Middle Ages*, trans. B.G. Babington (London: Trübner & Co., 1859), p. 354; revised. Latin.

In the month of June of the same year [1212] a certain boy, by occupation a shepherd, of a village named Cloyes near the town of Vendôme, said that the Lord had appeared to him in the form of a poor pilgrim, had received bread from him, and had delivered letters to him to be taken to the king of the French. When he came, together with his fellow shepherd boys (*cum coaevis suis pastoribus*), nearly thirty thousand people assembled around him from all parts of France. While he stayed at St. Denis, the Lord worked many miracles through him, as many have witnessed. There were also many other boys who were held in great veneration by the common multitude in many places because they were also believed to work miracles, to whom a multitude of boys gathered wishing to proceed to the holy boy (*sanctus puer*) Stephen under their guidance. All acknowledged him as master and prince over them. At length the king [Philip II], having consulted the masters of [the University of] Paris about this gathering of boys, commanded them to return to their homes; and so this childish enthusiasm was as easily ended as it had begun. But it seemed to many that, by means of such innocents gathered of their own accord, the Lord would do something great and new upon the earth, which issued far otherwise.

2. From the chronicle of Alberic, monk of Trois-Fontaines, written c. 1232 with later interpolations.

Source: "Child-Pilgrimages" trans. Robert H. Cooke, pp. 355–56; revised. Latin.

There happened this year [1212] a practically miraculous expedition of young children (*infantes*) coming together from everywhere. They came first from the regions around the castle of Vendôme to Paris, and when they were about thirty thousand strong, they went to Marseilles as if wishing to go cross the sea and fight against the Saracens. But coarse and bad men joined them and so corrupted the whole army that, some perishing in the sea, some being put up for sale, few of so great a multitude returned home. But the pope gave a command to those who had escaped these fates that when they were old enough, they should go across the sea as crusaders. Now the betrayers of these children (*infantes*) are said to have been Hugh Ferreus [i.e., Hard-hearted] and William Porcus [i.e., Pig], merchants of Marseilles. Since they were ship captains, they should have carried them over the sea without payment for God's sake, as they had promised them. They filled seven large ships with them, and when they had come after two day's sailing to the island of Saint Peter-at-the-Rock, which is called Recluse, a tempest arose, two ships were lost, and all the children aboard those ships were drowned. It is said that after some years, Pope Gregory IX [1227-41] built the church of the New Innocents on the island and appointed twelve prebendaries; and the bodies of the children, which the sea threw up there, are in that church and to this day they are shown uncorrupted to pilgrims. But the betrayers succeeded in taking the other five ships to Bougie and Alexandria, and there they sold all those children to Saracen princes and merchants, from whom the caliph bought for himself four hundred, all of them clerics and among whom were eighty priests, because he wished to keep them separate from the others; these he treated more honorably than was his wont. It is that caliph of whom I have earlier spoken who studied at Paris in the habit of a cleric, and learned fully all that is known among us, and he now lately has left off sacrificing camel's flesh. When the Saracen princes assembled at Baghdad that same year that the children were sold, they martyred eighteen of the children in their presence by various methods when they would not abandon the Christian faith; they carefully raised the rest of them in slavery. One of these clerics, who was one of those the caliph bought, saw this and faithfully reported that he had never heard that a single one of these children had renounced their Christianity. But the two betrayers Hugh Ferreus and William Porcus afterwards went to Mirabel, the prince of the Saracens of Sicily, and wished to plan the betrayal of the Emperor Frederick [II]; but by the grace of God the emperor triumphed over them, and hanged Mirabel, his two sons, and those two traitors from the same gallows. Eighteen years after this expedition, he who reported this added that Mascemuch of Alexandria still had seven hundred of them, no longer children but full-grown men.

The German Phase

3. From the Royal Chronicles of Cologne, written c. 1216.

Source: trans. J. Shinners from *Cronicae Regiae Coloniensis, Continuatio Prima*, ed. G.H. Pertz, *Monumenta Germaniae Historica*, Scriptorum 24 (Hanover, 1879), pp. 17-18. Latin.

An absolutely marvelous thing occurred that same year [1212], all the more marvelous since such a thing was unheard of in the world. For around Easter and Pentecost from all over Germany and France with no encouragement or preaching but driven by unknown inspiration many thousands of children (*pueri*) from six years old all the way to young manhood (*ad virilem etatem*) abandoned the plows and wagons they drove, or the cattle they herded, or whatever else they had at hand, and – though their unwilling parents, kinfolk, and friends tried to hold them back – suddenly ran one after the other and undertook a crusade. In groups of twenty, fifty, or a hundred, with their banners aloft they began heading for Jerusalem. Many people asked them by whose counsel or encouragement they had subjected themselves to this kind of life, especially since for quite some years before many kings, more dukes, and countless people going at it with their mighty hands had returned with the business unfinished; but they were still just youngsters (*adhuc etate puerili*) with neither the power nor strength to do anything, and so everyone judged them to be foolish and imprudent for attempting to do this. They answered briefly: they made themselves obedient to divine assent in this. Thus, whatever God wanted them to do they would endure gladly and with a compliant heart. And so making a little progress on the way, some turned back at Mainz, some at Piacenza, some at Rome. Others reached Marseilles, but whether they crossed the sea or what became of them is uncertain. But one thing is sure: of the many thousands who had set out, barely a few returned home.

4. From the Annals of Piacenza of Johannes Codagnellus, written c. 1220.

Source: trans. J. Shinners from *Annales Placentini Guelfi*, ed. G.H. Pertz, *Monumenta Germaniae Historica*, Scriptorum 18 (Hanover, 1863), p. 426. Latin.

On the following [Monday], August 20 [1212], a certain German boy (*puer*) called Nicholas who had taken the crusader vow passed through Piacenza hurrying to set out across the sea. He was accompanied by a great and countless multitude of German boys, babies at the breast, women, and girls (*puerorum et infantium lactantium, mulierum et puellarum*) who had also vowed to crusade with the sign of the Lord's cross. For it was said this boy had received a message from an angel that he and his following should recapture the Lord's sepulcher from the hands and the power of the iniquitous and villainous Saracens.

5. From the chronicle of William of Andres, written in the late 1220s-early 1230s.

Source: trans. J. Shinners from *Willelmi Chronica Andrensis*, ed. G.H. Pertz, *Monumenta Germaniae Historica*, Scriptorum 24 (Hanover, 1879), p. 754. Latin.

An infinite multitude of children (*parvuli*), with no advice either from within or without, gathered together from various cities, castles, towns, and villages, and hurried toward the Mediterranean Sea. When their parents or others asked them where they wanted to go, as if led by the same spirit each and every one said, "To God!"

6. From the annals of Albert, Abbot of Stade, written between 1232-40.

Source: trans. J. Shinners from *Annales Alberti Abbatis Stadensis*, ed. G.H. Pertz, *Monumenta Germaniae Historica*, Scriptorum 16 (Hanover, 1859), p. 355.

Around this time, children (*pueri*) without a master, without a leader ran together with eager steps from all the towns and cities of every region to parts beyond the sea. When people asked them where they were running, they said, "To Jerusalem, to seek the Holy Land." The parents of many of them confined them at home, but in vain; for they smashed their locks or walls and escaped. Pope [Innocent III] heard rumors about them and, sighing, said, "These children reproach us, for while we sleep they race to recover the Holy Land." Even now it is unknown what happened to them. But many of them returned home, and when they were asked the reason for their journey, they said they did not know. Also, at this same time naked women saying nothing ran together through the towns and cities.

7. From the Ebersheim Chronicle, written in the 1230s.

Source: trans. J. Shinners from *Chronicon Ebersheimense*, ed. G.H. Pertz, *Monumenta Germaniae Historica*, Scriptorum 23 (Hanover, 1874), p. 450. Latin.

Unheard of events appeal to us from their outset, challenging us to preserve their memory. A certain little boy (*puerulus*) named Nicholas, who came from the region of Cologne, spurred on a great gathering of children (*pueri*) through some unknown counsel, claiming that he could walk across the waves of the sea without wetting his feet and could provide sufficient provisions for those following him. The rumor of such a marvelous deed resounded through the cities and towns, and however many heard him, boys or girls (*masculi quam puelle*), they abandoned their parents, marked themselves as crusaders, and prepared to cross the sea. And so throughout all Germany and France an infinite number of serving-boys, handmaids, and maidens (*servulorum, ancillarum et virginum*) followed their leader and came to Vienne, which is a city by the sea [*sic*]. There they were taken aboard some ships, carried off by pirates, and sold to the Saracens. Some who tried to return home wasted away with hunger; and many girls who were virgins when they left were pregnant when they returned. Thus, one can clearly see that this journey issued from the deception of the devil because it caused so much loss.

8. From the Annals of Marbach written c. 1240.

Source: "Child-Pilgrimages" trans. Robert H. Cooke, p. 357; revised. Latin.

At this time [1212] a frivolous expedition occurred, as children and foolish people (*pueris et stultis hominibus*) marked themselves as crusaders without any discretion, more out of curiosity than for their salvation. People of both sexes, boys and girls alike, not just youngsters but also grown ups (*non solum minores sed etiam adulti*), married women with virgins, set out with empty purses, not only through all Germany, but also through parts of France and Burgundy. Their parents and friends could use no means to restrain them for they used every effort to join that expedition, so that everywhere in the villages and the fields they left their tools and whatever they had in hand at the time and joined the bands as they passed by. And just as we are often a crowd easily prone to belief when faced with such novelties, many thought that this happened not through some foolheadedness but through divine inspiration and a certain piety, and so they aided them with provisions, furnishing them food and other necessities. But when the clergy and some of the others of sounder mind spoke against it and judged the expedition to be in vain and useless, the laity vehemently objected, saying that the clerics were unbelievers, and that they opposed this more out of their envy and greed than for its truth and righteousness. But since no affair that begins without the balance of reason and the strength of counsel has a good end, after this stupid multitude reached the regions of Italy, they were separated and scattered through the cities and towns; many were kept by the inhabitants of the land as servants and handmaids. Others are said to have reached the sea where they were carried off by the sailors and mariners and transported to other distant parts of the world. But the rest came to Rome where they saw that they could go no further since they were supported by no authority. At last they realized that their effort was frivolous and empty. Still, they were by no means absolved from the vow to take the cross, except the boys under the age of discretion and those who were oppressed by old age. Thus deceived and perplexed, they began their return. Those who had once passed through the land in crowds and never without a song of encouragement among their troops, now returned singly and silently, barefoot and famished, held in scorn by everyone; and many virgins had been raped and had lost the flower of their chastity.

9. From the Deeds of Trier, written c. 1242.

Source: trans. J. Shinners from *Gestorum Treverorum Continuatio IV,* ed. G.H. Pertz, *Monumenta Germaniae Historica*, Scriptorum 24 (Hanover, 1879), pp. 398-99. Latin.

Many marvelous things happened in the world in [the archbishop Theodoric's] time. The first one of which that comes to mind, marvelous and unheard of in the whole world, happened a few months before [Theodoric's] election. For children (*pueri*) gathered together from all the towns and villages of Germany, and, as if by divine inspiration, they met in each place, united into a troop, and headed for the road to Jerusalem as if they meant to recapture the Holy Land. The leader and head of this journey was Nicholas, a boy (*puer*) from Cologne, who bore over him a cross having the shape of the Greek letter *tau*, which was put forward as a mark of his holiness and miraculous qualities, though it was hard to tell what kind of material or metal it was made of. When the children arrived at Brindisi, the local bishop, sensing something underhanded, did not permit them to cross the sea. For Nicholas's father sold them to the heathens, and this happened from the evil deed of demons. Because of this, the boy himself died, and his father met a violent death back in Cologne. Even more of the children died; for when they were on their way people generously aided them, but on their journey back home they gave them nothing.

What kinds of people join the Children's Crusade? What are their motives? Are they perceived by these various chroniclers as pious? Which of these various accounts seem the most credible?

67. THE SHEPHERDS' CRUSADE (1251)

Like the Children's Crusade, the rising of the pastoureaux *or shepherds in the spring of 1251 was another brief burst of mass piety aimed at recapturing the Holy Land. Just the year before, the saintly King Louis IX's expedition to Egypt, the Seventh Crusade, had ended disastrously when the king himself and many of his nobles were taken captive and held for ransom. Surely distress over this royal catastrophe fueled some of the enthusiasm for the Shepherds' Crusade. Unlike the Children's Crusade, however, this movement turned violent, anti-clerical, and anti-Semitic. The Hungarian leader described here was actually an apostate Cistercian monk named Jacob. As popular support for him mounted, his delusions of power grew more extravagant until finally he claimed the right to absolve sins and was said to have married women to multiple husbands. Based on an eyewitness report, this account is by Matthew Paris (c. 1200-59) one of the great medieval historians, though his allegiances and exaggerations are apparent here. Another Shepherds' Crusade was mounted in France in 1320; much like the rising of 1251 in inspiration, leadership, and its anti-clerical turn, it too was a misdirected effort that ended in failure.*

Source: trans. J. Shinners from Matthew Paris, *Chronica Majora*, v. 5, ed. Henry R. Luard, Rolls Series v. 57 (London: Longman, 1880), pp. 246-54. Latin.

Note a certain marvel about those in France who said that they were shepherds about to conquer the Holy Land

In the same days as the above [1251], the Enemy of the human race, trusting that "the Jordan may run into his mouth," [Job 40:18] since now the Sultan of Babylon drank from it, when he saw that the Christian faith staggered as it staggered even in parts of sweet Gaul, endeavored to stir up a new kind of deception. There was a sixty-year-old man from the land of Hungary (from his earliest years the worst Christian apostate) who had most richly imbibed the deceitful conjuring tricks of magicians from the sulphurous pit of Toledo, and had also been made a home-born slave and disciple of Mohammed by the Sultan of Babylon, whose servant he was. He promised [the Sultan] for sure that he would deliver to him for capture an infinite multitude of Christians so that, with France made vacant and its king bereft, the gateway to Christian climes would be more easily cast open to the Saracens. Thus this imposter (who spoke French, German, and Latin) wandered around here and there preaching without papal license or the patronage of any prelate, falsely claiming that he had received the following command from the Blessed Mary, Mother of the Lord: that he should call together all shepherds of sheep and other animals, to whom, he said, the heavenly hosts had granted that they, in their humility and simplicity, would win back the Holy Land from the power of the infidels with all their slaves – for God was displeased by the knightly pride of the French [nobility]. His eloquence added credence to his words, and he always kept one hand gripped tight in which he falsely claimed he held a letter and orders from the Blessed Virgin. Any of the shepherds he called to him left their sheep, herds, and horses behind, and, without asking their lords or their parents or giving concern to their provisions, followed him step by step.

(Of course he employed that sort of evil-doing that had been used once before in France by one still beardless and a boy [Stephen of Cloyes], who, about forty years before, had made fools of all the people of France, calling together an infinite multitude of boys who followed in his footsteps singing. And, what is remarkable, locks and bolts could not restrain them, nor the commands, blandishments, or favors of their fathers or mothers call them back. By this same delusion Robert the Bugger ["*Bugre*" or Robert le Bougre, whose nickname identifies him as a former Cathar heretic or "Bulgar," was an overzealous Dominican inquisitor], a false friar of the Order of Preachers, was said to have made fools of an infinite number, to have surrendered these harmless fools to the fire [in 1239 he burned 183 alleged heretics in one day], and to have seriously destroyed the secular power of the king of France, whom he had attracted to this undertaking. But I have related this in more detail elsewhere.)

This good-for-nothing and all those following him took the cross [vowed to go on crusade]. And there were many who showed him favor and even gave him aid, saying that often "God has chosen the weak things of the world to put to shame the strong" [1 Cor. 1:18], "nor does the Almighty take pleasure in the legs of a man" [Ps. 146 (147):10] or accept the preeminent as his army and his strength. Thus Queen Blanche [of Castile], the regent of the French, hoping that they would capture the Holy Land and avenge their children, hovered over them with grace and favor. And so their numbers swelled immensely, so much so that the war banners they made for themselves were reckoned at a hundred thousand or more. On his banner their master had affixed a lamb bearing a pennant: the lamb as a sign of innocence and humility, the pennant decorated with a cross as a sign of victory....

The continuation of the affair of the said shepherds

So rogues, exiles, outlaws, and excommunicates – all of whom in France are wont to be called the *ribauld* in the vernacular – flocked together to their company, so that with their master's banner and likewise those of his generals, they now had five hundred ensigns waving over a numberless army.

They carried swords, double-headed axes, spears, poniards, and daggers, so that now they looked more like worshipers of Mars than of Christ. Soon all but raving, they contracted illicit marriages. In their sermons the generals and their master, who dared to preach even though they were laymen, strayed outrageously from the articles of the Christian faith and the standards of plain truth. And if anyone contradicted them they savagely attacked him with arms rather than with appeals to reason or authority. When their exalted leader, surrounded on every side by armed men, preached to them, he denounced all religious orders except for their own conventicle, condemning especially the Friars Preachers and Minors, calling them vagabonds and hypocrites. He claimed that the Cistercian monks were the most grasping lovers of sheep [because their wealth came from selling wool] and land; the Black monks [Benedictines] were gluttons and haughty; the canons were semi-secular and voracious meat eaters; bishops and their officials hunted only after money and abounded in all kinds of ostentation. But he preached such unrepeatable slander about the Roman Curia that they clearly appeared to be heretics and schismatics. Yet due to their hatred and contempt of the clergy, people hearing this nonsense applauded it favorably, though what they heard was very dangerous.

The upheaval at Orleans

Arriving with great pomp and strength at Orleans, they entered the city on St. Barnabas's Day [June 11] against the wishes of the bishop and all the clergy, but with the willing approval of its citizens. When their leader with his town crier's voice like a miracle-working prophet had announced [the topic of] his sermon (or more precisely, when he had decreed it like a tyrant) the people in an infinite multitude came to him. But the bishop of the city, greatly dreading this deadly danger, forbade any of his clergy on pain of anathema to listen to his eloquent words or follow in his footsteps, charging that all these things were the snares of the devil. For now even laymen were condemning his violent threats and commands. Nevertheless, some of the clergy from the schools, rashly crossing over the line of the bishop's prohibitions, could not stop themselves from turning their itching ears to such unheard-of novelties, not because they wanted to embrace their errors, but because they wanted to examine this insolence. Of course it was strange and absurd that laymen – indeed, common people – spurning papal authorization should preach so boldly in public in a city such as this where a university thrived, and bend the hearts and ears of so many of the people to their impostures. There were, however, five hundred standard-bearers there; for that reason the clergy of saner counsel hid in their houses, tightly shutting their doors with locks and bolts, not without fear of an upheaval.

When the aforesaid master had stepped out into the open about to make his sermon, without announcing his theme he started babbling, bellowing back unrepeatable insults. Now one scholar standing at a distance, bearing himself boldly, burst out with these words: "O worthless heretic and enemy of truth, you are lying off the top of your head, deceiving innocent people with your false and fraudulent chattering." He had barely finished saying this when one of these vagabonds rushed over, raised up a pointed axe, and split his head in two so that the wounded man uttered not another word. An uproar erupted and those – whom up until now we called shepherds (*pastores*) but now should be called wolves in sheep's clothing (*impostores*) and forerunners of Antichrist – sprang up en masse hostilely against the clergy of Orleans. They rushed armed against the unarmed; smashing doors and windows they plundered their precious books and burned them. Under the conniving eyes of the people of the city who dissembled or, more truly said, consented (for which reason they deserve to be called dog-like), they slaughtered many and drowned many in the Loire. Some they just wounded, others they looted. When those who had hidden shut up in their houses saw this, they departed secretly by night in small groups. The whole university was driven out, and it was ascertained that about twenty-five clerics, besides being afflicted with various injuries, had met a wretched death. Moreover the bishop and those who had hidden to avoid being involved in similar calamities had endured their many abuses with losses. But the shepherds withdrew, fearing that they would encounter insurrection breaking out in the city and a war would commence against them. However the bishop, not wanting to be compared to a dog whose bark is worse than his bite, put the city under interdict since its citizens were blameworthy and had disgraced themselves by giving the shepherds permission to enter the city and by consenting and cooperating with them.

This clamor and complaint reached the ears of the Lady Blanche and her magnates, especially the prelates. But the queen modestly replied, "The Lord knows I believed that these people in their simplicity and holiness would win a victory in the Holy Land. But since they are deceivers let them be excommunicated, captured, and destroyed." And so all these mercenaries were excommunicated and denounced as such. But before this sentence was published, these charlatans arrived at Bourges and the gates of the city were thrown open to them with the consent of the citizens. Disobeying the archbishop's prohibition, the greater part of them entered and the rest remained within the stone walls around the vineyards outside the city. For there were so many of them that no city could receive them all comfortably; and many of their army were spread over several provinces. In fact, even Paris [the largest city in France] perceived the damage that would result in admitting them. When the chief of these deceivers promised that he would give a sermon in public and perform astounding miracles, a countless multitude of people flocked from everywhere so that they could hear what was unheard-of until then and see what had never been seen before. But when that traitor asserted some absurdities and the miracles he promised were exposed as fake, one man in the crowd – a butcher carrying a double-headed axe – struck him on the head and sent him with his brains knocked out to hell. His body was tossed unburied at a crossroads to be gnawed. When the news had spread that all of these people, their supporters, and those who listened to them were excommunicated, they were dispersed and everywhere beheaded like rabid dogs.

In a similar way, when some of their conventicle came to Bourdeaux, the gates were locked by order of Count Simon de Montfort and they were kept out. When they sought entrance the Count asked, "On whose authority do you do this?" They answered, saying, "We hold out the authority not of the pope or a bishop, but of Almighty God and Blessed Mary, his Mother, which is greater." After the count heard this, rightly taking it as foolishness, he offered this reply: "All of you depart as fast as you can or I will call together my whole army with the commune of this city and its neighbors, violently attack you, and chop off your heads."

How the second charlatan perished

When these wretches had heard this, thunderstruck, they became like mortar without sand fleeing in every direction every man for himself, and as they dispersed they were exposed to many perils. Their leader and master secretly slipped away, hired a boat, and tried to head for the heathen lands he had come from. But some sailors recognized him as a traitor and the ally of the aforementioned man from Hungary whom the people of Bourges had killed. They bound the wretch hand and foot and threw the vagabond into the Garonne. Thus evading Scylla, he fell into Charybdis. In his packsack they found not only money but quite a few letters written with freakish characters in Arabic and Chaldean, and poisonous powders for making many kinds of potions. The gist of some of the letters, as was later ascertained, was that the Sultan had enthusiastically urged him to undertake this with the promise of great reward; the main point of the other letters was that he was to surrender innumerable people to the Sultan. And so these two conjurers perished, entangled in Satan's snares.

How the third charlatan perished

A third man, however, presuming to go to England and landing at Shoreham, received at his command more than five hundred shepherds, plowmen, swineherds, oxherds, and other people of this ilk. But when it was soon broadcast that they had been excommunicated and that the Hungarian, who was their chief teacher, and his companion had been killed and their accomplices dispersed, their situation pretty much fell apart. However, after they arrived at Minster [?] their leader set up to preach there. But when he started making odd claims – indeed, insane ones – his audience rose up against him. While they flocked together to grab their weapons, he fled into some woods; but he was quickly apprehended and was not only dismembered, but chopped to pieces. His abandoned corpse was an easy meal for the crows.

Then after many of their followers realized that they had been seduced and recognized their own wretchedness, the penance was enjoined on them that they cast off the crosses which they had accepted at the hands of traitors, reaccept them from the hands of good men, and rightly complete their pilgrimage. Arriving in the Holy Land, they were made clients of the king of France after his ransom, as is told in what follows. For they said that their masters had taught them that they were going to liberate the king of the French, and for that reason all of them had earnestly taken the crusader oath.

Dom Thomas, from the land of Normandy, was a monk of Sherborne, a discerning and eloquent man. He had been appointed to transact some difficult business for the king in the lands across the sea at that time. He was seized by some shepherds against whom he had delivered a sermon and held for eight days. Because he would not agree with their comments, he was cudgeled most severely. Barely escaping from them one night, he went to the king [Henry III] at Winchester and described step by step for the king all these things and more about their tricks, in the hearing of he himself who wrote this down. On the spot this writer [Matthew Paris] more fully recorded them straight from the mouth of the narrator who had discussed them since they were worthy of belief.

A reflection on this matter

Serious-minded men and discerning prelates of deep understanding said that never since the time of Mohammed had so fearful a pest crept into Christ's church, especially since, because of the misfortune that befell the king of France, the Faith in the kingdom of the French began to waver.

To what does Matthew Paris attribute the appeal of the leaders of the Shepherds' Crusade? What impression would they have made on the citizens of the towns they visited? Are their motives discernible from Matthew's account?

68. THE FRANCISCAN SALIMBENE ON THE "GREAT HALLELUIA" (1233)

The Franciscan Salimbene de Adam (1221-c. 1289) wrote his vast chronicle between 1283 and 1288 for the instruction of his niece Agnes, a Poor Clare nun in Parma, though clearly he had a wider audience in mind as well. Heavily interlaced with scriptural quotations (even more so than most medieval chronicles) and morally didactic asides, the chronicle recounts his own eventful life, the history of the burgeoning Franciscan order, and the hot-button issues of thirteenth-century Italian politics. In these two excerpts he first describes the widespread Italian spiritual awakening called the "Great Halleluia" and then recounts the popular veneration of a Cremonese wine carrier. Notice that Salimbene was only twelve years old when the "Great Halleluia" began.

Source: trans. Joseph L. Baird, *The Chronicle of Salimbene de Adam* (Binghamton, NJ: Medieval & Renaissance Texts and Studies, 1986), pp. 47-56, 512-14. Latin.

1. Concerning the time of the Halleluia.

This [1233] was the time of the Halleluia, as it was later to be called, a time of happiness and joy, gladness and rejoicing, praise and jubilation, of quiet and peace, with all weapons laid aside. During this time, the people of the city and the country "young men and maidens ... the old with the younger" [Ps. 148 (149):12], even the knights and soldiers sang songs and divine hymns. And this spirit of devotion was abroad in all the cities of Italy. As I myself saw in my native city of Parma, for example, every parish devised a banner to be borne in holy processions, on which was depicted the martyrdom of its own particular saint, as, for instance, the flaying of St. Bartholomew on the banner of the parish where his church is situated – and likewise with all the others. Moreover, huge companies of men and women, boys and girls, came to the city from the villages round about with their own banners, so that they might be able to hear the preachers and give praise to God. And they sang with "voice of a god, and not of a man" [Acts 12:22], and they walked about as men saved, in fulfillment of the prophetic words: "All the ends of the earth shall remember, and shall be converted to the Lord: And all the kindreds of the Gentiles shall adore in his sight" [Ps. 21 (22):28]. And all men carried about with them tree branches and lighted candles. Furthermore, there was preaching at evening, morning, and noon, according to the prophecy: "Evening and morning, and at noon, I will speak and declare: and he shall hear my voice. He shall redeem my soul in peace from them that draw near to me: for among many they were with me" [Ps. 54 (55):18-19]. And the crowds of people made stops in the churches and in the squares, lifting up their hands to God in praise and blessing forever and ever; truly, they could not cease from divine praise because they were so inebriated with divine love. And blessed was he who could do the most good works and could best praise God. There was no anger in them, no disturbance, no discord, no rancor. They did all things peacefully and benevolently, so that they might say with the prophet, Isaiah [chapter] 65: "Because the former distresses are forgotten, and because they are hid from" our "eyes." And it is no wonder, for they drank from the sweet wine of the spirit of God, which having once tasted "everything of the flesh becomes insipid," as preachers interpret Proverbs 31: "Give strong drink to them that are sad: and wine to them that are grieved in mind: Let them drink, and forget their want, and remember their sorrow no more." Furthermore, Jeremiah's words in Lamentations 3 are appropriate to these events: "Let us search our ways, and seek and return to the Lord. Let us lift up our hearts with our hands to the Lord in the heavens." They truly did all these things, as I saw with my own eyes, fulfilling the teaching of the Apostle in I Timothy 2: "I will therefore that men pray in every place, lifting up pure hands, without anger and contention." Yet as the Wise Man teaches in Proverbs 11: "where there is no governor, the people shall fall." Thus lest you think this verse fulfilled in these people, let us speak of their leaders.

Concerning Brother Benedict, who began the spiritual movement in the time of the Halleluia.

At the very beginning of the Halleluia, Brother Benedict, called the Brother of the Horn, came to Parma. He was a simple and unlettered man, but a man of pure and honorable life. Brother Benedict was from the valley of Spoleto or, perhaps, from the vicinity of Rome, and I saw him and knew him well at Parma and, later, at Pisa. He was associated with no religious order, but lived by himself and strove to please God alone; he was, however, a very good friend of the Friars Minor. He seemed like a second John the Baptist, going before the Lord "to prepare unto the Lord a perfect people" [Luke 1:17]. On his head he wore an Armenian hat. He had a long black beard, and he carried a small horn of copper or brass which he blew loudly, sending forth a sound sometimes sweet, sometimes awesome. He was girded with a leather girdle, and his outer garment, which reached to his feet, was black as sack cloth. His toga was made like a cloak, on both sides of which was a huge, wide cross, long and red, reaching from his neck all the way to his feet, like a priestly chasuble. Dressed in this manner and carrying his horn with him, he would go into the churches and the squares, preaching and praising God, followed by great multitudes of children bearing branches of trees and lighted candles. Quite often I used to see him standing on the wall of the episcopal palace, then under construction, preaching and praising God. And he would begin his praises in this way, speaking in the vernacular: "Praise and blessing and glory be to the Father!" And the children would repeat it after him with a loud voice. Then he would repeat himself, adding "to the Son!" And the children would answer again, singing the words. Then a third time he would cry out the words, adding, "to the Holy Spirit!" And afterward, "Halleluia, Halleluia, Halleluia!" Then he would give a blast on his horn, before he began to preach, sounding forth praise to God. After preaching he would hail the Blessed Virgin in the following manner:

> Ave Maria, merciful and pure,
> Full of Grace, Serene Virgin!
> The Lord with you, and you with me!
> Blessed art thou among women,
> You who brought forth the peace of mankind
>   and the glory of angels!
> And blessed is the fruit of your womb,
> Christ, who brought it about through grace
> That we might be co-heirs with him, etc.

Concerning the notable preachers who were famous at the time of the Halleluia, and first of all about those who were Dominicans. Concerning Brother John of Vicenza, and the canonization of St. Dominic.

Let us speak now about the notable preachers who were famous at the time of this spiritual movement, and first of all we shall speak of two men of the Dominican Order. The first of these is Brother John of Bologna, a native of Vicenza; the second, Brother Jacopino of Reggio, who was born at Parma. The Blessed Dominic was not yet canonized, but lay hidden under the earth, as is sung in the liturgical song:

> The grain lies hidden,
> The star is darkened,
> But the Creator of all things
> Commands the bones of Joseph to spring forth

And the star to shine forth
For the salvation of the people.

And so it was that St. Dominic [d. 1221] had been buried for some twelve years without the matter of his sainthood being raised, but on the initiative of the aforementioned Brother John, who was preaching in Bologna at the time of the spiritual awakening, his canonization was effected. The bishop of Modena, later Cardinal William, lent his assistance to John in this matter. This Bishop William was from the Piedmont, and I once saw him preaching and saying mass during Easter in the church of the Friars Minor at Lyons, when Pope Innocent [IV] and the Curia were there. And since he was a great friend of the Dominicans, he exhorted them about Dominic, saying, "The Friars Minor have their saint, and you ought to have one too, even if you have to make him out of straw." Brother John was a man with little learning but with a great ambition for working miracles. And at the time of the Halleluia, he engaged in a great preaching campaign between Castelleone and Castelfranco.

About Brother Jacopino of Parma (also called Jacopino of Reggio) and his activities.

Brother Jacopino of Reggio, a native of Parma, was a learned man and a teacher of theology. As a preacher, he was eloquent, gracious, and impressive; as a man, he was lively, benevolent, charitable, friendly, courteous, magnanimous, and generous. During the time of the great war, we were once traveling companions for the whole journey from Parma to Modena, though each of us had his own assigned companion. During the time of this spiritual movement, Jacopino enjoyed special grace in his preaching, performing many good works. In this same year the Dominicans began construction on the church of Jesus Christ in Reggio, and the first stone, consecrated by Bishop Nicholas, was laid on the feast of St. James. In order to build this great church, men and women from every level of society came to Reggio – knights and soldiers, as well as farmers and townspeople. They carried the stones, sand, and cement in great bags upon their backs; and he who could carry the most counted himself blessed. They laid the foundations for the cloisters and the church, built part of the walls, and, at the end of the third year, brought their enterprise to completion. This work was supervised by Brother Jacopino. This Brother Jacopino held a great preaching service between Calerno and Sant' Ilario in the bishopric of Parma, on the lower side of the highway. To this service flocked a great throng – men and women, boys and girls, from Parma, from Reggio, from the mountains and valleys, and from the fields and remote villages. It happened that a certain poor woman who was with child brought forth a son at this service, and in response to

Brother Jacopino's exhortation, the people lavished gifts on her. One woman gave sandals, another a shirt, another a dress, and yet another swaddling clothes, so much so that her donkey was loaded with gifts; besides all this, she received a hundred imperial soldi from the men. I heard this a long time after from someone who had been present, as I was traveling with him through that area. And, besides, I have heard it from many other people....

Concerning the preachers of the Order of the Friars Minor; first of all, Brother Leo, to whom the director of a certain orphanage appeared after his death.

Among the Friars Minor, Brother Leo of Milan was a famous and worthy preacher, and he was a successful and hardy opponent of heresy. After many years of service as Provincial Minister in the Order of the Friars Minor, he became archbishop of Milan. He was a man of quite extraordinary courage. Once, for example, he marched alone at the head of the army of Milan as it engaged in battle against the Emperor. Then he crossed the river and remained there holding up the battle standard, totally alone, for the Milanese had seen the imperial army ready for battle and were afraid to cross with him. Again, this Brother Leo once heard the confession of a director of an orphanage in Milan, a man of noble family, renowned for his great holiness. And as the director was breathing his last, Leo made him promise to return after his death and report to him about the state of his soul. He promised to do so gladly. And after the director had died about Vespers, Brother Leo requested two Brothers (who had been his special companions when he was Provincial Minister) to watch with him that evening from the gardener's cell in a corner of the garden. And while the three of them were watching, Brother Leo grew drowsy, and, wishing to sleep, he asked his companions to wake him if they heard anything. Then suddenly they heard someone coming, crying out from great pain, and they saw what appeared to be a ball of fire falling from heaven. And it fell upon the roof of the cell, like a falcon swooping down to seize a duck. Whereupon, Brother Leo woke up. And since the apparition continually cried out, "Alas, alas!" Brother Leo asked him how it was with his soul. He replied that he was damned, because once, out of pure indignation, he had allowed some illegitimate children entrusted to the orphanage to die unbaptized, because he wished to spare his institution labor and expense. When Brother Leo asked him why he had not confessed this sin, he replied that it was because he had either forgotten it or had not thought it necessary to confess. Then Brother Leo said to him, "You have nothing to do with us. Get away from us! Go your own way!" Thus wailing and crying out, he went away. Brother Leo also did many good works in the time of the spiritual movement, later known as the Halleluia....

How these worthy preachers met together and drew up plans for their sermons.

Particular note should be made of the fact that at the time of the spiritual movement these worthy preachers met together and drew up plans for their sermons, that is to say, with respect to the place, the day, the hour, and the theme. And each one said to the other, "Hold fast what we have made firm." And they did precisely what they had arranged among themselves. And thus it was that preaching from a specially constructed platform in the square of Parma, Brother Gerard [of Modena] would suddenly cover his head with his hood and sink deep in thought like a man in profound meditation upon God, and thereby keep the people waiting in suspense in the midst of his sermon. Then after a long delay with the people gazing in wonder, he would remove the hood and begin to speak once more. Then beginning with the solemn words of Apocalypse 1, he would declare, "'I was in the spirit on the Lord's day,' and I heard our beloved John of Vicenza preaching in Bologna on the shore of the River Reno. There was a great multitude before him, and his sermon began: 'Blessed is the nation whose God is the Lord: the people whom he hath chosen for his inheritance'" [Ps. 32 (33):12]. Brother Gerard did this not only in Parma, but, in fact, in many other places. Sometimes he would use Brother Jacopino as his example, and all the other preachers would do the same with him. The people in the audience were amazed and, stirred by curiosity, sent messengers to find out the truth. Once these facts were verified, they marveled beyond measure, and, as a result, many men renounced the world and entered the Order of the Minorites or the Dominicans. All manner of good works were accomplished at various places during the time of the spiritual movement, as I saw with my own eyes.

About the rascals and tricksters who were active during the time of the Halleluia.

There were also during the time of the Halleluia just as many rascals and tricksters who wilfully sought to "lay a blot on the elect" [Ecclus. 11:33].

About Master Boncompagno the Florentine.

Among their number was Boncompagno the Florentine, a noted grammarian in Bologna and the author of books on the art of letter writing. This man was a notorious trickster, in the fashion of the Florentines, and he wrote a poem deriding Brother John of Vicenza. I can't recall either the beginning or the end of the poem, since I read it so long ago and did not commit it to memory, because I really didn't care for it. Here, however, are some of the words that I recall:

Old John John enhances
As he leaps and as he dances.
All of you who seek the sky
Must dance, and dance, and fly!
This one leaps and that one dances,
Every boy and maiden prances,
The young men dance with all the girls,
Even the duke of Venice whirls.

And since Brother John was known as a worker of miracles, Master Boncompagno sought to ape his behavior, and so he predicted to the Bolognese that, before their very eyes, he would fly high into the air. What can one say? News of his claim soon spread throughout Bologna. And so on the appointed day the entire populace congregated, "man and woman, young and old" [Josh. 6:21], at the foot of the mountain called Santa Maria in Monte. Boncompagno had constructed wings for himself, and he stood on top of the mountain looking down at them. And after they had been gazing at each other for a long period of time, he shouted down to them audaciously, "Go, with God's blessing, and let it suffice that you have looked upon the face of Boncompagno." Then they all departed, realizing full well that he had been mocking them the whole time. Now since this Boncompagno was an accomplished writer, he sought a position, on the advice of friends, at the papal court, hoping to be rewarded for his great talent. Yet he never succeeded in this, and years later he returned to Florence so poor that he was constrained to end his days in an institution. The Wise Man in Ecclesiastes speaks of such matters in chapter 9: "I saw that under the sun, the race is not to the swift, nor the battle to the strong, nor bread to the wise, nor riches to the learned, nor favor to the skilful: but time and chance in all." See also Ecclesiasticus 26: "At two things my heart is grieved, and the third bringeth anger upon me: A man of war fainting through poverty: and a man of sense despised: And he that passeth over from justice to sin, God hath prepared such an one for the sword."

About the foolish behavior of John of Vicenza, who was of the Order of the Dominicans.

After a time, Brother John of Vicenza became so taken with himself on account of the honors bestowed on him for his eloquent preaching that he actually believed himself capable of working miracles without the help of God. And this, of course, was the worst kind of stupidity, as the Lord says in John 15: "without me you can do nothing." The same kind of judgment may be found in Proverbs 26: "As he that casteth a stone into the heap of Mercury, so is he that giveth honor to a fool." And when his fellow Brothers criticized this foolishness, John retorted: "It was I who exalted your Dominic, who had lain hidden under the earth for twelve years, and if you don't quieten down, I will destroy your saint for you, and publish your own affairs to all the world." And since they were no match for him, they had to put up with him until his death. Once when John had just had his beard shaved in a convent of the Friars Minor, he felt it a great slight that the friars did not gather his hair to preserve as relics.

The pranks of Brother Detesalve of the Order of Friars Minor.

Yet Brother Detesalve of Florence, a Friar Minor, could have stood up well to John of Vicenza, answering "a fool according to his folly" very well indeed "lest he imagine himself to be wise" [Prov. 26:5]. For he was a great prankster, as Florentines naturally are. Once when visiting the convent of the Dominicans where John of Vicenza was, he accepted lunch only on the condition that they would give him a piece of Brother John's tunic as a relic. And they did indeed give him a large piece of the tunic. Then after his meal, Detesalve withdrew to relieve his bowels and, afterward, wiped himself with the tunic and threw it down the privy. And then taking a stick, he began to stir up the excrement, shouting, "Alas, Alas, help me, Brothers! I have lost the relic of a saint in the privy, and I am searching for it." And just as they bent their heads over the privy holes, he stirred all the harder so that they might receive the full brunt of the stench. Repulsed by this malodorous mess, they blushed in shame, realizing that they had been fooled by such a prankster.

Again, when Detesalve had once been ordered to go and install himself in the convent at Penne in Apulia, he went instead to the infirmary, and, undressing himself, he cut open the pillow and hid himself all day in bed among the feathers (*pennis*). And when he was finally discovered, he insisted that he had already complied with the command. As a result of this trick, the command was revoked, and he was not required to go to Penne.

On another occasion when Detesalve was walking in Florence during the winter, he slipped on the ice and fell flat, upon which those great pranksters, the Florentines, gathered round him and began to laugh at his expense. And one of them derisively inquired whether he would not like something more underneath him, to which Detesalve retorted, "Yes, your wife." The gathering of Florentines, far from taking this reply amiss, as one might have expected, commended him, saying, "He should be blessed, for he is one of us."

Some people say, however, that this incident happened to another Florentine, a Friar Minor named Paul Thousand-flies....

2. [Later in his chronicle, Salimbene relates the story of the popular canonization of a local worker at Cremona.]

In this year occurred the deceptive miracles of a man named Albert, who was a wine carrier, or brentator, *in Cremona.*

In that same year [1279] took place the deceptive miracles of a man from Cremona named Albert, a man who had been a wine carrier (*portator*), a wine drinker (*potator*) and indeed also a sinner (*peccator*). After this man's death, according to common report, God performed many miracles in Cremona, Parma, and Reggio: in Reggio in the church of St. George and St. John the Baptist; in Parma in the church of St. Peter, which is near Piazza Nuova. And all the *brentatores*, that is, the wine carriers of Parma congregated in the church, and blessed was that man who could touch them or give them something. Women did the same. And the people formed societies, parish by parish, and marched in procession through the streets to the church of St. Peter, where the relics of this man Albert were preserved. In their march they carried crosses and standards, and sang as they marched along. And they brought purple cloth, samite, canopies, and much money to the church. Later, the wine carriers divided all these things up among themselves. And when the parish priests saw this, they had this Albert painted in their churches so that they would receive better offerings from the people. And at this time, his image was painted not only in the churches, but also on many walls and porticoes of cities villages, and castles. This, however, is expressly against the laws of the church, for no man's relics are supposed to be held in reverence unless he is first approved of by the church and written in the catalogue of saints; in similar manner, a man is not to be depicted as a saint before he has been canonized by the church. Those bishops, therefore, who allow such abuses to be practiced in their diocese merit removal from office; that is, they should have the dignities of the episcopal office taken away from them. But there is nobody to correct those errors and abuses. And so the words of Zachariah [11:17] are appropriate for every bishop who allows such things to go on: "O shepherd, and idol, that forsaketh the flock: the sword upon his arm and upon his right eye: his arm shall quite wither away, and his right eye shall be utterly darkened." Yet whoever refused to take part in such celebrations was considered to be simply envious or even heretical.

Because of this man Albert, some wicked men insulted the Friars Minor and Preachers, but God quickly "showed them to be liars" who wished to accuse them.

Some men of secular life said to the Friars Minor and Preachers with a loud, clear voice, "You think that nobody can work miracles but your own saints, but you are clearly deceived, as has been made clear through Albert." But God quickly blotted out the slander against his servants and friends by showing "them to be liars that had accused" them [Wis. 10:14] and by punishing those who "lay a blot on the elect" [Ecclus. 11:33]. For a certain man came to Parma from Cremona bearing what he claimed to be a relic of this saint Albert, that is to say, the little toe of the right foot; and all the citizens of Parma gathered together, from the highest to the lowest, men and women, "young men and maidens ... the old with the younger" [Ps. 148 (149):12], clerks and lay, and men of all religious orders. Then in a large procession, singing as they went, they carried that toe to the cathedral of Parma, the church of the glorious Virgin. And when they had placed the toe on the high altar, Lord Anselm of San Vitale, canon and vicar of the bishop, came forward and kissed it. But he smelled the stench of garlic and told the other clerks. Then they all discovered that they had been deceived and confounded, for their "relic" turned out to be a clove of garlic. And thus the Parmese were tricked and mocked, because they "walked after vanity, and are become vain" [Jer. 2:5]. Moreover, since this man Albert was buried in a church in Cremona, the Cremonese wished to show that God would work infinite miracles through him, and so large numbers of infirm men came there from Pavia and the other parts of Lombardy that "they might be delivered from their infirmities" [Acts 5:15]. And many noble ladies came with their sons to Cremona from Pavia for devotional reasons, hoping to report the complete healing of their bodies, but "there was none that would answer" [Isa. 66:4] a word, or "opened the mouth, or made the least noise" [Isa. 10:14]. Thus Jeremiah 14 says: "Are there any among the graven things of the Gentiles that can send rain or can the heavens give showers?" Thus it is that a sinner or an infirm man goes badly astray by casting aside true saints and by praying to one who cannot intercede for them, as is written in the book of Wisdom 13: "For health he maketh supplication to the weak, and for life prayeth to that which is dead, and for help calleth upon that which is unprofitable: And for a good journey he petitioneth him that cannot walk: and for getting, and for working, and for the event of all things he asketh him that is unable to do anything."

The citizens of Cremona, Parma, and Reggio were made fools of through this Albert the wine carrier, whom they believed to be holy. The same is true of the Paduans through Antonio Pellegrino, and the Ferrarese through Armanno Punzilovo. And all these things were displeasing to God.

Take note and consider well that just as the citizens of Cremona, Parma, and Reggio were made fools of at this time through this Albert the wine carrier, so had been in previous times the Paduans through Antonio Pellegrino, and the Ferrarese through Armanno Punzilovo. "But they were not of the seed of those men by whom salvation was brought to Israel," I Machabees 5. Thus the Lord says, John 5: "I am come in the name of the Father, and you receive me not: if another shall come in his own name, him you will receive." Truly, the Lord came not only in his own person, but in the blessed Francis [of Assisi], the blessed Anthony [of Padua], St. Dominic, and their sons. And sinners should believe in them in order to merit salvation. And if they do not so, they will be punished, as the Apostle says, II Thessalonians 2: "Because they receive not the love of truth, that they might be saved. Therefore God shall send them the operation of error, to believe lying: That all may be judged who have believed the truth, but have consented to iniquity."

The many reasons for this iniquity.

Here are many reasons for the devotion to this Albert: because the infirm wished to regain their health, because the curious merely wanted to see novelties, because the clerks had envy toward the modern religious orders, and because the bishops and canons wished to gain money. This latter reason is made clear in the bishop and the canons of Ferrara, for they were greatly enriched through Armanno Punzilovo. Another reason is that the exiled of the Imperial party hoped to arrive at a peace settlement with their fellow citizens through these new miracles, so that they might come again into their own and not have to travel through the world as vagabonds.

What noteworthy details of mid-thirteenth-century religious life does Salimbene offer here? What motives appear to drive lay people's devotions in this account? Who counts as "holy" in these stories?

69. PIOUS RESPONSES TO THE BLACK DEATH IN TOURNAI (1349)

The Black Death was the greatest natural catastrophe of the Middle Ages. Spreading from the Asiatic steppe, it hit Constantinople in 1347 and reached Italy the same year (probably carried by Italian merchants), where it rapidly swept across Europe, decimating large areas while leaving others unscathed. By late 1349 it had done its worst damage; by 1351 it had ebbed away. While historians still debate its death toll (and lately even its cause), most modern estimates suggest that about a third of Europe's population was carried off. Whatever the precise numbers, in barely three years, millions of people died quite suddenly and painfully of a highly contagious pathogen which medieval medicine was helpless to fight. Though some people caught the plague and survived, most victims were dead several days after the onset of symptoms. The reactions of the people of Tournai in what is now modern Belgium shed light on how a crisis – here the onslaught of epidemic disease – could affect religious perceptions and practices. Gilles le Muisis (1272-1352), abbot of the monastery of St. Martin at Tournai, left an extensive account of the course of the plague in Flanders. Writing in 1350, the 78-year-old abbot reported how the plague reached Tournai in late August, peaked in September, and tapered off by early November. In that brief time, he claimed that it killed 25,000 in Tournai alone, a figure improbably high for a fairly small medieval city. In the following excerpt from his chronicle, he describes portents of impending disaster, the annihilation of local Jews suspected of causing the epidemic, the arrival of penitent companies in Tournai, and how the people of Tournai reacted to them.

Source: trans. J. Shinners from J.-J. de Smet, *Chronica Aegidii li Muisis* in *Recueil des Chroniques de Flandre, Corpus Chronicorum Flandriae* (Brussels: M. Hayes, 1841), v. II, pp. 340-61, with some corrections from Henri LeMaître, *Chronique et Annales de Gilles le Muisit*, Société de l'Historie de France (Paris: Librairie Renouard, 1906), v. 323, pp. 221-52. Latin.

Three authorities agree [with the earlier prophecy of Master Jean de Murs (c. 1295-1348/49)] that religious sects would be destroyed, kingdoms change, prophets appear, the people rise up, novel rituals [appear], and finally [there would be] a horrid and fearful blast of winds.

In the year 1345 and in the following years 1346, 1347, and 1348, many things happened, so it appears, that the above prophecies foretold, which those then living saw come to pass. Under the year 1349, I intend to mention how the destruction of the Jews came about, the death of people from an epidemic, the arrival of people doing public penance and scourging themselves, and many other things. But it is my concern to lend credence to the above prophecies or to the predictions of astrologers and mathematicians only insofar as belief allows, always bearing in mind the Roman See and the Catholic faith.

From Christmas to Easter of 1349 I can write little about the rule of Louis [II of Male], Count of Flanders [1346-84] because the Flemish people are rash and fickle; nevertheless, the count reigned the whole time, and dispensed much justice – public and private – upon the weavers, fullers, and the others who bore themselves badly in the wars, according to what I have heard from many trustworthy people.

And I, Abbot Gilles, take stock of the many things worth recounting for the year 1349, and consider also that long ago I compiled, organized, and wrote a certain treatise about many ancient matters concerning the lord bishops of Tournai, the town itself, and the wars between the kings of France and England and Flanders from long past. In this treatise, many things are included up to today, the time of the young Louis, Count of Flanders, who married the daughter of the Duke of Brabant and came into Flanders. The Flemish people welcomed the count and countess peacefully and continually not just for a day but for several days interspersed. From the time of their arrival, the country of Flanders was quiet, and there was little news about the wars between the kings of England and France. Merchants went safely to their markets, though the devalued currency circulating in France weakened their trade. As a result, everyone in common – rich, middling, and poor – complained bitterly about and were afflicted by the shortage of grain, wine, and all other victuals since those who worked profited little or not at all. A measure of grain sold for thirty sous of devalued coin, and wine for two sous; everything cost more because of the devalued currency.

In 1349 there were many reports and widespread rumors that the Jewish race was trying to destroy the Christian people, if they could, by casting poison into springs, wells, and water supplies.

 In addition, from spreading rumors and the reports of travelers and merchants who routinely visited these distant lands, there was reliable news about a mortality that began in the East and had spread over the Indies and all the territories of the Christians, pagans, Saracens, and other peoples, from the east to the north and the south. It was so bad that in many places a third, in many other places a quarter to a half of the people died; in many areas only one or two in ten were left alive. In a number of places the fields and vineyards lay uncultivated. Astrologers were saying that this disaster was caused by the conjunction of certain planets and stars which corrupted the air; this corruption of the air generated a malady, which they called an epidemic.

There were widespread rumors that in the cities, towns, hamlets, castles, and country villages of Hungary, Germany, and the duchy of Brabant, people were stirring one another up and gathering in groups of sometimes two hundred, sometimes three hundred, sometimes five hundred or more depending on the locality's population. For thirty-three days they went through their lands twice a day, barefoot, naked but for breeches, wearing hoods, and whipping themselves with scourges until the blood flowed. Finally they arrived in Flanders. But I want to point out that I cannot prove the truth of this matter, how and why it began, and what its purpose was, since I have found no one who could give me information about these things. Later I intend to mention the deeds I myself have seen and heard.

The seizure and destruction of the Jews.

In 1349 the Jews were all seized and put into jails and prisons wherever they lived. The reason for their arrest was the grave suspicion that they were maliciously attempting to destroy the Christian people by poison; that, whenever they could, they had secretly tossed poison into wells, springs, and water supplies. They did this in many places, or so news and rumor in general had it. Furthermore, there were some members of their religion – discerning and learned astrologers – who made predictions for them that, according to the course of the stars, at a future time there would be death on a large scale. Because of this prediction, they hoped to achieve their evil purpose more surely and insidiously. They also saw by the course of the stars that one religious sect would be destroyed – they hoped that it would be the Christian one. They further predicted that people would appear wearing red crosses, which set them wondering whether their own sect would be destroyed. They said many other things that it would take too long to repeat.

Now in the kingdom of France since the time of St. Louis the king [1226–70] there had been few if any Jews. But in other kingdoms and regions all those who were found there were seized, so it is said, and it was put to them what they intended to do. Many of them denied it, but others confessed their plan. I cannot say in truth what happened to them in distant regions, but it was rumored that all over Germany and in other regions they were either burned, beheaded, or killed in various other ways. It is a fact that in the counties of Lotharingia and Bari all who were found there were burned.

In the duchy of Brabant, in the town called Brussels, lived the Duke of Brabant [John III, 1312–55] and his eldest son. In that town was one very wealthy Jew. This man had known the duke for a long time, and the duke loved him very much and confided in him, since this Jew pretended that he was baptized. Seeing men arriving in the town doing penance and carrying red crosses, he went to the duke and said, "My lord, because these men have appeared doing such things, it is a certainty that I and the whole Jewish sect will be destroyed wherever we are found." The duke told him, "Don't be afraid. I don't know a man alive who would try to destroy you." But he responded, "O good duke, you cannot undo this, for it is ordained from on high."

In the town there were a large number of Jews. The duke, out of friendship for this Jew and for a price, aimed to defend them and guard them from death. But the commune and the inhabitants of the town, hearing the rumor about the poison, went to the duke's son wishing to have all the Jews destroyed, but not daring to do this since his father, the duke, wanted to protect them. Yet in spite of his father's wish, this eldest son, out of his love for the Catholic faith, goaded them on and ordered them to kill them all: afterwards he would make peace between them and his father. So the town's commune and its inhabitants sought out the Jews everywhere, slaughtering whomever they could find. It was reported that more than six hundred people were slain, but the wealthy Jew was captured alive. He acknowledged that he had received baptism unfaithfully, had consented to spreading the poison, and that the Jews had intended to do this because they trusted the message of the stars, hoping that the Jews would prevail. He also acknowledged that he had unworthily received the body of our Lord Jesus Christ at the altar three times; he then sent these three hosts to the Jews living in Cologne, who had pricked them and blood flowed from them [see Doc. 18]. He admitted many other horrible things, which the knights and other faithful people assisting them reported. (I say this by word of mouth, since I was not present.) Finally he was sentenced and burned. During that time in many towns in the duchy of Brabant and in other counties and duchies, justice was rendered against them.

I should not omit what happened in the city of Cologne [in 1349], which is the metropolitan see. In this city there were a large number of Jews. They had an area set aside for them and streets where they lived separated from the Christians. It happened that many Jews, fleeing other places where they were being put to death, came to Cologne and stayed there with other Jews. Thus, there was a vast multitude of Jews there. Seeing this, the citizens and inhabitants of Cologne took counsel and, as in other places, decided to destroy them. But the Jews protected themselves, searching out and arming themselves with the weapons that they held as pledges for loans made to Christians. Many resisted manfully. The citizens and other inhabitants were not strong enough to overcome them; they hesitated to set their houses on fire since that might burn down the whole city. But it happened that the butchers and many others from the city feigned sympathy for the Jews and allied themselves with them. One day the Jews prepared to attack with the help of these people; but the Christians, knowing this, held back and there was a huge battle there. Through God's will the Jews were defeated. They generally say that more than 25,000 Jews were slain; but many of the Christians were cut down and died. The Jewish neighborhood and its dwellings were pulled down; its houses were burned to ashes. The Christians took this victory.

What has been written above about the destruction of the Jews – how and in what manner they were destroyed in which places – must suffice for my readers since on the feast of All Saints [Nov. 1] 1349 news about them ceased. And if those who told me these stories were speaking the truth, then I am not fabricating in putting this into writing. But if the contrary proves true, posterity should not put the blame on me because I did not witness this event, I was told about it.

In the year 1349 sometimes people spoke falsely, sometimes truthfully. But it seems appropriate to me to make some mention of things that happened that are not true or are doubtful.

Since one cannot avoid evil unless it is first recognized, and since the human senses are prone to sin from the age of adolescence, and since men and women easily believe often dubious things professing them to be true, some things that happen ought not be regarded as true, since a thing is designated by its end, and if its end is good, the whole thing is good. But many things happen that on the face of it appear to be true.

In 1349 in the village called Houtaing near Tournai there was a girl about fourteen years old. She said that while she was watching her parents' cows she often saw certain people – women – dressed in white clothing, who spoke to her. She told her father, mother, and brothers and sisters what these people said to her and about the writings they showed her, teaching her lessons about [the magic power of] words and herbs. The girl began to work wonders, so much so that great numbers of people feeble, blind, or paralyzed poured around her, putting unthinking faith in her. She came to the notice of the bishop, the reverend father Lord Jean [de Pratis], at that time bishop of Tournai, who sent his official to her (accompanied by the dean of the cathedral of Notre Dame at Tournai and by lawyers and other skilled and learned clerics) to examine her and the works she had done. They reported that the girl was a half-wit who knew nothing, not even the Our Father and the Hail Mary, though she was impetuous in her words and in her answers to them. But since crowds of men and women alike were putting faith in the girl's deeds and calling what she said and did miraculous, the lord bishop, after careful and serious deliberation, silenced the girl and her parents, and ordered them to stop their undertaking. Obeying him, they ceased, and immediately there were no more rumors about her.

That same year in the village of Beclers near Tournai in the diocese of Cambrai there was a married woman who was being paid to nurse another woman's infant. This woman said that one night while her husband was away she got up before dawn to tend to some necessities. Going back to her room, she saw, so it seemed, a great light over the sleeping infant, and, thoroughly terrified, she heard, or so it seemed to her, a voice saying to her, "I am the Blessed Mary and I give notice to you and to all people that my Son is angry and there is a great disturbance upon his people." When morning came this woman sought the advice of her curate who took her to Tournai where she spoke to the dean of the cathedral, to Brother Gerard de Mur, and to Brother Robert de Paris, who examined her and found no validity to her story though there had been great rumor and various opinions among the people about this. She effectively dropped the whole matter.

Also that year in the parish church of Blessed Mary Magdalene at Tournai there was great excitement among the men and women because an image of the crucified Lord Jesus Christ in the church, which many saw, was said to have sweated and a large number of drops had fallen from it. This was reputed to be a miracle and a great part of the town poured into the church to see it. This opinion held sway for a few days, but in a brief time it was completely disregarded and forgotten.

In that year too, after these other events, in the leper-house of Vaulx outside the town walls there happened to be a certain image of the glorious Virgin. Many men and women maintained that they had seen it sweating and crying. This rumor instantly swept through the town and without interruption a huge crowd of people came there. Egging each other on in turn, they professed that the glorious Virgin had worked a miracle there. Such things happened at Tournai and in many other places. The people for the most part believed in them, reputing them to be miracles. It would take too long to describe such matters to those disinclined to believe quickly; therefore let this suffice for future [readers], and let them reflect on such things, since perhaps other people have made mention of them in their writings.

A narrative about those people who – through the cities, towns, hamlets, castles and other places, in companies now numbering a hundred, now two or three hundred, now more numerous still – banded together and went about doing public penance in 1349.

God knows how to change his verdicts if you know how to correct your mistakes. I would have been oppressed had I not known your mercy, Lord; for you said, "I desire not the death of the wicked, but that the wicked turn from his way, and live" [Ezek. 33:11]. And you, O good Jesus, said with your own holy and blessed mouth, "Learn from me for I am meek and humble of heart" [Matt. 11:29]. And "Come to me all you who labor and are burdened, and I will give you rest" [Matt. 11:28]. Therefore let sinners look into their heart, and may he who has stumbled look inward so that he may rise up, and let he who has sinned cease, because this is true contrition, and its definition is to weep for the past and, by weeping, to sin no more. For the time to repent is nigh, and when it comes to time, we have only the present. So let sinners hurry to penance while they have time.

[*Underlined in red:*] *Penance, however, should be prudent, reasonable, within proper limits, and undertaken at the will of a superior having the power to enjoin penance; because what is done without the authority and will of a superior should be regarded as presumptuous and vainglorious, not compensatory.*

In 1349, therefore, those living heard and saw marvelous things, and it seems appropriate to me to make it known to all future generations, since at the time all sane-minded people were absolutely dumbfounded by the various things that happened and by the changes in the times and in the people. It is a fact that at the beginning of the year, just after Lent and immediately before Easter Sunday, everyone – men and women, cleric and lay – fell into such a disordered state of every excess that it was a horrible thing to see, especially for those who remembered bygone times. This happened the world over and it would be hard to put it into words; for what can I say about the way people dressed and adorned themselves? Men wore clothes so close-fitting and short that their crotches were visible underneath, which was shameless. Lewd and lascivious women gladly looked at them nonetheless, since all human acts tend toward lust.

And what should I say about the lewd women? They copied the image and likeness of men in their dress and adornments, wearing dresses so tight that their close fit revealed the shapes of their naked bodies. They decorated their heads with wigs and with hair shaped into beast-like horns, and then they walked through the streets and lanes to their churches. Whenever the occasion arose they went to funerals, divine services, sermons, and any other place dressed as if they were attending a wedding feast. Through such fashions they seemed to be goading men on to look at them, not only by the way they dressed but by everything they did. They had no regard for the scripture that says "She is chaste whom no one has sought after," since through a nod, a laugh, a glance, they provoked men. It would take too long to describe their lewdness, their lustful songs, their fashion-bound dancing, music-making, and fads. Sad to say, I cannot totally exclude the clergy from these abuses, woe to the church! It seems that the time has arrived about which it is said: "as are the people, so are the priests" [Isa. 24:2]. The change in things is everywhere apparent, and everyone should reflect on this in his or her heart and make a decision about it. For the holy virgin Hildegard of Bingen [1098-1179] says in one of her letters to a clergyman, "They too have a voice, but they do not shout; they are given work but they do not do it: they want glory without merit and merit without work." But let him who wants glory cut himself off from his property. Let him who craves merit with God produce the work fit for it. For an overseer looks down from on high; hidden yet watchful, he is a strong yet merciful judge.

How utterly incredible! And I dare say that although the noble classes – men and their wives, and their sons and daughters – and some of the lower nobility and their offspring acted in the manner just mentioned, people of inferior station and poor people not only wanted but tried to act this way too. It happened that children, young people, and women, seeing these novelties, wanted to imitate them, so much so that the clothes on their backs and the jewels that many men and women wore in public were worth more than the houses they lived in. And so the vices mushroomed: pride, greed, anger, envy, gluttony, and lust and things of their ilk. But preachers – prelates and genuinely holy men, religious mendicants and learned men – seeing the world so universally snared in the vices, preached in churches and other fitting places, constantly proclaiming the Divine Word, praising virtue and damning vice. Yet they had little success, for as it is written: "the people sat down to eat, and drink, and they rose up to play" [Exod. 32:6], and examples do more good than words. The people's heart was not right with God; but he is merciful and will be kind toward sins. And that year he showed this, because the Most High changed his hand. As the vices boiled hot and swelled, the Lord summoned a fitting remedy. For after the aforementioned news about the destruction of the Jews, news grew about the penitents which I will mention. In Tournai there was no rumble of news except about the condemnation of the Jews and about the ritual of penitence that had already begun in Flanders. Yet people were not paying any attention to it the way they later did so that they would not have to correct their vices. But at the beginning of August or thereabout, people in some of the parishes started falling sick and dying.

The first appearance in Tournai of people doing penance.

That year [1349] on the feast day of the Assumption of the glorious Virgin [Aug. 15], it happened that around dinnertime about two hundred people arrived from the town of Bruges. They gathered in the town square. Immediately the news was all over town so that everyone went there. They came in large gangs to the square because they had heard the news and now aimed to see what was happening. In the meantime the people from Bruges had prepared themselves and started performing their ritual, which they called penitence. Everyone, men and women alike, who had never seen such a sight, began to suffer with these people and feel the pain of their penitence; they gave thanks to God for such penitence, which they considered most severe. The people from Bruges stayed in the town that whole day and night. The next day, which was a Sunday, they gathered at the monastery of St. Martin where they performed their penitential exercise, and then after dinner they went back out into the square. During those two days, the whole community felt compassion for these penitents, though there were differences of opinion. Some sane-minded people did not commend them; others could not approve their deed more highly.

On the following Tuesday, a common procession of the cathedral's dean and chapter, the clergy, and all the people went to our monastery of St. Martin, where the Franciscan brother Gerard de Mur preached the word of God about the coming plague. Preaching splendidly, rebuking the vices, and condemning the habits of men and women, he reprimanded them most sharply. But at the end of his sermon he neglected to pray for penitents like those from Bruges; consequently, the greater part of the audience was indignant and for that whole week people griped variously about him. That same week a great company of around 450 came from Ghent, and another company of about 300 from the town of Sluis on the sea, plus another company of 400 from around Dordrecht, who did the same kind of public penance twice a day, sometimes in the town square, sometimes in the courtyard of the monastery of St. Martin.

That Saturday, the feast of the beheading of John the Baptist [Aug. 29], a band of about 180 people came from Liège accompanied by a Dominican friar. On that day and the next – a Sunday – they remained doing their penance like the others. The friar obtained a license from the dean and chapter to preach the word of God in the same place where Brother Gerard had preached, at the monastery of St. Martin of Tournai. News about this spread throughout the city. Such a multitude of men and women gathered there as Tournai had never seen – there was scarcely a place in the monastery to put them all. The Dominican friar began to preach on the text "Unless the grain of wheat falls into the ground and dies, etc." [John 12:24]. Speaking about many things, he came to about the middle of his sermon. Then he got down to the matter of those with whom he had come who were doing penance. He called their company Red Knights; he accused the mendicant friars of preaching against the piety of those undertaking penance and said that for as many as they persuaded to stop, they persuaded an equal number to take up penance. He called such friars scourges and Antichrists, even comparing the blood of those they called the Red Knights to the blood of our Lord Jesus

Christ – or so many understood him to say. He also said that, since the shedding of our Savior's blood, there had not been such a noble outpouring of
blood as there was from those who now shed it while scourging themselves.
He said many other things that bordered on error, which some who were
there wrote down. When he finished his sermon the community was pleased
beyond measure and nearly all of them began to gripe against the mendicant
orders and even against all the clergy.

But the dean and chapter who, since the see was vacant [Bishop Jean de
Pratis had died of plague early that summer.], were acting in the capacity of
the bishop, convoked a gathering of religious mendicants and learned men,
together with those who had transcribed the words of the friar's sermon and
many other judicious and respected men. They consulted with them about the
propositions and statements in the friar's sermon and they deliberated over it.
Then they issued a proclamation that all the clergy and other religious and all
the people should assemble on that coming Tuesday in order to make a procession barefoot and shirtless; the procession should go as far as the parish church
of St. Catherine and then return to the monastery of St. Martin where the
word of God would be preached. In the procession the lord dean and another
canon priest would carry the most holy sacrament of the Body of our Lord
Jesus Christ. And so they all assembled at the monastery; but it was not like it
had been the preceding Sunday, for Brother Robert, an Austin friar, preached
the word of God. Taking for his subject the deaf-mute healed by our Lord
Jesus Christ [Mark 7:32-36], he expounded it most eloquently and ingeniously,
praising the virtues and reproaching the vices. At the end of his sermon, when
he was making the customary commendations and prayers, he neglected to
pray for those doing public penance. Afterwards he said, "O good folk, I was
charged to speak to you about the brother who preached here last Sunday, for
he spoke words that touched on the faith, expressing various opinions and,
among other things, making a comparison between the blood of our Lord
Jesus Christ and those people who are scourging themselves in public." But
before he could make his point, against all reason and custom some people
rose up shouting "Sir, you are badly informed. The friar did not say this in his
sermon." And instantly all the men and women started protesting and shouting, all at once saying that the friar had not said this in his sermon. Imposing
silence with great difficulty, however, Brother Robert spoke, wishing to calm
the people: "I told you what my charge was, but you hold to the opposite
view. Still, don't let keeping the faith displease you, for it's time for you to
observe peace and tranquility among everyone." But his soothing words had
little effect because the people stood up grumbling and egging each other on,
saying that these things were typical of the mendicant orders. And that whole
day there was huge unrest throughout the town over the mendicant orders and

the clergy in general. But on the following Sunday there was another common procession at the monastery. There, with the mayors and town leaders present, Brother Robert delivered a sermon which calmed the people down a bit.

It should not be overlooked that this same rascal Dominican preached things similar to what he said at Tournai and more at the town of Valenciennes, so that afterwards some scholarly clerics opposed him; but because of the company with which he traveled, they abandoned their effort to change his ways.

How those at Tournai, like others, prepared themselves to perform public penance.

Our Savior, the Lord Jesus Christ, when he washed the feet of his disciples at the Last Supper, said to them, "I have given you an example, that as I have done to you, so you also should do" [John 13:15]. This is the path of humility. And if we should follow the example of good people, we should especially follow our Creator's example, for actions speak louder than words, and the words and examples of our Savior Jesus Christ are all any of us need as a remedy. Thus, many of the people of Tournai who saw the method of penance of the visiting penitents began to grow so devout that about 565 men or so gradually gathered together and made a mutual pact with the permission of the town's leaders. They proposed to leave the town and follow the example of the other penitents for thirty-three days once they had made all their necessary arrangements. They departed the town on a Monday [Sept. 7], the eve of the feast of the birth of the glorious Virgin; but before they left they performed their first act of penance in the town square, where a huge crowd of people had gathered. Leaving the city, they traveled toward Lille. On the day they returned – a Saturday [Oct. 10], the day after the feast of the martyr St. Denis – they did their penance in the town square. The next day on Sunday the whole company went to Mont-Saint-Aubert, performing their usual ritual both coming and going. It is true that it was rumored that, when they left, they went through France all the way to Soissons; but how they traveled, through what places or towns they passed, and how they behaved themselves it is not my concern to know or to describe – let them render their own account to God and the world. Their leaders and captains were prudent men elected by the consent of the whole company: the knight Jean de Liancourt, Jean Mackes, Jean Wauckiers, and Jacob de Maulde representing Willem Pestiel at the behest of the mayors and town leaders. The prior of the house of Austin friars, accompanied by a fellow friar, went with them with two other secular priests to hear confessions and administer the sacraments if needed. And one of the canons of St. Nicholas-de-Prés, called Gilles the monk, kept company with them by his own choice.

In a marvelous and indescribable way, lay men and women reached such levels of piety during that time that it is scarcely believable. For many men and women by divine instinct – may God give it – changed their manner of dress and their adornments, and many women changed their hairstyles, casting off their horns and knots; they dropped their accustomed swear words that deform Jesus Christ and his Passion, the Virgin Mary, and all the saints; they abandoned dice-playing and their other games where the dice roll; they completely forsook dancing, lewd songs, and many trivial and dishonorable things that were their wont. Even rumors about men and women fornicating and committing adultery stopped circulating. And may the God of Israel preserve this goodwill and give us the grace of perseverance. For it is commendable that, due to those doing penance and to their example, many people forgave or excused ongoing quarrels between them; this happened at Tournai and in many other places.

It is also noteworthy that, although there was a great movement of people doing penance during that time, this did not occur anywhere in France nor in other more northern kingdoms and territories except in Flanders, Hainaut, Brabant, and other places lying westward.

While I was writing the above, the prediction of Master Jean de Murs came to mind: how he said that, where there was a conjunction of stars and planets among other things, there would be destruction of religious sects, an uprising of the people, new kinds of rituals, and an epidemic. It seems to me that in 1349 these things happened for the most part, just as we have heard and seen at Tournai; for the Jews, wherever they were found among Christians, were destroyed through various tortures. Furthermore, the advent of penitence and those doing penance stirred people everywhere to great dissension since some people maintained that their deeds should not be condoned because they had not received approval from the Roman curia. The king of France even had his *baillis* publicly proclaim everywhere that no one should admit these penitents. I also heard from a trustworthy person that he had seen at Avignon two thousand such penitents from Germany who wished to have their practices and those of others endorsed by the pope and curia. At the end of the day they were told that they should leave, otherwise they would face ecclesiastical censure; and so the next day and the day following all of them disappeared.

Due to these things and others that reason dictated, churchmen and other sane-minded and learned men held that, according to the Catholic faith, since the church had not consented and canon law prohibited it, their practices should not be approved. But the people – both men and women alike, those ignorant of Scripture, high-born and low – approved the practice beyond measure, especially in the regions mentioned above. And so there was remarkable and pointless dissension, and people everywhere blamed the mendicant orders in particular for setting up obstacles against them. But who could doubt that this was a new kind of ritual since they did their penance in churches, monasteries, and other holy places, where by law no violent shedding of blood whatsoever is allowed? And even when divine services or private masses were being said in churches, they paid no attention and did not interrupt their ritual. The greater part of the common people approved more of their penitential rites than they did of the divine services, calling them praiseworthy. Since there was such a transmutation of bad into good with their advent, as described above, churchmen who held to their conviction were quite often laughed at. Such was the common people's opinion that they claimed that miracles happened in many places by virtue of their penitence.

Since a man does not know whether he is more worthy of love than hate, therefore God is our judge, for the Lord's judgments are a great deep [Ps. 35 (36):7]. I hesitate, for this ritual now grew (and grows) so much in many places through companies or people banding together who perform such novelties and practices contrary to approved custom, that it is horrible to contemplate or speak of. For – omitting other towns, villages, and places – I refer only to Tournai, since, when these penitents first arrived, they performed penance there for thirty-three days. But now, banding together through the parishes, they perform their ritual both on the Sabbath and on feast days in the cathedral church of Notre Dame and in other churches, often interrupting divine services though the clergy do not dare criticize them due to pressure from the community. And what is more, it has spread and is a remarkable novelty because these penitents had a remarkable beginning. It is no longer proper to approach the cathedral canons and parish curates to collect the bodies of the dead, carry them to cemeteries, and bury them (as is reasonable and customary) since now the companies of penitents with cross and candle collect them, carry them, and bury them – and often induce those dying to make donations to them customarily given to curates, chaplains, hospitals, or the poor. And I dare say that from their arrival before Christmas of 1349, these and many other things have happened in Tournai.

And since man sees the surface but God sees into the heart, since the things I have mentioned are unusual novelties, and since our Savior said, "Pass no judgment before the time" [1 Cor. 4:5], I therefore commit to Divine Wisdom and Majesty the advantage and honor of Holy Mother Church, the practices of faith and Christianity, and the progress of souls. For I do not know how to describe or entrust to the future such innovations and the things that happened in these days.

The numbers of people, the names of their towns, and when they arrived as mentioned above, as it was reported to me.

On September 12, 120 people came from Tienen in Brabant; that same day, 80 came from the town of Sluis.

On the eve [Sept. 7] of the feast of the birth of the Blessed Mary, about 50 came from Damme.

On the feast of the birth of the Blessed Mary [Sept. 8] about 200 came from Enghien.

The day after the feast, about 160 came from the town of Namur, and about 150 from Bruges.

On the eve of the procession at Tournai [Sept. 7] about 80 came from Nieuwpoort. That same day, about 52 came from the town of Eeklo; about 300, in two companies, from Bruges; and about 100 from Damme.

On the day of the procession, about 50 came from Cassel.

The day after the procession about 250 came from Sluis; about 100 from the town of Deynze; and about 60 from Diksmuide.

On the eve of the feast of St. Matthew [Sept. 20], about 240 came from the town of Mons-en-Hainaut.

That same day, about 300 came from Oudenaarde; about 120 from Genappe; and about 200 from Lille.

On the feast of St. Matthew [Sept. 21], about twenty women came from Flanders, whipping themselves in same way as the men, but uncovering only their backs.

The Sunday after the feast of St. Matthew [Sept. 27], about 200 came from the town of Maubeuge; that same day, about 300 came from Bailleul in Flanders.

On October 3, the eve of the feast of St. Francis, about 450 came from Valenciennes.

Note that I learned from some of the leaders chosen by the penitents that those joining the penitent companies promised to do and observe to the best of their ability the following things (which were first read to them) for as long as they lived, otherwise they were not admitted. First, those joining made this promise, saying, "We swear to avoid every occasion of sin to the best of our ability, and to make general confession and contrition for all the sins we remember. We swear to make a last testament or some provision for our possessions, to pay or assign our debts, and to make restitution for borrowed goods. We will be peaceful, make amends, and show kindness. We will lay down our bodies and possessions to defend, maintain, and guard the rights of the holy church in its honor, liberty, faith, doctrine, and law. Recognizing that we are all created from the same kind of matter, redeemed by one ransom, endowed with one gift, we should address each other as 'brother' and no one shall call his comrade by his given name." Those joining should seek permission from their curate and receive their cross from him; they should seek permission from their lawful wives; and they should make themselves obedient to another's [authority]. They should discipline themselves for thirty-three and a half days, sitting on an uncushioned chair, sleeping without bed-clothes or pillows, keeping silent unless given permission to speak, receiving charity but seeking it from no one, entering houses only with the permission of their hosts, and upon entering or leaving saying five Our Fathers and five Hail Marys. Every morning they should say fifteen Our Fathers and fifteen Hail Marys, and fifteen more later on: five while kneeling before dinner, five after dinner, and five at night. They should wash their hands while kneeling on the ground before dinner, and they should not speak at the table unless given permission. "You shall not swear oaths on the Lord's Passion, nor blaspheme for the rest of your life insofar as you can. Every Friday you shall keep a Lenten fast if you can and you shall have life [Luke 10:28]; and on Good Friday you shall scourge yourself at three times only during the day and night for the length of time it takes you to say five Our Fathers and five Hail Marys. If any of our brothers disagrees with another brother, calling him a liar or quarrelsome, he will make amends at the discretion of our confessors. You shall not bear arms, nor fight in battle for anyone other than your true Lord. No one will be entrusted with [carrying] the [processional] cross while walking, sitting, or lying down who does not have a tunic or a hood. No one, healthy or ill, may depart the company without permission, nor sit at table without permission. No one shall scourge himself so much that he becomes sick or dies. You should give alms to the poor to the extent you can. No one should refuse alms given to him out of love of God, unless he is rich or a nobleman. You should persistently fix your heart and mouth in praise and penance and pray for all holy Christianity that God will put an end to this plague and be lenient to us for our sins. If anyone violates these measures or complains about them, he should amend himself at the discretion of a superior confessor, and he who is found persevering to the end is privileged by God's grace to reign in glory. If any of the brothers quits during a session of public scourging, each of them shall be obliged to scourge himself for the length of time it takes to say fifteen Our Fathers and fifteen Hail Marys. We wish each one to be required to put his penitential habit and his scourge on his bed, in order to keep in mind the passion of our Lord Jesus Christ. You should especially require yourself to abstain from all meat for the rest of your life, to keep your marriage vows sacred, and not to swear in vain. Also, everyone should be careful not to eat meat on Wednesday."

All of these things that the initiates promised obviously appear to be honest and devout things if their heart matched their words, if they persevered, and if Holy Mother Church consented and gave her authority. Since God – who says, "Without me, you can do nothing" [John 15:5] – alone knows the secrets of the heart [Ps. 43 (44):22], it is not my concern to approve or reprove them. As Augustine says, "I neither praise nor condemn daily [reception of communion]." And wise Seneca says "Praise little, blame even less." Thus, I yield judgment to God most high and to Holy Mother Church since if something is good in its end, everything coming from it will be good. It is, nevertheless, my intention to write an account for the future's notice because no one in past times has ever seen the penitents' methods, the way they dressed, and how they acted while doing penance. Many people have written or spoken about where and why this movement began, but I have never been able to get sure proof from anyone about these questions. I can only record what happened in Tournai since I do not know the truth of what happened in distant places.

Here was the procedure when companies of two or three hundred, sometimes more, sometimes less, had gathered. It was their practice to wear over their clothes a sleeveless tunic called a *cloche* [a bell-shaped cloak] in the vernacular. On the front of the tunic was a red cross on the breast and a similar cross on the back. It was cut on one side and hanging there were lashes (*scorpiones*) – what we call scourges (*scorgies*) in the vernacular – that had three tips on them, each iron tip spiked with four needle-like points. They wore hoods on their heads and on top of them a cap on which was sewn a red cross front and back; they carried penitentiary staves in their hands. Entering the town they carried a cross, banners, and wax torches as they were able, some more, some fewer, and they went in order, singing in their native language – Flemings in Flemish, Brabantines in German, French in French. When they arrived before the image of Blessed Mary in the cathedral church they stopped singing. Afterwards they assembled in the town square or in the courtyard of St. Martin's. They went into a private room or some other fitting place and stripped off their clothes and shoes, leaving someone behind to look after them until they returned. Then they came to the place with their heads covered by their hoods and the caps over them, their feet bare, and their bodies naked except for a cloth covering, like the kind bakers wear when they work. They wrapped this garment, which reached to the ground, completely around them over their breeches and cinched it at their waist. In their hands they held their scourges. When they reached a suitable street, it was their custom to process carrying crosses and banners following each other in order according to their numbers and the size of the place. Then they started forming a circle and singing chants in their native language, which appointed singers began while the others responded in unison. Chanting and responding they made a circle and the chanters and responders whipped themselves. The hymn was such that they were required to prostrate themselves three times. When they reached the first verse, they all fell to the ground at the same time and, stretching their arms out at their sides, made the shape of a cross. Getting up on their knees, they variously tormented themselves with the scourges, so much so that those seeing them were astonished and wept and felt compassion for their suffering. They did this a second and a third time, the chanters (who were curates or religious mendicants of the various orders) singing in the middle of the circles that each led. After they had finished making these circles and punishing themselves with prostrations and beatings, after they had ended their chanting, they all knelt and one of the priests among them offered commendations and prayers, just as if he were in church at funeral rites or the end of a sermon. All of them stayed kneeling until he had finished his commendations and prayers. It was most pious and terrible for those present to see what prostrations and punishments they inflicted on themselves. When everything was over, they stood up and, singing about the Blessed Virgin in their own language, they went back and put on their clothes. Many finished their chants before the image of the Blessed Virgin in some other place prior to dressing. One should not overlook that some bands underwent various kinds of torments, some more than others. After all this was done, they all went, rich and poor alike, into the town's streets, hoping that someone would invite or ask them to his house. Those who received invitations or summons went with the permission of their superiors, who remained with those uninvited until they had been asked to someone's house. None of them could eat or stay at one place more than once; they could stay longer at their own expense, but they had to obey the above ordinances. When the weather was pleasant and dry, they performed this ceremony in the public streets; when it rained, they did it in churches, cloisters, or other covered places. What sane person, according to the predictions of Master Jean de Murs, would not say that these things were a new kind of ritual and an advent of prophets?

Concerning the devotion of the people of Tournai – men, women, and outsiders – at the feast of the procession which is customarily celebrated on the day of the exaltation of the Holy Cross [Sept. 14]; in these days there was a terrible plague in the town that grew worse daily.

I dare say in all honesty that in my whole life I have not known, heard of, or seen such peace and such piety among the whole people on the night and day of the [annual] procession as there were this year. Bear in mind that two hundred and fifty or more men had gathered at Tournai, mutually associating and coming together, so that on the day of the procession and on the following eight days they did penance in the manner of those who had departed Tournai. Everyone who arrived met with Brother Robert, a lector at the house of Austin friars, who was their leader for these nine days. But it was his order that each day they make a circuit of the town without a cross, banners, or tapers, all of them wearing (as was explained above) a hood on their heads, and over that a black cap without a cross, holding scourges in their hands, barefoot and naked except for a breechcloth over which they wore a cloth garment tied at the waist, as described above. On the day of the procession they gathered in the church of Blessed Mary where they heard mass in St. Louis's chapel; during the whole mass two candles burned. When it was time for the procession to exit the church and go around the town, those who had prepared took off their clothes and put on the penitential garb. As was the custom, first came the mendicant clergy, then the companies of canons and monks, then a company of citizens – called squires – carrying the reliquary of the Blessed Mary in the usual way. They were barefoot and bore themselves devoutly. Behind these, led by Brother Robert, followed the band of penitents two by two without any ornaments, dressed in the aforementioned way and whipping themselves with scourges as much as their appointed leaders permitted so that they would not inflict too much pain or shed blood unduly. Of the two candles in the church, one was left burning before the Blessed Virgin's image, the other at the entrance to the cloister until the whole procession had returned and then each one was put back in its proper place.

The course of the eight days following the procession was such that each morning they assembled in the chapel of St. Michael and heard mass with two candles burning. After mass they undressed in the refectory, put on their penitential garb as mentioned, and, going down the steps, went before the image of the Blessed Virgin where, kneeling, they said the Our Father and the Hail Mary. And then walking two by two they circled the town whipping themselves as mentioned while the two candles were left in the aforesaid spots. Returning in the same order, everyone put their clothes back on and then went about their business.

When the nine days of processions ended, on the tenth day the greater part of the band heard morning mass dressed in their penitential habits and then went to Mont-Saint-Aubert and returned bearing themselves most devoutly and whipping themselves a little bit. I cannot find the words to describe the devotion of the people during those days, since many of them performed this penance going to Mont-Saint-Aubert over the space of thirty-three days.

Nor should one forget that in those days in the country of Hainaut and in the surrounding parishes there was a great movement of all the people, because they came in parish groups and bands carrying the cross, banners, and candles to Mont-Saint-Aubert, and the word of God was preached there. I have heard from those who were present that one day more than ten thousand people came together there.

Future readers should realize that if I wanted to record all the things going on around the penitents during that time and what was happening day to day, I would neither have the know-how nor the ability to do it. I believe and maintain that many people have been recording these deeds in both Latin and French; I have recorded what I have seen and heard.

Note that in that year Christmas was on a Friday, which was the beginning of the year according to style of the Roman curia. Thus it was a jubilee year and the indulgence ordained by the lord Pope Clement VI began [see Doc. 64.1]. Many evils ceased; and many things were reported that I do not think it right to pass on to the future until the truth about them is known. I thus put an end to my account.

That same year [in fact, 1350], in the first week of Lent, the town's governors proclaimed in the public square that everyone should cease performing public penance voluntarily undertaken; anyone doing otherwise would be banished for the rest of his days. The king also proclaimed that everyone should cease under pain of death and loss of goods, since the king declared [the penitents] a sect in his letters. This was also done with the common consent of the lord bishop of Tournai, the deans, the chapter, and the governors of the town. For in the second week of Lent on the eve of the feast of St. Peter's Chair [Feb. 22] in the cathedral church of Notre Dame, Tournai, the word of God was preached. With a huge number of people gathered there, the curate of St. Piat gave a sermon. He proclaimed the mandate of the lord pope about the penitents, but he did not show a copy of the bull itself, which caused people to complain greatly. In his sermon the curate announced a general indulgence issued from Rome at the basilicas of the blessed apostles Peter and Paul by the lord pope and his college. From that day these penitents, with great grumbling, reluctantly stopped.

How did the crisis of the Plague affect popular piety? Which elements of this account seem to be routine religious practices and which a reaction to the crisis? How did the Plague affect relations between clergy and laity? What features of the crisis most rivet Abbot Gilles's attention? What or whom does he think caused the Plague?

CHAPTER NINE: ERROR

Wherever there is orthodoxy, there will be error, willing or unintended. As conscientious as church leaders tried to be about educating both the clergy and the laity in basic Christian doctrine, their efforts were always uphill. Because the church's tools and opportunities for catechetical instruction were limited and its target audience often isolated and poorly educated, the typical medieval believer had a shaky grasp of what was orthodox, what was mistaken, and what was downright heretical. By and large the religious life of ordinary people, lay and clergy alike, was a pretty sturdy fabric of basic Christian dogma colorfully interwoven with strands of extra-Christian belief and local adaptations of Christianity, many of which would have failed theological scrutiny. Unintentional error could be undone through diligent preaching and correction. But stubbornly held error – heresy – threatened to undermine the deepest roots of Christian living. If allowed to spread unchecked, it put at stake the eternal fate of trusting, but deluded, Christian souls. Where it surfaced, church leaders aggressively moved, with varying degrees of success, to stamp it out.

Fig. 9.1. Masquerading

Men masked as animals and women dance a round dance to the tune of a gittern. Such folk rituals celebrating nature, which tapped deep into the pre-Christian roots of medieval culture, were vital components of popular religion despite the efforts of church leaders to eradicate them. Reproduced in Charles Knight's *Old England: A Pictorial Museum of Regal, Ecclesiastical, Baronial, Municipal, and Popular Antiquities* (London: Charles Knight & Co., 1845) v. I, p. 308, after a mid-fourteenth-century Flemish manuscript now in the Bodleian Library, Oxford, Bodeleian MS 264, f. 21v.

70. BURCHARD OF WORMS'S *CORRECTOR AND DOCTOR* (c. 1008-12)

Burchard of Worms's Corrector and Doctor *offers a memorable glimpse of some of the pre- or extra-Christian beliefs that were staples of popular religion to the never-ending exasperation of churchmen. Burchard (d. 1025) was elected bishop of Worms in 1000. Around 1008 he compiled an important early collection of canon law in twenty books called the* Decretum *(not to be confused with Gratian's work of the same name from the mid-twelfth century). He titled the nineteenth book of this work* Corrector et Medicus *since it was designed for priests in their role as spiritual doctors correcting and curing the sickness of souls. Following the lead of earlier penitential handbooks compiled to aid priests in administering confession, it adhered to the notion of "tariffed penance," a fixed term of penance (usually fasting) for any particular sin no matter the varying characters and circumstances of the penitents and their sins (compare Doc. 4). Burchard culled most of the sins and their penances in his collection from older peniten-tials, some dating back to the seventh century. So the sometimes startling popular beliefs and practices he equipped his priests to tackle in confession may not always paint an accurate picture of the state of popular Christianity in his own day. Still, some of his more detailed descriptions – for example, the witch Hulda, the rain-making ceremony, and various love potions – arguably come from his own first-hand encounters with the current folk practices in his diocese. While all the sins in Burchard's penitential concern the failure to meet the demands of Christian living, the complete work is too long to include here. Translated below are those sections that deal explicitly with sins that stray from Christian orthodoxy into extra-Christian beliefs and magic. The various topics Burchard covers are framed as questions for priests to ask penitents.*

Source: trans. J. Shinners from Burchard's *Decretorum Liber Decimus Nonus* in F.W.H. Was-serschleben, *Die Bußordnungen der abendländischen Kirche* (Halle: Verlag Graeger, 1851; rpt. Graz, 1958), pp. 643-65, with additions from J.-P. Migne, *Patrologiae Cursus Completus*, Series Latina (Paris: Migne, 1880), CXL, cols. 949-76. Latin.

This book is called the Corrector or Doctor because it is full of correctives for bodies and medicines for souls, and it teaches every priest, even one with little education, how he can come to the aid of anyone: someone in holy orders, a secular person, rich or poor, a boy, a young man, an old man, a decrepit man, someone healthy or sick, people of every age, and of either sex....

Concerning the Magical Arts

52. Have you violated a grave, by which I mean, after you see someone buried have you gone at night, broken open the grave, and taken his clothes? If you have, you should do penance for two years on the appointed fast days.

52a. Have you consulted magicians, inviting them into your house to look for some lost article using magical arts, or to purify the house; or, following pagan practice, have diviners divined something for you, so that you might ask them about the future as you would a prophet; or have you invited to you those who cast lots, or those who hope to foretell the future for you by lots, or those who pay regard to auguries or incantations? If you have, you should do penance for two years on the appointed fast days.

53. Have you observed pagans customs which, as if by hereditary right and with the devil's aid, fathers pass on to their sons even in these times: for instance, have you worshiped the elements, that is, the moon or sun, or the course of the stars, the new moon, or the waning moon whose light you hope to restore by your noise-making or aid? Have you used those elements to try to bring you help or to help others, or have you consulted the new moon before building something or getting married? If you have, you should do penance for two years on the appointed fast days, for it is written: "Whatever you do in word or deed, do it all in the name of our Lord Jesus Christ" [Col. 3:17].

53a. Have you observed the first of January using pagan rites, so that you did something more on that day because it was the new year than you would normally do either before or after it, by which I mean to say that on that day have you either set your table with stones or food-offerings, or led singers and dancers through the neighborhoods and streets, or sat on the roof of your house with your sword circumscribed with signs in order for you to see and know there what will happen to you in the coming year? Or have you sat at a crossroads on a bullskin in order to know your future? Or have you made loaves of bread to be cooked in your name the night before so that, if they rise well and are firm and tall, from this you foresee that your life will be prosperous in the coming year? If so, because you have abandoned God your creator and turned to idols and such vain things and have become an apostate, you should do penance for two years on the appointed fast days.

54. Have you tied knots or made incantations or other various enchantments that wicked men, swineherds, oxherds, and sometime hunters do while they sing devilish chants over bread, herbs, and certain foul bandages, and either hide these in a tree or throw them where crossroads meet in order

either to free their animals or dogs from pestilence or loss or to cause the loss of someone else's? If you have you should do penance for two years on the appointed fast days.

55. Have you been present at or approved of those foolish things that women do while doing their wool-work or weaving, who, when they start their weaving, hope that they can make it come about either with incantations or with their first steps that the threads of both the warp and the woof get so tangled together that unless some opposing diabolical incantations again intervene, the whole weave will fail? If you have been present at or approved of such, you should do penance for thirty days on bread and water.

56. Have you collected medicinal herbs using other incantations besides the Creed or the Lord's Prayer, that is, singing the "I believe in God" or the "Our Father"? If you have done this, you should do ten days of penance on bread and water.

57. Have you gone to any place to pray other than a church or some other religious place that your bishop or your priest showed you; for example, to springs, rocks, trees, or crossroads; and have you burned candles or small torches there to venerate that place, have you brought bread or some other offering there, have you eaten there, or sought anything there for the health of the body or the soul? If you have done this or approved of it, you should do penance for three years on appointed fast days.

On Divination

58. Have you practiced divination by looking in books or tablets as many are used to doing who presume to divine things in psalters, Gospel books, or books like this? If you have, you should do ten days of penance on bread and water [see Doc. 48.4].

59. Have you ever believed or taken part in this kind of faithlessness: that enchanters and those who say that they can summon up storms are able by demonic incantations either to stir up storms or influence men's minds? If you have believed or taken part in this, you should do penance for one year on the appointed fast days.

60. Have you ever believed that there is a kind of woman who can do what certain women, deceived by the devil, claim they must do by necessity or command; namely with a band of devils transformed into the shape of women (which the foolish rabble calls Hulda the Witch) on some nights they must ride on various beasts and number themselves in this assembly? If you have believed or taken part in this sort of faithlessness, you should do penance for one year on the appointed fast days....

64. Have you believed or taken part in this kind of lack of faith: that there is a type of woman who can influence men's minds using spells and incantations; that is, she can change a man's hatred into love or love into hatred, or can either destroy or steal a man's possessions using her enchantments? If you have believed or taken part in this, you should do penance for one year on the appointed fast days....

Concerning Impiety

78. Have you neglected to receive the Body and Blood of the Lord at the four proper times of the year, namely Holy Thursday, Easter Sunday, Pentecost, and Christmas; and have you not abstained from sexual intercourse during the whole of Lent and both seven days after the aforesaid times, and five days before receiving the sacred Body of the Lord? If you have neglected this, you should do twenty days of penance on bread and water.

78a. Have you refused to attend mass or prayers or to make an offering to a married priest, by which I mean have you not wished to confess your sins to him or receive the Body and Blood of the Lord from him because you thought he was a sinner? If you have done so, you should do penance for one year on the appointed fast days.

More concerning the Magical Arts

78b. Have you believed or taken part in this kind of faithlessness that some wicked women, turning back to Satan and seduced by the illusions and phantasms of demons, believe and proclaim: in the night hours they ride on certain animals with the pagan goddess Diana and a countless multitude of women, and they cross a great span of the world in the stillness of the dead of night, and they obey her commands as if she were a noble lady, and on some nights they are called to her service? Oh, if only these women alone perished in this faithlessness and did not lead many along with them down into the utter wreck of their inconstancy! For a countless multitude, deceived by this false belief, believe these things are true and stray from true faith by believing them; they turn back to pagan error when they consider that anything is divine or godly outside the one God. But the devil transforms himself into the figure and likeness of various people, and he deceives the mind that he holds captive with dreams, sometimes showing it joyful things, sometimes sad things, sometimes unknown people, and leads it off the straight and narrow. Though only the spirit experiences this, the unfaithful mind believes that it happens to the body, not the spirit. For who is not led out of himself in dreams and nocturnal visions and sees many things sleeping which he never saw awake? But who is so stupid and dimwitted to think that all these things which happened only in the mind also happened to the body? When the prophet Ezechiel saw and heard visions from the Lord in his spirit, not his body, this is what he said: "Immediately," he says, "I was in the spirit" [e.g., Ezek. 37:1]. And Paul is not so bold as to say that he was taken up in body [2 Cor. 12:2]. Thus, it should be publicly announced to everyone that anyone who believes these or similar things loses his faith, and he who does not have right faith with God belongs not to him, but to him in whom he believes – that is, the devil. For it is written about our Lord: "All things were made through him, and without him was made nothing" [John 1:3]. If you have believed these worthless things, you should do penance for two years on the appointed fast days.

79. Have you observed the funeral wake; that is, have you been present at vigils over the bodies of the dead where Christian bodies are watched over with pagan rites? Have you sung devilish songs there or danced those dances there that pagans devised at the devil's instruction? Have you gotten drunk there and dissolved into laughter and, putting aside all piety and feelings of charity, have you seemed to rejoice at the death of your brother? If you have, you should do penance for thirty days on bread and water.

Concerning Superstition

80. Have you made diabolical amulets or markings as certain people are used to doing at the devil's inspiration, or [employed magical] herbs or amber? Or have you honored Thursday as Jove's [i.e., Thor's] day? If you have done or approved of such, you should do forty days of penance on bread and water.

81. Have you conspired with other plotters against your bishop or his adjutants, by which I mean to say have you ridiculed or derided your bishop's or priest's teachings or orders? If you have, you should do penance for forty days on bread and water.

82. Have you eaten any offerings made to idols, that is, from offerings left in certain places at the tombs of the dead, or offered at springs, trees, rocks, or at crossroads; or have you carried stones to cairns, or put wreaths (*capitis ligaturas*) on the crosses set up at crossroads? If you have done or approved of such, you should do penance for thirty days on bread and water.

More concerning the Magical Arts

83. Have you put you son or daughter on your rooftop or on your oven in order to gain some remedy for their illness, or have you burned grain

where a dead man has lain, or tied a dead man's belt in knots in order to harm someone, or have you clapped together over a corpse the combs which little women use to tease wool, or after a corpse has been carried from its house, have you cut the cart that carried it in half and had the corpse carried between the two halves of the cart? If you have done or approved of such, you should do penance for twenty days on bread and water.

84. Have you done or approved of this sort of foolishness which stupid women are accustomed to do who, when the cadaver of a dead man is still lying in his house, run to some water and quietly bring along a jug filled with it; and when the dead man's body is lifted up, they pour some of this water underneath the bier, and they take care while the body is being carried out of the house that it is lifted no more than knee-high, which they do for purposes of some sort of healing? If you have done or approved of such, you should do penance on bread and water for ten days.

85. Have you done or approved of what some people do to a killed man when he is buried? They put a special ointment in his hand, as if his wound can be healed after death by this ointment, and they bury him in this way with the ointment. If you have, you should do penance for twenty days on bread and water.

86. In any work you have undertaken, have you done or said anything using sorcery or the magic arts when you should have invoked God's name? If you have, you should do penance for ten days on bread and water.

87. Have you done the sort of things pagans did and still do on the first of January, going about [masquerading] as a little stag or a calf? If you have done so, you should do penance for thirty days on bread and water.

88. Have you disparaged or cursed someone out of envy? If you have, you should do penance for seven days on bread and water.

89. Have you done what many people do? They scrape the area in their house where they normally make the fire and put grains of barley on the still warm spot; if the grains pop, there will be danger; if they lie there, there will be good fortune. If you have, you should do penance for ten days on bread and water.

90. Have you done what some people do when they visit anyone sick? As they approach the house where the sick person is lying, if they see any rock lying nearby they turn it over and look underneath it to see if anything alive is there. If they find a worm, a fly, an ant, or anything moving, then they claim that the sick person will recover; but if they find nothing moving, they say the person is going to die. If you have done or believed this, you should do twenty days of penance on bread and water.

91. Have you made tiny shooting bows or shoes for little boys and thrown them down your cellar or into your shed for satyrs or gnomes (*pilosi*) to play

with so that they will bring you other people's goods and make you richer? If you have, you should do penance for ten days.

92. Have you done what some people do on the first of January, that is, seven days after the Lord's birth? On that holy night at the devil's urging they wind thread, spin, and sew, doing all the work they can begin because of the new year. If you have, you should do penance for forty days on bread and water....

Concerning Forbidden Foods

115. Have you eaten a body scab to gain health, or have you drunk a solution of those little worms called lice, or drunk human urine, or eaten any feces to gain health? If you have, you should do penance for ten days on bread and water.

116. Have you eaten carrion, that is, animals that you discovered dead that have been mauled by wolves or dogs? If you have, you should do penance for ten days on bread and water.

117. Have you eaten birds that a hawk caught and you did not first kill them with any arrow bolt? If you have, you should do penance for five days on bread and water.

118. Have you eaten birds or animals that got strangled in nets and you found them dead that way? Unless you were compelled by famine to do this, you should do penance for ten days on bread and water.

119. Have you eaten fish you found dead in the water? Unless you found it dead this way on the same day that it was caught by fishermen, you should do penance for three days on bread and water....

More concerning sacrilege

124. Have you burned down a church or approved of this? If you have, restore the church and distribute your worth (that is, your wergeld) to the poor, and do fifteen years of penance on the appointed fast days.

125. Have you held back offerings for the dead because you did not want to hand them over to the church? If you have, you should do penance for one year on the appointed fast days.

126. Have you celebrated Easter, Pentecost, or Christmas in any place other than that city to which you are subject, unless you were prevented by some infirmity? If you have, you should do penance for ten days on bread and water....

More concerning Impiety

131. Have you done what some people are accustomed to do? After eating they go to mass stuffed with food and staggering from wine and dare to receive the sign of peace offered by the priest for the people. If you have, you should do three days of penance on bread and water.

132. Have you received the Body and Blood of the Lord after eating something no matter how little? If you have, unless you did it once during childhood, or you received it as the viaticum, you should do penance for ten days on bread and water.

133. Have you done what some people are accustomed to do? When they come into church, at first they move their lips a little as if they were praying, this for the sake of those standing or sitting about; but they quickly move on to telling stories and gabbling, and when the priest greets them and calls them to prayer, they return to their stories and say no responses or prayers. If you have, you should do penance for ten days on bread and water....

Concerning Unbelief

137. Have you believed what some people are accustomed to? When they are going on any journey, if a crow flies from their left to their right and caws to them, they hope that it means their journey will be prosperous. And when they are anxious about where to lodge, if that bird called a mouse-catcher (*muriceps*) – because it catches mice and is named for what it eats – flies across the path before them, they entrust themselves more to this augury and omen than to God. If you have done or believed this, you should do five days penance on bread and water.

138. Have you believed what some people are accustomed to? When they have need to go somewhere before daybreak, they do not dare, saying that it is now the next day, and it is forbidden to go out before the cock crows, and that it is dangerous because unclean spirits have more power to do harm before cockcrow than after, and that the cock's crowing is better able to repel and settle these spirits than that Divine Mind which resides in man through faith and the sign of the cross. If you have done or believed this, you should do penance for ten days on bread and water.

139. Have you believed what some people are accustomed to? That those beings which are popularly called the Fates either exist or that they can do what they are believed to do: namely when anyone is born, at that point they have the power to shape him into whatever they want, so that whenever he wants he can be transformed into a wolf, which common stupidity calls a *weruvoff*, or into any other shape? If you have believed this (which never did

or could occur since the divine image can never be transformed into another form or likeness by anyone other than Almighty God) you should do penance for ten days on bread and water.

140. Have you believed what some people are wont to believe: that there are wild women – whom they call *silvaticae* and say they are corporeal – and when they wish, they reveal themselves to their lovers, and they say that they amuse themselves with them; and also when they wish, they hide themselves and vanish? If you have believed this, you should do ten days of penance on bread and water.

In all the above things priests ought to exercise great discretion that they distinguish between someone who has sinned publicly and should do public penance, and someone who has sinned privately, and has confessed voluntarily.

Although all the above questions should be put commonly to men and women, the ones that follow particularly pertain to women.

Concerning Women's Vices

141. Have you done what some women are accustomed to do during certain times of the year? You prepare a table in your house and put your food and drink on it with three knives so that if those Three Sisters (which ancient posterity and ancient stupidity called the Fates) should come, they can take repast there; and have you removed from the Divine Piety his power and name and given them to the devil, by which I mean that you have believed those who you say are the Sisters can help you either now or in the future? If you have done or approved of such, you should do penance for one year on the appointed fast days....

147. Have you done what certain women are used to doing who, when they are fornicating and they want to kill their embryo, take action as the uterus is conceiving and, using their enchantments (*maleficia*) and their herbs, they abort it so that either the conceived child is killed or knocked loose, or if they have not yet conceived, they take action to prevent conception? If you have done, approved of, or taught such, you should do penance for ten years on the appointed fast days. But one ancient decree removes such women from church for the rest of their life. For whenever a woman prevents conception, she is guilty of homicide. Nevertheless it makes a great difference if the woman is poor and does this because of the hardship of raising the child or because she is a prostitute and does this to conceal her sins. But in the Council of Lérida [546] it is thus ordered for those who abort their infants conceived in adultery:

148. For those who have wrongfully conceived by committing adultery

and either try to kill the child as it is being born or crush it in its mother's womb with some potions, holy communion is offered to both adulterers, that is, the father and the mother, after a seven-year course [of abstinence]; nevertheless, they should dwell every moment of their life in tears and humility.

149. Have you given something to or shown to anyone how she could abort or kill her conceived child? If you have, you should do penance for seven years on the appointed fast days.

150. Have you aborted your conceived child before quickening? If you have, you should do penance for one year on the appointed fast days. If you have done this after it was instilled with a spirit, you should do three years of penance on the appointed fast days.

151. Have you willingly killed your newborn son or daughter? If you have, you should do penance for twelve years on the appointed fast days and never be without penance.

152. Have you neglected your infant and through your fault it died without being baptized? If you have, you should do penance for one year on the appointed fast days, and never be without penance.

153. Have you mixed any lethal potion and killed anyone with it? If you have, you should fast for one quarantine [carina, or forty days] with seven years penance subsequently, and you should never be without penance. If you wished to kill someone by poison and did not succeed, you should do penance for one year on the appointed fast days.

154. Have you tasted your husband's semen in order to make his love for you burn greater through your diabolical deed? If you have, you should do seven years of penance on the appointed fast days.

155. Have you drunk holy oil to subvert a judicial ordeal (judicium Dei), or have you done anything or taken counsel with others to do anything using herbs, words, wood, gemstones, or anything else foolishly believed in, or have you had something concealed in your mouth, sewn into your clothing, or tied around you, or contrived any other trick that you believed could subvert God's judgment? If you have, you should do seven years of penance on the appointed fast days.

156. Have you done what certain women are accustomed to do and firmly believe, I mean to say that if their neighbor has an abundance of milk or honeybees, they believe that with their enchantments and charms they can shift this abundance of milk or honey — which they saw that their neighbor had before they did — to themselves and their own animals or to whomever they wish with the devil's aid. If you have, you should do penance for three years on the appointed fast days.

157. Have you believed what certain women are wont to believe: that whatever house they enter, with a word, look, or sound they claim they can

cast the evil eye and destroy goslings, the chicks of peafowl, chicks, and even piglets and the offspring of other animals? If you have done or believed this, you should do penance for one year on the appointed fast days.

158. Have you believed what many women turning back to Satan believe and assert to be true: you believe that in the stillness of a quiet night, with you gathered in your bed with your husband lying at your bosom, you are physically able to pass through closed doors and can travel across the span of the earth with others deceived by a similar error? And that you can kill baptized people redeemed by Christ's blood without using visible weapons and then, after cooking their flesh, can eat it and put straw, wood, or something like this in place of their hearts, and, though you have eaten them, you can bring them back to life and grant them a stay during which they can live? If you have believed this, you should do penance for forty days (that is, a quarantine) on bread and water with seven years of penance subsequently.

159. Have you believed what some women are wont to believe: that in the stillness of a quiet night while your doors are shut, you along with other minions of the devil rise up into the sky all the way to the clouds and fight there with others and that you wound them and they wound you? If you have believed this, you should do penance for two years on appointed fast days.

160. Have you done what some women are accustomed to do? They take a live fish and put it in their vagina, keeping it there for a while until it is dead. Then they cook or roast it and give it to their husbands to eat, doing this in order to make the men be more ardent in their love for them. If you have, you should do two years of penance on the appointed fast days.

161. Have you done what some women are accustomed to do? They lie face down on the ground, uncover their buttocks, and tell someone to make bread on their naked buttocks. When they have cooked it, they give it to their husbands to eat. They do this to make them more ardent in their love for them. If you have, you should do two years of penance on the appointed fast days.

162. Have you put your baby next to the fire and then someone else puts a pot of water on the fire which boils over the pot onto the baby killing it? You, who should keep a child under your care for seven years, should do three years of penance on the appointed fast days; the person who put the water into the pot is innocent.

163. Have you done what some women do carrying out the devil's lessons? They study the footprints and tracks Christians make when walking, and then they take some sod from their footprints and examine it, hoping to bear away their health or life. If you have, you should do five years of penance on the appointed fast days.

164. Have you done what some women are used to doing? They take their menstrual blood, mix it into food or drink, and give it to their men to eat or drink to make them love them more. If you have done this, you should do five years of penance on the appointed fast days.

164a. Have you done what some women are wont to do? They take a man's skull, burn it, and give the ashes to their husbands to drink for health. If you have, you should do one year of penance on the appointed fast days.

164b. Have you eaten or drunk any animal's blood? If you have, you should do penance for five days on bread and water.

165. Have you done what some women are accustomed to do? I speak of those who have bawling babies. They dig a hole in the ground and make a tunnel through to the other side; then they pull their baby through the hole and say that this stops the baby's crying. If you have done or approved of such, you should do five days of penance on bread and water.

166. Have you done what some women are accustomed to do inspired by the devil? When any infant dies without baptism, they take the baby's corpse, put it in some secret spot, and impale its little body with a stake, saying that if they did not do so, the infant would rise from the dead and cause many people harm. If you have done, approved of, or believed in such, you should do penance for two years on the appointed fast days.

167. Have you done what some women are accustomed to do filled with the devil's boldness? When a woman is due to give birth and is unable, while she is struggling vainly to give birth, if she dies from her birth pangs, they impale the mother and her child into the ground with a stake in the same grave. If you have done or approved of such, you should do penance for two years on appointed fast days.

168. Have you involuntarily overlain your baby, or smothered it by the weight of your [bed] clothes, and did you do this after it was baptized? If you did, you should do forty days of penance (that is, a quarantine) on bread, water, vegetables, and beans; and you should abstain from marital relations until the forty days is up. Afterwards you should do penance on the appointed fast days for three years and keep three forty-day fasts each year. If the baby was overlain before it was baptized you should do penance for the next forty days as prescribed above and then for five years.

169. If you have found your baby overlain next to you where both you and your husband were lying and it is not apparent whether its father or you smothered it or whether it died on its own, you should not be carefree or without penance. For in these cases there should be a great regard for piety because, though nothing evil was willed, someone did die. Nevertheless, because of your negligence, you should do penance for forty days on bread and water. But if it is clear that you were the cause of the infant's death – not

willingly, but through negligence – you should do penance for three years on the appointed fast days, one of these on bread and water; and during the term of the penance you should keep yourself away from all luxuries....

171. Have you done what some women are wont to do? When a baby is newborn, immediately baptized, and dies, when they bury it, they put a wax paten with a Host in its right hand and in its left hand they put a wax chalice with wine in it and then they bury it. If you have, you should do ten days penance on bread and water.

172. Have you done what some adulterous women do? As soon as they find out that their lovers wish to take lawful wives, they use some sort of evil art to extinguish the men's sexual desire so that they are useless to their wives and unable to have intercourse with them. If you have done this or taught others to, you should do penance for forty days on bread and water.

173. Have you taken your child to be baptized at other than the legitimate times, that is, Easter Saturday and Pentecost Saturday, unless the child's ill-health requires otherwise? If you have, you should do ten days penance on bread and water.

174. Have you neglected to visit the sick, have you not gone to those in prison, and have you not ministered to them? If you have not, you should do penance for ten days on bead and water.

175. Have you eaten meat during Lent? If you have, you should abstain from eating any meat for the course of that year.

176. Have you eaten any food from Jews or from other pagans that they prepared for you? If you have, you should do penance for ten days on bread and water.

177. Have you done what certain people are used to doing? When they go to church, on the way there they flaunt their vanities and talk about idle things, and they give no thought to anything that has to do with what is useful for the soul. When they enter the porch of the church where the bodies of the faithful are buried, they trample on the tombs of their neighbors without reflecting that this will be their future, and they make no mention of them nor pour forth prayers to the Lord on their behalf as they should. If you have neglected this, you should do penance for ten days on bread and water, and take care that you not let this happen again. But whenever you enter the porch of a church, you should pray for them and ask those holy souls whose bodies rest there that they intercede before God for your sins insofar as they can.

178. Have you done any work on the Lord's Day? If you have, you should do penance for three days on bread and water.

179. Have you done what some women are accustomed to do? They take off their clothes and smear honey all over their naked body. With the honey

on their body they roll themselves back and forth over wheat on a sheet spread on the ground. They carefully collect all the grains of wheat sticking to their moist body, put them in a mill, turn the mill in the opposite direction of the sun, grind the wheat into flour, and bake bread from it. Then they serve it to their husbands to eat, who then grow weak and die. If you have, you should do penance for forty days on bread and water.

180. Have you done what certain women are accustomed to do? When they have had no rain and need it, they gather together many young girls and put one small virgin in charge as their leader. They strip her and lead the naked girl outside the village where they find the henbane plant, called *belisa* in German. They make the nude virgin dig up the henbane with the little finger of her right hand and then make her tie it by its roots with some string to the little toe of her right foot. All the other maidens, each holding a single branch in her hand, lead the virgin dragging the plant behind her into a nearby river where they sprinkle river water on the virgin from their branches; by their incantations, they thereby hope to get rain. With the naked virgin turning and changing her footsteps to resemble the [sideways] walk of a crab, they lead her back from the river to the village in their hands. If you have done or approved of such, you should do penance for twenty days on bread and water.

Judging by Burchard's descriptions, were the people of his diocese Christian? To what kinds of sins were they prone? What kind of situations made them turn to magic? Does Burchard believe in magic? What is his image of women?

71. THE INQUISITOR BERNARD OF GUI ON SORCERY (c. 1323)

In the wake of the rapid spread of Cathar heretics through southern France, Pope Gregory IX expressly set up procedures for the papal inquisition in the early 1230s to root out and suppress heresy. (It should not be confused with the fifteenth-century, royally sponsored Spanish Inquisition directed at first against Jews and Muslim converts to Christianity.) The inquisition's practical powers and its effectiveness were never as sweeping as some later historians would claim, but that it existed at all testifies to how seriously churchmen took organized challenges to established Christian doctrine. The Dominican Bernard of Gui (c. 1261-1331) was papally appointed as inquisitor of Toulouse in 1307, a post he held until 1324. Around 1323 he composed a manual to aid his fellow-inquisitors (typically his fellow-Dominicans or Franciscans) titled the Technique for the Work of Inquest into Heretical Depravity. *It first explained the mechanics of the inquisition: its procedures of arrest, investigation, sentencing and commutation, and the legal powers of inquisitors. Then it offered a detailed description, based on Bernard's experience and his research into older sources, of the various heresies and errors spread about southern France in the thirteenth and fourteenth centuries such as the Cathars, Waldensians, Pseudo-Apostles, Beguines, Jews, and sorcerers. The following list of questions to be put to suspected witches exposes a range of popular magical beliefs and practices that comfortably co-existed with Christianity in most medieval communities. It is fruitful to compare it to Burchard of Worms's similar list compiled 200 years earlier.*

Source: trans. J. Shinners from G. Mollat and G. Drioux, *Bernard of Gui's Manuel de l'Inquisiteur* [*Practica officii Inquisitionis heretice pravitatis*] (Paris: Edouard Champion, 1927), v. 2, pp. 20-25. Latin.

1. The following concerns sorcerers, diviners, and invokers of demons. The plague and error of sorcerers, diviners, and invokers of demons assume many and multiple forms in various lands and places according to the varied fabrications and false and vain information of superstitious people who resort to the spirits of error and the teachings of demons.

2. Questions for sorcerers, diviners, and invokers of demons. Examining a sorcerer, diviner, or invoker of demons, he should be asked what and how many kinds of sorcery, divination, or invocations he knows and from whom he learned them.

Next, getting down to particulars, consider the quality and the condition of the persons, since one should not ask the same questions of everyone equally or employ a single method: men should be interrogated one way, women another. Questions may be formulated according to the following list, namely:

What they know or have known or have done about children or infants on whom spells were cast or who were bewitched.

Also, inquire about lost or damned souls.

Also, about catching thieves [through sorcery].

Also, about [causing] marital concord or discord [through sorcery].

Also, about curing sterility.

Also, about those who give others hair, nail-clippings, or the like to eat.

Also, about [investigating] the state of the souls of the departed [through sorcery].

Also, about predicting events in the future.

Also, about fairies who, as they say, go about by night and bring good luck.

Also, enchantments or conjurations by means of incantations of fruit, plants, cords, or other things.

Also, to whom they taught these charms or conjurations, and from whom they heard or learned them.

Also, what they know about curing the sick through conjuring or incantations.

Also, what they know about collecting herbs while kneeling towards the east and saying the Lord's Prayer.

Also, what they enjoin about pilgrimages, masses, offerings of candles, and almsgiving.

Also, what to do to find lost objects or to discover hidden things.

Also, inquire especially into those things that smack of any possible superstition, irreverence, or insult towards the church's sacraments, most especially toward the sacrament of the Lord's Body, and also toward divine worship and sacred places.

Also, inquire about the practice of retaining the Eucharist, or of stealing chrism or holy oil from the church.

Also, inquire about baptizing figurines made of wax or other material, how they are baptized, and to what purposes or end.

Also, inquire about the practice of making lead figurines, how they are made, and to what purpose.

Also, from whom they learned or heard such things.

Also, how long they have used such practices.

Also, who and how many came to them seeking consultations, especially within the last year.

Also, if they were ever forbidden to use such practices and by whom, and if they abjured such practices and promised never to practice or use them again.

Also, if after making such an abjuration or promise, they returned to these practices.

Also, if they believed what others taught them was true.

Also, what goods, gifts, or payments they have or received for such services.

What daily concerns do these magical practices address? What type of religious abuses concern Bernard in this list? Does he believe in sorcery?

72. THE SPURIOUS SAINT GUINEFORT
(MID-1200s)

Popular distortions of Christian belief seldom arose maliciously. Most often, Christian people of good will and deep piety simply stumbled into error as they tried to adapt what they knew of Christian doctrine to their local customs and folklore. When lives and times are hard, people – medieval and modern alike – turn for relief to what they think will best work, leaving theologians and historians to sort out the finer points about what is orthodox and what is not. The strange case of the dog saint Guinefort nicely illustrates what happened when sincere Christian lay people collided with equally sincere clergy. Étienne de Bourbon (c. 1180-1262) studied at the University of Paris where he joined the budding Dominican Order. Appointed a papal inquisitor around 1235, he traveled across France, especially the Rhône valley, investigating and preaching against heresy. Near the end of his life he began writing a treatise on the seven gifts of the Holy Spirit. Though he died before he finished the book, he filled it with dozens of exempla *(or moral anecdotes to use in sermons) culled from his own experiences and from other standard collections. While the example he relates here is an extreme case of how popular Christianity could create unlikely saints when the need arose, pre-Christian belief also informed some aspects of St. Guinefort's cult: both the story of a dog guarding a child from a serpent and the fear of demons substituting changelings for human babies have deep roots in Indo-European folklore. According to the thirteenth-century theologian William of Auvergne, fauns (like the ones dwelling in Guinefort's woods) were the sons of incubi. They were woodland demons with corporeal bodies, horns, and goat's feet – a description gleaned from the fauns of classical mythology. Despite Étienne de Bourbon's zeal, remnants of Guinefort's cult survived intact in the woods near Châtillon-sur-Chalaronne about 25 miles north of Lyon until near the end of the nineteenth century. Jean-Claude Schmitt has studied the Guinefort legend in depth in* The Holy Greyhound *(trans. Martin Thom; Cambridge, 1983).*

Source: trans. J. Shinners from Étienne de Bourbon's *Tractatus de diversis materiis praedicalibus*, ed. A. Lecoy de la Marche in *Anecdotes historiques, légendes et apologues tirés du recueil inédit d'Etienne de Bourbon* (Paris, 1877), pp. 325-28. Latin.

... I should mention those contemptible superstitions, some of which are an insult to God, others to our neighbor. Superstitions affront God when they attribute divine honors to demons or some other creature, as does idolatry, or as do those wretched women who practice divination and seek favor by worshiping elder trees, making offerings to them, scorning churches and the relics of the saints, and seeking cures by carrying their children there or to anthills or other places.

This is what they did recently in the diocese of Lyon. When I went there to preach against divination (*sortilegia*) and hear confessions, many women confessed that they had taken their children to Saint Guinefort. I thought he was some holy man, so I asked about him and eventually learned that he was a *dog* – a greyhound – who died in this way: In the diocese of Lyon near the nun's village called Neuville-les-Dames in the territory of the lord of Villars-en-Dombes, there was a castle belonging to a lord who had an infant boy with his wife. One day the lord and his lady had gone from the manor and so had the nurse, leaving the baby alone in his cradle. A large serpent entered the house, winding its way toward the baby's cradle. But the greyhound, which was in the room, saw it and swiftly attacked it, chasing it under the cradle. Biting at the snake as the snake bit back, the dog knocked the cradle over. Finally the dog killed the snake and tossed it away from the baby's cradle. But the cradle and the floor around it were stained with the snake's blood, as were the dog's mouth and face as it stood near the cradle, injured by the snake. When the nurse came in and saw this, she thought the dog had killed and devoured the baby and she let out a great wail. The boy's mother heard this and came running. She saw and thought the same thing and she screamed too. The knight also came in. Thinking the same thing as the women, he unsheathed his sword and killed the dog. Then, going over to the baby, they found him unharmed sleeping sweetly. Looking around, they found the dead snake ripped apart by the dog's teeth. Realizing the truth of the matter and grief-stricken that they had so unjustly killed such a helpful dog, they threw it down a well which was near the castle's entrance, piled a big heap of rocks over it, and planted trees nearby in memory of the dog's deed.

But by divine will, the castle fell into ruin and the land around it was reduced to wasteland devoid of inhabitants. The country people, however, hearing of the dog's noble deed and how, though innocent, he was slain for an act that should have won him honor, visited the place, venerated the dog as a martyr, and invoked him for their illnesses and other needs. Many people were seduced and deluded there by the devil, who used this to lead them into error; but women especially took their weak or sickly children there. They brought along an old woman who lived in a fortified town about a league from there who taught them how to perform the ritual, to make offerings to demons and summon them, and who led them to the site. When they got there, they made an offering of salt and some other things, and they draped the child's baby clothes on the surrounding bushes. They stuck a needle in the trunk of one of the trees growing over the spot, and – with the mother on one side and the old woman on the other – they tossed the naked child back and forth nine times through the fork between the two trunks of two trees. While doing this they used a demonic invocation to summon the fauns (*fauni*) inhabiting the forest of Rimite to take the sickly or weak child (which they said belonged to the fauns) and to return theirs to them (which the fauns had abducted) fat and full, alive and well. After they did this, these homicidal mothers took the naked child and put it on the straw from its crib at the bottom of the tree. From fire they had carried there they lit two inch-long candles on both ends and stuck them [on the needle?] on the trunk overhead. Then they withdrew far enough away so that they could neither see the baby nor hear it crying and waited until the candles burned out. With these candles left burning like this, many children were set on fire and killed, as some people there told us. One woman also told me that after she had called on the fauns and withdrawn, she saw a wolf coming out of the forest and heading for her baby which the wolf (or the devil in its shape, as she said) would have devoured if her motherly love, taking pity, had not intervened. When they returned to the child, if they found it still alive they carried it to the rushing waters of a nearby river called the Chalaronne in which they dipped the child nine times – and it had to have a strong heart not to die on the spot or shortly after.

We went to this place, however, and called together the people of the area and preached against this practice. We had the dead dog exhumed and the sacred grove of trees cut down; then we had the trees and the dog's bones alike burned to ashes. We had the lords of the land issue an edict for the confiscation and sale of the property of those who should henceforth come to this place for that purpose.

What is the connection between the story of Guinefort and the rituals the women performed at the forked trees? How would you interpret the meaning of the ritual actions done at the trees? How well did Christianity penetrate into the village of Neuville-les-Dames?

73. AN ENGLISH BISHOP OVERSEES POPULAR PIETY (1296, 1299)

The case of the veneration of St. Guinefort was extreme, but church officials regularly had to cope with less extravagant outbursts of piety born of the popular yearning for miracles. Christians of all stripes, from bishops to peasants, believed in the miraculous; but as the power of the institutional church advanced, it grew diligent about investigating, endorsing, and controlling people's religious enthusiasms to keep them from straying into error. Here, Bishop Oliver Sutton of the large English diocese of Lincoln intervenes to quash two unauthorized nascent cults.

Source: trans. J. Shinners from *The Rolls and Registers of Bishop Oliver Sutton*, ed. Rosalind M.T. Hill, Lincoln Record Society, vv. 48 and 64 (Hereford, 1954, 1969), v. III, pp. 143-44, 176; v. VI, pp. 186-87. Latin.

1. Oliver, by divine permission bishop of Lincoln, etc. to the archdeacon of Buckingham sends greetings, etc. A short while ago a clamorous report reached us that some people were presuming openly and publicly to celebrate divine services without legitimate license in a certain private chapel newly constructed at the manor of Hambleden belonging to the nobleman Edmund, Earl of Cornwall [1249-1300]. And spurred on by certain superstitious fantasies and vain fabrications, they were unlawfully venerating that utterly profane place as if it were sacred. Of even greater concern, we discovered that many people from various areas, out of a false sense of devotion, were flocking to that place for the sake of pilgrimage, pretending that miracles of healing happened there. In order to reach a sure and clear decision about these events, we personally visited the site and, by questioning the clergy and the people and gathering evidence, we found that we were correct in our suspicion. But even though these things against the honor and position of the church through our negligence were egregiously undertaken to whatever degree out of zeal and respect for the lord earl, still, we neither do nor would wish to incur divine disfavor for any reason, or, by dissembling, open the way for other like-minded people to exceed [this transgression]. Thus, compelled by the legal requirement to make what we consider is the necessary correction, we have ordered that this should be done in this matter: Since, according to the decrees of the holy fathers, masses may only be celebrated in places consecrated by a bishop or where he permits them to be celebrated, firmly enjoining you by virtue of your obedience and under pain of excommunication, we order you that without delay you most expressly forbid divine services to be celebrated henceforth in that private chapel when the said lord earl is absent unless legitimate authority intervenes to allow it. Furthermore, since it is not fitting for people to frequent a place such as this for the sake of veneration because of the rash claim of miracles which have not been approved by the church, we order you as above that you forbid them from going there. We desire you to certify to us in writing by the feast of Pentecost [May 13] how you have carried out our mandate and how it was obeyed by others. Dated at Nettleham, April 9, 1296, the sixteenth year of our episcopacy. (Afterwards another letter went out relaxing this interdict, as appears on the last page of the nineteenth gathering [of the bishop's register].)

2. Oliver, bishop etc., to the archdeacon of Buckingham sends greetings, etc. We imposed a ban that, when the lord earl was not present, divine services were not to be celebrated in the private chapel recently constructed at the manor of Hambleden belonging to the nobleman, Edmund, Earl of Cornwall, to which many sick people flocked out of a false sense of devotion or seeking to recover their health through a miracle; and we forbade on pain of excommunication that there henceforth be any unlawful congregations of this sort there. But now that these gatherings have ceased, as we have learned, we have been led to concede that the said lord earl may have divine services celebrated by a chaplain supported at his own expense in the said chapel furnished, so it seems, for this purpose without prejudice to any law up until the next feast of St. Andrew [Nov. 30]. To this end we order you freely to permit divine services to be celebrated according to the abovementioned form. Farewell. Dated at Stow Park, August 20, 1296, the seventeenth year of our episcopacy.

3. Oliver, by divine permission bishop, etc., to the archdeacon of Buckingham or his official sends greetings, etc. A trustworthy report has reached us that many people of inconstant faith, out of a false sense of devotion, have been flocking from various areas to a certain well situated in a field at Linslade for the sake of pilgrimage, claiming that miracles of healing have happened there; and they have been venerating the spot with offerings and other acts. Also, to the danger of their souls and the pernicious example to others, they have been recklessly allowed to do this by those, afflicted by the vice of greed, who are known to hold the spiritual governance of the parish church of Linslade. Since, therefore, no profane place should be visited by people for the sake of veneration on account of a brash claim of miracles which have not been approved by the church, we, in accordance with our office, wish to abolish this error. We strictly order you that in every church in the archdeanery of Buckingham, on every Sunday and feast day until the next feast of the Assumption of the glorious Virgin [Aug. 15], during mass you should solemnly and publicly forbid visits to or gatherings at this site under pain of excommunication; and all those whom you shall indict for doing this you should take care to reprimand in such a way that their punishment will be an example to those venturing to do likewise. And since it is reported that the vicar of the church of Linslade has encouraged the people of this area in their error because he profits from their offerings – coveting money, so it seems, more than he cares for the salvation of souls – we order you to issue him a peremptory citation that on the next court day after the coming feast of St. Margaret the virgin [July 21], wherever we then happen to be in our diocese he must personally appear before us because of his egregious transgression to hear, receive, and perform what justice recommends. And you should certify

to us in a letter on the said day what you have done in this matter and the name of the vicar. Dated at Buckden, June 26, A.D. 1299.

74. POPULAR HERESY IN TWELFTH-CENTURY LE MANS (c. 1115)

Before the pastoral organization of the church was well established, there was always a danger that gullible people might follow some silver-tongued wandering preacher down the path of error before church leaders could intercede. Ironically, the rise of popular heresies in the early twelfth century was probably spurred in part by the church's own housecleaning undertaken in the two preceding centuries. The tenth-century renewal rippling forth from the Cluny-Gorze reforms of monastic life and the subsequent eleventh-century Gregorian papal reforms aimed at stamping out simony and clerical marriage now held the clergy to a higher standard of life. Those clergy who failed to meet it were apt to become the objects of lay criticism. Coupled to this anti-clerical bent among some lay people was the irresistible idea of the apostolic life, a return to a purer Christianity uncorrupted by wealth and secular influence that found an eager following whenever it surfaced in the Middle Ages (witness St. Bernard of Clairvaux, St. Francis, and Peter Waldes – see Docs. 8 and 9) or in any other age. While the movements they led were neither as widespread nor as durable as the later Cathar and Waldensian sects, several strong-willed and spellbinding heresiarchs were notorious in the first decades of the twelfth century. The career and criticisms of Henry of Le Mans (or Lausanne), apparently a renegade cleric of some sort, are typical. Typical too are the allegations of gross sexual indecency leveled at him by the monk – probably an eyewit- ness – who wrote the following account. Henry was eventually arrested in 1135. He recanted and was packed off to a monastery, but soon escaped and resumed his career. Some of his ideas ultimately found their way into Waldensian doctrine.

Source: trans. R.I. Moore, *The Birth of Popular Heresy* (London: Edward Arnold, 1975), pp. 34-38. Latin.

At about this time [c. 1115] a hypocrite appeared in the neighborhood whose behavior, perverted morals, and detestable teaching showed that he deserved, like a parricide, to be punished with scorpions. He was a wolf in sheep's clothing, with the haggard face and eyes of a shipwrecked sailor, his hair bound up, unshaven, tall, and of athletic gait, walking barefoot even in the depths of winter, a young man ready to preach, possessed of a fearful voice. His clothes were shabby, and his life eccentric: he had lodgings in the houses of the towns, his home in the doorways, and his bed in the gutters. But why go on? His reputation for unusual holiness and learning rested not on the merit of his character but on falsehood, not on his morals or piety, but on rumor. Women and young boys – for he used both sexes in his lechery – who associated with him openly flaunted his excesses, and added to them by caressing the soles of his feet and his buttocks and groin with tender fingers. They became so excited by the lasciviousness of the man, and by the grossness of their own sins, that they testified publicly to his extraordinary virility, and said that his eloquence could move a heart of stone to remorse, and that all monks, hermits, and canons regular ought to imitate his pious and celibate life. They claimed that God had blessed him with the ancient and authentic gift of the prophets, and he saw in their faces, and told them of sins which were unknown to others.

When this man's reputation began to grow in our area the people, with characteristic frivolity and predictable consequences, were delighted. They longed for his meetings all day and every day, so that they could know his heresy better and become more closely entangled in it. They often seek most eagerly what will do them most harm. As time passed it got worse. Deciding to tame our people with his snake-like speech, he sent to the bishop two disciples who resembled him in their dress and way of life, just as our Savior had sent his people ahead of him. When they reached the outskirts of the city [of Le Mans] on Ash Wednesday, the whole people, longing for the wickedness that was offered to them, received them as though they were the angels of the lord of the universe. They carried a standard in the way that [teachers] bear staves, a cross with wrought iron fixed at the top, and their bearing and manner suggested some sort of penitent. The bishop, a man of great piety, received them gently and devoutly. Not anticipating the wiles of the Trojan horse, he greeted them cheerfully and generously, and although he was about to set out for Rome ordered his archdeacons to allow the false hermit Henry (for that was the heretic's name) to enter the city peacefully and preach to the people.

When he entered the city the mob in its usual way applauded the novelty, preferring the unknown to the familiar. Was it surprising? They believed that his righteousness was even greater than his fame which was constantly inflated by gossip. Blinded by his schism and faction, and by personal corruption, many of the clerics pandered to the mob and prepared a platform from which the demagogue could address the crowds of people who followed him. When he spoke to them, with the clerics sitting weeping at his feet, his speech resounded as though legions of demons spoke through his open mouth. He was certainly remarkably eloquent. His words stuck in the minds of the people just as freshly taken poison when it has been forced into the limbs spreads its strength through the vitals and, with inexorable hatred of life, twists and bends to attack them unceasingly.

His heresy turned people against the clergy with such fury that they refused to sell them anything or buy anything from them and treated them like gentiles or publicans. Not content with pulling down their houses and throwing away their belongings, they would have stoned and pilloried them if the count and his men had not heard of their wicked and vicious exploits, and suppressed them by force instead of by reason, for a monster admits no argument. Some of the clergy who were left in the city, Hugh D'Osell, William Who-won't-drink-water (*Qui-non-bibit-aquam*) and Payn Aldricus obtained access to him one day to negotiate with him, and were viciously beaten and had their heads rolled in the filth of the gutter; they were scarcely able to escape alive from the attack of these brutal people, and when they did get away their departure had the appearance of flight. Once they had been caught they would not have escaped from the danger at all if they had not found shelter with the count and his knights, for as we have said the count resisted the heresy of the city, and did not shrink from the defense of the clergy.

The clergy, since they did not dare to address the heretic in person, sent him the following letter:

"Our church received you and your friends peaceably and honorably when you came dressed as a sheep, concealing the wiles of a hungry wolf underneath. In thought and deed it treated you with brotherly charity, expecting that you would advise the people faithfully on the salvation of their souls, and sincerely sow the seed of the word of God in their hearts. You have perversely returned anger for peace, slander for respect, hatred for charity, curses for blessings, and have presumed to disturb the church of God with your heresy. You have sown discord between clergy and people, and repeatedly incited a seditious mob to attack Mother Church with swords and clubs. You have offered us the kiss of Judas and called us and all clergy heretics, to our public injury. Worse still you have said pernicious and infidel things against the Catholic faith, which a faithful Christian would shudder to repeat. Therefore, by the authority of the one and undivided Trinity, and of the whole orthodox church, of St. Mary mother of God, of St. Peter the prince of the apostles, and his present vicar Pope Paschal, and of your bishop Hildebert, we forbid you and your associates in your evil and damnable heresy to preach again anywhere in the diocese of Le Mans, in private or in public, or to presume to propagate your perverse and absurd teachings. If you defy this authority and open your evil jaws once more then by the same authority we excommunicate you and all your accomplices, followers, and associates, and he whose divinity you have not ceased to contravene will have you delivered on the day of judgment to eternal damnation."

He would not accept the letter, but William Musca delivered it to him in person. The people who were standing around threatened to kill him, because he bravely heaped reproaches on Henry in public so that he could be seen. Henry nodded his head at each sentence of the letter, and replied in a clear voice, "You are lying." If it had not been for the count's steward, under whose protection he had come, William would not have returned to the church alive.

After this he summoned a sacrilegious meeting at the [monasteries] of St. Germain and St. Vincent, where he pronounced a new dogma, that women who had not lived chastely must, naked before everybody, burn their clothes and their hair. No one should accept any gold or silver or goods or wedding presents with his wife, or receive any dowry with her: the naked should marry the naked, the sick marry the sick, and the poor marry the poor, without bothering about whether they married chastely or incestuously. While they followed his instructions he admired the beauty of the women, and discussed which ones had fairer skin or better figures than the others. In spite of this the people subjected their every wish and deed to his command.

If he wanted it, gold and silver flowed to him in such quantity that he seemed to be the sole master of everybody's wealth. He accepted a great deal openly, but spared his greed in case he should seem avaricious. All the same he kept a lot for himself and gave very little for the clothes which, as we have said, had been burnt. On his advice many of the young men married the corrupt women, for whom he bought clothes to the value of four soldi, just enough to cover their nakedness. But the true judge destroyed the work of the heretic, and showed that this was the sort of tree that produces leaves rather than fruit. The young men who had married worthless women at his behest were soon driven by the poverty or debauchery of their wives to flee the city, leaving the women destitute, and while the men coupled with others in adultery the women whom they had left behind hoped to remarry illegally. Of those who entered into matrimony at his urging, and there were many of them, neither men nor women showed fidelity or respect towards their spouses. None of the women who had promised to renounce fornication when they destroyed their clothes were able to restrain themselves, and adding to their crimes daily they relapsed into a worse condition than ever.

After he had behaved in this way for some time the scoundrel heard that the bishop, who, as we said, had made a journey to Rome, was returning and withdrew to the village of St. Calais. He stayed there and in other towns nearby, and far from desisting from his wickedness daily discovered some new iniquity. On the holy day of Pentecost, when the true faithful devote the whole day to divine offices, this most evil of men, accompanied by a young cleric whose evidence later revealed his wantonness, went secretly at night to the house of a certain knight, and there caroused all day until mid-day in bed with the mistress of the house. Neither the fear of God nor shame before men could moderate his lasciviousness, until he had blazoned the enormity of his crimes to people far and wide.

When the bishop entered the city on his return, surrounded by a great retinue of his clergy, he made the sign of the living God over his people, and blessed them with fatherly solicitude. But they blasphemed bitterly, and rejected his episcopal sign and benediction.

"We want none of your ways," they cried, "We don't want your blessing. Bless the dirt! Sanctify filth! We have a father, a bishop, and a defender greater than you in authority, fame, and learning. These wicked clerics of yours here opposed him, and contradicted his teaching. They have hated it and rejected it as sacrilege because they are afraid that their crimes will be revealed by his prophetic spirit. They wrote letters attacking his heresy and his bodily unchastity. Their sins will be speedily turned against them when they presume so audaciously to forbid his heavenly preaching of the word of God."

The bishop took pity on the errors and ignorance of his people, and bore the insults which they hurled at him calmly, praying that God would restrain this mixture of heresy and excitement and prevent it from creating a schism in his church. God allowed a sudden fire to burn down a large part of the suburbs of the city, so that temporal loss might cause them to cast aside their evil beliefs, and call upon his holy name, the name of the living God.

A few days later the bishop went to the heretic and by divine authority brought his impiety under control. The bishop opened their conversation by asking how he had made his profession, but he did not know what a profession was, and kept silent. Trying again, the bishop asked what [holy] orders he had, and he replied, "I am a deacon." "Well then," said the bishop, "tell us whether you have been to mass today." "No." "Then let us recite the morning hymns to the Lord."

When they did so Henry showed himself ignorant of the daily office. Then to make his ignorance absolutely clear, the bishop began to sing the usual psalms to the Virgin, and Henry knew neither the lines themselves nor the sequence. So, blushing furiously, he revealed what kind of a life he had led, the worth of his teaching, and the extent of his presumption. He was only a vagabond, quite without knowledge and wholly given to lechery, who had [gained fame] by preaching to the people and [dice-playing].

When Henry's frivolity and impiety had been established the bishop forbade him by his apostolic authority to remain any longer within the bishopric, and told him to take himself off somewhere else and leave us alone. Thus convicted by the bishop's efforts he fled to disturb other regions and infect them with his poisonous breath, unless his reputation should precede him. Hildebert took every precaution to calm by reason and humility the popular fury which Henry had seditiously stirred up against the clergy, for the people had become so devoted to Henry that even now his memory can scarcely be expunged, or their love for him drawn from their hearts.

What was Henry's appeal? What was his message? Why did authorities turn against him?

75. HERESY AND ORTHODOXY IN A FRENCH VILLAGE (1320)

The episcopal register of Jacques Fournier, bishop of Pamiers (1318-25) and later Pope Benedict XII (1334-42), contains a remarkably comprehensive record of his investigation of 114 suspected heretics carried out in his diocese between 1318 and 1325. Most of the suspects were accused of embracing the dualist heresy of the Cathars (called Manichaeans in this document), which had erupted in the area late in the twelfth century and had been largely suppressed only by armed force in the early years of the thirteenth century. But pockets of resistance lingered on for another century, as Fournier's register makes abundantly clear. These documents reached a wide audience in 1975 when the French historian Emmanuel Le Roy Ladurie published his book, Montaillou *(translated into English in 1978), a close examination of one village's experience with heresy based on the transcripts of Fournier's inquisitions. The following excerpt from the register reveals the procedures of an ecclesiastical court of investigation as it gradually amassed evidence against Guillaume Austatz, a wealthy peasant farmer from the village of Ornolac just a few miles south of Montaillou in the French Pyrenees. Guillaume was the village* bayle, *the local count's legal and fiscal overseer. More importantly, it displays an extraordinary range of details about the daily religious life, orthodox and not so orthodox, of French peasants who, at least in this case, seemed to be talking constantly to each other about religious matters.*

Source: trans. J. Shinners from Jean Duvernoy, *Le Registre d'Inquisition de Jacques Fournier, Évêque de Pamiers (1318-1325)*, v. 1 (Toulouse: Éduard Privat, 1965), pp. 191-213. Latin.

Witnesses against Guillaume Austatz of Ornolac for the Crime of Heresy

In the year of the Lord 1320, May 11, Gaillarde, wife of Bernard Ros of Ornolac (sworn as a witness and questioned because the said Guillaume Austatz had spoken certain heretical words) said that about four years ago she was in her house at Ornolac, and Alazaïs, the wife of Pierre Mounié of the same place, was there with her. The said Guillaume arrived along with some other people whose names she says she does not recall. When they had gathered around the hearth in the house, they started talking about God and about the General Resurrection. Among other things, they said that God really needed to be great in power and strength since each human soul would return to its own body at the General Resurrection. Hearing this, Guillaume said, "And do you believe that God made as many human souls as there are men and women? Surely not! For when at death souls exit the human bodies they have been in, they steal into the bodies of children who have just been born; as they leave one body, they enter into another one." For, as he said, if each human soul were to reclaim the very same body it had been in, since the world has lasted for many years, the whole world would be filled up with souls – so much so, as he said, that they couldn't be contained in the area between Toulouse and the Mérens Pass. For although souls are quite small, so many people have existed that their souls could not be contained within that space. When she heard these words, Alazaïs took the witness in her arms and held her closely. And when, after a while, Guillaume left the witness's house, Alazaïs said to her, "O godmother, these are evil words that Guillaume spoke," and the witness said that they were strong words.

Asked why she had concealed these words for such a long time, she said that she had not believed they were as serious as they are, but, goaded by her conscience, she had revealed them this year to the priest Bernard Petron, who was staying at Ornolac, so that he could counsel her what to do about them. And this priest, so she said, advised her to reveal the words to the lord bishop of Pamiers. So, led by her conscience, as she said, she reported these words to the bishop.

Asked if she had seen Guillaume take communion or doing the other things which good and faithful Christians are accustomed to do, she responded that for the past twelve years she had lived in the village of Ornolac and she had never seen Guillaume take communion, not even when he was sick or on the feast days when people usually receive communion, though she had seen him going into the church. And she should know since, as she said, his mother-in-law is her sister. She said moreover that Guillaume, while he lived at Lordat where he was born, used to practice usury; but after he moved to Ornolac, he practiced no usury that she knew of.

Asked if she deposed the previous testimony out of hate, love, fear, or bad will, instructed, or suborned, she said no, but because it is the truth, as she said above.

In the same year on May 26, the said Gaillarde, wife of the said Bernard Ros, cited on the same day, appeared before the lord bishop in the episcopal see at Pamiers and was received by the lord bishop as a witness against Guillaume Austatz concerning some matters touching on the Catholic faith.

Swearing an oath as a witness, she said and deposed that this year, around the feast of the nativity of St. John the Baptist [June 24], some money and some other things had been stolen from her which she had kept in a certain chest that had been broken into. The witness went to the said Guillaume (who was then and is now the *bayle* of Ornolac) and requested him to carry out his office, search for the thief, and to do what needed to be done for her to get her stolen things back. When he was unwilling to listen to her about her case, weeping and wailing she went to the church of Our Lady of Montgauzy to get a miracle from her to recover her money and property. In order to better get the miracle, she girded the candle on Blessed Mary's altar [probably by tying a string around it which she would later use to make a wick for another candle to be offered at the altar]. When she got back to Ornolac, she again asked Guillaume to investigate the theft, but he did not want to bother himself with it. The witness told him he should search for the money and things stolen from her just as he had searched for grain stolen from him that year. He told her that he had looked for the grain because he would have recognized it had he found it, but he wouldn't recognize her stolen money and property, as she said. And she said, "I put my trust in Blessed Mary of Montgauzy. I visited her and asked her to restore my stolen money and property; and I asked her to take revenge against those who stole from me if they don't restore them." Then Guillaume told the witness in the presence of some other people whose names she does not recall (except for Julien de Ornolac from Ornolac), that Blessed Mary did not have the power to restore the witness's money and things. When she said that yes she did, and that what he had said was bad, and also that the Blessed Mary would avenge her, Guillaume said Blessed Mary did not kill people or commit murders.

Also she said that, on some day which she could not recall around Easter this year, she had heard from Alazaïs Mounié, her godmother, that when Alazaïs was depressed because in a short space of time she had lost her four sons, Guillaume, seeing her so sad and depressed, asked her why she was so sad. She said to Guillaume: "Why shouldn't I be this sad and depressed since I lost my four handsome boys in such a short time?" He responded to her: "You shouldn't weep over this because you'll get them back without a doubt." And when she told Guillaume that she believed she would see them and get them back in paradise, not in this world, Guillaume told Alazaïs that, in fact, she would regain her dead sons in this world because, so he said, when she got pregnant, the soul of one of her sons or her other children would be reincarnated in her baby – and this would happen with the souls of her other dead sons each time Alazaïs got pregnant.

Also the witness said that, although Guillaume seemed to be in good health during last Lent since he went about his business and there had been no sickness in his house or in others, still the same, on many days during Lent Guillaume ate meat prepared for him in his house. The witness heard it commonly said in Ornolac that Guillaume was likewise eating meat all during Lent. She knew nothing else nor had she heard anything except what she had deposed. Asked if she had given this testimony at someone's request or for money, etc., she said no.

Also, she said that two years ago she was talking with Alazaïs de Bordas of Ornolac, and they mentioned Guillaume. Then Alazaïs said, "Here's what kind of man Guillaume is: the other day while we were in a skiff crossing the Ariége, which was flooded, we were absolutely terrified we were going to sink – I especially so since I was pregnant. And when I mentioned this to Guillaume Austatz, he said it would have mattered little to him whether he died then, for he would be just as dead one way as another."

This testimony or deposition was made in the year and on the day mentioned above in the presence of Frère Gaillard de Pomiès of the Dominican house at Pamiers, Pierre de Verdier, archdeacon of Majorca, and Master Guillaume Pierre Barthe, the lord bishop's notary, who took and recorded the said deposition.

The year and day as above, Alazaïs, wife of Pierre Mounié of Ornolac, sworn as a witness and asked about the above matters, said that about four years past, she went to the house of Gaillarde, wife of Bernard Ros of Ornolac, and there in Gaillarde's house she found both Guillaume Austatz of Ornolac and some other person whose name she does not recall nor even whether it was a man or a woman. When they had gathered around the hearth, they started talking about the end of the world and the General Resurrection to come. At that point it seemed to her that Guillaume said that folks were stupid since they believed each human body had its own soul that would be restored to it at the Resurrection. But this wasn't true, so he said, for when a soul exited one body, it stole into another one, because, as he said, if there were as many human souls as there were bodies, the world would be overflowing with human souls. When the witness heard these words, she was dumbfounded and she took Gaillarde in her arms. After Guillaume left, she embraced her again, saying, "Holy Mary, what bad things that fellow says!" And Gaillarde responded that they really were bad words. Then the witness said that she had not wanted to be there. Asked whether Guillaume led a good life, she answered that many people said he was a usurer. Still, she had seen him receive communion. Asked whether Guillaume comes from a heretical family, she said yes, since his mother and dead sister had been incarcerated at [the ecclesiastical prison at] Carcassone, and his sister's husband had absconded due to the crime of heresy. Asked if her testimony had been deposed at someone's request, for money, or out of hate, love, fear, bad will, instructed, or suborned, she said that it had not, but because it is the truth.

The same year, July 25, the said Alazaïs, wife of Pierre Mounié, again appeared and offered testimony after she had been told to swear to tell the truth as a witness. She said that about two years ago she had lost her four sons one after the other and was terribly sad and depressed over this. One day when Guillaume had come back from his fields, he saw her standing in the doorway of her house looking quite depressed, and he asked her why she was so sad. She told him it was because she had so suddenly lost her four handsome boys. Guillaume told her not to be sad about this, for she would get her four dead sons back. And when she told Guillaume that she believed she would see her dead sons and get them back in paradise but not in this world, Guillaume told her that, on the contrary, she would get them back in this very world. For when she got pregnant the souls of her four dead sons would be reincarnated in the sons she conceived and carried in her womb; and in that way she would recover her dead sons in this world. Asked about those present, she said she did not recall that anyone was present except herself and Guillaume. Asked about the time and place, she answered as above.

Also she said that this year, on what day she did not recall, but after the [Waldensian] heretics Raymond de la Côte and the woman Agnes had been burned, she and Guillaume were standing near the door of his house and Guillaume said that the bishop of Pamiers was a proud and harsh man. She said that a man who had great power could do much. And then Guillaume said that if Raymond and Agnes had been listened to and had had an audience, just as the bishop did, the bishop would be worthier of burning than Raymond and Agnes. And when the witness said that it was not theirs to judge this, Guillaume quickly went inside his house.

Also she said she had heard from Julien de Ornolac that when Gaillarde, wife of Bernard Ros of Ornolac, had complained to Guillaume Austatz, the *bayle*, about some things stolen from a chest she had and Guillaume was unwilling to search for them, she said she had asked Blessed Mary of Montgauzy to put it into the hearts of the thieves to return the stolen goods to her or to take revenge on them for her. Guillaume told her, in the hearing of Julien, that Blessed Mary wasn't able to cause the return of the stolen goods to Gaillarde.

Also, she said that this year Guillaume, though he was strong, healthy, and able to work, ate meat all during Lent up to the feast of Palm Sunday. She herself saw him do this on several days. And one day when Guillaume's brother, Bernard Austatz of Lordat, came to Ornolac and criticized Guillaume for eating meat on Fridays and Saturdays and during Lent, Guillaume, who at that moment had a bowlful of meat in front of him, told his brother, who was getting up to leave after just a short time, that he wasn't going to shove the bowl down his throat. This is what the witness saw and heard, so she said. She also said that Ornolac's priest sent Alazaïs de Bordas to tell Guillaume that he was not pleased that he was eating meat during Lent since he was healthy and able to work. She said nothing else pertinent. Asked if she had said these things at someone's request, for money, or out of hate, instructed, or suborned, she said no, but because it is the truth. This deposition was given in the year and on the day and in presence of the same people as above.

Raymond Barrau, priest of Ornolac, sworn on the holy Gospels concerning the said Guillaume, said that this year during Easter Week he was in the house of Mathende de Alzen, and Guillaume Austatz was also there as well as two other people whose names he does not recall, so he said. Guillaume started talking about the fact that Ornolac's assistant priest, Bernard, had told the parishioners they had given much less in offerings this Easter Day than they usually did, and he upbraided them for this. Then Guillaume suggested that priests could not compel anyone to offer more than what was customary, that it was sufficient for people to give one strip of cloth, or a torte, or even a piece of straw, and that people couldn't be coerced to do this. He said nothing else pertinent. Asked if he had said these things at someone's request, for money, or out of hate, he said no, but because it is the truth.

The year and day as above, Alazaïs, wife of Pierre de Bordas of Ornolac, sworn as a witness and asked about the above matters against Guillaume Austatz pertaining to the Catholic faith, said that two years ago around the feast of Pentecost her husband was clearing the weeds from his crops which he owned across the Ariége. One day the witness and some others had returned from her husband's fields across the river, which was swollen, in a skiff. She had been greatly afraid crossing the Ariége, and as she stood in Guillaume's house still thoroughly shaken and afraid, he asked her why she was standing there like that. She told him she had been absolutely terrified the skiff would sink. And Guillaume said to her, "Why were you afraid? It should matter little to you whether you died there or elsewhere." When she answered that it was no small matter to die suddenly and without confession rather than to die with confession and the other things that a good Christian should have, Guillaume was silent and offered no reply to these words. Asked who was present when Guillaume said these words to her, she said she did not remember since the other people in Guillaume's house were going here and there about the house doing their work.

Also she said that this year when the heretic Raymond de la Côte was condemned by the bishop for heresy and later burned, Guillaume told the witness and Gaillarde, wife of Bernard Ros of Ornolac, in Guillaume's house that Raymond de la Côte, if they had listened to and understood his reasons, would not have been condemned or burned, and that it was evil for them to treat him this way since he was a good cleric.

She also said that she had heard it said in the village of Ornolac that when Gaillarde, the wife of Bernard Ros, had lost some money and some other items through theft, and Guillaume as the *bayle* was unwilling to search for them, Gaillarde told Guillaume that Blessed Mary of Montgauzy, to whom she had gone, would recover her money and goods and take revenge against the thieves. Guillaume told her that Blessed Mary wasn't able to cause the return of her property nor was she able to restore it to her.

Also she said and testified that last year (on what day she did not recall) when she was bargaining for cloth in Guillaume's house, they were talking about the dead and about the good that their souls had in the other world. Guillaume said and asserted that the soul of any man or woman who had good in this world could not have good in the next, and whoever suffered evil in this world could not suffer evil in the next, since, so he said, it was fitting that they should have good or evil either in this world or the next. Asked about those present, she said herself and Barchinona, wife of the late Bernard de Bordas; but the witness does not know if Barchinona heard this and she said nothing else pertinent. Asked if she deposed the previous testimony out of hate, at someone's request, for money, suborned or under others' instructions, she responded no, but because it is true, so she said.

The year and day as above, Julien de Ornolac, named after the place Ornolac, was sworn as a witness and questioned about the above matters and other things touching on the Catholic faith against Guillaume Austatz. He said he knew nothing, except that this year around the feast of the nativity of John the Baptist he heard him saying that Blessed Mary could not cause the return of some things stolen from Gaillarde, wife of Bernard Ros. Gaillarde herself said this in the witness's presence. Asked about the aforementioned matters, he said he knew nothing. Asked if he deposed the above induced or suborned by hate, money, or love, he said no, but because it is the truth, so he said.

The year and day as above, Barchinona, wife of the late Bernard de Bordas of Ornolac, was sworn as a witness and questioned about the above matters and other things touching on the Catholic faith against Guillaume Austatz. She said that once, while they were in the yard of his house, she heard him say that after a man or woman died, he or she would not afterwards resurrect. Asked about the time, she said she does not remember. Asked who was present, she says she does not remember.

Also she said she frequently heard Guillaume say that men and women who have good things in this life can have nothing but evil in the next world; and those who have evil now will not have evil but good in the future life.

She also said that at the feast of the apostles Philip and James [May 1], the day that the heretic Raymond de la Côte was burned, she heard Guillaume saying that Raymond was a good man, and if the lord bishop of Pamiers had listened to his arguments, he would not have been burned.

Also she said she heard him say that it was enough that they made offerings in church worth only a quarter of a penny, and they were not obliged nor could they be compelled to offer more.

Also she said that this year during Lent he ate meat for five weeks, even though he could have abstained for some part of that time without any risk to his health since he was going about taking care of his business around his house, at the threshing-floor, and throughout the village. She said nothing else relevant. Asked if she had deposed the above at someone's request, for money, out of hate, love, under instruction, or suborned, she said no, but because it is the truth, as she said.

The year as above, July 27, Pierre de Bordas of Ornolac was sworn as a witness and asked to tell the truth plainly and fully about the above matters and others touching on the Catholic faith against Guillaume Austatz. He said that this year, after the heretic Raymond de la Côte was burned by the lord bishop of Pamiers and the inquisitor of Carcassone, when the news reached Ornolac, the witness; his wife, Alazaïs; Barchinona, the wife of the late Bernard de Bordas; and Guillaume Austatz were sitting at the table eating when Guillaume said that the heretic Raymond who had been burned was a good cleric, one of the better people in all Christendom. And it would have been better for [the region of] Sabarthès if the bishop of Pamiers had been burned instead of Raymond. Asked whether he heard Guillaume saying that this heretic was a good Christian and a holy man, and that, if he had been treated justly, he would not have been burned, he said that he does not recall. Asked if, when Guillaume said these words – that it would have been better for Sabarthès for the lord bishop to have been burned than the heretic – he agreed or disagreed with him or chastised him for these words, he responded that he said nothing to him, though it seemed to him that he had spoken badly, so he said.

Also he said he frequently heard Guillaume say that every human soul passed through the fire of purgatory before it came to the kingdom of heaven. He said this was so even for souls of children who died immediately after baptism. Guillaume said that he had heard this, though he did not say from whom. Asked who was present when Guillaume said these words, he said he does not recall. Asked where this happened, he said the village of Ornolac, though he does not remember whether it was outside on the street or in a house. He wished to say nothing more, though he was carefully questioned.

The Confession of the Converted Heretic Guillaume Austatz

In the year of the Lord 1320, July 15, it came to the attention of the reverend father in Christ, Lord Jacques [Fournier], by God's grace bishop of Pamiers, that Guillaume Austatz of Ornolac in the diocese of Pamiers, had said and asserted before many people: that each human soul does not have its own body, but when it exits from one body, it steals into another body; and that even at the resurrection not every soul will resume its own body. He also said that each soul will not be rewarded or punished in the body it dwelled in, and that he personally did not trust that his soul would be saved or damned. He also said that, if each soul had its own body and was not reincarnated into another body, even though souls were very small, still the land of Sabarthès would be filled up from Toulouse all the way to the Mérens Pass – giving to understand through this that souls are corporeal. He also said that Raymond de la Côte, the heretic condemned this year by the lord bishop and the inquisitor of Carcassone, was a good Christian, and that what he taught was true. He also said that the church was not able to compel anyone to offer any specific thing at mass, but that it sufficed to offer a straw to the priest. Through these things it was apparent that he was a believer, favorer, and harborer of the Manichaean heretics and a member of their sect. The lord bishop informed himself about these matters and, wishing to question this man about them and other things pertaining to the Catholic faith, about which he was vehemently suspect, he cited him by his letters to appear on this day. Guillaume, appearing before the lord bishop and Frère Gaillard de Pomiès (the lord inquisitor of Carcassone's deputy), was asked by the same simply and not under oath if he had said, taught, or believed the aforesaid heretical words. He responded no.

The same lord bishop, wishing to lead him back to faith and free him from danger, gave him some time (until early tomorrow evening) to think about the aforesaid; and because Guillaume said that his enemies made these denunciations, the lord bishop asked him who he thought his enemies were, and Guillaume answered that the priest and assistant priest of Ornolac were, and no one else.

The next day at early evening the said Guillaume appeared before the lord bishop in his episcopal chambers, assisted by Frère Gaillard de Pomiès, and made a physical oath that he would tell the truth plain and simple without any falsehoods intermixed about the aforesaid heretical articles and other matters pertaining to the Catholic faith, both insofar as they concerned him as the defendant and others, living or dead, as witnesses. After the articles contained in the preceding were explained to him again in the vernacular, he responded to the first article that he had never said nor did he believe that each human soul does not possess its own body.

To the second article he said he had not said or believed that the human soul, when it exits from its body, enters at that point or later into another body.

To the third article he said he believes that the human soul will rise and resume the flesh and bones it occupied in this life, and he never said or believed otherwise, so he said.

To the fourth article he said that at the General Judgment, a soul will be punished or rewarded in the body it occupied in this life, and he had never said or believed otherwise, so he said.

To the fifth article he said he had never said that if each human being who ever was, is, or will be had his own soul, then the land between Toulouse and the Mérens Pass would be filled up with the souls of the people of Sabarthès, past and present.

To the sixth article he said that he had never said that Raymond de la Côte was a good Christian.

To the seventh article he said that, repeating a statement he heard from a man from Chateauverdun (who was repeating a statement of the Romans), he had indeed said that the church could not compel anyone to make a specific offering, but that it sufficed to offer anything, no matter how small. But the man had not said that he believed this or was trying to discourage anyone from making agreeable or proper offerings. Asked the name of the man from Chateauverdun, he said that he did not know. Asked when he heard the man say these words, he said this year. Asked who else was present, he said he did not remember. Asked if had seen heretics, believed in them, harbored them, or favored them, he said no.

Since the above information made it clear that the said Guillaume had neither told the truth about nor confessed the aforesaid heretical articles, the lord bishop arrested him and ordered him to be incarcerated immediately at the castle of Allemans by his deputies, ordering him not to leave the castle without the lord bishop's permission.

The same year as above, August 11, Guillaume Austatz standing for judgment at the residence of the episcopal see of Pamiers before the lord bishop assisted by Frère Gaillard de Pomiès, said and confessed that three or four years ago – he did not really remember the time or day – he was in his house at Ornolac, and [either] Bartholomette, the wife of Arnaud d'Urs of Vicdessos, who was then staying at his house, or Alazaïs, wife of Pierre de Bordas, had lost a son whom she had discovered lying dead next to her in bed. But he did not remember, so he said, which of the two women had lost her son. And when this woman wept and wailed over the death of her son, and he saw and heard her, he said to the woman that she should not weep or wail because

God would give that dead son's soul to the next child, boy or girl, that she conceived and bore, or else his soul will be in a good place in the next world. Asked what he understood it to mean when he said God would return the dead son's soul to whatever boy or girl the woman conceived or bore in the future, he said that he understood through these words that amends would be made to the woman with another child, and, so he said, though these words meant nothing, he said them anyway just as they came to his head. Asked if he had heard anyone saying that souls exiting human bodies reenter other human bodies, or if he had ever believed this or believed it still, he said he had never heard it from anyone, nor had he believed it, nor did he believe it now. Asked if he had ever said the same words or words to that effect to any person or persons except to Bartholomette or Alazaïs, he said he did not recall saying such words or words to that effect.

Also he said that around a year and a half ago he was in the village common of Ornolac and with him there, as he recalled, were Raymond de Ornolac, Pierre Doumenc, Pons Barrau, Guillaume de Aspira, Pierre de Gathlep, Bertrand de Ville, Raymond Benet the Younger, and some others he did not recall, so he said. Someone from among them, he did not remember who, started talking about the location of the souls of the dead, asking what place could hold as many souls as there were people who had died every day. Guillaume replied that they were received into paradise. And when those standing around asked him if paradise was so huge a place that it could hold every soul, he said that it was huge–so huge that if a house were made that occupied the whole area between Toulouse and Mérens, paradise would still be a bigger place and could hold many souls in it.

The same year as above, August 28, standing for judgment at the episcopal see of Pamiers before the lord bishop assisted by the said Frère Gaillard de Pomiès (the deputy of the lord inquisitor of Carcassone), Guillaume Austatz said and confessed that two and a half years ago or so, on the day that the said lord bishop first visited Sabarthès and the church of St. Martin of Ussat, the son of Alazaïs Mounié of Ornolac and also some other boy were burned by a fire that they had [accidentally] set in the house of Bernard Mounié. And when the said Alazaïs was crying over the loss of her son, Guillaume came over and visited Alazaïs at her house to console her about her son's death. While comforting her he said, "Godmother, don't weep and wail, for you can still get back the souls of your dead children." Alazaïs said that yes, she would get them back in paradise. He told her that in fact she would get them back in some son or daughter whom she would conceive and bear, for she was still young; and if she didn't get them back in a son or daughter, she would regain them in paradise.

The same year as above, August 29, standing for judgment at the aforesaid see before the said bishop assisted by the said Frère Gaillard de Pomiès, Guillaume Austatz said and confessed that eight years ago or so, as he recalled, his mother, Guillemette de Austatz, was cited for the crime of heresy by the lord inquisitor of Carcassone. When he heard this, he went on a market day to Lordat to be with his mother who had to go to Carcassone. And in his mother's house at Lordat they sat alone together by the fire and, as he said, he asked his mother if she thought she was guilty of heresy since she had been cited by the lord inquisitor. She said yes. And then he said to her, "How? Have you met heretics?" And she said yes: Pierre Authié and Prades Tavernier at Arnaud de Albiès's house in Lordat. And when he asked her why and how she had gone to that house to see these heretics, she said that late one evening she was standing at the door of her house, and Guillemette (the wife of the surgeon Arnaud Teisseire of Lordat and the daughter of the heretic Pierre Authié) arrived with Raymond Sabatié of Lordat. Then Raymond said to Guillaume's mother, "Come join Guillemette de Teisseire." She said "Gladly," so they went together (namely his mother, Guillemette, and Raymond) and went inside Albiès's house to a room where the heretics were. When they were at the door to the room, Raymond asked Guillaume's mother if she would like to see some holy men, and, quickly opening the door, they entered and found there the heretics Pierre Authié and Prades Tavernier, whom first Guillemette and next Raymond reverenced in a heretical fashion. When these two had greeted the heretics, they told Guillaume's mother she should adore them in the same way they had. Guillemette told her that this master [Pierre] was her [Guillemette's] father, and they taught her how she should adore them. And so his mother, after they had instructed her, reverenced the heretics. After this adoration, they stayed there with the heretics, and Pierre Authié preached to them. This heretic told them among other things that when children's souls exit after their death, they enter by stealth into the bodies of children who were generated and conceived after the death of the first children. This happens after the mother of the dead children conceives and bears other children.

This heretic also told her—as his mother told him—that not every human soul had its own body, because if this were the case, the world could scarcely contain as many souls as there are people living now and people once alive in the past. For although souls were very small, still, there have been so many people living and dead that they could hardly be contained in the world if each soul had its own body and entered into no other body except the one it originally had.

Also his mother told him, as she recalled, that the heretic told them that after death the human body would not rise and be reanimated; and she told him many other things that he said he did not remember. After the sermon that the heretic preached to these people, he gave them bread blessed by him. His mother, however, did not eat the bread, but slipped it into a crack, so she said.

After his mother had told him these things, he said to her, "Did you believe – *do* you believe that what this heretic said was true?" She said she neither believed nor disbelieved. He asked her if she had seen other heretics and whether she had given them anything. She said she had not seen them except the one time, but that she had given them things: twice she sent them a gallon of wine and a loaf of bread by way of Mengarde, the daughter of Arnaud de Albiès, because Mengarde had looked for bread and wine for the heretics but could find none for sale in Lordat. That night Guillaume and his mother spoke no more about the matter, and the next morning he went with her to Carcassone, talking to her along the way about these things.

Also he said that when Raymond Sabatié was arrested for heresy and jailed at Montgrenier, he had pledged himself for the fifty Toulouse sous which they paid on his behalf. He went to Lordat to speak with Pierre Sabatié, Raymond's son. When he got there, he took Pierre outside the village and asked him if his father, who was being held at Montgrenier, was guilty of heresy. He said yes. He also asked him if his mother Fabrisse and he himself were guilty, and he said yes. Then he asked Pierre, "How did this happen?" Pierre told him that his father and mother had kept Pierre Authié hidden in the cellar of their house. Pierre and his mother and father had heard from this heretic that some would be saved from among all kinds of people, Christians, Jews, and pagans; and that paradise could be obtained through his hands and those of his sect; and that as many would be saved who embraced their faith as those from any other sect or manner of living. He also said that human souls would be slower to gain paradise more for this than for any other reason: because men persecuted those of his sect. Pierre Authié's sister Fabrisse, the wife of Raymond Sabatié, said the same things or words to that effect to Guillaume. And [Pierre's] sister told him this in that very house.

Guillaume also said that a good twenty years ago or so, while talking with Raymond Sabatié about some sermon that a priest had given in the village of Lordat, he himself praised the sermon. Raymond told him that if he would like, he would give him a good sermon, and he began to lay out the Gospels to him. Hearing this, Guillaume told him he did not want to listen, and he swore by his head – so he said – that, because of words like this, Raymond would come to a bad end. Yet at that point he did not tell him anything heretical because Guillaume did not want to continue the conversation, so he said. And, so he said, from the time he heard the three heretical articles from his mother (namely that souls of dead children enter the bodies of other children newly conceived, that not every human soul has its own body since there are and have been so many more human bodies than souls that the whole world would be filled up with souls, and that people will not rise after they have died and been buried) he began to wonder whether what his mother told him about these three articles was true. Sometimes it seemed true, other times false. But for two or three years, so he said, he absolutely believed that what his mother told him about these three articles she learned from Pierre Authié was true. And during the time when he believed these things, it seemed to him that once, in the house of Gaillarde, wife of Bernard Ros, when they were talking about the souls of the dead and saying there were as many of them as there were people now dead or alive, he had said that not every human soul has its own body, but when a human soul leaves a human body after its death, it steals into another body newly conceived or born; for if each soul had its own body so that there were as many souls as there were bodies, since the world had lasted so long, the souls could scarcely be contained in the whole world.

Asked if there were any other people present besides Gaillarde when he said these words, he answered that he did not recall anyone else.

Also while he believed these things, many times and places he told Bartholomette, wife of Arnaud d'Urs of Vicdessos, and Alazaïs Mounié of Ornolac that they would yet get the souls of their dead children back in this world, because they could still conceive children, and in conceiving them, the souls of their dead children would reenter them. Asked if he had said any other words or words to this effect, he said he did not remember.

The same year as above, August 30, standing for judgment at the episcopal see of Pamiers before the lord bishop assisted by the said Frère Gaillard de Pomiès (the deputy of the lord inquisitor of Carcassone), Guillaume Austatz said and confessed that around six or seven years ago (he did not remember the time or the day well), one day he was in the cemetery of the church of Ornolac, and near the front of the church between the middle and the front, a grave was being dug to bury some dead person whose name he does not recall. They were pulling many human bones from the grave. Seeing these bones, he said to the many other people present (whose names he does not recall since most of the people in the village were there): "They say the souls of dead people return to the same flesh and bones of the people they originally dwelled in. How is it possible for a soul to return to these bones right here where it once was?" Asked if he had ever believed it was impossible for human bodies to rise, he said yes – for almost that whole day, because he had made that comment. Yet sometimes he did not believe how this could be possible. But for almost two years after he had heard from his mother that the heretic Pierre Authié had told her, among other things, that dead bodies would not rise, he wavered and he wondered whether there would be a resurrection of the dead or not. Sometimes he agreed with one side of the argument, sometimes with the other. At times, so he said, he did not believe there would be a resurrection, agreeing more with his mother, though he did not believe it totally. Other times he believed the opposite, because this was what he heard preached in church, and also because Guillaume de Alzinhac – a priest from Carbonne who once in a while stayed at his mother's house in Lordat and who had taught him when he was young and living with his mother at Lordat – told him there would be a future resurrection of dead men and women.

On the day he said these words in the cemetery (namely "How is it possible that, after death, the soul returns to the flesh and bones of the person it inhabited while he was alive?") he talked about them on his way home and he said the same words or words to that effect when he got home as he had said in the cemetery. And he continued believing this – that the resurrection of dead men and women was impossible. Asked about those present, he said the brothers Pierre and Jean Bordas; Barchinona, wife of the late Bernard de Bordas; and his own late wife Guillemette. He seemed to recall that he said these words in the yard of his house.

He also said that during the time he believed that human souls leaving one body entered into another body, he thought that the future resurrection would take place like this: if one soul entered in succession into many bodies, then only this soul, without entering another body, would reenter the last body it had left. And so only this last person would rise. Neither that soul nor any others would reenter the other bodies it had previously inhabited – and without a doubt, all these other bodies would not rise. Asked how many other bodies a soul leaving one body could enter in succession, he said his mother told him a soul could enter seven to nine bodies in turn, or so the heretic Pierre Authié had taught her. Guillaume believed this for the whole time that he believed that human souls exiting human bodies could enter into others. Asked if he believed the words of Pierre Authié and his sister Fabrisse (namely that some would be saved from among all of mankind's faiths – Christian, Jews, and pagans; that paradise could be gained more through the hands of the heretic Pierre Authié and others of his sect than through any other sect or faith; and that human souls were more hindered in gaining paradise because others persecuted the members of Pierre Authié's sect than for any other cause) he said no. Asked if he believed that one could save his soul in Pierre Authié's sect or faith, he said no. Asked if he had sent or given anything to Pierre Authié or other heretics of his sect, he said no. Asked if he had seen, reverenced, given blessing to, or eaten bread blessed by them, he said he had not seen them since they left the land of Sabarthès and went to Lombardy, nor had he adored them, given them blessing, or eaten any bread blessed by them. Asked if he had said and believed that those having riches and earthly goods in this world were unable to have them in the future world of the kingdom of heaven, he said he had indeed said that those having riches and earthly goods in this world could not enter the kingdom of heaven, just as a camel could not pass through the eye of a needle [Matt. 19:24]. But though he had not at the time specifically announced his opinion (since this is what was generally said about all rich people) still, then and now he understood and understands that people say this about those rich people who acquire their wealth unjustly or in a bad way, not about those rich people who possess or acquire their wealth justly and in a good way. In the same way, he said some poor people will be saved and others will perish.

Asked if he said or believed that all human souls that enter the kingdom of heaven must first pass through the fire of purgatory, he said he indeed clearly said all souls entering paradise first pass through the fire of purgatory. But he had always maintained and believed in his heart, though he had not said it out loud, that the souls of baptized children and also the souls of the martyrs and the saints did not pass through the fire of purgatory.

On August 30, standing for judgment at the episcopal see of Pamiers before the lord bishop assisted by the said Frère Gaillard de Pomiès (the deputy of the lord inquisitor of Carcassone), Guillaume Austatz said and confessed that this year, after the heretic Raymond de la Côte was burned in the village of Allemans, one Sunday the men of Ornolac (namely Pons Barrau, Guillaume de Aspira, Pierre Doumenc, Bernard de Ville, Guillaume Forsac, Raymond de Ornolac, all of them from Ornolac) were in the village common next to the elm tree there, and they were talking about the burning of the heretic. Guillaume arrived and said, "I'll tell you this for a fact: this fellow they burned was a good cleric – there was none better in these parts except the bishop of Pamiers. He constantly argued with the bishop and he disagreed with him, but he believed in God, Blessed Mary, and all the saints, and in the seven [sic] articles of faith, and he was a good Christian. And since he believed all these things, it was a great injustice to burn him." The men asked him why he was burned considering he was a good cleric and a good Christian, and he replied it was because he said the pope could not absolve sins and he denied purgatory – that is why he was burned.

Also he said that before he said these words in the village common of Ornolac, Raymond de Nan, who was staying with Pierre Mir, the canon of Foix, came to his house at Ornolac and told him, in the hearing of Pierre Bordas, Arnaud Pere, and Guillaume Garaud of Chateauverdun, that a man had been burned at the village of Allemans by the bishop of Pamiers. People said he was a good cleric, and that he had disagreed with the bishop but believed in God, Blessed Mary, all the saints, and the seven articles of faith, and was a good Christian, and it was a great injustice to burn him. When Guillaume heard this, he suggested that "it would have been better for Sabarthès if the bishop of Pamiers had been burned instead of this man, for afterwards he wouldn't make us spend our money." By this he understood not that the bishop was a heretic, but that the bishop demanded a tithe on sheep called *carnelages* from the people of Sabarthès. This was why he said it would have been better for the lord bishop to be burned than the heretic. Asked if he then believed or still believes it would have been better for Sabarthès if the bishop had been burned instead of the heretic Raymond de la Côte, he said he believed it then when he spoke these words, and he held that opinion for fifteen days; but after fifteen days he did not believe it nor does he now. He was asked – when he believed it was better for Sabarthès to burn the lord bishop of Pamiers instead of the heretic since the bishop exacted the tithe of sheep from Sabarthès – whether he believed or still believes the bishop can justly demand the tithe. He said he thought the bishop could justly demand the tithe. He was asked, since he believed the bishop could justly demand the tithe, whether he believed the people of Sabarthès acted justly in refusing to pay the tithe. He said that although the bishop exacted the tithe according to law, the people of Sabarthès also justly refused to pay the tithe according to their customs. Asked why he believed it was better to burn the bishop than the heretic, since, when he said this, he thought the lord bishop justly demanded the tithe from the people of Sabarthès, he responded that he said this because of the expenses the lord bishop cost the people of Sabarthès.

He was asked if, when he said the heretic Raymond de la Côte was a good Christian and was unjustly burned, he knew that he had been condemned by the lord bishop and the inquisitor of Carcassone as a heretic and had been judged a heretic. He said he did indeed know that Raymond had been condemned as a heretic by the bishop and the inquisitor; still, it did not seem to him or to others with whom he spoke that he was a heretic since he believed in God, Blessed Mary, all the saints, and the seven articles of faith. This was why it seemed to him that Raymond was a good Christian and had been unjustly condemned. But later, when they considered that the lord bishop and the inquisitor would not have burdened themselves with so great a sin as killing a man unless it was just, it seemed to them that – although to some small degree they had unjustly condemned him – still, in some measure they had acted justly. He was asked whether, after he had heard it said – as he confessed – that Raymond had been condemned as a heretic since he did not believe the pope could absolve sins and he denied that purgatory existed, he then believed and still believes that Raymond had been justly condemned as a heretic for denying these two articles. He said that at the time he spoke these words, he did not believe that the heretic should have been condemned for not believing the two articles; but before then and after then he believed and still believes he was justly condemned as a heretic for denying the two articles. However, for fifteen days he remained convinced that he had been unjustly condemned for denying the articles. He was asked whether, at the time he believed Raymond had been unjustly condemned as a heretic for denying the two articles, he thought that to say the pope could not absolve sins and to deny that purgatory existed in the next world were heresies. He said that for those fifteen days he did not believe it was heresy to say the pope could not absolve sins and that purgatory did not exist. But before and after those fifteen days, he believed and still believes that to deny these two articles is heresy, and also that someone denying these articles should be justly condemned as a heretic.

The year as above, September 1, the said Guillaume Austatz appeared for judgment at the episcopal see before the lord bishop assisted by Frère Gaillard de Pomiès, the deputy of the lord inquisitor of Carcassone. He said and confessed that about five years ago he was at home, and Pierre Bordas and his wife Alazaïs and Barchinona Bordas were there. They started talking about the salvation of souls. He said that, if it were true what the priests say – namely that if someone wanted to be saved, it was necessary for him to confess all his sins, and, if he could, to restore or return everything he had taken from other people against their will – not ten out a hundred people will be saved. Better yet, not ten out of a thousand. For people do not confess their sins very well, either because they have forgotten them or because they are embarrassed to confess them; and they take lots of things from other people. So only a few out of many will be saved, if what the priests say is true. Asked if he then believed and still believes that when priests say these two things they are telling the truth, he said yes. Asked whether he believed he would be damned for eternity if he died and had not wanted to confess that he had knowingly committed simple fornication or loaned money at interest or had failed to return interest that he had received if he could, he said that he did.

Also, he had said he believed that if each soul had its own body, the world could scarcely hold these souls since, though they were very small, there were so many of them that they would fill up the world. From this it appeared that he believed souls were material. He was asked if he thought human souls were material and had physical parts: hands, feet, and other parts. He said that at the time he had said this, he believed human souls had the physical shape of a man or woman and parts resembling the human body. But now he believed human souls were spirits without parts resembling the human body.

He was asked whether he believed the saints dwelling in paradise could help people living in this world; he said yes. He was asked whether he had ever said otherwise. He said that this year around Pentecost, when Gaillarde Ros had lost five sous stolen from a chest, she complained to him that since he was the local *bayle*, and since he had not immediately discovered who had committed the theft, she had asked Blessed Mary of Montgauzy to expose the thief. He said to Gaillarde, "And don't you think Blessed Mary would commit a greater sin if she revealed the person who stole the four [*sic*] sous from you? For wouldn't the thief be thrown into confusion and brought to justice [with the risk of capital punishment] by this than if Blessed Mary didn't return the four sous to you?" But he said this, so he said, as a joke, not really believing Blessed Mary would sin if she revealed the thief. He also did not think it would be a sin if she revealed the wrongdoer, or even if he were sentenced to death or killed by order of his superior.

He was asked if he had ever confessed the aforesaid heresies to a priest or in any other way. He said no, because he had not believed he had sinned by believing them and persisting in that belief. But now he realized that he had been gravely at fault for believing these errors, and he humbly begged absolution for the sentence of excommunication he incurred for believing them. He said he was prepared to perform any penance and suffer any penalty the lord bishop and the inquisitors enjoined on him for these things. But he was obliged that if he later recalls any other crime beyond that which he had confessed, or also if he remembers that someone else living or dead had committed this crime, as quickly as he can he will reveal this to the bishop, his successors, or the lord inquisitor of Carcassone. And the lord bishop, seeing his humility and contrition, absolved him in the church's due form from the sentence of excommunication he incurred for believing these heresies, provided that he fully confessed them and that he now and forevermore believes what the Roman Church preaches and teaches. But before granting him this absolution, he received from him an abjuration and oath as follows:

There Guillaume Austatz abjured all heresy, belief in, support of, defense of, harboring of, approval of the sect, life, or faith of, agreement with, and every other kind of participation with Manichaeans or Waldensians, etc. ... otherwise his absolution is not valid.

This was done in the presence of the said lord bishop, Frère Gaillard, Frère Arnaud de Caslar (both of the Order of Preachers at Pamiers), and Master Guillaume Pierre Barthe, the lord bishop's notary, who recorded and wrote the preceding. And I, Rainaud, faithfully corrected all of it against the original copy.

The year as above, September 3, standing for judgment at the episcopal see of Pamiers before the lord bishop assisted by the said Frère Gaillard de Pomiès (deputy of the lord inquisitor of Carcassone), Guillaume Austatz heard the bishop read to him in the vernacular everything he confessed above.

Asked whether everything he confessed against himself and against others in the above confession was true, he said yes. He said he wished and wishes to stand firm in this confession, seeking mercy that he be not judged upon the above matters; and he finished his business, and sought to be given a sentence and mercy for the above matters.

The year as above, March 7, the said Guillaume being cited, etc. ... finished his business. And the aforesaid lord bishop and the inquisitor assigned Guillaume a day to hear his definitive sentence, namely the Sunday [March 16] nearest the Ides of March, at the hour of terce in the Dominican house at Pamiers.

This was done the year and day as above, in the presence of Frère Gaillard de Pomiès, Frère Arnaud de Caslar (both of the Order of Preachers at Pamiers); Frère David, monk of Fontfroide; and me, Guillaume Pierre Barthe, the lord bishop's notary, and Barthélemy Adalbert, the lord inquisitor's notary, both of whom recorded the aforesaid.

On the Sunday assigned to the said Guillaume Austatz, he appeared in the churchyard of St. John the Martyr and sentence was rendered to him by the lord bishop and the lord inquisitor in this manner: "May all know, etc...." Look for this sentence in the Sentence Book of the inquisition of heretical depravity, which sentence was issued against the said Guillaume Austatz on Sunday, March 2 in the said churchyard.

And I, the aforesaid Rainaud, faithfully corrected all of this against the original copy.

How religious are these people? How well informed about Christianity are they? What religious topics interest them? Do you think Guillaume Austatz was a heretic or merely confused? Is the case against him, based on the testimony of his neighbors, solid? What details of the daily religious life of the villagers of Ornolac strike you as illuminating?

76. HERESY AND ORTHODOXY IN AN ENGLISH TOWN (1429)

England underwent only one major outburst of heresy in the Middle Ages: the wave of Lollardy that swept through the country in the late fourteenth and early fifteenth century, partly inspired by the writings of the priest John Wycliffe (c. 1330-84). Though they did not completely reject basic Christian theology as did the Cathars, the Lollards — apparently named from a Dutch word for "mumbler" (of prayers) — launched stinging criticisms against clerical wealth and privilege, the sacraments, and the veneration of saints and their images. At the heart of their belief was the word of God: one of Lollardy's hallmarks was the production of English translations of the Bible, usually discouraged by church authorities. Lollards came particularly from the literate lower ranks of urban tradesmen, artisans, and the unbeneficed clergy. William White, mentioned below in Margery Baxter's deposition, was a former priest and an enormously influential Lollard missionary who preached throughout the diocese of Norwich until he was arrested, tried, and burned for heresy in 1428 by Bishop William Alnwick. John Waddon, originally from Kent, was White's associate who died at the stake with him. Margery was a devoted disciple of White and had once harbored the fugitive heretic and helped disseminate his writings secretly. Like the transcript of Guillaume Austatz's trial above, the two following depositions tell us as much about ordinary people's orthodox beliefs as they do about doctrinal deviations.

Source trans. J. Shinners from Norman P. Tanner (ed.), *Heresy Trials in the Diocese of Norwich, 1428-31. Camden Fourth Series*, v. 20 (London: Royal Historical Society, 1977), pp. 43-51, 89-92. Latin.

1. On April 1, 1429 Johanna Clifland, wife of William Clifland, who lives in the parish of St. Mary the Less in Norwich, being cited, appeared in person before the reverend father and lord in Christ William, by the grace of God bishop of Norwich [1426-36], holding court in his palace chapel. At the command of the bishop she placed her hand on God's holy Gospels and swore that she would tell the truth about any and all questions asked of her that concerned matters of faith.

After swearing this oath, Johanna Clifland said that on the Friday [January 28] before the most recent feast of the Purification of the Blessed Mary, Margery Baxter, the wife of William Baxter the wright, recently living at Martham in the diocese of Norwich, was sitting and sewing near the fireplace with the witness in the witness's room. In the presence of the witness and her servants Johanna Grymell and Agnes Bethom, she told the witness and her servants that they should never swear oaths, saying in English: "Dame, beware of the bee, for every bee will sting; and therefore see that you swear neither by God nor by Our Lady nor by any other saint; and if you do the contrary the bee will sting your tongue and poison your soul."

Then the witness said Margery asked her what she did daily in church. The witness told her that as soon as she entered, after kneeling before the cross it was her habit to say five Our Fathers in honor of the crucifix and the same number of Hail Marys in honor of Blessed Mary, the Mother of Christ. Then Margery scolded her and told the witness, "You act badly by kneeling like that and praying before images in these churches, because God has never been in such a church, and he never has gone forth from heaven nor will he ever. And he will not give or offer you any more merit for the genuflectings, and adorations, and prayers that you do in these churches than a lit candle hidden away under the cover of a baptismal font can give any light to people inside a church at nighttime. For you should show no more honor to the images in a church or the images of the crucifix than you'd show to the gallows your brother had been hanged on." In English she said: "Ignorant craftsmen hew and carve such crosses and images out of sticks, and after that ignorant painters deck them out with colors. If you want to see Christ's true cross, I'll show it to you right here in your own house." The witness replied that she would love to see the true cross of Christ. And then Margery said "Look," and she stretched out her arms from her sides saying to the witness, "here is Christ's true cross; this is the cross you should look at and adore every day in your own house. In fact, you waste your time when you go to churches to adore or pray before any images or dead crosses."

Then the witness said Margery asked her what she believed about the sacrament of the altar. And the witness answered her, so she said, saying she believed that after the consecration, the sacrament of the altar is the true body of Christ in the form of bread. Then Margery told her, "You're wrong to believe that. If every such sacrament were God and the true body of Christ, there would be an infinite number of gods since every day a thousand or more priests consecrate a thousand such gods, and then they eat these gods and, having eaten them, they excrete them from their rear ends into foul, stinking privies where you can find these substitute gods if you want to poke around. Know for sure that, with God's grace, what you call the 'sacrament of the altar' will never be my God because priests falsely and deceptively set up that sacrament in the church to lure simple people into idolatry since that sacrament is only material bread."

Then, when the witness asked Margery about him, she said that the Thomas [Becket] of Canterbury whom people call "Saint" Thomas of Canterbury was a false traitor and was damned to hell because he endowed churches with possessions to their harm, and he encouraged and supported many heresies in the church that seduced simple people. So if God is blessed, this Thomas was and is cursed, and if Thomas was and is blessed, then God is cursed. And these false priests who say that Thomas patiently suffered his death before the altar are lying because, just like a false and foolish traitor, running for his life he was killed at the cathedral door.

Next the witness said that, when she asked her, Margery said that the accursed pope, the cardinals, archbishops, bishops, and specifically the bishop of Norwich and other rulers who generally support and sustain heresies and idolatry against the people will shortly have the same or worse fate that "the cursed Thomas of Canterbury had, for they falsely and cursedly deceive the people with their false idol-worshiping and their laws meant to extort money from simple people to support their own pride, luxury, and idleness. And you should know that God's vengeance will quickly come against those who so cruelly killed God's most holy sons and teachers – I mean the holy father Abraham, William White, that holiest and most learned teacher of divine law, and John Waddon and other followers of Christ's law [i.e., the Bible]." In fact this vengeance would have already struck that Caiaphas [see Matt. 26:3], the bishop of Norwich, and his ministers, who are the devil's members, except that the pope had sent false indulgences to these parts which Caiaphas's agents had falsely procured in order to persuade people to make pious processions for their realm and church, an indulgence that misleads simple people into damnable idolatry.

Next the witness said that the aforesaid Margery told her that no child or infant born of Christian parents ought to be baptized in water according to the common custom since such a child had been sufficiently baptized in its mother's womb. So the image-worshiping and idolatry these false and accursed priests do when they dip babies in fonts in churches is done solely to wrench money from people in order to maintain these priests and their concubines.

Next the witness said Margery told her there that the consent of mutual love alone between a man and a woman sufficed to make the sacrament of marriage; no other exchange of words or ceremonies in a church were necessary.

Next she said Margery told her that no faithful man or woman was obliged to fast during Lent, Ember Days, Fridays, the vigils of saints, or other days indicated by the church; and that anyone could eat meat or any other kind of food during these times and on these days; and that on fast days it was better for someone to eat scraps of meat left over from Thursday than to go to the market and run up debts buying fish; and that Pope Sylvester [(314-35), supposedly the recipient of the "Donation of Constantine"] had started Lent.

Next Margery told her that William White, who was falsely condemned for heresy, is a great saint in heaven and a most holy teacher ordained and sent by God; and that every day she prayed to Saint William White, and would continue to pray to him every day of her life so that he would deign to intercede for her before God in heaven; and that William White told Margery, so the witness asserted, that Margery should follow along with him to his place of punishment because then she would see how he would perform many miracles since he wished to convert people by his preaching and make them rise up and kill all the traitors who stood against him and his teaching, which was Christ's law. Margery told the witness she had in fact gone to the place where William White had been killed to see what he would do, and she saw that when William White wanted to preach God's word to the people while he stood at the stake where he was burned, one devil, a disciple of Caiaphas the bishop, struck William White on his lips and then stuck his hand over the holy teacher's mouth so that he couldn't possibly preach God's will.

Next the witness said the aforesaid Margery taught her and told her never to make a pilgrimage to Mary of "Falsingham" [the famous shrine at Walsingham] nor to any other saint or any other place.

The same Margery also said that the wife of Thomas Mone is a woman very discreet and learned in the teachings of William White, and that Richard Belward's nephew was a good teacher and had first instructed her in his teachings and opinions.

The witness also said Margery asked her and her servant Johanna to come secretly at night to Margery's house, and there they could hear her husband read the law of Christ to them, the law written in a book [the Bible] which her husband read to her at night; and she said her husband is an excellent teacher of Christianity.

Margery also said that she had spoken with Johanna West, a woman living near the churchyard of St. Mary-in-the-Marsh, about the law of Christ, and that Johanna is on the good road to salvation.

Furthermore, Margery said this to the witness: "Johanna, from your expression it looks like you plan to reveal what I've told you to the bishop." And the witness swore that she wished never to reveal her counsels in this regard unless Margery gave her cause to do so. Then Margery told her: "If you accuse me to the bishop, I'll do to you what I did to this Carmelite friar from Yarmouth who was the wisest friar in the land." The witness asked her what she had done to the friar. Margery answered that she had spoken with the friar, upbraiding him because he begged for his living and telling him that it wasn't an act of charity to do good to someone or give him aid unless he himself wanted to take off his friar's habit and get behind a plow to work for a living, which would be more pleasing to God than following the way of life of some of these friars. Then the friar asked her whether she had anything else to tell him or teach him. So Margery, as the witness said, explained the Gospels to him in English. After that, the friar left Margery, so the witness said. Later this friar accused Margery of heresy. But Margery, hearing that the friar had denounced her, accused him of wanting to have sex with her, and since she would not give in to him, he accused her of heresy. Margery said this was the reason her husband wanted to kill the friar. Out of fear the friar shut up and left these parts in shame.

Margery also told the witness she had often made false confessions to the dean of St. Mary-in-the-Fields [in Norwich] so that he would think she led a good life. Because of this, he often gave Margery money. Then the witness asked her whether she had confessed all her sins to a priest. Margery told her she had never done harm to any priest, so she had never wanted to confess to a priest or be obedient to any priest, since a priest had no power to absolve anyone from sins; and in fact priests sinned more grievously every day than other people. Margery also said that every man and woman who shared Margery's opinion were good priests, and that the holy church exists only wherever all those people were who believed as she did. For that reason, Margery said she was obliged to confess only to God, not to any priest.

Next Margery told the witness that people honor the devils that fell from heaven with Lucifer who, when they fell to earth, entered into the statues standing in churches. They have dwelled in them since then and are still hiding in them, so that people who adore statues are committing idolatry.

Next the witness said Margery informed her that holy water and blessed bread [unconsecrated bread given at mass in lieu of the Host] were just trifles with no power, and that every church bell should be pulled down and destroyed, and that all those who set up bells in churches are excommunicated.

Margery also said that even if she were convicted of Lollardy, she shouldn't be burned because she, so the witness said, had and still has a charter of salvation (*cartam salvacionis*) in her womb.

Next Margery said she had won a judgment against the lord bishop of Norwich, and Henry Inglese, and the lord abbots associated with them.

Next the witness said she had sent Agnes Bethom, her servant, to Margery's house on the Saturday after last Ash Wednesday. Margery wasn't home but Agnes found a bronze kettle on the fire, and boiling inside it were a piece of salt pork [in violation of the Lenten fast] and oat flour – so Agnes reported to the witness....

On October 7, 1429 Margery confessed her heresy and was sentenced to be flogged four times on four consecutive Sundays as she did public penance walking bareheaded, barefoot, dressed only in a shift, and carrying a one-pound candle around her parish church. Bishop Alnwick later dispensed her to wear a shoe on her bad foot. She was to do the same penance twice at the market in Acle, and then appear twice before the bishop at Norwich cathedral to do public penance.

2. On October 23, 1429, at my residence in Norwich in the presence of me, John Excester, notary undersigned, and of farmer Thomas Hard of South Creake, farmer Robert Merlowle of South Creake, and farmer James Crakeshild of South Creake, William Colyn, a skinner born in Snettisham and residing in South Creake, arrested on suspicion of heresy under the authority of the reverend father and lord in Christ, Lord William, by the grace of God bishop of Norwich, said, asserted, and admitted that:

About fourteen years ago Sir Thomas Baxter, then the parish chaplain of South Creake, enjoined the following penance on the said William for his sins revealed to him during confession: namely to say five Our Fathers and five Hail Marys kneeling before the image of the Blessed Mary of Pity in the said church. And because this William asserted and said to the chaplain that it would be better for him to say the five Our Fathers and Hail Marys before God in the sacrament of the altar (and in fact he said his penance before the sacrament of the altar instead of before the image of pity), he was reputed to be a Lollard.

Next he says that he remarked to the Lady Le Straunge, who was the mother of [Sir] Edmund Oldhall, that he would rather kiss the Lady Le Straunge's feet than the feet of Our Lady of Walsingham, and that he would rather that the foot of Our Lady of Walsingham be grievously injured than the Lady Le Straunge's foot suffer the tiniest hurt.

Next he says he himself said these words to John, the vicar of South Creake publicly in the tavern: "Sir Vicar, I'll tell you one thing – the human race is more indebted to the second person of the Trinity, the Son, than to the Father; because the Father created the first man, who caused the fall of the human race, while Christ, the Son of God, redeemed the human race through his suffering and death, and restored it to its original life."

Next he says that he himself said in the presence of Thomas Hardy of Creake and some others that he would rather touch a woman's private parts than the sacrament of the altar.

On Monday, March 20, the aforesaid year, before the reverend father and lord in Christ, Lord William by the grace of God bishop of Norwich, holding court in the hall of his manor at Thornage, the aforesaid William Colyn, skinner – previously arrested for heresy because he held, believed, and affirmed the errors and heresies described below – appeared. The lord had the articles written below put to him. He responded to these articles as is fully described below. Then present there were master William Ascogh, bachelor in sacred theology; John Sutton, bachelor of law; and John Willy, notary public.

First, that no honor should be shown to the images in church, nor should the statue of Blessed Mary of Walsingham – a block of wood – be adored at all. The said William Colyn denies this article.

Next, when the churchwardens of South Creake church were asking the parishioners to contribute toward painting the images in the church, the said William Colyn told them that he would sooner give twelve pence to burn an image than a halfpenny to paint one. When this article was put to the said William, he recalled it and admitted it under law.

Next we have proposed, said, and articulated to you that within our diocese you have held, believed, and asserted that you would rather go all the way to Walsingham to see the king of England than go to the door of your house to see the sacrament of the altar. When this article was put to the said

William, he remembered it and admitted it under law.

Also, that you asserted that you would rather see a woman's private parts than the sacrament of the altar. When this article was put to him, the said William said and admitted under law that what he had said was that he would rather *touch* a woman's private parts than the sacrament of the altar.

Also, that you held and asserted that all women should be held in common. He admits he said he wished marriage were annulled for some set period of time.

Also, that you held and asserted that confession should be made only to God, not to a priest. When this article is put to him, he denies it.

Also, that you held and asserted that from the time of Christ's Incarnation no soul has entered heaven. When this article is put to him, he denies it.

Also, that you held, asserted, and affirmed that all men are more indebted to the Son, Christ, than to the Father since the Father created the first man, Adam, who was the cause of the fall of the human race; and Christ, the Son of God, redeemed the human race through his suffering and death, and restored it to its original life. He admits that the human race is more indebted to the Son than the Father because the Son redeemed us all.

The reverend father received from William Colyn an oath sworn on the holy Gospels that he would perform penance for his aforementioned faults confessed, as stated above, before the same father. This is the penance: he shall offer before the high altar of the said church of South Creake one large candle worth forty pence; on every Sunday for as long as the candle lasts, he shall hold it before the high altar during the elevation of the Host at mass; with his head, legs, and feet bare, wearing only a short tunic or shift, for four days he shall walk in solemn procession in the manner of a public penitent around the church, carrying the said candle in his hands. When these things have been done, the said William swears on the holy Gospels that henceforward he will never hold heresies, errors, or other opinions contrary to the determination of the Holy Roman Church, nor will he sustain, support, or give counsel, aid, or support to heretics; and if he knows any heretics or persons suspected of heresy, he will report them as fast as he can to the said father or his vicar general. Finally, the same father declared that if in the future he is criminally convicted of these or other heresies, he will be burned.

Compare Margery's and William's trials to Guillaume Austatz's above. Of the three, who has fallen into the most serious error? Which of the three would church authorities judge most dangerous? How religious are townspeople in this transcript in comparison to the villagers of Ornolac? How well informed about Christianity are they? What religious topics interest them? What details of the daily religious life of the people of Norfolk strike you as illuminating?

CHAPTER TEN: DEATH AND JUDGMENT

The popular medieval tale of the Three Dead and the Three Living tells how three handsome young noblemen out riding stumble upon the reeking corpses of three dead men. Recoiling in horror at their rotting flesh, the three nobles ask the corpses who they were. "As you are, so once we were," they reply, "and as we are so shall you be." Commonplace in literature from the thirteenth century and in art from the fourteenth century onwards, the story aptly captures how much death haunted medieval people. Vexed by plague and war, as the death-dealing centuries of the later Middle Ages wore on, death became an even greater fixation for popular devotion. For death brought judgment, and judgment too easily brought hell or, at the very least, long suffering in purgatory. More and more, medieval religion sought a means of release from the agony of death and the spiritual punishment that followed. Masses, prayers, alms, and especially indulgences to aid the souls of the dead were the mainstay of devotions from the fourteenth century onward — so much so that historian A.N. Galpern has called later medieval Christianity "in large part a cult of the living in service of the dead."

Fig. 10.1. Doomsday

Carved on the façades of cathedrals or painted on the walls of village churches, the Last Judgment was an unnerving image always before the eyes of ordinary Christians. An etching (by Guillaumde after Viollet-le-Duc's drawing) of the reliefs on the tympanum of the west portal of the church of St. Urbain, Troyes shows Christ flanked by four angels, two holding the sun and the moon, two sounding the last trumpet. Below him sit the twelve apostles. Under them to the left and right, Mary and John the Evangelist plead for sinners. At bottom left, Abraham gathers the souls of the saved in the folds of his cloak. Next to him, two angels separate the souls and crown the saved. In the two remaining panels, devils haul away the damned – among them a mitered bishop and a crowned king – and toss them down a literal mouth of hell. Across the bottom of the portal, the dead rise from their tombs. Reproduced in M. Viollet-le-Duc's *Dictionnaire raisonné de l'architecture française du XIe au XVIe siècle* (Paris: A. Morel, 1868), v. 7, p. 428.

77. THE *DIES IRAE* (MID-THIRTEENTH CENTURY)

A sequence from the requiem mass and the most famous hymn of the Middle Ages, the Dies irae *has been attributed with some reliability to the Franciscan Thomas of Celano (c. 1190-1260), author of the earliest life of St. Francis of Assisi (see Doc. 9). In it he depicts the anxiety of a terror-stricken soul as the Last Judge returns to earth at Doomsday. The dirge-like plainchant to which it was traditionally set is now so ingrained in the western musical imagination that the briefest wisp of its melody evokes death and damnation. Hector Berlioz used it in his* Symphonie fantastique *(1830) as did Liszt, Saint-Saëns, Rachmaninoff, and contemporary film composers John Williams and Howard Shore, among others. Irons's famous translation from the mid-nineteenth century stays very true to the original Latin, even precisely preserving its rhyme and driving meter.*

Source: trans. William J. Irons in *Hymns Ancient and Modern, Standard Edition* (London: William Clowes and Sons, 1922), pp. 459-61; slightly revised. Latin.

Day of wrath and doom impending,
David's word with Sybil's blending!
Heaven and earth in ashes ending!

O, what fear man's bosom rendeth,
When from heaven the Judge descendeth,
On whose sentence all dependeth!

Wondrous sound the trumpet flingeth,
Through earth's sepulchers it ringeth,
All before the throne it bringeth.

Death is struck, and nature quaking,
All creation is awaking,
To its Judge an answer making.

Lo! the book exactly worded,
Wherein all hath been recorded;
Thence shall judgment be awarded.

When the Judge his seat attaineth,
And each hidden deed arraigneth,
Nothing unavenged remaineth.

What shall I, frail man, be pleading?
Who for me be interceding,
When the just are mercy needing?

King of majesty tremendous,
Who does free salvation send us,
Fount of pity, then befriend us!

Think, kind Jesus! my salvation
Caused thy wondrous Incarnation;
Leave me not to reprobation.

Faint and weary, thou hast sought me,
On the Cross of suffering bought me;
Shall such grace be vainly brought me?

Righteous Judge! for sin's pollution
Grant thy gift of absolution,
Ere that day of retribution.

Guilty, now I pour my moaning,
All my shame with anguish owning;
Spare, O God, thy suppliant groaning!

Through the sinful Mary [Magdalene] shriven,
Through the dying thief forgiven,
Thou to me a hope hast given.

Worthless are my prayers and sighing,
Yet, good Lord, in grace complying,
Rescue me from fires undying.

With thy sheep a place provide me,
From the goats afar divide me,
To thy right hand do thou guide me.

When the wicked are confounded,
Doomed to flames of woe unbounded,
Call me with thy saints surrounded.

Low I kneel with heart-submission,

See, like ashes, my contrition;
Help me in my last condition!

Ah! that day of tears and mourning!
From the dust of earth returning,
Man for judgment must prepare him;

Spare, O God, in mercy spare him!
Lord all-pitying, Jesu blest,
Grant them thine eternal rest.

78. THE KNIGHT OWEIN'S JOURNEY THROUGH ST. PATRICK'S PURGATORY (1184)

The notion of purgatory as a way station for Christian souls who still had penance left to do for their sins before they reached heaven emerged by the twelfth century, driven largely by lay people's enthusiasm for it. Mediating, as it did, the soul's earlier stark fate of either heaven or hell, purgatory offered hope to ordinary, fallible Christians; for while the pains of purgatory were unspeakable by earthly comparison, eventually the soul was purged and entered heaven. The tale of the knight Owein's journey through the otherworld was the most famous medieval account of purgatory. In fact, the site of his journey really exists: the Station Island in Lough Derg in Donegal, where legend said St. Patrick had been harassed by demons while at prayer. An ancient monastic center, by the twelfth century it was a destination for pilgrims eager to visit the entrance to the otherworld. Owein's journey is related in the Tractatus de Purgatorio Sancti Patricii *written in 1184 by the English Cistercian H. de Saltrey, who said that Gilbert, a monk of Louth abbey in Lincolnshire, told him the story, though its details are assembled from oral tradition and other vision literature, including a tenth-century collection of lives of St. Patrick. Owein's journey was enormously popular; over a hundred manuscripts of the Latin text, and at least 150 copies of its translation into all the major languages of Europe survive. It was, in fact, probably among the sources that inspired Dante's* Inferno. *Though the cave on Station Island purporting to be the entrance to purgatory was sealed by church authorities in 1780, barefoot pilgrims doing penance still visit it today.*

Source: trans. Jean-Michel Picard in *Saint Patrick's Purgatory, A Twelfth-Century Tale of a Journey to the Other World*, intro. Yolande de Pontfarcy (Dublin: Four Courts Press, 1985), pp. 50-71. Latin.

Chapter 4. In this our time, that is in the days of King Stephen [1135-54], it happened that a knight called Owein, who is the subject of this narrative, came for the purpose of confession to the bishop in whose diocese this Purgatory was located. And as the bishop was scolding him on account of his sins and telling him that he had seriously offended God, he cried aloud the inner contrition of his heart and vowed to carry out a suitable penance at the bishop's pleasure. And as the bishop wanted to impose a penance according to the measure of his sin, Owein answered: "Since you declare that I have so greatly offended my Creator, I will take on a penance more arduous than any penance. For in order to be worthy of receiving the remission of my sins, I will, with your encouragement, enter Saint Patrick's Purgatory." The bishop warned him against undertaking this but, a knight of courageous heart, he did not agree with this dissuasion. So, in order to deflect him from his intention, the bishop told him of the very great number of men who died there. But he could not sway the heart of a true penitent and a true soldier by any terror. The bishop advised him to take the holy orders of monks or canons but the knight answered that he would on no account do so until he had entered this Purgatory.

The bishop, seeing the steadfastness of his contrition, sent through him a letter to the prior of this place in order that he admit him to the Purgatory according to the custom of the penitents. When he arrived there the prior, on learning his purpose, set out for him the danger and loss suffered by many, in order to divert his heart from this intention. But the knight, remembering that he had gravely offended God and truly repenting, overcame the prior's caution by the fervor of his penitence. So, the prior admitted him to the church, where according to the custom, he devoted himself to prayer and fasting for fifteen days. When these were completed he was led to the Purgatory by the brothers and the neighboring clergy, as it has been written above. There all kinds of unbearable torments were enumerated and the prior attempted to dissuade him from carrying out his penance in this way. But since the knight persevered firmly in his purpose the prior addressed him in these words: "You are now about to enter the Purgatory in the name of the Lord. You will walk for some time through an underground cavern until you emerge in a large field where you will find a hall built with wonderful art. When you enter it you will immediately be met by messengers from God who will explain carefully what will be done to you or what you will suffer. They will then depart and leave you alone there and demons will arrive soon afterwards to tempt you. We understand it happens thus from those who have entered before you. As for you, be constant in the faith of Christ."

The knight, who had in his breast a manly heart, does not fear the danger that he was told had engulfed others. And the man who, armed with an iron sword, had taken part in the battles of men, now armed with faith, hope, and justice, confident in God's mercy and stronger than iron, hurls himself boldly into a battle with demons. First he commended himself to the prayers of all and raising his right hand he impressed upon his forehead the sign of the holy cross, then resolutely and cheerfully went in through the door. Thereupon, the prior locked it from outside and returned to the church with the procession.

Chapter 5. The knight, wishing to undertake a novel and unusual act of chivalry, went on boldly through the pit for a very long time, alone but confident in God. As the darkness grew more and more dense he soon lost sight of any light. At last, as he went along the cavern a tiny glimmer began to shine weakly from the opposite direction. It was not long before he had arrived at the aforementioned field and hall. But there the light was shining only as it shines on earth in winter after sunset. As regards the hall, it did not have solid walls but was built on all sides with columns and arches like a monk's cloister. After walking around it for a long time, marveling at its wonderful structure, he entered and what he saw within the sacred precincts was far more wonderful. He sat for some time in the hall, casting his eyes here and there and greatly admiring its magnificence and beauty.

He had been sitting by himself for a while when there came into the building fifteen men who looked like monks recently shorn [i.e., tonsured] and dressed in white clothes. They greeted him in the name of the Lord and sat beside him. And, while the others kept silent, one who appeared to be a kind of prior and their leader addressed him in these words: "Blessed be Almighty God who strengthened your good intention in your heart; may he perfect the good that he started in you. Since you have come to the Purgatory to be purified of your sins you are perforce compelled to act manfully or else you will die body and soul because of your inaction. For soon after our departure this building will be filled with unclean spirits who will inflict grave torments on you and will threaten to carry out more severe ones. They will promise to lead you unharmed to the door through which you entered if you agree to turn back; they will try to see if you can be deceived even by this ruse. If you are in any way either defeated by the agony of their tortures or terrified by their threats or taken in by their promises and if you offer them your consent, you will die body as well as soul as I have said. If however you firmly and faithfully place absolute hope in God so that you do not yield to their tortures, threats, or promises but steadfastly despise them as being nothing, not only will you be purified of all your sins but you will even see the torments which are in store for sinners and the place of rest in which the just rejoice. Always remember God and when they torture you call upon the Lord Jesus Christ, for through the invocation of his name you will immediately be delivered from the torture. Now we cannot stay any longer, but we commend you to Almighty God." And so, the man gave the knight his benediction and they withdrew.

Chapter 6. Thus instructed for a new kind of chivalry, the knight, who in the past had bravely fought men, is now ready to give battle bravely to demons. Shielded by Christ's arms he waits to see which of the demons will first challenge him to a fight. He is arrayed with the breastplate of justice; as a head bears a helmet, his spirit is crowned with the hope of victory and eternal salvation and he is protected by the shield of faith. Also, he holds the sword of the spirit which is the word of God: he piously invokes the Lord Jesus Christ to protect him with his royal battlements and prevent him from being overcome by his relentless enemies. Divine mercy did not fail him because it cannot fail those who trust in God.

So, as we said, while the knight was sitting alone in the hall, anticipating with an intrepid heart the fight with the demons, he suddenly heard a loud roar resounding around the building as if the entire earth was shaking. It seemed to him that if all the men and all the animals of earth, sea, and sky, together and in a single surge created a great uproar, they would not make a louder noise. Thus, had he not been protected by divine power and instructed to great advantage by these men, he would have lost his mind from the terrible noise.

After the horror of hearing such a noise there followed the more horrible material sight of demons. For, before his eyes, a countless multitude of hideously misshapen demons began to rush into the hall from all sides and, laughing and mocking him, they greeted him and said as if to disgrace him: "The other men who serve us do not come to us until after their death. That is why we must recompense you with a greater reward because you desired so much to honor our company – which you served eagerly and with dedication – that you did not want to wait until the day of your death like the others, but you wished to give us at the same time your body and your soul while still alive. You have done this in order to receive a greater reward from us: now you will receive in plenty what you deserve. For you came here to endure torments for your sins; so, you will obtain from us what you were looking for, namely pains and afflictions. Yet, because up to now you have served us, if you agree to our advice and turn back willingly, as a favor we will bring you unharmed to the door through which you entered so that you may continue to enjoy being alive in the world and not lose completely everything that is pleasant to your body." They promised these things because they wanted to deceive him either by terror or by flattery. But, a true soldier of Christ, he was not shaken by terror nor seduced by flattery, and he scorned with determination those who terrified him and those who flattered him by answering absolutely nothing.

So the demons, when they saw that they were spurned by the knight, growled at him in a horrific way. Then they built the pyre of an enormous fire in the very hall and pushed the knight bound hand and foot into the blaze and, howling, they dragged him with iron hooks backwards and forwards through the flames. When he was first thrown into the fire he felt a deep torment, but the man of God, protected by the battlements of his King as well as previously instructed by the aforementioned men, did not in the least forget the weapons of spiritual chivalry. For as his enemies roasted him in the blaze, he invoked the name of pious Jesus and he was immediately liberated from the fire. This was their first attack. When the name of the most pious Savior was invoked aloud the whole blazing pyre was quickly extinguished in such a way that not even a spark could be found. When the knight saw this he became more daring and he firmly resolved that in the future he would not fear those whom he saw he could overcome so easily through the invocation of the holy name.

Chapter 7. So the demons left the hall and dragged the knight with them, howling and making a terrible uproar. As they emerged they separated; some of them, however, dragged the knight for a long time across a waste land. The soil was black and the land dark and he could not see anything besides the demons who were pulling him. A burning wind was blowing which could barely be heard but which seemed nonetheless to pierce his body with its harshness. They dragged him towards the land where the sun rises in midsummer. When they arrived there, as if having gone to the end of the world, they started to turn towards the right and to make their way through a very wide valley facing south, that is towards the place where the sun rises in midwinter. As they were leaving this place he began to hear the most pitiful cries and laments and moans, as if made by the masses of the whole earth and the nearer he approached the clearer the cries could be heard.

At last, hauled by the demons, the knight arrived at a very large and very long plain filled with misery and pain. He could not see the further end of this plain on account of its very great length. The plain was full of human beings of both sexes and all ages who were lying naked on the ground on their bellies, stretched out by burning iron nails driven into the ground through their hands and feet. One could see them at times eating the earth because of the pain or else shouting pathetically "Mercy, mercy!" or "Pity!", with moans and lamentations. But there was nobody in the place who knew how to have mercy or pity. The devils could be seen running in every direction between them and above them and did not cease beating them with the hardest of whips. The devils said to him "You will experience the feeling of the tortures you see here if you do not agree to our advice: that is that you give up your purpose and turn back. And if you are willing to do this we will lead you peacefully to the door through which you entered and we will allow you to depart unharmed." And when he refused to do it, they stretched him on the ground and tried to transfix him with nails, like the others. But since he invoked the name of Jesus, they did not succeed in this attempt.

Chapter 8. Withdrawing from this plain they dragged the knight to another one full of greater misery. Similarly, this plain was packed with human beings of both sexes and all ages, pinned to the ground. However, there was a difference between these and the poor wretches of the other plain, precisely because the others had their bellies held to the ground but these were held fast on their backs. Flaming dragons were sitting on some of them lacerating them with their burning teeth in a pitiful way as if they were eating them. Fiery snakes encircled other people's necks, arms, or entire bodies and, pressing their heads against the chests of the poor wretches, they sank the burning fangs of their mouths into their hearts. One could see also toads of wonderful size and as if made of fire sitting on the chests of some and burying their hideous muzzles there as if trying to pull out their hearts. And those who were thus pinned and tormented never ceased crying and moaning. Also, the devils ran between them and above them and tortured them by beating them violently with whips. He could not see the end of this plain on account of its length, only the limits of its breadth by which he arrived and departed, for he had passed through these fields crosswise. The devils said "You will suffer the tortures you see unless you agree with us to turn back." And as he was scorning them they tried as previously to pin him with nails but they were not able to do so when they heard the name of Jesus.

Chapter 9. So, departing from there, the devils led the knight to a third plain filled with suffering. This plain was also full of people of both sexes and all ages. They were lying on the ground pinned by white-hot iron nails. They were covered by so many nails from the tops of their heads to the toes of their feet that you would not have found a free space big enough to be covered by the tip of one finger. Moreover they could hardly utter a sound in order to cry, but, as best they could, they made a noise like men who are about to die. Like the others they were also seen to be naked and they were tortured by an alternately freezing and burning wind and by the whips of the devils. "You will suffer these tortures," the devils said, "if you do not agree with us to turn back." And as they wanted to nail him down when he scorned their counsel, he invoked the name of Jesus Christ and they were not able to do anything more to him in this place.

Chapter 10. So, dragging the knight away from there, they arrived at a fourth plain full of fires and where all kinds of tortures were found. Some were hanging from blazing chains by the feet, others by the hands, others by the hair, others by the arms, others by the legs, with their heads turned upside down and immersed in sulphurous flames. Some were suspended in fires with iron nails stuck in their eyes, or ears or nostrils or throats or breasts or genitals. Others were burning in furnaces of sulphur; yet others were frying as if on pans; others were roasting on a fire, skewered on blazing spits which were turned by demons. Others were dripping with various molten metals and moreover they were all beaten with whips by demons running in every direction. There one could see all the kinds of torture that one could imagine. Also Owein saw some of his former companions there and he recognized them well. No human language is adequate to express the moans and cries of the wretches and the wailing that he heard. Moreover, these plains were full not only of tortured men but also of torturing demons. But when they wanted to torture him there, he invoked the name of Jesus Christ and remained unharmed.

Chapter 11. After moving away from this place, there appeared in front of them a wheel of fire wonderfully big, the spokes and rim of which were surrounded by hooks of fire. From every single one of these, men were dangling, transfixed. While one half of this wheel stood up in the air, the other half was buried beneath the earth. And the flames of a hideous and sulphurous fire rose from the earth around the wheel and roasted those hanging on it in a most pitiful way. The demons said to him: "You will suffer what these suffer unless you are willing to turn back. But first you will see what they endure." So the devils placed themselves opposite one another on either side of the wheel and driving iron rods between the spokes of the wheel they spun it with such speed that his eyes were not in the least able to distinguish those hanging on it one from another. For on account of its great speed, its movement appeared to be a complete circle of fire. And they threw him onto the wheel and he was lifted rotating into the air, but as he invoked the name of Christ he came down unharmed.

Chapter 12. So, proceeding from there the devils dragged the knight towards a large building which was smoking dreadfully. Its width was great but its length was so immense that he could not see its farthest points. While they were still some distance away he stopped, afraid to go further because of the extreme heat emanating from the building. The devils said to him: "Why are you slowing down? What you see here are the baths and whether you like it or not, you will walk up there and take a bath with the others." And they started to hear the most miserable cries and lamentations coming from this building. As he was brought inside he saw a frightful and horrific sight. For the floor of this building was full of round pits which were joined so close together that one could barely, if at all, walk between them. All the pits were full of all sorts of bubbling liquids and metals in which a great number of people of both sexes and all ages were immersed. Some of them were fully immersed, others up to the eyebrows, others up to the eyes, others up to the lips, others up to the neck, others up to the navel, others up to the thighs, others up to the knees, others up to the calves. Some were held only by one foot, others by only one hand or by both. "Now," said the devils, "you will have a bath with these." And lifting the knight, they tried to throw him into one of the pits. But when they heard the name of Christ, they abandoned their effort.

Chapter 13. Then, leaving this place, they went on towards a mountain on which he saw naked people of both sexes and all ages, hunched up and squatting on their haunches. Their multitude was so great that all those he had seen before now seemed a small number to him. They were all turned, terrified, towards the north wind as if waiting for death. And as the knight was wondering what this wretched crowd was expecting, one of the devils said to him: "Maybe you are wondering what this crowd is awaiting with such terror. Unless you consent willingly to turn back, you will know what it is they are expecting in such a state of trembling." The devil had barely finished his sentence when suddenly a whirlwind came from the north carrying away even the demons and the knight they were leading and all the people. It hurled them, crying and moaning miserably, far away to another part of the mountain into a fetid and icy river in which they suffered the most unbelievable cold. And as they tried to come out of the waters, demons, running on the surface, constantly plunged them back in. But the knight, remembering his Helper, invoked his name and found himself without delay on the opposite bank.

Chapter 14. But the devils, not yet tired of ill-treating the soldier of Christ, came to him and dragged him towards the south. And suddenly he saw in front of him a horrible flame stinking of foul sulphur which shot up as if from a well. It seemed to hurl people of both sexes and all ages, naked and blazing like sparks of fire, high into the air and as the flames lost their driving force, they kept falling back into the well and the fire. As he was getting nearer, the devils said to the knight: "This well, belching flames, is the entrance to hell. This is our home. And since you have served us up to now, you will stay with us here forever. And if you once enter here you will perish both in body and soul for all eternity. If however you agree with us you will be able to return to your home unharmed." But as he was confident in God's help he despised their promise. The devils then threw themselves into the well, dragging the knight with them. And as he went down deeper he found the well to be wider but he also suffered the pain more intensely. It reached the point of being so intolerable that he almost forgot the name of his Savior. However, under God's inspiration, he returned to his senses as best he could and shouted the name of Jesus Christ. Immediately the force of the flame projected him up into the air with the others and when he came down, he stood alone for some time beside the well. While he stood there, having withdrawn from the opening and not knowing which way to turn, other devils who were unknown to him came out of the well. They said to him: "Why are you standing here? Our companions told you that this was meant to be hell. They were lying. It is our habit always to lie so that we can deceive through lies those we cannot dupe through truth. This is not hell. But now, we will bring you to hell."

Chapter 15. So, dragging the knight away with a great and horrible commotion, they arrived at a very wide and stinking river. It was entirely covered with what looked like the flames of a sulphurous fire and it was full of demons. They told him: "We'll have you know that hell is under this burning river." A bridge stretched above the river before him. And the demons said to the knight: "You must cross this bridge. As for us, we will set in motion winds and whirls and throw you into the river from the bridge. And our companions there will capture you and plunge you into hell. However, we want to test you first to see if it is safe for you to cross it." So, taking hold of his hand, they escorted him onto the bridge. There were three things on this bridge which were most frightening for those who crossed it: first, it was so slippery that, even if it had been very wide, one could scarcely, if at all, get a foothold on it; secondly, it was so narrow and thin that apparently one could barely, if at all, stand or walk on it; thirdly, it stretched so high in the air that even to lift one's gaze to its height seemed horrible. And they said: "If you would yet agree with us to turn back you will be able to go home, safe even from this dangerous situation." Thinking to himself of the many dangers from which his most pious Defender had saved him, the faithful soldier of Christ invoked his name and started to advance cautiously on the bridge. As he felt nothing slippery under his feet, he moved forward more firmly, confident in God. And the higher he climbed, the wider he found the bridge. And after a little time, the width of the bridge had increased so much that it would even have taken two carts going in opposite directions. Then, the devils who had led the knight to this point, not having the strength to proceed further, stood at the foot of the bridge as if waiting for him to fall. But when they saw him crossing freely, they shook the air with such a clamor that the horror of it seemed to him more unbearable than any of the pains he had previously endured at their hands. However, realizing that they were stationary and had not the power to go further, and remembering his pious Guide, he went on more assuredly. The demons who were running backwards and forwards above the river threw their hooks at him, but he escaped unharmed. Finally, moving forward steadily, he saw that the width of the bridge had increased so much that he could barely look down on the water on either side.

Chapter 16. So as the knight went on, now free from all harassment from the devils, he saw in front of him a big wall which rose high in the air. This wall was a wonder and the ornamentation of the masonry was beyond compare. In the wall he saw a closed door adorned with various metals and precious stones, glittering with a wonderful brightness. As he was getting nearer, yet still at a distance of about half a mile, the door opened in front of him and a fragrance pouring from it wafted up to him. It seemed so sweet that, if all the world was turned into spices, it would not surpass the intensity of this sweetness. He gathered so much strength from this sweet fragrance that he thought he would now be able to sustain, without any strain, the tortures he had suffered. And looking inside the door, he saw a land suffused with a very strong light, surpassing the splendor of the sun, and he wished to go inside. Happy is the man for whom such a door opens! And the knight did not fail to understand who had allowed him to arrive there. He was still at some distance when a procession came to meet him with crosses, banners, candles and what looked like branches of golden palms. As far as he could judge, he had never seen a procession so big and so fine on earth. There he saw people of every religious order. He saw that they were arrayed in sacred garments corresponding to their rank: some were dressed as archbishops, others as bishops, others as abbots, canons, monks, priests and the ecclesiastics of all the orders in the holy church. Also everyone, clerics and lay people alike, seemed to be dressed in the type of clothes in which they had served God in this world. They greeted the knight with great respect and joy and bringing him with them to the harmonious sounds of a chorus unknown on earth, they entered through the door.

When the chorus had finished and the procession had dispersed, two persons who looked like archbishops came forward separately and welcomed him into their company and took him with them as if to show him the land and its glorious beauty. As they spoke to him, they first blessed God who had strengthened his soul with such constancy in the torments. Then they led him through a beautiful land and, wandering here and there, he gazed upon many lovelier and more delectable sights than he or the most skilled of men could describe in speech or in writing. The land was flooded with such a brightness that, as the light of a lamp is overpowered by the splendor of the sun, likewise it seemed that the brightness of the midday sun would look dark in the dazzling light of this wonderful land. Because of its immensity, he was not able to know what were the limits of the land except for the part where the door through which he entered was located. But the whole land seemed to consist of beautiful and verdant fields adorned with the different flowers and fruits of many-shaped plants and trees, on the fragrance of which, as I said, he would have lived for ever, had he been at liberty to remain. Night never obscured it because the splendor of the purest of skies irradiated it with eternal brightness.

There, he saw such a great multitude of people of both sexes that he reckoned that no one in this world had ever seen so many people. They were divided into communities, some accommodated in one place, others in other places. However, whenever they wished, some of them moved joyfully from their own group to that of others and their visits were joyfully returned, and so it was that they rejoiced in seeing each other and they were carried away with happiness at visiting each other. In places, choirs were ranged beside other choirs and together were singing out the praises of God in a chorus of sweet harmony. And, as one star differs from another in brightness, there was a harmonious difference in the beautiful brightness of their faces and their clothing. For some seemed to be arrayed in a golden raiment, others in a silver one, others in green, purple, jacinth, azure and dazzling white. However, the type of their clothes was the same as they used to wear in this world and indicated to the knight the office or rank each had held on earth. And so it looked as if the different colors of their dress had the splendor of different types of brightness. Some were walking like crowned kings, others were carrying golden palms in their hands. The sight of these just people, so numerous and so excellent, in this peaceful place, was delightful to the knight, as was the sound of their smooth and ineffably sweet harmony. From everywhere he could hear the chorus of the saints singing out the praises of God. Each individual rejoiced in his own felicity but they all exulted at the joy of each of the others. The land was filled with a fragrance so sweet that its inhabitants seemed to live on it. And all those who saw the knight were blessing God and congratulating each other on his coming as if it was their brother who had been delivered from death. It looked somewhat as if a new jubilation was taking place because of his coming. Everyone was exulting and the melody of the saints was echoing from everywhere. There he felt neither heat nor cold, nor did he see what could in any way offend or do any harm whatsoever. There everything was peaceful, everything was calm, everything was pleasant. In this place of rest he saw many more things than any man could ever tell or put in writing.

After this the archbishops said to the knight: "Now, brother, with the help of God, you have seen what you wished to see. For, as you came, you saw the torments of hell and here you saw the place of rest of the just. Blessed be the Creator and Redeemer of all who inspired you with such an intention and thanks to whom you showed perseverance when you went through the torments. Now, dearest one, we want you to know what the places of torture you saw are meant to be and also this land of such great beatitude."

Chapter 17. "Now, this land is the earthly paradise, from which the first man, Adam, was expelled for the sin of disobedience. And after he had, through his disobedience, disdained to submit to God, he was no longer able to look upon the incomparably supreme joys that you now see. For here he had listened attentively to the words of God himself, in the purity of his heart and the greatness of the inner vision; here he had been able to enjoy fully the sight of the blessed angels. But after the fall from such beatitude because of his disobedience, he also lost the light of reason in which he had been bathed. And since he did not understand this while he was in favor, he was likened to beasts of burden and became similar to them.

"And because of his sin of disobedience the whole of his posterity was like himself subjected to the sentence of death. O hateful crime of disobedience! But our most pious God, moved by goodness, decided that his Son, our Lord Jesus Christ, should become incarnate for the sake of the wretchedness of mankind. When we received the faith of Christ through baptism, we were freed from all sins, sins in act as well as original sin, and we became worthy of returning to this land. But, because after receiving the faith we have very frequently sinned through our weakness, we had to obtain remission of our sins through penance. For the penance we received either before our death or at the point of death and that we did not carry out during our lives, we repaid after the dissolution of the flesh by undergoing tortures in the places of punishment which you have seen, some of us for a long period, others for a shorter time. We all came through these places to this haven of peace. O incalculably horrible transition! Similarly, all those whom you saw in every place of punishment, except the ones who are kept down inside the mouth of the infernal well, will be saved in the end and will come to this place of rest after being purified. Even today purified people have arrived and we have welcomed them as we welcomed you, and admitted them here with joy.

"But none of those who are in torment knows for how long he will be tortured. Yet, through masses, psalms, prayers and alms, whenever they are made for them, their torments are alleviated or else they are converted into lesser and more tolerable ones until they are completely freed by such favors. But when they come to this place of rest, they do not know how long they are going to stay. For none of us can know, in respect of himself, how long he is to remain here. And as the length of their stay in the places of punishment is given according to the number of their sins, likewise we who are here will stay in this place of rest more or less according to our good merits. And although we are completely free from torments we are not yet worthy of rising to the higher joy of the saints. Yet none of us knows the day and the starting point of our advancement to a better state. And now, as you see, we live in great peace, but after the time limit laid down for each of us we will move to a greater peace. For each day our community in some way increases or decreases since every single day people ascend both from the torments to us and from us to the heavenly paradise."

Chapter 18. Having said this, they took the knight with them to the top of a mountain and they ordered him to look up and to tell them what kind of color the sky above appeared to him. He answered them: "It appears to me similar to gold glowing in a furnace." "This," they said, "is the gate of the heavenly paradise, through which those of us who are chosen enter heaven. And we must also let you know that once a day the Lord feeds us with celestial food. Soon, by gift of God, you will see what this food is like and how delicious it is when you taste it with us." This speech was barely finished when something like a flame of fire came down from the sky and covered the whole land. And, separating as if into rays, it came down over everyone's head and finally entered completely into them. It even came down over the knight among the others and entered into him. From it he felt such a delicious sweetness both in his heart and in his body that he was hardly able to make out whether he was alive or dead, so extreme was the sweetness. But this hour also passed quickly. "This is the food," they said, "with which once a day, as we were saying, God feeds us. But those among us who are taken into heaven enjoy this food endlessly.

Chapter 19. "But since you have seen in part what you wished to see, that is the rest of the blessed and the torments of the sinners, you must now return the same way you came. And if from now on you lead a sober and holy life, you can be sure not only of this rest, but also of the celestial mansion. But if, God forbid, you stain your life again with the seductions of the flesh, you have now seen for yourself what kind of tortures are in store for you. So, go back without fear. For whatever was out there to terrify you on your way in will be afraid even to appear in front of you on your way back." When he heard these words, the knight became frightened and in the greatest sorrow started to beg the archbishops not to force him to leave such bliss for the tribulations of this world. But they said: "It will not be as you asked but as has been arranged by the One who alone knows what he has prepared for everyone." So, full of sorrow and feeling miserable, he went out rather reluctantly and, after receiving their benediction, returned, sad but undaunted, on the same path he had come, and the door was closed.

Chapter 20. Having left the paradise, as we said, the knight was lamenting the fact that he was forced to leave such bliss to go back to the misery of this life, but he went back the way he came. On his way back some devils running in every direction were getting ready to frighten him but, at the sight of him, they fled into the air like terrified birds. Moreover, the tortures could not harm him in any way. As he came to the hall mentioned above, in which the devils had first assailed him, the fifteen men who had appeared to him in the first place and instructed him, suddenly stood in front of him. Praising God and congratulating him on his victory they said: "Hurrah, brother, now we know that you have been purified of all your sins through the torments which you have courageously endured and overcome. And now the light of dawn is already shining in your country. So, climb up as quickly as possible, for if the prior of the community, when he comes to the door with the procession after the solemn service of mass, does not find you are back, he will doubt your return and will leave immediately, closing the door." So, he received their benediction and went up without delay. And at the very moment when the prior opened the door, the knight appeared coming from the inside. The prior greeted him with great joy and led him to the church where it had been arranged that he would devote another fifteen days to prayer....

What are more memorable here: the pains of purgatory or the joys of paradise? What lessons about the afterlife does Owein's journey teach its audience? What elements of the story would explain its popularity? Compare Owein's tale to Thurkill's vision of hell (Doc. 37) and Walchelin's vision of purgatory (Doc. 40).

79. LAST WILLS AND TESTAMENTS (1377-83)

Medieval last wills were usually made by testators on their death beds. Since scribes and notaries followed legal formulas in composing them, since those attending the dying urged them not to omit certain standard (and often obligatory) pious bequests, since pious undertakings could be limited by income, and since imminent death tends to focus the mind on the hereafter and how to get there, wills cannot be taken as ironclad indicators of a testator's routine religious leanings. Still, when their bequests veer even slightly from standard formulas, they can throw some useful light on what devotions preoccupied a Christian in life and especially near death. For instance, the pilgrimages mentioned here that Katherine Rokelond posthumously launched on her behalf to some of the major shrines of England (Canterbury, Walsingham, Bromholm, Bury St. Edmund's) suggest that they held a valuable place in her devotional life. Katherine and the two other testators below were all fairly prosperous, allowing them freer rein with their pious bequests.

Source: trans. J. Shinners from Norwich, Norfolk Record Office, Norwich Consistory Court Register Heydon, ff. 144r; 211r, 213v. Latin.

1. In the name of God. Amen. I, Katherine Rokelond, living at Heigham near Norwich, on the fifteenth before the kalends of September [Aug. 18], the year of the Lord 1377, establish my testament in this manner: First, I bequeath my soul to almighty God, the Blessed Virgin Mary, and all the saints; and my body to be buried at the parish church of Heigham. Also I bequeath twenty pounds of wax [for candles] to burn around my body on the day of my burial. Also I bequeath 40 pence to the main altar of the aforesaid church [for unpaid tithes]. Also I bequeath 30 pence to the rector of the aforesaid church for celebrating [my funeral]. Also I bequeath 12 pence to the parish clerk of the aforesaid church for his labor [in writing and registering her testament]. Also I bequeath 6 shillings 8 pence for making repairs to the aforesaid church. Also I bequeath 2 shillings to Sir [*dominus*, here a title of respect] Geoffrey Canyard, chaplain. Also I bequeath 2 shillings to Sir Adam, chaplain. Also I bequeath to Benedict Barber one folding table with a cutting spade and other implements from my garden. Also I bequeath to the wife of the aforesaid Benedict ten pounds of wool, a spinning-wheel, wool card, poke, and other things needed for wool-working. Also I bequeath two silver spoons to the daughter of the said Benedict. Also I bequeath one plain pair of red clogs to Emma Geye of Heigham. Also I bequeath one plain pair of blue clogs to the wife of John Horn. Also I bequeath one cart made of cypress to Margery Messager. Also to my three godsons I bequeath 3 shillings to be divided in equal portions. Also I bequeath one pair of silver [rosary] beads with

a gold brooch to the cathedral church of the Holy Trinity at Norwich. Also I bequeath one gold ring to the chapel of the Blessed Mary of Walsingham [England's chief Marian shrine]. Also I bequeath one ring with a stone called a sapphire to the chapel of the Blessed Mary of Arnelingham in Yarmouth. Also I bequeath a silver ring to the church of Bromholm [site of a miracle-working crucifix]. Also I bequeath and wish that at my expense one man [as her proxy] should go on pilgrimage to St. Thomas at Canterbury, offering there one penny at his shrine and one penny at the head of St. Thomas; also one penny at [the shrine of] St. Augustine of Canterbury. Also one penny at Walsingham and one penny at Kelling. Also one penny at [the shrine of] St. Edmund at Bury. Also I bequeath for making repairs to the church of St. James at Norwich one copper pot, and Bartholomew Barker is to be delivered of the same. Also I bequeath for making repairs to the parish church of St. Margaret in Norwich one copper pot with a ring, and Gilbert Gronge is to be delivered of the same. Also I bequeath 13 shillings 4 pence to all my executors for their labor. Also I bequeath to Francis Horner of Holt one lined fur coat with a hood and two silver spoons. Also at the coming Christmas, I bequeath five marks to Sir Thomas to celebrate one year of [memorial] masses. Also I bequeath 20 shillings to each of the mendicant orders of friars of the city of Norwich. Also I bequeath 6 pence to each bed of the hospital of St. Giles and the Norman's Hospital. Also I bequeath to Robert Popy of Westwick one long trestle table and a copper bowl closed with a lock. Also I bequeath twopence to each sick person at the gates of the city of Norwich. Also I bequeath and wish that from the money received [in rent] from my tenement called "Cornerplace" in the parish of St. Benedict of Westwick in Norwich one suitable chaplain should celebrate mass for three years ongoing in the parish church of Heigham for my soul and the souls of all the faithful departed. And to carry out this testament and pay my debts, I bequeath all my tenements existing within the franchise of the city of Norwich and its suburbs to be sold by my executors named below whom I make, ordain, and appoint: Robert Kenton, rector of the church of Heigham; Robert Botcher; and John Medilton of the same place, so that they should dispose and ordain from all my goods movable and immovable as well as houses, gardens, and other things belonging to me inside and outside the city of Norwich as it will seem to them to please God and profit my soul. Dated the day and year given above.

2. In the name of the Father, and of the Son, and of the Holy Spirit. Amen. I, Roger de Wylasham, knight, being of sound mind and good memory, on Sunday, the feast of the Finding of the Holy Cross [May 3] in the year of the Lord 1383 establish my testament in this manner: First, I bequeath my soul

to almighty God, to the Blessed Virgin Mary, and to all the saints; and my body to be buried in the church of Thurston under the arch between the said church and the chapel of St. James. Also I bequeath 3 shillings 4 pence to the main altar of the same church [for unpaid tithes]. Also I bequeath 3 shillings 4 pence to the main altar of the church of Runhall and 46 shillings 8 pence for the repair of that same church. Also I bequeath 6 shillings 8 pence to the main altar of the church of Mattishall and five marks for the repair of that church's bell tower. Also I bequeath 20 shillings for the repair of the church and the bell tower of the church of Willisham. Also I bequeath 6 shillings 8 pence to the Prioress of [the convent of] Carrow. Also 3 shillings 4 pence to each professed nun and 2 shillings to each nun not yet professed of that aforesaid convent. Also I wish that within a month after my death, my executors have one thousand masses celebrated for me and for all the souls to whom I am bound. And the rest of all my goods, except those bequeathed above, I give and assign to my wife, Katherine, to Robert de Kenton, Walter de Gilderford, and the chaplain Roger Cristion, the which Katherine, Robert, Walter, and Roger, I in fact appoint as executors of this my testament, whom I ask that they keep it in mind to pay my debts and fulfill my will to the best of their ability as it seems best to expedite my soul. Dated the day and year given above.

3. In the name of God. Amen. I, Anabilla Maloysel, once the wife of John de Holveston, establish my testament on the Tuesday [July 16] immediately before the feast of St. Margaret the virgin in the year of the Lord 1383 in this manner: I bequeath my soul to God, to Blessed Mary, and to all the saints, and my body to be buried among the friars of the convent of St. Augustine, Norwich, next to the aforesaid John, once my husband. Also I bequeath 20 shillings to be spent for my funeral on the day of my burial. Also 20 shillings to the same brothers. Also 20 shillings for relief of the poor on the day of my burial. Also I bequeath 13 shillings 4 pence to the [cathedral] church of the Holy Trinity, Norwich. Also 6 shillings 4 pence for the repair of the church of St. Peter Haveringland. Also I bequeath 3 shillings 4 pence to William, parish chaplain of the church of the Holy Cross. Also I bequeath one dosser and my best bench-cover with six cushions to William Doff of Holveston, my son. Also to the same William six silver spoons. Also to the same William one complete set of priest's vestments with an alb made of fustian. Also to [the priest] Sir Giles, my son, one silver cup with a lid. Also to the same person, my red psalter. Also I bequeath to Margery, my goddaughter, my one best bed with a tapestry. Also my two best gowns with hoods to the said Margery. Also one white psalter with one pair of amber [rosary] beads to Petronilla de Henstede. Also one russet tunic to Alice Jugg. Also my pewter

vase to Margery de Enges, my sister. Also I give and bequeath the rest of all my goods to my executors to carry out faithfully this my testament; and I appoint these as my executors, namely Richard Spicer of Orford; William de Worsted, citizen of Norwich; William de Holveston, my son; and the chaplain Giles de Holveston, my son. Also I bequeath one gold ring with one stone called a diamond to the image of St. Mary of Walsingham. Also 3 shillings, 4 pence to the Friars Preachers of Norwich; also 3 shillings, 4 pence to the Friars Minor of the same city; also 3 shillings, 4 pence to the Friars Carmelites of the same city.

What conclusions about these testators' piety do you draw from their wills? Do any of their religious bequests seem out-of-the-ordinary or unorthodox? Does what they owned reveal anything about their religious interests? Insofar as these wills might reflect their last thoughts, what concerns them?

80. A SERMON FOR ALL SOULS' DAY (c. 1400)

This sermon for All Souls' Day (November 1), composed for the general use of parish clergy by the English curate John Myrc, rehearses briefly and vividly the late medieval preoccupation with death and deliverance from purgatory.

Source: modernized. J. Shinners from Theodor Erbe, [*John*] *Myrc's Festial, A Collection of Homilies*, Pt. 1, Early English Text Society, Extra Series 96 (1905), pp. 269–71. Middle English.

A Sermon for All Souls' Day

Good men and women, as you well know, the day after All Hallow's Eve is always the day of the mass for all the souls that are in purgatory in God's prison and have great need to be helped. Thus, just as holy church on that day worships all the saints of heaven generally together hoping to be helped by them, so too on Souls' Mass Day holy church bears in mind and sings and reads generally for all the souls in purgatory, having full belief in our ability to release them from their pain, some in full, some in part. Thus each Christian man and woman should help this day the souls that are in pain, as they may and will; for the least prayer that is made for them gives them ease. Even though a man just says "God have mercy on all Christian souls," he will be in charity and out of deadly sin. Thus, you should know that three things most help souls out of their suffering: devout praying, almsgiving, and masses.

Devout praying greatly helps a person's soul. For just as a lord who has a man in constraints sometimes releases him partly and sometimes completely at the request of his good servant, so God, at the prayer of his good servant, releases a soul that the servant has prayed for, sometimes in part and sometimes completely. To show you how greatly good prayers help the souls, I'll tell you this example that I find written in the book called *The Golden Legend* (see Doc. 32):

There was a man who had a house by the churchyard so that his door opened toward the church. It was his custom to say the psalm *De profundis* [Ps. 129 (130)] for all Christian souls whenever he walked by either side of the churchyard. One day it happened that he was pursued by enemies as he hurried home. But when he came to the churchyard he thought to himself "Now it's time for me to say the *De profundis*," and so he knelt down and prayed. And suddenly all the churchyard rose up full of corpses, each one holding the tool of his trade in his hand, and they rushed against his enemies. And when his enemies saw this they cried to God for mercy. These men and he were always afterwards more devout about praying for the souls. Thus devout prayer greatly helps souls.

Also almsgiving greatly helps them. For just as water quenches fire before our eyes, almsgiving quenches the fire that burns them in their pain. And if alms are offered for those who are already in heaven who have no need of them, they are put into the treasury of holy church and at God's bidding are dealt out among those to whom he assigns them. And the souls that are thereby helped fully thank the souls for whom the alms were given. Thus you should know that almsgiving greatly helps souls, for saints have often heard devils wailing and yelling when souls were delivered from their hands through almsgiving and good prayers. And so in olden times good men and women on this day would buy bread and distribute it for the souls of their beloved, hoping to get a soul out of purgatory with each loaf. There are some people who still do this, but too few, more is the pity. I read in the same book *The Golden Legend*:

A knight riding out to battle asked his cousin to sell his horse if he died in battle and use the money for alms for his soul. But when the knight was killed, his cousin liked the horse and took it for his own use. Soon after, the knight appeared to his cousin and said, "Since you didn't do with my horse as I asked you, you have made me stay in purgatory for eight days. But God will take vengeance on you: your soul will go to hell; mine will go to bliss." Then suddenly a horrible noise of lions and bears and wolves was heard in the air which grabbed this man bodily and carried him away never to be heard of again.

The third help that souls have is the singing of masses, for whenever any soul appears to men, he always wants and begs to have masses said for him. For just as food and drink comfort a man when he is feeble, so the sacrament of the mass comforts and strengthens the souls that it is said for.

I read also in the same book that a bishop suspended a priest because he only knew how to say the requiem mass, which he celebrated every day as he could. Then one high holy day as this bishop rode toward the church for matins, when he came to the churchyard a great number of dead bodies rose up around him and said to him: "You sing no masses for us and now you have taken away our priest from us. See that this is amended or in truth you shall be dead." This bishop was so aghast that he immediately sent for the priest and requested him to say mass as he always had, and he himself did the same as often as he could thereafter.

In the same book we find how the fishermen of St. Thibaud [Theobald] during the autumn harvest caught a great block of ice in their nets and took it to the saint since he was gouty, and they used it to quench the great heat in his feet. Then he heard a voice speaking to him from within the ice and it said, "I am a soul that drew my penance here, and if you would sing thirty masses back to back I would be delivered of my penance." Then this good man said he would. And so when he had said a number of these masses, the stirrings of the devil came to him and told him how all the town was fighting, and each was ready to slay the other, and he must go to them and stop them. And he did. Soon afterwards he began the masses again and when he had said half of them there came another devil and told him how enemies had come and were besieging the town and he must go and intervene. And so he left off with his masses. Soon after he began them yet again. And when he had sung all the masses but the last, word came that all his palace and the town were on fire, and he must help himself or else he would be burned up. Then he said: "Even though everything should burn, I hope with the help of God that I will sing this last mass." And when he had finished the mass, the fire was discovered to be a fantasy of the devil and nothing else. And the ice melted away and the soul was helped.

And so we pray to Jesus that he will help all the souls that we are bound here to pray for. Amen.

What lesson does this sermon teach? How effective are its examples in putting its point across?

81. THE *ART OF DYING WELL* (c. 1430-35)

One of the chief obsessions of medieval Christians was the need to make a "good death"
— one accompanied by confession to a priest to cleanse the soul, holy communion to fill
it with grace, and extreme unction (the sacrament of the last anointing, now called the
anointing of the sick) accompanied by prayers and meditations to prepare it for its oth-
erworldly journey. Sudden death was a terrifying prospect since it left the soul unready
and uncleaned: if it was too stained by sin, it meant eternal damnation. The Ars bene
moriendi *(Art of Dying Well)* was an enormously popular booklet that circulated
throughout Europe beginning in the early fifteenth century. Over 300 manuscripts, half
of them in Latin, the rest in various vernaculars, still survive, and there were many
more printed versions — first in block books, then in moveable type — beyond that.
The tract was a pastiche based chiefly on a treatise on dying written by the theologian
and chancellor of the University of Paris Jean Gerson (1363-1429). Gerson's treatise
seems to have been passed around at the Council of Constance (1414-18) where an
anonymous author, probably a Dominican, made this abridgment. Delegates returning
from the council to their homelands then helped spread the *Art of Dying Well across*
Europe. Two versions of the book circulated in the fifteenth and later centuries. The
edition of the shorter version translated here (from Latin) was produced by a German
scribe perhaps in Augsburg c. 1470. His text was accompanied by eleven block print
woodcuts commonly found in all editions of the treatise.

Source: trans. J. Shinners from an anonymous block print *Ars Bene Moriendi*, ed. Benjamin
Pifteau (Paris: Delarue, n.d. [1880?, 1889?]). Latin.

The Art of Dying

Although, according to the Philosopher [Aristotle] in the third book of his
Ethics, of all terrible things, the death of the body is the most terrible, it is
in no way comparable to the death of the soul. Consider Augustine, who
says that the loss of one soul is greater than the loss of a thousand bodies.
Or consider Bernard [of Clairvaux], who says that everything in the world
combined is not equal in value to the price of one soul. The death of the soul
is thus more terrible and detestable insofar as the soul is more noble and more
precious than the body. Since, therefore, the soul is so precious, the Devil,
who seeks its eternal death, harasses a mortally ill person with special temptations. It is thus of the utmost importance that a person take heed of his soul
so that it is not destroyed at his death. To this end, it is especially needful for
everyone frequently to contemplate the art of dying, which is the present intent, and to bear in mind one's deathbed illness. As Gregory [the Great] says,
"he will greatly rouse himself to doing good works who always bears in mind

his end. For if one gives prior thought to a future misfortune, he will be able to bear it more easily." According to this reasoning, when future things are made manifest, they are more lightly borne. Yet it is exceedingly rare for someone to prepare himself for death in a timely way, since everyone thinks that he is going to live longer than he does, never believing that he is about to die suddenly – a belief surely inspired by the Devil. Consequently, many people, through such vain hope, have neglected themselves, and so they die unprepared. Thus, one should never give a sick person too much hope that he will regain his physical health. For according to the Chancellor of Paris [Jean Gerson], because of such false consolation and the unrealistic hope of recovery, a man often gains damnation more than anything else. Therefore, one should point out to someone dying those things that are necessary for salvation. First, he should believe what a good Christian is obliged to believe and take heart that he is dying in the faith of Christ and in unity with and obedience to the church. Second, he should realize that he has gravely offended God and grieve because of this. Third, he should propose really to amend his ways and never to sin again if he should recover. Fourth, for God's sake he should be forgiving to those who have offended him and seek forgiveness from those he has himself offended. Fifth, he should make restitution for things he has taken. Sixth, he should recognize that Christ died for him and that he cannot be saved except by the merit of Christ's passion for which he should give thanks to God insofar as he can. If he can respond with a clear conscience to these things, it is a sign that he shall be among the number of those worthy of salvation. After this, he should be led carefully through the church's required sacraments: First, that with true contrition he has made a complete confession, receiving devoutly the other sacraments of the church. But whoever has not had someone ask or inform him about these matters should examine himself about them, considering whether he is disposed as described above. And whoever is so disposed, let him commit himself totally to Christ's passion, constantly holding it in mind and meditating on it. For through this, all of the Devil's temptations, especially those against faith, are overcome. One should note that those near death face more serious temptations than they have ever had before. And, as will become clear below, there are five temptations against which the Angel will counsel five useful encouragements. But in order for this material to be fruitful to everyone, and so that no one will be barred from contemplating it but may learn from it how to die well, it is offered to them both in writing, to serve the literate, and in pictures, to serve the literate and illiterate alike. Since the words and pictures correspond to each other, readers have a mirror, as it were, in which they may see the past and future as well as the present. Who wishes to die well, therefore, should carefully consider this and what follows.

The Devil's Temptations over Faith

Faith is the whole foundation of salvation, and without it no one at all can be saved, as Augustine attests when he says, "faith is the basis of every good and the beginning of human salvation." And Bernard says, "faith is the beginning of human salvation; without it no one can be numbered among the sons of God; without it every human work is in vain." The Devil, the enemy of the whole human race, therefore tries with all his might to completely turn someone mortally ill from faith, or he tries at least to make him question it, saying, "You wretch. You have made a big mistake. It is not as you believe or as the preacher says. Hell is overcome [through Jesus's harrowing of hell]. No matter what a person does – even if he kills someone or kills himself through excessive penance, as some have done, or he adores idols as the kings of the pagans and many pagan people do – in the end is it not all the same? For no one returns from the dead to tell you the truth [about the afterlife] and so your faith is nothing." With these words and words like them, the Devil really strives to turn dying people from faith, because he truly knows that if the foundation crumbles everything built on it will crumble. Nevertheless, the Devil cannot force a man into any temptation or influence him in any way to consent to it (so long as he has the use of his reason) unless he wants to give in to it of his own free will, which surely he ought to be on guard against above all. Thus, the apostle Paul says, "God is faithful and will not permit you to be tempted beyond your strength, but with the temptation will also give you a way out that you may be able to bear it " [1 Cor. 10:13].

The Angel's Good Encouragement about Faith

Against the Devil's first temptation, the Angel offers good encouragement, saying, "O man, do not believe the Devil's pernicious suggestions, for he is a liar. Through lies he deceived our First Parents. Do not in the least doubt your faith even though you cannot understand it through your senses or your intellect. If you could understand it, it would have no merit. For according to Gregory, 'faith for which human reason can offer proof is worthless.' But remember the words of the holy fathers – namely Paul, who says in the eleventh chapter of his epistle to the Hebrews, 'Without faith it is impossible to please God' [Heb. 11:5]. And the third chapter of John's Gospel says, 'He who does not believe is already judged' [John 3:18]. And St. Bernard says, 'faith is the firstborn of the virtues'; he also says that Mary was more blessed for bearing Christ in faith than in his flesh. Bear in mind also the faith of those ancient men of faith Abraham, Isaac, and Jacob, and some of the Gentiles: Joab, the harlot Rahab [Heb. 11:31], and others like them; and also the apostles and the steadfast martyrs, confessors, and virgins. For all the ancients and moderns have been made pleasing through faith. Through faith St. Peter walked upon the waters; St. John drank the poison offered to him without harm; through faith Alexander the Great prayed and joined together the Caspian Mountains [thus imprisoning Gog and Magog]. And so, with the merit of God's blessing, you will receive faith with which you should resist the Devil bravely and firmly believe all the church's commandments because the holy church is ruled by the Holy Spirit and cannot err." Notice that as soon as a sick person feels himself tempted against faith, he should think first how necessary faith is since without it no one can be saved. Second, he should think how useful it is since it makes all things possible. As the Lord says, "All things are possible to those who believe" [Mark 9:22]. And also, "All things whatever you ask for in prayer, believe that you shall receive" [Mark 11:24]. With the grace of God, then, a sick person may easily resist the Devil. This is why it is also good to recite the Creed in a loud voice to someone dying and to repeat it many times so that the sick person is stirred to constancy in faith, and demons, who cannot bear hearing it, are driven away.

The Devil's Temptations over Despair

Second, the Devil tempts a sick person through despair, which is contrary to the hope and trust a person should have in God. For when a sick person is racked by physical suffering, then the Devil heaps pain on pain mainly by bringing up his unconfessed sins to lead him into despair, saying, "You wretch! Look at your sins, so great that you will never find pardon for them. You should say with Cain, 'My iniquity is greater than any pardon I may deserve' [Gen. 4:13]. Look how you have disobeyed God's commandments. For you have not loved God above all things; you have borne injury to other people. And you surely know that no one is saved who hasn't kept God's commandments, because the Lord said 'If you will enter into life, keep the commandments' [Matt. 19:17]. But you thrived on pride, avarice, lust, gluttony, wrath, envy, and sloth even though you've heard it preached that someone can be damned for just one mortal sin. Furthermore, you haven't performed the seven works of mercy, which the Lord will particularly look for on the Last Day, as he himself remarked, saying 'to those on his left hand, "Depart from me into the everlasting fire.... For I was hungry, and you did not give me to eat; I was thirsty and you gave me no drink, etc."' [Matt. 25:41-42]. And James said likewise: 'For judgment will be without mercy to him who has not shown mercy on earth' [James 2:13]. Consider also how many people there are laboring vigilantly night and day who still dare not presume that they are saved, since 'man knows not whether he be worthy of love or hatred' [Eccles. 9:1]. So no hope of salvation is left to you." Through these words and words like them, the Devil leads someone into despair since it should be shunned above all evils because it offends God's mercy, which alone saves us. The prophet attests, "The mercies of the Lord that we are not consumed" [Lam. 3:22]. And Augustine says, "Each person sunk in sin, if he despairs of receiving true pardon, utterly loses God's mercy; for nothing offends God more than despair."

The Angel's Good Encouragement against Despair

Against the Devil's second temptation, the Angel gives good encouragement, saying, "O man, why do you despair? For even if you had committed as many robberies, thefts, and murders as there are drops of water in the sea or grains of sand [Ecclus. 18:8]; even if you were the only one in the world who had sinned; even if you had never done penance for these sins before or confessed them; even if you had never had any opportunity to confess them, still you should not despair, because in such a case a contrite heart alone is enough. The psalm says, 'A contrite and humble heart, O God, you will not despise' [Ps. 50 (51):19]. And Ezechiel says, 'At whatever hour a sinner bemoans his sin, he shall be saved' [Ezek. 33:12,19]. Thus, Bernard says, 'God's kindness is greater even than man's Fall'; and Augustine says, 'God can be more merciful than man can sin.' Even in a case where you know that you deserve to be numbered among the damned, you should not at all despair. For despair accomplishes nothing except to offend the most holy God even more, to make other sins worse, and to stretch eternal pain into infinity. Even Christ was crucified for sinners, not for the just, as he himself attested, saying 'I have not come to call the just, but sinners' [Luke 5:22]. You may take an example from Peter's denial of Christ, from Paul's persecution of the church, from the tax collectors Paul and Zacchaeus [Luke 19:7], the sinner Mary Magdalene, the woman taken in adultery, from the good thief hanging on the cross next to Jesus, from St. Mary of Egypt, etc." Note that as soon as a sick person senses that he is tempted by despair, he should consider that it is worse and more damnable than all other sins, and that it should never be allowed, regardless of the sin. For, as Augustine says, "Judas sinned more by despairing than did the Jews by crucifying Christ." Second, he should consider how useful and necessary hope is, which, according to St. John Chrysostom, is the anchor of our salvation, the bedrock of our life, and the guide which leads us along the path to heaven. So hope should never be abandoned, no matter what the sin.

The Devil's Temptation over Impatience

Third, the Devil tempts a sick person through impatience, which is born of serious illness, saying "Why do you endure this terrible suffering which is unbearable for any creature and utterly useless to you? Despite what your faults deserve, it is not right to demand such suffering from you, for it is written [in canon law], 'follow the more benign interpretation [of the law] when imposing punishments.' What is more aggravating, you get no sympathy, since who can doubt that this is beyond all reason? For although your friends say they have sympathy for you, in their hearts they want you to die, particularly because of the property you will leave behind. For after your soul has cast off the body, they are willing to sit watch over it for barely the space of a day in return for the property you leave behind." With these and like words the Devil tries to coax someone into impatience – which is contrary to the charity that requires us to love God over all things – to make him lose his merits. Note that the greatest possible physical distress afflicts those who are dying, especially those not dying from natural causes (which is rare, as clear experience teaches) but usually from unexpected causes, like a fever, an abscess, or some other serious, painful, and prolonged malady. Sickness causes such impatience and grumbling in most people, and especially in those unprepared to die or dying unfairly, that many people may seem to be out of their minds or irrational from excessively suffering in impatience, as often appears in many people. Consequently, it is very much the case that such people may fail particularly in true charity, as Jerome attests when he says, "If someone suffers sickness or accepts death with resentment, it is a sign that he does not love God enough." And Paul says, "charity is patient, is kind" [1 Cor. 13:4].

The Angel's Good Encouragement to Patience

Against the Devil's third temptation, the Angel gives good encouragement, saying, "O man, turn your soul from impatience through which the Devil seeks nothing but its harm with his deadly goading. For through impatience and grumbling your soul is lost, just as it is delivered through patience. So Gregory attests, who says, 'the kingdom of heaven is not for grumblers.' Therefore, do not let your suffering, which is mild compared to what you deserve, irk you since it is a sort of purgatory before death when you bear it properly: namely, both patiently and willingly with gratitude. For it is necessary to be grateful not only for those things that come as consolation but also for those that come as affliction, since, as Gregory says, 'the merciful God administers temporal punishment so that he will not inflict eternal revenge.'

And Augustine says, 'Lord, cut and burn here but spare me in eternity.' Therefore, let no hardships trouble you, for Christ reveals that he does not wish to forsake you. As Augustine says, 'The evils that afflict us here force us to turn to God. The pleasures of the flesh, therefore, make evident not the soul's salvation, but its eternal damnation.' According to Augustine, 'a clear sign of damnation is to acquire pleasurable things and be loved by the world.' And also, 'it is amazing that all the weights of the judgment scale [see Prov. 16:11] do not tilt up in consolation for all the people worthy of eternal damnation; it is more amazing still that all the weights do not tilt up as a threat for all those worthy of eternal salvation.' Therefore, drive impatience away from you as if it were a virulent disease, and take up patience as an impenetrable shield by which all the soul's enemies are easily overcome, and contemplate Christ and all the saints who were most patient even unto death." Note that when a sick person feels himself tempted by impatience, he should consider first how harmful impatience is, since, by making him restless and perturbed, it turns him away from God; for the Lord asks, "Upon whom shall my spirit rest if not upon the calm and the humble of heart?" Second, he should consider how diligently patience must be protected, first because it is necessary. As Paul says, "you have need of patience" [Heb. 10:36]. And "Did not the Christ have to suffer these things before entering into his glory" [Luke 24:26]? And Gregory says, "Never fail to protect concord through patience." Second, because it is useful. Thus, the Lord says, "By your patience you will win your souls" [Luke 21:19]. And Gregory says, "It is of more merit to bear hardships than to sweat over good works." And he says, "We can be martyrs without suffering the ordeal of torture if we truly keep patience in our heart." And Solomon says, "The patient man is better than the valiant: and he that rules his spirit, than he that takes cities" [Prov. 16:32].

The Devil's Temptation over Vainglory

Fourth, the Devil tempts a sick person through his own self-satisfaction, which is spiritual pride (with which he especially harasses devout, religious, and blameless people). For when he cannot lead a man to swerve from faith either through despair or impatience, then he attacks him with his own self-satisfaction, throwing such thoughts as these against him like darts: "Oh how firm you are in your faith, and how strong in hope, and how constantly patient you are during your illness. Oh how many good works you busy yourself with! You should take special pride because you are not like other people who committed countless sins but still reached the heavenly kingdom by a single groan [of contrition]. The kingdom of heaven cannot, therefore, rightfully be denied you because you properly fought for it. Accept, therefore, the crown prepared for you and the most excellent throne which you have gained ahead of others." Through these and similar words, the Devil most insistently strives to lead someone into spiritual pride or self-satisfaction. Take note that one should particularly avoid this kind of pride: first, because through it, someone makes himself like the Devil since it is pride alone that makes an angel into a devil. Second, because through it someone appears to commit blasphemy since he presumes to have acquired by himself the good that God gave him. Third, because his self-satisfaction can grow so great that he can be damned for it. Thus, Gregory says, "He who builds himself up remembering the good deeds he has done falls before the author of humility." And Augustine says, "the man who has justified himself or presumed himself to be justified, falls."

The Angel's Good Encouragement against Vainglory

Against the Devil's fourth temptation, the Angel gives good encouragement saying, "Wretched man. Why do you take pride in ascribing your constancy in faith, hope, and patience to yourself when it should be ascribed to God alone since you have nothing good from yourself? The Lord says, 'without me, you can do nothing.' And elsewhere it is written, 'you should not lay claims for yourself, or boast, or insolently exalt yourself, or presume anything about yourself, or ascribe anything good to yourself.' And the Lord says, 'he who exalts himself shall be humbled' [Luke 14:11]. And also, 'unless you become like little children, you will not enter the kingdom of heaven' [Matt. 18:3]. Humble yourself, therefore, and you will be exalted. As the Lord says, 'he who humbles himself will be exalted' [Luke 14:11]. And Augustine says, 'if you humble yourself, God will descend upon you; if you exalt yourself, God will withdraw from you.' Turn your mind, therefore, from pride, which transformed Lucifer, once the most beautiful of the angels, into the ugliest of the devils, and which cast him from the heights of heaven into the depths of hell, and which was also the cause of all sin. Thus, Bernard says, 'pride is the beginning of all sin and the cause of all perdition.' Also, 'take away this vice and, with little effort, all the other vices are cut back.'" Consequently, take special note that whenever a dying person feels himself tempted by pride, he ought to think first that pride so offends God that for its sake alone he banished the noblest creature Lucifer and all his cohorts from heaven and damned them for eternity. Bearing this in mind he should humble himself and belittle himself by recalling his sins since he does not know whether he is worthy of hatred or love. For this reason, he should especially follow St. Anthony's example, to whom the Devil said, "Oh Anthony, you have vanquished me; for when I want to exalt you, you belittle yourself; when I want to belittle you, you raise yourself up." Second, he ought to ponder that humility pleases God so much that, mainly because of it, the glorious Virgin Mary conceived God and was thereby exalted over all the choirs of angels.

The Devil's Temptation over Avarice

The Devil's fifth temptation is avarice, which especially harasses secular and worldly people, and is an excessive preoccupation with temporal and external things like wives or carnal friends or worldly riches and other things that people have greatly loved during their lives. The Devil especially vexes someone at the end of his life with avarice, saying, "O wretch! Now you will leave behind all those worldly goods that you have gathered together with great worry and effort – including your wife, your children, your kinfolk, your dearest friends, and all the other desirable things of the world whose company still matters to you and which would be of such great comfort and even an opportunity for great good." The Devil holds out these and similar words about avarice to a dying man so that through his love and greed for worldly things he may turn from the love of God and his own salvation. For this reason, take particular note that one should be very careful when someone is dying not to remind him of his carnal friends, wife, children, riches, and other earthly possessions, except insofar as his spiritual health demands or requires it. Otherwise it would be singularly dangerous if he were recalled away from matters of his spirit and salvation – which should be the inward and outward focus for all men especially at that moment – back towards those miserable temporal and worldly things which should be removed from the memory and the mind with great care at that moment since it is surely terribly dangerous to be occupied with them then.

The Angel's Good Encouragement against Avarice

Against the Devil's fifth temptation, the Angel gives good encouragement saying, "O man, turn your ears from the Devil's lethal suggestions by which he tries to provoke and harass you. Put completely behind you all earthly things, whose memory in any event cannot bring you salvation and is a great obstacle. Remember the words of the Lord to those who cling to these things: 'Every one of you who does not renounce all that he possesses, cannot be my disciple' [Luke 14:33]. And again, 'if anyone comes to me and does not hate his father and mother, and wife and children, and brothers and sisters, yes, and even his own life, he cannot be my disciple' [Luke 14:26]. But to those who renounce these things he says, 'and everyone who has left house, or brothers, or sisters, or father, or mother, or wife, or children, or

lands, for my name's sake shall receive a hundredfold, and shall possess life everlasting' [Matt. 19:29]. Be mindful also of Christ's poverty as he hung on the cross for you, willingly forsaking his most beloved mother and his dearest disciples for your salvation. Consider also how many holy men, having heard him, followed him in this contempt for worldly things. Come to your blessed Father; receive the kingdom prepared for you from the beginning of the world. Impress upon your mind these things and totally reject all the transitory things of the world as if they were poison. Turn your whole heart to voluntary poverty so that the kingdom of heaven will be owed to you as the Lord promised, saying, 'blessed are the poor in spirit, for theirs is the kingdom of heaven' [Matt. 5:3]. And, putting your whole faith in God, give yourself entirely to him who will bestow eternal riches on you." Note that when a sick person feels that he is being tempted by avarice or love of earthly things, he should first consider that love of worldly goods separates him from God because it shuts off the love of God, as Gregory attests who says, "The more anyone is cut off from heavenly love, the more he delights here below in created things." Second consider how voluntary poverty makes a person holy and leads him to heaven, as the Lord says, "Blessed are the poor in spirit for theirs is the kingdom of heaven."

If the sufferer still has his wits, let him pour forth prayers, first beseeching God that, through his inexpressible mercy and the power of his passion, he may deign to receive him. Second let him diligently call on the glorious Virgin Mary as his mediatrix. Then let him invoke all the angels – especially his guardian angel – and the apostles, the martyrs, confessors, and virgins, particularly those he venerated and loved before he fell sick, and let their pictures be shown to him, along with images of the crucifix and the Blessed Virgin Mary. Let him then say this verse: "Lord, thou has broken my bonds; I will sacrifice to thee the sacrifice of praise" [Ps. 115 (116):16]. For according to Cassiodorus, this verse is considered to be so powerful that people's sins are remitted if it is said with true confession when dying. Also let him say

Fig. 10.2. A good death (facing page)

As he contemplates the crucifixion and a priest helps him hold a lighted taper, four angels receive the dying man's little soul at the upper left by while a cluster of saints – including the penitent Mary Magdalene holding a spice pot (Mark 16:1) – looks on. Vanquished devils depart raging in Latin (from left to right): "Spes nobis nulla" – "There's no hope for us;" "Animam amisimus" – "We've lost his soul;" "Heu insanio" – "Oh! I am raving;" "Furore consumor" – "I'm consumed with rage;" and "Confusi sumus" – "We are confounded." Reproduction of the last xylographic woodcut in the *Ars moriendi* from Pifteau's facsimile edition (Paris: Delarue, n.d.).

three times these words or similar ones, which are ascribed to blessed Augustine: "May the peace of our Lord Jesus Christ, and the power of his passion, and the sign of the holy cross, and the purity of the most Blessed Virgin Mary, and the blessing of all the saints, and the protection of the angels, and the prayers of all the elect be between me and all my enemies visible and invisible in this the hour of my death." Finally, let him say, "Into thy hands I commend my spirit" [Ps. 30 (31):6, Luke 23:46]. But if the sick person does not know how to say these prayers, let someone from among those attending him say them near him in a loud voice, or tell him the pious stories that he always loved to hear. Let him pray, though, with his heart and desire if he knows how to and is able. But alas, there are few people who faithfully aid their neighbors in dying by questioning them, admonishing them, and praying for them, especially since mortally ill people themselves do not want to die yet, and so the souls of the dying are often pitiably put in jeopardy.

How insightful about death and dying is this tract? Does it idealize death or treat it realistically? Would it comfort its readers or frighten them? What assumptions does it make about the depth of the Christian beliefs of a dying person?

82. BURIAL OF THE DEAD (c. 1425)

This brief description of the rituals surrounding an ideal burial, excerpted from a collection of early fifteenth-century English sermons, draws its details mostly from Johannes Belethus's Rational of the Divine Services, *a twelfth-century work outlining liturgical practice.*

Source: modernized J. Shinners from Edward H. Weatherly, *Speculum sacerdotale*, Early English Text Society, Original Series, No. 200 (London: H. Milford, Oxford University Press, 1936), pp. 233-35. Middle English.

.... And when a man lies in his last sickness and draws near the hour of his death, he should be laid down upon the ground on ashes or on chaff to signify that he is ashes and to ashes he shall return [Gen. 3:19]. This is done after the manner of St. Martin [of Tours], who as an example laid on ashes and died there. The passion of our Lord, or else a part of the passion, ought to be read before the dying person if he is literate in order to steer him to compunction; the cross ought to stand at his feet, and his face should be turned upward so that he is looking into heaven.

When he is dead, bells ought to be rung so that the hearers may pray for him. They should be rung for a woman twice. Why? Because she caused a difference and an otherness in that time [in paradise] when she created alienation and division between God and man. For a man they should be rung three times. Why? Because man was created first and woman was created from man. For Adam was made first and formed of the earth, the woman came out of Adam, and mankind came from them both; thus, there was a trinity. The bells ought to be rung for a cleric as many times as the number of his holy orders [out of seven], and at the final time they should be tolled so that the people know for whom they ring.

Also the bells should be rung when he is borne to the church and when he is borne from the church to the burying place. The body should be washed before it is wrapped in cloths. The priest should come to the house and say orisons and prayers, praying to God and his saints to take that soul and bring it to the joy of heaven. There are many perfect souls which, as soon as they pass from their bodies, flee up into heaven; there are some that are utterly evil so that they go down into hell; and there are some in the middle between these two ways – for them such commendation and prayers are to be made.

When the body is washed and wrapped in cloths, then it should be borne to the church to have masses sung. In some churches each man in the choir is given a candle in one hand and a wafer in the other, which he offers to the priest after the Gospel.

The dead person should be borne to the earth by those who are most like him in order, craft, or degree: if he is a priest, he should be borne by priests, and so on. When he is put into the earth, the priest should cast holy water over him so that devils will not come to him, for they greatly dread holy water. For devils used to cause frenzies in the bodies of the dead to cause them the shame in death that they could not cause them in life. And scents would be cast in to ward off the evil smell of the dead that would perhaps be noticed. The [char]coals [mixed into the grave dirt] signify that the earth may not be used for ordinary purposes. And ivy or laurel, which are evergreens and do not fade, are strewn in the grave to signify that those who die observing the commandments of God and in perfection shall have life evermore without fail or fading; for though all such men are dead in body, they live in soul....

INDEX OF TOPICS

Topics are listed by document number and, in some cases, by books and sections or chapters within that document. Thus, 41.2 is a reference to document 41, ghost stories, story 2. If the topic appears several times within a document, no section or chapter number is given. Thus, 41 is a simple reference to ghost stories.

SOURCES

Chapter One

1. Basic Christian Prayers: the Hail Mary and the Sign of the Cross from Herbert Thurston, *Familiar Prayers, Their Origin and History* (Westminster, MA: Newman Press, 1953), pp. 12, 103.

2. The Fourth Lateran Council from H.J. Schroeder in *Disciplinary Decrees of the General Councils* (London: Herder, 1937), pp. 237-39, 251-52, 255-57, 259-60, 280-81, 286-87, 290-91.

8. The religious life of Peter Waldes from Walter L. Wakefield and Austin P. Evans, *Heresies of the High Middle Ages* (New York: Columbia University Press, 1969), pp. 200-02; reprinted with permission.

9. The religious life of St. Francis from Placid Hermann (ed.), Thomas of Celano, *Saint Francis of Assisi* (Chicago: Franciscan Herald Press, 1963), pp. 5-27; reprinted with permission.

11. The religious life of a Spanish peasant from William A. Christian, Jr., *Apparitions in Late Medieval and Renaissance Spain* (Princeton, NJ: Princeton University Press, 1981), pp. 153-56; reprinted with permission.

Chapter Two

12. *The Play of Adam (Ordo Representacionis Ade)* trans. Carl J. Odenkirken (Brookline, MA: Classical Folia Editions; Leiden: Brill, 1976) pp. 43-109.

13. St. Francis of Assisi and the Christmas crèche from Placid Hermann (ed.), Thomas of Celano, *Saint Francis of Assisi* (Chicago: Franciscan Herald Press, 1963), pp. 75-78; reprinted with permission.

14. The Passion Narrative from Giovanni de' Cauli's *Meditations on the Life of Christ* from Isa Ragusa and Rosalie Green (eds.), *Meditations on the Life of Christ, An Illustrated Manuscript of the Fourteenth Century* (Princeton, NJ: Princeton University Press, 1961), pp. 317-19, 327-38, 345-47; reprinted with permission.

16. Two hymns for the feast of Corpus Christi from Joseph Connelly, *Hymns of the Roman Liturgy* (Westminster, MA: Newman Press, 1957), pp. 124-26.

17. Catherine of Siena on receiving the Eucharist from Vida Scudder, *Saint Catherine of Siena as seen in her Letters* (London: J.M. Dent, 1926), pp. 199-205.

Chapter Three

20. Four antiphons of the Virgin from Joseph Connelly, *Hymns of the Roman Liturgy* (Westminster, MA: Newman Press, 1957), pp. 44-47.

23. The *Cantigas de Santa Maria* of Alfonso X, cantiga 228 from John E. Keller in *Mediaeval Age: Specimens of European Poetry from the Ninth to the Fifteenth Century*, ed. Angel Flores (New York: Dell, 1963), pp. 278-79; reprinted with permission.

26. The *Obsecro te* from Roger S. Wieck in *Time Sanctified, The Book of Hours in Medieval Art and Life* (New York: George Braziller, 1988), pp. 163-64; reprinted with permission.

27. An apparition of the Virgin Mary in Castile from William A. Christian, Jr., *Apparitions in Late Medieval and Renaissance Spain* (Princeton, NJ: Princeton University Press, 1981), pp. 27-32; reprinted with permission.

Chapter Four

28. The traveling relics of Laon cathedral from John F. Benton (ed.) and C.C. Swinton Bland (trans.) in *Self and Society in Medieval France, The Memoirs of Abbot Guibert of Nogent* (New York: Harper & Row, 1970), pp. 191-97; reprinted with permission.

29. Accommodating pilgrims at the church of St.-Denis from Erwin Panofsky (ed.), *Abbot Suger on the Abbey Church of St.-Denis and Its Art Treasures* (2nd ed., Gerda Panofsky-Suerel; Princeton, NJ: Princeton University Press, 1946, 1979), pp. 87-89; reprinted with permission.

31. Bishop Hugh of Lincoln's devotion to relics from Decima. L. Douie and Hugh Farmer (eds.), Adam of Eynsham's *Magna Vita Sancti Hugonis* (London: Thomas Nelson, 1962), v. 2, pp. 167-71; reprinted with permission.

32. St. Mary Magdalene and St. Nicholas from the *Golden Legend* from William G. Ryan, Jacobus de Voragine's *Golden Legend, Readings on the Saints* (Princeton: Princeton University Press, 1993), v. 1, pp. 21-27, 374-83; reprinted with permission.

Chapter Five

40. The young priest Walchelin's purgatorial vision from Marjorie Chibnall, *The Ecclesiastical History of Odericus Vitalis* (Oxford: Clarendon Press, 1973), v. 4, pp. 237-51; reprinted with permission.

43. Bernardino of Siena on witchcraft and superstition from Helen J. Robins in Nazareno Orlandi (ed.), *Bernardine of Siena, Sermons* (Siena: Tipografia Sociale, 1920), pp. 163-76.

44. The *Malleus Maleficarum* on superstitious practices from *The Malleus Maleficarum of Heinrich Kramer and James Sprenger*, trans. Montague Summers (New York: Dover Publications, 1971; reprint of the 1928 edition [London: John Rodker]), pp. 188-92; reprinted with permission.

45. A Necromancer's Love Spell from Richard Kieckhefer, *Forbidden Rites: A Necromancer's Manual of the Fifteenth Century* (University Park: Pennsylvania University Press, 1997), pp. 87-88; reprinted with permission.

Chapter Six

46. Advice to a young wife on mass and confession from W.P. Barret in Eileen Power, *The Goodman of Paris, A Treatise on Moral and Domestic Economy by a Citizen of Paris* (New York: Harcourt, Brace and Co., 1928), pp. 54-65; reprinted with permission.

49. Jacob of Voragine on the Greater and Lesser Rogations from William G. Ryan, Jacobus de Voragine's *Golden Legend, Readings on the Saints* (Princeton, NJ: Princeton University Press, 1993), v. 1, pp. 285-89; reprinted with permission.

52. Ceremony for the exclusion of a leper from *The Medieval Hospitals of England*, trans. Rotha Mary Clay (London: Frank Cass, 1909); Appendix A, pp. 273-76, from A. Jefferies Collins, *Manuale ad Usum Percelebris Ecclesiae Sarisburiensis* (Chichester: Henry Bradshaw Society, 1960), v. 91, pp. 182-85; reprinted with permission.

53. Christian charms: to cure muscular cramps from J.E. Anderson in Marc Bloch, *The Royal Touch: Sacred Monarchy and Scrofula in England and France* (London: Routledge & Kegan Paul, 1973), p. 96; reprinted with permission.

Chapter Seven

54. Rule for the Franciscan Third Order from Benen Fahy, *The Writings of St. Francis of Assisi* (Chicago: Franciscan Herald Press, 1964), pp. 168-75; reprinted with permission.

58. Guillaume de Deguileville's *Pilgrimage of Human Life* from Eugene Clasby, *The Pilgrimage of Human Life* (New York: Garland Publishing, 1992), pp. 3-9, 80-83, 147-52; reprinted with permission.

60. Geert Grote preaches the Modern Devotion from John Van Engen in *Devotio Moderna, Basic Writings* (New York: Paulist Press, 1988), pp. 92-97; reprinted with permission.

61. A spiritual regimen for a fifteenth-century gentleman from W.A.

Pantin, "Instructions for a Devout and Literate Layman" *in Medieval Learning and Literature, Essays Presented to Richard William Hunt*, ed. J.J.G. Alexander and M.T. Gibson (Oxford: Clarendon Press, 1976), pp. 398-400; reprinted with permission.

63. Popular proverbs from Richard Jente, *Proverbia Communia, A Fifteenth-Century Collection of Dutch Proverbs*, Indiana University Publications Folklore Series No. 4 (Bloomington: Indiana University, 1947), pp. 110-304, passim; reprinted with permission.

Chapter Eight

65. Pious church-builders at Chartres cathedral from G.G. Coulton, *Life in the Middle Ages* (Cambridge: Cambridge University Press, 1910; rpt. 1967), v. II, pp. 18-22; reprinted with permission.

68. The Franciscan Salimbene on the "Great Halleluia" from Joseph L. Baird, *The Chronicle of Salimbene de Adam* (Binghamton, NY: Medieval & Renaissance Texts and Studies, 1986), pp. 47-56, 512-14; reprinted with permission.

Chapter Nine

74. Popular heresy in twelfth-century Le Mans from R.I. Moore, *The Birth of Popular Heresy* (London: Edward Arnold, 1975), pp. 34-38; reprinted with permission.

Chapter Ten

78. The knight Owein's journey through St. Patrick's Purgatory from Jean-Michel Picard in *Saint Patrick's Purgatory, A Twelfth-Century Tale of a Journey to the Other World*, intro. Yolande de Pontfarcy (Dublin: Four Courts Press, 1985), pp. 50-71; reprinted with permission.

The publisher has made every effort to locate all copyright holders of the texts published in this book and would be pleased to hear from any party not duly acknowledged.